SECOND
EDITION

Drugs, Society, and Criminal Justice

Charles F. Levinthal

Hofstra University

PEARSON

Boston   New York   San Francisco

Mexico City   Montreal   Toronto   London   Madrid   Munich   Paris

Hong Kong   Singapore   Tokyo   Cape Town   Sydney

Senior Editor: *Dave Repetto*
Series Editorial Assistant: *Jack Cashman*
Production Supervisor: *Beth Houston*
Editorial Production Service: *Andrea Cava*
Composition Buyer: *Linda Cox*
Manufacturing Buyer: *Debbie Rossi*
Electronic Composition: *NK Graphics*
Photo Researcher: *Poyee Oster*
Cover Administrator: *Linda Knowles*

For related titles and support materials, visit our online catalog at www.ablongman.com.

Between the time website information is gathered and then published, it is not unusual for some sites to have closed. Also, the transcription of URLs can result in typographical errors. The publisher would appreciate notification where these errors occur so that they may be corrected in subsequent editions.

ISBN-10: 013513806X
ISBN-13: 9780135138069

Printed in the United States of America

10 9 8 7 6 5 4 3 2 1   VHP 11 10 09 08 07

Credits appear on page 413, which constitutes an extension of the copyright page.

For
Beth, David, and Brian

CONTENTS

Contents ■ **vii**

PREFACE

Drugs, Society, and Criminal Justice, Second Edition, is designed for students in sociology and criminal justice courses that focus on issues of drug use, misuse, and abuse. As the title indicates, a special emphasis is on the sociological aspects of drug-taking behavior and the relationship between drugs and crime (Chapter 13) and the criminal justice system (Chapter 14). The book is adapted from *Drugs, Behavior, and Modern Society,* Fifth Edition, in order to fit more closely the interests of sociology and criminal justice instructors and students.

Both textbooks have the same aim: To introduce the basic facts and major issues concerning drug-taking behavior in a straightforward, comprehensive, up-to-date, and reader-friendly manner. A background in biology, sociology, psychology, or chemistry is not necessary. The only requirement is a sense of curiosity about the range of chemical substances that affect our minds and our bodies and an interest in the challenges these substances bring to our society and our daily lives.

As you proceed through *Drugs, Society, and Criminal Justice,* a central theme will be apparent: The social problems surrounding drug misuse and abuse are not someone else's concern but rather everyone's concern. Like it or not, the decision to use drugs today is one of life's choices, regardless of our racial, ethnic, or religious background, how much money we have, where we live, how much education we have achieved, whether we are male or female, or whether we are young or old. The potential for drug misuse and abuse is a problem facing all of us. Our entire society is involved.

Another particularly important overarching theme in understanding the relationship between drug use and the American criminal justice system is the enormous diversity that exists among drugs that affect the mind and the body. We must educate ourselves not only about illicit street drugs such as cocaine, amphetamines, heroin, hallucinogens, and marijuana but also about legally available drugs such as alcohol and nicotine. We must be aware of the increasing usage of anabolic steroids and other performance-enhancing drugs, as well as problems associated with prescription medications and dietary supplements. *Drugs, Society, and Criminal Justice* addresses the entire range of drugs used and abused in America today.

Features

The chapters in *Drugs, Society, and Criminal Justice* are organized in four major sections:

- Part 1 (Chapters 1–3): Drugs and Society: Past and Present
- Part 2 (Chapters 4–9): Legally Restricted Drugs in Our Society
- Part 3 (Chapters 10–12): Legal Drugs in Our Society
- Part 4 (Chapters 13–15): Drug Abuse and Drug Policy

As you will see, discussions of particular drugs have been grouped not in terms of their pharmacological characteristics but rather in terms of their access to the general public and the societal attitudes toward their use. The last section concerns itself with crime and the criminal justice system, as well as approaches toward education and treatment.

A number of special features throughout the book will enhance your experience as a reader and serve as learning aids.

Quick Concept Checks

Sometimes, when the material gets complicated, you want to have a quick way of finding out if you understand the basic concepts being explained. I have included from time to time a Quick Concept Check, where you can see in a minute or two where you stand. Some of the Checks will be in matching format; others will be an interpretation of a graph or diagram. In some cases, you will be asked to apply the principles you have learned to a real-world situation.

Portraits

The Portrait feature in each chapter takes you into the lives of individuals who have either influenced our thinking about drugs and society or have been impacted by drug use and abuse. Some of them are known to the public at large, but many are not. In any case, the Portraits put a human face on the discussion of drugs, society, and criminal justice. They remind us that throughout this book we are dealing with issues that affect real people in all walks of life, now and in the past. Some examples of Portraits are the following:

- Eliot Ness and the Untouchables (Chapter 2)
- Nora D. Volkow—Imaging the Face of Addiction in the Brain (Chapter 3)
- Barry Tuttle and Russell Fitch—The Two Sides of OxyContin (Chapter 5)
- Timothy Leary—Whatever Happened to Him? (Chapter 6)
- Patricia White, GHB, and the "Perfect" Crime (Chapter 8)
- Bill W. and Dr. Bob—Founders of Alcoholics Anonymous (Chapter 11)
- Sigmund Freud—Nicotine Dependence, Cigars, and Cancer (Chapter 12)
- Pablo Escobar—Formerly Known as the Colombian King of Cocaine (Chapter 13)

Drugs . . . in Focus

There are many fascinating stories to tell about the role of drugs in our society, along with the important facts and serious issues surrounding drug use. While some of the Drugs . . . in Focus features summarize information that you can refer to at a later time when the need arises, several of them represent an interesting sidelight look on a question that you might have wondered about. Some examples of Drugs . . . in Focus features are the following:

- Abraham Lincoln, Depression, and Those "Little Blue Pills" (Chapter 2)
- What Happened to the Coca in Coca-Cola? (Chapter 4)
- Endorphins in Our Lives: A Psychosocial Perspective (Chapter 5)
- Strange Days in Salem: Witchcraft or Hallucinogens? (Chapter 6)
- Can You Control a Marijuana High? (Chapter 7)
- Resistol and *Resistoleros* in Latin America (Chapter 8)
- Suspension Penalties for Steroid Use in American Professional Sports (Chapter 9)
- THG and the War on Performance-Enhancing Drugs (Chapter 9)
- Alcohol, Security, and Spectator Sports (Chapter 10)
- The Sociology of Alcoholics Anonymous (Chapter 11)
- Introducing Light and Luscious Camel No. 9 (Chapter 12)

- Drug Smuggler Profiles (Chapter 14)
- Alcohol 101 on College Campuses (Chapter 15)

Help Lines

Information of a more personal nature is provided in the Help Line features. You will find important facts that you can use to recognize the signs of drug misuse or abuse and ways you can respond to emergency drug-taking situations, as well as warnings about risk situations. At the end of each Help Line, there is a web site that can be of further assistance to you. Examples of some features are the following:

- The Possibility of a Drug–Drug or Food–Drug Combination (Chapter 1)
- Cocaine after Alcohol: The Risk of Cocaethylene Toxicity (Chapter 4)
- Emergency Guidelines for a Bad Trip on LSD (Chapter 6)
- MDMA Toxicity: The Other Side of Ecstasy (Chapter 6)
- The Symptoms of Steroid Abuse (Chapter 9)
- Emergency Signs and Procedures in Acute Alcohol Intoxication (Chapter 10)
- The TWEAK Alcoholism Screening Instrument for Pregnant Women (Chapter 11)
- Ten Tips on How to Succeed When Trying to Quit Smoking (Chapter 12)

Drug Trafficking Updates

When you are reading about drugs and criminal justice, it is important that you understand the current intelligence reports collected by law enforcement agencies in the United States, as well as around the world, regarding the patterns of illicit drug trafficking. Drug Trafficking Update features provide important information about cocaine, methamphetamine, heroin, LSD, MDMA (Ecstasy), and PCP.

Other Features

Additional learning aids are a running glossary positioned on the page where new terminology is first introduced and, when necessary, a pronunciation guide for difficult-to-pronounce drug names and terms. At the end of each chapter, a summary allows an easy review of the chapter's main points. An alphabetized list of key terms previously presented in the running glossary is

An Invitation to Readers

I welcome your reactions to *Drugs, Society, and Criminal Justice*, Second Edition. Please send any comments or questions to the following address: Dr. Charles F. Levinthal, Department of Psychology, Hofstra University, Hempstead, NY 11549. You can also fax them to me at (516) 463-6052 or e-mail them to me at PSYCFL@hofstra.edu. I hope to be hearing from you.

Acknowledgments

In the course of writing this book, I have received much encouragement, assistance, and expert advice from a number of people. I have benefited from their sharing of materials, knowledge, and insights. In particular, I acknowledge the contributions of Dr. Brent Paterline, Associate Professor of Criminal Justice at North Georgia College & State University, who provided a valuable reorganization of chapters from my earlier book, *Drugs, Behavior, and Modern Society*, Fourth Edition, new material in Chapter 2, as well as original drafts of Chapters 3, 13, and 14. Rusty Payne of the Office of Public Affairs, Drug Enforcement Administration, U.S. Department of Justice, Washington DC, provided updated statistical information that greatly enhanced Chapters 13 and 14. I am particularly appreciative of the assistance and guidance of the Honorable Sol Wachtler, Chief Judge, New York State Court of Appeals (ret.) and the Honorable Judy Harris Kluger, Deputy Chief Administrative Judge, New York, for material in Chapter 14. Frank Jordan and Bruna DiBiase of the New York State Office of Court Administration, and David Heslin and David Kelly of the Kings County (Brooklyn) N.Y. District Attorney's Office were immensely helpful in providing updated material on drug courts and other problem-solving court programs. Elizabeth Crane of the Substance Abuse and Mental Health Services Administration, U.S. Department of Health and Human Services, Washington DC, provided expanded statistical data from the Drug Abuse Warning Network program.

I am quite fortunate to have worked with a superb team at Allyn and Bacon. I am especially indebted to my editor, Dave Repetto, and my production supervisor, Beth Houston. Their professionalism and friendship are appreciated. I also want to acknowledge the efforts of project editor and copyeditor Andrea Cava, photo researcher Poyee Oster, and proofreader Debbie Prato, who have contributed so much to the editorial production aspects of this book.

A number of manuscript reviewers, whose identities had been kept secret from me up to now, made invaluable suggestions as I worked on the revision of this book. Now I know their names, and I thank each of them for their help: James A. Gazell, San Diego State University; Frank E. Norton, Bowie State University; and Brian C. Renaver, Portland State University.

As always, my family has been a continuing source of strength and encouragement. I will always be grateful to my wife, Beth, and our wonderful sons, David and Brian, for their love and understanding.

Charles F. Levinthal

chapter 1

An Introduction to Drug Use and Abuse

Mike was seventeen, a high school junior—an age when life can be both terrific and terrifying. He looked at me with amazement, telling me by his expression that either the question I was asking him was ridiculous or the answer was obvious. "Why do kids do drugs?" I had asked.

"It's cool," he said. "That's why. Believe me, it's important to be cool. Besides, in my life, drugs just make me feel better. Smoking a little weed, mellowing out with some Perks or a little Vicodin, spinning with some Addies—it's a way of getting away from 'stuff.' And you know that everybody does it. At least all of my friends do it. It's easy to get them. All you need to know is where to go."

The meeting was over. But as he started to leave, Mike seemed to notice the concern on my face. "Don't worry about me," he said. "I can handle it. I can handle it just fine."

After you have completed this chapter, you will understand

- Basic terminology concerning drugs and drug-taking behavior
- The ways drugs enter and exit the body
- Factors determining the physiological impact of drugs
- The distinction between physical and psychological dependence
- The DAWN statistics as a measure of drug toxicity
- Club drugs and dietary supplements, as well as prescription and over-the-counter (OTC) drug abuse

Today, more than ever, drugs affect our daily lives. It is difficult to pick up a newspaper or watch television without finding a report or program that concerns drug use or some issue associated with it. We are continually bombarded with news about drug-related arrests of major drug dealers and ordinary citizens, as well as news about drugs intercepted and confiscated at our borders and in the towns and cities of America.

More important, in your personal life, you have had to confront the reality of drugs in your community. In school, you have been taught the risks involved in drug use, and very likely you have had to contend with social pressure to share a drug experience with your friends or the possibility of drugs being sold to you. According to a recent national survey, about one in five males and about one in eight females in the United States between the ages of twelve and seventeen have been approached in the past month by someone selling drugs. To some of you, these official statistics might appear to be underestimates.

It is not uncommon for high school students on a Monday morning to boast about how drunk they got over the weekend. For some, regular consumption of alcohol begins in junior high school or earlier, in a nation where twenty-one is the minimum legal age for obtaining alcoholic beverages. Binge drinking continues to be a significant problem on college campuses nationwide. Experimentation and, in some cases, regular use of stimulants, marijuana, inhalants from common household products, performance-enhancing agents to build muscle mass, and mind-altering substances of all sorts seem commonplace.

Cigarette smoking among young people continues to be a major societal problem, even though it is illegal for those younger than eighteen years old to purchase tobacco products. The public health concern about underage cigarette smoking centers on the fact that an estimated 80 percent of all adults in the United States who presently smoke on a regular basis started by the age of eighteen.

Whether we like it or not, the decision to use drugs of all types and forms, legally sanctioned or not, has become one of life's choices in American society and in communities around the world.

Social Messages about Drug Use

Unfortunately, we live in a social environment that sends mixed messages with respect to drug use. The appearance of Joe Camel, the Marlboro Man, and the Virginia Slims Woman in print advertisements for cigarettes may be increasingly distant memories, but at one time they were dominant images that conveyed the attractiveness of smoking to the public, particularly to young people. They are gone now as a result of federal regulations established in 1998. For decades, warning labels on cigarette packs and public-service announcements have cautioned us about the serious health hazards of tobacco use. Yet cigarette smoking remains glamorized in movies when we see popular actors and actresses smoking as part of their roles. Beer commercials during telecasts of football games and other athletic events are designed to be entertaining and to associate beer drinking with a desirable lifestyle of friendship, sex, and romance, but we are expected to "know when to say when."

Prominent political figures, including a former U.S. president (Bill Clinton) and a former U.S. vice-president (Al Gore), as well as a host of public officials on a local or national level, have admitted their experiences with marijuana earlier in their lives. Yet the position of the U.S. government on marijuana is that it is an illegal substance, officially classified since 1970 as a drug with a high potential for abuse and no accepted medical use, in the same category as heroin. Experiences with alcohol abuse and alcoholism abound, even as we hear reports that moderate alcohol drinking actually may be beneficial to our health. Anti-drug campaigns in the media are created to discourage young people from becoming involved with drugs. At the same time, we observe a continuing stream of sport figures, entertainers, and other high-profile individuals engaging in drug-taking behavior. Even though careers are frequently jeopardized and, in some instances, lives are lost as a result, powerful pro-drug-use messages continue to influence us. These messages come from the entertainment industry and Internet sources.[1]

An accused drug user is led away by an agent in a DEA windbreaker on a residential street in Billings, Montana, far away from the urban communities usually associated with drug use.

These facts, as confusing and often contradictory as some of them are, represent the present-day drug scene. The purpose of this book is to answer your questions and address your concerns about drugs and behavior in our society. In the chapters that follow, two general themes related to drugs will become clear. The first theme is that the diversity in the types of available drugs is immense. A quick glance at the contents of this book will show you the wide range of substances that will be covered. Some of you might have expected to see only the "classic" street drugs: cocaine, heroin, LSD, and marijuana. The coverage of others may be surprising: inhalants in common household products, anabolic steroids, prescription pain medication, and nicotine. You will see two chapters on the subject of alcohol, by far the most pervasive drug abuse problem in our society. As you will discover, communities in this country and around the world have had as many problems contending with legal drugs as with illegal ones.

The second theme is that drug use needs to be considered not merely as a "young people's issue" but rather as one that encompasses every segment of our society. The availability of drugs and the potential for drug abuse present a challenge for people of all ages, from the young to the elderly. The effects are being felt in the workplace and retirement communities as well as on street corners, in school yards, and on college campuses. The personal and social problems associated with drugs extend in one way or another to men and women of all ethnic and racial groups, geographic regions, and socioeconomic levels. No group should believe themselves exempt from this scourge.[2]

In the chapters that follow, we will explore the issues of legal and illegal drugs in the United States from a number of perspectives. As we will see, understanding the biological and psychological foundations of drug use is immensely important. We need to know how drugs are administered into the body, how they are eliminated from the body, as well as their specific effects on the brain. Equally important, however, is an understanding of the social history of drug use. We need to know the reasons why drug-taking behavior has been so pervasive a phenomenon over the many centuries of human history and the reasons why drug-taking behavior remains so compelling for us in our society today. Finally, we need to know the ways in which our society has responded to problems associated with drug use. A particular focus will be on the development of a criminal justice system in the United States that has been designed to reduce the negative impact of drugs on personal and community levels (see Chapters 13 and 14).

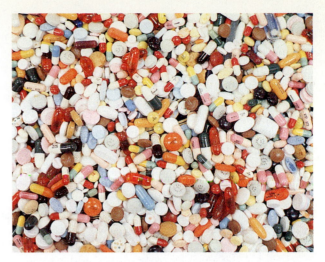

The problems associated with drug abuse and misuse in our society extend beyond the use of illegal drugs. We also need to be concerned with the abuse and misuse of legally available substances such as alcohol and nicotine, as well as prescription and over-the-counter medications.

Looking at Drugs and Society

There are two basic ways in which we can look at the subject of drugs and society. First, we can examine the psychological and sociological effects of consuming certain types of drugs. The focus is on the study of specific substances that alter our feelings, our thoughts, our perceptions of the world, and our behavior. These substances are referred to as **psychoactive drugs** because they influence the functioning of the brain and hence our behavior and experience. Examples that often receive the greatest amount of attention are officially defined in the United States as **illicit** (illegal) **drugs**: heroin, cocaine, and marijuana, as well as club drugs such as Ecstasy, LSD, PCP, ketamine, and GHB. Other equally important psychoactive substances, however, are **licit** (legal) **drugs,** such as alcohol, nicotine, and caffeine. In the cases of alcohol and nicotine, legal access carries a minimum-age requirement.

Second, we can focus on the social circumstances that lead to drug-taking behavior. We will examine the

psychoactive drugs: Drugs that affect feelings, thoughts, perceptions, or behavior.

illicit drugs: Drugs whose manufacture, sale, or possession is illegal.

licit drugs: Drugs whose manufacture, sale, or possession is legal.

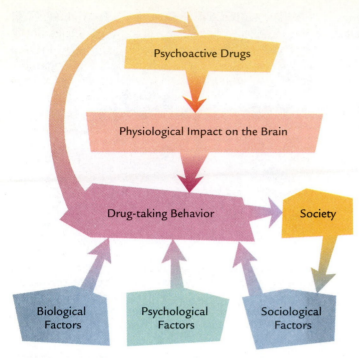

FIGURE 1.1

Understanding the interplay of drug-taking behavior and society.

possibility that drug use is, at least in part, a consequence of how we feel about ourselves in relationship to our parents, to our friends and acquaintances, to events occurring around us, and to the community in which we live. An exploration into the reasons why some individuals engage in drug-taking behavior, while others do not, will be a primary topic in Chapters 2 and 3.

Understanding the interplay between drug-taking behavior and society (Figure 1.1) is essential when we consider the dangerous potential for drug use to become **drug dependence.** As many of us know all too well, a vicious circle can develop in which drug-taking behavior fosters more drug-taking behavior in a spiraling pattern that is often extremely difficult to break. Individuals showing signs of drug dependence display intense cravings for the drug and, in many cases, require

drug dependence: A condition in which an individual feels a compulsive need to continue taking a drug. In the process, the drug assumes an increasingly central role in the individual's life.

drug: A chemical substance that, when taken into the body, alters the structure or functioning of the body in some way, excluding those nutrients considered to be related to normal functioning.

increasingly greater quantities to get the same, desired effect. They become preoccupied with their drug-taking behavior and eventually feel that their lives have gotten out of control.

Current research on drug dependence points to the need for us to examine the issue on both a biological level and a sociological level. First, the use of psychoactive drugs modifies the functioning of the brain, both at the time during which the drug is present in the body and later when the drug-taking behavior stops. Drug dependence, therefore, produces long-lasting brain changes. As one expert has put it, a "switch" in the brain seems to be thrown following prolonged drug use. It starts as a voluntary behavior, but once that switch is thrown, a pattern of drug dependence takes over. Second, drug dependence is a result of a complex interaction of the individual and his or her environment. We cannot fully understand the problem of drug dependence without being aware of the social context in which drug-taking behavior occurs. As you will see in Chapter 15, the recognition that drug dependence can be defined in terms of biological and social components has important implications for treatment.[3]

Which drugs have the greatest potential for creating drug dependence? How can someone escape drug dependence once it is established? What factors increase or decrease the likelihood of drug-taking behavior in the first place? What is the relationship between drug-taking behavior and crime? What impact have social policies and our system of criminal justice had on drug-taking behavior? These are some of the important questions to be considered as we examine the impact of drugs and drug-taking behavior on our lives.

A Matter of Definition

Considering the ease with which we speak of drugs and drug use, it seems as if it should be relatively easy to define what we mean by the word **drug.** Unfortunately, there are significant problems in arriving at a clear definition. The standard approach is to characterize a drug as *a chemical substance that, when taken into the body, alters the structure or functioning of the body in some way.* In doing so, we are accounting for examples such as medications used for the treatment of physical disorders and mental illnesses, as well as for alcohol, nicotine, and the typical street drugs. Unfortunately, this broad definition also could refer to ordinary food and water. Because it does not make much sense for nutrients to be considered drugs, we need to refine our definition, adding the phrase, *excluding those nutrients considered to be related to normal functioning.*

Bear in mind, however, that we may still be on slippery ground. We can now effectively eliminate the cheese in your next pizza from consideration as a drug, but what about some exotic ingredient in the sauce? Sugar is safely excluded, even though it has significant energizing and therefore behavioral effects on us, but what about the cayenne pepper that burns your tongue? Where do we draw the line between a drug and a nondrug? It is not an easy question to answer.

We can learn two major lessons from this seemingly simple task of defining a drug. First, there is probably no perfect definition that would distinguish drugs from nondrugs without leaving a number of cases that fall within some kind of gray area. The best we can do is to set up a definition, as we have, that handles most of the substances we are likely to encounter.

The second lesson is more subtle. We often make the distinction between drugs and nondrugs not in terms of their physical characteristics but rather in terms of whether the substance in question has been *intended to be used primarily as a way of inducing a bodily or psychological change.*[4] By this reasoning, if the pizza maker intended to put that spice in the pizza to make it taste better, the spice would not be considered a drug; it would simply be another ingredient in the recipe. If the pizza maker intended the spice to intoxicate you or quicken your heart rate, then it might be considered a drug (Drugs...in Focus).

Ultimately, the problem is that we are trying to reach a consensus on a definition that fits our intuitive sense of what constitutes a drug. We may find it difficult to define pornography, but (as has been said) we know it when we see it. So it may be with drugs. Whether we realize it or not, when we discuss the topic of drugs, we are operating within a context of social and cultural values, a group of

Drugs . . . in Focus

Defining Drugs: Olive Oil and Curry Powder?

An ever-increasing number of reminders about the blurriness of the distinction between drugs and nondrugs come from recent research on the chemical properties of specific foods we eat on a daily basis. For example, in 2005 it was found that freshly pressed olive oil contains large amounts of oleocanthal, a compound that inhibits the activity of cyclooxygenase enzymes in the identical manner as ibuprofen, a popular nonsteroid anti-inflammatory medication. Essentially, olive oil reduces inflammation in the body in a drug-like manner. By this definition, olive oil could be classified as a drug.

The discovery provides a biochemical clue toward understanding the well-documented but puzzling health benefits of a Mediterranean (olive-oil-based) diet, which leads to a lower risk of cancer, heart disease, and other chronic disorders, despite its heavy emphasis on fat and salt.

Another example is the understanding we have of the biologically active compounds in turmeric, a common ingredient in most commercial curry powders as well as the basis for the bright yellow color in many yellow mustards. The active ingredient of turmeric, called curcumin, has been credited with several medicinal benefits. Curcumin

apparently has antioxidant, anti-inflammatory, antiviral, antibacterial, and antifungal properties with potential benefits in the treatment of cancer, diabetes, arthritis, Alzheimer's disease, and other chronic disorders. In 2005 alone, nearly 300 technical and scientific papers referenced the drug-like activity of curcumin, three times the number reported in 2000. If the regulatory hurdles established by the U.S. Food and Drug Administration with respect to long-term safety can be overcome, curcumin could provide an inexpensive alternative approach to several mainstream pharmaceuticals currently available as prescription drugs.

As we continue to learn more about the therapeutic effects of common foods and spices on the body, the customary exclusion of nutrients in a definition of drugs becomes increasingly problematic. In the future, we might be hearing someone say that they are taking olive oil or curry powder for "medicinal reasons."

Source: Beauchamp, Gary K; Keast, Russell S. J.; More, Diane; Lin, Jianming; Pika, Jana; Han, Qiang; Lee, Chi-Ho; Smith, Amos B.; and Breslin, Paul A. S. (2005). Phytochemistry: Ibuprofen-like activity in extra-virgin olive oil. *Nature, 437,* 45–46. Stix, Gary (2007, February). Spice healer. *Scientific American,* pp. 66–69.

shared feelings about what kind of behavior (that is, what kind of drug-taking behavior) is right and what kind is wrong. As we will see in Chapter 2, these values have manifested themselves over the years in social legislation and a criminal justice system for the purpose of regulating the use of specific drugs and specific forms of drug-taking behavior.

The judgments we make about drug-taking behavior even influence the terminology we use when referring to that behavior. When we speak of "drug misuse" and "drug abuse," for example, we are implying that something wrong is happening, that a drug is producing some harm to the physical health or psychological well-being of the drug user or to society in general.

But what criteria do we use to decide whether a drug is being misused or abused? We cannot judge on the basis of whether the drug is legal or illegal, since the legality of a psychoactive drug may depend more on historical and cultural circumstances than on its chemical properties. Tobacco, for example, has deeply rooted associations in American history, dating to the earliest colonial days. Although it is objectionable to many individuals and harmful to the health of the smoker and others, tobacco is nonetheless legally available to adults. Alcohol is another substance that is legal, within the bounds of the law, even though it can be harmful to individuals who become inebriated and potentially harmful to others who may be affected by the drinker's behavior.

Instrumental and Recreational Use of Drugs

Given the differences in attitudes toward specific drugs across cultures and societies, it is useful to look closely at the relationship between drugs and behavior in terms of the intent or motivation on the part of the user. Depending on the intent of the individual, drug use can be categorized as either instrumental or recreational.[5]

By **instrumental use,** we mean that a person is taking a drug with a specific socially approved goal in mind. The user may want to stay awake longer, fall asleep more

> **instrumental use:** Referring to the motivation of a drug user who takes a drug for a specific purpose other than getting "high."
>
> **recreational use:** Referring to the motivation of a drug user who takes a drug only to get "high" or achieve some pleasurable effect.
>
> **drug misuse:** Drug-taking behavior in which a prescription or nonprescription drug is used inappropriately.

quickly, or recover from an illness. If you are a medical professional on call over a long period of time, taking a drug with the goal of staying alert is considered acceptable by most people. Recovery from an illness and achieving some reduction in pain are goals that are unquestioned. In these cases, drug-taking behavior occurs as a means toward an end that has been defined by our society as legitimate.

The legal status of the drug itself is not the issue here. The instrumental use of drugs can involve prescription and nonprescription (over-the-counter) drugs that are licitly obtained and taken for a particular medical purpose. Examples include an antidepressant prescribed for depression, a cold remedy for a cold, an anticonvulsant drug to control epileptic seizures, or insulin to maintain the health of a person with diabetes. The instrumental use of drugs also can involve drugs that are illicitly obtained, such as an amphetamine that has been procured through illegal means to help a person stay awake and alert after hours without sleep.

In contrast, **recreational use** means that a person is taking the drug not as a means to a socially approved goal but for the purposes of acquiring the effect of the drug itself. The motivation is to enjoy a pleasurable feeling or positive state of mind. Whatever happens as a consequence of the drug-taking behavior is viewed not as a means to an end but as an end unto itself. Drinking alcohol and smoking tobacco are two examples of licit recreational drug-taking behavior. Involvement with street drugs, in the sense that one's goal is to alter one's mood or state of consciousness, falls into the category of illicit recreational drug-taking behavior (Figure 1.2).

Although this four-group classification scheme is helpful in understanding the complex relationship between drugs and behavior, there will be instances in which the category might be debated. Drinking an alcoholic beverage, for example, is considered as recreational drug-taking behavior under most circumstances. If it is recommended by a physician for a specified therapeutic or preventative purpose (see Chapter 10), however, the drinking might be considered instrumental in nature. You can see that whether drug use is judged to be recreational or instrumental is determined in no small part by the attitudes of the society in which the behavior takes place. As mentioned earlier, these attitudes have a direct influence on drug-regulation laws that are enacted.

Misuse and Abuse of Drugs

How do misuse and abuse fit into this scheme? **Drug misuse** typically applies to cases in which a prescription or nonprescription drug is used inappropriately. Many

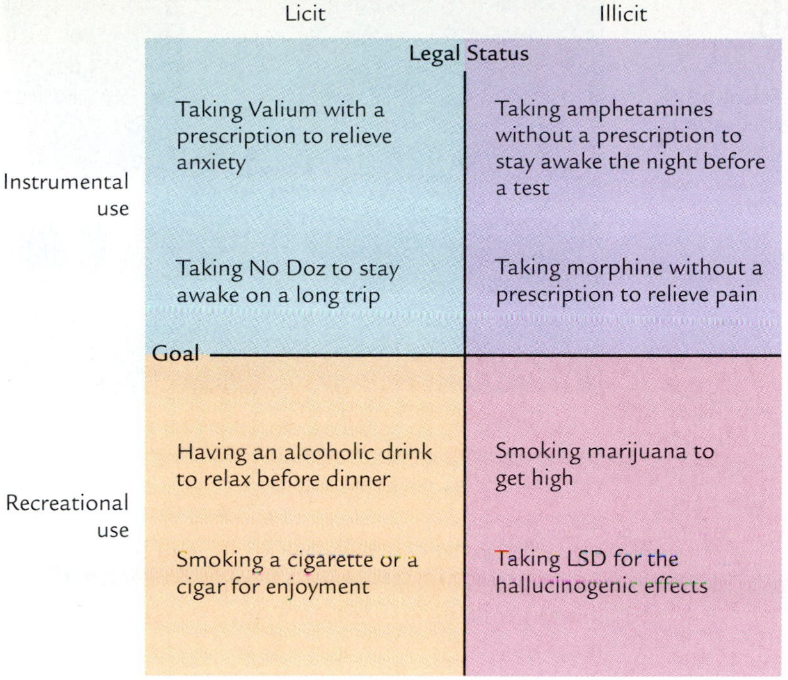

Figure 1.2

	Licit	Illicit
Instrumental use	Taking Valium with a prescription to relieve anxiety	Taking amphetamines without a prescription to stay awake the night before a test
	Taking No Doz to stay awake on a long trip	Taking morphine without a prescription to relieve pain
Recreational use	Having an alcoholic drink to relax before dinner	Smoking marijuana to get high
	Smoking a cigarette or a cigar for enjoyment	Taking LSD for the hallucinogenic effects

Legal Status (top); *Goal* (left)

FIGURE 1.2

Four categories of drug-taking behavior, derived from combinations of the user's goal and the drug's legal status.

Source: Expanded from Goode, Erich (2005). *Drugs in American Society* (6th ed.). New York: McGraw-Hill, p. 16.

instances of drug misuse involve instrumental goals. For example, drug doses may be increased beyond the level of the prescription in the mistaken idea that if a little is good, more is even better. Or doses may be decreased from the level of the prescription to make the drug supply last longer. Drugs may be continued past the time during which they were originally needed; they may be combined with some other drug; or a prescription drug might be shared by family members or lent to a friend even though the medical conditions may differ among them.

Drug misuse can be dangerous and potentially lethal, particularly when alcohol is combined with drugs that depress the nervous system. Drugs that have this particular feature include antihistamines, antianxiety drugs, and sleeping medications. Even if alcohol is not involved, however, drug combinations can still represent serious health risks, particularly for the elderly, who often take a large number of separate medications. This population is especially vulnerable to the hazards of drug misuse.

In contrast, **drug abuse** is typically applied to cases in which a licit or illicit drug is used in ways that produce some form of physical, mental, or social impairment. The primary motivation for individuals involved in drug abuse is recreational. *We should remember that drugs with abuse potential include not only the common street drugs but also legally available psychoactive substances such as caffeine and nicotine (stimulants), alcohol and inhaled solvents (depressants), as well as a number of prescription drugs designated for medical purposes but used by some individuals exclusively on a recreational basis.* In Chapter 5 we will examine recent concerns about the abuse of pain medications, known as narcotic analgesics, that contain synthetic opiates or opiate derivatives and are marketed under such brand names as Vicodin, OxyContin, Percodan, Demerol, and Darvon. In these particular cases, the distinction between drug misuse and drug abuse is particularly blurry. When there is no intent to make a value judgment as to the motivation or consequences of a particular type of drug-taking behavior, that behavior will simply be referred to, in the chapters that follow, as drug use.

Inevitably, decisions over whether a particular form of drug-taking behavior is categorized as drug use, abuse, or misuse take into account the potentially harmful physiological effects of the drug in question, as well as its potentially harmful psychological effects. It is important, therefore, to begin with an examination of the ways in which drugs have an effect on the body. What is the impact of the manner in which a drug is administered? What is the impact of timing factors on the overall effect of a drug? How do we measure its potential harmfulness? These are some of the questions we will now address.

drug abuse: Drug-taking behavior resulting in some form of physical, mental, or social impairment.

How Drugs Enter the Body

Some of you might have heard of the classic public-service announcement, which aired frequently on television in the late 1980s:

This is your brain (view of egg held in hand).

This is drugs (view of sizzling frying pan).

This is your brain on drugs (view of egg frying in pan).

Any questions?[6]

Giving the viewer considerable "food for thought," its impact was immediate: Don't do drugs because they fry your brain. The creators of this message were speaking metaphorically, of course. In effect, they were saying that there are certain classes of drugs that have a devastating impact on the human brain. Therefore, stay away from them.

Clearly, psychoactive drugs affect our behavior and experience through their effects on the functioning of the brain. Therefore, our knowledge about drugs and their effects is closely connected with the progress we have made in our understanding of the ways drugs work in the brain. A reasonable place to start is to answer the question: How do drugs get into the body in the first place?

There are four principal routes through which drugs can be delivered into the body: *oral administration, injection, inhalation,* and *absorption through the skin or membranes.* In all four delivery methods, the goal is for the drug to be absorbed into the bloodstream. In the case of psychoactive drugs, a drug effect depends not only on reaching the bloodstream but also on reaching the brain.

Oral Administration

Ingesting a drug by mouth, digesting it, and absorbing it into the bloodstream through the gastrointestinal tract is the oldest and easiest way of taking a drug. On the one hand, oral administration and reliance upon the digestive process for delivering a drug into the bloodstream provide a degree of safety. Many naturally growing poisons taste so vile that we normally spit them out before swallowing; others will cause us to be nauseous, and the drug will be expelled through vomiting.

In the case of hazardous substances that are not spontaneously rejected, we can benefit from a relatively long absorption time for orally administered drugs. Most of the absorption process is accomplished between five and thirty minutes after ingestion, but absorption is not

Orally consumed drugs are absorbed into the brain relatively slowly, though for a liquid beverage containing alcohol, the opposite applies: It is easily absorbed.

usually complete for as long as six to eight hours. Therefore, there is at least a little time after accidental overdoses or suicide attempts to induce vomiting or pump the stomach.

On the other hand, the gastrointestinal tract contains a number of natural barriers that may prevent certain drugs that we *want* absorbed into the bloodstream from doing so. We first have to consider the degree of alkalinity or acidity in a drug, defined as its pH value. The interior of the stomach is highly acidic, and the fate of a particular drug depends upon how it reacts with that environment. Weakly acidic drugs such as aspirin are absorbed better in the stomach than highly alkaline drugs such as morphine, heroin, or cocaine. Insulin is destroyed by stomach acid, so it cannot be administered orally, whereas a neutral substance such as alcohol is readily absorbed at all points in the gastrointestinal tract.

If it survives the stomach, the drug needs to proceed from the small intestine into the bloodstream. The membrane separating the intestinal wall from blood capillaries is made up of two layers of fat molecules, making it necessary for substances to be *lipid-soluble,* or soluble in fats, to pass through. Even after successful absorption into blood capillaries, however, substances still must pass through the liver for another "screening" before being released into the general circulation. There are enzymes in the liver that destroy a drug by metabolizing (breaking down) its molecular structure prior to its excretion from the body. There is a further barrier separating the circulatory system from brain tissue, called the *blood-brain barrier,* which determines a drug's psychoactive effects.

As a result of all these natural barriers, orally administered drugs must be ingested at deliberately elevated dose levels to allow for the fact that some proportion of the drug will not make it through to the bloodstream. We can try to compensate for the loss of the drug during digestion, but even then we may be only making a good guess. The state of the gastrointestinal tract changes constantly over time, making it more or less likely that a drug will reach the circulatory system. The presence or absence of undigested food and whether the undigested food interacts with the chemical nature of the drug are examples of factors that make it difficult to make exact predictions about the strength of the drug when it finally enters the bloodstream.

Injection

A solution to the problems of oral administration is to bypass the digestive process entirely and deliver the drug more directly into the bloodstream. One option is to inject the drug through a hypodermic syringe and needle.

The fastest means of injection is an **intravenous** (i.v.) injection, since the drug is delivered into a vein without any intermediary tissue. An intravenous injection of heroin in the forearm, for example, arrives at the brain in less than fifteen seconds. The effects of abused drugs delivered in this way, often called *mainlining*, are not only rapid but extremely intense. In a medical setting, intravenous injections provide an extreme amount of control over dosage and the opportunity to administer multiple drugs at the same time. The principal disadvantage, however, is that the effects of intravenous drugs are irreversible. In the event of a mistake or unexpected reaction, there is no turning back unless some other drug is available that can counteract the first one. In addition, repeated injections through a particular vein may cause the vein to collapse or develop a blood clot.

With **intramuscular** (i.m.) injections, the drug is delivered into a large muscle (usually in the upper arm, thigh, or buttock) and is absorbed into the bloodstream through the capillaries serving the muscle. Intramuscular injections have slower absorption times than intravenous injections, but they can be administered more rapidly in emergency situations. Our exposure to intramuscular injections comes early in our lives when we receive the standard schedule of inoculations against diseases such as measles, diphtheria, and typhoid fever. Tetanus and flu shots are also administered in this way.

A third injection technique is the **subcutaneous** (s.c. or sub-Q) delivery, in which a needle is inserted into the tissue just underneath the skin. Because the skin has a less abundant blood supply relative to a muscle, a subcutaneous injection has the slowest absorption time of all the injection techniques. It is best suited for situations in which it is desirable to have a precise control over the dosage and a steady absorption into the bloodstream. The skin, however, may be easily irritated by this procedure. As a result, only relatively small amounts of a drug can be injected under the skin compared with the quantity that can be injected into a muscle or vein. When involved in drug abuse, subcutaneous injections are often referred to as *skin-popping*.

All injections require a needle to pierce the skin, so there is an inherent risk of bacterial or viral infection if the needle is not sterile. The practice of injecting heroin or cocaine with shared needles, for example, promotes the spread of infectious hepatitis and AIDS. If administered orally, drugs do not have to be any more sterile than the foods we eat or the water we drink.

Inhalation

Next to ingesting a drug by mouth, the simplest way of receiving its effects is to inhale it in some form of gaseous or vaporous state. The alveoli within the lungs can be imagined as a huge surface area with blood vessels lying immediately behind it. Our bodies are so dependent upon the oxygen in the air we breathe that we have evolved an extremely efficient system for getting oxygen to its destinations. As a consequence of this highly developed system, the psychoactive effect of an inhaled drug is even faster than a drug delivered through intravenous injection. Traveling from the lungs to the brain takes only five to eight seconds.

One way of delivering a drug through inhalation is to burn it and breathe in the smoke-borne particles in the air. Drugs administered through smoking include nicotine from cigarettes, opium, tetrahydrocannabinol (THC) from marijuana, free-base cocaine, crack cocaine, and crystallized forms of methamphetamine. Drugs such as paint thinners, gasoline, and glues also can be inhaled because they evaporate easily and the vapors travel freely through the air. In medical settings, general anesthetics are administered through inhalation, since the concentration of the drug can be precisely controlled.

The principal disadvantage of inhaling smoked drugs, as you probably expect, arises from the long-term hazards of breathing particles in the air that contain not only the active drug but also tars and other substances produced by the burning process. Emphysema, asthma,

intravenous (i.v.): Into a vein.
intramuscular (i.m.): Into a muscle.
subcutaneous (s.c. or sub-Q): Underneath the skin.

Drugs . . . in Focus

Ways to Take Drugs: Routes of Administration

Oral Administration (by Mouth)

- Method: By swallowing or consuming in eating or drinking
- Advantages: Slow absorption time; possibility of rejecting poisons and overdoses
- Disadvantages: Slow absorption time; no immediate effect
- Examples: Medications in pill form, marijuana (baked in food), amphetamine and methamphetamine, barbiturates, LSD (swallowed or licked off paper), PCP, opium, methadone, codeine, caffeine, alcohol

Injection (by Hypodermic Syringe)

Intravenous Injection

- Method: By needle positioned into a vein
- Advantages: Very fast absorption time; immediate effects
- Disadvantages: Cannot be undone; risks of allergic reactions
- Examples: PCP, methamphetamine, heroin, methadone, morphine

Intramuscular Injection

- Method: By needle positioned into a large muscle
- Advantages: Quicker to administer than an intravenous injection
- Disadvantages: Somewhat slower absorption time than an intravenous injection; risk of piercing a vein by accident
- Examples: Vaccine inoculations

Subcutaneous Injection

- Method: By needle positioned underneath the skin
- Advantages: Easiest administration of all injection techniques

- Disadvantages: Slower absorption time than an intramuscular injection; risk of skin irritation and deterioration
- Examples: Heroin and other narcotics

Inhalation (by Breathing)

Smoking

- Method: By burning drug and breathing smoke-borne particles into the lungs
- Advantages: Extremely fast absorption time
- Disadvantages: Effect limited to time during which drug is being inhaled; risk of emphysema, asthma, and lung cancer from inhaling tars and hydrocarbons in the smoke; lung and throat irritation over chronic use
- Examples: Nicotine (from tobacco), marijuana, hashish, methamphetamine, ice, free-base cocaine, crack cocaine, PCP, heroin, and opium

Vaporous Inhalation

- Method: By breathing in vapors from drug
- Advantages: Extremely fast absorption time
- Disadvantages: Effect limited to time during which drug is being inhaled; lung and throat irritation over chronic use
- Examples: Surgical and dental anesthetics, paint thinners, gasoline, cleaning fluid

Absorption (through Skin or Membranes)

- Method: By positioning drug against skin, inserting it against rectal membrane, snorting it against mucous membranes of the nose, or placing it under the tongue or against the cheek so it diffuses across into bloodstream
- Advantages: Quick absorption time
- Disadvantages: Irritation of skin or membranes
- Examples: Cocaine, amphetamine, methamphetamine, nicotine, snuff tobacco, coca leaves

Drugs consumed by inhalation are absorbed extremely quickly, aided by a very efficient delivery system from lungs to brain.

and lung cancer can result from smoking in general (see Chapter 12). There is also the possibility in any form of drug inhalation that the linings leading from the throat to the lungs will be severely irritated over time.

Absorption through the Skin or Membranes

Drug users over the ages have been quite creative in finding other routes through which drugs can be administered. One way is to sniff or snort a drug in dust or powder form into the nose. Once inside the nose, it adheres to thin mucous membranes and dissolves through the membranes into the bloodstream. This technique, referred to as an **intranasal** administration, is commonly used in taking snuff tobacco or cocaine. Prescription medications are becoming increasingly available in nasal-spray formulations, avoiding the need for needle injections or difficult-to-swallow pills.

Snuff tobacco, chewing tobacco, and cocaine-containing coca leaves also can be chewed without swallowing over a period of time or simply placed in the inner surface of the cheek and slowly absorbed through the membranes of the mouth. Nicotine chewing gums, available for those individuals who wish to quit tobacco smoking, work in a similar way. Nitroglycerin tablets for heart disease patients are typically administered **sublingually**, with the drug placed underneath the tongue and absorbed into the bloodstream.

At the opposite end of the body, medicines can be placed as a suppository into the rectum, where the suppository gradually melts, and the medicine is absorbed through thin rectal membranes. This method is less reliable than an oral administration, but it may be necessary if the individual is vomiting or unconscious.

Another absorption technique involves a **transdermal patch,** which allows a drug to slowly diffuse through the skin without breaking the skin surface. Transdermal patches have been used for long-term administration of nitroglycerin, estrogen, motion-sickness medication, and more recently, nicotine. Newly developed procedures to enhance the process of skin penetration include the promising technique of administering low-frequency ultrasound, which allows large molecules such as insulin to pass through the skin. Insulin administration is an especially interesting application because, until now, the only effective way of getting it into the bloodstream has been through needle injection. Alternative methods under development include small silicon chip patches containing a grid of microscopic needles that painlessly pierce the skin and allow the passage of large molecules into the bloodstream. Other techniques involve a mild electric current that propels the medication through the skin or the application of medication with special compounds that help the medication slip through skin pores.[7]

Drugs...in Focus summarizes the various ways drugs can be administered into the body.

How Drugs Exit the Body

Having reviewed how a drug is absorbed into the bloodstream and, in the case of a psychoactive drug, into the brain, we now will consider the ways in which the body eliminates it. The most common means of elimination is through excretion in the urine after a series of actions in the liver and kidneys. Additionally, elimination occurs through excretion in exhaled breath, feces, sweat, saliva, or (in the case of nursing mothers) breast milk.

---

intranasal: Applied to the mucous membranes of the nose.

sublingual: Applied under the tongue.

transdermal patch: A device attached to the skin that slowly delivers the drug through skin absorption.

The sequence of metabolic events leading to urinary excretion begins with a process called **biotransformation,** chiefly through the action of specific enzymes in the liver. The products of biotransformation, referred to as **metabolites,** are structurally modified forms of the original drug. Generally speaking, if these metabolites are water-soluble, they are passed along to the kidneys and eventually excreted in the urine. If they are less water-soluble, then they are reabsorbed into the intestines and excreted through defecation. On rare occasions, a drug may pass through the liver without any biotransformation at all and be excreted intact. The hallucinogenic drug *Amanita muscaria* is an example of this kind of drug (see Chapter 6).

A number of factors influence the process of biotransformation and urinary excretion and, in turn, the rate of elimination from the body. For most drugs, biotransformation rates will increase as a function of the drug's concentration in the bloodstream. In effect, the larger the quantity of a drug, the faster the body tries to get rid of it. An exception, however, is alcohol, for which the rate of biotransformation is constant no matter how much alcohol has been ingested (see Chapter 10).

The activity of enzymes required for biotransformation may be increased or decreased by the presence of other drugs in the body. As a result, the effect of one drug may interact with the effect of another, creating a potentially dangerous combination. An individual's age also can be a factor. Because enzyme activity in the liver declines after the age of forty, older people eliminate drugs at a slower pace than do younger people. We will look at the consequences of drug interactions and individual differences in the next section of this chapter.

Finally, it is important to point out that drugs are gradually eliminated from the body at different rates simply on the basis of their chemical properties. In general, if a drug is fat-soluble, the rate will be slower than if a drug is water-soluble. On average, we can look at the rate of elimination of a particular drug through an index called its **elimination half-life,** the amount of time it takes for the drug in the bloodstream to decline to 50 percent of its original equilibrium level. Many drugs such as cocaine and nicotine have half-lives of only a few hours; marijuana and some prescription medications are examples of drugs with much longer half-lives.[8] Understanding the variation in the elimination rates of drugs and their metabolites is extremely important in the development of drug-testing procedures to detect drug-taking behavior, a topic to be examined in Chapter 9.

Factors Determining the Physiological Impact of Drugs

The type of delivery route into the bloodstream, as has been discussed, places specific constraints upon the effect a drug may produce. Some drug effects are optimized, for example, by an oral administration, whereas others require more direct access to the bloodstream.

Other factors must be considered as well. If a drug is administered repeatedly, the timing of the administrations plays an important role in determining the final result. If two drugs are administered close together in time, we also must consider how these drugs might interact with each other in terms of their acute effects. Repeated administrations of a drug may produce a diminished physiological or psychological effect.

Finally, it is possible that two identical drugs taken by two individuals might have different effects by virtue of the characteristics of the drug user at the time of administration.

Timing

All drugs, no matter how they are delivered, share some common features when we consider their effects over time. There is initially an interval (the **latency period**) during which the concentration of the drug is increasing in the blood but is not yet high enough for a drug effect to be detected. How long this latency period will last is related generally to the absorption time of the drug. As the concentration of the drug continues to rise, the effect will become stronger. A stage will be reached eventually when the effect attains a maximum strength, even though the concentration in the blood continues to rise. This point is unfortunately the point at which the drug may produce undesirable side effects. One solution to this problem is to administer the drug in a time-release form. In this approach, a large dose is given initially to enable the drug effect to be felt; then smaller doses are

biotransformation: The process of changing the molecular structure of a drug into forms that make it easier to be excreted from the body.

metabolite (me-TAB-oh-lite): A by-product resulting from the biotransformation process.

elimination half-life: The length of time it takes for a drug to be reduced to 50 percent of its equilibrium level in the bloodstream.

latency period: An interval of time during which the blood levels of a drug are not yet sufficient for a drug effect to be observed.

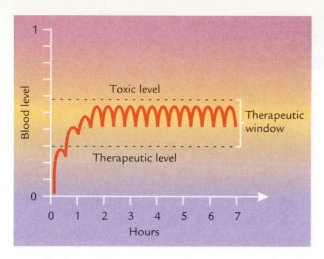

FIGURE 1.3

The therapeutic window. Time-release drugs are formulated to administer the drug in small amounts over time to stay between the therapeutic level and the toxic level.

Drug Interactions

Two basic types of interactions may occur when two drugs are mixed together. In the first type, two drugs in combination may produce an acute effect that is greater than the effect of either drug administered separately. In some cases, the combination effect is purely *additive.* For example, if the effect of one drug alone is equivalent to a 4 and the effect of another drug is a 6, then the combined additive effect is equivalent to a value of 10. In other cases, however, the acute combination effect is *hyperadditive*, with the combined effect exceeding the sum of the individual drugs administered alone, as in the two drugs in the first example combining to a value of 13 or more. Any hyperadditive effect produced by a combination of two or more drugs is referred to as **synergism.** In some synergistic combinations, one drug may even double or triple the effect of another. It is also possible that one drug might have no effect at all unless

programmed to be released at specific intervals afterward to postpone, up to twelve hours or so, the decline in the drug's concentration in the blood. The intention is to keep the concentration of the drug in the blood within a "therapeutic window," high enough for the drug to be effective while low enough to avoid any toxic effects. When drugs are administered repeatedly, there is a risk that the second dose will boost the concentration of the drug in the blood too high before the effect of the first dose has a chance to decline (Figure 1.3).

it is taken simultaneously with another. This special form of synergism is called **potentiation;** it is as though a drug with no effect at all by itself, when combined with a drug having an effect of 6, produces a result equivalent to a 10. The danger of such interactions is that the combined effect of the drugs is so powerful as to become toxic. In extreme cases, the toxicity can be lethal.

synergism (SIN-er-jih-zum): The property of a drug interaction in which the combination effect of two drugs exceeds the effect of either drug administered alone.

potentiation: The property of a synergistic drug interaction in which one drug combined with another drug produces an enhanced effect when one of the drugs alone would have had no effect.

HELP LINE

The Possibility of a Drug–Drug or Food–Drug Combination

It would be impossible to list every known drug–drug interaction or food–drug interaction. Nonetheless, here are some examples. Any adverse reaction to a combination of drugs or a combination of a drug with something eaten should be reported to your physician immediately. An awareness of adverse interactions is particularly important for elderly patients, who tend to be treated with multiple medications. The best advice is to ask your physician whether alcohol, specific foods, or other medications might either increase or decrease the effect of the medication that is being prescribed.

Hyperadditive Effects

Alcohol with barbiturate-related sleep medications, cardiovascular medications, insulin, anti-inflammatory medications, antihistamines, painkillers, antianxiety medications

Septra, Bactrim, or related types of antibiotics with Coumadin (an anticoagulant)

Tagamet (a heartburn and ulcer treatment medication) with Coumadin

Aspirin, Aleve, Advil, Tylenol, or related painkillers with Coumadin

Plendil (a blood pressure medication) and Procardia (an angina treatment), as well as Zocor, Lipitor, and Mevacor (all cholesterol-lowering medications), with grapefruit juice

Lanoxin (a medication for heart problems) with licorice

Lanoxin with bran, oatmeal, or other high-fiber foods

Antagonistic Effects

Morphine/heroin with naloxone or naltrexone

Norpramin or related antidepressants with bran, oatmeal, or other high-fiber foods

Soy products and certain vitamin K–rich vegetables such as broccoli, cabbage, and asparagus with Coumadin

Possible Toxic Reactions

Internal bleeding by a combination of Parnate and Anafranil (two types of antidepressants)

Elevated body temperature by a combination of Nardil (an antidepressant) with Demerol (a painkiller)

Excessive blood pressure or stroke by a combination of Parnate, Nardil, or other monoamine oxidase inhibitors (MAOIs) used to treat depression with cheddar cheese, pickled herring, or other foods high in tyramine

Agitation or elevated body temperature by a combination of Paxil, Prozac, Zoloft, or related antidepressants with Parnate, Nardil, or other monoamine oxidase inhibitors (MAOIs) used to treat depression

Irregular heartbeat, cardiac arrest, and sudden death by a combination of Hismanal or Seldane (two antihistamines) with Nizoral (an antifungal drug)

Note: The hyperadditive effects of grapefruit on certain medications can be dangerous or useful under certain circumstances. If grapefruit enhances the effect of the cholesterol-reducing medication Lipitor, for example, it is possible that drinking grapefruit juice might allow the patient to take less Lipitor (reducing costs and possible side effects) and still receive the same level of benefit. Combinations of this kind, however, should be administered only under the close supervision of one's physician.

Where to go for assistance:

www. medscape/ druginfo/ druginterchecker

Register free and check out any combination of prescription or OTC drugs for potential adverse interactions.

Sources: Graedon, Joe, and Graedon, Teresa (2000, October 16). Say "aaah": The people's pharmacy; drugs and foods can interact adversely. *Los Angeles Times*, p. 2. Graedon, Joe, and Graedon, Teresa (1995). *The people's guide to deadly interactions.* New York: St. Martin's Press. Sørensen, Janina M. (2002). Herb-drug, food–drug, nutrient–drug, and drug–drug interactions: Mechanisms involved and their medical implications. *Journal of Alternative and Complementary Medicine, 8,* 293–308.

In the second type of interaction, two drugs can be *antagonistic* if the acute effect of one drug is diminished to some degree when administered with another, a situation comparable to a drug with the effect of 6 and a drug with the effect of 4 combining to produce an effect of 3.

Later chapters discuss drugs that are totally antagonistic to each other, in that the second exactly cancels out, or neutralizes, the effect of the first. Help Line provides some examples of drug–drug combinations and food–drug combinations that can present significant problems.

Having overdosed on pure heroin, the driver in the car had already died, and the passenger would die soon afterward. The police found a needle injected through the driver's pants leg. The two men had just cashed their paychecks and bought the drugs.

Tolerance Effects

Legend has it that in the first century B.C., King Mithridates VI of Pontus, a region of modern-day Turkey near the Black Sea, grew despondent following a series of defeats by the Romans and decided to commit suicide by poison. The problem was that no amount of poison was sufficient, and the grim task had to be completed by the sword. It turned out that Mithridates, having lived in fear of being poisoned by his rivals, had taken gradually increasing amounts of poison over the course of his life to build up a defense against this possibility. By the time he wanted to end his life by his own hand, he could tolerate such large doses that poisoning no longer presented any threat to his life. This royal case is the first recorded example of drug tolerance. In fact, the phenomenon originally was called *mithridatism*, and several celebrated poisoners of history, including the notorious Lucretia Borgia in the early sixteenth century, were later to use the same defensive strategy.[9]

The concept of **tolerance** refers to the capacity of a drug dose to have a gradually diminished effect on the user as the drug is taken repeatedly. Another way of viewing tolerance is to say that over repeated administrations a drug dose needs to be increased to maintain an equivalent effect. A common illustration is the effect of caffeine in coffee. When you are first introduced to caffeine, the stimulant effect is usually quite pronounced; you might feel noticeably "wired" after a 5-ounce cup of coffee, containing approximately 100 mg of caffeine. After several days or perhaps a few weeks of coffee drinking, the effect

is greatly diminished; you may need to be on the second or third cup by that time, consuming 200 to 300 mg of caffeine, to duplicate the earlier reaction. Some individuals who drink coffee regularly have developed such high levels of tolerance to caffeine that they are able to sleep comfortably even after several cups of coffee, whereas individuals with more infrequent ingestions of caffeine end up awake through the night after a single cup.

Tolerance effects, in general, illustrate the need for us to look at the *interaction* between the actual amount of the drug taken and other factors involved in the drug-taking behavior. For example, as already noted, the number of previous times the drug has been used is crucial; repetition is what tolerance is all about. Another important factor, however, is the setting within which the drug-taking behavior occurs. There is strong evidence that tolerance is maximized when the drug-taking behavior occurs consistently in the same surroundings or under the same set of circumstances.[10] We speak of this form of tolerance as **behavioral tolerance.**

To have a clear idea of behavioral tolerance, we first have to understand the processes of Pavlovian conditioning, upon which behavioral tolerance is based. Suppose that you consistently heard a bell ring every time you had a headache. Previously, bells had never had any negative effect on you. The association between the ringing bell and the pain of the headache, however, would become strong enough that the mere ringing of a bell would now give you a headache, perhaps less painful than the ones you had originally but a headache nonetheless; this effect is Pavlovian conditioning at work.

A pioneering study by the psychologist Shepard Siegel showed a similar phenomenon occurring with drug-taking behavior. In his experiment, one group of rats was injected with doses of morphine in a particular room over a series of days and later tested for tolerance to that dose in the same room. Predictably, they displayed a lessened analgesic effect as a sign of morphine tolerance. A second group was tested in a room other

> **tolerance:** The capacity of a drug to produce a gradually diminished physiological or psychological effect upon repeated administrations of the drug at the same dose level.
>
> **behavioral tolerance:** The process of drug tolerance that is linked to drug-taking behavior occurring consistently in the same surroundings or under the same circumstances. Also known as *conditioned tolerance.*

than the one in which the injections had been given. No tolerance developed at all. They reacted as if they had never been given morphine before, even though they had received the same number of repeated injections as the first group.

In a more extreme experiment, Siegel tested two groups of rats that were administered a series of heroin injections with increasingly higher dosages. Eventually, both groups were surviving a dosage level that would have been lethal to rats experiencing the drug for the first time. The difference in the groups related to the environment in which these injections were given. One group received these injections in the colony room where they lived. When the second group was receiving the injections, they were in a room that looked quite different and were hearing 60-decibel "white noise." Siegel then administered a single large dose of heroin, normally a level that should have killed them all. Instead, rats administered this extremely high dosage in the *same room* in which they had received the earlier heroin injection series showed only a 32 percent mortality rate. When the room was different, the mortality rate doubled (64 percent). In both groups, more rats survived than if they had never received heroin in the first place, but the survival rate was influenced by the environment in which the heroin was originally administered.

Siegel explained the results of his studies by assuming that environmental cues in the room where the initial injections were given elicited some form of effect *opposite* to the effect of the drug. In the case of heroin, these compensatory effects would partially counteract the analgesic effect of the drug and protect the animal against dying from potentially high dosage levels.

The phenomenon of behavioral tolerance, also referred to as *conditioned tolerance* because it is based on the principles of Pavlovian conditioning, explains why a heroin addict may easily suffer the adverse consequences of an overdose when the drug has been taken in a different environment from the one more frequently encountered or in a manner different from his or her ordinary routine.[11] The range of tolerated doses of heroin can be enormous; amounts in the 200- to 500-mg range may be lethal for a first-time heroin user, whereas amounts as high as 1800 mg may not even be sufficient to make a long-term heroin user sick.[12] You can imagine how dangerous it would be if the conditioned compensatory responses a heroin addict had built up over time were suddenly absent.

Behavioral tolerance also helps to explain why a formerly drug-dependent individual is strongly advised to avoid the surroundings associated with his or her past drug-taking behavior. If these surroundings provoked a physiological effect opposite to the effect of the drug through their association with prior drug-taking behavior, then a return to this environment might create internal changes that only drugs could reverse. In effect, environmentally induced withdrawal symptoms would increase the chances of a relapse. The fact that conditioning effects have been demonstrated not only with respect to heroin but with alcohol, cocaine, nicotine, and other dependence-producing drugs as well makes it imperative that the phenomenon of behavioral tolerance be considered during the course of drug abuse treatment and rehabilitation.[13]

Cross-Tolerance

If you were taking a barbiturate (a sedation-producing drug that acts to depress bodily functioning) for an extended length of time and you developed a tolerance for its effect, you also might have developed a tolerance for another depressant drug even though you have never taken the second one. In other words, it is possible that a tolerance effect for one drug might automatically induce a tolerance for another. This phenomenon, referred to as **cross-tolerance,** is commonly observed in the physiological and psychological effects of alcohol, barbiturates, and other depressants. As a result of cross-tolerance, an alcoholic will have already developed a tolerance for a barbiturate, or a barbiturate abuser will need a greater amount of an anesthetic when undergoing surgery.

Individual Differences

Some variations in drug effects may be related to an interaction between the drug itself and specific characteristics of the person taking the drug. One characteristic is an individual's weight. In general, a heavier person will require a greater amount of a drug than a lighter person to receive an equivalent drug effect, all other things being equal. It is for this reason that drug dosages are expressed as a ratio of drug amount to body weight. This ratio is expressed in metric terms, as milligrams per kilogram (mg/kg).

Another characteristic is gender. Even if a man and a woman are exactly the same weight, differences in drug effects still can result on the basis of gender differences in body composition and sex hormones. Women have, on

cross-tolerance: A phenomenon in which the tolerance that results from the chronic use of one drug induces a tolerance effect with regard to a second drug that has not been used before.

level of estrogen and progesterone in women. Whether gender differences exist with regard to drugs other than alcohol is presently unknown.

Another individual characteristic that influences the ways certain drugs affect the body is ethnic background. About 50 percent of all people of Asian descent, for example, show low levels of one of the enzymes that normally breaks down alcohol in the liver shortly before it is excreted. With this particular deficiency, alcohol metabolites tend to build up in the blood, producing a faster heart rate, facial flushing, and nausea.[15] As a result, many Asians find drinking to be quite unpleasant.

Ethnic variability can be seen in terms of other drug effects as well. It has been found that Caucasians have a faster rate of biotransformation of antipsychotic and antianxiety medications than Asians and, as a result, end up with relatively lower concentrations of drugs in the blood. One consequence of this difference is in the area of psychiatric treatment. Asian schizophrenic patients require significantly lower doses of antipsychotic medication for their symptoms to improve, and they experience medication side effects at much lower doses than do Caucasian patients. Since other possible factors such as diet, life-style, and environment do not account for these differences, we can speculate that these differences have a genetic basis.[16]

In some cases, differences in the physiological response to a particular drug can explain differential patterns of drug-taking behavior. For example, researchers have found recently that African Americans have a slower rate of nicotine metabolism following the smoking of cigarettes relative to whites. This finding might be the reason why African Americans, on average, report smoking fewer cigarettes per day than whites. If we assume that an equivalent level of nicotine needs to be maintained in both populations, fewer cigarettes smoked but a higher level of nicotine absorbed per cigarette will produce the same effect as a greater number of cigarettes smoked but a lower nicotine level absorbed per cigarette. Consequently, African American smokers may be taking in and retaining relatively more nicotine per cigarette and, as a result, not having to smoke as many cigarettes per day.[17]

Psychological Factors in Drug-Taking Behavior

This chapter has pointed out that certain physiological factors such as weight and gender must be taken into account to predict particular drug effects. Yet, even if we

average, a higher proportion of fat, due to a greater fat-to-muscle ratio, and a lower proportion of water than men. When we look at the effects of alcohol consumption in terms of gender, we find that the lower water content (a factor that tends to dilute the alcohol in the body) in women makes them feel more intoxicated than men, even if the same amount of alcohol is consumed.

Relative to men, women also have reduced levels of enzymes that break down alcohol in the liver, resulting in higher alcohol levels in the blood and a higher level of intoxication.[14] We suspect that the lower level of alcohol biotransformation may be related to an increased

controlled these factors completely, we would still frequently find a drug effect in an individual person to be different from time to time, place to place, and situation to situation. Predictions about how a person might react would be far from perfect.

A good way of thinking about an individual's response to a particular drug is to consider the drug effect to be a three-way interaction of the drug's pharmacological properties (the biochemical nature of the substance), the individual taking the drug (set), and the immediate environment within which drug-taking behavior is occurring (setting). Whether one or more of these factors dominate in the final analysis seems to depend upon the dosage level. Generally speaking, the higher the drug dose, the greater the contribution made by the pharmacology of the drug itself; the lower the dose, the greater the contribution of individual characteristics of the drug-taker or environmental conditions.[18]

Expectation Effects

One of the most uncontrollable factors in drug-taking behavior is the set of expectations a person may have about what the drug will do. If you believe that a drug will make you drunk or feel sexy, the chances are increased that it will do so; if you believe that a marijuana cigarette will make you high, the chances are increased that it will. You can consider the impact of negative expectations in the same way; when the feelings are strong that a drug will have no effect on you, the chances are lessened that you will react to it. In the most extreme case, you might experience a drug effect even when the substance you ingested was completely inert—that is, pharmacologically ineffective. Any inert (inactive) substance is referred to as a **placebo** (from the Latin, "I will please"), and the physical reaction to it is referred to as the *placebo effect.*

The concept of a placebo goes back to the earliest days of pharmacology. The bizarre ingredients prescribed in ancient times to treat various diseases were effective to the extent that people *believed* that they were effective, not from any known therapeutic property of these ingredients. No doubt, the placebo effect was strong enough for physical symptoms to diminish. During the Middle Ages, in one of the more extreme cases of the placebo effect, Pope Boniface VIII reportedly was cured of kidney pains when his personal physician hung a gold seal bearing the image of a lion around the pope's thigh.[19]

placebo (pla-SEE-bo): Latin term translated "I will please." Any inert substance that produces a psychological or physiological reaction.

The likelihood of a placebo effect is maximized when the patient highly regards the expertise of the physician prescribing a drug. This placebo effect will often increase the benefits of a drug with known therapeutic properties.

It would be a mistake to think of the placebo effect as involving totally imaginary symptoms or totally imaginary reactions. Physical symptoms, involving specific bodily changes, can occur on the basis of placebo effects alone. How likely is it that a person will react to a placebo? The probability will vary from drug to drug, but in the case of morphine, the data are very clear. In 1959, a review of studies in which morphine or a placebo was administered in clinical studies of pain concluded that a placebo-induced reduction in pain occurred 35 percent of the time. Considering that morphine itself had a positive result in only 75 percent of the cases, the placebo effect is a very strong one.[20]

Unfortunately, we cannot predict with certainty whether a person will react strongly or weakly to a placebo. We do know, however, that the enthusiasm or lack of enthusiasm of the prescribing physician can play a major role. In one study that varied the attitude of the physician toward a particular medication, negative attitudes toward the medication resulted in the least benefits, whereas positive attitudes resulted in the most.[21]

It is not at all clear how the placebo effect is accomplished. In the case of pain relief, there is evidence that we have the natural ability to increase the levels of endorphins in the bloodstream and the brain from one moment to the next, but the nature of our ability to alter other important substances in our bodies is virtually unknown. Recent studies have documented a 33 percent increase in lung capacity among asthmatic children who inhaled a bronchodilator containing a placebo instead of medication and the development of skin rashes in people who have been exposed to fake poison ivy, to name a few examples of placebo-induced physiological reactions. Placebo research forces us to acknowledge the potential for psychological control over physiological processes in our bodies.[22]

Drug Research Methodology

Given the power of the placebo effect in drug-taking behavior, it is necessary to be very careful when carrying out drug research. For a drug to be deemed truly effective, it must be shown to be better not only in comparison to a no-treatment condition (a difference that could conceivably be due to a placebo effect) but also in comparison to an identical-looking drug that lacks the active ingredients of the drug being evaluated. For example, if the drug under study is in the shape of a round red pill, another round red pill without the active ingredients of the drug (called the *active placebo*) also must be administered for comparison purposes.

The procedures of these studies also have to be carefully executed. Neither the individual administering the drug or placebo nor the individual receiving the drug or placebo should know which substance is which. Such precautions, referred to as **double-blind** procedures, represent the minimal standards for separating the pharmacological effects of a drug from the effects that arise from one's expectations and beliefs.[23] We will return to the issue of interactions between drug effects and expectations when we consider alcohol intoxication in Chapter 10.

Physical and Psychological Dependence

When we refer to the idea of dependence in drug abuse, we are dealing with the fact that a person has a strong compulsion to continue taking a particular drug. Two possible models or explanations for why drug dependence occurs can be considered. The first is referred to as physical dependence, and the second is referred to as psychological dependence. The two models are not mutually exclusive; the abuse of some drugs can be a result of both physical and psychological dependence, whereas the abuse of others can be a result of psychological dependence alone.

Physical Dependence

The concept of **physical dependence** originates from observations of heroin abusers, as well as of those who abuse other opiate drugs, who developed strong physical symptoms following heroin withdrawal: a runny nose, chills and fever, inability to sleep, and hypersensitivity to pain. For barbiturate abusers in a comparable situation, symptoms include anxiety, inability to sleep, and sometimes lethal convulsions. For chronic alcoholics, abstention can produce tremors, nausea, weakness, and tachycardia (a fast heart rate). If severe, symptoms may include delirium, seizures, and hallucinations.[24]

While the actual symptoms vary according to the drug being withdrawn, the fact that we observe physical symptoms at all suggests very strongly that some kind of physical need, perhaps as far down as the cellular level, has developed over the course of drug abuse. It is as if the drug, previously a foreign chemical, has become a normal part of the nervous system, and its removal and absence become abnormal.

From this point of view, it is predictable that the withdrawal symptoms would involve symptoms that are opposite to effects the drug originally had on the body. For example, heroin can be extremely constipating, but eventually the body compensates for heroin's intestinal effects. Abrupt abstinence from heroin releases the processes that have been counteracting the constipation, and the result of withdrawal is diarrhea. You may have noticed a strong resemblance between the action–counteraction phenomena of withdrawal and the processes Siegel has hypothesized as the basis for behavioral tolerance.

Psychological Dependence

The most important implication of the model of physical dependence, as distinct from psychological dependence, is that individuals involved in drug abuse continue the drug-taking behavior, at least in part, *to avoid the feared consequences of withdrawal*. This idea can form the basis for a general model of drug dependence only if physical

double-blind: A procedure in drug research in which neither the individual administering nor the individual receiving a chemical substance knows whether the substance is the drug being evaluated or an active placebo.

physical dependence: A model of drug dependence based on the idea that the drug abuser continues the drug-taking behavior to avoid the consequences of physical withdrawal symptoms.

withdrawal symptoms appear consistently for every drug considered as a drug of abuse. It turns out, however, that a number of abused drugs (cocaine, hallucinogens, and marijuana, for example) do not produce physical withdrawal symptoms, and the effects of heroin withdrawal are more variable than we would expect if physical dependence alone were at work.

It is possible that drug abusers continue to take the drug not because they want to avoid the symptoms of withdrawal but because they crave the pleasurable effects of the drug itself. They may even feel that they need the drug to function at all. This is the way one heroin addict has expressed it:

> I'm just trying to get high as much as possible.... If I could get more money, I would spend it all on drugs. All I want is to get loaded. I just really like shooting dope. I don't have any use for sex; I'd rather shoot dope. I like to shoot dope better than anything else in the world.[25]

Many heroin abusers (between 56 and 77 percent in one major study) who complete the withdrawal process after abstaining from the drug have a relapse.[26] If physical dependence were the whole story, these phenomena would not exist. The withdrawal symptoms would have been gone by that time, and any physical need that may have been evident before would no longer be present.

When we speak of **psychological dependence**, we are offering an explanation of drug abuse based not upon the attempt of abusers to avoid unpleasant withdrawal symptoms but upon their continued desire to obtain pleasurable effects from the drug. Unfortunately, we are faced here with a major conceptual problem: The explanation by itself is circular and tells us basically nothing. If I were to say, for example, that I was taking cocaine because I was psychologically dependent upon it, then I could as easily say I was psychologically dependent upon cocaine because I was abusing it. Without some *independent* justification, the only explanation for the concept of psychological dependence would be the behavior that the concept was supposed to explain!

Fortunately, there is independent evidence for the concept of psychological dependence, founded chiefly

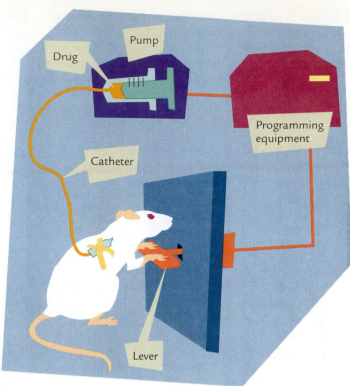

FIGURE 1.4

A simplified rendition of how drugs are self-administered in rats. The rat's pressure on a lever causes the pump to inject a drug through a catheter implanted into its vein.

upon studies showing that animals are as capable of self-administering drugs of abuse as humans are. Using techniques developed in the late 1950s, researchers have been able to insert a catheter into the vein of a freely moving laboratory animal and arrange the equipment so that the animal can self-administer a drug intravenously whenever it presses a lever (Figure 1.4). It had been well known that animals would engage in specific behaviors to secure rewards such as food, water, or even electrical stimulation of certain regions of the brain. These objectives were defined as positive reinforcers because animals would learn to work to secure them. The question at the time was whether animals would self-administer drugs in a similar way. Could drugs be positive reinforcers as well?

The experiments showed clearly that animals would self-administer drugs such as cocaine and other stimulants despite the fact that these drugs would not ordinarily produce physical symptoms during withdrawal. In one study, rats pressed the lever as many as 6,400 times for one administration of cocaine; others were nearly as eager for administrations of amphetamines.[27] Interestingly, a number of other drugs were

> **psychological dependence:** A model of drug dependence based on the idea that the drug abuser is motivated by a craving for the pleasurable effects of the drug.

aversive, judging from the reluctance of animals to work for them. Hallucinogens such as LSD, antipsychotic drugs, and antidepressant drugs were examples of drugs that animals clearly did not like.[28]

By connecting the concept of psychological dependence to general principles of reinforcement, it is possible for us to appreciate the powerful effects of abused drugs. When presented with a choice of pressing levers for food or for cocaine, cocaine wins hands down even to the point of an animal starving to death.[29] When comparing the effects of heroin with cocaine, the differences are dramatic:

> Those rats that self-administer heroin developed a stable pattern of use, maintained their pretest weight, continued good grooming behavior, and tended to be in good health. Their mortality rate was 36 percent after thirty days. Those self-administering cocaine … exhibited an extremely erratic pattern of use, with "binges" of heavy use alternating with brief periods of abstinence. They lost 47 percent of their body weight, ceased grooming behavior, and maintained extremely poor physical health. After thirty days, 90 percent were dead.[30]

In the final analysis, from the standpoint of treating individuals who abuse drugs, it might not matter if there is physical dependence or psychological dependence going on. According to many experts in the field, the distinction between physical and psychological dependence has outgrown its usefulness in understanding the motivation behind drug abuse. Whether the discontinuation of an abused drug does induce major physical withdrawal symptoms (as in the case of heroin, alcohol, and barbiturates) or does not (as in the case of cocaine, amphetamines, and nicotine), the pattern of compulsive drug-taking behavior in all instances is remarkably similar. If the pattern of behavior is similar, then there can be common strategies for treatment.[31]

Psychiatric Definitions

Most health professionals use guidelines published by the American Psychiatric Association as a kind of official standard for defining problems associated with drug-taking behavior. Generally speaking, these problems, which range from the ingestion of a drug of abuse (including alcohol) to the experience of side effects of a medication, are collectively referred to as *substance-related disorders*. The fourth edition (text revision) of the association's *Diagnostic and Statistical Manual of Men-*

tal Disorders (DSM-IV-TR or simply DSM-IV, for short), published in 2000, identifies two specific behavioral conditions: **substance dependence** and **substance abuse** (Table 1.1).

Two features of the DSM-IV guidelines are worth noting. First, the guidelines consist of a listing of behavioral criteria to be used for the diagnosis (identification) of substance dependence or substance abuse. There is no discussion of why these problems have arisen or what circumstances produced them, only their behavioral features. The position of the American Psychiatric Association is that a judgment of whether a person has a problem of dependence or abuse should depend on the behavior of that person, not the chemical that is being consumed. Second, the broader term "substance" has been substituted for the word "drug" in the guidelines primarily because there is often confusion in the public mind in deciding what is defined as a drug and what is not, particularly in the instance of alcohol or nicotine use.[32]

The Problem of Drug Toxicity

When we say that a drug is toxic, we are referring to the fact that it may be dangerous, poisonous, or in some way interfering with a person's normal functioning. Technically, any substance, no matter how benign, has the potential for **toxicity** if the **dose,** the amount in which the substance is taken, is high enough. The question of a drug's safety, or its relative safety when compared to other drugs, centers on the possibility that it may be toxic at relatively low doses. We certainly do not want people to harm themselves accidentally when taking the drug in the course of their daily lives. When there is a possibility that the *short-term* effects of a particular drug will trigger a

substance dependence: A diagnostic term used in clinical psychology and psychiatry that identifies an individual with significant signs of a dependent relationship upon a psychoactive drug.

substance abuse: A diagnostic term used in clinical psychology and psychiatry that identifies an individual who continues to take a psychoactive drug despite the fact that the drug-taking behavior creates specific problems for that individual.

toxicity (tox-IS-ih-tee): The physical or psychological harm that a drug might present to the user.

dose: The quantity of drug that is taken into the body, typically measured in terms of milligrams (mg) or micrograms (µg).

TABLE 1.1

Criteria for substance dependence and substance abuse according to the DSM-IV

SUBSTANCE DEPENDENCE	SUBSTANCE ABUSE
At least three out of the following must apply within a twelve-month period:	At least one of the following must apply within a twelve-month period:
1. Tolerance. The person has to take increasingly large doses of the drug to get the desired effect. Or else the person experiences a diminished effect from the same amount of the drug.	1. Recurrent substance use resulting in a failure to fulfill major role obligations at work, school, or home. Examples include repeated absences from work, suspensions or expulsions from school, or neglect of children or one's household.
2. Withdrawal. When the drug is stopped, there are psychological or physiological withdrawal symptoms. Or else the substance is taken to relieve or avoid these symptoms.	2. Recurrent drug use in situations in which use is physically hazardous.
3. Unintentional overuse. The person repeatedly takes more of the drug or takes it over a longer period of time than he or she intended.	3. Recurrent substance-related legal problems, such as an arrest for disorderly conduct or drug-related behavior. Symptoms of the disturbance must have persisted for more than a month or occurred over a longer period of time.
4. Persistent desire or efforts to control drug use. The person tries to quit and repeatedly relapses into further drug use.	4. Continued drug use despite the knowledge of persistent social, occupational, psychological, or physical problems that would be caused or made more difficult by the use of the drug.
5. Preoccupation with the drug. The person spends a great deal of time in activities necessary to obtain the substance, use it, or recover from its effects.	*Important:* The person must have never met the criteria for substance dependence for this particular drug.
6. The reduction or abandonment of important social, occupational, or recreational activities in order to engage in drug use. A person quits a job, neglects a child, or gives up other important activities.	
7. Continued drug use despite major drug-related problems. A person repeatedly arrested for drug possession still maintains the drug habit, or a person with serious lung disease continues to smoke cigarettes, for example.	
Symptoms of the disturbance must have persisted for more than a month or occurred repeatedly over a longer period of time.	

Source: Adapted from the *American Psychiatric Association: Diagnostic and statistical manual of mental disorders. Text Revision.* (4th ed.). Washington, DC: American Psychiatric Association, 2000. Reprinted with permission from the *Diagnostic and statistical manual of mental disorders* (4th ed.), Text revision. Copyright 2000. American Psychiatric Association.

toxic reaction, then this drug is identified as having some level of **acute toxicity.**

To understand the principle of toxicity in general, we need to examine an S-shaped graph called the

acute toxicity: The physical or psychological harm a drug might present to the user immediately or soon after the drug is ingested into the body.

dose-response curve: An S-shaped graph showing the increasing probability of a certain drug effect as the dose level rises.

effective dose: The minimal dose of a particular drug necessary to produce the intended drug effect in a given percentage of the population.

dose-response curve (Figure 1.5a). Let us assume that we have the results of data collected from laboratory tests of a hypothetical sleep-inducing drug. Increases in the dose level of the drug are producing the desired sleep-inducing effect in an increasingly large percentage of a test population of mice. At 10 milligrams (mg), 50 percent of the population has fallen asleep; at 50 mg, 100 percent has done so. There is always some variability in individual reactions to any drug; some mice may be internally resistant to the drug's effect, whereas others may be quite susceptible. Any one animal may fall asleep with an extremely low dose or a dose of 50 mg, so we have to think of the **effective dose** (ED) of a drug on a test population in terms of probabilities, from 0 to 100 percent.

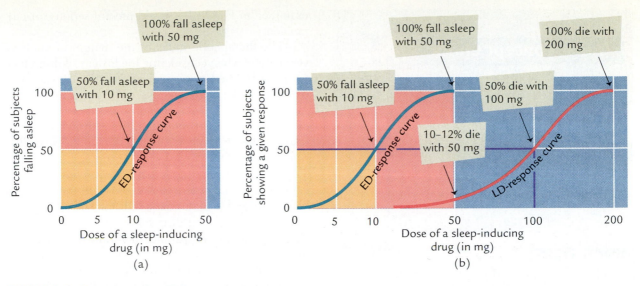

FIGURE 1.5

(a) An effective dose-response curve, and (b) an effective dose-response curve (left) alongside a lethal dose-response curve (right).

For example, the ED50 of a drug refers to the effective dose for 50 percent of the population; ED99 refers to the effective dose for 99 percent of the population. In this case, the ED numbers refer to the drug's effect of producing sleep. The same drug may be producing other effects (muscular relaxation, for instance) at lower doses; these drug effects would have their own separate dose-response curves. It is a good idea to remember that we are looking at the properties of a drug *effect* here, not the properties of the drug itself.

Now we can look at Figure 1.5b, where the effective dose-response curve is represented along with another S-shaped dose-response curve, also gathered from laboratory testing, in which the "response" is death. It makes sense that the second curve should be shifted to the right because the **lethal dose** (LD) generally involves greater amounts of a drug than the amounts necessary to produce an effect.

Emphasis should be placed on the word "generally" because the lethal dose-response curve overlaps with the effective dose-response curve in this example. While a 100-mg dose has to be taken to kill 50 percent of the test population, it can be seen that a dose of as little as 50 mg (or less) is lethal for at least a few of them. The LD50 of a drug refers to the lethal dose for 50 percent of the population; LD1 refers to a relatively lower dose that is lethal for 1 percent of the population.

It is useful to combine the effective and lethal doses of a drug in a ratio to arrive at some idea of that

drug's toxicity. The ratio of LD50/ED50 is called the **therapeutic index.** If the LD50 for a drug is 450 mg and the ED50 is 50 mg, then the therapeutic index is 9. In other words, you would have to take nine times the dose that would be effective for half the population to incur a 50 percent chance of dying.

It can be argued, however, that a 50 percent probability of dying represents an unacceptably high risk even for a drug that has genuine benefits. To be more conservative in the direction of safety, the ratio of LD1/ED99 is often calculated. Here we are calculating the ratio between the dose that produces death in 1 percent of the population and the dose that would be effective in 99 percent. This second ratio, called the **margin of safety,** should be as high as possible. The higher the ratio, the safer, or less toxic, is the drug. It can be seen that the margin of safety for the hypothetical drug

lethal dose: The minimal dose of a particular drug capable of producing death in a given percentage of the population.

therapeutic index: A measure of a drug's relative safety for use, computed by the ratio of the lethal dose for 50 percent of the population over the effective dose for 50 percent of the population.

margin of safety: The ratio of a lethal dose for 1 percent of the population to the effective dose for 99 percent of the population.

Understanding Dose-Response Curves

Check your understanding of dose-response curves and the toxicity of drugs by answering the following question.

The following three sets of dose-response curves show the effective and lethal responses to three drugs A, B, and C.

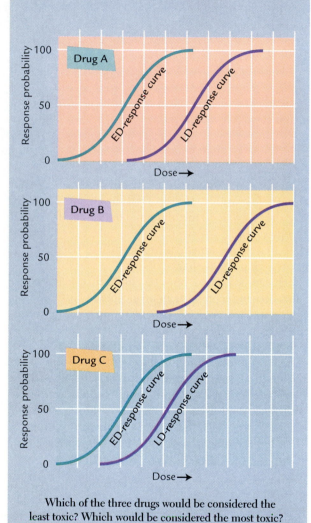

Which of the three drugs would be considered the least toxic? Which would be considered the most toxic?

Answer: The second set of curves (B) refers to the least toxic drug. The third set of curves (C) refers to the most toxic drug.

examined in Figure 1.5 would present serious toxicity problems.

The therapeutic index or the margin of safety is very helpful when considering the toxicity of drugs that are manufactured by recognized pharmaceutical companies and regulated by the U.S. Food and Drug Administration (FDA), keeping in mind the possibility that a person might intentionally or unintentionally take a higher-than-recommended dose of the drug. But what about the toxicity risks in consuming illicit drugs? The reality of street drugs is that the buyer has no way of knowing what he or she has bought until the drug has been used, and then it is frequently too late.

Few, if any, illicit drug sellers make a pretense of being ethical businesspeople; their only objective is to make money and avoid prosecution by the law. Frequently, the drugs they sell are diluted with either inert or highly dangerous ingredients. Adulterated heroin, for example, may contain a high proportion of milk sugar as a harmless filler and a dash of quinine to simulate the bitter taste of real heroin, when the actual amount of heroin that is being sold is far less than the "standard" street dosage. At the other extreme, the content of heroin may be unexpectedly high and may lead to a lethal overdose, or else it may contain animal tranquilizers, arsenic, strychnine, insecticides, or other highly toxic substances. Cocaine, LSD, marijuana, and all the other illicit drugs available to the drug abuser, as well as look-alike drugs that are unauthorized copies of popular prescription medications, present hidden and unpredictable risks of toxicity. Even if drugs are procured from a friend or someone you know, these risks remain. Neither of you is likely to know the exact ingredients. The dangers of acute toxicity are always present.

Given the uncertainty that exists about the contents of many abused drugs, what measure or index of acute toxicity can we use to evaluate their effects on individuals in society? The natural tendency is to look first to the news headlines; think of all the well-known public individuals who have died as a direct consequence of drug misuse or abuse (Drugs...in Focus). Such examples, however, can be misleading. Celebrities are not necessarily representative of the drug-using population in general, and the drugs prevalent among celebrities, because of their expense, may not represent the drugs most frequently encountered by the rest of society. To have some idea of the toxic effects of psychoactive drugs in a broader context, we have to turn to the institutions that contend with drug toxicity on a daily basis: the emergency departments of hospitals around the country.

Drugs . . . in Focus

Acute Toxicity in the News: Drug-Related Deaths

The following famous people have died either as a direct consequence or as an indirect consequence of drug misuse or abuse.

Name	Year of Death	Age	Reasons Given for Death
Marilyn Monroe, actress	1962	36	Overdose of Nembutal (a sedative-hypnotic medication); circumstances unknown
Lenny Bruce, comedian	1966	40	Accidental overdose of morphine
Judy Garland, singer and actress	1969	47	Accidental overdose of sleeping pills
Janis Joplin, singer	1970	27	Accidental overdose of heroin and alcohol
Jimi Hendrix, singer and guitarist	1970	27	Accidental overdose of sleeping pills
Elvis Presley, singer and actor	1977	42	Cardiac arrhythmia suspected to be due to an interaction of antihistamine, codeine, and Demerol (a painkiller), as well as Valium and several other tranquilizers
John Belushi, comedian and actor	1982	33	Accidental overdose of heroin combined with cocaine
David A. Kennedy, son of U.S. senator Robert F. Kennedy	1984	28	Accidental interaction of cocaine, Demerol, and Mellaril (an antipsychotic medication)
Len Bias, college basketball player	1986	22	Cardiac-respiratory arrest from accidental overdose of cocaine
Don Rogers, professional football player	1986	23	Cardiac-respiratory arrest from accidental overdose of cocaine
Abbie Hoffman, antiwar and political activist	1989	52	Suicide using phenobarbital combined with alcohol
River Phoenix, actor	1993	23	Cardiac-respiratory arrest from accidental combination of heroin and cocaine
Jonathan Melvoin, keyboardist for the Smashing Pumpkins rock band	1996	34	Accidental overdose of heroin
Chris Farley, comedian and actor	1998	33	Accidental overdose of heroin and cocaine
Dee Dee Ramone, bassist for the Ramones rock band	2002	49	Accidental overdose following an injection of an undisclosed drug of abuse
Steve Bechler, Baltimore Orioles pitcher	2003	23	Multiple organ failure due to heatstroke, suspected to be related to the use of Xenadrine RFA-1, a weight-control dietary supplement containing ephedra
Bobby Hatfield, singer, the Righteous Brothers	2003	63	Heart failure following overdose of cocaine
Robert Pastorelli, actor	2004	39	Accidental overdose of heroin
Mitch Hedberg, comedian	2005	37	Heart failure, related to heroin and cocaine use
Anna Nicole Smith, model and actress	2007	39	Accidental overdose of the sedative-hypnotic choral hydrate, with intestinal flu and bacterial infection being contributing factors

Note: Celebrities whose drug-related deaths have been attributed to the toxicity of alcohol alone or nicotine, tars, or carbon monoxide in tobacco products are not included in this listing.

Sources: Various media reports.

Emergency medical service (EMS) crews frequently have to deal with drug-related cases.

The DAWN Reports

The U.S. government currently gathers data concerning drug-related medical emergencies in major metropolitan hospitals through a program called the **Drug Abuse Warning Network (DAWN)**. Two basic types of information are reported. The first concerns the number of times an individual visits an emergency department (ED) for any reason that is connected to recent drug use. These **drug-related ED visits** involve a wide range of drug-related situations: suicide attempts, malicious poisoning, overmedication, and adverse reactions to medications, as well as the use of illicit drugs, the use of dietary supplements, and the nonmedical use of prescription or over-the-counter (OTC) drugs. The second type of information concerns the number of drug-related deaths, as determined by a coroner or medical examiner.[33]

Approximately one out of seven ED visits in the United States in 2005 was associated with either drug misuse or abuse. Nearly one-third (31 percent) of all drug-related ED visits involved illicit drugs only, while 27 percent involved prescription or OTC medications alone, and 7 percent involved a combination of illicit drugs and medications (Figure 1.6).[34]

The proportion of drug-related ED visits involving alcohol use shown in Figure 1.6 requires some explanation. First, statistics about ED visits *related to the use of alcohol alone* are restricted in the DAWN reporting system to such use by individuals younger than twenty-one years of age. In other words, such medical emergencies are resulting, by definition, from underage drinking. DAWN statistics are not collected for ED visits involving alcohol use alone by individuals who are twenty-one years or older. There is a very good reason for this exclusion. If all emergencies related to alcohol use alone were reported, the numbers would far exceed those related to any other drug. Considering the fact that more than 240,000 individuals in the United States are injured in driving-while-intoxicated (DWI) automobile accidents and individuals by the hundreds of thousands incur alcohol-related personal injuries each year (see Chapter 10), the examination of ED visits related to other circumstances would be obscured if all alcohol-related ED visits were included.

Second, an important message in the ED-visit statistics is the considerable toxicity resulting from *alcohol-in-combination*. This term refers to the use of alcohol in conjunction with another drug, regardless of one's age. More than one-fourth (28 percent) of drug-related ED

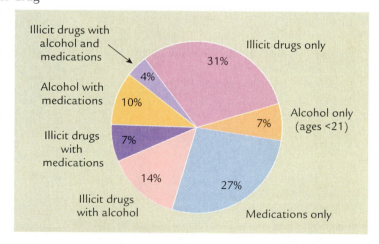

FIGURE 1.6

Drug-related ED visits in 2005, by type of drug involvement.

Source: Substance Abuse and Mental Health Services Administration (2007). *Drug Abuse Warning Network, 2005:* National estimates of drug-related emergency department visits. Rockville, MD: Office of Applied Studies, Substance Abuse and Mental Health Services Administration, Table 1.

Drug Abuse Warning Network (DAWN): A federal program in which metropolitan hospitals report the incidence of drug-related lethal and nonlethal emergencies.

drug-related ED visit: An occasion on which a person visits an emergency department (ED) for a purpose that is related to recent drug use.

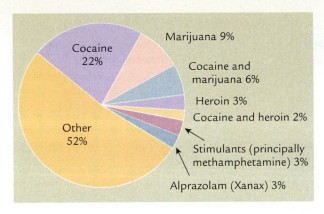

FIGURE 1.7

Frequency of drugs reported in alcohol-in-combination ED cases in 2005.

Note: More than 340 drugs are represented in the "Other" category of alcohol-in-combination ED cases.

Source: Substance Abuse and Mental Health Administration (2007). *Drug Abuse Warning Network, 2005: National estimates of drug-related emergency department visits.* Rockville MD: Office of Applied Studies, Substance Abuse and Mental Health Administration, pages 8, 29, and Table 6.

visits involve some use of alcohol in combination with an illicit drug, with a prescription or OTC medication, or with an illicit drug and a medication. As Figure 1.7 shows, a large number of alcohol-in-combination ED visits involve either cocaine or marijuana or a combination of the two together. A much smaller proportion involves heroin, stimulants (principally methamphetamine), and alprazolam (brand name: Xanax), which are used in the treatment of anxiety. The remainder, more than 50 percent of the total, are spread among a wide variety of illicit drugs or medications, including OTC medications such as acetaminophen (brand name: Tylenol) and ibuprofen (brand names: Advil, Motrin, among others).[35]

Emergencies Related to Illicit Drugs

What types of illicit drugs are most likely to result in an ED visit? In 2005, of the approximately 817,000 illicit-drug-related ED visits, the largest number of cases involved cocaine, followed by marijuana, heroin, and stimulants (principally methamphetamine), in that order. The use of MDMA (Ecstasy), PCP, LSD, and other hallucinogens each accounted for a considerably smaller number of cases. In general, patients in 2005 were twice as likely to be male than female in ED visits involving illicit drugs, with the ratio increasing to about six to one in cases involving LSD.[36]

Drug-Related Deaths

Current DAWN statistics on instances of drug-related deaths in the United States are not reported on a nationwide basis but instead in terms of individual metropolitan areas. Because the population levels of these areas vary widely, overall interpretations of these statistics have to be made with great care. For example, the almost identical level of opiate-drug involvement (Figure 1.8) in drug-related deaths in Washington DC and San Diego, with an approximately 2:1 ratio in their respective populations, is indicative of a relatively greater opiate-drug problem in San Diego rather than an equivalent concern in these two cities. In addition, each metropolitan area has a somewhat different drug problem "profile." Cocaine use, for example, is prominently reported in drug-related deaths in most metropolitan areas surveyed in the DAWN report but plays a relatively minor role in drug-related deaths in Louisville, Kentucky.

Yet, despite these problems in examining drug-related deaths across metropolitan areas in the United States, a number of generalizations can be made.

- In nearly all metropolitan areas surveyed in the DAWN report, opiate drugs (predominantly heroin but also including morphine and methadone) and cocaine are the two most frequently reported drugs. In the six representative metropolitan areas shown in Figure 1.8, opiate drugs exceed cocaine in terms of the degree of involvement in a drug-related death. Alcohol (chiefly alcohol in combination with some other drug but also including alcohol ingested by someone younger than 21 years old) is commonly in third place.

- Typically, medications used to treat anxiety and depression are either the fourth or fifth most frequently reported drugs in drug-related death cases. However, the presence of these categories of licit drugs in the "top five" listing should be interpreted carefully. The amounts ingested in these circumstances either far exceed the recommended dosage levels or have been combined with one or more other drugs.

- In general, it is far more common for drug-related deaths to be a result of multiple-drug (polydrug) use than from single-drug use. Nonetheless, Figure 1.8 clearly shows that a substantial number of deaths result from the single-drug use of opiates and cocaine. In the cases of alcohol, antianxiety medication, and antidepressant medication, it is extremely unusual for a death to result from the use of any of these drugs alone.

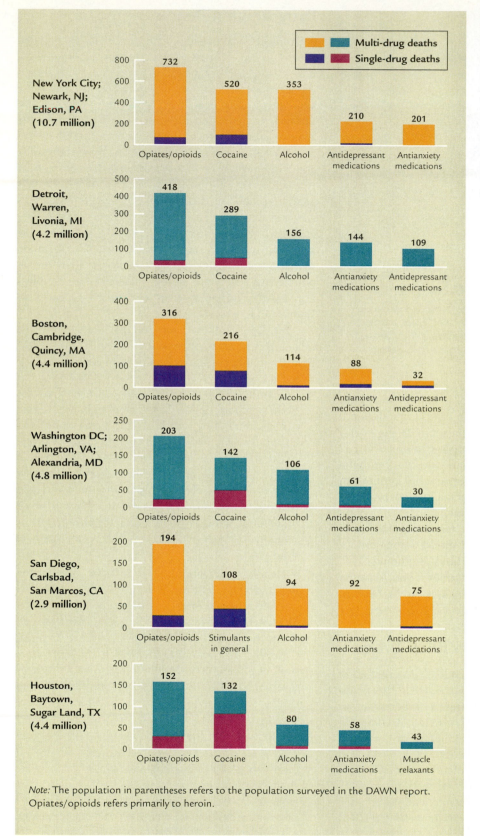

FIGURE 1.8

Drug-related deaths in 2003:
A tale of six cities.

Source: Substance Abuse and Mental Health Services Administration (2005). *Drug Abuse Warning Network, 2003: Area profiles of drug-related mortality.* Rockville MD: Office of Applied Studies, Substance Abuse and Mental Health Services Administration, pp. 52–53, 62–63, 64–65, 80–81, 98–99, and 106–107.

Note: The population in parentheses refers to the population surveyed in the DAWN report. Opiates/opioids refers primarily to heroin.

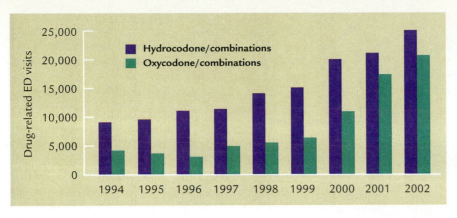

FIGURE 1.9

Trends in drug-related ED visits involving hydrocodone and oxycodone, 1994–2002.

Note: Under a new DAWN reporting system initiated in 2004, there were approximately 42,000 ED visits due to the use of hydrocodone/combinations and 36,000 ED visits due to the use of oxycodone/combinations.

Source: Substance Abuse and Mental Health Administration (2004, July). Oxycodone, hydrocodone, and polydrug use, 2002. *DAWN Report,* p. 1. Substance Abuse and Mental Health Services Administration (2006). *Drug Abuse Warning Network, 2004: National estimates of drug-related emergency department visits.* Rockville MD: Office of Applied Studies, Substance Abuse and Mental Health Services Administration, Table 13.

- Marijuana is far less prominent in drug-related deaths and, when there are reports of its involvement, it is almost exclusively in the context of multiple-drug rather than single-drug use.

- Methamphetamine use as a cause of a drug-related death is largely underestimated in the DAWN statistics, due to the emphasis on reports from large metropolitan areas rather than smaller, rural areas in the United States, where methamphetamine is a significant public health concern (see Chapter 4).[37]

Judging Drug Toxicity from Drug-Related Deaths

The finding that the use of heroin (and other opiate drugs) or cocaine alone is frequently involved in drug-related deaths is particularly striking when you consider the fact that heroin and cocaine users constitute a relatively small proportion of the total number of illicit drug users, and certainly in terms of the general population. The fact that there are more instances of heroin use in drug-related deaths than instances of cocaine use underestimates the potential lethality of heroin, since there are far fewer heroin users than cocaine users in the United

States. In contrast, the rare association of marijuana with drug-related deaths is actually overstating its potential lethality, given its widespread use within a much larger group of people.

In short, a judgment about the relative toxicity of illicit drugs requires an understanding of how frequently a particular drug is used in the general population. All other facts being equal, if one illicit drug produces twice as many deaths as a second drug but the number of users of the first drug is twice that of the second, then the toxicity levels of the two drugs should be considered equivalent.

Demographics and Trends

By examining DAWN statistics from 1980 to 2005, we can arrive at some idea of the changes that have taken place in the frequency of medical emergencies over the years. For example, a dramatic increase in the number of cocaine-related emergencies occurred in the 1980s as a result of the rise of cocaine abuse and crack cocaine abuse. A decade later, an upturn in heroin-related emergencies took place during the 1990s, as the purity of available heroin increased and the availability of heroin use without a needle injection caused heroin-related emergency rates to rise.

In the mid-1990s, significant concerns emerged about the increase in ED visits arising from the use of two classes of drugs. The first consisted of illicit club drugs that included Ecstasy, GHB, ketamine, LSD, and methamphetamine. The second class of drugs that raised health concerns during this period included opiate-based prescription pain medications, also known as *narcotic analgesics.* Figure 1.9 shows the sharp rise in medical emergencies related to oxycodone (brand name: Percodan) and hydrocodone (brand name: Vicodin).[38]

From Acute Toxicity to Chronic Toxicity

Through the DAWN reports, we can appreciate the extent of acute toxicity involved in the ingestion of a particular drug, but we are unable to get an illuminating picture of the negative consequences of using a particular drug over a long period of time. Examples of

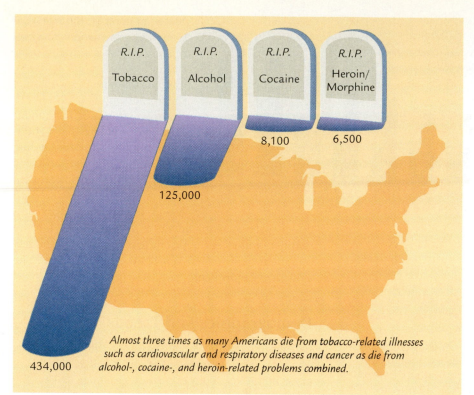

FIGURE 1.10

U.S. deaths per year from tobacco, alcohol, and other drug use.

Source: National Institute on Drug Abuse (1994, September/ October). *NIDA Notes,* p. 5.

R.I.P. Tobacco
R.I.P. Alcohol
R.I.P. Cocaine
R.I.P. Heroin/ Morphine

8,100
6,500
125,000
434,000

Almost three times as many Americans die from tobacco-related illnesses such as cardiovascular and respiratory diseases and cancer as die from alcohol-, cocaine-, and heroin-related problems combined.

chronic toxicity can be found in a wide range of psychoactive drugs, either legally or illegally obtained. Ironically, it is the chronic use of alcohol and tobacco, both of which are legally available in our society, that causes by far the greatest adverse health effects. As we will see in Chapters 10 and 12, the number of people who die each year as a result of drinking alcohol or smoking tobacco far outstrips the number of fatalities from the abuse of illicit drugs (Figure 1.10).

A number of important issues with respect to drug-taking behavior will be examined in the chapters ahead. What exactly are the problems associated with *chronic* drug use? What is the most productive way of looking at drug dependence in general? How has our society responded to the problems of drug-taking behavior over the years? How successful have we been in dealing with these problems? What new strategies are there to handle drug-related problems in a more effective way?

Looking to the Future and Learning from the Past

What does the future hold with respect to drug use and abuse in our society? Where should we direct our concerns? Predictions are always tricky to make, but with regard to drug-taking behavior in general, there are historical patterns that can serve as guides.

Old Drugs, New Drugs

One certainty is that the use and abuse of specific drugs will continue to come into and fall out of favor. New drugs will appear on the scene, and others may reappear like ghosts from the past, sometimes in new forms and involving new faces in the drug underground. As one researcher has pointed out, "There is always something old and something new in the U.S. drug scene."[39]

For example, as cocaine declined in popularity in the United States during the 1990s, heroin reemerged as a major drug of abuse. During this time, heroin was distributed not only in an injectable form but also in a more potent blend that could be snorted like cocaine or smoked like crack. On the one hand, these new forms of drug-taking behavior circumvented the traditional need for a hypodermic syringe and the associated dangers of being infected by nonsterile needles. As a result, the possibility of becoming infected with hepatitis or the virus responsible for acquired immunodeficiency syndrome

chronic toxicity: The physical or psychological harm a drug might cause over a long period of use.

(AIDS) was avoided. On the other hand, new populations of people formerly turned off to heroin because of their fear of needles were introduced to it for the first time.[40]

LSD and other hallucinogens, once the darlings of the psychedelic generation in the 1960s, staged a comeback during this period of time as well. In recent years, as mentioned earlier, prescription painkillers—traditionally the primary medical option for pain management in the treatment of cancer, arthritis, and a host of other physical disorders—have become increasingly popular drugs of abuse.[41]

Club Drugs

A serious concern in today's drug scene has been the popularity of *club drugs,* a term referring to substances typically ingested at all-night dance parties ("raves"), dance clubs, and bars. Examples of club drugs include MDMA (Ecstasy), GHB, ketamine, Rohypnol, methamphetamine, and LSD. When used in combination with alcohol, as they often are, these drugs carry considerably increased health risks beyond their own individual toxicities. Since many club drugs are colorless, tasteless, and odorless, they can be slipped unobtrusively into drinks by individuals who want to intoxicate or sedate others. The potential danger of sexual assault, therefore, is a major problem.[42] Drugs . . . in Focus examines the major features of these six club drugs. A more detailed discussion will follow in Chapter 4 (methamphetamine), Chapter 6 (LSD, MDMA, and ketamine), and Chapter 8 (GHB and Rohypnol).

Dietary Supplements

Another phenomenon that has attracted considerable concern has been the increasing prominence of herbal and nonherbal products, packaged and marketed as **dietary supplements,** that purport to enhance mood, energize the mind, or relieve feelings of anxiety. While clearly not as problematic as illicit drugs such as heroin and hallucinogens or club drugs, the fact remains that these products need to be closely examined for their potential to create as well as resolve health problems. It is estimated that dietary supplements are used for medicinal purposes on a regular basis by 20 to 30 percent of the U.S. population. In the vast majority of cases, people are taking supplement preparations without any communication with a physician or other health professional.[43] In addition, herb-based dietary supplements are now commercially available in products such as iced tea, soft drinks, fruit juices, and yogurts. Sales of food and drink products that promise bene... basic nutrition presently exceed $40 billion ye... year.[44]

Since dietary supplements are not officially clas... fied as drugs, governmental regulations for them are different from those that apply to prescription and over-the-counter medications. The Dietary Supplement Health and Education Act of 1994 requires that supplement labels contain the statement that any claims made by the manufacturer "have not been evaluated by the U.S. Food and Drug Administration." In effect, this disclaimer allows these products to be marketed and sold in the United States without the rigorous process of review and evaluation that assures the consumer that they are safe to take and effective for medicinal purposes. Some examples of such dietary supplements are androstenedione, creatine, gingko biloba, ginseng, and St. John's wort.

What medical claims can be made for these preparations? On the one hand, the 1994 law clearly prohibits manufacturers from making any claim that refers to a form of disease. On the other hand, a federal ruling in 2000 stipulated that certain common physical conditions associated with different stages of life such as aging, adolescence, pregnancy, and menopause are not diseases, and, therefore, dietary supplement claims for helping these conditions are allowed. Uncommon or more serious conditions associated with these life stages would still be considered diseases, and supplement labels are required to indicate that the products are not intended to "diagnose, treat, cure, or prevent" these particular conditions.

Unfortunately, the distinction between disease and non-disease can be difficult to make. For example, manufacturers can now claim that certain supplements may be able to treat muscle pain but are prohibited from mentioning joint pain because the latter is a symptom of arthritis. They can claim to treat "mild memory loss associated with aging" but not more severe memory problems associated with Alzheimer's disease. Federal officials admit that, at best, it is a difficult line to draw. At worst, there are serious concerns that consumer protections are being compromised. As one critic has

---

dietary supplements: Commercial preparations derived from vitamins, amino acids, or herbal extracts. Dietary supplement manufacturers are permitted to claim that these products can help with certain physical conditions associated with different stages of life, but they cannot be used to diagnose, treat, cure, or prevent physical disease.

Drugs . . . in Focus

Facts about Club Drugs

MDMA (methylenedioxymethamphetamine)

- Street names: Ecstasy, XTC, X, E, Adam, Clarity, Lover's Speed, Hug Drug, Euphoria, M&M
- Variations: MDA (methylenedioxyamphetamine), MDEA (methylenedioxyethylamphetamine)
- Forms: Tablet or capsule
- Drug type: Stimulant and hallucinogen
- Behavioral effects: Appetite suppression, excitation, perceptual distortions
- Physiological effects: increased heart rate and blood pressure, dehydration
- Length of effect: 3 to 6 hours
- Toxicity: Marked increase in body temperature; possible heart attack, stroke, or seizure (see Chapter 6)

GHB (gamma-hydroxybutyrate)

- Street names: Grievous Bodily Harm, G, Liquid X, Liquid Ecstasy, Georgia Home Boy
- Variations: Gamma-butyrolactone (GBL)
- Forms: Clear liquid, tablet, capsule, or white powder
- Drug type: Depressant
- Behavioral effects: Intoxication, euphoria, sedation, anxiety reduction
- Physiological effects: Central nervous system depressant, stimulation of growth-hormone release
- Length of effect: Up to 4 hours
- Toxicity: Overdoses produce drowsiness, loss of consciousness, impaired breathing, coma, potential death. GHB greatly potentiates the sedative action of alcohol (see Chapter 8).

Ketamine

- Street names: K, Special K, Vitamin K, Cat Valiums
- Variations: None
- Forms: Liquid, white powder snorted or smoked with marijuana or tobacco, intramuscular injection
- Drug type: Hallucinogen
- Behavioral effects: Dream-like state of consciousness, hallucinations
- Physiological effects: Increased blood pressure, potential seizures, and coma
- Length of effect: 1 hour
- Toxicity: Impaired attention and memory, impaired motor coordination, disorientation (see Chapter 6)

Rohypnol (flunitrazepam)

- Street names: Roofies, Rophies, Roche, Rope, Forget-me pill
- Variations: None
- Forms: Tablet dissolvable in beverages
- Drug type: Antianxiety drug
- Behavioral effects: Sedation
- Physiological effects: Decreased blood pressure, visual disturbances, gastrointestinal disturbances
- Length of effect: 8 to 12 hours
- Toxicity: Anterograde amnesia (loss of memory for events experienced under its influence). Rohypnol effects are greatly potentiated by alcohol (see Chapter 8).

Methamphetamine

- Street names: Speed, Ice, Meth, Crystal, Crystal Meth, Crank, Fire, Glass, Ice, Rock Candy
- Variations: Amphetamines, with varying degrees of similarity
- Forms: Many forms; methamphetamine can be smoked, snorted, injected, or orally ingested.
- Drug type: Stimulant
- Behavioral effects: Increased alertness and energy
- Physiological effects: Increased heart rate and blood pressure, decreased appetite
- Length of effect: Several hours
- Toxicity: Possible heart attack or cardiovascular collapse, seizures, cerebral hemorrhage, and coma (see Chapter 4)

LSD (lysergic acid diethylamide)

- Street names: Acid, Boomers, Yellow Sunshines, Barrels, Blotters, Cubes, Domes, Lids, Wedges
- Variations: Hallucinogens, with varying degrees of similarity
- Forms: Crystalline material soluble in water
- Drug type: Hallucinogen
- Behavioral effects: Distortions of visual perceptions, distortions of time and space
- Physiological effects: Increased heart rate and blood pressure, sweating, tremors
- Length of effect: 30 to 90 minutes, though effects might last several hours
- Toxicity: Numbness, nausea (see Chapter 6)

Sources: Brands, Bruna, Sproule, Beth, and Marshman, Joan (1998). *Drugs and drug abuse: A reference text.* Toronto: Addiction Research Foundation. National Institute on Drug Abuse (1999, December). *Community Drug Alert Bulletin: Club Drugs.* Bethesda, MD: National Institute on Drug Abuse.

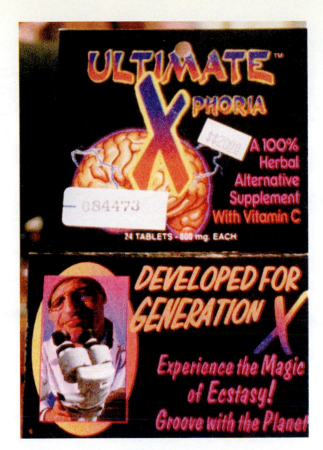

Herb-based dietary supplements such as Ephedra offer a tempting prospect of increased energy and euphoria but also carry significant health risks.

expressed it, the new regulations mean that "consumers at the beginning of the twenty-first century are about at the same place as consumers at the end of the nineteenth century."[45]

Beyond the potential risks associated with the instrumental use of dietary supplements, however, are the risks associated with the use of these products (particularly the herbal varieties) for recreational purposes by those individuals seeking a so-called natural herbal high. For example, a product that claims to increase alertness also may produce extreme euphoria, disorientation, and dangerous cardiovascular changes.

Prescription and Over-the-Counter (OTC) Drug Abuse

While the prevalence rates among young people for several categories of illicit drugs have shown steady declines since their most recent peaks in the late 1990s (see Chapter 2), the recreational use of prescription and over-the-counter (OTC) drugs has remained at relatively high levels. Approximately 10 percent of high school seniors and 7 percent of tenth graders in 2006 reported using the prescription pain medication hydrocodone (brand name: Vicodin) for nonmedical reasons in the past year and approximately 4 percent of high school seniors and tenth graders reported using the sustained-release form of oxycodone (brand name:

PORTRAIT   Nicholas and the Dextromethorphan High

Nicholas, sixteen years old, began using dextromethorphan to get high in late 2006. At first, he took two Coricidin HBP Cough and Cold pills a day and later increased his intake to eight a day, then sixteen. When his lunch money allowance to pay for his drug supply ran out, he shoplifted. At one point, he began to experience hallucinations at school.

By early 2007, his mother (pictured) was desperate. She pleaded with local drugstores to keep the cold remedies away from her son and other teenagers who were engaged in dextromethorphan abuse. "My son is going to die from these pills," she said.

The day after Nicholas's mother had made her plea with drugstore managers, Nicholas was charged with petty larceny for allegedly stealing fourteen boxes of Coricidin, worth about $168. If he had been convicted, he would have faced up to a year in jail.

The case of Nicholas and other similar cases has spurred Suffolk County, New York, to ban the sale of medicines containing dextromethorphan to anyone eighteen years old or younger. This regulatory legislation has made the county the first New York municipality to impose a ban of this kind, placing it at the forefront of

a nationwide movement to prevent minors to purchase these products and use them for recreational purposes.

In the meantime, Nicholas was released from custody and committed to a drug rehabilitation facility, after his mother declared her son a danger to himself.

Source: Schuster, Karla (2007, June 28). Cold remedy ban. *Newsday*, p. A50. Lam, Chau (2007, April 19). Sick over teen's use of medicine for high. *Newsday*, p. A2.

OxyContin). From 2002 to 2006, recreational use levels in these age groups have remained either steady or increased. The use over the past year of sedative-hypnotic drugs such as barbiturates (Chapter 8) among high school seniors has gradually risen from 3 percent in 1993 to 7 percent in 2005, with only a small decline in 2006. In addition, approximately 7 percent of high school seniors reported in 2006 taking OTC cough-and- cold medications that contain the cough suppressant dextromethorphan in the past year for the purpose of getting high, a practice commonly referred to as "robo-tripping" or "skittling." The easy availability of dextromethorphan for people of all ages and the increased risk of brain damage, seizure, and death associated with high doses of dextromethorphan are elements of great concern in today's drug scene (see Portrait).[46]

Summary

A Matter of Definition

- Psychoactive drugs are those drugs that affect our feelings, perceptions, and behavior. Depending on the intent of the individual, drug use can be considered either instrumental or recreational.

- Drug abuse refers to cases in which a licit or illicit drug is used in ways that produce some form of impairment. Drug misuse refers to cases in which a prescription or nonprescription drug is used inappropriately.

How Drugs Enter the Body

- There are four basic ways to administer drugs into the body: oral administration, injection, inhalation, and absorption through the skin or membranes. Each of these presents constraints on which kinds of drugs will be effectively delivered into the bloodstream.

How Drugs Exit the Body

- Most drugs are eliminated from the body through urinary excretion. Drugs are broken down for elimination by the action of enzymes in the liver. An index of how long this process takes is called the elimination half-life.

Factors Determining the Physiological Impact of Drugs

- The physiological effect of a drug can vary as a factor of the time elapsed since its administration, the possible combination of its administration with other drugs, and finally the personal characteristics of the individual consuming the drug.

- Some characteristics that can play a definite role in the effect of a drug include the individual's weight, gender, and racial or ethnic background.

- Two important issues need to be understood in looking at the physiological effect of drugs: the extent to which drugs pass into the bloodstream and from the bloodstream to the brain and the extent to which tolerance effects occur over repeated administrations of a given drug.

Psychological Factors in Drug-Taking Behavior

- Although the physiological actions of psychoactive drugs are becoming increasingly well understood, great variability in the effect of these drugs remains, largely because of psychological factors.

- The most prominent psychological factor is the influence of personal expectations on the part of the individual consuming the drug. The impact of expectations on one's reaction to a drug, a phenomenon called the placebo effect, is an important consideration in drug evaluation and research.

Physical and Psychological Dependence

- Drugs can be viewed in terms of a physical dependence model, in which the compulsive drug-taking behavior is tied to an avoidance of withdrawal symptoms, or a psychological dependence model, in which the drug-taking behavior is tied to a genuine craving for the drug and highly reinforcing effects of the drug on the user's body and mind.

Psychiatric Definitions

- The American Psychiatric Association currently recognizes two major conditions associated with drug-taking behavior: substance dependence and substance abuse. The broader term "substance" is used instead of "drug," because there is often confusion in the public mind in deciding what is defined as a drug and what is not.

The Problem of Drug Toxicity

- A drug's harmful effects are referred to as its toxicity. Acute toxicity can be measured in terms of a drug's therapeutic index or its margin of safety, each of which can be computed from its effective and lethal dose-response curves.

The DAWN Reports

● Drug Abuse Warning Network (DAWN) statistics, which reflect drug-related lethal and nonlethal emergencies in major metropolitan hospitals in the United States, offer another measure of acute drug toxicity. In general, DAWN statistics show that cocaine and narcotic drugs are both highly toxic and that many emergencies involve drugs being taken in combination with alcohol. There are also recent concerns for the increasing number of emergencies associated with club drugs and opiate-based pain-relief medications.

Looking to the Future and Learning from the Past

● Predictions regarding future patterns of drug abuse and drug-taking behavior in general are largely founded on patterns from the past. New drugs will undoubtedly come on the scene; old drugs that are currently out of favor will regain popularity.

● A serious concern in recent years has been the emergence of a group of drugs referred to as club drugs. They include MDMA (Ecstasy), GHB, ketamine, Rohypnol, methamphetamine, and LSD. They have their own individual toxicity profiles, with considerable health risks when used in combination with alcohol.

● Herbal or nonherbal products, marketed as dietary supplements, have been under increasing scrutiny with respect to possible toxic effects. Since dietary supplements are not officially classified in the United States as drugs, governmental regulations for them are different from those that apply to prescription and over-the-counter medications.

● Relatively high prevalence rates for recreational use of prescription drugs and over-the-counter (OTC) drugs among young people have raised serious concerns. Examples of abused drugs in this category include pain medications such as Vicodin and OxyContin, sedative-hypnotic drugs such as barbiturates, and dextromethorphan in popular cough-and-cold remedies.

Key Terms

acute toxicity, p. 22
behavioral tolerance, p. 15
biotransformation, p. 12
chronic toxicity, p. 30
cross-tolerance, p. 16
dietary supplements, p. 31
dose, p. 21
dose-response curve, p. 22
double-blind, p. 19
drug, p. 4
drug abuse, p. 7

Drug Abuse Warning Network (DAWN), p. 26
drug dependence, p. 4
drug misuse, p. 6
drug-related ED visit, p. 26
effective dose, p. 22
elimination half-life, p. 12
illicit drugs, p. 3
instrumental use, p. 6
intramuscular, p. 9
intranasal, p. 11

intravenous, p. 9
latency period, p. 12
lethal dose, p. 23
licit drugs, p. 3
margin of safety, p. 23
metabolite, p. 12
physical dependence, p. 19
placebo, p. 18
potentiation, p. 13
psychoactive drugs, p. 3
psychological dependence, p. 20

recreational use, p. 6
subcutaneous, p. 9
sublingual, p. 11
substance abuse, p. 21
substance dependence, p. 21
synergism, p. 13
therapeutic index, p. 23
tolerance, p. 15
toxicity, p. 21
transdermal patch, p. 11

Endnotes

1. Centers for Disease Control and Prevention (2003). Tobacco use among middle and high school students—New Hampshire, 1995–2001. *Morbidity and Mortality Weekly Report, 52*, 7–9. Forman, Robert F. (2003). Availability of opioids on the Internet. *Journal of American Medical Association, 290*, 889. Grube, Joel W. (1995). Television alcohol portrayals, alcohol advertising, and alcohol expectancies among children and adolescents. In Susan E. Martin (ed.), *The effects of the mass media on the use and abuse of alcohol* (NIAAA Research Monograph 28). Bethesda, MD: National

Institute on Alcohol Abuse and Alcoholism, pp. 105–121. Ifill, Gwen (1992, March 30). Clinton admits experiment with marijuana in 1960's. *New York Times*, p. A13. Substance Abuse and Mental Health Services Administration (2004). Availability of illicit drugs among youths. *The NSDUH Report*. Rockville, MD: Office of Applied Studies, Substance Abuse and Mental Health Services Administration, p. 2. Slater, Michael D.; Rouner, Donna; Murphy, Kevin; Beauvais, Frederick; Van Leuven, James; and Rodríguez, Melanie Domenech (1996). Male adolescents' reactions to

TV beer advertisements: The effects of sports content and programming context. *Journal of Studies in Alcohol*, 57, 425–433. Zwarun, Lara, and Farrar, Kirstie M. (2005). Doing what they say, saying what they mean: Self-regulatory compliance and depictions of drinking in alcohol commercials in televised sports. *Mass Communication and Society*, 8, 347–371.

2. Butterfield, Fox (2002, February 11). As drug use drops in big cities, small towns confront upsurge. *New York Times*, pp. A1, A18. Substance Abuse and Mental Health Services Administration (2001, November 23). Substance use among older adults. *The NHSDA Report*. Rockville, MD: Office of Applied Statistics, Substance Abuse and Mental Health Services Administration.

3. Leshner, Alan I. (1998, October). Addiction is a brain disease—and it matters. *National Institute of Justice Journal*, 2–6.

4. Jacobs, Michael R., and Fehr, Kevin O'B. (1987). *Drugs and drug abuse: A reference text*. Toronto: Addiction Research Foundation, pp. 3–5.

5. Goode, Erich (2005). *Drugs in American society* (6th ed.). New York: McGraw-Hill College, pp. 15–26.

6. Public-service message, "Frying Pan." Partners for a Drug-free America, New York, 1987.

7. Drug patch for Parkinson's (2007, May 14). *Newsday*, p. A32. Drugmakers trying to retire the needle (2002, September 24). *New York Times*, p. F7. Mitragotri, Samir, Blankschtein, Daniel, and Langer, Robert (1995). Ultrasound-mediated transdermal protein delivery. *Science*, 269, 850–853.

8. Hawks, Richard L., and Chiang, C. Nora (1986). Examples of specific drug assays. In Richard L. Hawks and C. Nora Chiang (Eds.), *Urine testing for drugs of abuse* (NIDA Research Monograph 73). Rockville, MD: National Institute on Drug Abuse, pp. 84–112. Julien, Robert M. (2001). *A primer of drug action* (9th ed.). New York: Worth, pp. 27–31. McKim, William A. (2000). *Drugs and behavior: An introduction to behavioral pharmacology* (4th ed.). Upper Saddle River, NJ: Prentice-Hall, pp. 1–25.

9. Lankester, E. Ray (1889). Mithridatism. *Nature*, 40, 149.

10. Siegel, Shepard (1990). Drug anticipation and the treatment of dependence. In Barbara A. Ray (ed.), *Learning factors in substance abuse* (NIDA Research Monograph 84). Rockville, MD: National Institute on Drug Abuse, pp. 1–24.

11. Siegel, Shepard (1975). Evidence from rats that morphine tolerance is a learned response. *Journal of Comparative and Physiological Psychology*, 89, 489–506. Siegel, Shepard; Hinson, Riley E.; Krank, Marvin D.; and McCully, Jane. (1982). Heroin "overdose" death: Contribution of drug-associated environmental cues. *Science*, 216, 436–437.

12. Brecher, Edward M., and the editors of *Consumer Reports*. (1972). *Licit and illicit drugs*. Mount Vernon, NY: Consumers Union.

13. Siegel, Shepard (1999). Drug anticipation and drug addiction. The 1998 H. David Archibald Lecture. *Addiction*, 94, 1113–1124.

14. Frezza, Mario; DiPadova, Carlo; Pozzato, Gabrielle; Terpin, Maddalena; Baraona, Enrique; and Lieber, Charles S. (1990). High blood alcohol levels in women: The role of decreased gastric alcohol dehydrogenase activity and first-pass metabolism. *New England Journal of Medicine*, 322, 95–99.

15. Nakawatase, Tomoko V., Yamamoto, Joe, and Sasao, Toshiaki (1993). The association between fast-flushing response and alcohol use among Japanese Americans. *Journal of Studies on Alcohol*, 54, 48–53.

16. Goodman, Deborah (1992, January–February). NIMH grantee finds drug responses differ among ethnic groups. *ADAMHA News*, pp. 5, 15.

17. Perez-Stable, Eliseo J.; Herrera, Brenda; Jacob III, Peyton; and Benowita, Neal L. (1998). Nicotine metabolism and intake in black and white smokers. *Journal of the American Medical Association*, 280, 152–156.

18. Goode, Erich (1999). *Drugs in American society* (5th ed.). New York: McGraw-Hill College, p. 9.

19. Kornetsky, Conan (1976). *Pharmacology: Drugs affecting behavior*. New York, Wiley, p. 23. Morris, David B. (1999). Placebo, pain, and belief: A biocultural model. In Anne Harrington (ed.), *The placebo effect: An interdisciplinary exploration*. Cambridge, MA: Harvard University Press, pp. 187–207. Shapiro, Arthur K., and Shapiro, Elaine (1997). *The powerful placebo: From ancient priest to modern physician*. Baltimore: Johns Hopkins University Press.

20. Beecher, H. K. (1959). *Measurement of subjective responses: Quantitative effects of drugs*. New York: Oxford University Press.

21. Benedetti, F. (2002). How the doctor's words affect the patient's brain. *Evaluation and the Health Professions*, 25, 369–386. Schindel, L. E. (1962). Placebo in theory and practice. *Antibiotica et Chemotherapia*, Advances, 10, 398–430. Cited in Kornetsky, *Pharmacology*, p. 36.

22. Blakeslee, Sandra (1998, October 13). Placebos prove so powerful even experts are surprised. *New York Times*, pp. F1, F4. Christensen, Demaris (2001, February 3). Medicinal mimicry: Sometimes, placebos work—but how? *Science News*, 74–75, 78. De la Fuente-Fernández, R., and Stoessl, A. J. (2002). The biochemical bases for reward: Implications for the placebo effect. *Evaluation and the Health Professions*, 25, 387–398. Flaten, Magne Arve, Simonsen, Terje, and Olsen, Harald (1999). Drug-related information generates placebo and nocebo responses that modify the drug response. *Psychosomatic Medicine, 61,* 250–255. Levinthal, Charles F. (1988). *Messengers of paradise: Opiates and the brain*. Anchor Press/Doubleday. Talbot, Margaret (2000, January 9). The placebo prescription. *New York Times Magazine*, pp. 34–39, 44, 58–60.

23. Quitkin, Frederic M. (1999). Placebos, drug effects, and study design: A clinician's guide. *American Journal of Psychiatry*, 156, 829–836.

24. Blum, Kenneth. (1991). *Alcohol and the addictive brain*. New York, Free Press, p. 17.

25. Pinel, John P. J. (2003). *Biopsychology* (5th ed.). Boston: Allyn and Bacon, p. 398.

26. Simpson, D. Dwayne, and Marsh, Kerry L. (1986). Relapse and recovery among opioid addicts 12 years after treatment. In Frank M. Tims and Carl G. Leukefeld (Eds.), *Relapse and recovery in drug abuse* (NIDA Research Monograph 72). Rockville, MD: National Institute on Drug Abuse, pp. 86–103. Simpson, D. Dwayne, and Sells, Saul B. (1982). Effectiveness of treatment for drug abuse: An overview of the DARP research program. *Advances in Alcohol and Substance Abuse, 2*, 7–29.

27. Halikas, James A. (1997). Craving. In Joyce H. Lowinson, Pedro Ruiz, Robert B. Millman, and John G. Langrod (Eds.), *Substance abuse: A comprehensive textbook* (3rd ed.). Baltimore: Williams and Wilkins, pp. 85–90. Pickens, Roy, and Thompson, Travis (1968). Cocaine-reinforced behavior in rats: Effects of reinforcement magnitude and fixed-ratio size. *Journal of Pharmacology and Experimental Therapeutics, 161*, 122–129.

28. Hoffmeister, F. H., and Wuttke, W. (1975). Psychotropic drugs as negative reinforcers. *Pharmacological Reviews, 27*, 419–428. Yokel, R. A. (1987). Intravenous self-administration: Response rates, the effect of pharmacological challenges and drug preferences. In Michael A. Bozarth (Ed.), *Methods of assessing the reinforcing properties of abused drugs*. New York: Springer-Verlag, pp. 1–34.

29. Johanson, Chris E. (1984). Assessment of the abuse potential of cocaine in animals. In John Grabowski (Ed.), *Cocaine: Pharmacology, effects, and treatment of abuse*. Rockville, MD: National Institute on Drug Abuse, pp. 54–71.

30. Quotation from Goode, Erich. (1989). *Drugs in American society* (3rd ed.). New York: McGraw-Hill, p. 49. Data from Bozarth, Michael A., and Wise, Roy A. (1985). Toxicity associated with long-term intravenous heroin and cocaine self-administration in the rat. *Journal of the American Medical Association, 254*, 81–83.

31. Goode, Erich. *Drugs*, pp. 11–18. Stewart, Jane, De Wit, Harriet, and Eikelboom, Roelof (1984). Role of unconditioned and conditioned drug effects in the self-administration of opiates and stimulants. *Psychological Review, 91*, 251–268.

32. American Psychiatric Association (2000). *Diagnostic and statistical manual. Text Revision* (4th ed.). Washington, DC: American Psychiatric Association, pp. 191, 197, and 199.

33. Substance Abuse and Mental Health Services Administration (2007). *Drug Abuse Warning Network, 2005: National estimates of drug-related emergency department visits*. Rockville MD: Office of Applied Studies, Substance Abuse and Mental Health Services Administration. Substance Abuse and Mental Health Services Administration (2005). *Drug Abuse Warning Network, 2003: Area profiles of drug-related mortality*. Rockville, MD: Office of Applied Studies, Substance Abuse and Mental Health Services Administration.

34. Substance Abuse, *National estimates of drug-related emergency department visits*, Table 1.

35. Ibid.

36. Ibid, Table 2.

37. Substance Abuse, *Area profiles of drug-related mortality*, pp. 52–53, 62–63, 64–65, 80–81, 98–99, and 106–107.

38. Substance Abuse and Mental Health Administration (2004, July). Club drugs, 2002 update. *DAWN Report*, p. 3. Substance Abuse and Mental Health Administration (2004, July). Oxycodone, hydrocodone, and polydrug use, 2002. *DAWN Report*, p. 1.

39. Inciardi, James A. (2002). *The war on drugs III*. Boston: Allyn and Bacon, p. 69.

40. Hernandez, Daisy (2003, March 23). Heroin's new generation: Young, white, and middle class. *New York Times*, p. 34. Office of National Drug Control Policy (1998, Winter). *Pulse check: Trends in drug abuse, January–June 1998*, Washington, DC: Office of National Drug Control Policy. Sabbag, Robert (1994, May 5). The cartels would like a second chance. *Rolling Stone*, pp. 35–37. Wilkinson, Peter (1994, May 5). The young and the reckless. *Rolling Stone*, pp. 29, 32.

41. Colliver, James D.; Kroutil, Larry A.; Dai, Lanting; and Gfroerer, Joseph C. (2006). *Misuse of prescription drugs: Data from the 2002, 2003, and 2004 National Surveys on Drug Use and Health*. Rockville, MD: Office of Applied Studies, Substance Abuse and Mental Health Services Administration. Substance Abuse and Mental Health Services Administration (2004, September). Narcotic analgesics, 2002 update. *The DAWN Report*. Rockville, MD: Office of Applied Studies, Substance Abuse and Mental Health Services Administration, pp. 1–8.

42. Substance Abuse and Mental Health Services Administration (2004, July). Club drugs, 2002 update. *The DAWN Report*. Rockville, MD: Office of Applied Studies, Substance Abuse and Mental Health Services Administration, pp. 1–4.

43. Brody, Jane E. (2003, February 4). Herbal and natural don't always mean safe. *New York Times*, p. F7. De Smet, Peter (2002). Herbal remedies. *New England Journal of Medicine, 347*, 2046–2056. Hurley, Dan (2007, January 16). Diet supplements and safety: Some disquieting data. *New York Times*, p. F5. Straus, Stephen E. (2002). Herbal medicines—What's in the bottle? *New England Journal of Medicine, 347*, 1997–1998.

44. Barnes, Julian E., and Winter, Greg (2001, May 27). Stressed out? Bad knee? Relief promised in a juice. *New York Times*, pp. 1, 18.

45. Dietary supplement claims: FDA eases restrictions; consumer advocates wary of harmful effects (2000, January 6). *Newsday*, p. A22. Quotation by Bruce Silverglade. Fontanarosa, Phil B., Rennie, Drummond,

and DeAngelis, Catherine D. (2003). The need for regulation of dietary supplements—Lessons from ephedra. *Journal of the American Medical Association, 289*, 1568–1570. Shekelle, Paul G.; Hardy, Mary L.; Morton, Sally, C.; Maglione, Margaret; Mojica, Walter A.; et al. (2003). Efficacy and safety of ephedra and ephedrine for weight loss and athletic performance: A meta-analysis. *Journal of the American Medical Association, 289*, 1537–1545.

46. Johnston, Lloyd D.; O'Malley, Patrick M.; Bachman, Jerald G.; and Schulenberg, John E. (2007). *Monitoring the Future national results on adolescent drug use. Overview of key findings, 2006.* Bethesda, MD: National Institute on Drug Abuse, Table 2.

chapter 2

The History of Drug Use and Drug Legislation

After you have completed this chapter, you will understand

- The origins and history of drugs and drug-taking behavior
- How early movements toward drug regulation were often fueled by racism or fear of a minority group
- America's tolerant attitude toward drug use from 1960 to 1980
- President Nixon's war on drugs
- The renewed interest in drug regulation during the 1980s
- Present-day statistics on drug use in the United States
- America's drug debate

If the Chinaman cannot get along without his "dope," we can get along without him.

—*American Pharmaceutical Association, 1902*

Most of the attacks upon white women of the South are the direct result of the cocaine-crazed Negro brain. . . . Negro cocaine fiends are now a new Southern menace.

—New York Times, *February 8, 1914*

Liquor traffic is un-American, pro-German, crime-producing, food-wasting, youth-corrupting, home-wrecking, and treasonable.

—*The Anti-Saloon League, 1918*

Under marijuana, Mexicans become very violent, especially when they become angry, and will attack an officer even if a gun is drawn on him. They seem to have no fear; I have also noted that under the influence of this weed they have enormous strength and that it will take several men to handle one man, while under ordinary circumstances one man could handle him with ease.

—A Texas police officer, 1927

The use of consciousness-altering drugs has been a part of human life in almost every culture and in every age of history. Psychoactive drugs have been used in the context of religious rituals, health care, celebration, and recreation. In most societies, the use of some drugs has been permitted, whereas the use of other drugs has been prohibited, often depending on the type of drug that is being used, the drug's effects, and who is using the drug. Understanding the history of drug use and our efforts to control drug abuse is important because knowledge of the past provides the basis for our understanding of drug abuse in our society now and in the future.

The United States has an extensive history in the use and abuse of drugs, and over the years, our views toward certain drugs have fluctuated between enthusiastic acceptance and passionate rejection. Heroin, marijuana, cocaine, and numerous other drugs all have had periods of popularity and periods of disapproval. In the late 1800s, for example, America experienced an epidemic of cocaine use. This was followed by a rejection in the early 1900s and a reemergence in the second half of the 1970s, followed by another period of rejection in the 1980s. Understanding these historical swings helps us make sense of our current attitudes and policies toward present-day drug use.

As we will see in this chapter, American drug control policy also has had its own historical swings. Drug control policies have not always been founded on rational decisions based on empirical data. Sometimes, decisions on which drugs to outlaw and which to legalize have been based on fear, hysteria, politics, and racism, with the legal prohibition of a particular drug associated with fear of a given drug's effect on a threatening minority group. Some of these fears, as we will see in more detail later, include the belief that cocaine would cause southern African Americans to rape white women, opium would facilitate sexual contact between Chinese and white Americans, marijuana would incite violence among Latinos, and alcohol abuse would lead to particularly disruptive behavior among Italian and Irish immigrants. This chapter provides an overview of drug use and drug legislation from early times to the present day. In addition, we will examine current patterns of drug use in the United States, among young people and the population at large.

Drugs in Early Times

Try to imagine the circumstances under which a psychoactive drug might have been discovered accidentally. Thousands of years ago, perhaps hundreds of thousands of years ago, the process of discovery would have been as natural as eating, and the motivation as basic as simple curiosity. In cool climates, next to a cave dwelling may have grown a profusion of blue morning glories or brightly colored mushrooms, plants that produce hallucinations similar to LSD. In desert regions, yellow-orange fruits grew on certain cacti, the source of the hallucinogenic drug peyote. Elsewhere, poppy plants, the source of opium, covered acres of open fields. Coca leaves, from which cocaine is made, grew on shrubs along the mountain valleys throughout Central and South America. The hardy cannabis plant, the source of marijuana, grew practically everywhere.[1]

It is entirely possible that some of the curiosity of humans was inspired by observing the unusual behavior of animals as they fed on these plants. Within their own experience, somewhere along the line people made the connection between the chewing of willow bark (the source of modern-day aspirin) and the relief of a headache or the eating of the senna plant (a natural laxative) and the relief of constipation.

Of course, some of these plants made people sick, and many were sufficiently poisonous to cause death. The plants that had the strangest impact, however, were the ones that produced hallucinations. Having a sudden vision of something totally foreign to everyday experiences must have been overwhelming, like a visit to another world. Individuals with prior knowledge about such plants, as well as about plants with therapeutic powers, would eventually acquire great power over others in the community. This knowledge was the beginning of **shamanism**, a practice among primitive societies dating back, by some estimates, more that 40,000 years,

shamanism: The philosophy and practice of healing in which the diagnosis or treatment is based on trance-like states, either on the part of the healer (shaman) or the patient.

in which an individual called a **shaman** acts as a healer through a combination of trances and plant-based medicines, usually in the context of a local religious rite. Shamans still function today in remote areas of the world, often alongside practitioners of modern medicine, and hallucination-producing plants still play a major role in present-day shamanic healing.[2]

With the development of centralized religions in Egyptian and Babylonian societies, the influence of shamanism would gradually decline. The power to heal through a knowledge of drugs passed into the hands of the priesthood, which placed a greater emphasis on formal rituals and rules than on hallucinations and trances.

The most extensive testament to the development of priestly healing during this period is a 65-foot-long Egyptian scroll known as the **Ebers Papyrus,** named after the British Egyptologist who acquired it in 1872. This mammoth document, dating from 1500 B.C., contains more than eight hundred prescriptions for practically every ailment imaginable, including simple wasp stings and crocodile bites, baldness, constipation, headaches, enlarged prostate glands, sweaty feet, arthritis, inflammations of all types, heart disease, and cancer. More than a hundred of the preparations contained castor oil as a natural laxative. Some contained the "berry of the poppy," which is now recognized as referring to opium. Other ingredients were quite bizarre: lizard's blood, the teeth of swine, the oil of worms, the hoof of an ass, putrid meat with fly specks, and crocodile dung (excrement of all types being highly favored for its ability to frighten off the evil spirits of disease).[3]

How successful were these strange remedies? It is impossible to know because records were not kept on whether or not patients were cured. Although some of the ingredients, such as opium and castor oil, had true medicinal value, it may be that much of the improvement from these concoctions was psychological rather than physiological. In other words, improvement in the patient's condition resulted from the *belief* on the patient's part that he or she would be helped, a phenomenon known as the **placebo effect** (see Chapter 1).

Along with substances that had genuine healing properties, other psychoactive drugs were put to other uses. In the early Middle Ages, Viking warriors ate the mushroom *Amanita muscaria*, known as "fly agaric," and experienced increased energy, which resulted in wild behavior in battle. They were called "Berserkers" because of the bear skins they wore, and reckless, violent behavior has come to be called "berserk." Later, witches operating on the periphery of Christian society created "witch's brews," which were said to induce hallucinations and a

In a wide range of world cultures throughout history, hallucinogens have been regarded as having deeply spiritual powers. Under the influence of drugs, this modern-day shaman communicates with the spirit world.

sensation of flying. The brews were mixtures made of various plants such as mandrake, henbane, and belladonna. The toads that they included in their recipes did not hurt either: We know now that the sweat glands of toads contain a chemical related to DMT, a powerful hallucinogenic drug, as well as bufotenine, a drug that raises blood pressure and heart rate (see Chapter 6).[4]

Drugs in the Nineteenth Century

By the end of the nineteenth century, the medical profession had made significant strides with respect to medical healing. Morphine was identified as the active

shaman (SHAH-men): A healer whose diagnosis or treatment of patients is based at least in part on trances. These trances are frequently induced by hallucinogenic drugs.

Ebers Papyrus: An Egyptian document, dated approximately 1500 B.C., containing more than 800 prescriptions for common ailments and diseases.

placebo (pla-CEE-bo) effect: Any change in a person's condition after taking a drug, based solely on that person's beliefs about the drug rather than on any physical effects of the drug (see Chapter 1).

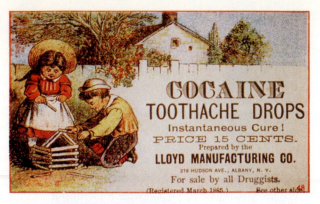

In the latter part of the nineteenth century in the United States, cocaine was a popular ingredient in over-the-counter medications. These products were totally unregulated, and customers included children as well as adults.

ingredient in opium, a drug that had been in use for at least three thousand years, and had become the physician's most reliable prescription to control the pain of disease and injury. Invention of the syringe made it possible to deliver morphine directly and speedily into the bloodstream.

Morphine became a very popular treatment for pain during the Civil War, a time during which a surgeon's skill was often measured by how quickly he could saw off a wounded patient's limb. Following the war, morphine dependence among Civil War veterans was so common that it was called the "soldier's disease" or the "army disease." After the Civil War, doctors also recommended morphine injections for women to treat the pain associated with "female troubles," and by the late 1890s, morphine dependence among women made up almost half of all cases of drug dependence in the United States (see Chapter 5).[5]

Cocaine, having been extracted from South American coca leaves, was also a drug in widespread use in Europe and North America and was taken quite casually in a variety of forms. The original formula for Coca-Cola, as the name suggests, contained cocaine until 1903, as did Dr. Agnew's Catarrh Powder, a popular remedy for chest colds. In the mid-1880s, Parke, Davis, and Company (since 2002, merged with Pfizer, Inc.) was selling cocaine and its botanical source, coca, in more than a dozen forms, including coca-leaf cigarettes and cigars, cocaine inhalants, a coca cordial, and an

laissez-faire (LAY-say FAIR) (Fr.): The philosophy of exerting as little governmental control and regulation as possible.

injectable cocaine solution.[6] A Viennese doctor named Sigmund Freud, who was later to gain a greater reputation for his psychoanalytical theories than for his ideas concerning psychoactive drugs, called cocaine a "magical drug." Freud would later reverse his position when a friend and colleague became dependent on cocaine (see Chapter 4).[7]

During the nineteenth century, America's public attitude toward drug use was one of **laissez-faire,** roughly translated from the French as "allow [people] to do as they please," which means that there was little regulation or control of drugs. In fact, the United States was the only major Western nation that allowed the unlimited distribution, sale, and promotion of psychoactive drugs. The result was a century of widespread medicinal and recreational drug use that has been described as a "dope fiend's paradise."[8]

There were two major factors that explain why there were no major drug control policies during this period. First, unlike many European nations, the United States did not have any agencies regulating the medical field, and because doctors and pharmacists were unlicensed, it was not difficult to call oneself a doctor and distribute drugs. The American Medical Association (AMA) was established in 1847, but only a fraction of practicing health professionals were members during the 1800s. Doctors of this era had no choice but to rely upon untested and potentially toxic drugs to treat both physical and psychological disorders (Drugs . . . in Focus). A second factor was the issue of states' rights. During the nineteenth century, the prevailing political philosophy was a belief in the strict separation of state and federal powers, especially in southern states. Therefore, the regulation of drugs was left to the states, most of which had few, if any, drug laws. For the federal government to pass laws limiting the use of any drug would have been seen as a serious challenge to the concept of states' rights.[9]

Drug Regulation in the Early Twentieth Century

By 1900, the promise of medical advances in the area of drugs was beginning to be matched by concerns about the dependence that some of these drugs could produce. Probably the two most important factors that fueled the movement toward drug regulation in the beginning of the twentieth century were (1) the abuse of patent medicines and (2) the association of drug use with minority groups. Between 1890 and 1906, numerous

Drugs . . . in Focus

Abraham Lincoln, Depression, and Those "Little Blue Pills"

It is well known to historians that Abraham Lincoln suffered from long bouts of melancholy, a condition that would today be diagnosed as major depression. What is less known is that Lincoln had been advised by his physician to take what he called his "little blue pills" to help him elevate his mood.

A few months into his presidency, in 1861, however, Lincoln stopped taking these pills, complaining that they made him "cross." During the late 1850s, Lincoln had experienced episodes of bizarre behavior that included towering rages and mood changes that appeared out of nowhere or were responses to innocuous and sometime trivial circumstances. It is reasonable to assume that the symptoms were, as Lincoln himself surmised, due to the "little blue pills."

It is a good thing that Lincoln made this decision. The medication he was taking was a common nineteenth-century remedy for depression, called *blue mass*. It consisted of licorice root, rosewater, honey, sugar, and rose petals. But the main ingredient in these blue-colored pills, about the size of peppercorns, was approximately 750 micrograms of mercury, a highly toxic substance. At the common dosage level of two or three pills per day, individuals ingested nearly nine thousand times the amount of mercury that is considered safe by current health standards.

If Lincoln had continued to take blue mass for his depression, he undoubtedly would have continued to experience the behavioral and neurological symptoms common to chronic mercury poisoning as he led the nation during the Civil War. Fortunately, the symptoms of mercury poisoning in Lincoln's case were reversible after he stopped taking blue mass. Lincoln would suffer from severe bouts of depression until his death in 1865, but America was spared what might have been a catastrophe of historic proportions.

Postscript: Mercury poisoning was quite common throughout the nineteenth century, as this substance's toxic properties had not yet been discovered or fully appreciated. Hat makers were particularly susceptible to mercury toxicity because they would routinely rub mercury into the felt material of hats to preserve them for commercial sale, absorbing the substance through their fingers. Symptoms of severe mood swings and eventually dementia were commonly observed among people in this profession and eventually became the basis for the expression "mad as a hatter."

Source: Hirschhorn, Norbert, Feldman, Robert G., and Greaves, Ian (2001, Summer). Abraham Lincoln's blue pills: Did the 16th President suffer from mercury poisoning? *Perspectives in Biology and Medicine*, pp. 315–322.

---

patent medicines were sold that included such ingredients as alcohol, opium, morphine, cocaine, and marijuana.

The term "patent medicine" is misleading. Generally, one thinks of a patented product as one that is registered with the government, providing the producers with the exclusive right to sell that product. However, patent medicines around the turn of the twentieth century were not registered with the federal government or any other agency, and their formulas were often kept secret. Manufacturers did not have to list the ingredients of patent medicines on the bottle label or the package in which they were sold. One of the most popular methods of marketing patent medicines was the traveling medicine show, which included magicians and other performers, and culminated with a "pitch man" who convinced the gathering crowd to buy his patent medicine.[10]

As the popularity of patent medicines grew, so did drug abuse. Unlike many of today's drug abusers, the typical nineteenth-century abuser was a white middle- or upper-class housewife who became dependent upon a patent medicine. In response to the growing number of drug-dependent Americans, President Theodore Roosevelt proposed a federal law that would regulate misbranded and adulterated foods, drinks, and drugs. This proposal was met with strong opposition from the business sector, which was making a good profit from the patent medicine industry. Public opinion swayed in Roosevelt's direction after Upton Sinclair published *The Jungle* in 1906, a novel that exposed the unsanitary conditions of the meat packaging industry in Chicago. The

patent medicine: A drug or combination of drugs sold through peddlers, shops, or mail-order advertisements.

book depicted how diseased cattle and hogs, as well as human body parts, were included in packaged food and how much of the meat sold to the general public included undesirable parts of animals sometimes scraped from slaughterhouse floors. Congress responded by passing the 1906 Pure Food and Drug Act, which required all packaged foods and drugs to list the ingredients on the label of the product.

The new law did not prevent drugs from being sold, but it did mandate that the proportion of drugs in patent medicines had to be listed. Thus cocaine, alcohol, heroin, and morphine could still be in patent preparations as long as they were listed as ingredients. Following the enactment of the Pure Food and Drug Act, however, the amount of patent medicines bought and used by Americans was greatly reduced.[11]

Drug Regulation, 1914–1937

By the second decade of the twentieth century, calls for expanded drug regulatory legislation were spurred in large part by a growing prejudice against minority groups in America that were believed to be involved in drug use. As we will see, this social phenomenon impacted upon the eventual prohibition of opium and heroin, cocaine, and marijuana, as well as the temporary prohibition of alcohol.

The movement toward federal drug control legislation, in general, was first met with resistance from southern politicians, who believed that such actions were yet another intrusion of the federal government into state affairs. In order to overcome this resistance from southerners, a propaganda campaign was launched that associated African Americans with cocaine. Southern newspapers began printing stories of the cocaine-induced raping of white women and demonstrations of superhuman strength.[12] One of the most incredible myths was that cocaine made African Americans unaffected by .32 caliber bullets, a claim that is said to have caused many southern police departments to switch to .38 caliber revolvers. The propaganda campaign was successful. Southerners became more afraid of African Americans than of an increase in federal power and offered their support for the Pure Food and Drug Act and later the Harrison Act of 1914.[13]

Another example of how racism became interwoven with drug policy was the identification of Chinese workers with the smoking of opium. After the Civil War, the United States had imported Chinese workers to help build the rapidly expanding railroads. The Chinese

This late nineteenth-century illustration of young working girls in a New York City opium den was part of a widespread media campaign at the time to outlaw the smoking of opium.

brought with them the habit of smoking opium, which many Americans believed led to prostitution, gambling, and overall moral decline. When the railroads were finished, Chinese workers began to migrate into western cities such as San Francisco. Working for low wages, the Chinese, some Americans feared, would take jobs from whites and the "big bosses" of business would use cheap Chinese labor as a means of preventing union organization. Hostility and violence against the Chinese became common. The first anti-drug legislation in the United States was an ordinance enacted in 1875 by the City of San Francisco prohibiting the operation of opium dens—establishments in which the smoking of opium occurred. Other states followed San Francisco's lead by prohibiting opium smoking, and in 1887, Congress prohibited the possession of smokable opium by Chinese citizens.[14]

The Harrison Act of 1914

The origins of the landmark Harrison Act of 1914 can be traced back to the concern over Chinese opium use. While many Americans detested the Chinese and their habit of smoking opium, at the same time, the U.S.

government wanted to open up trade with China. China refused to purchase American goods, however, because of the poor treatment of Chinese people in the United States. To increase its influence in China and to improve its trade position, the United States initiated several international conferences to attempt to control the worldwide production and distribution of narcotics, especially opium. Recognizing the enormous population of opium abusers within their own country, Chinese leaders were eager to participate in such conferences. At an international conference held in the Hague in 1912, the United States was accused of maintaining a double standard. According to its critics, the U.S. government was attempting to pass international agreements to regulate the drug trade while at the same time having no domestic control of drug production and distribution within its own borders. In response, on December 17, 1914, Congress passed the Harrison Act, named after its sponsor, Representative Francis Burton Harrison of New York.[15]

The Harrison Act was designed to regulate drug abuse through government taxation and became the basis for narcotics regulation in the United States for more than a half-century. The act required anyone importing, manufacturing, selling, or dispensing cocaine and opiate drugs to register with the Treasury Department, pay a special tax, and keep records of all transactions. Because the act was a revenue measure, enforcement was made the responsibility of the Department of the Treasury and the commissioner of the Internal Revenue Service.

Cocaine was not defined as a narcotic under the law, but it became lumped together with opiates and often was referred to as a narcotic as well. Although application of the term to cocaine was incorrect ("narcotic" literally means "stupor-inducing," and cocaine is anything but that), the association has unfortunately stuck. Later, several restricted drugs, including marijuana and the hallucinogen peyote, also were officially classified as narcotics without regard to their pharmacological characteristics. Today, many people still think of any illegal drug as a narcotic, and for many years, the bureau at the Treasury Department charged with drug enforcement responsibilities was the Bureau of Narcotics, and its agents were known on the street as "narks."

The Harrison Act did not make opiates and cocaine illegal. Physicians, dentists, and veterinarians could prescribe these drugs "in the course of their professional practice only." What this phrase meant was left to a good deal of interpretation. The Treasury Department viewed the maintenance of patients on these drugs, particularly opiates, as beyond medical intentions, and the Supreme Court upheld this interpretation. Between 1915 and 1938, thousands of physicians in the United States were found to be in violation of the law. Eventually, physicians stopped issuing prescriptions for drugs now covered under the Harrison Act. As a result, a new class of criminal was created, driving individuals to seek drugs through the black market. In what would become a continuing and unfortunate theme in the history of drug law enforcement legislation, the Harrison Act failed to reduce drug-taking behavior. Instead, it created a new lucrative market for organized crime.

Alcohol and the Prohibition Era

Since the 1800s, there had been movements for the prohibition of alcohol in the United States (see Chapter 10), and although several states had passed anti-alcohol measures, prohibitionists were never quite able to gain national support for their movement. World War I, however, changed public sentiment, particularly with respect to a prominent minority group. During the war, anti-immigrant sentiment began to flourish, especially against German Americans, who were prominent in the business of making beer. Prohibitionists launched a campaign to convince Americans that the production of beer was part of a German plot to undermine America's willpower and deplete the cereal grains that were needed to make food for the soldiers in Europe. Prohibitionists were typical rural white Protestants, antagonistic toward Irish and Italian immigrants who were gaining political power in metropolitan areas such as Chicago and New York. To many who were behind the movement, prohibition represented a battle between America's Protestant rural towns and America's "sinful," immigrant-filled cities.[16]

In January 1919, Congress passed the Eighteenth Amendment, which outlawed the manufacture and sale of alcohol, except for industrial use. Nine months after the amendment was passed, it was followed by passage of the Volstead Act, authored by Congressman Andrew Volstead of Minnesota. The Volstead Act provided for the federal enforcement of the Eighteenth Amendment by creating a Prohibition Bureau under control of the Treasury Department. Unfortunately, agents of the Prohibition Bureau developed a reputation as being inept and corrupt. Some viewed the bureau as a training school for bootleggers because agents frequently left law enforcement to embark upon their own criminal enterprises. One of the Prohibition Bureau's heroes, Eliot Ness, became famous for organizing a team of agents known as "The Untouchables," named because of their reputation for honesty and refusal to take bribes. Eliot Ness and his Untouchables were eventually able to arrest one of the most famous organized crime figures of the time, Al Capone (Portrait).[17]

Prohibition failed to produce an alcohol-free society and spurred numerous problems. Many citizens had little regard for the new law and continued to consume alcohol in underground nightclubs and bars known as **speakeasies** or "blind pigs." Alcohol itself became dangerous to consume. Before prohibition, large companies and the government controlled the manufacture of alcohol. During prohibition, criminal organizations and "moonshiners," who sometimes added dangerous adulterants to their alcohol, controlled the manufacture and distribution of alcohol. Adulterants in black-market alcohol, such as kerosene, were known to cause paralysis, blindness, and even death. The sale of black-market alcohol made small-time gangsters into millionaires. Notorious bootlegger Al Capone, for example, made over $6 million per year in untaxed income.

The "Roaring Twenties" became one of the most lawless periods in American history. The court system was stretched beyond its limits. By the time **Prohibition** ended, nearly 800 gangsters in the city of Chicago alone had been killed in bootleg-related killings. Overall disregard for the law had become common. A jury hearing a bootlegging case in Los Angeles, for example, was itself put on trial after they drank the evidence! The jurors argued that they had simply sampled the evidence to determine whether or not it contained alcohol, which they determined it did. The defendant charged with bootlegging had to be acquitted because the evidence in the case had been consumed.[18]

In the late 1920s a group of wealthy businessmen, many of whom were the heads of large U.S. corporations, formed the Association Against Prohibition. Their primary goal was to reduce the amount of income taxes they were paying. Before Prohibition, taxes on alcohol had been one of the primary sources of revenue for the federal government. The Depression, which began in 1929, increased the need for greater tax revenues. Because of the need for new tax revenue and the overall disregard for Prohibition, the Eighteenth Amendment was repealed in 1933 by the Twenty-first Amendment.[19]

Over time, regulatory control over alcohol was returned to the states. In 1966, the last "dry" state, Mississippi, became "wet." Later in the 1970s, thirty states lowered the legal drinking age to eighteen, but in the 1980s, concerns began to be raised over the large number of young people dying in alcohol-related traffic accidents. Congress responded by authorizing the Transportation Department to withhold federal highway funds for any state that did not raise the minimum drinking age to twenty-one. This mandate made twenty-one the uniform drinking age across the United States.

Marijuana and the Marijuana Tax Act of 1937

As with opium, cocaine, and alcohol, public concerns about marijuana did not surface until the drug was linked to a minority group—namely, migrant Mexican workers. During the 1920s, Mexican laborers emigrated to the United States to perform jobs that white workers refused to do, such as picking cotton, fruit, and vegetables on large farms in the Southwest. Some of the Mexican workers would smoke marijuana as a drug of entertainment and relaxation. When the Depression struck the United States, many white workers would take just about any job they could get, and public opinion supported sending the Mexican workers home. Many white laborers in the Southwest began to band together and form organizations such as the "Key Men of America" and the "American Coalition," whose goal was to "Keep America American." Leaders of these organizations believed that marijuana and the problems with Mexican immigration were closely connected, and many southwestern police chiefs agreed. Newspaper stories began to circulate telling of how marijuana made users become sexually excited and violently insane.[20]

The first commissioner of the newly formed Federal Bureau of Narcotics (FBN), Harry J. Anslinger, saw the marijuana issue as a way to gain national attention and extend the power of FBN. Congressional committees heard testimony from Anslinger, who relied on sensational tales of murder, insanity, and sexual promiscuity that were brought on by marijuana, referred to as the "killer weed." Movies produced and released in the 1930s, such as *Reefer Madness* (now a cult classic on many university campuses) and *Marihuana: Weed with Roots in Hell*, supported Anslinger's propaganda campaign by depicting innocent young people committing terrible acts under the influence of marijuana (see page 170). The result was the Marijuana Tax Act of 1937, which did not outlaw marijuana but required that a tax be collected on its manufacture and sale. Each time marijuana was sold, the seller had to pay a tax of as much as $100 per ounce for a transfer tax stamp. Failure to possess

speakeasies: Business establishments that sold liquor illegally during the Prohibition era.

Prohibition: A period between 1920 and 1933 in the United States when alcohol manufacture and sale was illegal.

Shortly after graduating from the University of Chicago with a degree in business administration and political science, Eliot Ness accepted an appointment as an agent with the U.S. Treasury Department's Prohibition Bureau during a time when bootlegging was rampant throughout the nation. The Chicago branch of the Prohibition Bureau had a reputation for being corrupt, and it was difficult to find an honest law enforcement agent working in the city. Ness developed a reputation for his reliability and honesty and was given the job of assembling and leading a team to go after the liquor operations of famous gangster Al Capone. Capone was one of the most powerful and successful bootleggers in the country and operated thousands of illegal distilleries, breweries, and speakeasies.

Ness was given the personnel records of the entire Prohibition Bureau, from which he was to select a small team of reliable agents. Ness selected nine men. One of Ness's first operations was to close down eighteen of Capone's operations in Chicago in one night. The raids were all scheduled to occur simultaneously at nine thirty at night so that they could make a clean sweep before the news got out to Capone. Ness's men led the raiding parties,

and given the poor reputation of the average prohibition agent, Ness's men made sure that none of the men in the raiding parties had the opportunity to make a telephone call before the raid. With a sawed off shotgun in his arms, Ness and his men charged through the front door, yelling, "Everybody keep his place! This is a federal raid!" The operation was a success. Eighteen stills were shut down, and fifty-two people were arrested. Over the coming months, Ness and his team closed down numerous illegal stills and breweries worth an estimated $1 million.

Capone, feeling the pinch of Ness's operations, believed that every man had his price and made several attempts to bribe Ness and his men, but he had no success. In one instance, a man threw an envelope filled with cash into a car driven by one of Ness's men. Ness's agents caught up with the car and threw the money back into the gangster's car. Ness took advantage of this event to call a press conference to talk about Capone's failed bribery attempt. Ness wanted Capone's organization to realize that there were still law enforcement agents who could not be bought. The press conference was carried by newspapers all over the country, one

of which coined the term "The Untouchables."

Ness's war with Capone came to an end when Al Capone was convicted of tax evasion. Capone, with his extravagant life-style, had not filed an income tax return for several years, and even though his lawyers continually warned him of his vulnerability to the Internal Revenue Service (IRS), Capone always felt that he was above the law. Some have claimed that Ness was an egomaniac who craved the spotlight and used his crusade against Capone to gain attention. Ness responded to the issue of his motivation by explaining why he took the job: "Unquestionably, it was going to be highly dangerous. Yet I felt it was quite natural to jump at the task. After all, if you don't like action and excitement, you don't go into police work. And what the hell, I figured, nobody lives forever!" Many years later, Ness and his unit's exploits became a household word through the popular TV series *The Untouchables* and the 1987 film starring Kevin Costner.

Sources: Heimel, Paul W. (1997). *Eliot Ness: The real story.* Coudersport, PA: Knox Books. Kobler, John (1971). *The life and world of Al Capone.* New York: G. P. Putnam's Sons.

---

such a stamp was a federal offense, and not surprisingly, tax stamps were rarely issued (see Chapter 7). This effectively made marijuana illegal, and the drug was prohibited in this manner until the Controlled Substance Act of 1970.

Drugs and Society from 1945 to 1960

In the recreational drug scene of post–World War II United States, smoking was considered romantic and sexy, as one could observe by going to the movies and

seeing the hero and heroine lighting up their cigarettes. It was the era of the two-martini lunch, when social drinking was at its height of popularity and acceptance. Cocktail parties dominated the social scene. There was little or no public awareness that alcohol or nicotine consumption could be considered drug-taking behavior.

However, the general perception of certain drugs such as heroin, marijuana, and cocaine was simple and negative: They were considered bad and illegal, and "no one you knew" had anything to do with them. Illicit drugs were seen as the province of criminals, the urban poor, and nonwhites.[21] The point is that during

James Dean was one of many Hollywood actors and actresses in the 1950s whose smoking was part of their glamorous screen image.

The Return of Drug Tolerance, 1960–1980

During the 1960s, the basic premises of American life—the beliefs that working hard and living a good life would bring happiness and that society was stable and calm—were being undermined by the reality of the Vietnam war. The large adolescent and college-aged cohort born after World War II, often referred to as the "baby boomers" or "hippie" generation, was challenging many accepted cultural norms and the established hierarchy. Many young people were searching for new answers to old problems, and their search led to experimentation with drugs that their parents had been taught to fear. The principal symbol of this era of defiance against the established order, or indeed against anyone over thirty years old, was marijuana. No longer would marijuana be something foreign to middle America. Marijuana, as well as new drugs such as LSD, became associated with the sons and daughters of white middle-class families. Illicit drug use, once a problem associated with minority populations, inner cities, and the poor, was now too close to our personal lives for us to ignore.

Along with the turbulence of the period came a disturbing increase in heroin abuse across the country. In the early 1970s, reports surfaced estimating that up to 15 percent of the American troops returning home from Vietnam had been heroin abusers. Organized crime groups

this period, a whole class of drugs was outside the mainstream of American life. Furthermore, an atmosphere of fear and suspicion surrounded people who took such drugs. Commissioner Anslinger in the 1950s accused the People's Republic of China of selling opium and heroin to finance the expansion of Communism. Drug abuse now became un-American, and Congress became convinced that penalties for illicit drug use were too lenient. Congress passed the Boggs Act in 1951 that increased the penalties of previously enacted marijuana and narcotics laws. Under the Boggs Act, marijuana and narcotics were lumped together under uniform penalties, which provided for a minimum sentence of two years for first-time offenders and up to ten years for repeat offenders. Later, Congress passed the Narcotics Control Act of 1956, which further increased the penalties for drug violations. The sale of heroin to individuals under the age of eighteen, for example, was made a capital offense. The Narcotics Control Act also authorized the FBN and customs agents to carry firearms and serve search warrants. The basis of these laws was the belief that strict drug laws and an increase in drug-law enforcement would curb future drug demand.

The famous Woodstock Festival concert drew an estimated 500,000 people to a farm in upstate New York in the summer of 1969. According to historian David Musto, "It was said that the (use of marijuana) at the gigantic Woodstock gathering kept peace—as opposed to what might have happened if alcohol had been the drug of choice."

established the **French connection,** in which opium grown in Turkey was converted into heroin in southern French port cities, smuggled into America, and then sold on the streets of major cities. A new form of crudely processed heroin from Mexico, known as "black tar," was beginning to be sold throughout western United States. Heroin abuse increased in many inner cities, and heroin abuse was later connected to a rise in the crime rate, specifically a growing number of robberies and burglaries committed by heroin abusers to get money to buy drugs.[22]

For President Richard Nixon, elected in 1968, illicit drug use became a major political issue. He declared a "total war on drugs," ordering his senior staff to make the reduction of drug abuse one of their top priorities. In 1970, the Nixon administration persuaded Congress to pass the Comprehensive Drug Abuse Prevention and Control Act, popularly known as the "Controlled Substance Act." The act was passed to consolidate the large number of diverse and overlapping drug laws as well as the duplication of efforts by several different federal agencies.

The act established five schedules for the classification of drugs, based upon their approved medical uses, potential for abuse, and potential for producing dependence (Table 2.1). These categories define the extent to which various drugs are authorized to be available to the general public in the United States. Schedules I and II refer to drugs presenting the highest level of abuse potential, and Schedule V refers to drugs presenting the least. All drugs, except those included under Schedule I, are available legally on either a prescription or nonprescription basis.

Under the system of controlled substance schedules, drugs that are considered more dangerous and more easily abused are subject to progressively more stringent restrictions on their possession, the number of prescriptions that can be written, or the manner in which they can be dispensed. In the case of Schedule I drugs (heroin, LSD, mescaline, and marijuana, for example), no acceptable medical use has been authorized by the U.S. government, and availability of these drugs is limited to research purposes only. As a result of the 1970 Controlled Substance Act, the control of drugs is placed under federal jurisdiction regardless of state regulations.

The 1970 act also shifted the administration of drug enforcement from the Treasury Department to the Justice Department, creating the Drug Enforcement Administration (DEA). The DEA was given the control of all drug-enforcement responsibilities, except those related to ports of entry and borders, which were given to the U.S. Customs Service. DEA agents were to conduct drug investigation, collect intelligence about general trends in drug trafficking and drug production,

TABLE 2.1
Summary of controlled substance schedules

SCHEDULE I

High potential for abuse and no accepted medical use. Research use only, and drugs must be stored in secure vaults. Examples: marijuana, LSD, mescaline.

SCHEDULE II

High potential for abuse. Some accepted medical use, though use may lead to severe physical or psychological dependence. No prescription renewals are permitted, and the drugs must be stored in secure vaults. Examples: cocaine, amphetamines, opium, morphine, codeine, methadone.

SCHEDULE III

Some potential for abuse. Accepted medical use, though use may lead to low to moderate physical or psychological dependence. Up to five prescription renewals are permitted within six months. Examples: phencyclindine (PCP), some barbiturates.

SCHEDULE IV

Low potential for abuse. Accepted medical use. Up to five prescription renewals are permitted within six months. Examples: diazepam (Valium), phenobarbital.

SCHEDULE V

Minimal abuse potential. Widespread medical use. Minimal controls for selling and dispensing. Examples: prescription cough medicines and preparations with small amounts of narcotics.

and coordinate efforts among federal, state, and local law enforcement agencies. The DEA's mission today remains both domestic and foreign. Agents are stationed in foreign countries, and although they do not possess arrest powers, they act as liaisons with foreign law enforcement agencies. Both the DEA and the Federal Bureau of Investigation (FBI) share responsibility for enforcement of the Controlled Substance Act of 1970, and the director of the DEA reports to the director of the

French connection: A term referring to the supply route of heroin in the 1960s from Turkey (where opium poppies were grown) to port cities in France (where heroin was manufactured) to cities in the United States (where heroin was distributed).

FBI, who in 1982 was given responsibility for supervising all drug-law enforcement efforts and policies.

President Nixon also believed that reducing the supply of drugs from overseas sources could curb drug abuse in the United States. In the 1970s, the federal government estimated that 80 percent of the heroin reaching the United States was produced from opium poppies grown in Turkey. As mentioned earlier, the opium was shipped to southern French port cities, where it was converted to heroin and then later smuggled into the United States. In an attempt to reduce the amount of heroin coming into the United States, the Nixon administration threatened to cut off aid to Turkey if that country did not put an end to the export of opium. Nixon also promised Turkey millions of dollars in aid to make up for the subsequent losses resulting from reduced poppy cultivation. Initially, this action did lead to a shortage of heroin on American streets in 1973. The decline in heroin production, however, did not last long. In 1974, Mexico became a primary source of opium production, and in response, the U.S. government began to finance opium eradication programs in Mexico (see Chapter 14).[23]

Another response of the Nixon administration to drug abuse, particularly with regard to the increase in heroin dependence, was to finance a number of treatment programs for drug dependents. These treatment programs ranged from inpatient detoxification and therapeutic communities to newly created methadone outpatient programs. Methadone is a long-acting opiate that is taken orally in order to prevent heroin withdrawal symptoms for up to twenty-four hours (see Chapter 5). Methadone maintenance programs were designed to wean heroin abusers off of heroin by allowing them to have a better chance at employment and ending the need to commit crimes to maintain their abuse. After an initial report of the drug's success in 1966, methadone's popularity quickly spread. Methadone maintenance programs represented the first time that the federal government made a commitment to drug-abuse treatment in the community.

By 1972, some of the Nixon administration's anti-drug programs appeared to be working. There was a national network of methadone treatment centers, and successful eradication efforts. Turkey had agreed to stop growing opium, and Mexico was cooperating with U.S. law enforcement. The price of heroin was up, the purity level was down, and there was a decrease in the number of drug overdose cases. When President Gerald Ford took the White House in 1974, however, the nation's attention was diverted from drug abuse to other issues, such as unemployment, inflation, and an energy crisis. Illicit drug use was no longer an important issue. Ford's policy toward illicit drug use was based on the attitude that drug abuse was here to stay, but government actions could contain the problem. The administration also believed that some drugs were more dangerous than others and that anti-drug policies should be directed at controlling the supply and demand of those drugs which posed the greatest threat to society.

President Jimmy Carter, elected in 1976, was more tolerant toward drug use than Ford and even favored decriminalization of the possession of small amounts of marijuana. President Carter stated: "Penalties against possession of a drug should not be more damaging to an individual than the use of the drug itself, and where they are, they should be changed. Nowhere is this more clear than in the laws against the possession of marijuana in private for personal use."[24] By 1978, eleven states followed Carter's lead and decriminalized small amounts of marijuana. California and Oregon made possession of one ounce or less of marijuana a citable misdemeanor with a maximum penalty of $1,000, and there were no increased penalties for recidivists.[25] Relaxed attitudes toward drugs reached a peak in 1979. An astounding 53 percent of high school seniors in 1979 reported using an illicit drug over the previous twelve months, compared with 37 percent of high school seniors in 2006.[26]

Renewed Efforts at Control, 1980–2000

With the decade of the 1980s came significant changes in the mood of the country in the form of a social and political reaction to earlier decades. If the media symbol formerly had been the "hippie," now it was the "yuppie," a young, upwardly mobile professional. The political climate became more conservative in all age groups. With regard to drugs, the concern about heroin dependence was being overshadowed by a new fixation: cocaine. At first, cocaine took on an aura of glamour and (because it was so expensive) became a symbol of material success. The media spotlight shone on a steady stream of celebrities in entertainment and sports who used cocaine. Not long after, however, the harsh realities of cocaine dependence were recognized. The very same celebrities who had accepted cocaine into their lives were now experiencing the consequences; many of them were in rehabilitation programs, and some had died from cocaine overdoses. To make matters worse, in 1985, a new form of cocaine called "crack," smokeable and cheap, succeeded in extending the problems of cocaine dependence to the inner cities of the United States, to segments of American society that did not have the financial resources to afford cocaine itself. In the glare of intense media attention, crack dependence soon took on all the aspects of a national nightmare.

In the 1970s, there had been generally a lack of public interest and even some tolerance of drug use. As mentioned earlier, in several U.S. states there was even a trend toward deregulation. In the 1980s, however, the lack of public interest in drug use began to shift as grass-roots groups began to demand that something be done about "America's drug problem." During the presidency of Ronald Reagan, drug abuse became a major political and social issue. President Reagan declared an all-out war on drugs, and First Lady Nancy Reagan launched her "Just Say No" campaign, which focused mostly on white middle-class children who had not yet tried drugs. Reagan's war on drugs focused on a policy of controlling the supply of drugs by increasing the budgets of drug enforcement agencies and providing foreign aid to such countries as Colombia, Peru, Bolivia, and Mexico. Demand was to be reduced by enacting laws that imposed some of the harshest penalties ever for drug-law violators.

With popular sentiment once again turned against drugs, Congress rewrote virtually all of the nation's drug laws in record time. In 1984, Congress passed the Comprehensive Crime Control Act, which increased the penalties for violations of the Controlled Substance Act and expanded asset-forfeiture law, allowing both local and federal drug enforcement agencies to keep most of the money made from the sale of seized assets (see Chapter 14). Two years later, Congress passed the Anti-Drug Abuse Act of 1986, which placed mandatory minimum sentences for federal drug convictions, eliminating a judge's discretion in pronouncing a sentence. Different mandatory minimum sentences were to be given for possession of powder and crack cocaine. The new law imposed a prison sentence of five to forty years for possession of 500 grams of cocaine or 5 grams of crack cocaine. This mandatory sentence could not be suspended, nor could the offender be paroled or placed on probation. The Anti-Drug Abuse Act of 1986 also created a "kingpin" statute under which the heads of drug trafficking organizations could receive mandatory life imprisonment if convicted of operating a continuing criminal enterprise.

One of the most important drug laws passed in the 1980s was the Anti-Drug Abuse Act of 1988. This legislation created a cabinet-level Director of National Drug Control Policy, often referred to in the media as the "Drug Czar," whose job was to coordinate federal activities with respect to both drug supply and demand reduction. The first director was former Education Secretary William J. Bennett, who believed that individual users of drugs should accept moral responsibility for their behavior. Bennett believed that drug laws should be strict so that drug users would understand that involvement in the illegal drug trade has clear consequences. The law created harsher penalties for the possession of drugs; penalties for selling drugs to minors were enhanced; and the act reinstated the death penalty for anyone convicted as a "drug kingpin" or anyone convicted of a drug-related killing. The act also addressed alcohol use, especially the problem of drunk driving, by providing federal money to states that instituted tough penalties for drunk drivers. Lastly, the act addressed the issues of drug use in schools and in the workplace by requiring educational institutions and businesses to establish a system to ensure that students and workers remained drug-free. This provision later established the basis for drug testing in schools and in the workplace.

The wave of anti-drug legislation in the 1980s (Drugs . . . in Focus) profoundly changed America's criminal justice system. Law enforcement budgets increased as more officers had to be hired to enforce drug laws. The number of drug violators increased to the highest level ever, and courts became backlogged with drug case after drug case. The number of inmates in U.S. prisons and jails rose nearly 100 percent from 1985 to 1996, and the budget for prisons increased by more than 160 percent.[27] Prison building became one of the biggest public works businesses in America, with both the federal and state governments building hundreds of new prisons across the country. Fortunately, by the end of the 1990s, the extent of crack abuse had greatly diminished, crime rates had begun to fall, and rates of illicit drug use began to decline. It is still being debated, however, to what extent these changes were due to the "get tough" policy on drugs or how much were due to an overall aging of the U.S. population or other sociocultural factors.

The 1990s and the beginning of the twenty-first century can be characterized by a general lack of political interest in drug abuse. During his first term office from 1992 to 1996, President Bill Clinton placed little emphasis on drug abuse and reduced the staff of the Office of National Drug Control Policy by 83 percent, a move that he ascribed to keeping his campaign promise to reduce the White House staff by 25 percent. As the 1996 election approached and a rise in marijuana use among youth became publicized, Clinton began to be criticized for his overall neglect of America's drug problem. In response, Clinton declared his own war on drugs and appointed a retired four-star military general, Barry McCaffrey, to be his "Drug Czar." Clinton urged Congress to appropriate a $100 million increase in the

Drugs... in Focus

A History of American Drug Legislation

1794 A federal tax on whiskey leads to the Whiskey Rebellion in western Pennsylvania (see Chapter 11).

1868 Pharmacy Act of 1868 requires registration of those dispensing drugs.

1875 The Anti-Opium Smoking Act is passed in San Francisco.

1906 Pure Food and Drug Act requires all packaged foods and drugs to list the ingredients on the label of the product.

1914 The Harrison Narcotic Act is designed to regulate addiction and drug abuse through government taxation.

1919 Congress passes the Eighteenth Amendment, which outlaws the manufacture and sale of alcohol, except for industrial use.

1933 Congress passes the Twenty-first Amendment, which repeals the Eighteenth Amendment.

1937 The Marijuana Tax Act places a tax on the manufacture and sale of marijuana.

1951 The Boggs Act increases the penalties for drug offenses.

1956 Selling heroin to someone under the age of eighteen can result in the death penalty.

1970 Comprehensive Drug Abuse Prevention and Control Act, popularly known as the Controlled Substance Act, establishes five schedules for the classification of drugs based upon their approved medical uses, potential for abuse, and potential for producing dependence.

1984 Congress passes the Comprehensive Crime Control Act, which enhances the penalties for violations of the Controlled Substance Act and expands asset-forfeiture law, allowing both local and federal drug enforcement agencies to keep the majority of the money made from the sale of seized assets.

1986 Congress passes the Anti-Drug Abuse Act of 1986, which places mandatory sentences for federal drug convictions, eliminating a judge's discretion in pronouncing a sentence.

1988 The Anti-Drug Abuse Act of 1988 increases penalties for drug offenses involving children and creates a cabinet-level position of Director of National Drug Control Policy, often referred to in the media as "Drug Czar."

1996 Arizona Proposition 200 and California Proposition 215 are passed, which legalize the use of marijuana for medicinal purposes within these two states (see Chapter 7).

1996 Comprehensive Methamphetamine Control Act increases the penalties for trafficking and manufacture of methamphetamine and its precursor chemicals.

2000 GHB (gamma-hydroxybutyrate) is added to the list of Schedule I controlled substances.

2003 The Illicit Drug Anti-Proliferation Act, aimed at the promoters of "raves," holds persons more accountable for knowingly renting, leasing, or maintaining any place where drugs are distributed or manufactured.

2004 Anabolic Steroid Control Act of 2004 adds several new steroids and steroid precursors to the list of controlled substances.

2004 The Food and Drug Administration (FDA) issues regulations prohibiting the sale of dietary supplements containing ephedrine.

2005 The Combat Methamphetamine Epidemic Act establishes nationwide sales restrictions on precursor chemicals and law enforcement initiatives for the seizure of domestic methamphetamine laboratories.

---

budget for drug interdiction, and he increased foreign aid to stop the supply of drugs at their source. In addition, he signed the Comprehensive Methamphetamine Control Act into law in 1996. Designed to curb the use of methamphetamine, this act increased the penalties for trafficking and manufacture of methamphetamine and its precursor chemicals.

The Globalization of Drug Regulation, 2001–Present

After the events of September 11, 2001, the war on terrorism became a more pressing matter for President George W. Bush than the war on drugs, and an effort was made to

2002, Bush changed the U.S. strategy by granting the Colombian government the funding to combat drug trafficking and terrorism, two struggles that in the eyes of the Bush administration had become one. Colombia was awarded an all-time high of $650 million in U.S. aid to begin a unified campaign against drug trafficking and the activities of groups designated as terrorist organizations.[28] On the domestic side, President Bush asked for an increase in the drug treatment and prevention budgets. Recently, several U.S. states have attempted to rid themselves of the mandatory sentencing laws, and others are focusing on treatment rather than enforcement by starting drug courts and community treatment centers. As a new generation confronts the drug question, only time will tell if America will continue with the "get tough" policy of the past or turn to a policy that focuses on drug-abuse treatment, education, and prevention.

Present-Day Attitudes toward Drugs

Attitudes toward drug-taking behavior at the beginning of the twenty-first century are quite different from those that prevailed even as recently as twenty years ago. First, there is a far greater awareness today that a wide range of psychoactive drugs, whether they are licit or illicit, qualify as substances with varying levels of potential for misuse and abuse. The "war on drugs," declared officially in 1971 and still ongoing today in the United States, is no longer a war on a particular drug, such as heroin in the 1970s or cocaine in the 1980s. As a society, we need to be concerned with "designer drugs." These new compounds, referred to as *structural analogs*, are created by altering the chemical structure of existing illicit drugs while mimicking their psychoactive effects. We also need to address the widespread personal and social difficulties created by the abuse of alcohol, steroids, inhalants, and nicotine, as well as the misuse of prescription drugs and dietary supplements. In short, the battles being waged today are against a wide range of drug misuse and abuse involving licit as well as illicit substances.

A second difference in attitude toward drug-taking behavior is related to the history of such behavior in our society since the late 1960s. It is important to recognize that in 1980, about two-thirds of high school seniors had reported illicit drug use (principally marijuana smoking) at some time in their lives. They were born toward the end of the "baby boom" generation (technically defined as those born between 1946 and 1964) and were the first group to have grown up during the explosion of drug

combine the two problems into one all-encompassing policy. During the Clinton presidency, aid to Colombia had risen to a previously unprecedented level of $88 million. This money, however, was tightly restricted to police and counterdrug efforts and was not intended to support Colombia's war against insurgent groups. In

experimentation. Now, as the parents of teenagers at the beginning of the twenty-first century, they face the difficult challenge of dealing with the present-day drug-taking behavior of their children. The question has arisen as to whether parents would be able to discourage such behavior in their sons and daughters without appearing hypocritical if they themselves were part of the drug scene at an earlier time in their lives. Interestingly, a recent study has found no relationship between prior marijuana use among parents and marijuana use by their children.[29]

Patterns of Drug Use in the United States

How is it possible to obtain information that would give us a statistical picture of drug-taking behavior today? Assuming that we cannot conduct large-scale random drug testing, the only alternative we have is simply to ask people about their drug-taking behavior through self-reports. We encourage honesty and arrange the data-collection procedure so as to convince the respondents that their answers are confidential, but the fact remains that any questionnaire is inherently imperfect because there is no way to verify the truthfulness of what people say about themselves. Nevertheless, questionnaires are all we have, and the statistics on drug use are based on such survey measures (Drugs . . . in Focus).

One of the best-known surveys, referred to as the Monitoring the Future study, has been conducted every year since 1975 by the University of Michigan. Typically, nearly fifty thousand American students in the eighth, tenth, and twelfth grades participate in a nationally representative sampling each year, as well as more than seven thousand college students and young adults between the ages of nineteen and thirty-two (with the upper limit recently being extended to forty-five).

The advantage of repeating the survey with a new sample year after year is that it enables us to look at trends in drug-taking behavior over time and compare the use of one drug relative to another. We can assume that the degree of overreporting and underreporting stays relatively constant over the years and does not affect the interpretation of the general trends.

Since the surveys are conducted in schools, high school dropouts are unavailable as respondents. This group represents roughly 15 percent of the potential high school graduates each year, according to U.S. Census statistics. As a result, it is conceivable that the interpretation of specific prevalence rates for various forms of drug-taking behavior may be underestimated. Recent analyses by researchers at the University of Michigan have indicated that rates would be slightly higher if dropouts were included, particularly for the most dangerous drugs such as heroin, crack cocaine, and PCP, the use of which is highly correlated with educational aspirations and attainment. However, we can assume that this bias would be relatively constant over time, so an analysis of trends in prevalence rates from year to year can still be made.[30]

Survey questions concerning drug use have been phrased in four basic ways:

- Whether an individual has ever used a certain drug in his or her lifetime
- Whether an individual has used a certain drug over the previous year
- Whether an individual has used a certain drug within the previous thirty days
- Whether an individual has used a certain drug on a *daily* basis during the previous thirty days

You can see that these questions distinguish three important degrees of involvement with a given drug. The first question focuses on the extent of experimentation, including individuals who may have taken a drug only once or twice in their lives and who have stayed away from it ever since. The second and third questions focus on the extent of current but moderate drug use, while the fourth question focuses on the extent of heavy drug use. What do the numbers tell us?

Illicit Drug Use among High School Seniors

We are naturally concerned with any level of drug-taking behavior among U.S. high school seniors, but it is at least encouraging to know that 2006 statistics of drug use have declined from prevalence levels in the late 1990s and are substantially lower than they were at the end of the 1970s. In 2006, for example, 37 percent of high school seniors reported use of an illicit drug over the previous year, less than the 54 percent reporting such use in the peak year of 1979 (Figure 2.1). If we look specifically at marijuana use over the previous year, the senior sample reported 32 percent, a reduction from a level of 51 percent in 1979. Cocaine use over the previous year for seniors was 6 percent, about one-half the number reporting such behavior in the peak year of 1985. Recreational use of inhalants has held steady at

Drugs...in Focus

Measuring the Impact of Drugs on Our Society

A number of U.S. federal programs have been instituted to track the availability and use of licit and illicit drugs, the health consequences of drug-taking behavior, drug trafficking patterns, and drug-abuse treatment.

- **Drug Abuse Warning Network (DAWN) Program** Conducted by the Substance Abuse and Mental Health Services Administration, U.S. Department of Health and Human Services, to track admissions to emergency departments of major metropolitan hospitals and drug-related facilities. Reports are issued annually. (See Chapter 1.)

- **Monitoring the Future (MTF) Study** Conducted by the University of Michigan to track drug use and drug attitudes among secondary students, college students, and young adults. Annual reports of MTF findings are released in December through a press release. More extensive statistical information is published in the following year. (See page 54.)

- **Arrestee Drug Abuse Monitoring (ADAM) Program** Conducted by the National Institute of Justice, U.S. Department of Justice, to track the prevalence of methamphetamine, cocaine, heroin, and marijuana in the bloodstreams of adult and juvenile arrestees. Reports were issued up to

2003. The program has been suspended. (See Chapter 13.)

- **National Survey of Drug Use and Health (NSDUH) Study** Conducted by the Substance Abuse and Mental Health Services Administration, U.S. Department of Health and Human Services, to track drug use among individuals across the life span (age twelve or older). Reports are issued annually. (See pages 59–60.)

- **National Drug Threat Assessment (NDTA) Program** Conducted by the National Drug Intelligence Center, U.S. Department of Justice, to assess the trafficking patterns of illicit drugs into the United States. Reports are issued each year. (See Chapter 13.)

- **Pulse Check** Conducted by the Office of National Drug Control Policy to assess "street level" drug use through interviews with police, ethnographers, and treatment providers in major metropolitan areas. Reports are issued semiannually. (See Chapter 13.)

- **Treatment Episode Data Set (TEDS) Program** Conducted by the Substance Abuse and Mental Health Services Administration, U.S. Department of Health and Human Services, to track demographic and substance abuse characteristics of individuals admitted to (and discharged from) substance abuse treatment facilities. Reports are issued annually. (See Chapter 15.)

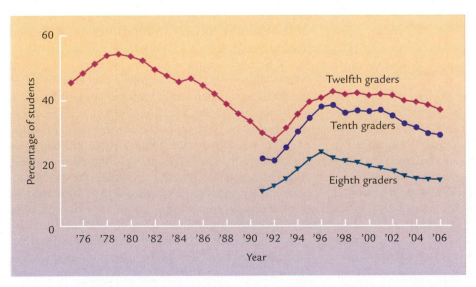

FIGURE 2.1

Trends in annual prevalence of illicit drug use among eighth, tenth, and twelfth graders.

Source: Johnston, Lloyd D.; O'Malley, Patrick M.; Bachman, Jerald G.; and Schulenberg, John E. (2007). *Monitoring the Future national results on adolescent drug use. Overview of key findings, 2006.* Bethesda, MD: National Institute on Drug Abuse, p. 12.

between 4 and 5 percent since 2000, about one-half the number reporting such behavior in the mid-1990s.

Nonetheless, the absolute percentages in 2006 were still substantial. They indicate that about four out of every ten high school seniors had used some form of illicit drug over the last twelve months, about one in three had smoked marijuana, about one in sixteen had used cocaine, and about one in twenty or so had used inhalants on a recreational basis. In 2006, about one in twenty-five had used Ecstasy. One in fifty seniors had used LSD, about one-fourth the prevalence rate in 1996, reflecting a steadily downward trend in the use of hallucinogens in general.[31]

Illicit Drug Use among Eighth Graders and Tenth Graders

Since 1991, we also have had extensive survey information about illicit drug use among students as early as the eighth grade. As Figure 2.1 shows, the upward trend in the percentages of drug use among eighth and tenth graders from 1991 to 1996 paralleled a similar trend among high school seniors. At the time, the data from these two groups reflected a level of drug involvement that was quite disturbing. Drug-abuse professionals were left to speculate as to the negative effect on still younger children, as they observed the drug-taking behavior of their older brothers and sisters. Fortunately, since 1996, the upward trend among the eighth graders in several categories has reversed its course substantially (Table 2.2), as has been the case among tenth graders to a somewhat lesser degree.[32] It is now expected that in the years ahead, as eighth graders progress through high school, their increasing disinclination toward drug use will be reflected in declining prevalence rates among older secondary school students.

Drugs among Youth in a Diverse Society

In looking at racial and ethnic differences in both illicit and licit drug use among adolescents in the University of Michigan survey, certain consistent patterns emerge. For nine major categories of drugs (marijuana, inhalants, hallucinogens, LSD, Ecstasy, cocaine, crack cocaine, non-injected heroin, and alcohol), drug use among African American seniors is lower than that among white students. In addition, levels of daily cigarette smoking and binge drinking among African American seniors are substantially below those of white students. A comparison of African American, Hispanic/Latino, and white

TABLE 2.2

Percentage of drug use among eighth graders, 2006

	2006	CHANGE SINCE 1996
Been drunk in past year	13.9	30% down
Marijuana in past year	11.7	36% down
Cocaine in past year	2.0	33% down
Amphetamines in the past year	4.7	48% down
Inhalants in past year	9.1	25% down
Use of cigarettes in previous 30 days	8.7	59% down
Daily use of cigarettes	4.0	61% down

Source: Johnston, Lloyd D.; O'Malley, Patrick M.; Bachman, Jerald G.; and Schulenberg, John E. (2007). Monitoring the Future national results on adolescent drug use. Overview of key findings, 2006. Bethesda, MD: National Institute on Drug Abuse, Tables 2, 3, and 4.

seniors (Table 2.3) shows that Hispanic/Latino seniors have the highest annual prevalence rates of use of inhalants, heroin, cocaine, and crack cocaine.[33]

Drug Use among College Students and Young Adults

The University of Michigan survey also allows a look at drug use among college students and young adults. Compared to high school seniors, college students report lower annual prevalence rates in the use of illicit drugs in general and in many illicit drug categories, with the exception of cocaine, non-LSD hallucinogens, and alcohol (see "Patterns of Alcohol Use").[34]

When you examine the drug-taking behavior of young adults (not necessarily college students) by tracking them at two-year intervals for as long as fourteen years after graduating from high school, an interesting pattern emerges. Evidently, the new freedoms of young adulthood initially lead to an increase in substance use for some individuals. Not surprisingly, those young adults who frequently go out at night for fun and recreation are the ones who are most likely to drink heavily, smoke heavily, and use illicit drugs. As these people grow older, these relationships weaken. The link between going out and cigarette smoking, for example, virtually disappears by the time they are in their late twenties and early thirties. On average, drug use at

TABLE 2.3

Percentages of white, African American, and Hispanic/Latino high school seniors who used a particular drug or engaged in a drug-related behavior in the past year

	WHITE	AFRICAN AMERICAN	HISPANIC/ LATINO
Marijuana	34.8	27.7	28.7
Inhalants	5.3	1.9	5.7
Hallucinogens	6.0	1.5	3.8
LSD	1.8	0.9	1.4
Ecstasy	4.0	1.8	3.0
Cocaine	5.8	1.6	6.5
Crack cocaine	1.9	1.0	3.1
Heroin (needle)	0.3	0.7	0.9
Heroin (no needle)	0.6	0.4	1.0
Binge drinking (in last two weeks)	30.4	11.4	23.3
Steroids	1.6	1.7	2.3
Daily cigarettes	15.3	5.7	7.0

Source: Johnston, Lloyd D.; O'Malley, Patrick M.; Bachman, Jerald G.; and Schulenberg, John E. (2007). Data from 2005 and 2006 surveys combined. *Monitoring the Future: National survey results on drug use, 1975–2006. Volume 1: Secondary school students 2006.* Rockville, MD: National Institute on Drug Abuse, Table 4.9.

these ages drops substantially from levels reported in high school, as young adults begin making personal commitments, marrying, and starting families. Not surprisingly, non-drug-using wives have a major influence in reducing their husbands' level of drug use. Personal setbacks such as divorces, however, produce an increase in drug use, often to the same levels as when they were in high school. In other words, in hard times, an individual will revert to old patterns of drug-taking behavior.[35]

Patterns of Alcohol Use

Not surprisingly, the prevalence percentages related to the use of alcohol are much higher than for illicit drugs. While 22 percent of high school seniors in 2006 reported use of illicit drugs in the previous month, about half (45 percent) drank an alcoholic beverage, with 27 percent reporting at least one instance of *binge drinking*, defined as having five or more drinks in a row in the previous two weeks. These figures are down substantially from those found in surveys conducted in 1980, when

72 percent of high school seniors reported that they had consumed alcohol over the previous month, and 41 percent reported binge drinking.

A partial explanation for the decline from 1980 to the present lies in the reduced accessibility to alcohol for this age group, with all U.S. states now having adopted a twenty-one-year-or-older requirement. Despite the long-term downward trend and a suggestion of further decline in alcohol use in recent years, however, the present level of alcohol consumption among high school seniors remains a matter of great concern. Alcohol consumption on a regular basis is widespread for individuals in this age group despite the fact that it is officially illegal for any of them to purchase alcoholic beverages. A significant decline in alcohol use and binge drinking among tenth graders occurred from 2000 to 2006.

The drinking habits of college students have shown relatively little change since the mid-1990s. In 2006, 69 percent of college students surveyed drank at least once in the previous month, and 40 percent reported an instance of binge drinking in the previous two weeks. Evidently, the "know when to say when" message, as promoted by major beer companies, has not gotten through.[36]

Patterns of Tobacco Use

Roughly 12 percent of high school seniors in 2006 had established a regular habit of nicotine intake by smoking at least one cigarette every day. In fact, nicotine remains the drug most frequently used on a daily basis by high school students, although present-day rates are substantially lower than those observed in 1977, when twice as many high school seniors (29 percent) smoked cigarettes. From the mid-1990s to about 2002, there had been a steady decline in smoking rates in eighth and tenth graders as well as seniors, owing to the national attention directed toward cigarette smoking among young people. As of 2002, this decline has virtually ceased. In 2006, about 6 percent of seniors, 3 percent of tenth graders, and 2 percent of eighth graders reported smoking at least a half-pack of cigarettes per day, a strikingly high level for these age groups considering the legal obstacles they face when attempting to obtain cigarettes.[37]

Somewhat fewer college students smoke cigarettes than high school seniors. The reason is not a matter of a change in smoking behavior from high school to college, but rather reflects differences between the two populations. Non-college-bound seniors are about three times more likely to smoke at least a half-pack of cigarettes per day than college-bound seniors. Therefore, the difference in smoking rates between seniors and college students is chiefly a result of excluding the heavier smokers in the survey as students progress from secondary to postsecondary education. In 2006, about 9 percent of college students smoked cigarettes on a daily basis, with about 5 percent smoking more than a half-pack per day.[38]

Perceived Risk and Drug Use

To understand the changing patterns of drug use among young people over the years and what trends might unfold in the future, it is helpful to look at their *perception of the risks involved in drug use* during the same span of time. A troubling trend reflected in the University of Michigan surveys during the 1990s was the steady decline in the percentages of high school students, college students, and young adults who regarded regular drug use as potentially dangerous. These responses contrasted with reports beginning in 1978 that had shown a steady increase in such percentages (Figure 2.2). A spokesperson for the 1996 Michigan survey offered one possible reason for this reversal:

This most recent crop of youngsters grew up in a period in which drug use rates were down substantially *from what they had been 10 to 15 years earlier. This gave youngsters less opportunity to learn from others' mistakes and resulted in what I call "generational forgetting" of the hazards of drugs.[39]*

Also troubling during much of the 1990s were changes in the way our society dealt with the potential risks of drug use. Drug abuse prevention programs in schools were scaled back or eliminated due to a lack of federal funding, parents were communicating less with their children about drug use, anti-drug public service messages were less prominent in the media than they were in the 1980s, and media coverage in this area declined. At the same time, the cultural influences of the music and entertainment industry were, at best, ambivalent on the question of drug-taking behavior, particularly with respect to marijuana smoking (see Chapter 7). All these elements can be seen as having contributed to the upward trend in drug use during this period.

The reciprocal relationship between perceived risk of harm in regular drug use and the likelihood of drug use itself is shown in Figure 2.2, in the case of marijuana smoking trends across a span of almost thirty years. For

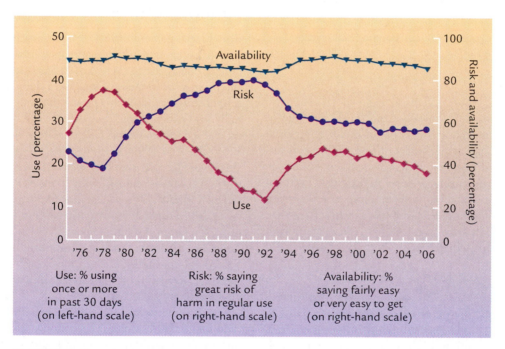

FIGURE 2.2

Trends in perceived availability, perceived risk of marijuana use, and prevalence of marijuana use in the past month for high school seniors.

Source: Johnston, Lloyd D.; O'Malley, Patrick M.; Bachman, Jerald G.; and Schulenberg, John E. (2007). *Monitoring the Future national results on adolescent drug use. Overview of key findings, 2006.* Bethesda, MD: National Institute on Drug Abuse, Tables 3, 7, and 13.

TABLE 2.4

Illicit drug use during the past year among persons in the United States aged 26 or older in 2006

	ESTIMATED NUMBERS OF USERS
Any illicit drug	19,552,000
Marijuana and hashish	12,860,000
Cocaine	3,399,000
Crack	1,113,000
Heroin	376,000
Hallucinogens	1,160,000
LSD	181,000
Ecstasy	591,000
Inhalants	531,000
Nonmedical use of any psycho-therapeutic medication (not including over-the-counter drugs)	9,058,000
Pain relievers	6,761,000
Tranquilizers	2,791,000
Stimulants	1,624,000
Sedatives	632,000
Any illicit drug other than marijuana	11,481,000

Source: Substance Abuse and Mental Health Services Administration (2007). *Results from the 2006 National Survey on Drug Use and Health: Detailed tables.* Rockville, MD: Office of Applied Studies, Substance Abuse and Mental Health Services Administration, Table 8.11A.

the most part, the percentages who consider marijuana smoking as presenting a great risk form a mirror image to the percentages who report smoking marijuana at least once in the previous month.

The relationship between a decline in prevalence rates and an increase in the perception of risk is particularly striking in the case of Ecstasy use over recent years. Following a moderate increase in the percentages of high school seniors reporting "great risk in trying Ecstasy once or twice" from 2000 to 2001, a dramatic increase in risk perception from 2001 to 2006 coincided with a major decline in Ecstasy use. It is reasonable that the perception of risk needed to rise to a critical level for that perception to have any effect on the incidence of drug use.[40]

Patterns of Illicit Drug Use in Adults Aged Twenty-Six and Older

A comprehensive examination of the prevalence rates of illicit drug use among Americans in several age groups across the life span has been accomplished by the National Survey on Drug Use and Health (formerly the National Household Survey on Drug Abuse). Table 2.4 shows the percentages of illicit drug use in 2006 among

persons aged twenty-six or older. About 10 percent of this population (about 19 million people) reported using an illicit drug over the past twelve months, about 7 percent (nearly 13 million people) used marijuana or hashish, and about 5 percent (about 9 million people) engaged in the nonmedical (recreational) use of a prescription-type pain reliever, tranquilizer, stimulant, or sedative. As with the results of the University of Michigan survey, however, there are some limitations to the interpretation of these estimates. Patients institutionalized for either medical or psychiatric treatment as well as homeless people are not included in the collection of sample data.[41]

Looking at the rates of various forms of drug-taking behavior across fifteen of the largest metropolitan statistical areas in the United States reveals a number of regional differences. San Francisco, Detroit, and Seattle were significantly higher than the national average

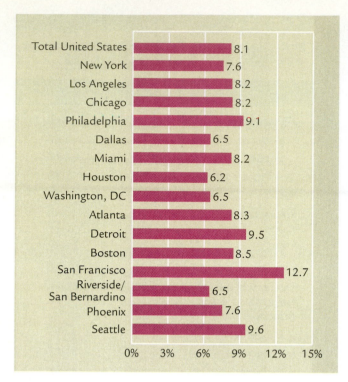

Total United States	8.1
New York	7.6
Los Angeles	8.2
Chicago	8.2
Philadelphia	9.1
Dallas	6.5
Miami	8.2
Houston	6.2
Washington, DC	6.5
Atlanta	8.3
Detroit	9.5
Boston	8.5
San Francisco	12.7
Riverside/San Bernardino	6.5
Phoenix	7.6
Seattle	9.6

0%   3%   6%   9%   12%   15%

FIGURE 2.3

Percentages of persons aged 12 or older reporting past month use of any illicit drug by metropolitan statistical areas: 2002–2005

Source: Substance Abuse and Mental Health Services Administration (2007, January 5). Substance use in the 15 largest metropolitan statistical areas: 2002–2005. *The NSDUH Report,* p. 2.

in terms of the rate of illicit drug use over the previous month (Figure 2.3). Regional differences with regard to binge drinking and regular cigarette smoking are shown in Figure 2.4.[42]

America's Drug Debate

If the history of drug-taking behavior teaches us anything, it is that some people will always be attracted to the drug experience. This certainty arises directly from the consciousness-altering character of psychoactive drugs themselves. For a certain duration, psychoactive drugs can make us feel euphoric, lightheaded, relaxed, or powerful, all of which undoubtedly feel good to most people. Other nonpharmacological ways of arriving at these states of mind exist, but drugs provide an easy and quick route. Some drugs also seem to increase our awareness of our surroundings and give

the impression that we are seeing or hearing things in a more intense way. No matter whether we are young or old, rich or poor, drugs can allow us to retreat from an often distressing world, to feel no pain.

Unfortunately, in every generation there will be young people who are alienated from their families and the community of adults around them, who seek some form of temporary release from an unhappy existence. There will be a younger generation seeking a form of rebellion against traditional values and adolescents who will use drugs in the context of having a good time with their friends.

Despite our best efforts to prevent drug abuse from happening, there will be young people who simply are willing to try anything new, including drugs. Their curiosity, to find out "what it's like," brings us full circle to the earliest times in human history, when we nibbled on the plants in the field just to find out what would happen. In the modern era, drug experimentation is neither a new nor a singular phenomenon; it can involve an alcoholic drink, an inhaled solvent from some household product, a cigarette, or an illicit drug.

Given the difficulties in reducing the problems of drug abuse in any sector of our population, some policymakers have naturally questioned the object of "zero tolerance" with regard to illicit drug-taking behavior—that is, an eventual eradication of illicit drug use in the United States. Opponents of zero tolerance argue that governmental efforts should focus instead on minimizing the various medical, psychological, and social costs associated with drug abuse rather than trying to eliminate such behavior entirely. This strategy has been called the "harm-reduction" approach.

Examples of harm reduction include needle-exchange programs to lower the incidence of infection among intravenous drug abusers, methadone maintenance programs for the treatment of heroin abusers, efforts to reduce the incidence of driving while under the influence of alcohol and other performance-interfering drugs, and the use of nicotine patches to avoid adverse effects of cigarette smoking, such as lung cancer and emphysema. A more controversial application of harm reduction is the suggestion that we should attempt to reduce the level of heavy drug use down to a level of occasional use, rather than no use at all. It is evident that public policy in the United States has been guided more by a "zero-tolerance" philosophy than by "harm-reduction." We will see the implications of this perspective in terms of specific drug-abuse programs in Chapters 14 and 15.

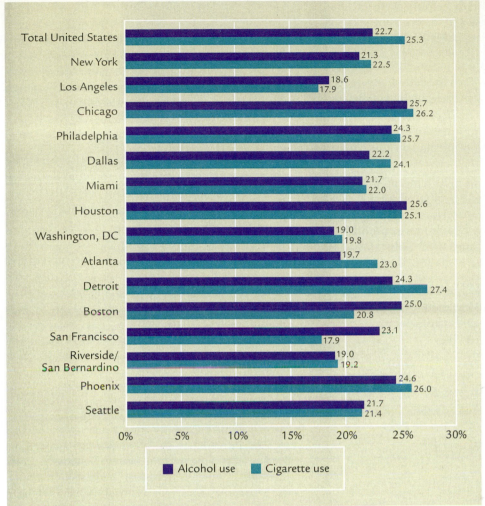

FIGURE 2.4

Percentages of persons aged 12 or older reporting past month binge alcohol use and cigarette use by metropolitan statistical areas: 2002–2005

Source: Substance Abuse and Mental Health Services Administration (2007, January 5). Substance use in the 15 largest metropolitan statistical areas: 2002–2005. *The NSDUH Report,* p. 3.

Summary

Drugs in Early Times

● Probably the earliest experiences with psychoactive drugs came from tasting naturally growing plants. Individuals with knowledge about such plants were able to attain great power within their societies.

● Ancient Egyptians and Babylonians in particular had extensive knowledge of both psychoactive and nonpsychoactive drugs. Some of these drugs had genuine beneficial effects, while others did not.

Drugs in the Nineteenth Century

● Medical advances in the 1800s allowed isolation of the active ingredients within many psychoactive substances. For example, morphine was identified as the major active ingredient in opium.

● During the nineteenth century, there was little regulation or control of drugs, and the U.S. government imposed no limitations on their distribution, sale, and promotion. The result was a century of widespread and uncontrolled medicinal and recreational drug use.

Drug Regulation in the Early Twentieth Century

● The effects of drug dependence began to become a social concern. The two most important factors that fueled the movement toward drug regulation in the beginning of the twentieth century were (1) the abuse of patent medicines and (2) the association of drug use with socially marginalized minority groups.

Drug Regulation, 1914–1937

- The Harrison Act of 1914 was the first of several legislative efforts to impose criminal penalties on the use of opiates and cocaine.

- Passage of the Eighteenth Amendment resulted in the national prohibition of alcohol in the United States from 1920 to 1933.

- The Marijuana Tax Act of 1937 required that a tax stamp be issued to anyone selling marijuana. Tax stamps, however, were rarely issued, making marijuana essentially illegal. The drug was prohibited in this way until the Controlled Substance Act of 1970.

Drugs and Society from 1945 to 1960

- During the 1940s and 1950s, the use of illicit drugs such as heroin, cocaine, and marijuana was outside the mainstream of American life.

- The Boggs Act of 1951 increased the penalties for drug violations and provided for a minimum sentence of two years for first-time offenders and up to ten years for repeat offenders.

The Return of Drug Tolerance, 1960–1980

- In the 1960s and 1970s, the use of marijuana and hallucinogenic drugs spread across the nation, along with an increase in problems related to heroin.

- The Comprehensive Drug Act of 1970 organized the federal control of drugs under five classifications called schedules. Now a drug is scheduled based upon a drug's approved medical uses, potential for abuse, and potential for producing dependence.

- In the 1970s, there was generally a lack of public interest and increasing tolerance of drug use. In some U.S. states, there was a decriminalization of marijuana.

Renewed Efforts at Control, 1980–2000

- A decline in heroin abuse in the 1980s was matched by an increase in cocaine abuse and the emergence of crack as a cheap, smokable form of cocaine.

- During the 1980s, a wave of federal drug legislation increased the penalties for the possession and trafficking of illicit drugs. As a result, the number of drug violators rose to the highest level ever, and courts became backlogged with drug cases. The number of inmates in U.S. prisons and jails rose nearly 100 percent from 1985 to 1996.

The Globalization of Drug Regulation, 2001–Present

- The 1990s and the beginning of the twenty-first century can be characterized by a general lack of political interest in drug abuse. After the events of September 11, 2001, the war on terrorism became a more pressing matter than the war on drugs.

Present-Day Attitudes toward Drugs

- It is now recognized that a wide range of psychoactive drugs, licit or illicit, qualify as potential sources of misuse and abuse.

- Individuals born toward the end of the "baby boom" generation were the first group to have grown up during the explosion of drug experimentation in the 1960s and 1970s. Now, as the parents of teenagers at the beginning of the twenty-first century, they face the difficult challenge of dealing with the present-day drug-taking behavior of their children. Interestingly, however, a recent study has found no relationship between prior marijuana use among the parents and marijuana use by their children.

Patterns of Drug Use in the United States

- Surveys of illicit drug use among high school seniors in 2006 have shown that four in every ten seniors used an illicit drug over the last twelve months, more than one in three smoked marijuana, one in sixteen used cocaine, and one in twenty-five had used Ecstasy or inhalants on a recreational basis. One in fifty seniors had used LSD.

- During the 1990s, marijuana use among high school seniors rose significantly, as did the use of other illicit drugs. Since 1997, however, there has been a steady decline in illicit drug use among eighth and tenth graders.

- Drug use in general and the use of individual psychoactive drugs vary greatly along racial and ethnic lines.

- The prevalence rate for alcohol use in the previous month among high school seniors in 2006 was 23 percent and among college students in 2005 was 69 percent. Roughly 12 percent of high school seniors smoked at least one cigarette every day in 2006.

- Over the last thirty years or so, the prevalence trends for regular drug use and perceived risk form an almost exact mirror image to each other. As perceived risk goes up, the level of regular drug use goes down.

America's Drug Debate

- Policymakers in the United States have recently begun to question the objective of zero tolerance with respect to illicit drug-taking behavior, shifting attention toward a harm-reduction approach in which the focus is on minimizing societal and personal problems associated with drug abuse rather than trying to eliminate drug abuse entirely.

Key Terms

Ebers Papyrus, p. 41
French connection, p. 49
laissez-faire, p. 42

patent medicine, p. 43
placebo effect, p. 41

Prohibition, p. 46
shaman, p. 41

shamanism, p. 40
speakeasies, p. 46

Endnotes

1. Caldwell, A. E. (1970). *Origins of psychopharmacology: From CPZ to LSD.* Springfield, IL: C. C. Thomas, p. 3. Muir, Hazel (2003, December 20; 2004, January 9). Party animals. *New Scientist,* pp. 56–59.

2. De Foe, Vincenzo (2003). Ethnomedical field study in northern Peruvian Andes with particular reference to divination practices. *Journal of Ethnopharmacology, 85,* 243–256. Del Castillo, Daniel (2002, November 22). Just what the shaman ordered. *The Chronicle of Higher Education,* p. A72. Metzner, Ralph (1998). Hallucinogenic drugs and plants in psychotherapy and shamanism. *Journal of Psychoactive Drugs, 30,* 333–341.

3. Bryan, Cyril P. (1930). *Ancient Egyptian medicine: The Papyrus Ebers.* Chicago: Ares Publishers. Inglis, Brian (1975). *The forbidden game: A social history of drugs.* New York: Scribners, pp. 11–36.

4. Grilly, David (1998). *Drugs and human behavior.* (3rd ed.). Boston: Allyn and Bacon, p. 2.

5. Sneader, Walter (1985). *Drug discovery: The evolution of modern medicines.* New York: Wiley, pp. 15–47. Stearns, Peter N. (1998). Dope fiends and degenerates: The gendering of addiction in the early twentieth century. *Journal of Social History, 31,* 809–814.

6. Bugliosi, Vincent (1991). *Drugs in America: The case for victory.* New York: Knightsbridge Publishers, p. 215.

7. Freud, Sigmund (1884). Über coca (On ca).*Centralblatt feur die gesammte Therapie.* Translated by S. Pollak (1884). *St. Louis Medical and Surgical Journal, 47.*

8. Brecher, Edward M. (1972). *Licit and illicit drugs.* Boston: Little, Brown, p. 3.

9. Musto, David F. (1987). *The American disease: Origins of narcotics control.* New York: Oxford University Press.

10. Young, James Harvey. (1961). *The toadstool millionaires: A social history of patent medicines in America before regulation.* Princeton, NJ: Princeton University Press.

11. Latimer D., and Goldberg, J. (1981). *Flowers in the blood: The story of opium.* New York: Franklin Watts.

12. Helmer, John (1975). *Drugs and minority oppression.* New York: Seabury Press.

13. Cloyd, Jerald W. (1982). *Drugs and information control: The role of men and manipulation in the control of drug trafficking.* Westport, CT: Greenwood.

14. Musto, *The American disease.* Latimer and Goldberg, *Flowers in the blood.*

15. Latimer and Goldberg, *Flowers in the blood.*

16. Cashman, Sean D. (1981). *Prohibition.* New York: Free Press. Coffey, Thomas M. (1975). *The long thirst: Prohibition in America, 1920–1933.* New York: Norton, pp. 196–198. Gusfield, Joseph R. (1963). *The symbolic crusade: Status politics and the American temperance movement.* Urbana, IL: University of Illinois Press. Sinclair, Andrew. (1962). *The era of excess: A social history of the prohibition movement.* Boston: Little, Brown.

17. Woodiwiss, Michael (1988). *Crime, crusaders and corruption: Prohibition in the United States, 1900–1987.* Totawa, NJ: Barnes and Noble.

18. Behr, E. (1996). *Prohibition.* New York: Arcade. *New York Times,* January 7, 1928.

19. Sinclair, Andrew (1962). *The era of excess.*

20. Musto, *The American disease.*

21. Helmer, *Drugs and minority oppression.* Schlosser, Eric (2003). *Reefer madness: Sex, drugs, and cheap labor in the American black market.* Boston: Houghton Mifflin, p. 245.

22. Musto, *The American disease.*

23. Marshall, Elliot (1971). Cold turkey: heroin. The source supply. *New Republic, 165,* 23–25.

24. Carter, James Earl, Jr. (1979). President's message to the Congress on drug abuse. *Federal Strategy for Drug Abuse and Drug Traffic Prevention,* pp. 66–67.

25. Himmelstein, Jerome L. (1983). *The strange career of marijuana: Politics and ideology of drug control in America.* Westport, CT: Greenwood.

26. Johnston, Lloyd D.; O'Malley, Patrick M.; Bachman, Jerald G.; and Schulenberg, John E. (2007a). *Monitoring the Future national results on adolescent drug use. Overview of key findings, 2006.* Bethesda, MD: National Institute on Drug Abuse, Table 2.

27. Bureau of Justice Statistics (1998). *U.S. Department of Justice sourcebook of criminal justice statistics.* Washington, DC: Bureau of Justice Statistics.

28. Adam, Isacson (2003). Washington's new war in Colombia: The war on drugs meets the war on terror. *NACLA Report on the Americas,* 36, pp. 5–11.

29. Astin, Alexander W.; Parrott, Sarah A.; Korn, William S.; and Sax, Linda J. (1997). *The American freshman: Thirty year trends.* Los Angeles: Higher Education Research Institute, UCLA. *Back to school 1999—National survey of American attitudes on substance abuse V: Teens and their parents* (1999, August). New York: The National Center on Addiction and Substance Abuse at Columbia University. Kandel, Denise B.; Griesler, Pamela C.; Lee, Gang; Davies, Mark; and Schaffsan, Christine (2001). *Parental influences on adolescent marijuana use and the baby boom generation: Findings from the 1976–1996 National Household Survey on Drug Abuse.* Rockville, MD: Office of Applied Studies, Substance Abuse and Mental Health Services Administration. Kluger, Jeffrey, and Ressner, Jeffrey (2006, January 23). Balding, wrinkled, and stoned. *Time,* pp. 54–56. What do you say when your child asks: Did you ever do drugs? (2005, October 3). *Alcoholism and Drug Abuse Weekly,* p. 5.

30. Johnston, Lloyd D.; O'Malley, Patrick M.; Bachman, Jerald G.; and Schulenberg, John E. (2007b). *Monitoring the future: National survey results on drug use, 1975–2006. Vol. I: Secondary school students 2006.* Bethesda, MD: National Institute on Drug Abuse. Johnston, Lloyd D.; O'Malley, Patrick M.; Bachman, Jerald G.; and Schulenberg, John E. (2007c). *Monitoring the future: National survey results on drug use, 1975–2006. Vol. II: College students and adults ages 19–45, 2006.* Bethesda, MD: National Institute on Drug Abuse.

31. Johnston, O'Malley, Bachman, and Schulenberg (2007a), *Monitoring the Future national results,* Tables 2, 3, and 4.

32. Ibid.

33. Johnston, O'Malley, Bachman, and Schulenberg (2007b), *Monitoring the Future, Vol. I,* Table 4-9.

34. Johnston, O'Malley, Bachman, and Schulenberg (2007c), *Monitoring the Future, Vol. II,* Table 2-2.

35. Bachman, Jerald G.; O'Malley, Patrick M.; Schulenberg, John E.; Johnston, Lloyd D.; Bryant, Alison L.; and Merline, Alicia C. (2002). *The decline of substance use in young adulthood: Changes in social activities, roles, and beliefs.* Mahwah, NJ: Lawrence Erlbaum Associates. Bachman, Jerald G.; Wadsworth, Katherine N.; O'Malley, Patrick M.; and Johnston, Lloyd D. (1997). *Smoking, drinking, and drug use in young adulthood: The impacts of new freedoms and new responsibilities.* Mahwah, NJ: Lawrence Erlbaum Associates. Leonard, Kenneth E., and Homish, Gregory G. (2005, Spring) Changes in marijuana use over the transition into marriage. *Journal of Drug Issues,* 409–430.

36. Johnston, O'Malley, Bachman, and Schulenberg (2007a), *Monitoring the Future national results,* Tables 3 and 4. Johnston, O'Malley, Bachman, and Schulenberg (2006c), *Monitoring the Future, Vol. II,* Tables 2-3 and 2-4.

37. Centers for Disease Control and Prevention (2006, June 9). Youth behavior surveillance, United States. *Mortality and Morbidity Weekly Report,* 55, 1–108. Johnston, O'Malley, Bachman, and Schulenberg (2007a), *Monitoring the Future national results,* Table 4.

38. Johnson, O'Malley, Bachman, and Schulenberg (2007b), *Monitoring the Future, Vol. I,* p. 30. Johnston, O'Malley, Bachman, and Schulenberg (2007c), *Monitoring the Future, Vol. II,* Table 2-4.

39. Johnston, Lloyd D. (1996, December 19). The rise in drug use among American teens continues in 1996. News release from the University of Michigan, Ann Arbor, pp. 6–7.

40. Johnston, O'Malley, Bachman, and Schulenberg (2007a), *Monitoring the Future national results,* Tables 2 and 7.

41. Substance Abuse and Mental Health Services Administration (2007). *Results from the 2006 National Survey on Drug Use and Health: National findings.* Rockville, MD: Office of Applied Studies, Substance Abuse and Mental Health Services Administration. Substance Abuse and Mental Health Services Administration (2007). *Results from the 2006 National Survey on Drug Use and Health: Detailed tables.* Rockville, MD: Office of Applied Studies, Substance Abuse and Mental Health Services Administration, Tables 8.11A and 8.11B.

42. Substance Abuse and Mental Health Services Administration (2007, January 5). Substance use in the 15 largest metropolitan statistical areas: 2002–2005. *The NSDUH Report,* pp. 2–3.

chapter **3**

Theoretical Perspectives on Drug Use and Abuse

After I got married and had kids, I wanted to quit smoking weed. I stopped smoking for two weeks and didn't have any withdrawal symptoms like the shakes or anything, but sometimes certain things would make me want to smoke again. Like if I heard an old Dead song or saw someone I used to get high with, I kind of had an urge to light up a joint. And every time I got drunk, I wanted to end the night with a bong hit. I still get high sometimes if I go out with some of my old friends, but I never tell my wife. She would kick me out of the house.

—*A twenty-seven-year-old marijuana user*

After you have completed this chapter, you will understand

- Biological perspectives on drug abuse
- Psychological perspectives on drug abuse
- Sociological perspectives on drug abuse
- The biopsychosocial model of drug abuse
- Risk factors and protective factors for drug use

Why do people take drugs? We all take drugs, of course, for genuine therapeutic reasons, to relieve ourselves of pain or symptoms that arise from a range of physical or psychological disorders. But why do people take drugs on a purely recreational basis? Is it for sheer pleasure, to escape from a life of boredom, to suppress feelings of sorrow and depression, to fit in with a group of friends, to relieve stress? There are so many different reasons why people use and abuse drugs that arriving at a satisfactory explanation presents an enormous challenge. The fact is that no one has developed a single theory that explains why some people are more prone to drug abuse than others, and, indeed, an effort to determine a single explanation probably is doomed to failure. As sociologist Erich Goode has commented, "Hardly any researcher in the field believes that one factor, and one alone, explains the phenomenon under investigation." Instead, we must be content with a variety of explanations, some having to do with drug-taking behavior in general and others having to do with the abuse of a specific drug.[1]

The oldest theory of drug abuse, and arguably the oldest theory to explain disapproved behavior in general, has its origin in demonology. Why would someone do something bad? Because "the devil made him do it." In the last two hundred years or so, we have moved away from believing that evil spirits invoke bad behavior, but this belief underlies the way many people still think about drug abuse. Drug abusers are sometimes considered to be individuals who are morally deficient, who, because of personal inadequacies, overindulgence, a weakness of will, or other character flaw, have given in to the clutches of a "fiendish dope peddler." A nonreligious version of this point of view is referred to as the **moral model** of drug abuse. According to the moral model, drug-taking behavior is simply a matter of personal choice, not a consequence of a biological defect, a psychological dysfunction, or a sociological misfortune. :

The implications can be profound with respect to the ways in which drug abusers are held responsible for their actions and the way the criminal justice system views drug-taking behavior. As drug counselors Gary Fisher and Thomas Harrison explain it

> A 1988 Supreme Court decision found that crimes committed by an alcoholic were willful misconduct and not the result of a disease.... Certainly, the

manner in which states [in the United States] deal with drunk driving violations may relate to the moral model. In states where violators are not assessed for chemical dependency and where there is no diversion to treatment, the moral model guides policy. If excessive alcohol use is the result of personal choice, then violators should be punished.[2]

As we will see, present-day positions on drug use and abuse have gone beyond the moral model. In this chapter, we will review theoretical explanations of drug use and abuse from three broad perspectives: biological, psychological, and sociological.

Biological Perspectives on Drug Abuse

When we theorize about the origins of drug abuse from a biological perspective, we are referring to specific physical mechanisms in specific individuals that influence the initial experience with drugs or an engagement in drug abuse over a period of time. Biological theories have focused primarily on genetic factors, physiological factors, and neurochemical systems in the brain.

Genetic Factors

As genetic research has advanced over the years, particularly since the completion of the mapping of the human genome in 2000, a great deal of attention has focused on the contribution that certain genetic traits make toward the abuse of a range of drugs. Environmental factors are also undoubtedly important. Recent studies have shown, however, that genetic factors play an equal or greater role. Studies of different strains of mice and rats, for example, have found that some have a genetic propensity to become dependent upon cocaine, whereas other strains are more susceptible to the dependence-producing effects of opiates.[3]

Most studies concerning genetic factors in humans have focused on alcoholic individuals, and a growing research literature indicates that alcoholism has a genetic component (see Chapter 11). Family studies have shown that children of alcoholics are four times more likely than other children to become alcoholics (Figure 3.1). Identical twins (those who have identical genetic compositions) are more likely to have a similar risk for alcoholism than fraternal twins, who share only half their genetic traits with each other. In addition, children who have at least one alcoholic biological parent

moral model: An explanation for drug use in which drug-taking behavior is attributed to personal inadequacies, overindulgence, a weakness of will, or other serious character flaw.

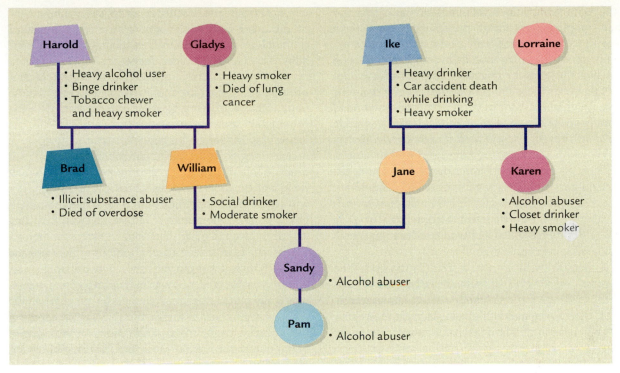

FIGURE 3.1

The genogram of two alcohol abusers, Pam and Sandy, reveals that alcohol and other substances have been abused for four generations, causing family problems and death throughout the family's history.

Source: Stevens, Patricia, and Submit, Robert L. *Substance abuse counseling: Theory and practice* (3rd ed.). Boston: Allyn and Bacon, p. 94.

and were adopted by nonalcoholic parents are three times more likely to have a problem with alcohol, even when they have been raised in a low-risk environment.[4]

The single gene that may be responsible for the emergence of alcoholism has not yet been identified, and it is believed likely that several genes play a role in determining the level of risk. Like diabetes and heart disease, alcoholism is considered to be genetically complex, distinguishing it from diseases such as cystic fibrosis, which results from the mutation of a single gene. Genes that play an important role in alcoholism may include genes associated with liver enzymes that metabolize (break down) alcohol, genes associated with depression and stress, and genes affecting the activity of specific neurotransmitters, such as serotonin and gamma-aminobutyric acid (GABA). One study, for example, found that college students with a particular variant of the serotonin gene consumed more alcohol per occasion, drank more often expressly to become inebriated, and engaged more frequently in binge drinking than students with another variant of the gene.[5]

Even so, we are not speaking of genetic factors producing these effects in a deterministic manner. In Erich Goode's words,

No researcher exploring the inherited link with alcoholism asserts that genetic factors comprise the only or even the principal factor in compulsive drinking. Rather, they posit a genetic predisposition toward alcoholism. Inheritance is one factor out of several. Alone, it does not "make" someone a compulsive, destructive drinker. In combination with other variables, genetic factors may facilitate or make the process more likely, however.[6]

Physiological Factors

One physiological factor hypothesized to be involved in drug abuse has to do with metabolic processes in the body. In the case of heroin abuse, for example, it has been proposed that chronic abusers may have a metabolic defect. Just as Type 1 diabetics have insufficient levels of insulin, heroin abusers may have a natural deficiency with respect to natural opiate-like chemicals in the brain that compels them to seek out heroin and other opiate drugs. From this perspective, heroin abusers are "normalizing" their body by virtue of their heroin abuse. A metabolic-defect theory has been posited as the basis for treatment of heroin-dependent individuals in which oral administrations of a synthetic opiate (methadone) in a medical setting are substituted for injections of heroin, a program that makes it possible for heroin abusers to avoid their former self-destructive lifestyle and turn to more appropriate social behaviors, such as steady employment and a more stable family life (see Chapter 5). Methadone maintenance treatment programs are designed to administer methadone to such individuals over an undetermined length of time because the metabolic defect with respect to opiates is considered to be irreversible.

A specific dysfunctional system in the body of a heroin abuser, however, has yet to be discovered. At present, the evidence for a metabolic defect is only circumstantial; heroin-dependent individuals appear to behave *as if* they have a metabolic imbalance with respect to opiates.[7]

Neurochemical Systems in the Brain

Amphetamines, cocaine, heroin, alcohol, and nicotine may be very different from a pharmacological standpoint, but the way people and animals react to them are remarkably similar. Use of these substances results in a pattern of compulsive behavior based on an intense craving for repeating the experience. The similarities among all of these drugs and across species are numerous enough to entertain the idea that there exists a common neurochemical system in the brain that links them all together (Drugs...in Focus).

It may not be a coincidence that there is a special area of the brain that animals will work hard to stimulate electrically. We cannot say how they are feeling at the time, but their behavior indicates that they want to "turn on" this region of their brains. Their compulsive efforts to receive this stimulation are unmistakable. Could there be a connection to the craving, the intense "rush," and compulsive drug-taking behavior associated with heroin, cocaine, amphetamines, or a host of other dependence-producing drugs?

Two of the key elements in the intensely rewarding effect of certain psychoactive drugs are the neurotransmitter dopamine and a group of neurons in the brain called the **nucleus accumbens.** When laboratory animals are administered amphetamines, heroin, cocaine, alcohol, or nicotine, there is a release of dopamine in the nucleus accumbens. Dopamine activity in the nucleus accumbens is closely linked to their subsequent behavior. Administration of any substance that interferes with the action of dopamine in this region eliminates the desire of animals to work for the self-administration of these abused drugs. While we cannot say, of course, that these animals no longer experience feelings of craving as a result, you will recall that self-administration behavior in animals closely parallels the pattern of human behavior that characterizes psychological dependence (see Chapter 1). Therefore, these studies can be used to understand the neural changes that occur as a consequence of drug abuse. Considering the evidence now in hand, a persuasive argument can be made that dopamine-related processes in the nucleus accumbens underlie the reinforcing effects of many abused drugs. Research also shows an involvement of the nucleus accumbens in compulsive gambling and eating disorders (Portrait, page 71).[8]

Research on the influence of dopamine in drug dependence has the potential to allow us to understand why some individuals may be more susceptible than others to drug-taking behavior. In one study, for example, twenty-three drug-free men with no history of drug abuse were given doses of methylphenidate (brand name: Ritalin), a psychoactive stimulant when ingested by adults. Twelve of the men experienced a pleasant feeling, nine felt annoyed or distrustful, and two felt nothing at all. Measurements of a subclass of dopamine receptors in the brains of these subjects showed a consistent pattern. *The men with the least concentration of dopamine receptors were the ones experiencing pleasant effects.* It is reasonable to hypothesize that those individuals with the fewest dopamine receptors might be the most vulnerable to drug abuse. Their drug-taking behavior might, in part, be a compensation for an inadequate number of dopamine receptors necessary to experience pleasurable feelings without drugs (Portrait).

Psychological Perspectives on Drug Abuse

Psychological perspectives on drug abuse typically draw on either psychoanalytic or nonpsychoanalytic theories of personality or the behavioral processes of human learning.

nucleus accumbens (NEW-clee-us ac-CUM-buns): A region of the brain considered to be responsible for the reinforcing effects of several drugs of abuse.

Drugs...in Focus

Understanding the Biochemistry of Psychoactive Drugs

Neurons are specialized cells in the nervous system, designed to receive and transmit information. There are an estimated 100 billion neurons in the brain, making the brain arguably the most complex organ of the body. Importantly, neurons are interconnected with other neurons, providing the basis for communication of information within the nervous system.

The typical neuron consists of three principal components: the *cell body*, the *dendrites*, and the *axon*. The cell body comprises the bulk of the neuron and contains the nucleus of the cell. Dendrites are short appendages or branches that extend out from the cell body to receive and respond to the activity of other neurons. The long appendage called the axon, in some cases, extends a great distance from the cell body. The axon carries information outward from the cell body to other neurons; dendrites carry information toward the cell body from other neurons.

When an electrical nerve impulse is generated, it is conducted down the axon until it reaches the axon's end-point. At this location, the axon diverges like the branches of a tree. At the terminal end of these branches are small button-like structures called *synaptic knobs*. The gap between a synaptic knob and the surface of another neuron is referred to as the *synapse*.

The transfer of information at the synapse is controlled by the activity of chemical molecules called **neurotransmitters,** which are stored in the synaptic vesicles and released into the synapse when the nerve impulse reaches the end-points of the axon. Special receptor sites on the other side of the synapse (typically embedded in the dendrites of another neuron) receive the neurotransmitters that have been released. Each receptor can be imagined as having an internal shape that is designed to match the external shape of the neurotransmitter, allowing the neurotransmitter and receptor to "fit together" like a key fitting into a lock. When the neurotransmitter has successfully locked into the receptor site (an event called *receptor binding*), an electrical change occurs in the surface of the receiving neuron. Neuron A has now communicated with neuron B.

The "message" of this communication takes one of two forms. It is either a messag[e] inhibit. Excitation makes the neuron emit a g of nerve impulses per second; inhibition makes the neuron emit a lesser number of nerve impulses per second.

Receptor binding by neurotransmitters, however, is not all of the story. After excitatory or inhibitory effects are produced, neurotransmitters return to the synaptic knob in anticipation of the arrival of another nerve impulse. The process of returning back is called *reuptake*. If reuptake is inhibited or blocked, neurotransmitters will remain in the receptor sites a bit longer than usual, resulting in a greater excitatory or inhibitory effect. Any drug that is a reuptake inhibitor of a given neurotransmitter will end up increasing that neurotransmitter's effect on receptors.

Here is a partial list of neurotransmitters that play a role in the effects of alcohol and other drugs:

- *Acetylcholine* influences heart rate, learning, and memory.
- *Dopamine* affects motor control, mood, and feelings of euphoria. Dopamine plays an major role in producing feelings of craving that encourage a continuing pattern of compulsive drug-taking behavior.
- *Serotonin* affects sensory perception, sleep, mood, and body temperature. Alterations in serotonin have been related to hallucinatory effects of such drugs as LSD and psilocybin. Abnormal levels of serotonin have been associated with depression and other mood disorders.

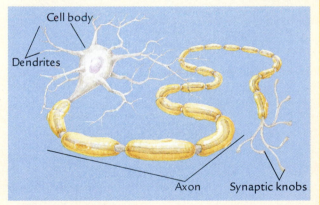

Cell body

Dendrites

Axon   Synaptic knobs

continued

neurotransmitters: Chemical substances that a neuron uses to communicate information at the synapse.

...ins are natural pain killers produced by the ...and bear a remarkable resemblance to morphine.

...orpinephrine influences sleep, blood pressure, ...heart rate, and memory. Along with serotonin, norpinephrine has been associated with the regulation of mood.

- *Gamma-aminobutyric acid (GABA)* influences levels of anxiety and general excitation in the brain. Antianxiety medications, often referred to as tranquilizers, stimulate GABA-releasing neurons, providing a reduction in feelings of stress and fear.

- *Glutamate* is the basis for the effects of PCP (angel dust) and ketamine. It is also involved in drug craving and the likelihood of drug-abuse relapse. Current development of new drugs that block glutamate receptors in the brain shows great promise for future drug abuse treatment.

Psychoanalytic Theories

Psychoanalytic explanations of drug abuse are derived from the work of Sigmund Freud (1856–1939), the founder of psychoanalysis, and focus on internal psychological disturbances that begin in early childhood. According to Freud, one's personality consists of three basic systems: the id, the ego, and the superego. The id, present at birth, consists of instinctual animal impulses or drives, such as hunger and sex. On an unconscious level, the id continually seeks pleasure, is self-serving, and disregards others who get in the way. At the time of birth and immediately thereafter, humans are essentially "all id." The ego, however, is the part of the personality that becomes conscious and rational. The ego develops when a child begins to recognize that he or she cannot "get away with everything," that his or her actions have specific consequences, and that fun-

> **psychoanalytic explanations:** Theoretical explanations based upon the writings of Sigmund Freud and those influenced by him. In terms of drug use and abuse, psychoanalytic concepts include subconscious processes that develop in early childhood, a fixation on the oral stage of development, expressions of power, and self-loathing.

Drugs...in Focus

Dopamine and Reinforcement: Both the Chicken *and* the Egg

The connection between dopamine and behaviors associated with abused drugs has been evident for some time, but until recently the exact relationship had not been determined. Research by Paul Phillips and his colleagues at the University of North Carolina, using a new technique that measures dopamine release at the nucleus accumbens every one-tenth of a second as a rat presses a lever to self-administer cocaine has shown that timing is everything.

When rats have been trained to self-administer cocaine only in a special test chamber, causing them to develop an association between cocaine and this particular environment, a brief pulse of dopamine is released just a few seconds before the animals become interested in approaching and pressing the lever. In other words, dopamine produces a priming effect for future drug-taking behavior. Dopamine levels continue to increase as the rats make the final approach to the lever and peak a few seconds after the lever press occurs. Other studies have shown that elevated dopamine levels last for several minutes after an injection of cocaine. Phillips's study is the first to show what happens beforehand, when drug-related cues are present.

The bottom line is that dopamine appears to represent both the "chicken" and the "egg" in drug dependence. The increased release of this neurotransmitter in the nucleus accumbens acts as a reward for the drug-taking behavior. Afterward, a release of dopamine triggers a pursuit of the same reward in environments previously associated with drug-taking behavior.

It is quite possible that drug-dependent individuals are victims of a similar vicious circle of environmental priming and behavioral reward—both processes controlled by dopamine signals in the brain. In later chapters, we will see the major impact of environmental cues in drug-taking behaviors with respect to a wide range of dependence-producing substances.

Sources: Nestler, Eric, J., and Malenka, Robert C. (2004, March). The addicted brain. *Scientific American*, pp. 78–85. Phillips, Paul E. M.; Stuber, Garret D.; Helen, Michael, L. A. V.; Wightman, R.; and Carelli, Regina, M. (2003). Subsecond dopamine release promotes cocaine seeking. *Nature, 422,* 614–618.

PORTRAIT

Nora D. Volkow—Imaging the Face of Addiction in the Brain

It is one thing to speculate about the effects of drug abuse on the brain, to assert that the transition from initially being a voluntary drug user to becoming a compulsive drug user is a matter of subtle but significant brain changes. It is quite another thing to show the physical effects themselves. But that is precisely what Nora D. Volkow and her associates at the Brookhaven National Laboratory in New York have done. Using a brain scanning technique called positron emission tomography (PET), neural activity in the human brain can be captured in graphic detail. Volkow and her colleagues have shown that chronic cocaine abuse leads to the loss of about 20 percent of the dopamine receptors in the nucleus accumbens. This effect appears to be long-lasting, enduring for up to four months after the last cocaine exposure, even though the cocaine abuser no longer has cocaine in his or her system. Volkow estimates that a comparable decline in dopamine receptors would take at least 40 years to accomplish in a drug-free brain.

It is not surprising that the nucleus accumbens, with its rich concentration of dopamine receptors, would be the site of this dramatic change. Dopamine and the nucleus accum-bens have been associated with feelings of reward and pleasure in a wide range of behavioral activities, from drug use to compulsive exercising to gambling. As Volkow says, "It is through activation of these circuits that we are motivated to do the things we perceive as pleasurable. If you have a decrease in dopamine receptors that transmit pleasurable feelings, you become less responsive to the stimuli such as food or sex, that normally activate them." The irony is that it may be precisely those individuals who have fewer dopamine receptors who may be inclined to engage in drug-taking behavior in the first place; the drug exposure evidently makes the deficit worse. As one drug researcher has put it, "In the end, [these people] could be much worse off biologically than when they started."

Following Volkow's pioneering work on brain imaging, other mysteries about drug abuse are being unlocked. For example, what creates the intense craving for specific drugs once an individual has been first exposed to them? The answer lies in the research of Anna R. Childress and her associates at the University of Pennsylvania. When chronic drug abusers were shown video segments of drug-associated paraphernalia (a pic-ture of a syringe or a mound of white powder), brain scans revealed a change in activity in an area of the limbic system. The connection between the limbic system and one's emotional behavior in times of stress makes it reasonable to hypothesize that this area of the brain, in this instance, would be involved in feelings of drug craving.

In 2003, Nora D. Volkow was appointed director of the National Institute of Drug Abuse (NIDA), the first woman to lead this federal agency in its history.

Sources: Childress, Anna Rose; Mozley, David; McElgin, William; Fitzgerald, Josh; Reivich, Martin; and O'Brian, Charles P. (1999). Limbic activation during cue-induced cocaine craving. *American Journal of Psychiatry, 156,* 11–18. National Institute on Drug Abuse (2003, January 23). Press release: Dr. Nora D. Volkow named new director of NIDA. Bethesda, MD: National Institute on Drug Abuse. Volkow, Nora D.; Wang, Gene-Jack; Fowler, Joanna S.; Logan, Jean; Gatley, Samuel J.; Hitzemann, Richard; Chen, A. D.; and Pappas, Naomi. (1997). Decrease in striatal dopaminergic responsiveness in detoxified cocaine-dependent subjects. *Nature, 386,* 830–833.

damental needs should and eventually will be satisfied in an appropriate context of socially approved behavior. The development of the superego represents the internalization of societal norms and serves as one's social conscience. As a person develops a superego, feelings of guilt and shame arise when social norms are violated.

Psychoanalytic theory asserts that a strong and healthy ego is ultimately the product of a delicate psychological balancing act in which everyday decisions are maintained in such a way as to minimize excessive out-of-control pressures from the id on the one hand and excessive pressures of guilt and anxiety from the superego on the other. You might notice a connection between the psychoanalytic viewpoint and the basic tenets of the moral model, discussed earlier.

Another psychoanalytic concept that may help explain drug abuse is the idea that most of us pass through (and advance beyond) an oral and narcissistic stage of development in infancy, a time when our basic needs of food, water, and feelings of security are satisfied orally. Drug abusers, however, are thought to be fixated on the oral stage well past infancy. Psychoanalyst Otto Fenichel theorized that individuals engage in drug abuse to satisfy an archaic oral longing, a sexual longing, a need for security, and a need for the maintenance of self-esteem. All of these needs, he argued, exist in the earliest years of life and, in drug abusers, continue to exert influence, resulting in an orally based pattern of drug-taking behavior.[10]

Some psychoanalytic theorists focus on the symbolism of "getting high" as an expression of power in the sense that the drug abuser is striving for superiority over others and, importantly, is attempting to rise above a self-deprecating sense of self. Other theorists view drug dependence in terms of an unconscious death wish, the ultimate form of self-loathing. The self-destructive lifestyle of drug abuse is viewed as a failure of ego functioning that, under normal and healthier circumstances, should promote self-care, self-protection, and self-esteem.[11]

Behavioral Theories

In contrast to a psychoanalytic theory that emphasizes internal struggles of human personality or primitive impulses and drives, **behavioral theory** emphasizes the role of learning through reinforcement. According to the behavioral point of view, practically all of human behavior is learned. In other words, drug-taking behavior leading to drug abuse and dependence is a consequence of having modified one's behaviors in specific ways and according to specific principles.

The overarching principle of behavioral theory is that any behavior that is followed by a reward (reinforcement) is more likely to be repeated in the future. Repeated rewards will result in a continuing pattern of behavior that can be weakened only when these reinforcers are removed (extinction) or other behaviors are now reinforced (counter-conditioning). Individuals using a drug with a high reinforcement potential typically report that they care more about obtaining and using the drug than just about anything else in their life. In this case, reinforcers related to drug-taking behavior exceed or overcome competing reinforcers, such as the benefits and satisfactions derived from a job, money, or friends and family.

While behavior theorists make the distinction between positive reinforcement (gained through the attainment of a pleasurable circumstance) and negative reinforcement (gained through the reduction of a painful or uncomfortable circumstance), the principle of reinforcement remains the same. The reinforcement of heroin abuse, therefore, can focus either on the re-experiencing of the euphoric feelings associated with heroin or on the relief from uncomfortable feelings associated with heroin withdrawal.

Which aspect of reinforcement is emphasized among drug abusers in general can determine the pattern of drug-taking behavior. Those guided by the positive reinforcement of the drug experience are often referred to as *euphoria seekers* and those guided by the negative reinforcement of withdrawal relief are referred to as *maintainers*. Euphoria seekers typically display a compulsive pattern of drug-taking behavior.[12]

In the case of heroin abuse, maintainers tend to consume just enough heroin to avoid the withdrawal symptoms that would occur if their pattern of heroin abuse were to cease. They try to stay within the conventionality of their social community as they "nurse" their habit along. Euphoria-seekers, however, are inclined to be so heavily into the pleasurable aspects of heroin that their lives have spiraled out of control. They have descended into a life-style dominated by the drug. Social conventionality is no longer possible. In Chapter 5, we will examine studies of heroin abusers (called chippers), who are classified as maintainers rather than euphoria-seekers. Clearly, their lives are extremely precarious—a testament to the power of heroin.[13]

Behavioral theorists also assert that specific cues or situations have the capability of stimulating powerful drug cravings brought on by memories of past pleasurable (reinforcing) experiences. Through a process of Pavlovian conditioning (see Chapter 1), drug users will associate drug use with certain visual cues, specific friends and situations, or even a song. Cigarette smokers, for example, commonly report that it is difficult to abstain from smoking when drinking alcohol, talking on the phone, or driving a car if these circumstances have been closely associated with smoking behavior. Some marijuana users report cravings after seeing paraphernalia used in smoking marijuana, such as a bong or pipe, while heroin injectors may crave heroin after viewing a hypodermic needle. The importance of Pavlovian conditioning was discussed in the context of behavioral tolerance in Chapter 1.

A visual image of white powder, resembling lines of cocaine, tends to elicit powerful feelings of craving among individuals with earlier experiences of cocaine abuse.

behavioral theory: An explanation of behavior based upon the effect of reinforcement on learned responses to one's environment.

Conditioned cues are very difficult to break and can present major obstacles to overcome on the path to drug-abuse recovery. Drug-abuse treatment efforts are often cut short by the appearance of cues that have played an important part in previous drug-taking behavior. Counseling professionals believe that it is essential that individuals break both their pharmacological and their psychological (behavioral) dependence on drugs to return to and maintain a drug-free life.

Non-psychoanalytic Personality Theories

Psychological explanations of drug abuse can also emphasize a constellation of personality traits that distinguish drug abusers from nonabusers, without reference to psychoanalytic concepts. A general theme is that antisocial personality disorder, anxiety, and depression are more common among drug abusers. Individuals with antisocial personality disorder are typically impulsive, sensation seeking, and immature. Individuals displaying these traits may be more prone to abuse drugs because of their increased need for stimulation, excitement, and immediate gratification. Sensation-seeking people are essentially risk-takers ("edgewalkers"), and drug use epitomizes risk-taking behavior, particularly in adolescence.[14]

Interestingly, as pointed out in Chapter 1, risk-seeking does not appear to be a pervasive element in the natural world. Our attraction to the use of hallucinogens such as LSD (see Chapter 6) as a means for altering one's conscious experience, for example, is not commonly shared by animals. While animals may self-administer drugs such as cocaine and other stimulants with a level of compulsiveness that matches the human experience, a number of other drugs are not attractive at all, judging from the animals' reluctance to work for their administration. Hallucinogens, in particular, are examples of drugs that animals clearly prefer to leave alone.[15]

Drug abusers typically demonstrate poor judgment, have difficulty learning from their mistakes, are emotionally insensitive to others, and are unable to form long-lasting relationships with other people. It is believed that anxiety and depression are immediate precursors to drug abuse, in that drugs elevate one's mood and relieve feelings of stress. In effect, individuals suffering from anxiety and depression are engaging in a pattern of self-medication. It is well known, however, that patterns of drug abuse can actually induce anxiety and depression or make matters worse (see Chapter 11 in the case of alcohol abuse).

While psychologists have studied specific personality traits that are more frequently observed in drug abusers, they have not been able to identify a unique set of personality traits for such individuals. For example, alcohol abusers tend to be more independent, nonconformist, and impulsive, but these same traits are also found in successful athletes.[16]

Sociological Perspectives on Drug Abuse

For sociologists, environmental and societal factors play an especially important role in drug use and abuse. The focus is a sharp contrast to the focus in the biological and psychological perspectives discussed so far:

> [The] most crucial factor . . . is not the characteristics of the individual, but the situations, social relations, or social structures in which the individual is, or has been, located. More specifically, it is the individual located within specific [social] structures.[17]

During the Vietnam war, for example, a large proportion of American troops used and abused heroin, which was available in Vietnam at extraordinarily high levels of purity. It is reasonable to assume that easy access to heroin in the context of being in a strange and dangerous environment encouraged them to turn to heroin for escape and relief (see Chapter 5). However, only one in eight soldiers continued to use heroin after returning home to a "normal" life. Evidently, the social context was crucial.[18]

Sociological perspectives on drug use and abuse will be represented by anomie or strain theory, social control or bonding theory, differential association theory, subcultural recruitment and socialization theory, and labeling theory.

Anomie/Strain Theory

In 1893, sociologist Emile Durkheim used the term **anomie** to describe the feelings of frustration and alienation that exist among individuals who see themselves as not being able to meet the demands of society.[19] Durkheim studied the effects of anomie as they pertained to suicide, while sociologist Robert Merton in 1968

> **anomie (AN-eh-MEE):** In sociological terms, feelings of frustration and alienation when individuals see themselves as not being able to meet the demands of society. Anomie theory is sometimes referred to as strain theory.

INHALANTS...
(Sprays / Aerosols / Glues)

EVIL SPIRITS THAT BREAK THE BONDS BETWEEN OURSELVES AND OUR ELDERS, DISRUPT THE CIRCLE OF OUR FAMILY SYSTEM, DESTROY THE HARMONY BETWEEN US AND ALL CREATION.

FOR OUR OWN SURVIVAL, THE SURVIVAL OF OUR FAMILY, OUR TRIBE AND THE INDIAN NATION, WE MUST RESIST THESE SPIRITS OF DEATH.

This prevention message focuses on inhalant abuse among American Indian children, adolescents, and young adults, addressing feelings of anomie through the sociocultural filter of their community.

applied the concept to other forms of deviant behavior, such as drug use. Merton believed that every society includes a set of cultural goals and means to achieve them (norms). In most cases, members of society can reach these cultural goals, or at least have some hope of reaching them, by following certain socially defined means. In the United States and other economically developed nations of the world, the primary cultural goal is economic success, and individuals aspire to reach this goal through the acceptable social norm of hard work. When someone is unable to obtain economic success, the result is a feeling of frustration and anomie. This sense of anomie or strain (hence the terms, anomie theory or strain theory) is highest among disadvantaged segments of the population, who experience high rates of crime and drug use in their everyday lives.[20]

Merton classified five possible adaptations or responses to anomie when someone is unable to achieve cultural goals through acceptable means. The five adaptations of conformity, innovation, ritualism, retreatism, and rebellion will be reviewed in the context of drug use and abuse.[21]

- In the first adaptation of *conformity*, individuals accept both culturally defined goals and the prescribed means for achieving them. They may find it necessary to scale down their aspirations, work hard, and save money, while continuing to follow legitimate paths. In this sense, conformity is not deviant behavior but rather an adjustment in their lives. It is also the most common mode of response when contending with anomie. This type of adaptation would lead to a decision not to use or abuse drugs that are outside the mainstream of our culture. It would not, however, discourage the use of alcohol or nicotine if drinking and tobacco smoking were acceptable drug-taking behaviors.

- In the second adaptation of *innovation*, individuals retain the dominant cultural goal of monetary success but choose to reject legitimate avenues of goal attainment. Unlike conformity, innovation involves illegal behavior. Aspiring to be a drug dealer in order to achieve economic success is an example of innovation.

- In the third adaptation of *ritualism*, individuals reject the goal of economic success (considering it unattainable) but continue to accept the means of working in legitimate areas of life. An example is the burnt-out factory worker who uses illicit drugs to get through the day without "making waves" and then goes home to get drunk or "stoned."

- In the fourth adaptation of *retreatism*, individuals reject both the goal of economic success and the means of hard work. They have, in effect, given up. Members belonging to this category include individuals who have developed a dependence on alcohol or other drugs. Retreatists can be viewed as double failures. First, they have been unable to find success through conformity. Second, they have not been able to find success as an innovator through criminal activity. Ironically, drug dependent individuals retreat in this way with the expectation that they are entering a seemingly undemanding world. The harsh reality, however, is that drug dependence itself sets off a never-ending series of brutal demands, on both a physical and psychological level. Perhaps only in the case of a Chinese opium smoker (see Chapter 5) would a retreatist adaptation approach the fantasy of a completely undemanding existence.

- In the fifth adaptation, *rebellion*, individuals not only reject both the goal of economic success and the means of working but also seek to overturn the social system and replace it with an alternate set of values. These individuals are the radicals and revolutionaries of society who break the law in an attempt to change it. An example is the rebellious youth of the "hippie" subculture of the 1960s. Their association with marijuana and LSD use and their involvement with a wide range of psychoactive substances were components of a political act of rebellion. The popular slogan of the time, "sex, drugs, and rock and roll," represented their rebellious response to the anomie they felt at the time.

It is conceivable that someone's personal adaptation to anomie might be a combination of the above possibilities.

A survey of more than 9,000 high school students in 1990 found that feelings of anomie or strain were important predictors of drug use. Students who have a negative response to questions such as, "When you are older, do you expect to own more possessions than your parents do now?" or to the statement, "My life is in my hands, and I am in control of it" were more likely to engage in drug-taking behavior.[22]

Anomie theory, however, does tend to oversimplify a complex problem. We know that people who have attained economic success have, at the same time, become dependent on drugs and alcohol. Rock stars and celebrities of all kinds, for example, have become dependent on drugs such as cocaine, heroin, alcohol, and prescription medication. In fact, celebrity status in our society encourages such involvement. Moreover, anomie theory fails to explain why one person chooses to be a ritualist, for instance, whereas another becomes an innovator. Finally, anomie theory disregards the influence of social factors such as peer group association, differential access to drugs, and the degree of attachment to one's community and family.

Social Control/Bonding Theory

A second major sociological perspective on drug use and abuse is **social control theory.** According to social control theorists, all human beings are, by nature, rule breakers. The bonds that people have to society and its moral code are what keep them from breaking the law and remaining socially controlled (hence the terms, social control theory or bonding theory). When an individual is strongly bonded to his or her family, religious affiliation, school, or community, that individual is less likely to engage in delinquent behavior. When these bonds become weakened, deviant behavior, such as drug use, results.

Treatment for drug-related problems is optimized when there is positive involvement from the family and the social bond of attachment is strengthened.

Social control theorists identify four social bonds that promote conformity: attachment, commitment, involvement, and belief.[23] *Attachment* refers to one's closeness to significant others, such as parents, peers, and teachers. Individuals will conform to social norms and refrain from drug use because they seek the approval of these significant individuals. *Commitment* refers to an individual's investment and pursuit in reaching conventional goals, such as the attainment of a good education and a satisfying job. *Involvement* refers to the extent to which one is associated with conventional activities within a school, community, or religious affiliation. *Belief* refers to how well an individual has internalized the moral values of society, such as honesty, perseverance, and respect for authority. Attention to social bonds is important in drug-abuse prevention and treatment (see Chapter 15).

Empirical tests of predictions made by social control theory with regard to drug use are mixed. Several studies have found that variables such as parental attachment and school attachment are related to lower rates of drug use among youths, whereas other studies have found that relationships with peers act as a more important predictor of drug use than attachment to one's family or school. In fact, the primary weakness of social control theory is that it underestimates the importance of the role of delinquent friends, while overestimating the importance

social control theory: A sociological theory of drug use based on weakened social bonds between an individual and social entities such as family, religious affiliation, school, and community. Social control theory is sometimes referred to as bonding theory.

of involvement in conventional social activities. Studies have consistently found that patterns of adolescent alcohol and drug use are strongly related to drug abusers having friends who also engage in this behavior. Yet there is no explanatory role for peers in social control theory.[24]

Differential Association Theory

The third major sociological perspective is **differential association theory.** Originally proposed by sociologist Donald Sutherland in 1939 as a general theory of deviance, differential association theory has served as a theoretical foundation for some of the most important research on illicit drug use. The basic premise of the theory is that deviant behavior such as drug use is learned in interactions and communications with other individuals. This learning takesplace within relatively intimate groups, such as family and friends. Significant others (parents and friends) often communicate pro-drug or anti-drug messages. When one's attitudes and beliefs favoring drug use exceed one's attitudes and beliefs against drug use, the likelihood increases that drug use will occur. In other words, if an adolescent has a greater number of friends who encourage and use drugs than friends who discourage and do not use drugs, he or she is more likely to engage in that behavior.[25]

From a differential association perspective, the process of learning to use drugs also involves learning the techniques to use drugs and learning how to enjoy the experience. First-time marijuana users, for example, must learn how to roll a "joint" and how to hold the marijuana smoke in their lungs for a period of time to obtain the drug's full effects (see Chapter 7). First-time heroin users must learn how to "cook" or prepare the heroin for intravenous injections by placing the drug in a spoon with water, then heating the substance with a lighter or match to liquify the heroin. Heroin users also must learn the correct method of injecting the drug without damaging their veins (see Chapter 5). Individuals who use LSD or MDMA (Ecstasy) for the first time may be frightened. Users may experience social withdrawal, anxiety, and paranoia. Peers often play an important role in calming novice users and in teaching them to focus on the positive aspects of the drug experience rather than the negative ones (see Chapter 6). These techniques are typically demonstrated in small, intimate groups. In fact, very few, if any, adolescents begin using drugs alone or with strangers present at the time.[26]

Identifying oneself as a drug user typically emerges from being immersed in a social network of friends who share a similar outlook in life. Some drug-using youths take part in a drug subculture that plays a pivotal role in teaching them about illicit drugs. A **subculture** is a subdivision within a dominant culture that has its own norms, beliefs, and values. It exists within the larger society, not apart from it. Several important American drug subcultures include the "hippie" subculture of the 1960s that promoted the use of marijuana and LSD or the rave subculture that has promoted the use of Ecstasy. Drug subcultures not only teach young users about the skills for successfully using drugs but also point out the way to obtain drugs, how to avoid getting "ripped off," and sometimes how to manufacture the drugs themselves. A strong sense of social bonding within a drug subculture provides the motivation for continued drug use (Drugs . . . in Focus).

Subcultural Recruitment and Socialization Theory

The fourth major sociological perspective draws on the assumptions of differential reinforcement theory but focuses more directly on the dynamic relationships that drug abusers have with respect to each other. According to proponents of **subcultural recruitment and socialization theory,** such as Erich Goode and Bruce Johnson, a selective interaction exists in which individuals are drawn to drug users because they recognize a compatibility of social values. As Goode has expressed it,

> *Even before someone uses a drug for the first time, he or she is "prepared for" or "initiated into" its use—or, in a sense,* socialized in advance—*because his or her values are already somewhat consistent with those of the drug subculture.*[27]

The social bonding of individuals in the subculture increases as a direct function of drug-taking behavior becoming more and more a central focus of their social interactions.

---

differential association theory: A sociological theory of drug use based upon the premise that drug-taking behavior is learned in interactions and communications with other individuals.

subculture: A subdivision within a dominant culture that has its own norms, beliefs, and values. An example is a drug subculture that provides the social bonding for continued drug use and abuse.

subcultural recruitment and socialization theory: A theoretical perspective on drug abuse that focuses on specific relationships that drug abusers have with respect to each other within a cohesive subculture and the changes that occur in this subculture over time.

The Private Language of a Drug Subculture

A powerful bond within a subculture is a common language that makes sense only for people within it and is virtually unintelligible to people on the outside. This communication system is largely hidden from the mainstream culture of the society at large. In the case of a marijuana drug subculture in New York City, a personal language provides a socially constructed way of talking, expressing, and interacting among marijuana users and distributors.

Sociologist Bruce Johnson and his associates have examined the importance of "argot" (invented slang) on maintaining the identity of the subculture as well as establishing boundaries with subcultures defined by other types of drugs. In their words, they "constitute important verbal threads that effectively connect participants." They can be standard words with special meanings or completely new words. Here are some examples:

- *Bambu*—marijuana rolling papers
- *One and a Dutch*—a single tabacco cigarette and a blunt (marijuana in a Dutch Master cigar shell)
- *Kind*—good-quality marijuana, shortened form for *kind bud*, shortened further to *kb*
- *Baked, crunked, blazed*—under the influence of marijuana

- *Beastin'*—rushing the process of smoking; not willing to wait one's turn and thus rushing everyone around them
- *Puff-puff-pass*—promoting equality among smokers in group settings, meaning each person takes two inhalations and then passes the marijuana to the next person, until everyone has smoked or the marijuana joint is finished

A private language is a characteristic feature of any deviant subculture, whether the focus is a particular illicit drug such as heroin, cocaine, or Ecstasy or a specialized illicit activity such as computer hacking.

Sources: Holt, Thomas (2007). Subcultural evolution? Examining the influence of on- and off-line experiences on deviant subcultures. *Deviant Behavior, 28,* 171–198. Furst, R. Terry; Johnson, Bruce D.; Dunlap, Eloise; and Curtis, Richard (1999). The stigmatized image of the "crack head": A sociocultural exploration of a barrier to cocaine smoking among a cohort of youth in New York City. *Deviant Behavior, 20,* 153–181. Johnson, Bruce D.; Bardhi, Flutura; Sifraneck, Stephen J.; and Dunlap, Eloise (2006). Marijuana argot as subculture threads: Social constructions by users in New York City. *British Journal of Criminology, 46,* 46–77. Quotation on page 46.

The dominant influence of peers, however, applies primarily to adolescent drug abuse, according to the studies of Denise Kandel. In later stages of drug abuse, when the drugs of choice change from a concentration on beer, wine, cigarettes, liquor, and marijuana to drugs such as cocaine and heroin, drug abusers tend to break away from a tightly focused subcultural group and move toward a set of less intimate relationships. At this point, there is typically a close relationship with only one drug-abusing friend, an individual who shares the same social attitudes, behaviors, and problems.[28]

Labeling Theory

The fifth major sociological perspective is **labeling theory.** Labeling theorists argue that virtually everyone has experimented with drugs at some time in his or her life. This experimentation is referred to as **primary deviance,** nonconformity that is temporary, exploratory, and easily concealed. Primary deviant acts, such as drug experimentation, often go unnoticed, and individuals who commit these acts do not generally regard themselves as deviants and are not labeled as such by others. Once the drug use is discovered and made public by others, however, the situation changes. At this point, drug users are labeled as deviant, and they are often seen

labeling theory: A sociological theory of drug use that emphasizes the process by which a drug user internalizes a newly acquired label of deviance and continues a pattern of drug-taking behavior that is based on the expectations of others.

primary deviance: Noncomformist behavior associated with drug experimentation. It is temporary, exploratory, and easily concealed from others.

in a new light by others as a "stoner" or "dope head." It becomes difficult for users to shed this new status.

Eventually, users begin to internalize the newly acquired label and continue to use drugs because others expect them to do so. In other words, the individual changes his or her self-perception to fit the expectations of others. Behavior now continues as **secondary deviance**, persistent nonconformity by the individual who has been labeled as deviant. Drug users who do not wish to be labeled as deviant may choose to keep their drug use covert or, in time, may become a member of a drug subculture.

According to labeling theorists, social class distinctions play a major role in determining whether an individual might be labeled in a negative manner. A businessman who drinks five vodka martinis at lunch, for example, is much less likely to be labeled as deviant than a factory worker who drinks five beers at lunch. As discussed in Chapter 2, policy decisions regarding which drugs to outlaw and which to legitimize have often been associated with an underlying fear of a minority group whose drug use has become labeled as socially deviant.[29]

Integrating Perspectives on Drug Abuse

Success in drug-abuse treatment rests upon the recognition that there are multiple pathways to drug abuse and dependence. For each individual, a specific combination of biological, psychological, and sociological factors play a role in getting that person to the point at which treatment is necessary. This integrated, combinational approach to treatment is referred to as the **biopsychosocial model** (Figure 3.2). The review of theoretical perspectives on drug abuse in this chapter has allowed us to consider viewpoints on an individual basis, but none of them alone provides the full picture of this complex problem.[30]

Risk Factors and Protective Factors

Researchers have asked high school seniors to report their personal reasons for taking drugs.[31] The most frequently occurring responses among the classes of 1983 and 1984 have included "to have a good time with my friends" (65 percent), "to experiment or see what it's like" (54 percent), "to feel good or get high"

secondary deviance: Persistent nonconformist behavior by an individual who has been labeled as deviant and whose deviant behavior (e.g., drug use) is based upon expectations of others.

biopsychosocial model: A theoretical perspective on drug use that recognizes the biological, psychological, and sociological factors underlying drug-taking behavior and encourages an integrated approach toward drug-abuse treatment.

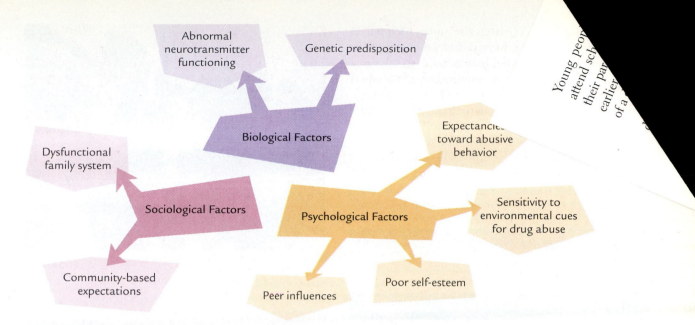

FIGURE 3.2

The biopsychosocial model asserts that there are multiple pathways to drug abuse.

Source: Modified from Margolis, Robert D., and Zweben, Joan E. (1998). *Treating patients with alcohol and other drug problems: An integrated approach.* Washington, DC: American Psychological Association, pp. 76–87.

(49 percent), and "to relax or relieve tension" (41 percent). These responses were similar to reasons given by the class of 1976 in earlier surveys, and there is no reason to suspect significant differences today.

These studies are interesting not only for the insights they have provided but also for the way they have been carried out. There was no theoretical perspective behind the question; the question was simply asked. In other words, the research was not theory-driven.

A large literature has accumulated that deals in a straightforward manner with the relationship between a given variable (pertaining to an individual's life-style, family makeup, environmental condition, etc.) and the likelihood that drug use will occur. Based on the information gained in such studies, we find it useful to consider that a given person has a certain degree of vulnerability with respect to drug-taking behavior. This vulnerability can be shaped by two separate groups of factors in a person's life. The first are **risk factors,** which make it *more likely* that a person will be involved with drugs; the second are **protective factors,** which make it *less likely* that a person will be involved with drugs.

Together, risk factors and protective factors combine to give us some idea about the likelihood that drug-taking behavior will occur. The emphasis, however, should be on the phrase "some idea." We still cannot know for certain which individuals would use drugs and which ones would not. Any predictions about drug use would be probabilistic, not deterministic.

Nonetheless, an understanding of risk factors and protective factors in general and knowledge about which factors apply to a given individual are useful pieces of information in the development of effective drug prevention programs. Identifying the population with the highest risk toward drug use is the first step toward allocating the necessary time, effort, and money to lower the chances that drug-related problems will occur.

Specific Risk Factors

Certain factors that may appear to be strong risk factors for drug-taking behavior in general (socioeconomic status, for example) turn out to have an association that is far from simple and may depend upon the particular drug under discussion. The most reliable set of risk factors consists of psychosocial characteristics that reflect a tendency toward nonconformity within society.

risk factors: Factors in an individual's life that increase the likelihood of involvement with drugs.

protective factors: Factors in an individual's life that decrease the likelihood of involvement with drugs and reduce the impact that any risk factor might have.

ple who take drugs are more inclined to
school irregularly, have poor relationships with
parents, or get into trouble in general. As discussed
sociologists refer to such individuals as members
a deviant subculture.[32]

The effects of being a participant in a socially
deviant subculture are highlighted by the increased
probability that an individual will display some level of
drug-taking behavior. For example, the odds of youths
aged twelve to seventeen using marijuana during the
past year are thirty-nine times greater among those who
had at least a few close friends who tried or used mari-

Peer influence is a major factor in predicting the extent of
drug-taking behavior during adolescence. It can represent
either a risk factor or a protective factor for drug abuse.

TABLE 3.1

Odds ratios for marijuana use over the past year as
related to specific risk factors

RISK FACTOR	ODDS RATIO
At least a few close friends tried or used marijuana	39
Was ever offered marijuana	27
Friends not very upset if tried marijuana 1–2 times	16
Marijuana easy to get	15
Friends not very upset if smoked marijuana once a month	14
Friends not very upset if smoked marijuana 1–2 times a week	11
Perception of not great risk for monthly marijuana use	10
Parents not very upset if smoked marijuana once a month	10
Was ever offered cocaine	8
Parents not very upset if tried marijuana 1–2 times	8
Friends not very upset if smoked 1+ packs of cigarettes per day	7
At least a few close friends smoked 1+ packs of cigarettes per day	7
Shoplifted in past year	7
Friends not very upset if had 5+ drinks 1–2 times a week	6
At least a few close friends had 5+ drinks 1–2 times a week	5
Participated in a gang fight in past year	5

Source: Substance Abuse and Mental Health Services Administration (2001). *Risk and protective factors for adolescent drug use: Findings from the 1997 National Household Survey on Drug Abuse.* Rockville, MD: Office of Applied Studies, Substance Abuse and Mental Health Services Administration, Table 3.2.

juana than among those who did not have such friends
(Table 3.1). To put this statistic in perspective, this "odds
ratio" is considerably higher than the twenty-seven times
greater likelihood of developing lung cancer after
decades of smoking more than a pack of cigarettes each
day (versus never smoking at all). However, it should be
pointed out that in the case of marijuana use we are
speaking of an increased *probability* that it will occur—
not necessarily a cause-and-effect relationship. In the
case of tobacco use and lung cancer, a causal link has
been clearly established (see Chapter 12).

The leading risk factors for marijuana use include
the potential approval/disapproval of friends and parents, the degree of marijuana availability, judgments
regarding the risks involved, and the inclination toward
other drug use or delinquent behavior. In general, as
the number of risk factors increases, so does the likelihood of drug use and drug involvement. As shown in
Table 3.1, a major grouping of risk factors relates to
peer influence. The importance of peer influence is
found across cultural groups; white, African American,
and Latino youngsters react in similar ways.[33] By contrast, economic hardship and parental abuse do not
appear to represent significant risk factors with regard
to the inclination to use drugs.[34]

Specific Protective Factors

Protective factors provide the basis for someone to have
stronger resistance against the temptations of drugs, to have
a degree of resilience against engaging in a drug-taking life-
style, despite the presence of risk factors in that person's
life.[35] It is important that we not see these protective factors

TABLE 3.2

Major protective factors for drug-taking behavior among adolescents

An intact and positive home environment
  Mother and father living together
  Close parental involvement and supervision in child's activities
  Strong parent–child attachment
  Parent's educational level at high school or greater
A positive educational experience
  High reading and math achievement levels
  A close attachment to teachers
  Aspirations/expectations to go to college
  Parent's aspirations/expectations for child to go to college
  Exposure to school-based prevention education
Conventional peer relationships
  Socially conforming attitudes among child's peers
  Parents with positive evaluations of child's peers
Positive attitudes and beliefs
  High self-esteem
  Involvement in religious activities and prosocial activities
  Closeness to an adult outside the family

Source: Adapted from Smith, Carolyn; Lizotte, Alan J.; Thornberry, Terence P.; and Krohn, Marvin D. (1995). Resilient youth: Identifying factors that prevent high-risk youth from engaging in delinquency and drug use. *Current Perspectives on Aging and the Life Cycle, 4,* 217–247.

as simply the inverted image, or the negation of, opposing risk factors. Rather, each group of factors operates independently of the other. One way of thinking about protective factors is to view them as a kind of insurance policy against the occurrence of some future event that you hope to avoid. The major protective factors are listed in Table 3.2.

Protective factors can serve as a buffering element among even high-risk adolescents, allowing them to have a greater degree of resilience against drug-taking behavior and a higher resistance to drug use than they would have had otherwise. In one study, protective factors were examined in one thousand high-risk male and female adolescents in the seventh and eighth grades, and information was collected on their drug use later in high school. As the number of protective factors increased, the resistance of these students to drug use increased as well. With six or more such factors in their lives, as many as 56 percent of the high-risk adolescents showed a resistance to drug use three years later. In contrast, with three or fewer factors, only 20 percent of the youths were drug-free.[36]

Recently, the concept of protective factors has been taken a step further. In research by the Search Institute in Minneapolis, as many as forty protective factors have been identified, referred to collectively as *developmental assets.*[37] Similar to the protective factors listed in Table 3.2, these developmental assets have been found to increase resistance not only to drug-taking behavior (such as problem alcohol use and illicit drug use) but to other high-risk behaviors (such as sexual activity and violence) as well (Figure 3.3).

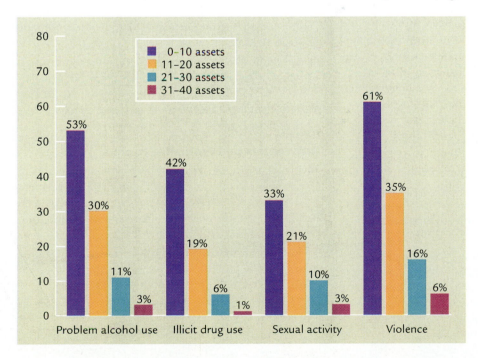

FIGURE 3.3

The percentages of four high-risk behaviors as a function of the number of developmental assets, based on responses of sixth- to twelfth-grade youth.

Source: Information courtesy of Search Institute, Minneapolis, Minnesota, 2000.

Biological Perspectives on Drug Abuse

- Biological perspectives on drug abuse refer to specific physical mechanisms in specific individuals that influence the initial experience with drugs or an engagement with drug abuse over a period of time. Theories from this perspective have focused on genetic factors, physiological factors, and neurochemical systems in the brain.

- Research on genetic factors has concentrated primarily on explanations for alcohol abuse and alcoholism. The consensus in this literature is that there is a genetic predisposition toward alcoholism.

- Physiological factors include metabolic deficiencies that set the stage for individuals to seek out drugs to "normalize" their bodies. A metabolic-defect concept has been applied to the study of heroin abuse.

- Research on the role of neurochemical systems in drug abuse have concentrated on the functioning of dopamine in the nucleus accumbens. Drug-taking behavior has been hypothesized to be a compensation for an inadequate number of dopamine receptors necessary to experience pleasurable feelings without drugs.

Psychological Perspectives on Drug Abuse

- Psychological perspectives on drug abuse draw on either theories of personality or the behavioral processes of human learning.

- Psychoanalytic theories of personality, derived from the writings of Sigmund Freud, focus on psychological disturbances that have their origin in early childhood. Concepts include the competition of id and superego processes for dominance in ego functioning, oral fixation in development, and self-destructive behavior as an expression of self-loathing.

- Behavioral theories emphasize the pivotal role of reinforcement in the learning of drug-taking behaviors. Behavioral theorists have studied the influence of positively reinforcing experiences inherent in the drug experience itself as opposed to negatively reinforcing experience of gaining relief from uncomfortable withdrawal symptoms in predicting the manner in which heroin is abused.

- Non-psychoanalytic personality theories consider the personality traits that distinguish drug abusers from nonabusers, without reference to psychoanalytic concepts. A central theme in these theories is the role of sensation-seeking among individuals as a predisposing characteristic for drug experimentation and abuse.

Sociological Perspectives on Drug Abuse

- Sociological perspectives emphasize the important role of environmental and social factors in drug use and abuse. Theories generated from a sociological perspective include anomie/strain theory, social control/bonding theory, differential association theory, subcultural recruitment and socialization theory, and labeling theory.

- Anomie/strain theorists assert that drug use and abuse result from feelings of frustration and alienation existing in individuals who see themselves as not being able to meet the demands of society. Adaptations to feelings of anomie include conformity, innovation, ritualism, retreatism, and rebellion.

- Social control/bonding theory identifies attachment, commitment, involvement, and belief as four social bonds that promote conformity and the disinclination to be a drug user.

- The basic premise of differential association theory is that drug use is learned in interactions and communications with significant others such as parents and friends.

- In subcultural recruitment and socialization theory, the focus is on the dynamic relationships among drug abusers as a cohesive group. In adolescent patterns of drug abuse, peer influence is the dominant factor in maintaining the subculture; in later stages, drug abusers tend to break away from a tightly focused subcultural group and move toward a set of less intimate relationships.

- Labeling theory emphasizes the process through which individuals continue to use drugs because others expect them to do so. Drug users who are labeled as deviant may "find comfort" in being a member of a drug subculture.

Risk Factors and Protective Factors

- Investigations of risk factors and protective factors in drug-taking behavior are not theory-driven. A relationship is sought between a given variable (an individual's lifestyle, family makeup, environmental condition, etc.) and the likelihood that drug use will occur.

- Risk factors for drug-taking behavior in adolescence include a tendency toward nonconformity within society and the influence of drug-using peers.

- Protective factors for drug-taking behavior include an intact home environment, a positive educational experience, and conventional peer relationships.

Key Terms

anomie, p. 73
behavioral theory, p. 72
biopsychosocial model, p. 78
differential association
    theory, p. 76

labeling theory, p. 77
moral model, p. 66
neurotransmitters, p. 69
nucleus accumbens, p. 68
primary deviance, p. 77

protective factors, p. 79
psychoanalytic explanations,
    p. 70
risk factors, p. 79
secondary deviance, p. 78

social control theory, p. 75
subcultural recruitment
    and socialization theory,
    p. 76
subculture, p. 76

Endnotes

1. Goode, Erich (2005). *Drugs in American society* (6th ed.). Boston: McGraw-Hill College. Quotation on p. 55.
2. Fisher, Gary L., and Harrison, Thomas C. (2000). *Substance abuse: Information for school counselors, social workers, therapists, and counselors.* Boston: Allyn and Bacon. Quotation on p. 57. Goode, *Drugs.* Miller, William R., and Hester, Reid K. (1995). Treatment for alcohol problems: Toward an informed eclecticism. In William R. Miller and Reid K. Hester (Eds.), *Handbook of alcoholism treatment approaches* (2nd ed.). Boston: Allyn and Bacon, pp. 1–11.
3. George, F. R., and Goldberg, S. R. (1989). Genetic approaches to the analysis of addictive processes. *Trends in Pharmacologial Science, 10,* 78–83. LeGrand, Lisa N.; Iacono, William G.; and McGue, Matt (2005, March–April). Predicting addiction. *American Scientist,* pp. 140–147.
4. Sher, Kenneth J. (1991). *Children of alcoholics: A critical appraisal of theory and research.* Chicago: University of Chicago Press.
5. Herman, Aryeh. I.; Philbeck, John W.; Vasilopoulos, Nicholas L.; and DePetrillo, Paolo B. (2003). Serotonin transport promoter polymorphism and differences in alcohol consumption behavior in a college study population. *Alcohol and Alcoholism, 38,* 446–449. Li, Ting-Ka (2000). Pharmacogenetics of responses to alcohol and genes that influence alcohol drinking. *Journal of Studies on Alcohol, 61,* 5–12. National Institute on Alcohol Abuse and Alcoholism (2003). *Is there a genetic relationship between alcoholism and depression?* Rockville, MD: National Institute on Alcohol Abuse and Alcoholism. Nurnberger, John I., and Bierut, Laura Jean (2007, April). Seeking the connections: Alcoholism and our genes. *Scientific American,* 46–53. Schuckit, Marc A., Mazzanti, C., and Smith, T. L. (1999). Selective genotyping for the role of 5-HT and GABA receptors and the serotonin transporter in the level of response to alcohol: A pilot study. *Biological Psychiatry, 45,* 647–651.
6. Goode, *Drugs.* Quotation on p. 56.
7. Goode, *Drugs,* pp. 56–57. Myerson, David J. (1969). Methadone treatment of addicts. *New England Journal of Medicine, 281,* 380. Prendergast, Michael L., and Podus, Deborah (1999, May 10). Methadone debate reflects deep-rooted conflicts in field. *Alcoholism and Drug Abuse Weekly,* p. 5.
8. Blakeslee, Sandra (2002, February 19). Hijacking the brain circuits with a nickel slot machine. *New York Times,* pp. F1, F5. Heidbreder, Christian A., and Hagan, Jim J. (2005). Novel pharmacotherapeutic approaches to the treatment of drug addiction and craving. *Current Opinion in Pharmacology, 5,* 107–108. Nestler, Eric J., and Malenka, Robert C. (2004, March). The addicted brain. *Scientific American,* pp. 78–85. Phillips, Paul E. M.; Stuber, Garret D.; Heien, Michael L, A. V.; Wightman, R. Mark; and Carelli, Regina. M. (2003). Subsecond dopamine release promotes cocaine seeking. *Nature, 422,* 614–618. Weiss, Freidbert (2005). Neurobiology of craving, conditioned reward, and relapse. *Current Opinion in Pharmacology, 5,* 9–19.
9. Volkow, Nora D.; Wang, Gene-Jack; Fowler, Joanna S.; Logan, Jean; Gatley, Samuel J.; Gifford, Andrew; Hitzemann, Robert; Ding, Yu-Shin; and Pappas, Naomi (1999). Prediction of reinforcing responses to psychostimulants in humans by brain dopamine D_2 receptor levels. *American Journal of Psychiatry, 156,* 1440–1443.
10. Fenichel, Otto (1945). *The psychoanalytic theory of neurosis.* New York: Norton. Fields, Richard (2004). *Drugs in perspective* (5th ed.). New York: McGraw-Hill Higher Education.
11. Fields, *Drugs in perspective.* Gottheil, Edward (ed.) (1983). *Etiological aspects of alcohol/drug abuse.* Springfield, IL: Charles C. Thomas. Stanton, M. Duncan, and Todd, Thomas C. (Eds.) (1982). *The family therapy of drug abuse and addiction.* New York: Guilford Press.
12. Goode, *Drugs,* pp. 57–60.
13. Goode, Erica (2001, May 22). For users of heroin, decades of despair. *New York Times,* p. F5. Hser, Yih-Ing; Hoffman, Valerie; Grella, Christine; and Anglin, M. Douglas (2001). A 33-year follow-up of narcotics addicts. *Archives of General Psychiatry, 58,* 503–508. McAuliffe, William E., and Gordon, Robert A. (1974). A test of Lindesmith's theory of addiction: The frequency of euphoria among long-term addicts. *American Journal of Sociology, 79,* 795–840. Zinberg, Norman E. (1984). *Drugs, set, and setting: The basis for controlled intoxicant use.* New Haven, CT: Yale University Press, pp. 46–81.

14. Cristie, Kimberly A.; Burke, Jack; Regier, Darrel A.; Rae, Donald S.; Boyd, Jeffrey H.; and Locke, Ben Z. (1988). Epidemiological evidence for early onset of mental disorders and higher risk of drug abuse in young adults. *American Journal of Psychiatry, 145*, 971–975. Fields, *Drugs in perspective*, p. 8. Lewis, C. E. (1984). Alcoholism, antisocial personality, narcotic addiction: An integrative approach. *Psychiatric Developments, 3*, 22–35. Meier, Richard F. (1989). *Crime and society*. Boston: Allyn and Bacon. Shedler, Jonathan, and Block, Jack (1990). Adolescent drug users and psychological health: A longitudinal inquiry. *American Psychologist, 45*, 612–630.

15. Yokel, Robert A. (1987). Intravenous self-administration: Response rates, the effect of pharmacological challenges and drug preferences. In Michael A. Bozarth (Ed.), *Methods of assessing the reinforcing properties of abused drugs*. New York: Springer-Verlag, pp. 1–34.

16. Kerr, John S. (1996). Two myths of addiction: The addictive personality and the issues of free choice. *Human psychopharmacology, 11*, 39–45. Ross, Helen E.; Glaser, Frederick B.; and Germanson, Teresa (1988). The prevalence of psychiatric disorders in patients with alcohol and other drug problems. *Archives of General Psychiatry, 45*, 1023–1031.

17. Goode, *Drugs*, p. 63.

18. Robins, Lee N. (1974). *The Vietnam drug user returns*. Special Action Office for Drug Abuse Prevention Monograph Series A, No. 2, Contract HSM-42–72–75.

19. Durkheim, Emile (1951). *Suicide* (translated by John Spaulding and George Simpson). New York: Free Press.

20. Agnew, Robert (1992). Foundation for a general strain theory of crime and delinquency. *Criminology, 30*, 47–87. Merton, Robert K. (1968). *Social theory and social structure*. New York: Free Press.

21. Merton, *Social theory*.

22. Lorch, Barbara D. (1990). Social class and its relationship to youth substance use and other delinquent behaviors. *Social Work Research Abstracts, 26*, 25–34.

23. Akers, Ronald L. (1992). *Drugs, alcohol, and society: Social structure, process, and policy*. Belmont CA: Wadsworth, pp. 8–9. Hirschi, Travis (1969). *Causes of delinquency*. Los Angeles: University of California Press.

24. Burkett, Steven R., and Warren, Bruce O. (1987). Religiosity, peer associations, and adolescent marijuana use: A panel study of underlying causal structures. *Criminology, 25*, 109–131. Durkin, Keith F., Wolf, Timothy W., and Clark, Gregory (1999). Social bond theory and binge drinking among college students: A multivariate analysis. *College Student Journal, 33*, 450–462. Durkin, Keith F.; Wolfe, Timothy; and Clark, Gregory A. (2005). College students and binge drinking: An evaluation of social learning theory. *Sociological Spectrum, 25*, 255–272. Guo, Jie; Hill, Karl J.; Hawkins, David; Catalano, Richard F.; and Abbott, Robert D. (2002). A developmental analysis of sociodemographic, family, and peer effects on adolescent illicit drug initiation. *Journal of the American Academy of Child and Adolescent Psychiatry, 41*, 838–846.

25. Sutherland, Edwin H. (1939). *Principles of criminology* (3rd ed.). Philadelphia: Lippincott.

26. Becker, Howard S. (1953). Becoming a marijuana user. *American Journal of Sociology, 59*, 235–242. Faupel, Charles E. (1991). *Shooting dope: Career contingencies of hard-core heroin users*. Hirsch, Michael L., Conforti, Randall W., and Graney, Carolyn, J. (2001). The use of marijuana for pleasure: A replication of Howard S. Becker's study of marijuana use. *Journal of Social Behavior and Personality, 5*, 497–510.

27. Goode, *Drugs*, pp. 71–74. Quotation on p. 71. Johnson, Bruce (1973). *Marijuana users and drug subcultures*. New York: Wiley-Interscience. Johnson, Bruce (1980). Toward a theory of drug subcultures. In Dan J. Lettieri et al. (Eds.), *Theories on drug abuse*, pp. 110–119.

28. Kandel, Denise B. (1973). Adolescent marijuana use: Role of parents and peers. *Science, 181*, 1067–1070. Kandel, Denise B. (1980). Developmental stages in adolescent drug involvement. In Dan J. Lettieri et al. (Eds.), *Theories on drug abuse*, pp. 120–127. Kandel, Denise B., and Mark Davies (1991). Friendship networks, intimacy, and drug use in young adulthood: A comparison of two competing theories. *Criminology, 29*, 441–467.

29. Becker, Howard S. (1963). *Outsiders: Studies in the sociology of deviance*. New York: Free Press. Erickson, K. (1962). Notes on the sociology of deviance. *Social Problems, 9*, 397–414. Lemert, Edwin M. (1951). *Social pathology*. New York: McGraw-Hill.

30. Margolin, Robert D., and Zweben, Joan E. (1998). *Treating patients with alcohol and other drug problems: An integrated approach*. Washington DC: American Psychological Association, pp. 76–87.

31. Johnston, Lloyd D., and O'Malley, Patrick M. (1986). Why do the nation's students use drugs and alcohol? Self-reported reasons from nine national surveys. *The Journal of Drug Issues, 16*, 29–66.

32. Goode, *Drugs*, pp. 68–71.

33. Substance Abuse and Mental Health Services Administration (2001). *Risk and protective factors for adolescent drug use: Findings from the 1997 National Household Survey on Drug Abuse*. Rockville, MD: Office of Applied Studies, Substance Abuse and Mental Health Services Administration, pp. 27–42. Watts, W. David, and Wright, Loyd S. (1990). The drug use–violent delinquency link among adolescent Mexican-Americans. In Mario De la Rosa, Elizabeth Y. Lambert, and Bernard Gropper (Eds.), *Drugs and violence: Causes, correlates, and consequences* (NIDA Research Monograph 103). Rockville, MD: National Institute on Drug Abuse.

34. Fawzy, F. L.; Coombs, R. H.; Simon, J. M.; and Bowman-Terrell, M. (1987). Family composition, socioeconomic status, and adolescent substance use. *Addictive Behaviors, 12*, 79–83.

35. Scheier, Lawrence M., Botvin, Gilbert J., and Baker, Eli (1997). Risk and protective factors as predictors of adolescent alcohol involvement and transitions in alcohol use: A prospective analysis. *Journal of Studies in Alcohol, 58,* 652–667. Scheier, Lawrence M., Newcomb, Michael D., and Skager, Rodney (1994). Risk, protection, and vulnerability to adolescent drug use: Latent-variable models of three age groups. *Journal of Drug Education, 24,* 49–82.

36. Smith, Carolyn; Lizotte, Alan J.; Thornberry, Terence P.; and Krohn, Marvin D. (1995). Resilient youth: Identifying factors that prevent high-risk youth from engaging in delinquency and drug use. In J. Hagan (Ed.), *Delinquency and disrepute in the life course.* Greenwich, CT: JAI Press, pp. 217–247.

37. Scales, Peter C., and Leffert, Nancy (1999). *Developmental assets: A synthesis of the scientific research on adolescent development.* Minneapolis: Search Institute. Search Institute (2001, February). *Profiles of student life: Attitudes and behavior.* Minneapolis: Search Institute.

chapter **4**

The Major Stimulants: Cocaine and Amphetamines

After you have completed this chapter, you will understand

- The history of cocaine
- How cocaine works in the brain
- Patterns of cocaine abuse
- Treatment programs for cocaine abuse
- The history of amphetamines
- How amphetamines work in the brain
- Patterns of methamphetamine abuse
- Stimulant treatment for attention deficit/hyperactivity syndrome (ADHD)

S. F. is a brilliant, young physician attending a case conference at a metropolitan medical center where he is a resident. He has been on call for thirty-six hours and cannot concentrate on the presentation. S. F. is lonely, depressed, and overworked. All he can think about is his fiancée, Martha, who is several hundred miles away. He knows that her father will not permit her to marry until he is able to support her, and with his loans and meager salary, that could take years. He excuses himself from the conference, takes a needle syringe from the nurses' station, and locks himself in a bathroom stall. He fills the syringe with cocaine and plunges the needle into his arm. Within seconds, the young doctor feels a rush of euphoria. His tears dry up; he regains his composure and quickly rejoins the conference.

—The date is 1884, the place is Vienna, and the doctor is Sigmund Freud.

The time, place, and identity of S. F. in this fiction-alized clinical vignette, based upon the facts of Freud's life, may have surprised you, but unfortunately the over-all picture of cocaine abuse is all too familiar.[1] The year could have been 1984 (or any other year in the past two decades or so) instead of 1884, and the individual involved could have been anyone twenty-eight years old, as Freud was at the time, or some other age. Freud was extremely lucky; he never became dependent upon cocaine, though a close friend did and millions of people have since Freud's time.

The story of cocaine is both ancient and modern. While its origins stretch back more than four thousand years, cocaine abuse continues to represent a major portion of the present-day drug scene. For this reason, it is important to understand its history, the properties of the drug itself, and the ways in which it has the ability to control and ultimately, in many cases, destroy a person's life.

This chapter will focus not only on cocaine but also on another group of stimulant drugs, referred to collec-tively as amphetamines. Although cocaine and amphet-amines are distinct in terms of their pharmacology (their characteristics as biochemical substances), there are enough similarities in their behavioral and physiological effects and patterns of abuse to warrant their being dis-cussed together. In general, cocaine and amphetamines represent the two major classes of psychoactive stimu-lants, drugs that energize the body and create feelings of euphoria.

The Social History of Cocaine

Cocaine is derived from small leaves of the coca shrub (*Erythroxylon coca*), grown in the high-altitude rain forests and fields that run along the slopes of the Peru-vian and Bolivian Andes in South America. Like many other psychoactive drugs, cocaine use has a long history. We can trace the practice of chewing coca leaves, which contain about 2 percent cocaine, back to the Inca civi-lization, which flourished from the thirteenth century until its conquest by the Spaniards in 1532, as well as to other Andean cultures dating back five thousand years. Coca was considered a gift from the god Inti to the Incas, allowing them to endure a harsh and physically demanding life in the Andes.[2]

> **cocaine:** An extremely potent and dependence-producing stimulant drug, derived from the coca leaf.

To this day, coca chewing is part of the culture of this region. It is estimated that about 2 million Peruvian men who live in the Andean highlands, representing 90 percent of the male population in that area, chew coca leaves.[3] These people, called *acullicadores*, mix their own blend of coca, chalk, lime, and ash to achieve the desired effects, whether it is to fight fatigue or social-ize with friends.[4]

This form of cocaine use among these people pro-duces few instances of toxicity or abuse. The reason lies in the very low doses of cocaine that chewed coca leaves pro-vide; in this form, absorption from the digestive system is slow, and relatively little cocaine enters the bloodstream and is distributed to the brain (see Chapter 1). A much more serious problem has been the introduction of a coca paste containing a much higher percentage of cocaine mixed with tobacco. It is called a *bazuco* and smoked as a cigarette. Making matters worse, dangerously high levels of kerosene, gasoline, and ether are involved in the coca-refining process and end up as adulterants in the cigarettes themselves.[5]

Cocaine in Nineteenth-Century Life

Coca leaves were brought back to Europe from the Spanish colonies soon after the conquest of the Incas, but their potency was nearly gone after the long sea voy-age. Perhaps, it was said at the time, the legendary effects of coca were merely exaggerations after all. Coca leaves were ignored for nearly three hundred years. By the late 1850s, however, the active ingredient of the coca plant had been chemically isolated. In 1859, Alfred Nie-mann, a German chemist, observed its anesthetic effect on his tongue and its bitter taste and named it "cocaine." Interest in the drug was renewed, and by the 1860s the patent medicine industry in the United States and Europe (see Chapter 2) had lost no time in taking advantage of cocaine's appeal.

Commercial Uses of Cocaine

By far the most successful commercial use of cocaine in the nineteenth century was a mixture of coca and wine invented in 1863 by a Corsican chemist and business-man, Angelo Mariani. We know now that the combina-tion of alcohol and cocaine produces a metabolite with an elimination half-life several times longer than cocaine alone, so the mixture tends to be quite intoxicating (see Help Line). No wonder "Vin Mariani" became an instant sensation. A long list of endorsements by celebri-ties accumulated over the next few decades from satisfied customers such as U.S. President William McKinley,

Cocaine after Alcohol: The Risk of Cocaethylene Toxicity

The risks of dying from cocaine arise from the drug's powerful excitatory effects on the body, such as abnormal heart rhythms, labored breathing, and increased blood pressure. The toxicity potential for any of these toxic reactions is, unfortunately, increased when alcohol is already in the bloodstream. The biotransformation of cocaine and alcohol (ethanol), when ingested in combination, produces a metabolite called *cocaethylene*. One effect of cocaethylene is a three- to fivefold increase in the elimination half-life of cocaine. As a result, cocaine remains in the bloodstream for a much longer time. More important, cocaethylene has a specific excitatory effect on blood pressure and heart rate that is greater than that produced by cocaine alone.

While the combination of alcohol and cocaine is associated with a prolonged and enhanced euphoria, it also brings an eighteen- to twenty-five-fold increased risk of immediate death. The fact that 62–90 percent of cocaine abusers are also abusers of alcohol makes the dangers of cocaethylene toxicity a significant health concern.

> **Where to go for assistance:**
>
> www.nida.nih.gov/MedAdv/00/NR6–26.html
>
> This web site is sponsored by the National Institute of Drug Abuse and contains a comprehensive examination of cocaine risks, including the combination of cocaine with alcohol.

Sources: Andrews, Paul (1997). Cocaethylene toxicity. *Journal of Addictive Diseases, 16*, 75–84. Harris, Debra S.; Everhart, E. Thomas; Mendelson, John; and Jones, Reese T. (2003). The pharmacology of cocaethylene in humans following cocaine and ethanol administration. *Drug and Alcohol Dependence, 72*, 169–182.

In the late nineteenth century, the Coca-Cola Company advertised its beverage in medicinal terms. A company letterhead of this period spoke of Coca-Cola as containing "the tonic properties of the wonderful coca plant."

Thomas Edison, the surgeon general of the U.S. Army, General Ulysses S. Grant, Sarah Bernhardt, Jules Verne, the Prince of Wales, the czar of Russia, and Popes Pius X and Leo XII. In a letter to Mariani, Frederic Bartholdi, the sculptor of the Statue of Liberty, wrote that if he had been drinking Vin Mariani while designing the statue, it would have been more than three times taller.[6] We can only assume that this comment was intended to be complimentary.

Meanwhile in the United States, Atlanta pharmacist John Pemberton promoted an imitation form of Vin Mariani that he called French Wine Cola. Shortly after, in 1885, as a concession to the American temperance movement, he took out the alcohol (see Chapter 10), added soda water, and reformulated the basic mixture to combine coca with the syrup of the African kola nut containing about 2 percent caffeine. Coca-Cola was born. Early advertisements for Coca-Cola emphasized the drink as a stimulating brain tonic that made you feel more productive and as a remedy for such assorted nervous ailments as sick headaches and melancholia (a word used at the time to mean depression).[7] The medicinal slant to the early promotion of Coca-Cola is probably the reason why soda fountains first appeared and continued for years to be located in drugstores.[8]

A number of competing brands with similar formulations sprang up with names such as Care-Cola, Dope

What Happened to the Coca in Coca-Cola?

Every day, in a drab factory building in a New Jersey suburb of Maywood, a select team of employees of the Stepan Company carries out a chemical procedure that has been one of the primary responsibilities of the company since 1903. They remove cocaine from high-grade coca leaves. The remainder, technically called "decocainized flavor essence" is then sent to the Coca-Cola Company as part of the secret recipe for the world's favorite soft drink.

Each year, the Stepan Company is legally sanctioned by the U.S. government (and carefully monitored by the DEA) to receive shipments of about 175,000 kilograms of coca leaves from Peruvian coca farms, separate the cocaine chemically, and produce about 1,750 kilograms of high-quality cocaine. Its annual output is equivalent to approximately 20 million hits of crack, worth about $200 million if it were to make it to the illicit drug market. Fortunately, the Stepan Company has an impeccable security record.

In case you are wondering what happens to the cocaine after it is removed from the coca leaves, it turns out that Stepan finds a legitimate market in the world of medicine. Tincture of cocaine is used regularly as a local anesthetic to numb the skin prior to minor surgical procedures such as stitching up a wound. Surgeons frequently use cocaine as a topical ointment when working on the nose or throat.

As a result, the Stepan Company essentially has it both ways. It is the exclusive U.S. supplier of cocaine for use in medical settings as well as decocainized coca for your next can of Coke. As a recent article in the *Wall Street Journal* has put it, "The two markets end up sending Stepan's products into virtually every bloodstream in America."

Sources: Inclardi, James A. (2002). *The war on drugs III.* Boston: Allyn and Bacon, p. 21. Miller, Michael W. (1994, October 17). Quality stuff: Firm is peddling cocaine, and deals are legit. *Wall Street Journal,* pp. A1, A14.

Cola, Kola Ade, and Wiseola.[9] Eventually, public pressure brought about official restrictions on the patent medicine industry, which, by the beginning of the twentieth century, was marketing more than fifty thousand unregulated products.[10] The Pure Food and Drug Act of 1906 specified that all active ingredients had to be listed on patent medicine labels. In Canada, the Proprietary and Patent Medicine Act of 1908 banned cocaine from patent medicines entirely, but in the United States no further restrictions on cocaine sales or use were imposed until the Harrison Act of 1914 (see Chapter 2).

The Coca-Cola Company, aware of the growing tide of sentiment against cocaine, changed the formula in 1903 from regular coca leaves to decocainized coca leaves, which eliminated the cocaine but retained the coca flavoring that remains to this day (Drugs . . . in Focus). The "pause that refreshed" America would henceforth be due only to the presence of sugar and caffeine.

The use of cocaine also was becoming a major factor in the practice of medicine. In the United States, William Halstead, one of the most distinguished surgeons of the time and one of the founders of Johns Hopkins Medical School, studied the effect of cocaine on anesthetizing nerves and whole limbs. In the process, he acquired a cocaine habit of his own (which was replaced several years later by a dependence on morphine). It was in Europe, however, that the psychological implications of cocaine were explored most extensively, ironically through the triumphs and tribulations of Sigmund Freud.

Freud and Cocaine

In 1884 Freud was a struggling young neurologist given to bouts of depression and self-doubt but nonetheless determined to make his mark in the medical world. He had read a report by a German army physician that supplies of pure cocaine could help soldiers endure fatigue and feel better in general. Freud secured some cocaine for himself and found the experience exhilarating; his depression lifted, and he felt a new sense of boundless energy. His friend and colleague Dr. Ernst von Fleischl-Marxow, taking morphine and enduring a painful illness, borrowed some cocaine from Freud and found favorable results as well.

Freud immediately saw the prospects of fame and fortune. In a letter to his fiancée, Martha Bernays, he

Understanding the Social History of Cocaine

Check your understanding of the history of cocaine by matching the names on the left with the identifications on the right. Be careful; some identifications may not match up with any of the names.

1. Angelo Mariani

2. John Pemberton

3. William Halstead

4. Sigmund Freud

5. Ernst von Fleischl-Marxow

a. Friend of Sigmund Freud; first documented case of cocaine psychosis

b. Developer of Coca-Cola, originally containing cocaine

c. Early advocate of restricting cocaine use in the United States

d. Cofounder of Johns Hopkins Medical School; early developer of cocaine to anesthetize nerves and whole limbs

e. A popular figure in present-day Peru

f. Early advocate of cocaine use; originator of psychoanalysis

g. Promoter of a popular coca-laced wine

Answers: 1. g   2. b   3. d   4. f   5. a

---

wrote: "If it goes well I will write an essay on it and I expect it will win its place in therapeutics by the side of morphium [morphine] and superior to it."[11]

Before long, Freud was distributing cocaine to his friends and his sisters and even sent a supply to Martha. In the words of Freud's biographer Ernest Jones, "From the vantage point of our present knowledge, he was rapidly becoming a public menace."[12] We can gain some perspective on the effect cocaine was having on Freud's behavior at this time through an excerpt from a personal letter to Martha:

Woe to you, my Princess, when I come. I will kiss you quite red and feed you till you are plump. And if you are forward you shall see who is the stronger, a gentle little girl who doesn't eat enough or a big wild man who has cocaine in his body [underlined in the original]. In my last severe depression I took coca again and a small dose lifted me to the heights in a wonderful fashion. I am just now busy collecting the literature for a song of praise to this magical substance.[13]

Within four months, his "song of praise" essay, "Über Coca" (Concerning Coca), was written and published.

Unfortunately, the sweetness of Freud's romance with cocaine soon turned sour. Freud himself escaped becoming dependent upon cocaine, though later in his life he clearly became dependent on nicotine (see Chapter 12). His friend, Fleischl, however, was not so lucky. Within a year, Fleischl had increased his cocaine dose to twenty times the amount Freud had taken and had developed a severe cocaine-induced psychosis in which he experienced hallucinations that snakes were crawling over his skin (a phenomenon now referred to as **formication**). Fleischl suffered six years of painful agony and anguish until his death.

The story of Freud's infatuation with cocaine and his later disillusionment with it can be seen as a miniature version of the modern history of cocaine itself.[14] Between 1880 and 1910, the public reaction to cocaine went from wild enthusiasm to widespread disapproval. As this chapter will later describe, a similar cycle of attitudes swept the United States and the world between 1970 and 1985.

Acute Effects of Cocaine

While the effects of cocaine on the user vary in degree with the route of administration, the purity of the dose, and the user's expectations about the experience, certain features remain the same. The most characteristic reaction is a powerful burst of energy. If the cocaine is injected intravenously, the extremely intense effect (often referred to as a "rush") is felt within a matter of seconds, peaking in three to five minutes and wearing off in thirty to forty minutes. If snorted through the nose, the effect begins in about three minutes, peaking after fifteen to twenty minutes, and wearing off in sixty to ninety minutes.

Users also experience a general sense of well-being, although in some instances cocaine may precipitate a panic attack.[15] When cocaine levels diminish, the mood

formication: Hallucinatory behavior produced by chronic cocaine or amphetamine abuse, in which the individual feels insects or snakes crawling either over or under the skin.

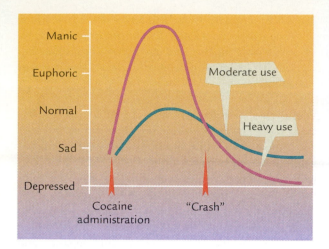

FIGURE 4.1

Ups and downs of a typical dose of cocaine.

The depiction of actor Al Pacino as a cocaine kingpin. The movie *Scarface* is an example of Hollywood's glamorization of cocaine during the early 1980s.

changes dramatically. The user becomes irritable, despondent, and depressed (Figure 4.1). These after-effects are uncomfortable enough to produce a powerful craving for another dose.

The depression induced in the aftermath of a cocaine high can lead to suicide. In 1985, during one of the peak years of cocaine abuse in the United States, as many as one out of five suicide victims in New York City showed evidence of cocaine in their blood at autopsy. The prevalence of cocaine use was greatest among victims who were in their twenties and thirties, and for African Americans and Latinos.[16] In a 1989 survey of teenage callers to the 800-COCAINE hotline, one out of seven reported a previous suicide attempt.[17] On the basis of these studies, cocaine use has become recognized as a significant risk factor for suicide attempts.

Cocaine's effect on sexual arousal is often cited as having been the basis for calling it "the aphrodisiac of the 1980s." On the one hand, interviews of cocaine users frequently include reports of spontaneous and prolonged erections in males and multiple orgasms in females during initial doses of the drug. On the other hand, cocaine's reputation for increasing sexual performance (recall Freud's reference in his letter to Martha) may bias users toward a strong expectation that there will be a sexually stimulating reaction, when in reality the effect is a much weaker one. As one cocaine abuser expressed it, "Everybody says that it's an aphrodisiac. Again, I think some people say it because it's supposed to be. I think that it's just peer group identification.... I never felt that way. I was more content to sit there and enjoy it."[18] The fact is that chronic cocaine use results in decreased sexual performance and a loss

of sexual desire, as the drug essentially takes the place of sex.

Cocaine produces a sudden elevation in the sympathetic branch of the autonomic nervous system. Heart rate and respiration are increased, while appetite is diminished. Blood vessels constrict, pupils in the eyes dilate, and blood pressure rises. The cocaine user may start to sweat and appear suddenly pale. The powerful sympathetic changes can lead to a cerebral hemorrhage or congestive heart failure. Cardiac arrhythmia results from cocaine's tendency to bind to heart tissue itself. As you may recall from Chapter 1, cocaine is frequently cited for involvement in drug-related deaths, as reported in DAWN statistics.[19]

Given the extreme excitatory effects of cocaine on bodily organs, it is not surprising that behavioral skills would be adversely affected. In a study of drivers showing reckless behavior on the road, those found to have been under the influence of cocaine were wildly overconfident in their abilities, taking turns too fast or weaving through traffic. One highway patrol officer called this behavior "diagonal driving. They were just as involved in changing lanes as in going forward." Yet they passed the standard sobriety tests designed to detect alcohol intoxication.[20]

Chronic Effects of Cocaine

Repeated and continued use of cocaine produces undesirable mood changes that can only be alleviated when the person is under the acute effects of the drug. Chronic cocaine abusers are often irritable, depressed, and paranoid. As was true in Fleischl's experience with cocaine, long-term abuse can produce the disturbing hallucinatory experience of formication. The sensation of "cocaine bugs" crawling on or under the skin can become so severe that abusers may scratch the skin into open sores or even pierce themselves with a knife to cut out the imaginary creatures. These hallucinations, together with feelings of anxiety and paranoia, make up a serious mental disorder referred to as **cocaine psychosis.**

When snorted, cocaine causes bronchial muscles to relax and nasal blood vessels to constrict; the opposite effects occur when the drug wears off. As the bronchial muscles contract and nasal blood vessels relax, chronic abusers endure continuously stuffy or runny noses and bleeding of nasal membranes. In advanced cases of this problem, the septum of the nose can develop lesions or become perforated with small holes, both of which present serious problems for breathing.

Medical Uses of Cocaine

When applied topically on the skin, cocaine has the ability to block the transmission of nerve impulses, deadening all sensations from the area. This local anesthetic effect of cocaine remains its only legitimate medical application. In procedures in which tubes are passed through the nose or throat, cocaine is applied on the membranes to ease the discomfort.

There are, however, potential problems in the use of cocaine even for these specific, beneficial circumstances. One danger is that cocaine may be inadvertently absorbed into the bloodstream, leading to possible cocaine abuse. Finally, the local anesthetic effects are brief because cocaine breaks down so rapidly. Synthetic drugs such as lidocaine (brand name: Xylocaine) have the advantage of acting as local anesthetics over a longer period of time, and because they do not have the euphoriant effects of cocaine, the abuse potential is reduced. Consequently, lidocaine and other similar drugs, by injection into the gums, are used widely as local anesthetics during dental procedures.

How Cocaine Works
in the Brain

Cocaine greatly enhances the activity of dopamine, and, to a lesser extent, norepinephrine in the brain. In the case of both neurotransmitters, the actual effect is to block the reuptake process at the synapse, so the neurotransmitters stimulate receptors longer and to a greater degree. Unlike the amphetamines (discussed later in this chapter), the structure of cocaine does not appear to resemble the structure of either norepinephrine or dopamine, so why cocaine should block their reuptake so effectively is not at all clear. Nonetheless, what has been determined is that the acute effect of euphoria experienced through cocaine is directly related to an increase in dopamine in the region of the brain that controls pleasure and reinforcement in general: the nucleus accumbens (see Chapter 3).

Chronic cocaine abuse, however, leads to the loss of about 20 percent of the dopamine receptors in this region of the brain over time. The depletion of dopamine receptors among long-term cocaine abusers has been observed up to four months after the last cocaine exposure, even though the cocaine abuser no longer has cocaine in his or her system. As a result, there is a tendency toward a decline in the experience of pleasure from any source. In fact, cocaine abusers frequently report that their craving for cocaine no longer stems from the pleasure they felt when taking it initially. Their lives may be in shambles and the acute effects of euphoria from cocaine may no longer be strong, but they still crave the drug more than ever. In other words, there is now a dissociation between "liking" and "wanting."[21]

One feature of cocaine is quite unlike that of other psychoactive drugs. While cocaine abusers over repeated cocaine exposures develop a pattern of drug tolerance to its euphoric effect, they develop a pattern of sensitization (a heightened responsiveness) with respect to motor behavior and brain excitation. This phenomenon, referred to as the **kindling effect,** makes cocaine particularly dangerous because cocaine has the potential for setting off brain seizures. Repeated exposure to cocaine can lower the threshold for seizures, through a sensitization of neurons in the limbic system over time. As a result of the kindling effect, deaths from cocaine overdose may occur from relatively low dose levels.[22]

cocaine psychosis: A set of symptoms, including hallucinations, paranoia, and disordered thinking, produced from chronic use of cocaine.

kindling effect: A phenomenon in the brain that produces a heightened sensitivity to repeated adminstrations of some drugs, such as cocaine. This heightened sensitivity is the opposite of the phenomenon of tolerance.

Present-Day Cocaine Abuse

The difficult problems of cocaine abuse in the United States and around the world mushroomed during the early 1970s and continue to the present day, though the incidence of abuse is down from peak levels reached around 1986. In ways that resembled the brief period of enthusiasm for cocaine in 1884, attitudes during the early period of this "second epidemic" were incredibly naive. Fueled by media reports of use among the rich and famous, touted as the "champagne of drugs," cocaine became synonymous with the glamorous life.

The medical profession at this time was equally nonchalant about cocaine. The widely respected *Comprehensive Textbook of Psychiatry* (1980) stated the following: "If it is used no more than two or three times a week, cocaine creates no serious problem. . . . At present chronic cocaine use does not usually present a medical problem."[23]

These attitudes began to change as the 1980s unfolded. The death of actor-comedian John Belushi in 1982, followed by the drug-related deaths of other entertainers and sport figures (see Drugs . . . in Focus, page 25) produced a reversal of opinion about the safety and desirability of cocaine. The greatest influence, however, was the arrival of crack cocaine on the drug scene in 1985, which will be examined in the next sections.

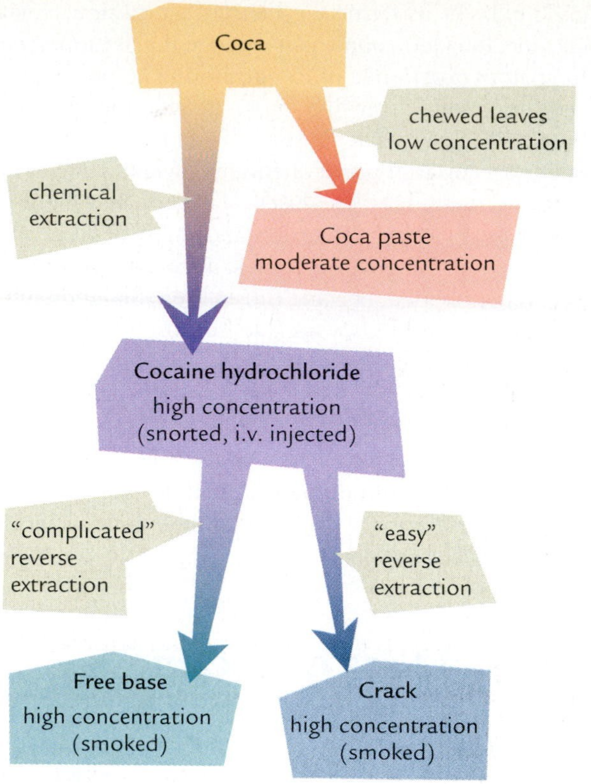

From Coca to Cocaine

To understand the full picture of present-day cocaine abuse, it is necessary to examine the various forms that cocaine can take, beginning with the extraction of cocaine from the coca plant itself (Figure 4.2). During the initial extraction process, coca leaves are soaked in various chemical solvents so that cocaine can be drawn out of the plant material itself. Leaves are then crushed, and alcohol is percolated through them to remove extraneous matter. After sequential washings and a treatment with kerosene, the yield is cocaine that is approximately 60 percent pure. This is the coca paste, which, as mentioned earlier, is combined with tobacco and smoked in many South American countries.

Cocaine in this form, however, is not water-soluble and therefore cannot be injected into the bloodstream. An additional step of treatment with oxidizing agents

cocaine hydrochloride: The form of cocaine that is inhaled (snorted) or injected into the bloodstream.

FIGURE 4.2

Steps in producing various forms of cocaine from raw coca.

and acids is required to produce a water-soluble drug. The result is a white crystalline powder called **cocaine hydrochloride,** about 99 percent pure cocaine and classified chemically as a salt.

When in the form of cocaine hydrochloride, the drug can be injected intravenously or snorted. The amount injected at one time is about 16 mg. Intravenous cocaine also can be combined with heroin in a highly dangerous mixture called a *speedball.*

If cocaine is snorted, the user generally has the option of two methods. In one method, a tiny spoonful of cocaine is carried to one nostril while the other nostril is shut, and the drug is taken with a rapid inhalation. In the other method, cocaine is spread out on a highly polished surface (often a mirror) and arranged with a razor blade in several lines, each containing from 20 to 30 mg. The cocaine is then inhaled into one nostril by means of a straw or rolled piece of paper. During the early 1980s, a $100 bill was a fashionable alternative, emphasizing the level of income necessary to be using cocaine in the first place.[24]

From Cocaine to Crack

Options beyond the intake of cocaine hydrochloride widened with the development of **free-base cocaine** during the 1970s and **crack cocaine** (or simply **crack**) during the mid-1980s. In free-base cocaine, the hydrochloride is removed from the salt form of cocaine, thus liberating it as a free base. The aim is to obtain a smokable form of cocaine, which, by entering the brain more quickly, produces a more intense effect. The technique for producing free-base cocaine, however, is extremely hazardous, since it is necessary to treat cocaine powder with highly flammable agents such as ether. If the free base still contains some ether residue, igniting the drug will cause it to explode into flames.

Crack cocaine is the result of a cheaper and safer chemical method, but the result is essentially the same: a smokable form of cocaine. Treatment with baking soda yields small rocks, which can then be smoked in a small pipe.[25] When they are smoked, a cracking noise accompanies the burning, hence the origin of the name "crack."

How dangerous is crack? There is no question that the effect of cocaine when smoked exceeds the effect of cocaine when snorted; for some users, it even exceeds the effect of cocaine when injected. Inhaling high-potency cocaine (the purity of cocaine in crack aver-

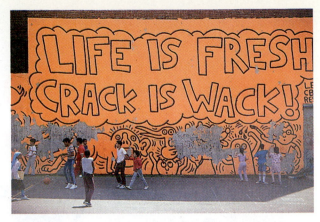

A message on a playground mural in the 1980s was a community's response to the desolation and misery resulting from crack cocaine abuse.

ages about 75 percent) into the lungs, and almost immediately into the brain, sets the stage for a pattern of psychological dependence. And at a price of $3 to $20 per dose, cocaine is no longer out of financial reach (Table 4.1). The answer is that crack is very dangerous indeed.

Beyond its effect on the user, however, is the effect on the society where crack is prevalent. Women who are crack abusers find that their drug cravings overwhelm their maternal instincts, resulting in the neglect of the basic needs of their children, either in postnatal or prenatal stages of life. In New York, for example, the number of reported cases of child abuse and neglect increased from 36,000 in 1985 to 59,000 in 1989, a change largely attributed to the introduction of crack. The enormous monetary profits from the selling of crack caused inner-city crime and violence to skyrocket (Figure 4.3).[26]

While crack abuse remains a problem, the number of new crack abusers has declined substantially, particularly in the inner-city communities of the United States. While 36 percent of all males over thirty-six years old who were arrested in New York in 1998 had used crack, little more than 4 percent of those fifteen to twenty years old had done so. A principal reason for this change in prevalence rates has been the present-day stigmatized image of the "crack head," considered by one's peers to be a social loser in his or her community.[27]

A detailed examination of present-day cocaine trafficking patterns can be found in Chapter 13.

TABLE 4.1

Street names for cocaine

TYPE OF COCAINE	STREET NAME
Cocaine hydrochloride (powder)	blow, C, coke, big C, lady, nose candy, snowbirds, snow, stardust, toot, white girl, happydust, cola, flake, pearl, Peruvian lady, freeze, geeze, doing the line
Free-base cocaine	freebase, base
Crack cocaine	crack, rock, kibbles and bits, crell
Crack cocaine combined with PCP (see Chapter 6)	beam me up Scottie, space cadet, tragic magic
Cocaine combined with heroin	speedball, snowball
Cocaine combined with heroin and LSD	Frisco special, Frisco speedball

Source: Bureau of Justice Statistics Clearinghouse (1992). *Drugs, behavior and crime.* Washington DC: Department of Justice, pp. 24–25.

free-base cocaine: A smokable form of cocaine.
crack cocaine or crack: A smokable form of cocaine.

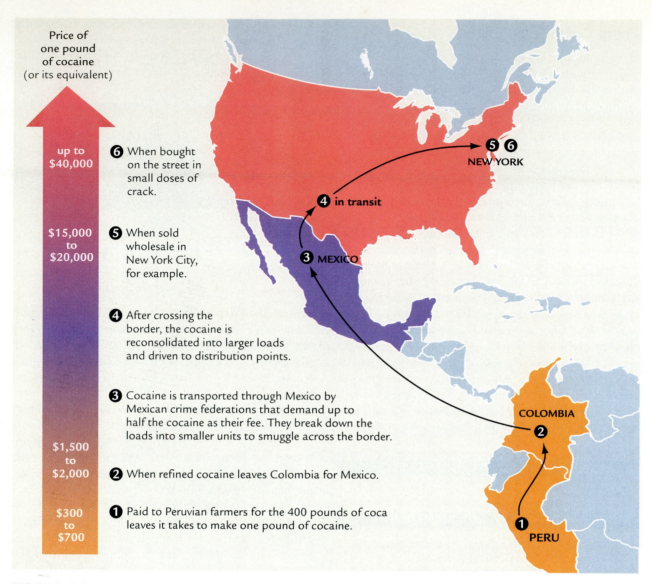

Price of one pound of cocaine (or its equivalent)

up to $40,000

6 When bought on the street in small doses of crack.

$15,000 to $20,000

5 When sold wholesale in New York City, for example.

4 After crossing the border, the cocaine is reconsolidated into larger loads and driven to distribution points.

3 Cocaine is transported through Mexico by Mexican crime federations that demand up to half the cocaine as their fee. They break down the loads into smaller units to smuggle across the border.

$1,500 to $2,000

2 When refined cocaine leaves Colombia for Mexico.

$300 to $700

1 Paid to Peruvian farmers for the 400 pounds of coca leaves it takes to make one pound of cocaine.

5 6 NEW YORK

4 in transit

3 MEXICO

COLOMBIA 2

1 PERU

FIGURE 4.3

From farm prices in Peru to current street prices as crack, the estimated value of cocaine escalates from as little as $300 for the 400 pounds of coca necessary to produce one pound of cocaine to $40,000 for the crack doses made from that pound of cocaine.

Source: New York Times, March 4, 1997, p. A20. Copyright © 1997 by The New York Times Company. Reprinted by permission. Information updated to 2006, courtesy of the Drug Enforcement Administration, Washington D.C.

Patterns of Cocaine Abuse

In 2006, the National Survey on Drug Use and Health estimated that approximately 35 million Americans aged 12 or older had used cocaine at some time in their lives, 6 million had used it during the past year, and 2.4 million had used it during the past month. Approximately 8.5 million Americans had used crack at some time in their lives, 1.5 million had used it during the past year, and 702,000 had used it during the past month.[28]

Although the present-day incidence of cocaine abuse in the United States is lower than it was during the 1980s, medical emergencies associated with cocaine use, as measured through the DAWN statistics, have increased dramatically. In 2005, there were approximately 448,481

Drugs . . . in Focus

Cocaine Contamination in U.S. Paper Currency

In recent years, a strange but reliable phenomenon has come to light with respect to the paper currency that Americans handle every day: the contamination of this currency with detectable levels of cocaine. In 2001, analyses were made of fifty randomly sampled one-dollar bills from five cities in the United States and Puerto Rico (Baltimore, Chicago, Denver, Honolulu, and San Juan). Detectable amounts of cocaine were found in an astounding 92 percent of these bills.

The explanation for this finding is based on the pattern of cocaine abuse and the present-day system of currency processing and distribution. Contamination is believed to begin with the handling of currency during cocaine trafficking (see Chapter 13) and with the rolling up of bills for cocaine snorting. The contaminated money is then transferred from bill to bill during automated counting in banks and other financial institutions. The extremely high incidence of cocaine-contaminated money is attributed to cross-contamination after the act of drug-taking behavior, rather than to the behavior itself. The lower incidence of contamination with respect to other illicit drugs such as methamphetamine or heroin is due largely to the relatively lower prevalence rates of abuse in general and the fact that currency is not as likely to be directly involved in their consumption.

Source: Jenkins, Amanda J. (2001). Drug contamination of U.S. paper currency. *Forensic Science International, 3,* 189–193.

---

cocaine-related ED visits reported by metropolitan hospitals. It is evident that emergency departments have borne a great burden in the acute care of cocaine abusers. Likewise, law-enforcement agencies have borne the burden of reducing the availabity of cocaine and cocaine-derivatives (Drugs . . . in Focus).[29]

Treatment Programs for Cocaine Abuse

One way of grasping the significant impact the cocaine-abuse problem is to look at the number of people who have wanted to get help. In 1983, a nationwide toll-free hotline, 1-800-COCAINE, was established as a twenty-four-hour service for emergency and treatment information. From 1983 to 1990, more than 3 million callers responded, averaging more than 1,000 per day.[30]

Yet we can see, through the statistics gathered from the hotline over the years, the changing face of cocaine abuse. In 1983, the typical cocaine abuser was college educated (50 percent), employed (83 percent), earning more than $25,000 per year (52 percent), and taking cocaine powder intranasally (61 percent). By 1988, however, the typical cocaine abuser had not gone to college (83 percent) and was earning less than $25,000 per year (80 percent). From 1983 to 1988, the percentage of individuals reporting an abuse of a free-base form of cocaine had more than doubled to 56 percent. In 1986 alone, one year after the introduction of crack, half of all calls to the hotline referred to problems of crack abuse.[31]

Treating cocaine abuse presents difficulties that are peculiar to the power of cocaine itself. This is the way one treatment expert has put it:

> *Coming off cocaine is one of the most anguished, depressing experiences. I've watched people talk about coming off freebase and one of the things I noticed was the nonverbal maneuvers they use to describe it. It looks like they're describing a heart attack. They have fists clenched to the chest. You can see that it hurts. They can recreate that hurt for you because it's a devastating event. They'll do almost anything to keep from crashing on cocaine. And on top of that they'll do just about anything to keep their supply coming. Postcocaine anguish is a strong inducement to use again—to keep the pain away.[32]*

The varieties of treatment for cocaine abuse all have certain features in common. The initial phase is detoxification and total abstinence: The cocaine abuser aims to achieve total withdrawal with the least possibility of physical injury and minimal psychological

PORTRAIT

PORTRAIT

Robert Downey Jr.—Trials and Tribulations

The parade of celebrities who have struggled against cocaine abuse is seemingly endless. Over the years, we have witnessed their personal triumphs and failures, seen some careers lost and occasionally careers regained. In 1986, the nation was galvanized by the untimely deaths of college basketball player Len Bias and professional football player Dan Rogers, within months of each other, as well as the death of comedian John Belushi four years earlier. In the 1990s, baseball players Doc Gooden and Darryl Strawberry captured headlines less often because of their athletic achievements and more frequently as a result of their struggles with substance abuse. Sometimes the battle has been won (Gooden), sometimes the battle continues (Strawberry). The death of actor River Phoenix in 1993 at the age of twenty-three, due to a combination of cocaine and heroin, underscored the ever-present risks of drug-taking behavior (Chapter 2).

The story of actor Robert Downey Jr., an Academy Award nominee for his portrayal of the title role in

Chaplin in 1992, has been an emotional roller-coaster ride, and we simply have to hold our breath as events unfold. In January 2003, Downey at the age of thirty-seven could remark, "I'm a little older. I'm mildly wiser. My frequent appearances on Court TV have brought me to another level than just always 'the acting guy.' . . . I think I've become very, I don't want to say real, but I'm very tangible to people." He made those comments while at the premiere of a new film, his first since completing a year-long court-ordered drug rehabilitation program in 2002. At the time, he was about one year into a three-year probation period, after pleading "no contest" to cocaine possession and being under the influence during a November 2000 arrest in a Palm Springs hotel.

In 1999, Downey had spent a year in prison after being convicted on charges of cocaine possession. Upon his release, Downey landed a major role in the successful *Ally McBeal* TV show, only to be fired from the series in 2000. His drug-abuse problems had first begun making headlines in 1996, when he was found

with cocaine, heroin, and a pistol in his car.

Today, with help from his friends and other sources of support, a new clean-and-sober Downey has managed to return to an active and varied career. His self-destructive life-style may be over. "I think," he has said, "part of my destiny has to be realizing that I'm not the poster boy for drug abuse. I'm just the guy who has a really strong sense of wanting home and wanting foundation and having not had it. I now choose to create it."

The clear message is that recovery is still possible even after multiple relapses. The key is treatment that is intensive, lengthy, and ongoing. Nonetheless, it is difficult to underestimate the magnitude of the problem that such individuals face. Willpower alone is not enough to overcome substance dependence.

Sources: Robert Downey Jr. cleans up (2005, October 26). CNN.com. Second quotation. Downey's back, older and "mildly wiser" (2003, January 21). First quotation. *Newsday*, p. A12. Lemonick, Michael D. (2000, December 11). Downey's downfall. *Time*, p. 97.

---

discomfort. During the first twenty-four to forty-eight hours, the chances are high that there will be profound depression, severe headaches, irritability, and disturbances in sleep.[33]

In severe cases involving a pattern of compulsive use that cannot be easily broken, the cocaine abuser needs to be admitted for inpatient treatment in a hospital facility. The most intensive interventions, medical supervision with psychological counseling, can be made in this kind of environment. The early stages of withdrawal are clearly the most difficult, and the recovering abuser can benefit from around-the-clock attention that only a hospital staff can give.

The alternative approach is an outpatient program, under which the individual remains at home but travels regularly to a facility for treatment. An outpatient program is clearly a less expensive route to take, but it works only

for those who recognize the destructive impact of cocaine dependence on their lives and enter treatment with a sincere desire to do whatever is needed to stop.[34]

For cocaine abusers who have failed in previous attempts in outpatient treatment or for those who are in denial of their cocaine dependence, an inpatient approach may be the only answer. For most abusers, it is important to stay away from an environment where cocaine and other drugs are prevalent and peer pressure to resume drug-taking behavior is intense. This factor is particularly crucial among adolescents:

Peer acceptance is of utmost importance to adolescents. In order to interrupt the addiction cycle, youth are cautioned to avoid drug-using friends. Since many addicted adolescents are alienated from the mainstream and what few friends they have are users, this challenge can appear overwhelming. Recovering adolescents often comment that they can't find friends who don't at least drink.[35]

A third alternative is a combined approach in which a shortened inpatient program, seven to fourteen days in length, is followed by an intensive outpatient program that continues for several months (Portrait).

Whether on an inpatient or outpatient basis, there are several approaches for treatment. One alternative is the self-help support group Cocaine Anonymous, modeled after the famous twelve-step Alcoholics Anonymous program (see Chapter 11). In this program, recovering cocaine abusers meet in group sessions, learn from the life experiences of other members, and gain a sense of accomplishment from remaining drug-free in an atmosphere of fellowship and mutual support. In another drug-treatment option, cocaine abusers meet with cognitive-behavioral therapists, who teach them new ways of acting and thinking in response to their environment. During the course of cognitive-behavioral therapy, cocaine abusers are urged to avoid situations that lead to drug use, recognize and change irrational thoughts, manage negative moods, and practice drug-refusal skills. While the success rates of both approaches are approximately the same for patients in cocaine-abuse treatment overall, some evidence suggests that a cocaine abuser's personal characteristics may affect the kind of treatment that will work best (Figure 4.4). Whatever the approach taken, however, it is clear that an intensive relearning

process has to go on because cocaine abusers often cannot remember a life without cocaine.[36]

Currently pharmacological approaches in cocaine-abuse treatment, as well as the combination of pharmacological and behavioral approaches, are being vigorously pursued. An extremely promising example of a purely pharmacological strategy is the development of the compound gamma-vinyl-GABA (GVG), currently available as an antiepileptic drug called Vigabatrin. Essentially, it has been established that GVG "short-circuits" the reinforcing effect of cocaine by preventing the sudden surge of dopamine in the brain when cocaine is administered. Animals that have become cocaine-dependent no longer self-administer the drug after taking GVG and are no longer attracted to locations that have been associated with cocaine in the past. In other words, GVG allows animals to resist the conditioned cues for chronic cocaine use. Recent evidence indicates that GVG is effective in a similar way in humans, and large-scale clinical trials are currently underway.[37]

The potential for relapse is a particularly challenging element among recovering cocaine abusers, primarily as a result of powerful conditioned cues that have been associated with the drug. A specialist in cocaine abuse rehabilitation tells this story: "A woman was doing well in treatment. Then one day she was changing her baby's diaper. She used baby powder and the sight of the white powder induced a tremendous craving for cocaine."[38] The development of any drug that reduces craving would be a great advance in the treatment of

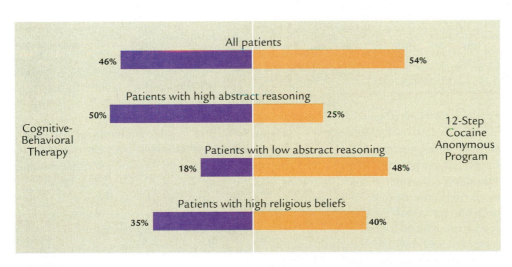

FIGURE 4.4

Percentage of patients achieving four consecutive weeks of cocaine abstinence, comparing two types of treatment.

Source: Adapted from Shine, Barbara (2000, March). Some cocaine abusers fare better with cognitive-behavioral therapy, others with 12-step programs. *NIDA Notes, 15* (1), 9.

cocaine dependence and in the prevention of problems associated with cocaine dependence.

The continuing investigation of treatment and prevention approaches to cocaine abuse reflects a general orientation toward reducing the negative impact of drug-taking behavior on the individual and society (the "demand" side), as opposed to reducing the availability of the drugs themselves (the "supply" side). The Drug Trafficking Update focuses on information regarding governmental efforts to disrupt the supply line of cocaine into the United States.

Amphetamines

One of humanity's fondest dreams is to have the power of unlimited endurance, to be able to banish fatigue from our lives, to be capable of endless energy as if we had discovered some internal perpetual-motion machine. We all have wanted, at some time in our lives, to be a super-hero. Cocaine, as we know, gives us that illusion. The remainder of this chapter will examine another powerful drug source for these feelings of invincibility: amphetamines. As we will see, the attractions and problems of abuse associated with cocaine and amphetamines are very similar.

amphetamine (am-FEH-ta-meen): A family of ephedrine-based stimulant drugs.

The Social History of Amphetamines

The origin of modern amphetamines dates back almost five thousand years to a Chinese medicinal herb called *ma huang (Ephedra vulgaris)* that was used to clear bronchial passageways during bouts of asthma and other forms of respiratory distress. According to Chinese legend, this herb was first identified by the Emperor Shen Nung, who also is credited with the discovery of tea and marijuana.

German chemists isolated the active ingredient of *ma huang* in 1887, naming it ephedrine. It was soon obvious that ephedrine stimulated the sympathetic nervous system in general. The pharmaceutical company Smith, Kline and French Laboratories marketed a synthetic form of ephedrine called **amphetamine** under the brand name Benzedrine in 1932 as a nonprescription CNS stimulant appetite suppressant and bronchial dilator.

During World War II, both U.S. and German troops were being given amphetamine to keep them awake and alert. Japanese kamikaze pilots were on amphetamine during their suicide missions. The advantages over cocaine, the other stimulant drug available at the time, were two-fold: Amphetamine was easily absorbed into the nervous system from the gastrointestinal tract, so it could be taken orally, and its effects were much longer lasting.

After the war, amphetamine use was adapted for peacetime purposes. Amphetamine, often referred to as "bennies," was a way for college students to stay awake to study for exams and for long-distance truck drivers to fight fatigue on the road. Truckers would take a "St. Louis" if they had to go from New York to Missouri and back or a "Pacific turnabout" if they needed to travel completely across country and back, without stopping to sleep.[39]

In the meantime, the word got around that amphetamine produced euphoria as well, and soon amphetamine began to be sought for recreational purposes. People found ways of opening up the nonprescription amphetamine inhalers, withdrawing the contents, and getting high by drinking it or injecting it intravenously. Since each inhaler contained 250 mg of amphetamine, there was enough for several powerful doses. During the early 1960s, injectable amphetamines could be bought with forged prescriptions or even by telephoning a pharmacy and posing as a physician. By 1965, amendments to federal drug laws tightened the supply of prescription amphetamines, requiring manufacturers, wholesalers, and pharmacies to keep careful records of amphetamine transactions, but amphetamines soon became available from illegal laboratories.[40]

Amphetamine abuse in the United States reached a peak about 1967, declining slowly over the 1970s as other drugs of abuse, notably cocaine, grew in popularity. By 1970, 10 percent of the U.S. population over fourteen years of age had used amphetamine, and more than 8 percent of all drug prescriptions were for amphetamine in some form.[41] For about two decades afterward, amphetamine abuse steadily faded from prominence in the drug scene. Cocaine and later crack cocaine became the dominant illicit stimulant of abuse. Only since the mid-1990s has amphetamine abuse resurfaced as a significant social concern.

The Different Forms of Amphetamine

To understand amphetamine abuse, both past and present, it is necessary to know something about the molecular structure of amphetamines themselves and their relationship to important neurotransmitters in the brain. As you can see at the top of Figure 4.5, amphetamine can be represented chiefly as carbon (C), hydrogen (H), and nitrogen (N) atoms, in a prescribed arrangement. What you are seeing, however, is only one version of amphetamine, the "right-handed" form, since amphetamine contains a "left-handed" version as well (imagine a mirror image of Figure 4.5). The more potent version is the right-handed form, called dextroamphetamine or **d-amphetamine** (brand name: Dexedrine). It is stronger than the left-handed form, called levoamphetamine or l-amphetamine, which is not commonly available. A modified form of d-amphetamine, formulated by substituting CH_3 (called a methyl group) instead of H at one end, is called **methamphetamine**. This slight change in

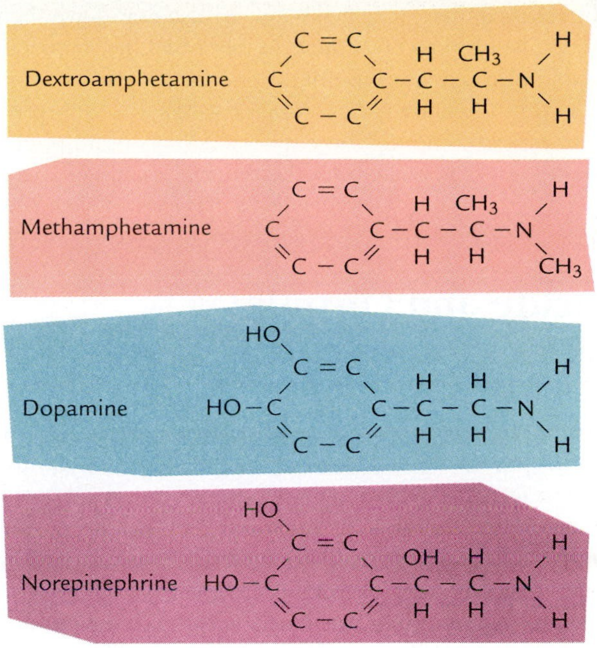

FIGURE 4.5

The molecular structure of dextroamphetamine, methamphetamine, dopamine, and norepinephrine.

the formula allows for a quicker passage across the blood-brain barrier. It is methamphetamine, often called *meth*, *speed*, or *crank*, that has been the primary form of amphetamine abuse in recent years.

How Amphetamines Work in the Brain

We can get a good idea of how amphetamines work in the brain by looking carefully at the molecular structures of dopamine and norepinephrine alongside d-amphetamine and methamphetamine in Figure 4.5. Notice how similar they all are, with only slight differences among them. Because of the close resemblance to dopamine and norepinephrine, it is not hard to imagine amphetamines increasing the activity level of these two neurotransmitters. Specifically, amphetamines cause increased amounts of dopamine and norepinephrine to

d-amphetamine: Shortened name for dextroamphetamine, a potent form of amphetamine, marketed under the brand name Dexedrine.

methamphetamine: A type of amphetamine, once marketed under the brand name Methedrine. Methamphetamine abusers refer to it as meth, speed, or crank.

be released from synaptic knobs and also slow down their reuptake from receptor sites. As described in Chapter 3, dopamine figures prominently in regions of the brain (notably the nucleus accumbens) associated with positive reinforcement. The euphoric effects of amphetamines, and the craving for them during abstinence, are considered to result from changes in dopamine activity.

Acute and Chronic Effects of Amphetamines

The acute effects of amphetamine, in either d-amphetamine or methamphetamine form, closely resemble those of cocaine. However, amphetamine effects extend over a longer period of time. For intervals of eight to twenty-four hours, there are signs of increased sympathetic autonomic activity such as faster breathing and heart rate as well as hyperthermia (increased body temperature) and elevated blood pressure. Users experience feelings of euphoria and invincibility, decreased appetite, and an extraordinary boost in alertness and energy. Adverse and potentially lethal bodily changes include convulsions, chest pains, and stroke. These serious health risks have, unfortunately, been reflected in the DAWN statistics, in which methamphetamine-related hospital emergencies have risen substantially from 1990 to 2005.[42]

Chronic effects of amphetamine abuse are both bizarre and unpleasant, particularly in the case of methamphetamine. Heavy methamphetamine abusers may experience formication hallucinations similar to those endured by cocaine abusers. They may become obsessed with the delusion that parasites or insects have lodged in their skin and so attempt to scratch, cut, or burn their skin in an effort to remove them. It is also likely that they will engage in compulsive or repetitive behaviors that are fixated upon ordinarily trivial aspects of life; an entire night might be spent, for example, counting the corn flakes in a cereal box.[43]

The most serious societal consequence of methamphetamine abuse is the appearance of paranoia, wildly bizarre delusions, hallucinations, tendencies toward violence, and intense mood swings. In the words of one health professional, "It's about the ugliest drug there is."[44] Because the symptoms have been observed with the chronic abuse of amphetamines of any type, they are referred to collectively as **amphetamine psychosis.** These "psychotic" effects, often persisting for weeks or even months after the drug has been withdrawn, so closely resemble the symptoms of paranoid schizophrenia that it has been speculated that the two conditions have the same underlying chemical basis in the brain: an overstimulation of dopamine-releasing neurons in those regions that control emotional reactivity.[45] A study of heavy methamphetamine users has shown changes in chemical metabolites in those regions of the brain that are associated with Parkinson's disease, suggesting that this group may be predisposed to acquiring Parkinson symptoms later in life, due to their methamphetamine exposure. Fortunately, however, recent evidence indicates that chemical changes in the brain in chronic methamphetamine users can be at least partially reversed by abstaining from the drug for a year or more.[46]

Patterns of Methamphetamine Abuse and Treatment

In the United States, the emergence of widespread methamphetamine abuse was intermingled with the marijuana and LSD scene during San Francisco's

Methamphetamine abuse produces an enormous increase in alertness and energy, but frightening hallucinations and compulsive behaviors also can occur.

amphetamine psychosis: A set of symptoms, including hallucinations, paranoia, and disordered thinking, resulting from high doses of amphetamines.

"Summer of Love and Peace" in 1967. Almost from the beginning, however, speed freaks—as methamphetamine abusers were called—whose behaviors were anything but loving or peaceful, became the outcasts of that society:

> These wild-eyed, manic burnout cases would blither on endlessly, rip off anything not welded in place, then go into fits of erratic and violent behavior.... They were shunned by other sorts of drug users, and ended up congregating with the only segment of the population who could stomach their company—other speed freaks.[47]

In the meantime, prescription amphetamines, widely administered during the 1960s for weight control and as a way to combat drowsiness, resulted in large numbers of abusers from practically every segment of society. Even though d-amphetamine was classified as a Schedule II drug in 1970 and the number of d-amphetamine prescriptions decreased by 90 percent from 1971 and 1986, the pills were still out there, and people found ways to continue an abusive pattern of drug-taking behavior.

Present-Day Patterns of Methamphetamine Abuse

As crack cocaine became increasingly associated with the urban poor and powder cocaine with upscale affluence in the 1980s, amphetamine abuse declined dramatically. In the 1990s, however, as crack cocaine and powder cocaine abuse began to diminish, methamphetamine abuse reemerged on the drug scene. Once identified with the countercultural 1960s, methamphetamine has become a major stimulant of abuse in the United States, with its popularity now concentrated among working-class people rather than among the poor or the affluent (Table 4.2).

> Methamphetamine ... made inroads among many blue-collar people because it did not carry the stigma of being a hard drug ... It's what people used to get them through a shift at the factory or keep up on a construction site.[48]

Administered by snorting, injecting, or smoking, methamphetamine has become one of the few drugs reported as equally or more prevalent than other illicit drugs in areas outside America's inner cities. In the early 1990s, distribution of methamphetamine was dominated by organized groups operating out of southern California and Mexico, with trafficking routes extending through

TABLE 4.2

Street names for amphetamines

TYPE OF AMPHETAMINE	STREET NAME
Amphetamine in general	bennies, uppers, ups, A, pep pills, white crowns, whites
Dextroamphetamine	dexies, cadillacs, black beauties
Methamphetamine*	meth, speed, Tina, crank, little whites, white crosstops, crystal meth, quill, yellow bam, zip, go fast, chalk, shabu, spoosh, get go
Smokable methamphetamine*	ice, crystal, crystal meth, L.A., L.A. glass, quartz, cristy, hanyak, Christina, Tina
Methcathinone (a synthetic analog of methamphetamine)	khat, cat, goob

*Slang terms often confuse smokable and nonsmokable forms of methamphetamine, so some street names may overlap the two categories.

Sources: Drug Enforcement Administration and the Office of National Drug Control Policy.

several U.S. states, including Arizona, Colorado, Iowa, Missouri, Nebraska, North Dakota, and Texas.

More recently, thousands of "homegrown" methamphetamine laboratories have proliferated in small towns and rural areas throughout the nation. They are typically situated in mobile homes, campers, vans, and easily hidden farm sheds, making their detection by law enforcement agencies extremely difficult. As of 2006, retail outlets have been required by federal law to limit the sales of numerous cold remedies (Sudafed, Tylenol Cold, among others) that contain pseudoepinephrine—an essential ingredient in the making of methamphetamine. Products that have formerly been "over-the-counter" (see Chapter 14) are now "behind-the-counter." Customers cannot buy more than the equivalent of approximately seventy 60 mg tablets per day and must provide photo identification upon purchase and sign a logbook recording the transaction. Because liquid anhydrous ammonia, commonly used as a farm fertilizer, is another ingredient in the making of methamphetamine, fertilizer dealers have installed security systems to protect their supplies from theft. Toxic residue from methamphetamine manufacture, approximately five pounds of waste for every one pound of methamphetamine produced, has seeped into the soil and contaminated rivers and streams. Increasing attention has been directed to children who have suffered

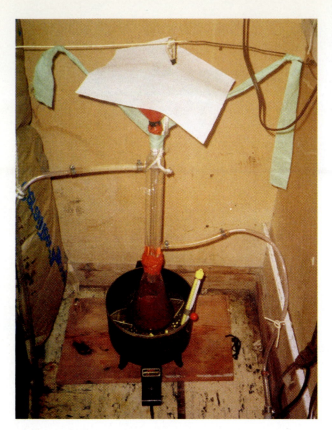

A device for making methamphetamine is shown during a raid in an Altamont, Tennessee, home. Like modern-day moonshine, the powerful stimulant is being produced by the bucketful in trailers and barns in rural areas of the United States.

from inhaling the toxic fumes emitted during the process of methamphetamine manufacture, from the risks of fire and explosions, and from abuse and neglect by methamphetamine-dependent parents (Drugs... in Focus).[49]

Methamphetamine has become a major club drug in New York, Los Angeles, and other cities (see Chapter 1). A smokable form of methamphetamine hydrochloride called **ice** (also referred to as *crystal meth*) is particularly dangerous. Its name originates from its quartz-like, chunky crystallized appearance. Ice appeared on the drug scene in Hawaii in the late 1980s, but its abuse did not expand to the mainland to a significant degree until the latter 1990s. The combination of a purity of 98 to 100 percent and a highly efficient delivery route through the lungs produces a high level of potential for dependence and a significant social problem. An association between methamphetamine abuse and increased high-risk sexual behavior among HIV-positive gay or bisexual men has raised public-health concerns.[50]

While both methamphetamine and cocaine are similar in their stimulant effects and both trigger a major release of dopamine in the brain, the pattern of drug-taking behavior for each type of drug has its own distinctive character. Methamphetamine abusers typically use the drug throughout their waking day, at two- to four-hour intervals, in a pattern that resembles taking medication. Cocaine abusers typically use the drug in the evening and nighttime rather than during the day, taking it in a continuous (binge-like) fashion until all the cocaine on hand has been exhausted. This latter pattern of drug-taking behavior fits the typical picture of the recreational user.

The duration of effect in the two drugs may help to explain the differences in usage. Methamphetamine effects generally last more than ten hours, and its elimination half-life is about twelve hours. Cocaine effects last about twenty to thirty minutes, and its elimination half-life is about one hour.

On tests that evaluate different forms of cognitive functioning, methamphetamine and cocaine abusers show significant differences in terms of the type of cognitive impairment that is produced. Methamphetamine abusers are impaired on tests of perceptual speed or manipulation of information, effects observed to a lesser extent among cocaine abusers. The greatest difference between the two groups is observed when tests require both speed and the manipulation of information.[51]

The course of methamphetamine withdrawal—and amphetamine withdrawal in general—is very similar to the course of events described earlier for cocaine. First, there is the "crash" when the abuser feels intense depression, hunger, agitation, and anxiety within one to four hours after the drug-taking behavior has stopped. Withdrawal from amphetamines, during total abstinence from the drug, takes between six and eighteen weeks, during which the intense craving for amphetamine slowly subsides.

As in cocaine-abuse treatment, there are inpatient and outpatient programs, depending on the circumstances and motivation of the abuser. Self-help groups such as Cocaine Anonymous can be useful as well, since the symptoms of amphetamine withdrawal and cocaine withdrawal are nearly identical. Unfortunately, relatively few methamphetamine abusers attempt treatment because they perceive themselves as

ice: A smokable form of methamphetamine hydrochloride. It is often referred to as crystal meth, due to its quartz-like appearance.

Drugs . . . in Focus

The Methamphetamine Epidemic Across America

The methamphetamine abuse epidemic in Watauga County, North Carolina, had gotten so bad that it has nicknamed itself "the county that never sleeps." Dozens of methamphetamine laboratories in the region were raided. Every fire emergency was treated as if it were a meth-lab fire.

Watauga County was not alone. A survey of more than 500 county sheriffs in the United States, conducted by the National Association of Counties in 2005, documented the alarming proportions of meth abuse across the country since 2000. Fifty-eight percent of sheriffs in the survey regarded methamphetamine abuse as the biggest drug problem they faced, ahead of concerns about heroin, cocaine, or marijuana.

The law enforcement and criminal justice challenges have been immense. In half of the counties surveyed, one in five current prison inmates had been incarcerated due to meth-related crimes. In 17 percent of the counties, more than half of the inmate population had been incarcerated for such crimes. A majority of sheriffs reported that meth use was the major contributing factor for increases in robberies or burglaries, domestic violence, and simple assaults. At the same time, only one in six counties reported that they had the financial resources to support a meth rehabilitation center or program.

The adverse impact on children has been of particular concern. There have been significant increases in cases in which children need to be placed out of the home as a result of neglect and abuse by parents who are meth abusers or a child's proximity to the hazards of meth labs. Nearly three-fourths of county child welfare officials in California and Colorado, for example, have reported increases in such cases since 2000. More than 69 percent of counties in Minnesota reported an increase in meth-related child placements between 2004 and 2005.

Two exacerbating factors have made it particularly difficult for children who are affected by the meth epidemic. First, meth abuse has been concentrated in mostly rural areas, where social service networks are ill-prepared to handle the increased numbers of foster children. Second, the chances of reunifying families torn apart by meth abuse has been considerably lower than in cases involving other forms of drug abuse, due to the high rate of relapse among meth abusers in treatment.

Recently, the picture of meth abuse in America has changed. In 2006, federal reports indicated a decline in the number of meth lab seizures, particularly in western U.S. states that were most dramatically affected by meth abuse. This decline might have been due to the restrictions on acquiring basic ingredients for meth production. The influx of illegal methamphetamine from Mexico, however, has increased. This new drug-trafficking pattern indicates that meth abusers in the United States might simply have shifted their reliance on domestic sources to foreign sources (see Chapter 13).

Sources: Combat Meth Act added to 2006 spending bill (2005, October 15). *Alcoholism and Drug Abuse Weekly*, p. 7. Doyle, Rodger (2006, August). The crystal crisis: Meth abuse moves eastward. *Scientific American*, p. 28. National Association of Counties (2005, July 5). The meth epidemic in America. Two surveys of U.S. counties: The criminal effect of meth on communities and the impact of meth on children. Washington DC: National Association of Counties. Reports suggest gain in fight on meth labs (2006, June 20). *New York Times*, p. A15. Substance Abuse and Mental Health Services Administration (2007, January 26). Methamphetamine use. *The NSDUH Report*. Washington DC: Office of Applied Studies, Substance Abuse and Mental Health Services Administration. Zernike, Kate (2005, July 11). A drug scourge creates its own form of orphan. *New York Times*, pp. A1, A15.

in control over their drug use. As a recent report has expressed it:

> This perception is particularly dangerous because the crossover from initial use to loss of control is rapid for meth users, and generally they have lost control long before they can acknowledge it. . . . This *attitude of denial makes it difficult to convince meth abusers to enter and stay in treatment.*[52]

Overall, methamphetamine abusers find it extremely difficult to become drug-free, and their relapse rate is one of the highest for any category of illicit or licit drug abuse (Drug Trafficking Update).

attention deficit/hyperactivity disorder (ADHD): A behavioral disorder characterized by increased motor activity and reduced attention span.

Medical Uses for Amphetamines and Similar Stimulant Drugs

While amphetamines in general continue to present potential problems of abuse, there are approved medical applications for amphetamines and amphetamine-like stimulant drugs in specific circumstances. Stimulant drugs are prescribed widely for elementary-school-age children diagnosed as unable to maintain sufficient attention levels and impulse control in school or as behaviorally hyperactive. These symptoms are collectively referred to as **attention deficit/hyperactivity disorder (ADHD).** When there is no evidence of hyperactivity, the designation is shortened to *attention deficit disorder (ADD).*

ADHD is the most common psychological disorder among children. It is estimated that 3 to 5 percent of all school-age children meet the criteria for ADHD. The prevalence rate is three times greater and the symptoms are generally more severe for boys than for girls. These children have average to above-average intelligence but typically underperform academically. As many as two-thirds of school-age children with ADHD have at least one other psychiatric disorder, including anxiety and depression.[53]

Despite the public image of ADHD as an exclusively childhood phenomenon, about 40 to 60 percent of ADHD children show symptoms that persist into adulthood. As adults, these individuals are ten times more likely to be diagnosed with an antisocial personality

Drug Trafficking Update
Methamphetamine

- **Origins:** Domestic small-scale production of methamphetamine, under intense law enforcement pressure and domestic sale restrictions for precursor chemicals, has declined substantially since 2005. In addition, importation of pseudoephedrine from Canada into the United States has been curtailed. Filling the void are "superlabs" in extremely remote rural areas in the United States, operated by Mexican criminal groups. Methamphetamine production within Mexico has increased sharply.

- **Points of Entry:** Methamphetamine is primarily produced domestically. Drug seizures frequently occur at the U.S.–Mexico border.

- **Traffickers:** Distribution of methamphetamine is now dominated by Mexican criminal groups, even in Midwestern states such as Iowa, Missouri, Illinois, and Ohio.

Note: Patterns of methamphetamine trafficking will be examined in more detail in Chapter 13.

Source: National Drug Intelligence Center (2006). *National Drug Threat Assessment 2007.* Washington DC: National Drug Intelligence Center, U.S. Department of Justice, pp. 6–9.

disorder, twenty-five times more likely to have been institutionalized for delinquency, and nine times more likely to serve a prison sentence.[54]

Stimulant Drug Treatment for ADHD

Commonly prescribed stimulant medications for the treatment of ADHD include oral administrations of dextroamphetamine (brand name: Dexedrine), a combination of dextroamphetamine and amphetamine (brand name: Adderall), pemoline (brand name: Cylert), and an amphetamine-like drug, methylphenidate (brand name: Ritalin).

Ritalin dominates the market in prescriptions written for ADHD. In this drug's original formulation, the rapid onset and short duration of Ritalin requires two administrations during a school day: one at breakfast and another at lunchtime, supervised by a school nurse. In the evening, blood levels of Ritalin decline to levels that permit normal sleep. Adderall has a longer duration of action, making it possible to administer a single dose and avoiding school involvement in treatment. In comparative studies, Ritalin and Adderall have been found to be equivalent in effectiveness.[55]

Recently, new drug treatments for ADHD have become available that are essentially variations of the traditional methylphenidate medication. They include a sustained-release formulation (Concerta), a formulation that produces an initial rapid dose of methylphenidate followed by a second sustained-release phase (Metadate), and a chemical variation of methylphenidate that allows for a longer duration of action (Attenade, Focalin). A methylphenidate patch, designed to release the drug through the skin slowly over a period of nine hours, was approved in 2006.

About 70 percent of the approximately 1 million children in the United States who take stimulants for ADHD each year respond successfully to the treatment. In 1999, a major study examining the effects of medication over a fourteen-month period found that medication was more effective in reducing ADHD symptoms than behavioral treatment and nearly as effective as a combined approach of medication and behavioral treatment.

One side effect of stimulant medications is a suppression of height and weight gains during these formative years, reducing growth to about 80 to 90 percent normal levels. Fortunately, growth spurts during the summer, when children are typically no longer taking medication (referred to as "drug holidays"), usually compensate for this problem.

Discontinuance, however, has to be carefully monitored. Symptoms such as lethargy, lack of motivation,

and, in some cases, depression can occur during this time. A more serious concern is the increased risk of cardiovascular disease due to the effects of stimulant drugs. In 2006, the FDA recommended a "black box" warning on ADHD medications as a guide for patients and physicians. Recent studies indicate that stimulant treatment for ADHD in childhood does not increase the risk for substance abuse later in life. In fact, the risks for future problems with alcohol and other drugs appear to be reduced.[56]

Until recently, the phenomenon of *reducing* hyperactivity with methylphenidate and related stimulant drugs, rather than increasing it, had been quite puzzling to professionals in this field. It is now known that orally administered methylphenidate and related stimulant drugs produce a relatively slow but steady increase in dopamine activity in the brain. This change in brain chemistry is hypothesized to have two effects that are beneficial to an individual with ADHD. First, increased dopamine may amplify the effects of environmental stimulation, while reducing the background firing rates of neurons. Thus, there would be a greater "signal-to-noise" ratio in the brain, analogous to having now a stronger radio signal received by a radio that no longer emits a large amount of background static. The behavioral effect would be an improvement in attention and decreased distractibility. Symptoms of ADHD may be a result of not having a sufficient "signal-to-noise" ratio in the processing of information for tasks that require concentration and focus. Second, increased dopamine may heighten one's motivation with regard to a particular task, enhancing the salience and interest in that task and improving performance. An individual might perform better on a task simply because he or she likes doing it. The slow rate of absorption achieved through oral administration (Chapter 1) avoids the emotional high that is experienced when stimulants are smoked, snorted, or injected.[57]

The theory that increased dopamine activity accounts for the reduction in ADHD symptoms, however, may be incomplete. In 2003, a selective norepinehrine reuptake inhibitor, atomoxetine (brand name: Strattera), was approved by the FDA for the treatment of ADHD in both children and adults. Since Strattera produces an increase in norepinephrine activity in the brain, it is possible that lowered norepinephrine levels may play a role in ADHD as well. Strattera has been marketed as a once-a-day non-stimulant medication that reduces ADHD symptoms by increasing norepinephrine levels—not dopamine levels—in the brain. The full story may be either that both norepinephrine and dopamine are jointly involved in

ADHD or that ADHD itself may be two separable disorders, one related to dopamine activity and the other related to norepinephrine activity. According to this hypothesis, the symptoms may overlap to such a degree that it is difficult to distinguish the two disorders on a strictly behavioral basis.

Ritalin and Adderall Abuse

In 1996, the Swiss pharmaceutical company Ciba-Geigy sent letters to hundreds of thousands of pharmacies and physicians in the United States, warning them to exert greater control over Ritalin tablets and prescriptions to obtain them. The alert came in response to reports that Ritalin was becoming a drug of abuse among young people, who were crushing the tablets and snorting the powder as a new way of getting a stimulant high. Many high school and college students are obtaining Ritalin and Adderall from classmates who have been prescribed these medications or through drug thefts of unsecured school offices. The drugs are crushed and snorted either for recreational use or to enhance school performance by being able to study late into the night (Drugs . . . in Focus).[58]

Other Medical Applications

Narcolepsy (an unpredictable and uncontrollable urge to fall asleep during the day) is another condition for which stimulant drugs have been applied in treatment. In 1999, modafinil (brand name: Provigil) was approved for treating narcolepsy. The advantage of Provigil over traditional stimulant treatments such as dextroamphetamine is that it does not present problems of abuse and produces fewer adverse side effects. Alternative medications for narcolepsy that do not work by stimulating the CNS are presently under development.[59]

There are also several amphetamine-like drugs available to the public, some of them on a nonprescription basis, for use as nasal decongestants. In most cases, their effectiveness stems from their primary action on the peripheral nervous system rather than on the CNS. Even so, the potential for misuse exists: Some continue to take these drugs over a long period of time because stopping their use may result in unpleasant rebound effects such as nasal stuffiness. This reaction, by the way, is similar to the stuffy nose that is experienced in the chronic administration of cocaine.[60]

Drugs . . . in Focus

Stimulant Medications as "Smart Pills"

When twenty-four-year-old Jeff Ewing was first prescribed Adderall to help him maintain his focus after a major automobile accident cost him a year at a midwestern university, he was surprised to find so many healthy students who were taking the same drug to help them study. Some of them were putting all of their study time into two nights, when it would have ordinarily required a week.

The misuse of stimulant medications such as Ritalin, Adderall, and Provigil is clearly on the rise in this population. An estimated 2.3 million adolescents in middle or high school are taking stimulant medications, sometimes called "smart pills" or "brain steroids," without a prescription. Approximately 9 percent of students in a New England liberal arts college reported in 2006 taking stimulants for nonmedical purposes. This pattern of drug-taking has not received much notice from law enforcement agencies or the FDA. As Richard Restak of the American Neuropsychiatric Association has put it, these drugs users are "an entirely different population of people—from the unmotivated to the supermotivated. . . . [They] may be at the top of the class, instead of the ones hanging around the corners."

Nonprescription stimulant drugs are purchased through illicit sources or obtained free from friends with legitimate prescriptions.

Sources: Carroll, Bronwen C., McLaughlin, Thomas J., and Blake, Diane R. (2006). Patterns and knowledge of nonmedical use of stimulants among college students. *Archives of Pediatric and Adolescent Medicine, 160,* 481–485. Machniak, Christofer, and Garreau, Joel (2006, June 19). "Smart pills" drug use on rise in classroom. *The Flint Journal,* www.cmarchiak@flintjournal.com. Students tapping pills for academic boost (2006, June 20). *Newsday,* p. B13, quotation.

Summary

The Social History of Cocaine

- Cocaine, one of the two major psychoactive stimulants, is derived from coca leaves grown in the mountainous regions of South America. Coca chewing is still prevalent among certain groups of South American Indians.

- During the last half of the nineteenth century, several patent medicines and beverages were sold that contained cocaine, including the original (pre-1903) formulation for Coca-Cola.

- Sigmund Freud was an early enthusiast of cocaine as an important medicinal drug, promoting cocaine as a cure for morphine dependence and depression. Soon afterward, Freud realized the strong dependence that cocaine could bring about.

Acute Effects of Cocaine

- Cocaine produces a powerful burst of energy and sense of well-being. In general, cocaine causes an elevation in the sympathetic autonomic nervous system.

Chronic Effects of Cocaine

- Long-term cocaine use can produce hallucinations and deep depression, as well as physical deterioration of the nasal membranes if cocaine is administered intranasally.

Medical Uses of Cocaine

- The only accepted medical application for cocaine is its use as a local anesthetic.

How Cocaine Works in the Brain

- Within the CNS, cocaine blocks the reuptake of dopamine and norepinephrine. As a result, the activity level of these two neurotransmitters in the brain is enhanced.

Present-Day Cocaine Abuse

- Compared with the permissive attitude toward cocaine use seen during the 1970s and early 1980s, attitudes toward cocaine use since the second half of the 1980s have changed dramatically.

- The emergence in 1986 of relatively inexpensive, smokable crack cocaine expanded the cocaine-abuse problem to new segments of the U.S. population and made cocaine abuse one of the major social issues of our time.

Treatment Programs for Cocaine Abuse

- Cocaine abusers can receive treatment through inpatient programs, outpatient programs, or a combination of the two. Relapse is a continual concern for recovering cocaine abusers.

Amphetamines

- Amphetamines, the second of the two major psychoactive stimulants, have their origin in a Chinese medicinal herb, used for thousands of years as a bronchial dilator; its active ingredient, ephedrine, was isolated in 1887.

- The drug amphetamine (brand name: Benzedrine) was developed in 1927 as a synthetic form of ephedrine. By the 1930s, various forms of amphetamines, specifically d-amphetamine and methamphetamine, became available around the world.

Acute and Chronic Effects of Amphetamines

- Amphetamine is effective as a general arousing agent, as an antidepressant, and as an appetite suppressant, in addition to its ability to keep people awake for long periods of time.

- While the acute effects of amphetamines resemble those of cocaine, amphetamines have the particular feature of producing (when taken in large doses) symptoms of paranoia, delusions, hallucinations, and violent behaviors, referred to as amphetamine psychosis. The bizarre behaviors of the "speed freak," the name given to a chronic abuser of methamphetamine, illustrate the dangers of amphetamine abuse.

Patterns of Methamphetamine Abuse and Treatment

- With the emphasis on cocaine abuse during the 1980s, amphetamine abuse was less prominent in the public mind. Recently, however, there has been a resurgence of amphetamine-abuse cases involving methamphetamine, particularly in nonurban regions of the United States.

- Treatment for methamphetamine abuse generally follows along the same lines as treatment for cocaine abuse.

Medical Uses for Amphetamines and Similar Stimulant Drugs

- Amphetamine-like stimulant drugs have been developed for approved medical purposes.

- Methylphenidate (brand name: Ritalin), atomoxetine (brand name: Strattera), and dextroamphetamine (brand name: Adderall) are three examples of drugs prescribed for children diagnosed with attention deficit/hyperactivity disorder (ADHD). Recently, there has been growing concern over the recreational use of these medications.

- Other medical applications for amphetamine-like drugs include their use as a treatment for narcolepsy and as a means for the temporary relief of nasal congestion.

Key Terms

amphetamine, p. 100
amphetamine psychosis, p. 102
attention deficit/hyperactivity disorder (ADHD), p. 106
cocaine, p. 88
cocaine hydrochloride, p. 94
cocaine psychosis, p. 93
crack cocaine or crack, p. 95
d-amphetamine, p. 101
formication, p. 91
free-base cocaine, p. 95
ice, p. 104
kindling effect, p. 93
methamphetamine, p. 101

Endnotes

1. Rosencan, Jeffrey S., and Spitz, Henry I. (1987). Cocaine reconceptualized: Historical overview. In Henry I. Spitz and Jeffrey S. Rosencan (Eds.), *Cocaine abuse: New directions in treatment and research.* New York: Brunner/Mazel, p. 5.

2. Inciardi, James A. (2002). *The war on drugs III.* Boston: Allyn and Bacon, p. 129. Inglis, Brian (1975). *The forbidden game: A social history of drugs.* New York: Scribner's, pp. 49–50. Montoya, Ivan D., and Chilcoat, Howard D. (1996). Epidemiology of coca derivatives use in the Andean region: A tale of five countries. *Substance Use and Misuse, 31,* 1227–1240.

3. Jaffe, Jerome (1985). Drug addiction and drug abuse. In Louis S. Goodman and Alfred Gilman (Eds.), *The pharmacological basis of therapeutics* (7th ed.). New York: Macmillan, p. 552.

4. Nahas, Gabriel G. (1989). *Cocaine: The great white plague.* Middlebury, VT: Paul S. Eriksson, pp. 154–162.

5. Kusinitz, Marc (1988). *Drug use around the world.* New York: Chelsea House Publishers, pp. 91–95.

6. Karch, Steven B. (1996). *The pathology of drug abuse* (2nd ed.). Boca Raton, FL: CRC Press, pp. 2–3. Nuckols, Caldwell C. (1989). *Cocaine: From dependency to recovery* (2nd ed.). Blue Ridge Summit, PA: Tab Books, p. x.

7. Brecher, Edward M., and the editors of *Consumer Reports* (1972). *Licit and illicit drugs.* Boston: Little, Brown, p. 270. Weiss, Roger D., and Mirin, Steven M. (1987). *Cocaine.* Washington DC: American Psychiatric Press, p. 6.

8. McKim, William A. (2000). *Drugs and behavior* (4th ed.). Upper Saddle River, NJ: Prentice Hall, p. 203.

9. Erickson, Patricia G.; Adlaf, Edward M.; Murray, Glenn F.; and Smart, Reginald G. (1987). *The steel drug: Cocaine in perspective.* Lexington, MA: D. C. Heath, p. 9.

10. Musto, David (1973). *The American disease: Origins of narcotic control.* New Haven, CT: Yale University Press.

11. Cole, John R. (1998). Freud's dream of the botanical monograph and cocaine the wonder drug. *Dreaming, 8,* 187–204. Quotation from Jones, Ernest (1953). *The life and work of Sigmund Freud.* Vol. 1. New York: Basic Books, p. 81.

12. Jones, *The life and work of Sigmund Freud,* p. 81.

13. Ibid., p. 84.

14. Brecher, *Licit and illicit drugs,* pp. 272–280.

15. Aronson, T. A., and Craig, T. J. (1986). Cocaine precipitation of panic disorder. *American Journal of Psychiatry, 143,* 643–645.

16. Marsuk, Peter M.; Tardiff, Kenneth; Leon, Andrew C.; Stajic, Marina; Morgan, Edward B.; and Mann, J. John (1992). Prevalence of cocaine use among residents of New York City who commited suicide during a one-year period. *American Journal of Psychiatry, 149,* 371–375.

17. Office of Substance Abuse Prevention (1989). *What you can do about drug use in America* (DHHS publication No. ADM 88–1572). Rockville, MD: National Clearinghouse for Alcohol and Drug Information.

18. Philips, J. L., and Wynne, R. D. (1974). A *cocaine bibliography—nonannotated.* Rockville MD: National Institute on Drug Abuse, 1974. Cited in Ernest L. Abel. (1985). *Psychoactive drugs and sex.* New York: Plenum Press, p. 100.

19. Kaufman, Marc J.; Levin, Jonathan M.; Ross, Marjorie H.; Lange, Nicholas; Rose, Stephanie L.; Kukes, Thellea J.; Mendelson, Jack H.; Lukas, Scott E.; Cohen, Bruce M.; and Renshaw, Perry F. (1998). Cocaine-induced cerebral vasoconstriction detected in humans with magnetic resonance angiography. *Journal of the American Medical Association, 279,* 376–380.

20. Experiment in Memphis suggests many drive after using drugs (1994, August 28). *New York Times,* p. 30.

21. Koob, George T.; Vaccarino, Franco J.; Amalric, Marianne; and Swerdlow, Neal R. (1987). In Seymour Fisher,

Allen Raskin, and E. H. Uhlenhuth (Eds.), *Cocaine: Clinical and biobehavioral aspects.* New York: Oxford University Press, pp. 80–108. Robinson, Terry E., and Berridge, Kent C. (2000). The psychology and neurobiology of addiction: An incentive-sensitization view. *Addiction, 95* (supplement), S91–S117. Volkow, Nora D.; Wang, Gene-Jack; Fowler, Joanna S.; Logan, Jean; Gatley, Samuel J.; Hitzemann, Richard; Chen, A. D.; and Pappas, Naomi. (1997). Decrease in striatal dopaminergic responsiveness in detoxified cocaine-dependent subjects. *Nature, 386,* 830–833.

22. Robinson, Terry E. (1993). Persistent sensitizing effects of drugs on brain dopamine systems and behavior: Implications for addiction and relapse. In Stanley G. Korenman and Jack D. Barchas (Eds.), *The biological basis of substance abuse.* New York: Oxford University Press, pp. 373–402. Weiss and Mirin, *Cocaine,* pp. 48–49.

23. Kaplan, Harold I., Freedman, Arnold M., and Sadock, Benjamin J. (1980). *Comprehensive textbook of psychiatry.* Vol. 3. Baltimore, MD: Williams and Wilkins, p. 1621.

24. Flynn, John C. (1991). *Cocaine: An in-depth look at the facts, science, history, and future of the world's most addictive drug.* New York: Birch Lane/Carol Publishing, pp. 38–46.

25. Ibid., p. 44.

26. Humphries, Drew (1998). Crack mothers at 6: Prime-time news, crack/cocaine, and women. *Violence against Women, 4,* 45–61. Massing, Michael (1998).*The fix.* New York: Simon and Schuster, p. 41. Singer, Lynn T.; Minnes, Sonia; Short, Elizabeth; Arendt, Robert; Farkas, Kathleen; Lewis, Barbara; Klein, Nancy; Russ, Sandra; Min, Meeyoung O.; and Kirchner, H. Lester (2004). Cognitive outcomes of preschool children with prenatal cocaine exposure. *Journal of the American Medical Association, 291,* 2448–2456.

27. Egan, Timothy (1999, September 19). A drug ran its course, then hid with its users. *New York Times,* pp. 1, 46. Furst, R. Terry; Johnson, Bruce D.; Dunlap, Eloise; and Curtis, Richard (1999). The stigmatized image of the "crack head": A sociocultural exploration of a barrier to cocaine smoking among a cohort of youth in New York City. *Deviant Behavior, 20,* 153–181.

28. Substance Abuse and Mental Health Services Administration (2007). *Results from the 2006 National Survey on Drug Use and Health: National findings.* Rockville, MD: Office of Applied Studies, Substance Abuse and Mental Health Services Administration, Tables G.1, G.3, and G.5.

29. Substance Abuse and Mental Health Administration (2007). *Drug Abuse Warning Network, 2005: National estimates of drug-related emergency department visits.* Rockville MD: Office of Applied Studies, Substance Abuse and Mental Health Administration, Table 2.

30. Gold, Mark S. (1990). *800–COCAINE.* New York: Bantam Books.

31. Nuckols, *Cocaine,* pp. 144–146. Lee, Felicia R. (1994, September 10). A drug dealer's rapid rise and ugly fall. *New York Times,* pp. 1, 22.

32. Nuckols, *Cocaine,* p. 42.

33. Ibid., pp. 71–72.

34. Weiss and Mirin, *Cocaine,* p. 125.

35. Fox, C. Lynn, and Forbing, Shirley E. (1992). *Creating drug-free schools and communities: A comprehensive approach.* New York: HarperCollins, p. 165.

36. Shine, Barbara (2000, March). Some cocaine abusers fare better with cognitive-behavioral therapy, others with 12-step programs. *NIDA Notes, 15* (1), 9–11.

37. Baclofen holds promise for cocaine treatment (2004, January 7). *Biotech Week,* p. 601. Brodie, Jonathan D.; Figueroa, Emilia; Laska, Eugene M., and Dewey, Stephen L. (2005). Safety and efficacy of gamma-vinyl GABA (GVG) for the treatment of methamphetamine and/or cocaine addiction. *Synapse, 55,* 122–125. Schiffer, Wynne K., Marsteller, Douglas, and Dewey, Stephen L. (2003). Sub-chronic low dose gamma-vinyl GABA (vigabatrin) inhibits cocaine-induced increases in nucleus accumbens dopamine. *Psychopharmacology, 168,* 339–343. Talan, Jamie (2004, November 23). Anti-seizure drug helps meth, cocaine addicts. *Newsday,* p. A26.

38. Barnes, Deborah M. (1988). Breaking the cycle of addiction. *Science, 241,* p. 1029. Whitten, Lori (2005, August). Cocaine-related environmental cues elicit physiological stress responses. *NIDA Notes, 20* (1), pp. 1, 6–7.

39. McKim, *Drugs and behavior,* p. 205.

40. Brecher, *Licit and illicit drugs,* pp. 282–283.

41. Greaves, George B. (1980). Psychosocial aspects of amphetamine and related substance abuse. In John Caldwell (Ed.), *Amphetamines and related stimulants: Chemical, biological, clinical, and sociological aspects.* Boca Raton, FL: CRC Press, pp. 175–192. Peluso, Emanuel, and Peluso, Lucy S. (1988). *Women and drugs.* Minneapolis: CompCare Publishing.

42. Facts about methamphetamine (1996). *NIDA Notes, 11* (5), 19. Substance Abuse, *Drug Abuse Warning Network.*

43. Goode, Erich (2005). *Drugs in American society* (6th ed.). New York: McGraw-Hill College, p. 276.

44. Bai, Matt (1997, March 31). White storm warning: In Fargo and the prairie states, speed kills. *Newsweek,* pp. 66–67. Quotation by Mark A. R. Kleiman, p. 67.

45. Goode, *Drugs in American society,* p. 276.

46. Ernst, Thomas; Chang, Linda; Leonido-Yee, Maria; and Speck, Oliver (2000). Evidence for long-term neurotoxicity associated with methamphetamine abuse: A 1H MRS study. *Neurology, 54,* 1344–1349. London, E. D.; Simon, S. L.; Berman, S. M.; Mandelkern, M. A. et al. (2004). Mood disturbances and regional cerebral metabolic abnormalities in recently abstinent methamphetamine abusers. *Archives of General Psychiatry, 61,* 73–84.

47. Young, Stanley (1989, July). Zing! Speed: The choice of a new generation. *Spin magazine,* pp. 83, 124–125.

Reprinted in Erich Goode (Ed.) (1992), *Drugs, society, and behavior 92/93*. Guilford, CT: Dushkin Publishing, p. 116.

48. Johnson, Dirk (1996, February 22). Good people go bad in Iowa, and a drug is being blamed. *New York Times*, pp. A1, A19. Quotation on p. A19.

49. Butterfield, Fox (2004, January 4). Across rural America, drug casts a grim shadow. *New York Times*, p. 10. Ebay bans pseudoephedrine sales (2005, October 17). *Alcoholism and Drug Abuse Weekly*, p. 7. Harris, Gardiner (2005, December 15). Fighting methamphetamine, lawmakers reach accord to curb sales of cold medicines. *New York Times*, p. A33. Jefferson, David J. (2005, August 5). America's most dangerous drug. *Newsweek*, pp. 41–48. Johnson, Dirk (2004, March 8). Policing a rural plague: Meth is ravaging the Midwest. *Newsweek*, p. 41. National Association of Counties (2006, January). *The meth epidemic in America*. Washington DC: National Association of Counties. Zernicke, Kate (2006, February 26). With scenes of blood and pain, ads battle methamphetamine in Montana. *New York Times*, p. 18.

50. Jacobs, Andrew J. (2004, January 12). The beast in the bathhouse: Crystal meth use by gay men threatens to reignite an epidemic. *New York Times*, pp. B1, B5. Shernoff, Michael (2005, July-August). Crystal's sexual persuasion. *The Gay & Lesbian Review*, pp. 24–26.

51. Zickler, Patrick (2001). Methamphetamine, cocaine abusers have different patterns of drug use, suffer different cognitive impairments. *NIDA Notes*, 16 (5), 11–12.

52. Drug and Alcohol Services Information System (2005, January 7). *The DASIS Report: Smoked methamphetamine, amphetamines: 1992–2002*. Washington DC: Office of Applied Studies, Substance Abuse and Mental Health Services Administration. Drug and Alcohol Services Information System (2006, February 1). *The DASIS Report: Methamphetamine/amphetamine treatment admissions in urban and rural areas: 2004*. Washington DC: Office of Applied Studies, Substance Abuse and Mental Health Services Administration. Gawin, Frank H., and Ellinwood, Everett H. (1988). Cocaine and other stimulants: Action, abuse, and treatment. *New England Journal of Medicine*, 318, 1173–1182. National Institute of Justice (1999, May). *Meth matters: Report on methamphetamine users in five western cities*. Washington DC: National Institute of Justice, U.S. Department of Justice. Quotation on p. xii.

53. Julien, Robert M. (2001). *A primer of drug action* (9th ed.). New York: Worth, pp. 207–213.

54. Julien, *A primer of drug action*, p. 208. Wilens, Timothy E. (2003). Drug therapy for adults with attention-deficit hyperactivity disorder. *Drugs*, 63, 2385–2411. Wilens, Timothy E.; Biederman, Joseph; Spencer, Thomas J.; and Prince, Jefferson (1995). Pharmacotherapy of adult attention deficit/hyperactivity disorder: A review. *Journal of Clinical Psychopharmacology*, 15, 270–279.

55. Julien, *A primer of drug action*, pp. 211–212.

56. Meyers, Laurie (2007, March). Empty bottles: Easing clients off meds. *Monitor on Psychology*, pp. 20–21. Nissen, Steven E. (2006, April 6). ADHD drugs and cardiovascular risks. *New England Journal of Medicine*, pp. 1445–1448. Taylor, Eric (1999). Commentary: Development of clinical services for attention-deficit/hyperactivity disorder. *Archives of General Psychiatry*, 56, 1088–1096. The MTA Cooperative Group (1999). A 14-month randomized clinical trial of treatment strategies for attention-deficit/hyperactivity disorder. *Archives of General Psychiatry*, 56, 1073–1086. Wilens, Timothy E.; Faraone, Stephen V.; Biederman, Joseph; and Gunawardene, Samantha (2003). Does stimulant therapy of attention deficit/hyperactivity disorder beget later substance abuse? A meta-analytic review of the literature. *Pediatrics*, 111, 179–185.

57. Julien, *A primer of drug action*, p. 211. Volkow, Nora D.; Wang, Gene.-Jack; Fowler, Joanna S.; Logan, Jean; Gerasimov, Madina; Maynard, Laurence; Ding, Yu-Shin; Gatley, Samuel J.; Gifford, Andrew; and Franceschi, Dinko (2001). Therapeutic doses of oral methylphenidate significantly increase extracellular dopamine in the human being. *Journal of Neuroscience*, 21 (121RC), 1–5.

58. Marks, Alexandria (2000, October 31). Schoolyard hustler's new drug: Ritalin. *Christian Science Monitor*, p. 1. Thomas, Karen (2000, November 27). Stealing, dealing and Ritalin: Adults and students are involved in abuse of drug. *USA Today*, p. D1.

59. Green, P. M. and Stillman, M. J. (1998). Narcolepsy. Signs, symptoms, differential diagnosis, and management. *Archives of Family Medicine*, 7, 472–478. Ricks, Delthia (2005, August 4). Work nights? So does a pill, study says. *Newsday*, p. A2. Tuller, David (2002, January 8). A quiet revolution for those prone to nodding off. *New York Times*, p. F7.

60. Julien, Robert M. (1998). *A primer of drug action* (8th ed.). New York: Freeman, pp. 141–143.

chapter **5**

Narcotics: Opium, Heroin, and Synthetic Opiates

Mary, age sixteen, is a self-described "garbage head"—she will ingest anything she thinks will give her a high. Recently, her drug of choice has been OxyContin. She downs a few pills with a shot of vodka, calling the combination "the sorority girl's diet cocktail" because it allows for a stronger state of intoxication and has fewer calories than alcohol alone.

After Mary had a tonsillectomy, her surgeon wrote a prescription for eighty tablets of OxyContin for postoperative pain. Mary took sixty of them over the next two weeks, averaging five a day.

Presently, Mary is in substance abuse treatment, focusing on the problem of prescription medication abuse. When asked whether he had read Mary's medical chart detailing her history of substance abuse before prescribing OxyContin, instead of alternatives such as acetaminophen, Mary's surgeon replied, sheepishly, "Well, I guess I wasn't thinking."[1]

There is no escaping the love-hate relationship we have about opium and the opiates that are derived from it. Here is a family of drugs that has the astonishing power to banish pain from our lives and at the same time the power to enslave our minds.

This chapter will concern itself with the medical uses and recreational abuses of opiate-derived and opiate-related drugs. Together, these drugs are referred to as **narcotics** (from the Greek word for "stupor"), in that they produce a dreamlike effect on the user and at higher doses induce a state of sleep. The most important characteristic of narcotic drugs, however, is that they have powerful analgesic properties; they greatly reduce feelings of pain.

As noted in Chapter 2, the term "narcotic" often has been used inappropriately to mean *any* illicit psychoactive drug or at least any drug that causes some degree of dependence, including such unlikely examples as cocaine and amphetamine. Even today, the term can be misleading, because other drugs having no relationship to opium are far more effective in inducing sleep (see Chapter 8). Nonetheless, we are stuck with this inexact terminology; it is not likely to disappear anytime soon.

Narcotic drugs, in general, are divided into three major categories. The first includes **opium** and three natural components that can be extracted from it: morphine, codeine, and thebaine (Figure 5.1). The second category includes opium derivatives that are created by making slight changes in the chemical composition of morphine. The best example of this type is heroin. Although technically an opiate derivative, heroin is commonly included with morphine, codeine, and thebaine, and collectively all four chemicals, along with opium itself, are referred to simply as **opiates.** The third category includes synthetic drugs that are not chemically related to morphine or any of its derivatives but nonetheless produce opiate-like effects that are behaviorally indistin-

guishable from the effects of opiates themselves. Drugs of this type are commonly referred to as **synthetic opiates** or *synthetic opiate-like drugs.* This last category is a result of a continuing effort to discover drugs that achieve the same degree of analgesia as opiates but without the potential for abuse.

Opium in History

Like cocaine, the origins of heroin and other opiates go back to the fields of faraway times and places. This particular story begins with the harvesting of raw opium in remote villages of Myanmar (formerly Burma), Laos, Thailand, Afghanistan, Mexico, Colombia, Peru, and other countries where the weather is hot and labor is cheap. The source is the opium poppy, known by its botanical name as *Papaver somniferum* (literally "the poppy that brings sleep"), an annual plant growing three to four feet high. Its large flowers are typically about four or five inches in diameter and can be white, pink, red, or purple. This variety is the only type of poppy that produces opium; common garden plants such as the red Oriental poppy or the yellow California poppy look similar but do not produce psychoactive effects.

The present-day method of opium harvesting has not essentially changed for more than three thousand years. When the petals of the opium poppy have fallen but the seed capsule of the plant underneath the petals is not yet completely ripe, laborers make small, shallow incisions in the capsules, allowing a milky white juice to ooze out. The next day, this substance will have oxidized and hardened by contact with the air. At this point, now reddish brown and having a consistency of heavy syrup, it is collected, plant by plant, onto large poppy leaves. Later, it will darken further and form small gumlike balls that look like tar, taste bitter, and smell like new-mown hay.[2]

Opium was first described in specific detail in the early third century B.C., but we can be fairly sure that it was used for at least a thousand years before that. A ceramic opium pipe has been excavated in Cyprus, dating from the Late Bronze Age, about 1200 B.C. Cypriot vases from that era depict incised poppy capsules. From evidence contained in the Ebers Papyrus writings (see Chapter 2), Egyptians were knowledgeable about the medicinal value of opium.[3]

In the second century A.D., Claudius Galen, the famous Greek physician and surgeon to Roman gladiators, recommended opium for practically everything. He wrote that it

---

narcotics: A general term technically referring to opiate-related or opiate-derived drugs. It is often mistakenly used to include several other illicit drug categories as well.

opium: An analgesic and euphoriant drug acquired from the dried juice of the opium poppy.

opiates: Any ingredients of opium or chemical derivatives of these ingredients. Opiates generally refer to opium, morphine, codeine, thebaine, and heroin.

synthetic opiates: Synthetic drugs unrelated to morphine that produce opiate-like effects.

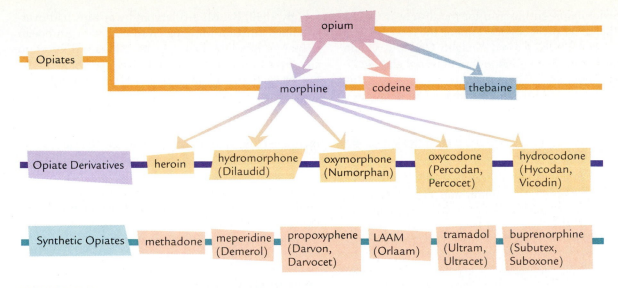

FIGURE 5.1

Major opiates, opiate derivatives, and synthetic opiates. (Note: Brand names are shown in parentheses.)

Sources: Physicians' desk reference (60th ed.) (2006). Montvale, NJ: Medical Economics Data. Raj, P. Prithvi (1996). *Pain medicine: A comprehensive review.* St. Louis: Mosby, pp. 126–153.

. . . resists poison and venomous bites, cures chronic headache, vertigo, deafness, apoplexy, dimness of sight, loss of voice, asthma, coughs of all kinds, spitting of blood, tightness of breath, colic, . . . jaundice, hardness of the spleen, . . . urinary complaints, fever, . . . leprosies, the troubles to which women are subject, melancholy, and all pestilences.[4]

Galen's enthusiasm for the instrumental use of opium is an early example of "over-prescribing." Interestingly, however, there are no records in ancient times that refer to the recreational use of opium, nor with any problems of opium dependence.[5]

Western Europe was introduced to opium in the eleventh and twelfth centuries by returning crusaders who had learned of it from the Arabs. At first, opium was used only by sorcerers as an ingredient in their potions. Later, during the first stirrings of modern medicine in Europe, opium began to be regarded as a therapeutic drug. In 1520, a physician named Paracelsus, promoting himself as the foremost medical authority of his day, introduced a medicinal drink combining opium, wine, and an assortment of spices. He called the mixture *laudanum* (derived from the Latin phrase meaning "something to be praised"), and before long the formula of Paracelsus was being called the stone of immortality. Even though Paracelsus himself denounced many of the doctrines of earlier physicians in history, he con-

tinued the time-honored tradition of recommending opium for practically every known disease.

In 1680, the English physician Thomas Sydenham, considered the father of clinical medicine, introduced a highly popular version of opium drink similar to that of Paracelsus, called Sydenham's Laudanum. For the next two hundred years or so, the acceptable form of taking opium among Europeans and later Americans would be in the form of a drink, either Sydenham's recipe or a host of variations.

A young harvester tends to his crop of opium poppies in the rugged mountains of Colombia.

Sydenham's enthusiasm for the drug was no less than that of his predecessors. "Among the remedies," he wrote, "which it has pleased Almighty God to give man to relieve his sufferings, none is so universal and so efficacious as opium."[6] The popularity of opium drinking eventually would lead to the emergence of opium as a recreational drug in Europe and the United States.

The Opium War

Sometime in the eighteenth century, China invented a novel form of opium use, opium smoking, which eventually became synonymous in the Western mind with China itself. However, for at least eight hundred years before that, the Chinese used opium only in a very limited way. They took it almost exclusively on a medicinal basis, consuming it orally in its raw state as a painkiller and treatment for diarrhea.

The picture changed dramatically in the eighteenth century for the basic reason that the British people had fallen in love with Chinese tea. British merchants wanted to buy tea and send it home, but what could they sell to China in exchange? The problem was that there were few, if any, commodities that China really wanted from the outside. In their eyes, the rest of the world was populated by "barbarians" with inferior cultures, offering little or nothing the Chinese people needed.

The answer was opium. In 1773, British forces had conquered Bengal Province in India and suddenly had a monopoly on raw opium. It was now easy to introduce opium to China as a major item of trade. Opium was successfully smuggled into China through local British and Portuguese merchants, allowing the British government and its official trade representative, the East India Company, to present a public image of not being directly involved in the opium trade. Huge quantities of opium, flooding into China from its southern port of Canton, found a ready market as a recreational drug in the form of opium smoking, and not surprisingly opium dependence soon became a major social problem. Despite repeated edicts by the Chinese emperor to reduce the use of opium within China or cut the supply line from India, the monster flourished.[7]

In 1839, tensions had reached a peak. In a historic act of defiance against the European powers, including Britain, an imperial commissioner appointed by the Chinese emperor to deal with the opium problem once and for all confiscated a shipment of opium and burned it publicly in Canton. Events escalated shortly after until open fighting between Chinese and British soldiers broke out. The Opium War had begun.

By 1842, British artillery and warships had overwhelmed a nation unprepared to deal with European firepower. In a humiliating treaty, China was forced to sign over to Britain the island of Hong Kong and its harbor (until the distant year of 1997), grant to British merchants exclusive trading rights in major Chinese ports, and pay a large amount of money to reimburse Britain for losses during the war. Despite these agreements, fighting broke out again between 1858 and 1860; this time the British soldiers and sailors were joined by French and American forces. Finally, in a treaty signed in 1860, China was required to legalize opium within its borders. The Opium War had succeeded in opening up the gates of China, much against its will, to the rest of the world.[8]

Opium in Britain

To the average Briton in the mid-1800s, the Opium War in China was purely a trade issue, with little or no direct impact upon his or her daily life. Nonetheless, opium itself was everywhere. The important difference between China and Britain with respect to opium was not in the *extent* of its consumption but in the *way* it was consumed. The acceptable form of opium use in Victorian England was opium drinking in the form of laudanum, whereas the Asian practice of opium smoking was linked to a perceived life-style of vice and degradation and associated with the very lowest fringes of society. The contrast was strikingly ironic. Opium dens, with all the evil connotations that the phrase has carried into modern times, were the places where opium was *smoked*; the respectable parlors of middle-class British families were the places where opium was *drunk*.

In a sense, opium was the aspirin of its day. Supplies were unlimited and cheaper than gin or beer; medical opinion was at most divided on the question of any potential harm; there was no negative public opinion and seldom any trouble with the police. As long as there were no signs of opium smoking, a chronic opium abuser was considered no worse than a drunkard. Nearly all infants and young children in Britain during this period were given opium, often from the day they were born. Dozens of laudanum-based patent medicines, with appealing names like Godfrey's Cordial, A Pennysworth of Peace, and Mrs. Winslow's Soothing Syrup, were used to dull teething pain or colic, or merely to keep the children quiet. The administration of opium to babies was particularly attractive in the new, industrial-age life-style of female workers, who had to leave their infants in the care of elderly women or young children when they went off to work in the factories.[9]

A nineteenth-century advertising card for Mrs. Winslow's Soothing Syrup, a popular opium remedy, was directed toward young mothers and their children.

Out of this climate of acceptance sprang a new cultural phenomenon: the opium-addict writer. Just as LSD and other hallucinogens were to be promoted in the 1960s as an avenue toward a greatly expanded level of creativity and imagination (see Chapter 6), a similar belief was spreading during this period with respect to opium. The leader of the movement was Thomas DeQuincey, and his book *Confessions of an English Opium Eater*, published in 1821, became the movement's bible. It is impossible to say how many people started to use opium recreationally as a direct result of reading DeQuincey's *Confessions*, but there is no doubt that the book made the practice fashionable.

Opium in the United States

In many ways, opium consumption in the United States paralleled its widespread use in Britain. In one survey of thirty-five Boston drugstores in 1888, 78 percent of the prescriptions that had been refilled three or more times contained opium. Opium poppies were cultivated in Vermont and New Hampshire, in Florida and Louisiana, and later in California and Arizona. It was not until 1942 that the growing of opium poppies was outlawed in the United States.

Women outnumbered men in opium use during the nineteenth century by as much as three to one. The principal reason for this gender difference lay in the social attitudes toward women at the time. Men could engage in the recreational use of alcohol in the time-honored macho tradition, but such use among women was not considered respectable. Only opium use, in the form of laudanum and similar products, was open to American women. As one researcher has expressed it, the consequence was that "husbands drank alcohol in the saloon; wives took opium at home."[10]

Throughout the 1800s, opium coexisted alongside alcohol, nicotine (in tobacco products), and cocaine as the dominant recreational drugs in America. As late as 1897, the Sears, Roebuck mail-order catalog was advertising laudanum for sale for about six cents an ounce, while other opium products were addressed specifically to the alcoholic. For example, Sears's "White Star Secret Liquor Cure" was advertised as designed to be added to the gentleman's after-dinner coffee so that he would be less inclined to join his friends at the local saloon. In effect, he would probably nearly fall asleep at the table, since the "cure" was opium. If customers became dependent on opium, perhaps as a result of the "liquor cure," fortunately they could order "A Cure for the Opium Habit," promoted on another page of the same catalog. Chances were good that the ingredients in this one included alcohol.[11] Opium habits often were replaced by cocaine habits (see Chapter 4) and vice versa.

Given the openness of opium drinking in the nineteenth-century United States, we can only surmise that the fanatical reaction against opium smoking was based on anti-Chinese prejudice. It is clear that intense hostility existed toward the thousands of Chinese men and boys brought to the West in the 1850s and 1860s to build the railroads. Since most of the Chinese workers were recruited from the Canton area, where opium trafficking was particularly intense, the practice of opium smoking was well known to them, and it served as a safety valve for an obviously oppressed society of men. In 1875 San

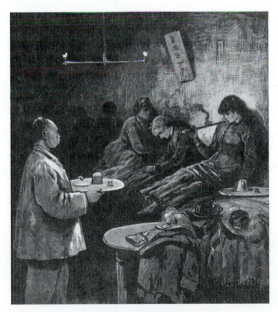

This late-nineteenth-century illustration of young working girls in a New York City opium den was part of a widespread media campaign at the time to outlaw the smoking of opium.

Francisco outlawed opium smoking for fear, to quote a newspaper of the time, that "many women and young girls, as well as young men of respectable family, were being induced to visit the dens, where they were ruined morally and otherwise."[12] No mention was ever made of any moral ruin arising from drinking opium at home.

A federal law forbidding opium smoking soon followed, whereas the regulation of opium use by any other means failed to receive legislative attention at that time. By the beginning of the twentieth century, however, the desire for social control of opium dens became overshadowed by the emergence of opium-related drugs that presented a substantially greater threat than smoked opium.[13]

Morphine and the Advent of Heroin

In 1803, a German drug clerk named Friedrich Wilhelm Adam Sertürner first isolated a yellowish white substance in raw opium that turned out to be its primary active ingredient. He called it morphium, later changed to **morphine,** in honor of Morpheus, the Greek god of dreams. For the first time, more than three-fourths of the total weight of opium (containing inactive resins, oils, and sugars) could be separated out and discarded. Morphine represented roughly 10 percent of the total weight of opium, but it was found to be roughly ten times stronger than raw opium. All the twenty-five or so opiate products that were eventually isolated from opium were found to be weaker than morphine and formed a far smaller proportion of opium. Besides morphine, other major opiate products were **codeine** (0.5 percent of raw opium) and **thebaine** (0.2 percent of raw opium), both of which were found to have a considerably weaker opiate effect.

In the scientific community, Sertürner's discovery was recognized as a major achievement of its time. It was not until 1856, however, with the invention of the hypodermic syringe, that morphine became a widely accepted medical drug. With the syringe it could be injected into the bloodstream rather than administered orally, bypassing the gastrointestinal tract and thus speeding the delivery of effects. The new potential of a morphine injection coincided with the traumas of the Civil War in the United States (1861–1865) and later the Franco-Prussian War in Europe (1870–1871).

Information about the syringe came too late for morphine injections to be widespread during the American conflict, but millions of opium pills and oral doses of morphine were distributed to soldiers injured in battle. It is not surprising that large numbers of soldiers became dependent on opiates and maintained the condition in the years that followed. After the Civil War, opiate dependence in general was so widespread among returning veterans that the condition was often called the "soldier's disease."[14]

Against the backdrop of increasing worry about opiate dependence, a new painkilling morphine derivative called **heroin** was introduced into the market in 1898 by the Bayer Company in Germany, the same company that had been highly successful in developing acetylsalicylic acid as an analgesic drug and marketing it as "Bayer's Aspirin." About three times stronger than morphine, and, strangely enough, believed initially to be free of morphine's dependence-producing properties, heroin (from the German *heroisch*, meaning "powerful") was hailed as an entirely safe cough suppressant (preferable to codeine) and as a medication to relieve the chest discomfort associated with pneumonia and tuberculosis. In retrospect, it is incredible that from 1895 to 1905, no fewer

morphine: The major active ingredient in opium.

codeine (COH-deen): One of the three active ingredients in opium, used primarily to treat coughing.

thebaine (THEE-bayn): One of three active ingredients in opium.

heroin: A chemical derivative of morphine. It is approximately three times as potent as morphine and a major drug of abuse.

Quick Concept Check 5.1

Understanding the History of Drugs

Check your understanding of the historical background for opiates and other psychoactive drugs discussed in earlier chapters by answering the following question. Imagine yourself to be living as a male adult in the year 1900. Check yes or no to indicate whether the following psychoactive drugs would be available to you.

1. heroin   ☐ yes   ☐ no
2. cocaine   ☐ yes   ☐ no
3. fentanyl   ☐ yes   ☐ no
4. d-amphetamine   ☐ yes   ☐ no
5. morphine   ☐ yes   ☐ no

Answers: 1. yes   2. yes   3. no   4. no   5. yes

than forty medical studies concerning injections of heroin failed to pick up on its potential for dependence! The abuse potential of heroin, which we now know exceeds that of morphine, was not fully recognized until as late as 1910.[15]

Why is heroin more potent than morphine? The answer lies in its chemical composition. Heroin consists of two acetyl groups joined to a basic morphine molecule. These attachments make heroin more fat-soluble and hence more rapidly absorbed into the brain. Once inside the brain, the two acetyl groups break off, making the effects of heroin chemically identical to that of morphine. One way of understanding the relationship between the two drugs is to imagine morphine as the contents inside a plain cardboard box and the heroin as the box with gift wrapping. The contents remain the same, but the wrapping increases the chances the box will be opened.

Opiates and Heroin in American Society

The end of the nineteenth century marked a turning point in the history of opium and its derivatives. Opiate dependence would never again be treated casually. By 1900, there were, by one conservative estimate, 250,000 opiate-dependent people in the United States, and the actual number could have been closer to 750,000 or more. If we rely upon the upper estimate, then we would be speaking of roughly one out of every hundred Americans, young or old, living at that time. Compare this figure with the 2006 estimate of 560,000 Americans (aged twelve or older) who have used heroin within the past year out of a current population nearly four times the population in 1900, and you can appreciate the impact opiate abuse was having on society in the early twentieth century.[16]

The size of the opiate-abusing population alone at that time probably would have been sufficient grounds for social reformers to seek some way of controlling these drugs, but there was also the growing fear that the problems of opiate abuse were becoming closely associated with criminal elements or the underworld. There was a gnawing anxiety that opiates were creating a significant disruption in American society. A movement began to build toward instituting some system of governmental regulation.

Opiate Use and Abuse after 1914

The Harrison Act of 1914 (see Chapter 2) radically changed the face of opiate use and abuse in the United States. It ushered in an era in which the abuser was

... no longer seen as a victim of drugs, an unfortunate with no place to turn and deserving of society's sympathy and help. He became instead a base, vile, degenerate who was weak and self-indulgent, who contaminated all he came in contact with and who deserved nothing short of condemnation and society's moral outrage and legal sanction.[17]

The situation, however, did not change overnight. Most important, the 1914 legislation did not actually ban opiate use. It simply required that doctors register with the Internal Revenue Service the opiate drugs (as well as cocaine and other coca products) that were being prescribed to their patients and pay a small fee for the right to prescribe such drugs. The real impact of the new law came later, in the early 1920s, as a result of several landmark decisions sent down from the U.S. Supreme Court. In effect, the decisions interpreted the Harrison Act more broadly. Under the Court's interpretation of the Harrison Act, no physician was permitted to prescribe opiate drugs for "nonmedical" use. In other words, it was now illegal for addicted individuals to obtain drugs merely to maintain their habit, even from a physician.

Without a legal source for their drugs, opiate abusers were forced to abandon opiates altogether or to turn to illegal means, and the drug dealer suddenly provided the only place where opiate drugs could be obtained. In 1924 a new law outlawed the importation of opium into the United States, if the opium was to be made into heroin. Since there was ordinarily no way of telling what the destination of imported opium might be, the presumption was always that its purpose was illegal. As a result, legitimate opium sources were cut off, and the importation of opium or any opium-related drug was now in the hands of the smuggler.

Heroin became the perfect black market drug. It was easier and more profitable to refine it from raw opium overseas and ship it into the country in small bags of odorless heroin powder than it was to transport raw opium with its characteristic odor. In addition, because it had to be obtained illegally, heroin's price tag skyrocketed to thirty to fifty times what it had cost when it was available from legitimate sources.[18]

With the emergence of restrictive legislation, the demographic picture also changed dramatically. No longer were the typical takers of narcotic drugs characterized as female, predominantly white, middle-aged, and middle-class, as likely to be living on a Nebraskan farm as in a Chicago townhouse. In their place were young, predominantly white, urban adult males, whose opiate drug of choice was intravenous heroin and whose drug supply was controlled by increasingly sophisticated crime organizations. In the minds of most Americans, heroin could be comfortably relegated to the fringes of society.[19]

Heroin Abuse in the 1960s and 1970s

Three major social developments in the 1960s brought the heroin story back into the mainstream of the United States. The first began in late 1961, when a crackdown on heroin smuggling resulted in a significant shortage of heroin on the street. The price of heroin suddenly increased, and heroin dosages became more adulterated than ever before. Predictably, the high costs of maintaining heroin dependence encouraged new levels of criminal behavior, particularly in urban ghettos. Heroin abuse soon imposed a cultural stranglehold on many African American and Latino communities in major U.S. cities.

A second development, beginning in the 1960s, affected the white majority more directly. Fanned by extensive media attention, a youthful counterculture of hippies, flower children, and the sexually liberated swept the country.

> *It was a time of unconventional fashions and anti-establishment attitudes. In unprecedented numbers, middle- and upper-class people experimented with illegal drugs to get high. They smoked marijuana; tried the new synthetic properties of amphetamines and barbiturates; rediscovered the almost forgotten product of the coca plant, cocaine; and, for the first time, people from the mainstream of American life began to experiment with derivatives of the opium poppy. Thus, heroin addiction made its insidious way back to the forefront of national concern.*[20]

Finally, disturbing news about heroin abuse began to appear that focused not only on Americans at home but also on American armed forces personnel stationed in Southeast Asia in connection with the Vietnam War. Faced with a combination of despair and boredom, a lack of definable military mission or objective, opposition at home to the conflict itself, and the unusual stresses of fighting a guerrilla war, many of these soldiers turned to psychoactive drugs as a way of coping. Reports beginning in the late 1960s indicated an increasingly widespread recreational abuse of heroin, along with alcohol, marijuana, and other drugs, among U.S. soldiers. One returning Vietnam veteran related the atmosphere of polydrug abuse at the time:

> *The last few months over there were unbelievable. My first tour there in '67, a few of our guys smoked*

Military involvement in Vietnam brought U.S. soldiers in contact with unusually potent doses of heroin and other psychoactive drugs.

> *grass, you know. Now the guys walk right in the hootch with a jar of heroin or cocaine. Almost pure stuff. Getting smack [heroin] is like getting a bottle of beer. Everybody sells it. Half my company is on the stuff.*[21]

With respect to heroin, the problem was exacerbated by the fact that Vietnamese heroin was 90 to 98 percent pure, compared to 2 to 10 percent pure in the United States at the time, and incredibly cheap to buy. A 250-mg dose of heroin, for example, could be purchased for $10, whereas the standard intravenous dose on the streets of a major U.S. city would amount to only 10 mg. A comparable 250 mg of highly diluted U.S. heroin would have cost about $500. With the purity of heroin supplies so high, most U.S. soldiers smoked or sniffed it to get an effect; some drank it mixed with alcohol, even though most of the drug was lost as it was filtered through the liver en route to the bloodstream.[22]

Beyond the concern about the soldiers overseas, there was also the worry that up to 100,000 Vietnam veterans would be returning home hopelessly dependent on heroin. It has been estimated from survey data that about 11 percent of Army returnees in 1971 were

the perspective of the heroin abuser. We have to be careful, however, to recognize that the specific effects are quite variable. The intensity of a response to heroin changes as a factor of (1) the quantity and purity of the heroin taken, (2) the route through which heroin is administered, (3) the interval since the previous dose of heroin, and (4) the degree of tolerance of the user to heroin itself. In addition, there are psychological factors related to the setting, circumstances, and expectations of the user that make an important difference in what an individual feels after taking heroin.[27] Nonetheless, there are several major effects that occur often enough to qualify as typical of the experience.

If heroin is injected intravenously, there is an almost immediate tingling sensation and sudden feeling of warmth in the lower abdomen, resembling a sexual orgasm, for the first minute or two. There is a feeling of intense euphoria, variously described as a "rush" or a "flash," followed later by a state of tranquil drowsiness that heroin abusers often call being "on the nod." During this period, lasting from three to four hours, any interest in sex is greatly diminished. In the case of male heroin abusers, the decline in sexual desire is due, at least in part, to the fact that narcotics reduce the levels of testosterone.[28]

An individual's first-time experience with heroin may be considerably unpleasant. Opiates in general cause nausea and vomiting, as the reflex centers in the brain are suddenly stimulated. Some first-time abusers find the vomiting so aversive that they never try the drug again; others consider the discomfort largely irrelevant because the euphoria is so powerful.

There are a number of additional physiological changes in the body. A sudden release of histamine in the bloodstream produces an often intense itching over the entire body and a reddening of the eyes. Heroin also will cause pupillary constriction, resulting in the characteristic "pinpoint pupils" that are used as an important diagnostic sign for narcotic abuse in general. As with sedative-hypnotic drugs (see Chapter 8), heroin also reduces the sensitivity of respiratory centers in the medulla to levels of carbon dioxide, resulting in a depression in breathing. At high doses, respiratory depression is a major risk factor that can result in death. Blood pressure is also depressed from heroin intake. Finally, a distressing, though nonlethal, effect of heroin is the slowing down of the gastrointestinal tract, causing a labored defecation and long-term constipation.[29]

How Opiates Work in the Brain

It is useful to view the neurochemical basis for a number of psychoactive drugs in terms of their influence upon specific neurotransmitters in the brain. For example, the stimulant effects of cocaine and amphetamine are related to changes in norepinephrine and dopamine (see Chapter 4). In the case of opiate drugs, however, as a result of major discoveries in the 1970s, it is clear that we are dealing with a more direct effect: the activation of receptors in the brain that are specifically sensitive to morphine.

During the 1960s, suspicions grew that a morphine-sensitive receptor, or a family of them, exists in the brain. One major clue came from the discovery that small chemical alterations in the morphine molecule would result in a group of new drugs with strange and intriguing properties. Not only would these drugs produce little or no *agonistic* effects—that is, they would not act like morphine—but they would instead act as *opiate antagonists*—that is, they would reverse or block the effects of morphine (Figure 5.2).

The most complete opiate antagonist to be identified, **naloxone** (brand name: Narcan), has turned out to

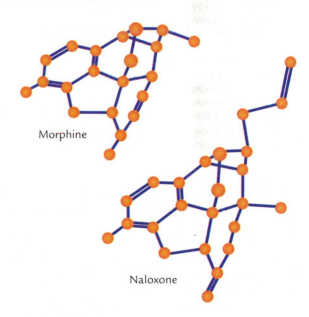

Morphine

Naloxone

FIGURE 5.2

Only minor differences exist between a morphine molecule and a naloxone molecule. Yet, naloxone is a complete antagonist to morphine.

naloxone (nah-LOX-ohn): A pure antagonist for morphine and other opiate drugs. Brand name is Narcan.

have enormous therapeutic benefits in the emergency treatment of narcotic-overdose patients. In such cases, intramuscular or intravenous injections of naloxone reverse the depressed breathing and blood pressure in a matter of a minute or so, an effect so fast that emergency department specialists view the reaction as "miraculous." The effect lasts for one to four hours. Higher doses of naloxone bring on symptoms that are similar to those observed following an abrupt withdrawal of narcotic drugs. Interestingly, in normal undrugged people, naloxone produces only negligible changes, either on a physiological or a psychological level. Only if morphine or other narcotic drugs are already in the body does naloxone have an effect.[30]

Beyond its practical application, the discovery of naloxone had theoretical implications as well. The argument went as follows: If such small molecular changes could so dramatically transform an agonist into an antagonist, then some receptor in the brain must exist in such a way that it can be easily excited or inhibited. The concept of a special morphine-sensitive receptor fulfilled these requirements.

The actual receptors themselves were discovered in 1973, precisely where you would have expected them to be: in the spinal cord and brain, where pain signals are known to be processed, and in the limbic system of the brain, where emotional behaviors are coordinated. In other words, it was clear that the analgesic and euphoric properties of morphine were due to stimulation of these receptors.

Why would these receptors exist in the first place? No one seriously considers the possibility that receptors in the brain have been patiently waiting millions of years in evolutionary history for the day that the juice of the opium poppy could finally slip inside them! The only logical answer is that we must be producing our own morphine-like chemicals that activate these receptors.

As a result of a series of important discoveries from 1975 to the early 1980s, three groups of natural morphine-like molecules have been identified: enkephalins, beta-endorphin, and dynorphins. Together, they are known as **endogenous opioid peptides,** inasmuch as they are (1) all peptide molecules (amino acids strung together like a

necklace), (2) opiate-like in function, and (3) produced within the nervous system. Unfortunately, this is such an unwieldy name that more frequently they are simply referred to as *endorphins.*

What can we then conclude about the effect of opiates on the brain? The answer, as we now understand it, is that the brain has the ability to produce its own "opiate-like" substances, called endorphins, and contains a special set of receptor sites to receive them. By an amazing quirk of fate, the opium poppy yields a similarly shaped chemical that fits into these receptor sites, thus producing equivalent psychological and physiological effects. Naloxone acts as an opiate antagonist because its structural features enable it to fit into these receptor sites, replacing the opiate molecules that have gotten in. The receptors themselves, however, are *inactivated* by naloxone. This is why naloxone can "undo" the acute effects of an opiate drug like heroin (Drugs . . . in Focus).

A long-acting form of naloxone, **naltrexone** (brand name: ReVia, previously marketed as Trexan), administered orally three times per week, has since been found to be a useful medication in the treatment of heroin abuse, mainly for patients who are highly motivated to stop their drug-taking behavior. Such patients include doctors, nurses, and other health professionals who must end a pattern of heroin abuse to retain their licenses and former heroin abusers on parole who are at risk of returning to prison if they suffer a relapse. Severe potential penalties need to be in place, should patients fall back into heroin abuse, because naltrexone has a major drawback as an agent for treatment: Naltrexone counteracts the powerful rewarding effects of heroin but does not help reduce the craving for it or the lingering effects of withdrawal.[31]

Patterns of Heroin Abuse

The dominant route of administration in heroin abuse is intravenous injection, usually referred to as either *mainlining* or *shooting.* Heroin also can be administered by a variety of other routes. Heroin smoking is popular in Middle Eastern countries and in Asia, but until very recently it has seldom been observed in the United States. Newcomers to heroin may begin their abuse either by snorting the drug through the nose or injecting it subcutaneously (skin-popping). Experienced heroin abusers may snort heroin to avoid using a needle or choose the subcutaneous route when they can no longer find veins in good enough condition to handle an intravenous injection. As mentioned earlier, an oral administration of heroin is

> **endogenous opioid peptides (en-DODGE-eh-nus OH-pee-oid PEP-tides)** also known as *endorphins:* A class of chemicals produced inside the body that mimic the effects of opiate drugs.
>
> **naltrexone (nal-TREX-ohn):** A long-lasting form of naloxone. Brand name prior to 1994 was Trexan, brand name has since been changed to ReVia.

Drugs... in Focus

Endorphins in Our Lives: A Psychosocial Perspective

From the discovery of endorphins in the 1970s, there emerged a new understanding not only of how pain is controlled in the brain but also of the role that opiate-like chemicals play in our daily lives. Here is a sampling of research findings that consider the psychosocial aspects of brain endorphins:

- *Pain and Stress.* Under stressful circumstances, people can become temporarily analgesic (relatively insensitive to pain) without the use of any external drugs. There are well-documented cases of soldiers who have ignored their injuries during the heat of battle, athletes who are unaware of their pain until the game is over, and individuals in primitive societies who endure painful religious rituals without complaint. Increased levels of endorphins may be a contributing factor in making these phenomena possible.

- *Acupuncture.* The Chinese technique of acupuncture, the inserting of needles into the skin at precisely defined points in the body, is completely reversible by naloxone. It is reasonable, therefore, to conclude that acupuncture produces increased levels of endorphins.

- *Labor and Childbirth Pain.* Endorphin levels measured in the placental bloodstream of pregnant women near to the time of childbirth are greatly elevated from levels normally present in nonpregnant women, reaching a peak during labor itself. It is believed that, as a result, women in labor are enduring less pain than they would have if endorphin levels were unchanged. Endorphins may protect them against an even greater amount of discomfort.

- *The "Runner's High."* Some studies have shown increased levels of endorphins among compulsive runners and other athletes. This increase could explain the euphoria, and in some instances analgesia, felt during strenuous physical exercise. Nonetheless,

there also are increased levels of adrenalin at the same time, which cannot be ruled out as contributing to this effect.

- *Anorexia.* Emaciated anorexic women have been found to have higher endorphin levels than control patients without anorexic symptoms. When body weight returns to normal, endorphin levels decline. Anorexic women often report feeling euphoric, particularly while engaging in physical exercise.

- *Chocolate Cravings.* Laboratory rats like chocolate, seemingly as much as humans do. In tasks in which they are trained to work for chocolate rewards, injections of naloxone make them less eager to perform the tasks. It is possible that at least a portion of the pleasure of eating chocolate is linked to the release of endorphins.

- *Separation Anxiety.* When morphine is administered to young animals, they become less inclined to cry when they are separated from their mothers. Naloxone, on the other hand, increases the incidence of separation cries. After low doses of morphine, pairs of rats are more inclined to engage in chasing, jostling, and "pinning" behaviors that constitute the rodent version of social play. Naloxone causes these behaviors to decrease. It is likely that endorphins serve to reinforce social attachment and other behaviors essential to the development of normal social interactions. Conversely, abnormal endorphin responses could contribute to the development of dysfunctional social behaviors.

Sources: Dum, J., and Herz, A. (1984). Endorphinergic modulation of neural reward systems indicated by behavioral changes. *Pharmacology, Biochemistry, and Behavior, 21,* 259–266. Panksepp, Jaak (2006). Emotional endorphenotypes in evolutionary psychiatry. *Progress in Neuropsychopharmacology and Psychiatry, 30,* 774–784. Levinthal, Charles F. (1988). *Messengers of Paradise: Opiates and the Brain. The struggle over pain, rage, uncertainty, and addiction.* New York: Anchor Press/Doubleday.

usually worthless because absorption is extremely poor. American soldiers in Vietnam who were abusing heroin often took the drug orally, but because of the extremely high purity of the heroin they were consuming, their effective dose levels merely equaled or only slightly exceeded levels found on American streets at the time (Drug Trafficking Update).

Tolerance and Withdrawal Symptoms

A prime feature of chronic heroin abuse is the tolerance that develops, but the tolerance effects themselves do not occur across the board with regard to all the responses commonly associated with heroin. Gastrointestinal effects of constipation and spasms do not show much tolerance at all, whereas the distinctive pupillary responses (the pinpoint feature of the eyes) eventually subside with chronic use. The greatest signs of tolerance are seen in the degree of analgesia, euphoria, and respiratory depression. The intense thrill of the intravenous injection will be noticeably lessened. The overall decline in heroin reactions, however, is dose-dependent. If the continuing dose level is high, then tolerance effects will be more dramatic than if the dose level is low.

The first sign of heroin withdrawal, a marked craving for another fix, generally begins about four to six hours after the previous dose and intensifies gradually to a peak over the next thirty-six to seventy-two hours, with other symptoms beginning from a few hours later (Table 5.1). The abuser is essentially over the withdrawal period in five to ten days, though mild physiological disturbances, chiefly elevations in blood pressure and heart rate, are observed as long as six months later. Generally, these long-term effects are associated with a gradual withdrawal from heroin rather than an abrupt one.

The overall severity of heroin-withdrawal symptoms is a function of the dosage levels of heroin that have been sustained. When dosage levels are in the "single digits" (less than 10 percent), the withdrawal symptoms are comparable to a moderate to intense case of the flu. In more severe cases, the withdrawal process can result in a significant loss of weight and body fluids. With recent increases in the purities of street heroin in the 1990s, the symptoms of withdrawal are greater. Only rarely, however, is the process of heroin withdrawal life threatening, unlike the withdrawal from barbiturate drugs (see Chapter 8).

TABLE 5.1

Symptoms of administering heroin and of withdrawing heroin

ADMINISTERING	WITHDRAWING
Lowered body temperature	Elevated body temperature
Decreased blood pressure	Increased blood pressure
Skin flushed and warm	Piloerection (gooseflesh)
Pupillary constriction	Tearing, runny nose
Constipation	Diarrhea
Respiratory depression	Yawning, panting, sneezing
Decreased sex drive	Spontaneous ejaculations and orgasms
Muscular relaxation	Restlessness, involuntary twitching and kicking movements*
Nodding, stupor	Insomnia
Analgesia	Pain and irritability
Euphoria and calm	Depression and anxiety

*Probably the source of the expression "kicking the habit."

Source: Adapted from Grilly, David M. (2006). *Drugs and human behavior* (5th ed.). Boston: Allyn and Bacon, p. 229.

It should not be surprising that withdrawal symptoms are essentially the mirror image of symptoms observed when a person is under the influence of heroin. If we are dealing with a group of endorphin-sensitive receptors that are, in the case of the heroin abuser, being stimulated by the opiates coming in from the outside, then it is reasonable to assume that over time, the production of endorphins would decline. Why produce stuff on your own when you are getting it from an external source? By that argument, withdrawal from heroin would then be a matter of cutting off those receptors from that external source, resulting in a reaction opposite to the one that would have occurred had the receptors been satisfied in the first place. Over a period of time, coinciding with the withdrawal period for a heroin abuser, we would expect that the normal production of endorphins would reestablish itself and there would be little or no need for the external supply of heroin.

The receptor explanation for heroin dependence sounds reasonable and does account for the presence of withdrawal symptoms, but unfortunately, it is an oversimplification for heroin abuse in general. We would expect that once the endorphin-sensitive receptors regain their natural supply of endorphins, heroin abuse should end, but we know that it does not.

In the case of heroin abusers, their tendency to continue taking heroin is propelled by a number of factors. There is, first of all, the combination of fear and distress associated with the prospect of experiencing withdrawal symptoms, along with a genuine craving for the effects themselves, reflecting the physical and psychological dependence that heroin brings.

In addition, as discussed in Chapter 1, long-term heroin abuse frequently produces such a powerful conditioned-learning effect that the social setting in which the drug-taking behavior has occurred takes on reinforcing properties of its own. Even the act of inserting a needle can become pleasurable. Some heroin abusers (called *needle freaks*) continue to insert needles into their skin and experience heroin-like effects even when there is no heroin in the syringe. In effect, the heroin abuser is responding to a placebo. Any long-term treatment for heroin abuse, as will be discussed in a later section, must address itself to a range of physical, psychological, and social factors to be successful.

The Lethality of Heroin Abuse

Considering the statistics of deaths and hospital emergencies associated with heroin abuse (see Chapter 1), you might be surprised that one would question the toxicity of heroin itself. To understand the toxicity of heroin, we first

Quick Concept Check 5.2

Understanding the Effects of Administering and Withdrawing Heroin

Without peeking at Table 5.1, check your understanding of the effects of heroin, relative to withdrawal symptoms, by noting whether the following symptoms are associated with administering heroin or withdrawing it.

SYMPTOM	ADMINISTERING	WITHDRAWING
1. coughing and sneezing		
2. skin flushed and warm		
3. decreased sex drive		
4. yawning and panting		
5. pain and irritability		
6. pupillary constriction		
7. increased blood pressure		
8. diarrhea		
9. analgesia		

Answers: 1. withdrawing   2. administering
3. administering   4. withdrawing   5. withdrawing
6. administering   7. withdrawing   8. withdrawing
9. administering

need to separate the effects of chronic heroin abuse from the drug's acute effects. From a long-term perspective with regard to one's physical health, heroin is considered relatively nontoxic, particularly when compared to several other drugs of abuse. As one expert has put it:

> Unlike alcohol, the amphetamines, and the barbiturates, which are toxic to the body over the long run with relatively heavy use, the narcotics are relatively safe. The organs are not damaged, destroyed, or even threatened by even a lifetime of narcotic addiction. There are no major malformations of the body, no tissue damage, no physical deterioration directly traceable to the use of any narcotic, including heroin.[32]

A notable exception, however, is found in the case of heroin administered through inhalation. Smoked heroin has been linked to leukoencephalopathy, an incurable neurological disease in which a progressive loss of muscle coordination can lead to paralysis and death, as well as kidney degeneration.[33]

On the other hand, it is abundantly clear that the practice of heroin abuse is highly dangerous and potentially lethal. The reasons have to do with situations resulting from the acute effects of the drug.

■ Heroin has a relatively small ratio of LD (lethal dose) to ED (effective dose). Increase a dose that produces a high in a heroin abuser by ten or fifteen times and you will be in the dosage range that is potentially fatal. As a result, death by overdose is an ever-present risk. If we take into account the virtually unknown potency of street heroin in any given fix, we can appreciate the hazards of a drug overdose. The "bag" sold to a heroin abuser may look like the same amount each time, but the actual heroin content could be anywhere from none at all to 90 percent. Therefore, it is easy to underestimate the amount of heroin being taken in.

■ The user risks possible adverse effects from any toxic substance that has been "cut" with the heroin. Adding to the complexity, deaths from heroin overdose are frequently consequences of synergistic combinations of heroin with other abused drugs such as stimulants like cocaine or depressants like alcohol, Valium, or barbiturates. In some cases, individuals have smoked crack as their primary drug of abuse and snorted heroin to ease the agitation associated with crack. In other cases, lines of cocaine and heroin are alternately inhaled in a single session, a practice referred to as "criss-crossing." In the DAWN reports (see Chapter 1), the combinations of heroin with cocaine or heroin with alcohol were frequently observed causes of heroin-related deaths. Relatively few heroin-related fatalities are due to the abuse of heroin alone. A listing of street names for heroin and heroin combinations is given in Table 5.2.

■ It is also possible that some heroin abusers develop unstable levels of tolerance that are tied to the environmental setting in which the heroin is administered. As a result of conditioned tolerance, a heroin dose experienced in an environment that has not been previously associated with drug taking may have a significantly greater effect on the abuser than the same dose taken in more familiar surroundings. Consequently, the specific effect on the abuser is highly unpredictable (see Chapter 1).

TABLE 5.2
Street names for narcotic drugs

TYPE OF NARCOTIC	STREET NAME
morphine	Big M, Miss Emma, white stuff, M, dope, hocus, unkle, stuff, morpho
white heroin	junk, smack, horse, scag, H, stuff, hard stuff, dope, boy, boot, blow, jolt, spike, slam
Mexican heroin	black tar, tootsie roll, chapapote (Spanish for "tar"), Mexican mud, peanut butter, poison, gummy balls, black jack
heroin combined with amphetamines	bombitas
heroin combined with cocaine	dynamite, speedball, whizbang, goofball
heroin combined with marijuana	atom bomb, A-bomb
heroin combined with cocaine and marijuana	Frisco special, Frisco speedball
heroin combined with cocaine and morphine	cotton brothers
codeine combined with Doriden (a nonbarbiturate sedative-hypnotic)	loads, four doors, hits

Sources: U.S. Department of Justice, Drug Enforcement Administration. (1986). *Special report: Black tar heroin in the United States*, p. 4. U.S. Department of Justice, Bureau of Justice Statistics Clearinghouse. (1992). *Drugs, crime, and the justice system*, pp. 24–25.

■ While the overriding danger of excessive amounts of heroin is the potentially lethal effects of respiratory depression, abusers can die from other physiological reactions. In some instances, death can come so quickly that the victims are found with a needle still in their veins, due to a massive release of histamine or an allergic reaction to some filler in the heroin to which the abuser was hypersensitive. Intravenous injections of heroin increase the risks of hepatitis or HIV infections, while unsterile water used in the mixing of heroin for these injections can be contaminated with bacteria.

■ An extra risk began to appear during the mid-1980s. In some forms of synthetic heroin illicitly produced in clandestine laboratories in the United States, manufacturers failed to remove an impurity called MPTP that destroys dopamine-sensitive neurons in the

The Secret and Dangerous Life of a Chipper

The man lives in a condo on the fashionable Upper East Side of Manhattan, drives an expensive car, takes vacations with his wife to Europe and the Caribbean, pulls down a six-figure salary as a company executive, and has been taking heroin for the last twenty years. Outwardly, he seems to have his life in firm control, and upon casual inspection he appears to be the model of the successful chipper. A closer look, however, reveals the elements of a struggle with forces he has yet to subdue.

His life has been an alternating cycle in which he would take heroin for a week or two, then stop for three weeks, and begin again. "For the first two weeks after I've stopped," he has said, "it does not occupy my thoughts in an overwhelming sense. But by the third week it is creeping in there and it just gets to the point when I want it. I

say: 'It's time. I've been good enough. I want my reward.' . . . The drug is an enhancement of my life. I see it as similar to a guy coming home and having a drink of alcohol."

Despite the facade of security, his life as a chipper is full of danger. After an overdose eleven years ago, he no longer injects his heroin, preferring to snort it from the corner of a credit card or the clip of a ballpoint pen. He buys his heroin from a friend who has been his supplier for years, but he runs the continual risk of being detected and losing his job. Sampling as potentially dependence-inducing a drug as heroin has to be an extremely risky business. One drug abuse expert has commented that it is a little like playing Russian roulette: "Not everyone will become addicted, but you can't predict who will and who won't."

Source: Treaster, Joseph B. (1992, July 22). Executive's secret struggle with heroin's powerful grip. *New York Times,* pp. A1, B4.

---

substantia nigra of the midbrain. As a result, young people exposed to this type of heroin acquired full-blown symptoms of Parkinson's disease that virtually identical in character to the symptoms observed in elderly patients suffering from a progressive loss of dopamine-sensitive neurons in their brains.

Heroin Abuse and Society

While society over the years has had to deal with the reality of drug abuse in many forms, many people still look upon heroin abuse as the ultimate drug addiction and the heroin abuser as the ultimate "dope addict." It is true that many heroin abusers fit this image: people driven to stay high on a four- to eight-hour schedule, committing a continuing series of predatory crimes.

Yet the actual picture of the present-day heroin abuser is more complex. A major study has shown that while robbery, burglary, and shoplifting accounted for 44 percent of an abuser's income and nearly two-thirds of that abuser's criminal income, a substantial amount of income came from either victimless crimes (such as pimping or prostitution) or noncriminal activity. Often a

heroin abuser would work in some capacity in the underground drug industry and be paid in heroin instead of dollars.[34]

A related question with regard to our image of the heroin abuser is whether controlled heroin abuse is possible. Is heroin abuse a situation that is, by definition, out of control? For most heroin abusers, the answer is yes. Yet for some individuals, heroin may not be a compulsion. The practice of controlled or paced heroin intake is referred to as **chipping,** and the occasional heroin abuser is known as a *chipper.*

An important study conducted by Norman E. Zinberg in 1984 analyzed a group of people who had been using heroin on a controlled basis for more than four years.[35] Over the course of one year, 23 percent reported taking heroin less than once a month, 36 percent reported taking it one to three times a month, and 41 percent reported taking it twice a week. Four years of exposure to heroin would seem to have been sufficient time to develop a compulsive dependence, but that did not happen. The observation that most compulsive heroin-dependent individuals never had any period of controlled use implies that controlled heroin abuse might not be

chipping: The taking of heroin on an occasional basis.

merely an early transitional stage that will eventually turn into uncontrolled heroin dependence.

The chipper and the classic heroin abuser seem to belong to two separate populations. What factors differentiate them? Zinberg's study showed that, unlike compulsive heroin abusers, occasional abusers tend to avoid heroin use in the presence of known addicts, rarely use heroin on a binge basis, and most often know the heroin dealer personally. Their motivations are different as well. Occasional abusers tend to use heroin for relaxation and recreation rather than to escape from difficulties in their lives or to reduce depression and anxiety (see Drugs...in Focus). From a behavioral standpoint the chipper appears to be avoiding the environmental influences (the social setting) that reinforce drug dependence.

While the Zinberg findings have provided support for the possibility of long-term heroin abuse on a controlled basis, newer evidence from studies of heroin abusers over more than three decades—a period of time much longer than that studied by Zinberg—indicates a somewhat darker scenario. A series of follow-up investigations during the 1970s, 1980s, and 1990s were carried out of nearly six hundred male heroin abusers who had been admitted to a compulsory drug-treatment program for heroin-dependent criminal offenders from 1962 to 1964. By 1996–1997, only 42 percent of the original sample, on average, about fifty-eight years old at the time, were available for interview. About 9 percent were of unknown status, and 49 percent had died. The most common cause of death (22 percent) was accidental poisoning from heroin adulterants or heroin overdose. Homicide, suicide, or accident accounted for 20 percent of the deaths, with the remainder being related to liver disease, cardiovascular disease, or cancer. Regarding the drug-taking behavior of the survivors, the researchers concluded that heroin dependence had been very difficult for them to avoid. As the principal investigator of the study has expressed it:

Although many of the survivors reported that they had been able to stop using heroin for extensive periods, fewer than half reported abstinence for periods of more than five years. Abstinence for five years sig-

nificantly reduced the likelihood of relapse, but even among those who achieved fifteen years of abstinence, a quarter still relapsed.[36]

Moreover, large proportions of these men were engaged in alcohol, cocaine, or amphetamine abuse as well.

Treatment for Heroin Abuse

For the heroin abuser seeking treatment for heroin dependence, the two primary difficulties are the short-term effects of heroin withdrawal and the long-term effects of heroin craving. Any successful treatment, therefore, must combine a short-term and long-term solution.

Opiate Detoxification

Traditionally, it has been possible to make the process of withdrawal from heroin, called **detoxification** ("detox"), less distressing to the abuser by reducing the level of heroin in a gradual fashion under medical supervision rather than by stopping "cold turkey" (a term inspired by the gooseflesh appearance of the abuser's skin during abrupt withdrawal). In medical settings, synthetic opiates such as **propoxyphene** (brand name: Darvon) or **methadone** have been administered to replace the heroin initially; then doses of these so-called transitional drugs are decreased over a period of two weeks or so.[37]

Methadone Maintenance

For the heroin abuser seeking out medical treatment for heroin dependence, the most immediate problem is getting the drug out of the abuser's system during detoxification with a minimum of discomfort and distress. As mentioned earlier, the naloxone and clonidine combination has been particularly important in speeding up withdrawal and reducing the severity of physiological symptoms.

After detoxification, however, the long-term problem of drug dependence remains. The craving for heroin persists, and the abuser most often has little choice but to return to a drug-oriented environment where the temptations to satisfy the craving still exist. Since the mid-1960s, one strategy has been to have a detoxified heroin abuser participate in a program in which oral administrations of the synthetic opiate methadone are essentially substituted for the injected

detoxification: The process of drug withdrawal in which the body is allowed to rid itself of the chemical effects of the drug in the bloodstream.

propoxyphene (pro-POX-ee-feen): A synthetic opiate useful in treating heroin abuse. Brand name is Darvon.

methadone: A synthetic opiate useful in treating heroin abuse.

heroin. This treatment approach, called **methadone maintenance,** was initiated in New York City through the joint efforts of Vincent Dole, a specialist in metabolic disorders, and Marie Nyswander, a psychiatrist whose interest had focused on narcotic dependence. Their idea was that if a legally and carefully controlled narcotic drug was available to heroin abusers on a regular basis, the craving for heroin would be eliminated, their drug-taking life-style would no longer be needed, and they could now turn to more appropriate social behaviors such as steady employment and a more stable family life.

For the Dole–Nyswander treatment program, now serving more than 100,000 former heroin abusers in the United States, methadone has definite advantages. First of all, since it is a legal, inexpensive narcotic drug (when dispensed through authorized drug-treatment centers), criminal activity involved in the purchase of heroin on the street can be avoided. Methadone is slower acting and more slowly metabolized so that, unlike heroin, its effects last approximately twenty-four hours and can be easily absorbed through an oral administration. Since it is a narcotic drug, methadone binds to the endorphin-sensitive receptors in the brain and prevents feelings of heroin craving, yet its slow action avoids the rush of a heroin high.

Typically, clients in the program come to the treatment center daily for an oral dose of methadone, dispensed in orange juice, and the dose is gradually increased to a maintenance level over a period of four to six weeks. The chances of an abuser turning away from illicit drug use are increased if the higher doses of methadone are made conditional upon a "clean" (drug-free) urinanalysis.[38]

The general philosophy behind maintenance programs is that heroin abuse is a metabolic disorder requiring a maintenance drug for the body, just as a diabetic patient needs a maintenance supply of insulin. In other words, the maintenance drug "normalizes" the drug abuser.

As a social experiment, methadone-maintenance programs have met with a mixture of success and failure. On the one hand, evaluations of this program have found that 71 percent of former heroin abusers who have stayed in methadone maintenance for a year or more have stopped intravenous drug taking, thus lessening the risk of AIDS. In a major study, drug-associated problems declined from about 80 percent to between 17 and 28 percent, criminal behavior was reduced from more than 20 percent to less than 10 percent, and there was a slight increase in permanent employment.[39] While attracting only a fraction of the heroin-dependent

community, methadone maintenance does attract those who perceive themselves as having a negligible chance of becoming abstinent on their own. It is reasonable to assume that we are looking at the potential rehabilitation of a hard-core subpopulation within heroin abusers.[40]

On the other hand, maintenance programs are not without problems. The first has to do with the moral question of opiate maintenance itself. Some critics have seen these treatments as a "cop-out" that perpetuates rather than discourages the sense of low self-esteem among heroin abusers, a system that serves the needs of society over the needs of the individual. Methadone programs, they argue, simply substitute one type of dependence with another, and the goal should eventually be abstinence from all drugs.[41]

Although maintenance programs do help many heroin abusers, particularly those who stay in the program over an extended period of time, there are strong indications that the programs do not help the overall vulnerability toward drug abuse in general. In other words, methadone blocks the yearning for heroin, but it is less effective in blocking the simple craving to get high. Alcohol abuse among methadone-maintenance clients, for example, ranges from 10 to 40 percent, suggesting that alcohol may be substituting for narcotics during the course of treatment, and one study found that as many as 43 percent of those who had successfully given up heroin had become dependent on alcohol. Cocaine and methamphetamine abuse can be problems as well. Unfortunately, urinanalysis tests may be scheduled too infrequently to allow identification of other patterns of drug abuse among clients in these programs.[42] Furthermore, methadone is sometimes diverted away from the clinics and onto the streets for illicit use. The availability of street methadone remains a matter of great concern.[43]

Alternative Maintenance Programs

Two alternative orally administered maintenance drugs for heroin abusers have been recently developed that may avoid the problems associated with the daily dosage approach of methadone programs. The first is the synthetic opiate **LAAM** (levo-alpha-acetylmethadol),

methadone maintenance: A treatment program for heroin abusers in which heroin is replaced by the long-term intake of methadone.

LAAM: A synthetic narcotic drug levo-alpha-acetyl-methadol used in the treatment of heroin abuse. Brand name is Orlaam.

marketed under the brand name Orlaam. The advantage of LAAM is a substantially longer duration, relative to methadone, so that treatment clients need to receive the drug only three times a week instead of every day.[44]

The second drug is the synthetic opiate **buprenorphine** (brand name: Subutex), also available as a three-times-a-week medication. Both medications have been shown to be useful in heroin-abuse treatment. To reduce the potential for buprenorphine tablets to be made into an injectable form and abused, buprenorphine is also available in combination with naloxone (brand name: Suboxone). If the tablets are crushed and dissolved into an injectable solution, the combined formulation triggers undesirable withdrawal symptoms.

The advantage of buprenorphine as a heroin-abuse treatment is that it can be prescribed by office-based physicians rather than being required to be dispensed through maintenance centers, as is the case with methadone or LAAM. When combined with naloxone, the abuse potential of buprenorphine is minimized and, while long-term blockage of opiate receptors occurs, there is less of an opiate "high."

Buprenorphine treatment substantially reduces the cost to public health clinics because it can be administered more widely in less-secured medical locations, such as primary care clinics and physicians' offices. It also reduces the inconvenience and stigmatization faced by treatment clients, particularly for teenage heroin abusers who would be disinclined to seek treatment at facilities that are associated with older people (Help Line, page 134).[45]

Behavioral and Social-Community Programs

To help deal with the tremendous social stresses that reinforce a continuation of heroin abuse, programs called **therapeutic communities** (Daytop Village, Samaritan Village, and Phoenix House are examples) have been developed, in which the abuser establishes

---

buprenorphine (BYOO-preh-NOR-feen): A synthetic opiate used in the treatment of heroin abuse. Brand names are Subutex and (in combination with naloxone) Suboxone.

therapeutic communities: Living environment for individuals in treatment for heroin and other drug abuse, where they learn social and psychological skills needed to lead a drug-free life.

multimodality programs: Treatment programs in which a combination of detoxification, psychotherapy, and group support is implemented.

---

temporary residence in a drug-free group setting and receives intensive counseling. Typically, counselors are former heroin abusers or former abusers of other drugs who have successfully given up drugs.

Other approaches have been developed that combine detoxification, treatment with naltrexone, psychotherapy, and vocational rehabilitation, under one comprehensive plan of action. These programs, called **multimodality programs,** are designed to focus simultaneously on the multitude of needs facing the heroin abuser, with the goal being a successful reintegration into society. As a continuing effort to help the recovering heroin abuser, there are also twelve-step group support programs such as Narcotics Anonymous, modeled after similar programs for those recovering from alcohol or cocaine dependence.[46]

Medical Uses of Narcotic Drugs

We have focused upon the acute effects of narcotic drugs in the context of heroin abuse, but it is also important to look at the beneficial effects that narcotic drugs can have in a medical setting (Table 5.3).

Beneficial Effects

Excluding heroin, which is a Schedule I drug in the United States and therefore unavailable even for medical use, narcotic drugs are administered with three primary therapeutic goals in mind: the relief of pain, the treatment of acute diarrhea, and the suppression of coughing. These applications are not at all new; they have been employed throughout the long history of opiate drugs.

The first and foremost medical use of narcotic drugs today is for the treatment of pain. For a patient suffering severe pain following surgical procedures or from burns or cancer, the traditional drug of choice has been morphine. Recently, pain treatment with fentanyl through a transdermal patch administration has been found to be more effective as an analgesic than morphine in an oral time-release administration. It is preferred by patients with chronic pain because the pain relief is achieved with less constipation and an enhanced quality of life.[47]

The second application capitalizes on the effect of opiates in slowing down peristaltic contractions in the intestines that occur as part of the digestive process. As noted earlier, one problem associated with the chronic abuse of heroin, as well as of other opiates, is constipation. However, for individuals with dysentery, a bacterial

TABLE 5.3

Major narcotic drugs in medical use

GENERIC NAME	BRAND NAME*	RECOMMENDED DOSE FOR ADULTS	GENERIC NAME	BRAND NAME*	RECOMMENDED DOSE FOR ADULTS
morphine	Avinza	30–120 mg (oral, combined immediate release, and time release)		Percocet	5 mg (oral) with acetaminophen
				Percodan	4.5 mg (oral) with aspirin
	Duramorph	5–10 mg (i.v.)	hydrocodone	Hycodan	5 mg (oral)
	Kadian	20–100 mg (oral, time release)		Vicodin	5 mg (oral) with acetaminophen
	MS Contin	15–200 mg (oral, time release)	methadone	Dolorphine	5–10 mg (oral, i.v., or s.c.)
			meperidine	Demerol	50–100 mg (oral, i.m., i.v.)
	Oromorph	15–100 mg (oral)	propoxyphene	Darvocet-N	50 mg (oral) with acetaminophen
	Oromorph SR	15–100 mg (oral, time release)			
				Darvon	65 mg (oral)
	Roxanol	10–30 mg (oral)	pentazocine	Talwin	12.5 mg (oral) with aspirin
codaine		30–60 mg (oral, i.m., or s.c.)	fentanyl	Duragesic	2.5–10 mg (time release by transdermal patch)
hydromorphone	Dilaudid	1–8 mg (oral, i.m., i.v., or s.c.)			
	Palladone	12–32 mg (oral, time release)		Actiq	"lollipop" form
			tramadol	Ultram	50–100 mg (oral)
oxymorphone	Numorphan	1–1.5 mg (i.m. or s.c.)		Ultracet	50–100 mg (oral) with acetaminophen
oxycodone	OxyContin	10–160 mg (oral, time release)			

*Only a portion of the brands are listed here. Some narcotic drugs are available only under their generic names or under either their generic or brand names.

Note: i.v. = intravenous; i.m. = intramuscular; s.c. = subcutaneous.

Source: Physicians' desk reference (61st ed.) (2007). Montvale, NJ: Medical Economics Data.

infection of the lower intestinal tract causing pain and severe diarrhea, this negative side effect becomes desirable. In fact, the control of diarrhea by morphine is literally life-saving, since acute dehydration (loss of water) from diarrhea frequently can be fatal. An added benefit is that it takes much less morphine to affect gastrointestinal activity than to produce analgesia, so dose levels can be smaller. A traditional treatment is the administration of a camphorated form of opium called **paregoric.**

The third application focuses on the effect of narcotic drugs to suppress the cough reflex center in the brain. In cases in which an **antitussive** (cough-suppressing) drug is necessary, codeine is frequently prescribed, either by itself or combined with other medications such as aspirin or acetaminophen (brand names: Tylenol, among others). As an alternative treatment for coughing, a nonaddictive, nonopiate drug, **dextromethorphan,** is available in over-the-counter syrups and lozenges as well as in combination with antihistamines. The "DM" designation in these cough-control preparations refers to dextromethorphan.

paregoric (PAIR-a-GORE-ik): A form of opium used medically for the control of gastrointestinal difficulties.

antitussive: Having an effect that controls coughing.

dextromethorphan (DEX-troh-meh-THOR-fan): A popular non-narcotic ingredient used in over-the-counter cough remedies.

Sustained-Release Buprenorphine: Ushering in a New Era

When buprenorphine (brand name: Subutex) and its combination with naloxone (brand name: Subuxone) were FDA-approved in 2002, a new era of heroin abuse treatment began. Since buprenorphine is only a partial activator of opiate-sensitive receptors in the brain, as opposed to full activators such as heroin and methadone, clients in treatment are more likely to discontinue their heroin intake without experiencing withdrawal symptoms, and the symptoms that do occur are considerably milder. At the same time, buprenorphine administration avoids the typical heroin effects of euphoria and respiratory depression. There is also no evidence of significant reduction of cognitive or motor performance in the course of long-term buprenorphine maintenance.

Typical buprenorphine therapy begins with an induction phase, in which buprenorphine is administered in a medically monitored setting following heroin abstention for 12–24 hours, while the individual is in the early stages of heroin withdrawal. In the stabilization and maintenance phases of treatment, buprenorphine dosage levels are adjusted on an individualized basis.

Two significant developments have, in recent years, expanded the social benefits of buprenorphine as a heroin-abuse treatment. First, a sustained-release version of buprenorphine, administered by injection at a treatment facility on a once-per-month basis, is now available. As a result, heroin abusers in treatment need to visit the physician's office only on a monthly basis. Second, new federal legislation enacted in 2007 allow certified physicians to treat up to 100 patients at any one time. Previous regulations had limited caseloads to no more than 30 patients.

Where to go for assistance:

www. buprenorphine. samhsa. gov/about. html

This web site, sponsored by the Substance Abuse and Mental Health Services Administration of the U.S. Department of Health and Human Services, provides extensive information on treatment options and a listing of available buprenorphine treatment locations. More than 800 physicians are certified for buprenorphine treatment in New York State alone.

Sources: Martin, Kimberly R. (2004, September). Once-a-month medication for heroin addiction? *NIDA Notes*, p. 9. Mitka, Mike (2003). Office-based primary care physicians called on to treat the "new" addict. *Journal of the American Medical Association, 290,* 735–738. Opioid detox study shows buprenorphine improves retention rate for teens (2005, October 10). *Alcoholism and Drug Abuse Weekly,* pp. 1–2. Substance Abuse and Mental Health Services Administration (2007, January/February). Buprenorphine: Patient limits increase. *SAMHSA Report,* p. 7.

Potential Adverse Effects

Given the many simultaneous effects of opiates on the body, it is natural that some concerns should be attached to their medical use, even though the overall effect is beneficial. For example, respiration will be depressed for four to five hours even following a therapeutic dose of morphine, so caution is advised when the patient suffers from asthma, emphysema, or pulmonary heart disease. Nausea and vomiting also can be a problem for patients receiving morphine, especially if they walk around immediately afterward. As a result, patients are advised to remain still, either sitting or lying down, for a short period following their medication. In addition, opiate medications decrease the secretion of hydrochloric acid in the stomach and reduce the pushing of food through the intestines, a condition that can lead to intestinal spasms. Finally, although opiates will have a sleep-inducing effect in high doses, it is not recommended that they be used as a general sedative-hypnotic treatment, unless sleep is being prevented by pain or coughing.[48]

Current Use and Abuse of OxyContin

Since the late 1990s, there has been a dramatic increase in cases in which prescription narcotic medications, developed with the intention to be used for the relief of pain, have been subject to abuse. While a variety of narcotic analgesics such as Vicodin, Darvon, Percodan, and Demerol have abuse potential, the most dramatic example has been the time-release form of oxycodone (brand name: **OxyContin**).

Since the drug was introduced in 1995, the availability of OxyContin has increased rapidly. This powerful

OxyContin: A time-release form of oxycodone, used in the treatment of chronic pain.

By 2000, Barry Tuttle's pain had become so excruciating that he was on the verge of suicide. A former salesman of plumbing supplies in North Plainfield, New Jersey, Tuttle (above left photo) had endured pulsating back pain for six years. Seven surgeries, endless doctor's appointments, thousands of pills, acupuncture, and other alternative treatments had all proved unsuccessful. When Tuttle began taking OxyContin, however, a relatively normal life-style returned. His perceived pain level (on a scale of 1 to 10, with 10 being the most horrible pain imaginable) was an acceptable 2 or 3—a dramatic improvement from his continual ratings of 8 or 9 before the advent of OxyContin. The drug had literally saved his life.

For every Barry Tuttle, however, there is a Russell Fitch (above right photo). Prescribed OxyContin following hip-replacement surgery, Fitch found that the drug was difficult to give up even after his recovery was complete. In 1999, this resident of rural Maine was convicted of selling guns to finance the purchase of a steady supply of OxyContin. In May 2001, while on parole for the firearms theft conviction, Fitch was charged with walking into a pharmacy with a gun and pushing a note across the counter that read: "Give me all your OxyContin or I will shoot you."

Fitch is not alone in his descent into criminal activity as a result of compulsive OxyContin abuse. Arrests have been made in all parts of the United States (the drug has been called the "rural heroin") for crimes ranging from simple theft to murder and drug trafficking, all related to the illicit abuse of this drug. At the same time, demands to remove OxyContin from the market until an abuse-reducing formulation is developed would return people like Barry Tuttle to a life of abject misery. From Tuttle's perspective, some individuals simply cannot handle any form of a powerful drug. Perhaps, in the absence of OxyContin, Fitch would have become dependent on something else. In Tuttle's words, "Drugs don't addict people. People addict people."

The problem is that it is difficult to predict which path a patient will follow. As a neurologist and pain-management specialist has expressed it, "A practicing physician has to be mindful that someone, even if they don't come with 'addict' written all over them, may be one. . . . The physician has to establish a relationship with the patient they're taking care of on a long-term basis."

Note: In May 2007, three top executives of Purdue Pharma, the company that makes OxyContin, pleaded guilty to criminal charges that, from 1995 to 2001, they had misled federal regulators, physicians, and patients about the potential for OxyContin to be an abused drug. The company agreed to $600 million in fines and other payments; the executives themselves were fined $34 million for their wrongdoing.

Sources: Adler, Jerry (2003, October 20). In the grip of a deeper pain. *Newsweek*, pp. 48–49. Meier, Barry (2003). *Pain killer: A "wonder" drug's trail of addiction and death.* New York: Rodale Press. Meier, Barry (2007, May 11). Narcotic maker guilty of deceit over marketing. *New York Times*, pp. A1, C4. Susman, Tina (2001, July 29). Good drug, bad drug: OxyContin eases pain, lures addicts. *Newsday*, pp. A6, A36. Quotations on p. A36.

analgesic drug for debilitating pain was promoted initially as being relatively safe from potential abuse and more acceptable to the general public because it lacked the social stigma associated with morphine. Its FDA-approved formulation permits OxyContin to be taken orally and absorbed slowly over a period of twelve hours, killing the pain without inducing a sudden feeling of euphoria. However, when OxyContin tablets are crushed and then either swallowed or inhaled as a powder, or injected after diluting the powder into a solution, the effect can be similar to that of heroin. Even with the prescribed formulation, some patients have suffered severe withdrawal symptoms, similar to those experienced during heroin withdrawal, when they abruptly stopped taking high-dosage levels of the medication. Since the mid-1990s, a dramatic increase in drug-related ED visits associated with narcotic analgesics (see Chapter 1) has been attributed largely to physical problems deriving from OxyContin abuse.[49]

OxyContin abusers vary widely across age groups, socioeconomic status levels, geographic locations, and gender. Particularly striking have been the outbreaks in the United States of OxyContin abuse and the criminal activity that is associated with obtaining it (when legitimate prescription access fails) in rural towns and small cities, places where traditional opiate-related abuse cases have been relatively rare. In 2006, almost 13 million Americans older than the age of twelve were estimated to have used a prescription pain reliever for nonmedical reasons in the past year. According to the University of Michigan survey, 4 percent of high-school seniors in 2006 reported nonmedical use of Oxycontin, and 10 percent reported nonmedical use of Vicodin during the previous

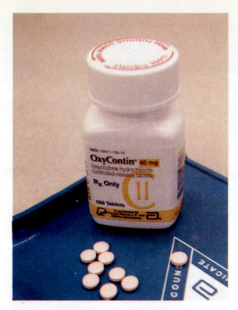

OxyContin pills. Generic versions of OxyContin (time-release oxycodone) were approved by the FDA in 2004. In 2006, approximately 1.3 million Americans older than twelve years of age reported taking OxyContin for nonmedical purposes over the past year.

year. Health officials suspect that the increased popularity of this form of drug abuse has been largely a response to the decreasing availability of Ecstasy (see Chapter 6).[50]

Recent efforts have been made to reduce Oxy-Contin abuse in a number of ways. An FDA-mandated warning label now states that the drug is as potentially addictive as morphine and that chewing, snorting, or injecting it could be lethal. Additionally, physicians are receiving special training in spotting potential abusers of narcotic analgesics in general. A reformulation, combining OxyContin and naloxone, is in development. In the future, if the tablet is crushed, instead of taken orally as an intact tablet, naloxone will be released and counteract the opiate-related effects. You may recall that a similar approach was taken in the case of one form of buprenorphine (Suboxone) to reduce its abuse potential. A limitation placed on the distribution of OxyContin as a medication, however, has been discouraged, since it would put into jeopardy hundreds of thousands of patients for whom OxyContin has been a godsend in their struggle with pain (see Portrait).[51] The dilemma of OxyContin use and its potential for abuse brings us back full circle to the ambivalence, mentioned at the opening of this chapter, that we feel about opiate-related drugs in general.

Summary

Opium in History

● A drug with a very long history, opium's medicinal and recreational uses stretch back approximately 5,000 years.

● During the nineteenth century, opium even figured in global politics as the instigating factor for the Opium War fought between China and Britain. At the time, opium use was widespread in Britain and the United States at all levels of society.

Morphine and the Advent of Heroin

● The discovery of morphine in 1803 as the principal active ingredient in opium revolutionized medical treatment of pain and chronic diseases.

● At the end of the nineteenth century, heroin was introduced by the Bayer Company in Germany. Initially, it was believed that heroin lacked the dependence-producing properties of morphine.

Opiates and Heroin in American Society

● The abuse potential of morphine and especially heroin was not fully realized until the beginning of the

twentieth century. Social and political developments in the United States after the passage of the Harrison Act in 1914 drove heroin underground, where it acquired a growing association with criminal life.

● Heroin abuse became associated with African American and other minority communities in urban ghettos after World War II; later, the drug revolution and the military involvement in Vietnam during the 1960s and 1970s brought the issues of heroin abuse to a wider population.

Effects on the Mind and the Body

● The effects of narcotic drugs such as heroin include euphoria, analgesia, gastrointestinal slowing, and respiratory depression.

● Respiratory depression is the major risk factor for heroin intake.

How Opiates Work in the Brain

● Since the 1970s, we have known that the effects of morphine and similar drugs are the result of the activation of morphine-sensitive receptors in the brain.

- Three families of chemical substances produced by the brain bind to these receptors. These chemicals are collectively known as endorphins.

Patterns of Heroin Abuse

- Chronic heroin abuse is subject to tolerance effects over time. Withdrawal effects include intense craving for heroin and physical symptoms such as diarrhea and dehydration.
- One of the major problems surrounding heroin abuse is the unpredictability in the content of a heroin dose.

Treatment for Heroin Abuse

- Treatment for heroin abuse includes short-term detoxification and long-term interventions addressing the continuing craving for the drug and physical dependence factors in the body.

- Methadone-maintenance programs focus primarily on the physiological needs of the heroin abuser, whereas therapeutic communities and support groups focus on a long-term reintegration into society.

Medical Uses of Narcotic Drugs

- In medical settings, narcotic drugs have been extremely helpful in the treatment of pain, in the treatment of dysentery, and in the suppression of coughing.
- Side effects of narcotic medication include respiratory depression, nausea, intestinal spasms, and sedation.
- There has been great concern since the late 1990s that narcotic analgesic medications have been diverted to nonmedical purposes and are subject to abuse. The most frequently abused drug of this type has been a time-release formulation of oxycodone (brand name: OxyContin).

Key Terms

antitussive, p. 133
black tar, p. 121
buprenorphine, p. 132
chipping, p. 129
codeine, p. 118
detoxification, p. 130
dextromethorphan, p. 133

endogenous opioid peptides, p. 124
fentanyl, p. 121
heroin, p. 118
LAAM, p. 131
methadone, p. 130
methadone maintenance, p. 131

morphine, p. 118
multimodality programs, p. 132
naloxone, p. 123
naltrexone, p. 124
narcotics, p. 114
opiates, p. 114
opium, p. 114

OxyContin, p. 134
paregoric, p. 133
propoxyphene, p. 130
synthetic opiates, p. 114
thebaine, p. 118
therapeutic communities, p. 132

Endnotes

1. Modified from Markel, Howard (2005, December 27). When teenagers abuse prescription drugs, the fault may be the doctor's. *New York Times*, p. F5.
2. Levinthal, Charles F. (1988). *Messengers of paradise: Opiates and the brain.* New York: Anchor Press/Double-day, p. 4.
3. Courtwright, David T. (2001). *Forces of habit: Drugs and the making of the modern world.* Cambridge MA: Harvard University Press, pp. 31–39. Merlin, M. D. (1984). *On the trail of the ancient opium poppy.* Cranbury, NJ: Associated University Press.
4. Scott, James M. (1969). *The white poppy: A history of opium.* New York: Funk and Wagnalls, p. 111.
5. Nencini, Paolo (1997). The rules of drug-taking: Wine and poppy derivatives in the ancient world. VIII. Lack of evidence of opium addiction. *Substance Use and Misuse,* 32, 1581–1586.
6. Levinthal, *Messengers of paradise*, pp. 3–25. Snyder, Solomon H. (1977). Opiate receptors and internal opiates. *Scientific American*, 236 (3), 44.
7. Beeching, Jack (1975). *The Chinese opium wars.* New York: Harcourt Brace Jovanovich, p. 23. Hanes, W. Travis III, and Sanello, Frank (2002). *The opium wars.* Napierville, IL: Sourcebooks.
8. Owen, David E. (1934). *British opium policy in China and India.* New Haven, CT: Yale University Press. Waley, Arthur (1958). *The opium war through Chinese eyes.* London: Allen and Unwin.
9. Fay, Peter W. (1975). *The opium war 1840–1842.* Chapel Hill: University of North Carolina Press, p. 11.
10. Brecher, Edward M., and the editors of *Consumer Reports* (1972). *Licit and illicit drugs.* Boston: Little, Brown, p. 17.

11. Kaplan, Eugene H., and Wieder, Herbert. (1974). *Drugs don't take people; people take drugs.* Secaucus, NJ: Lyle Stuart.
12. Brecher, *Licit and illicit drugs*, pp. 42–43.
13. Levinthal, *Messengers of paradise*, pp. 16–17.
14. Courtwright, David T. (1982). *Dark paradise: Opiate addiction in America before 1940.* Cambridge, MA: Harvard University Press, p. 47.
15. Inciardi, James A. (2002). *The war on drugs III.* Boston: Allyn and Bacon, p. 24. Terry, Charles E., and Pellens, Mildred. (1928/1970). *The opium problem.* Montclair, NJ: Patterson Smith.
16. Substance Abuse and Mental Health *Services Administration* (2007). *Results from the 2006 National Survey on Drug Use and Health: National findings.* Rockville, MD: Office of Applied Studies, Substance Abuse and Mental Health Services Administration, Table G.3.
17. Smith, Roger (1966). Status politics and the image of the addict. *Issues in Criminology*, 2 (2), 172–173.
18. Zackon, Fred (1986). *Heroin: The street narcotic.* New York: Chelsea House Publishers, p. 44.
19. McCoy, Alfred W., with Read, Cathleen B., and Adams, Leonard P. (1972). *The politics of heroin in southeast Asia.* New York: Harper and Row, pp. 5–6.
20. Zackon, *Heroin*, p. 45.
21. Bentel, David J., Crim, D., and Smith, David E. (1972). Drug abuse in combat: The crisis of drugs and addiction among American troops in Vietnam. In David E. Smith and George R. Gay (Eds.), *It's so good, don't even try it once: Heroin in perspective.* Englewood Cliffs, NJ: Prentice Hall, p. 58.
22. Karch, Steven B. (1996). *The pathology of drug abuse* (2nd ed.). Boca Raton, FL: CRC Press, p. 288. McCoy, *The politics of heroin*, pp. 220–221.
23. Robins, Lee N., David, Darlene H., and Goodwin, Donald W. (1974). Drug use by U.S. Army enlisted men in Vietnam: A follow-up on their return home. *American Journal of Epidemiology*, 99 (4), 235–249.
24. Greenhouse, Steven (1995, February 12). Heroin from Burmese surges as U.S. debates strategy. *New York Times*, p. 3.
25. Holloway, Lynette (1994, August 31). 13 heroin deaths spark wide police investigation. *New York Times*, pp. A1, B2. Leland, John (1996, August 26). The fear of heroin is shooting up. *Newsweek*, pp. 55–56. Quotation on p. 56.
26. Hernandez, Daisy (2003, May 23). Heroin's new generation: Young, white, and middle class. *New York Times*, p. 34. Johnston, Lloyd D.; O'Malley, Patrick M.; Bachman, Jerald G.; and Schulenberg, John E. (2007). *Monitoring the Future national results on adolescent drug use. Overview of key findings, 2006.* Bethesda, MD: National Institute on Drug Abuse, Table 1. Warrem (1996, October 26). Boycott groups: Klein ads carry scent of "heroin chic." *Christian Science Monitor*, p. 3. Thomson, Stephanie (2005, September 26). Heroin chic OK, cocaine use not. *Advertising Age*, pp. 3–4.
27. Winger, Gail, Hofmann, Frederick G., and Woods, James H. (1992). *A handbook on drug and alcohol abuse: The biomedical aspects.* New York: Oxford University Press, 1992, pp. 44–46.
28. Abel, Ernest L. (1985). *Psychoactive drugs and sex.* New York: Plenum Press, pp. 175–204.
29. Winger, Hofmann, and Woods, *Handbook on drug and alcohol abuse*, pp. 46–50.
30. Jaffe, Jerome H., and Martin, William M. (1985). Opioid analgesics and antagonists. In Alfred C. Gilman, Louis S. Goodman, Theodore W. Rall, and Ferid Murad (Eds.), *The pharmacological basis of therapeutics* (7th ed.). New York: Macmillan, pp. 491–531.
31. Levinthal, *Messengers of paradise*. Mathias, Robert (2003, March). New approaches seek to expand naltrexone use in heroin treatment. *NIDA Notes*, 17 (6), p. 8. Self, David W. (1998). Neural substrates of drug craving and relapse in drug addiction. *Annals of Medicine*, 30, 379–389.
32. Goode, Erich (1999). *Drugs in American society* (5th ed.). New York: McGraw-Hill, p. 328. Strang, J., Griffiths, P., and Gossop, M. (1997). Heroin smoking by "chasing the dragon": Origins and history. *Addiction*, 92, 673–684.
33. Karch, Steven B. (2002). *Pathology of drug abuse* (3rd ed.). Boca Raton, FL: CRC Press, p. 323.
34. Johnson, Bruce D.; Goldstein, Paul J.; Preble, Edward; Schmeidler, James; Lipton, Douglas S.; Spunt, Barry; and Miller, Thomas (1985). *Taking care of business: The economics of crime by heroin abusers.* Lexington, MA: Lexington Books.
35. Zinberg, Norman E. (1984). *Drug, set, and setting: The basis for controlled intoxicant use.* New Haven, CT: Yale University Press, pp. 46–81.
36. Hser, Yih-Ing; Hoffman, Valerie; Grella, Christine; and Anglin, M. Douglas (2001). A 33-year follow-up of narcotics addicts. *Archives of General Psychiatry*, 58, 503–508. Goode, Erica (2001, May 22). For users of heroin, decades of despair. *New York Times*, p. F5. National Institute on Drug Abuse (2001). 33-year study finds lifelong, lethal consequences of heroin addiction. *NIDA Notes*, 16 (4), 1, 5, 7. Quotation on p. 5.
37. Schuckit, Marc A. (1995). *Drug and alcohol abuse: A clinical guide to diagnosis and treatment* (4th ed.). New York: Plenum Press, pp. 155–162.
38. Stitzer, Maxine L.; Bickel, Warren K.; Bigelow, George E.; and Liebson, Ira A. (1986). Effect of methadone dose contingencies on urinalysis test results of polydrug-abusing methadone-maintenance patients. *Drug and Alcohol Dependence*, 18, 341–348.
39. Ball, John C.; Lange, W. Robert; Myers, C. Patrick; and Friedman, Samuel R. (1988). Reducing the risk of AIDS through methadone maintenance treatment. *Journal of Health and Social Behavior*, 29, 214–226. Maddux, James F., and Desmond, David P. (1997). Outcomes of methadone maintenance 1 year after admission. *Journal*

of *Drug Issues, 27,* 225–238. Rhoades, Howard M.; Creson, Dan; Elk, Ronith; Schmitz, Joy; and Grabowski, John (1998). Retention, HIV risk, and illicit drug use during treatment: Methadone dose and visit frequency. *American Journal of Public Health, 88,* 34–39. Sees, Karen L.; Delucchi, Kevin L.; Masson, Carmen; Rosen, Amy; Clark, H. Westley; Robillard, Helen; Banys, Peter; and Hall, Sharon M. (2000). Methadone maintenance vs 180-day psychosocially enriched detoxification for treatment of opioid dependence. *Journal of the American Medical Association, 283,* 1303–1310.

40. Hargreaves, William A. (1983). Methadone dose and duration for maintenance. In James R. Cooper, Fred Altman, Barry S. Brown, and Dorynne Czechowicz (Eds.), *Research on the treatment of narcotic addiction,* pp. 19–79. Kreek, Mary Jeanne (1991). Using methadone effectively: Achieving goals by application of laboratory, clinical, and evaluation research and by development of innovative programs. In Roy W. Pickens, Carl G. Leukefeld, and Charles R. Schuster (Eds.), *Improving drug abuse treatment* (NIDA Research Monograph 106), pp. 245–266.

41. Myerson, D.J. (1969). Methadone treatment of addicts. *New England Journal of Medicine, 281,* 380. Prendergast, Michael L., and Podus, Deborah (1999, May 10). Methadone debate reflects deep-rooted conflicts in field. *Alcoholism and Drug Abuse Weekly,* p. 5.

42. Kosten, Thomas R., Rounsaville, Bruce J., and Kleber, Herbert D. (1986). A 2.5 year follow-up of treatment retention and reentry among opioid addicts. *Journal of Substance Abuse Treatment, 3,* 181–189. Maddux, James F., and Desmond, David P. (1986). Relapse and recovery in substance abuse careers. In Frank M. Tims and Carl G. Leukefeld (Eds.), *Relapse and recovery in drug abuse* (NIDA Research Monograph 72). Rockville, MD: National Institute on Drug Abuse, pp. 49–71. Wasserman, David A.; Korcha, Rachel; Havassy, Barbara E.; and Hall, Sharon M. (1999). Detection of illicit opioid and cocaine use in methadone maintenance treatment. *American Journal of Drug and Alcohol Abuse, 25,* 561–571.

43. Faupel, Charles E. (1991). *Shooting dope: Career patterns of hard-core heroin users.* Gainesville: University of Florida Press, pp. 170–173. Gollnisch, Gernot (1997). Multiple predictors of illicit drug use in methadone maintenance clients. *Addictive Behaviors, 22,* 353–366. Substance Abuse and Mental Health Services Administration (2003, January). Narcotic analgesics. *The DAWN report.* Rockville, MD: Office of Applied Studies, Substance Abuse and Mental Health Services Administration, Figure 2. Substance Abuse and Mental Health Services Administration (2003). *Emergency department trends from the Drug Abuse Warning Network: Final estimates 1995–2002.* Rockville, MD: Office of Applied Studies, Substance Abuse and Mental Health Services Administration, Table 2.8.0.

44. Eissenberg, Thomas; Bigelow, George F.; Strain, Eric C.; Walsh, Sharon L.; Brooner, Robert K.; Stitzer, Maxine L.; and Johnson, Rolley E. (1997). Dose-related efficacy of levomethadryl acetate for treatment of opioid dependence: A randomized clinical trial. *Journal of the American Medical Association, 277,* 1945–1951.

45. Mitka, Mike (2003). Office-based primary care physicians called on to treat the "new" addict. *Journal of the American Medical Association, 290,* 735–738. Substance Abuse and Mental Health Services Association (2007, January/February). Buprenorphine: Patient limits increase. *SAMHSA Report,* p. 7.

46. Greenstein, Robert A., Fudala, Paul J., and O'Brien, Charles P. (1997). Alternative pharmacotherapies for opiate addiction. In Joyce H. Lowinson, Pedro Ruiz, Robert B. Millman, and John G. Langrod (Eds.), *Substance abuse: A comprehensive textbook* (3rd ed.). Baltimore, MD: Williams and Wilkins, pp. 415–425. Ward, Adrian; Kasinski, Kajetan; Pooley, Jane; and Worthington, Alan (Eds.) (2003). *Therapeutic communities for children and young people.* London: Kingsley Publishers.

47. Allan, Laurie; Hays, Helen; Jensen, Niels-Henrik; Le Polain de Waroux, Bernard; Bolt, Michiel; Royden, Donald; and Kalso, Eija (2001). Randomised crossover trial of transdermal fentanyl and sustained release oral morphine for treating chronic non-cancer pain. *British Medical Journal, 322,* 1154–1158.

48. Jaffe and Martin, Opioid analgesics and antagonists.

49. Kalb, Claudia (2001, April 9). Playing with pain killers. *Newsweek,* pp. 45–48. Meier, Barry, and Petersen, Melody (2001, March 5). Sales of painkiller grew rapidly but success brought a high cost. *New York Times,* pp. A1, A15. Rosenberg, Debra (2001, April 9). How one town got hooked. *Newsweek,* pp. 49–50. Tough, Paul (2001, July 29). The alchemy of OxyContin. *New York Times Magazine,* pp. 31–37, 52, 62–64.

50. Johnston, O'Malley, Bachman, and Schulenberg (2007), *Monitoring the Future national results,* Table 2. Leinwand, Donna (2005, April 22–24). Post-9/11 security cuts into Ecstasy: Youths turning to prescription drugs. *USA Today,* p. 1A. Leinwand, Donna (2005, April 22–24). Ecstasy's lost "its panache" among teens. *USA Today,* p. 3A. Drug and Alcohol Services Information System (2004, January 23). *The DASIS Report: Treatment admissions in urban and rural areas involving abuse of narcotic painkillers.* Washington DC: Office of Applied Studies, Substance Abuse and Mental Health Services Administration. Substance Abuse and Mental Health Services Administration (2007). *Results from the 2006 National Survey,* Table G.3.

51. Ammann, Melinda (2003, April). The agony and the ecstasy. *Reason,* pp. 28–34. Meier, Barry (2003, November 23). The delicate balance between pain and addiction. *New York Times,* pp. F1, F6.

chapter **6**

LSD and Other Hallucinogens

I was forced to interrupt my work in the laboratory in the middle of the afternoon and proceed home, being affected by a remarkable restlessness combined with a slight dizziness. At home I lay down and sank into a not unpleasant intoxicated-like condition, characterized by an extremely stimulated imagination. In a dreamlike state with eyes closed . . . I perceived an uninterrupted stream of fantastic pictures, extraordinary shapes with intense, kaleidoscopic play of colors.

—*Albert Hofmann, reflecting on his first encounter with LSD*
LSD: My Problem Child *(1980)*

After you have completed this chapter, you will understand

- The classification of hallucinogenic drugs
- The history of LSD
- Facts and fictions about LSD effects
- Prominent hallucinogens other than LSD
- The special dangers of MDMA (Ecstasy), phencyclidine (PCP), and ketamine

On an April afternoon in 1943, Albert Hofmann, a research chemist at Sandoz Pharmaceuticals in Basel, Switzerland, went home early from work, unaware that his fingertips had made contact with an extremely minute trace of a new synthetic chemical he had been testing that day. The chemical was **lysergic acid diethylamide (LSD)**, and as the opening passage indicates, Hofmann unknowingly experienced history's first "acid trip." Three days later, having pieced together the origin of his strange experience, he decided to try a more deliberate experiment. He chose a dose of 0.25 mg, a concentration that could not, so he thought, possibly be effective. His plan was to start with this dose and gradually increase it to see what would happen.

The dose Hofmann had considered inadequate was actually about five times greater than an average dose for LSD. As he later recalled his experience,

> My condition began to assume threatening forms Everything in my field of vision wavered and was distorted as if seen in a curved mirror. I also had the sensation of being unable to move from the spot.[1]

A little while later, his experience worsened:

> The dizziness and sensation of fainting became so strong at times that I could no longer hold myself erect, and had to lie down on a sofa. My surroundings had now transformed themselves in more terrifying ways. Everything in the room spun around, and the familiar objects and pieces of furniture assumed grotesque, threatening forms. . . . I was seized by the dreadful fear of going insane. I was taken to another place, another time.[2]

His experience then became pleasant:

> Kaleidoscopic, fantastic images surged in on me, alternating, variegated, opening and then closing themselves in circles and spirals. . . . It was particularly remarkable how every acoustic perception, such as the sound of a door handle or a passing automobile, became transformed into optical perceptions. Every sound generated a vividly changing image, with its own consistent form and color.[3]

Hofmann's vivid remembrances are presented here at length because they succinctly convey some of the major facets of a hallucinogenic drug experience: the distortions of visual images and body sense, the frightening reaction that often occurs when everyday reality is so dramatically changed, and the strange intermingling of visual and auditory sensations. These effects will be con-

sidered later in more detail as this chapter explores the bizarre world of hallucinogenic drugs.

Like many of the drugs that have been examined in the preceding chapters, hallucinogenic drugs such as LSD and several others have a story that belongs both in our contemporary culture and in the distant past. Hofmann worked in the modern facilities of an international pharmaceutical company, but the basic material on his laboratory bench was a fungus that has been around for millions of years. It has been estimated that as many as six thousand plant species around the world have some psychoactive properties.[4] This chapter will focus on a collection of special chemicals called *hallucinogenic drugs* or simply **hallucinogens**, often pharmacologically dissimilar to one another but with the common ability to distort perceptions and alter the user's sense of reality.

A Matter of Definition

Definitions are frequently reflections of the definer's attitude toward the thing that is being defined, and the terminology used to describe hallucinogens is no exception. For those viewing these drugs with a "positive spin," particularly for those who took LSD in the 1960s, hallucinogens have been described as *psychedelic*, meaning "mind-expanding" or "making the mind manifest." For others viewing these drugs with more alarm than acceptance, the popular descriptive adjectives have been *psychotomimetic*, meaning "having the appearance of a psychosis," *psychodysleptic*, meaning "mind-disrupting," or even worse, *psycholytic*, meaning "mind-dissolving." You can see that the description one chooses to use conveys a strong attitude, pro or con, with regard to these psychoactive substances.

As a result of all this emotional baggage, the description of these drugs as hallucinogenic, meaning "hallucination-producing," is probably the most even-handed way of defining their effects; that is the way they will be referred to in this chapter. Some problems, however, still need to be considered. Technically, a hallucination is the reported perception of something that does not physically exist. For example, a schizophrenic

lysergic acid diethylamide (LSD) (lye-SER-jik ASS-id di-ETH-il-la-mide): A synthetic, serotonin-related hallucinogenic drug.

hallucinogens (ha-LOO-sin-oh-jens): A class of drugs producing distortions in perception and body image at moderate doses.

might hear voices that no one else hears, and therefore we must conclude (at least the nonschizophrenic world must conclude) that such voices are not real. In the case of hallucinogens, the effect is more complicated because we are dealing with a perceived alteration in the existing physical environment. Some researchers have used the term *illusionogenic*, as a more accurate way of describing drugs that produce these kinds of experiences.

We also should be aware of another qualification when we use the term "hallucinogen." Many drugs that produce distinctive effects when taken at low to moderate dose levels turn out to produce hallucinations when the dose levels are extremely high. Examples of this phenomenon appeared in Chapter 4 with cocaine and amphetamines and will appear in Chapter 8 with inhalants. Here the category of hallucinogens will be limited to only those drugs that produce marked changes in perceived reality at relatively low dosages.

Classifying Hallucinogens

Most hallucinogens can be classified in terms of the particular neurotransmitter in the brain that bears a close resemblance to the molecular features of the drug. As shown in Table 6.1, hallucinogens fall into three principal categories: (1) those that are chemically similar to serotonin (LSD, psilocybin, morning glory seeds, DMT, and harmine), (2) those that are chemically similar to norepinephrine (mescaline, DOM, MDMA, and MDA), and (3) those that are chemically similar to acetylcholine (atropine, scopolamine, hyoscyamine, and ibotenic acid). In addition, a fourth category comprises a few hallucinogens (PCP and ketamine are examples) that are chemically unlike any known neurotransmitter; these drugs will be called miscellaneous hallucinogens. As Figure 6.1 indicates, several of these drugs have natural botanical origins.

TABLE 6.1

Major categories of hallucinogens

CATEGORY	SOURCE
Hallucinogens related to serotonin	
lysergic acid diethylamide (LSD)	a synthetic derivative of lysergic acid, which is, in turn, a component of ergot
psilocybin	various species of North American mushrooms
lysergic acid amide or morning glory seeds	morning glory seeds
dimethyltryptamine (DMT)	the bark resin of several varieties of trees and some nuts native to Central and South America
harmine	the bark of a South American vine
Hallucinogens related to norepinephrine	
mescaline	the peyote cactus in Mexico and the U.S. Southwest
2,5,-dimethoxy-4-methylamphetamine (DOM or more commonly STP)	a synthetic mescaline-like hallucinogen
MDMA (Ecstasy) and MDA	two synthetic hallucinogens
Hallucinogens related to acetylcholine	
atropine	*Atropa belladonna* plant, known as deadly nightshade, and the datura plant
scopolamine (hyoscine)	roots of the mandrake plant, henbane herb, and the datura plant
hyoscyamine	roots of the mandrake plant, henbane herb, and the datura plant
ibotenic acid	*Amanita muscaria* mushrooms
Miscellaneous hallucinogens	
phencyclidine (PCP)	a synthetic preparation, developed in 1963, referred to as angel dust
ketamine	a PCP-like hallucinogen

Source: Schultes, Richard E., and Hofmann, Albert (1979). *Plants of the gods: Origins of hallucinogenic use.* New York: McGraw-Hill.

FIGURE 6.1

Botanical sources for four hallucinogenic drugs: (a) *Claviceps tulasne* (ergot), (b) *Amanita muscaria* (ibotenic acid), (c) *Atropa belladonna* (atropine), (d) *Datura stramonium*, called jimsonweed (atropine, scopolamine, and hyoscyamine). They are shown the same size, when in actuality they are not.

Lysergic Acid Diethylamide (LSD)

The most widely known hallucinogen is LSD, which does not exist in nature but is synthetically derived from **ergot,** a fungus present in moldy rye and other grains. One of the compounds in ergot, lysergic acid, is highly toxic, inducing a condition called **ergotism.** Historians have surmised that widespread epidemics of ergotism (called St. Anthony's fire) occurred periodically in Europe during the Middle Ages, when extreme famine forced people to bake bread from infected grain (Drugs . . . in Focus).

In one particularly deadly episode in 944, an outbreak of ergotism claimed as many as forty thousand lives. The features of this calamity were two-fold. One form of ergotism produced a reduction in blood flow toward the extremities, leading to gangrene, burning pain, and the eventual loss of limbs. The other form produced a tingling sensation on the skin, convulsions, disordered thinking, and hallucinations.[5]

Even though the link between this strange affliction and ergot in moldy grain has been known since the 1700s, outbreaks of ergotism have continued to occur in recent times. A major one took place in a small French community in 1951. Hundreds of townspeople went totally mad on a single night:

> *Many of the most highly regarded citizens leaped from windows or jumped into the Rhône, screaming that their heads were made of copper, their bodies wrapped in snakes, their limbs swollen to gigantic size or shrunken to tiny appendages. . . . Animals went berserk. Dogs ripped bark from trees until their teeth fell out.*[6]

Albert Hofmann's professional interest in lysergic acid centered on its ability to reduce bleeding and increase contractions in smooth muscle, particularly the uterus. He was trying to find a nontoxic chemical version that would be useful in treating problems associated with childbirth. The LSD molecule was number twenty-five in a series of variations that Hofmann studied in 1938, and his creation was officially named LSD-25

ergot (ER-got): A fungus infecting rye and other grains.

ergotism: A physical and/or psychological disorder acquired by ingesting ergot-infected grains. One form of ergotism involves gangrene and eventual loss of limbs; the other form is associated with convulsions, disordered thinking, and hallucinations.

Strange Days in Salem: Witchcraft or Hallucinogens?

In the early months of 1692, in Salem, Massachusetts, eight young girls suddenly developed a combination of bizarre symptoms: disordered speech, odd body postures, and convulsive fits. They also began to accuse various townspeople of witchcraft. During the summer, in a series of trials, more than 150 people were convicted of being witches and 20 were executed. Accusations were also made in neighboring villages in the county and in Connecticut. Nothing approaching the magnitude of the Salem witch trials has since occurred in American history.

Over the years, a number of theories have attempted to account for these strange events: a case of adolescent pranks, general hysteria, or some kind of political scapegoating. An interesting and controversial speculation has been advanced that these girls were showing the hallucinogenic and convulsive symptoms of ergotism, acquired from fungus-infected rye grain. Arguments that support this theory include the following:

- Rye grain, once harvested, was stored in barns for months, and the unusually moist weather in the area that year could have promoted the growth of ergot

fungus during storage. Of twenty-two Salem households with some afflicted member, sixteen were located close to riverbanks or swamps.

- Children and teenagers would have been particularly vulnerable to ergotism because they ingest more food, and hence more poison, per body weight than do adults.

- The Salem girls as well as the accused "witches" frequently displayed hallucinatory behavior and physical symptoms common to convulsive ergotism.

The role of ergotism in the Salem witch trials of 1692 has been vigorously debated by both historians and pharmacologists. The readings listed below provide more information on this intriguing possibility.

Sources: In favor: Caporael, Linnda R. (1976). Ergotism: The Satan loosed in Salem? *Science, 192,* 21–26. Matossian, Mary K. (1982). Ergot and the Salem witchcraft affair. *American Scientist, 70,* 355–357. Matossian, Mary K. (1989). *Poisons of the past: Molds, epidemics, and history.* New Haven CT: Yale University Press, pp. 113–122. Against: Spanos, Nicholas P., and Gottlieb, Jack (1976). Ergotism and the Salem village witch trials. *Science, 194,* 1390–1394.

---

for that reason. He thought at the time that the compound had possibilities for medical use but went on to other pursuits, returning to it five years later in 1943, the year of his famous LSD experience.

The Beginning of the Psychedelic Era

Sandoz Pharmaceuticals applied for Food and Drug Administration (FDA) approval of LSD in 1953, and as was a common practice at the time, the company sent out samples of LSD to laboratories around the world for scientific study. The idea was that LSD might be helpful in the treatment of schizophrenia by allowing psychiatrists to gain insight into subconscious processes, which this drug supposedly unlocked. One of the researchers intrigued by the potential psychotherapeutic applications of LSD was the psychiatrist Humphrey Osmond of the University of Saskatchewan in Canada, who coined the word "psychedelic" to describe its effects and whose interest also extended to other hallucinogens such as mescaline.

In 1953, Osmond introduced the British writer Aldous Huxley to mescaline, and Huxley later reported his experiences, under Osmond's supervision, in his essay *The Doors of Experience.* Prior to 1960, LSD was being administered to humans under fairly limited circumstances, chiefly as part of research studies in psychiatric hospitals and psychotherapy sessions on the West Coast. As would be revealed later in court testimony in the 1970s, there were also top-secret experiments conducted by the Central Intelligence Agency (CIA), which was interested in LSD for possible application in espionage work. Word of its extraordinary effects, however, gradually spread to regions outside laboratories or hospitals. One of those who picked up on these events was a young clinical psychologist and lecturer at Harvard University named Timothy Leary.

Leary's first hallucinatory experience (in fact his first psychoactive drug experience of any kind, other than alcoholic intoxication) was in Mexico in 1960, when he ate some mushrooms containing the hallucinogen psilocybin. This is his recollection of his response:

> *During the next five hours, I was whirled through an experience which could be described in many extravagant metaphors but which was above all and without question the deepest religious experience of my life.*[7]

Back at Harvard, his revelations sparked the interest of a colleague, Richard Alpert (later to be known as Baba Ram Dass). The two men were soon holding psilocybin sessions with university students and whoever else was interested, on and off campus. At first these studies retained some semblance of scientific control. For example, a physician was on hand, and objective observers of behavior reported the reactions of the subjects. Later, these procedures were altered. Physicians were no longer invited to the sessions, and Leary himself began taking the drug at the same time. His argument was that he could communicate better with the subject during the drug experience, but his participation seriously undermined the scientific nature of the studies.

In 1961, Leary, Alpert, and other associates turned to LSD as the focus of their investigations, in their homes and other locations off the Harvard campus. Though these experiments were technically separate from the university itself, public relations concerns on the part of the academic community were mounting. Leary further aggravated the situation through his writings. In a 1962 article published in the *Bulletin of the Atomic Scientists*, he suggested that the Soviets could conceivably dump LSD into the water supply and, to prepare for such an attack, Americans should dump LSD into their own water supply so that citizens would then know what to expect. The U.S. government was not amused.

In 1963, after a Harvard investigation, Leary and Alpert were dismissed from their academic positions, making it the first time in the twentieth century that a Harvard faculty member had been fired. As you can imagine, such events brought enormous media exposure. Leary was now "Mr. LSD" (see Portrait), and suddenly the public became acquainted with a class of drugs that had been previously unknown to them.[8]

For the rest of the 1960s, LSD became not only a drug but also one of the symbols for the cultural revolt of a generation of youth against the perceived inadequacies of the established, older generation. Leary himself told his followers that they were "the wisest and holiest generation that the human race has ever seen" and advised them to "turn on to the scene, tune in to what's happening; and drop out—of high school, college, grade school . . . and follow me, the hard way."[9] The era has been described in this way:

> There were psychedelic churches, ashrams, rock festivals, light shows, posters, comic books and newspapers, psychedelic jargon and slang. Every middle-sized city had its enclaves, and there was a drug culture touring circuit. . . . Everyone had his own idea of what was meant by turning on, tuning in, and dropping out—his own set and setting—and the drug culture provided almost as many variations in doctrine, attitude, and way of life, from rational and sedate to lewd and violent, as the rest of society.[10]

To borrow the words of songwriter and singer Bob Dylan, "the times were a-changin'," but not always for the better. LSD became a battleground unto itself. In congressional hearings on LSD use by the nation's youth, scientists, health officials, and law-enforcement experts testified to a growing panic over the drug. Newspaper stories emphasized the dangers with alarmist headlines: "A monster in our midst—a drug called LSD" and "Thrill drug warps mind, kills," among them. Sandoz quietly allowed its LSD patent to lapse in 1966 and did everything it could to distance itself from the controversy. Hofmann himself called LSD his "problem child."

In 1966, LSD was made illegal, later becoming a Schedule I drug, with possession originally set as a misdemeanor and later upgraded to a felony. By the 1970s, LSD had become entrenched as a street drug, and taking LSD had become a component of the already dangerous world of illicit drugs. The story of LSD will be updated in a later section, but first

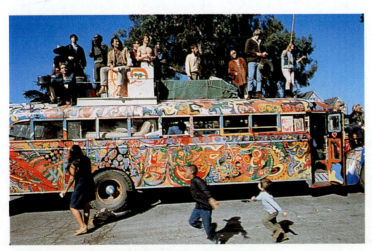

The multicolored images, inspired by the LSD experience, epitomized the psychedelic era of the 1960s.

it is important to understand the range of effects LSD typically produces.

Acute Effects of LSD

LSD is considered one of the most, if not *the* most, powerful psychoactive drugs known. Its potency is so great that effective dose levels have to be expressed in terms of micrograms, one-millionths of a gram, often called *mikes.* The typical street dose ranges from 50 to 150 micrograms, though sellers often claim that their product contains more. The effective dose can be as small as 10 micrograms, with only one-hundredth of a percent being absorbed into the brain. Compare these figures to the fact that a single regular-strength aspirin tablet contains 325,000 micrograms of aspirin, and you can appreciate the enormous potency of LSD.[11]

Taken orally, LSD is rapidly absorbed into the bloodstream and the brain, with effects beginning within thirty to sixty minutes. Once its concentration has peaked (in about ninety minutes), the elimination

half-life, or the time it takes for 50 percent of the drug to diminish in the bloodstream (see Chapter 1), is approximately three hours. Within five to twelve hours, LSD effects are over.[12]

Surprisingly, given its extreme potency, the toxicity of LSD is relatively low. Generalizing from studies of animals given varying doses of LSD, we can estimate that a lethal dose of LSD for humans would have to be roughly three hundred to six hundred times the effective dose, a fairly comfortable margin of safety. In 2005, the DAWN statistics showed that the ingestion of LSD represented about 0.1 percent of drug-related ED visits. To this day, there has been only one definitive case in which a death has been attributed solely to an LSD overdose.[13]

Street forms of LSD may contain color additives or adulterants with specific flavors, but the drug itself is odorless, tasteless, and colorless. LSD is sold on the street in single-dose "hits." It is typically swallowed in the form of powder pellets (microdots) or gelatin chips (windowpanes) or else licked off small squares of absorbent paper that have been soaked in liquid LSD (blotters). In the past, blotters soaked with LSD have been decorated with pictures of mystical symbols and signs, rocket ships, or representations of Mickey Mouse, Snoopy, Bart Simpson, or other popular cartoon characters.

LSD initially produces an excitation of the sympathetic autonomic activity: increased heart rate, elevated blood pressure, dilated pupils, and a slightly raised body temperature. There is an accompanying feeling of restlessness, euphoria, and a sensation that inner tension has been released. There may be laughing or crying, depending on one's expectations and the setting.[14]

Between thirty minutes and two hours later, a "psychedelic trip" begins, characterized by four distinctive features. The best way to describe these effects is in the words of individuals who have experienced them:[15]

- Images seen with the eyes closed.

   Closing my eyes, I saw millions of color droplets, like rain, like a shower of stars, all different colors.

- An intermingling of senses called **synesthesia**, which usually involves sounds appearing as hallucinatory visions.

Acid blotters with various designs.

I clapped my hands and saw sound waves passing before my eyes.

- Perception of a multilevel reality.

   I was sitting on a chair and I could see the molecules. I could see right through things to the molecules.

- Strange and exaggerated configurations of common objects or experiences.

   A towel falling off the edge of my tub looked like a giant lizard crawling down.

   When my girlfriend was peeling an orange for me, it was like she was ripping a small animal apart.

During the third and final phase, approximately three to five hours after first taking LSD, the following features begin to appear:

- Great swings in emotions or feelings of panic.

   It started off beautifully. I looked into a garden . . . and suddenly, it got terrible . . . and I started to cry. . . . And then, my attention wandered, and something else was happening, beautiful music was turned on. . . . Then suddenly I felt happy.

- A feeling of timelessness.

   Has an hour gone by since I last looked at the clock? Maybe it was a lifetime. Maybe it was no time at all.

- A feeling of ego disintegration, or a separation of one's mind from one's body.

   Boundaries between self and nonself evaporate, giving rise to a serene sense of being at one with the universe. I recall muttering to myself again and again, "All is one, all is one."

Whether these strong reactions result in a "good trip" or a "bad trip" depends heavily on the set of expectations for the drug, the setting or environment in which the LSD is experienced, and the overall psychological health of the individual.

Effects of LSD on the Brain

LSD closely resembles the molecular structure of serotonin. Therefore, it is not surprising that LSD should have effects on receptors in the brain that are sensitive

synesthesia: A subjective sensation in a modality other than the one being stimulated. An example is a visual experience when a sound is heard.

to serotonin (see Chapter 3). As a result of research in the 1980s, it turns out that the critical factor behind LSD's hallucinogenic effects lies in its ability to stimulate a special subtype of serotonin-sensitive receptors, commonly called S_{2A} receptors. In fact, all hallucinogens, even those drugs whose structures do not resemble serotonin, are linked together by the common ability to excite S_{2A} receptor sites. Drugs that specifically block S_{2A} receptors, leaving all other subtypes unchanged, will block the behavioral effects of hallucinogens. In addition, the ability of a particular drug to produce hallucinogenic effects is directly proportional to its ability to bind to S_{2A} receptors.[16]

Patterns of LSD Use

The enormous publicity surrounding Timothy Leary and his followers in the 1960s made LSD a household word. As many as fifty popular articles about LSD were published in major U.S. newspapers and magazines between March 1966 and February 1967 alone. By 1970, however, the media had lost interest, and hardly anything was appearing about LSD. Even so, while media attention was diminishing, the incidence of LSD abuse was steadily rising. In four Gallup Poll surveys conducted between 1967 and 1971, the percentage of college students reported to have taken LSD at least once in their lives rose dramatically from 1 to 18 percent.[17]

From the middle 1970s to the early 1990s, the numbers showed a steady decline. By 1986, the University of Michigan survey indicated that the lifetime incidence of LSD taking among high school seniors was 7 percent, down from 11 percent in 1975. By the end of the 1990s, prevalence rates were once again on the rise, reaching and later exceeding the levels of a quarter-century earlier. Since 1997, however, LSD use has declined substantially. About 3 percent of high school seniors in 2006 reported taking LSD at some time in their lives.

It should be noted that today's LSD users are different from those of a previous generation in a number of ways. Typical LSD users now take the drug less frequently and, because the dosage of street LSD is presently about one-fourth the level common to the 1960s and 1970s, they remain high for a briefer period of time. They also report using LSD simply to get high, rather than to explore alternative states of consciousness or gain a greater insight into life. For current users, LSD no longer has the symbolic or countercultural significance that it had in an earlier time.[18]

Facts and Fictions about LSD

Given the history of LSD use and the publicity about it, it is all the more important to look carefully at the facts about LSD and to unmask the myths. Six basic questions that are often asked about this drug are examined in the following sections.

Will LSD Produce a Dependence?

There are three major reasons why LSD is not likely to result in a drug dependence, despite the fact that the experience at times is quite pleasant.[19] First, LSD and other hallucinogens cause the body to build up a tolerance to their effects faster than any other drug category. As a result, one cannot remain on an LSD-induced high day after day, for an extended period of time. Second, LSD is not the drug for someone seeking an easy way to get high. As one drug expert has put it,

> The LSD experience requires a monumental effort. To go through eight hours of an LSD high—sensory bombardment, psychic turmoil, emotional insecurity, alternations of despair and bliss, one exploding insight upon the heels of another, images hurtling through the mind as fast as the spinning fruit of a slot machine—is draining and exhausting in the extreme.[20]

Third, the LSD experience seems to control the user rather than the other way around. It is virtually impossible to "come down" from LSD at will. Besides, the unpredictability of the LSD experience is an unpopular feature for those who would want a specific and reliable drug effect every time the drug is taken.

Will LSD Produce a Panic or a Psychosis?

One of the most notorious features of LSD is the possibility of a bad trip. Personal accounts abound of sweet, dreamlike states rapidly turning into nightmares. Perhaps the greatest risks are taken when a person is slipped a dose of LSD and begins to experience its effect without knowing that he or she has taken a drug. Panic reactions do occur, however, even when a person is fully aware of having taken LSD. Although the probability of having a bad trip is difficult to estimate, there are very few regular LSD abusers who have not experienced a bad trip or had a disturbing experience as part of an LSD trip. The best treatment for adverse effects is the companionship and reassurance of others throughout the period when LSD is active. Help Line includes some specific procedures for dealing with LSD panic episodes.

Despite the possibility of an LSD panic, there is no strong evidence that the panic will lead to a permanent psychiatric breakdown. Long-term psychiatric problems are relatively uncommon, with one study conducted in 1960 showing that there was no greater probability of a person's attempting suicide or developing a psychosis after taking LSD than when undergoing ordinary forms of psychotherapy.[21] The incidents that do occur typically involve people who were unaware that they were taking LSD, showed unstable personality characteristics prior to taking LSD, or were experiencing LSD under hostile or threatening circumstances.

The possible link between the character of LSD effects and symptoms of schizophrenia also has been examined closely. It is true that on a superficial level, the two behaviors show some similarities, but there are important differences. LSD hallucinations are primarily visual, best seen in the dark, and, as mentioned earlier, more accurately characterized as illusions or pseudohallucinations; schizophrenic hallucinations are primarily auditory, seen with open eyes, and qualify as true hallucinations. Individuals taking LSD are highly susceptible to suggestion and usually will try to communicate the experience to others; the schizophrenic individual is typically resistant to suggestion and withdrawn from his or her surroundings. Therefore, it is unlikely that LSD is mimicking the experience of schizophrenia.

Will LSD Increase Creativity?

The unusual visual effects of an LSD experience may lead you to assume that your creativity is enhanced, but the evidence indicates otherwise. Professional artists and musicians creating new works of art or songs while under the influence of LSD typically think that their creations are better than anything they have yet produced, but when the LSD has worn off, they are far less impressed. Controlled studies generally show that individuals under LSD *feel* that they are creative, but objective ratings do not show a significant difference from levels prior to the LSD.[22]

Will LSD Damage Chromosomes?

In March 1967, a study published in the prestigious scientific journal *Science* described a marked increase in chromosomal abnormalities in human white blood cells that had been treated with LSD in vitro (that is, the cells were outside the body at the time).[23] Shortly after, three other studies were reported in which chromosomal abnormalities in the white blood cells of LSD abusers were higher than those of people who did not use drugs, whereas three additional studies reported no chromosomal effect at all.

By the end of that year, a second study was published by the people whose report had started the controversy in the first place. They wrote that eighteen LSD abusers had two to four times the number of chromosomal abnormalities in their white blood cells, when compared with fourteen control subjects. Interestingly, the subjects in this study were not exactly model citizens. Every one of them had taken either one or more of amphetamines, barbiturates, cocaine, hallucinogens, opiates, or antipsychotic medication.

The picture was confused, to say the least. Not only were many of these studies unreplicable, but many were methodologically flawed as well. Most important, when studies actually looked at the chromosomes of *reproductive cells themselves* for signs of breakage from exposure to LSD, the results were either ambiguous or entirely negative. By 1971, after nearly a hundred studies had been carried out, the conclusion was that LSD did not cause chromosomal damage in human beings at normal doses, and that there was no evidence of a high rate of birth defects in the children of LSD users.[24] Yet, in the highly politicized climate of the late 1960s, the media tended to emphasize the negative findings without any scrutiny into their validity or relevance. The public image of LSD causing genetic damage still persists, despite the lack of scientific evidence. This is not to say, however, that there is no basis for exercising some degree of caution. Women should avoid LSD, as well as other psychoactive drugs, during pregnancy, especially in the first three months.[25]

Will LSD Have Residual (Flashback) Effects?

One of the most disturbing aspects of taking LSD is the possibility of reexperiencing the effects of the drug long after the drug has worn off, sometimes as long as several years later. These experiences are referred to as *hallucinogen persisting perception disorder*, or simply "flashbacks." The likelihood of LSD flashbacks is not precisely known. Some studies estimate its rate of incidence as only 5 percent, whereas others estimate it as high as 33 percent. It is reasonable to assume that the range of estimates is related to differences in the dosage levels ingested.

Flashback effects sometimes can be frightening and other times be quite pleasant; they can occur among LSD novices or "once-only" drug takers as well as among experienced LSD abusers. While they appear without warning, there is a higher probability that they will occur when the individual is beginning to go to sleep or has just entered a dark environment.[26]

Because they are not common to any other psychoactive drug, the reason why LSD flashbacks might occur is not well understood. It is possible that LSD has a peculiar ability to produce some biochemical changes that remain dormant for a period of time and then suddenly reappear or that some remnant of the drug has the ability to persist over extended periods of time. It is also possible that individuals who ingest LSD are highly suggestible to social reminders about the original exposure to LSD.

Whether LSD produces major long-term deficits in the behavior of the user remains largely unknown. Memory problems and visuospatial impairments have been reported in some studies but not confirmed in others. Unfortunately, several problems persist in research studies examining long-term effects of LSD. Often, they have included either individuals with a history of psychiatric disorders prior to LSD ingestion or regular users of other illicit drugs and alcohol. As a result, it has been impossible in these studies to tease apart the long-term effects of LSD alone.[27]

Will LSD Increase Criminal or Violent Behavior?

As will be noted in Chapter 13, it is very difficult to establish a clear cause-and-effect relationship between a drug and criminal or violent behavior. In the highly charged era of the 1960s, stories related to this question were publicized and conclusions were drawn without any careful examination of the actual facts. Take, for example, the 1964 case of a woman undergoing LSD therapy treatment who murdered her lover three days after her last LSD session.[28] The details of the case, overlooked by most subsequent media reports, reveal that the woman had been physically abused by the man, he had caused her to have an abortion, and the woman already had a serious mental disorder before going into treatment. The fact that the homicide took place well after the LSD had left her body indicates that the murder was not pharmacologically based (see Chapter 13). Other cases in which violent behavior appeared to be associated with an LSD experience turned out in fact to be associated with the use of other hallucinogenic drugs.

It is possible, however, that an individual can "freak out" on LSD. The effects of a euphoriant drug such as LSD can lead to a feeling of invulnerability. This feeling, in turn, can lead to dangerous and possibly life-threatening behavior. While we cannot reliably estimate the likelihood of these effects or pinpoint the circumstances under which they might occur, we should recognize that psychological reactions to LSD are inherently unpredictable, and caution is advised.

Psilocybin and Other Hallucinogens Related to Serotonin

The source of the drug **psilocybin** is a family of mushrooms native to southern Mexico and Central America. Spanish chroniclers in the sixteenth century wrote of "sacred mushrooms" revered by the Aztecs as *teonanacatl* (roughly translated as "God's flesh") and capable of providing extraordinary visions when eaten. Their psychoactive properties had been known for a long time, judging from stone-carved representations of these mushrooms discovered in El Salvador and dating back to as early as 500 B.C. Today, shamans in remote villages in Mexico and Central America (see Chapter 2) continue the use of psilocybin mushrooms, among other hallucinogenic plants, to provide healing on both physical and spiritual levels.[29]

Native use of these mushrooms disappeared from historical accounts until the late 1930s, when several varieties were identified. In 1955, a group of Western observers documented the hallucinogenic effects of the *Psilocybe mexicana* in a native community living in a remote mountainous region of southern Mexico. Three years later, samples worked their way to Switzerland, where Albert Hofmann, already known for his work on LSD, identified the active ingredient and named it

Psilocybe mexicana mushrooms, the source of psilocybin.

psilocybin. As was his habit, Hofmann sampled some of the mushrooms himself and wrote later of his reactions:

> *Thirty minutes after my taking the mushrooms, the exterior world began to undergo a Mexican character. . . . I saw only Mexican motifs and colors. When the doctor supervising the experiment bent over me to check my blood pressure, he was transformed into an Aztec priest.*[30]

We can never know whether the Aztec character of these hallucinogenic effects was a result of suggestion or that Aztec designs may have been inspired over the centuries by the effects of psilocybin.

Once ingested, psilocybin loses a portion of its molecule, making it more fat-soluble and more easily absorbed into the brain. This new version, called **psilocin,** is the actual agent that works on the brain. Since LSD and psilocin are chemically similar, the biochemical effects are also similar. Cross-tolerance will occur (see Chapter 1). If you develop a tolerance to LSD, you have become tolerant to psilocybin effects, and vice versa.[31]

Far less potent than LSD, psilocybin is effective at dose levels measured in the more traditional units of milligrams rather than micrograms. At doses of 4 to 5 mg, psilocybin causes a pleasant, relaxing feeling; at doses of 15 mg and more, hallucinations, time distortions, and changes in body perception appear. A psilocybin trip generally lasts from two to five hours, considerably shorter than an LSD trip.

Individuals who have experienced both kinds of hallucinogens report that, relative to LSD, psilocybin produces effects that are more strongly visual, less emotionally intense, and more euphoric, with fewer panic reactions and less chance of paranoia. On the other hand, experimental studies of volunteers taking high doses of psilocybin have established that the drug produces drastic enough changes in mood, sensory perception, and thought processes to qualify as a psychotic experience.

As with LSD, psilocybin (often called simply "shrooms") has become relatively easy to obtain as a drug of abuse. In 2006, about 44 percent of high school seniors reported that non-LSD hallucinogens (including "shrooms") were "fairly easy" or "very easy" to get, whereas about 29 percent felt the same way about LSD itself.[32]

psilocybin (SIL-oh-SIGH-bin): A serotonin-related hallucinogenic drug originating from a species of mushrooms.

psilocin (SIL-oh-sin): A brain chemical related to serotonin, resulting from the ingestion of psilocybin.

Drugs . . . in Focus

Bufotenine and the *Bufo* Toad

Bufotenine is a drug with a strange past. Found in a family of beans native to Central and South America, bufotenine is better known as a chemical that can be isolated from the skin and glands of the *Bufo* toad, from which it gets its name. As noted in Chapter 2, *Bufo* toads figured prominently in the magical potions of European witches. Evidence also exists that *Bufo* toads were incorporated into the ceremonial rituals of ancient Aztec and Mayan cultures. Largely as a result of these historical references, it has been widely assumed that bufotenine was the primary contributor to the psychoactive effects of these concoctions and that bufotenine itself is a powerful hallucinogen.

It turns out that these conclusions are wrong. The few studies in which human volunteers were administered bufotenine indicate that the substance induces strong excitatory effects on blood pressure and heart rate but no hallucinatory experiences. Some subjects report distorted images with high dosages of the drug, but this might well occur as oxygen is cut off from parts of the body, particularly the optic nerve carrying visual information to the brain. It is likely that whatever hallucinogenic effects *Bufo* toads may produce are brought on by another chemical also found in these toads that functions similarly to the hallucinogen DMT.

Despite the confusion as to which substance is responsible for its psychoactive properties, *Bufo* toads continue to fascinate the public. Wildly exaggerated and frequently unsubstantiated accounts of "toad licking" and "toad smoking" periodically circulate in the media. Reportedly, a small group calling themselves Amphibians Anonymous was formed in the late 1980s; the group's motto was "Never has it been so easy to just say no."

The bottom line, however, is that the dangers of consuming toad tissue are substantial. Besides the extreme cardiovascular reactions, toxic effects include a skin condition called **cyanosis** (literally, "turning blue"). Actually, the description may be an understatement. Skin color has been observed to be closer to an eggplant purple.

Sources: Horgan, J. (1990, August). Bufo abuse. *Scientific American*, pp. 26–27. Iniardi, James A. (2002). *The war on drugs III*. Boston: Allyn and Bacon, pp. 4–5. Lyttle, Thomas, Goldstein, David, and Gartz Jochen (1996). Bufo toads and bufotenine: Fact and fiction surrounding an alleged psychedelic. *Journal of Psychoactive Drugs, 28,* 267–290.

Lysergic Acid Amide (LAA)

In addition to their reverence for psilocybin mushrooms, the Aztecs ingested locally grown morning glory seeds, calling them *ololuiqui*, and used their hallucinogenic effects in religious rites and healing. Like many Native American practices, the recreational use of morning glory seeds has survived in remote areas of southern Mexico. In 1961, Albert Hofmann (once again) identified the active ingredient in these seeds as **lysergic acid amide (LAA)**, after having sampled its hallucinogenic properties. As the chemical name suggests, this drug is a close relative to LSD.

The LAA experience, judging from Hofmann's report, is similar to that of LSD, though LAA is only one-tenth to one-thirtieth as potent and the hallucinations tend to be dominated by auditory rather than visual images. Commercial varieties of morning glory seeds are available to the public, but suppliers have taken the precaution of coating them with an additive that causes nausea and vomiting, if eaten, to minimize their abuse.[33]

bufotenine (byoo-FOT-eh-neen): A serotonin-related drug obtained either from a bean plant in Central and South America or the skin of a particular type of toad.

cyanosis (SIGH-ah-NOH-sis): A tendency for the skin to turn bluish purple. It can be a side effect of the drug bufotenine.

lysergic acid amide (LAA) (lye-SER-jik ASS-id A-mide): A hallucinogenic drug found in morning glory seeds, producing effects similar to those of LSD.

dimethyltryptamine (DMT) (dye-METH-il-TRIP-ta-meen): A short-acting hallucinogenic drug.

Dimethyltryptamine (DMT)

The drug **dimethyltryptamine (DMT)** is obtained chiefly from the resin of the bark of trees and nuts native to the West Indies as well as to Central and South America, where it is generally inhaled as a snuff. An oral administration does not produce psychoactive effects. The similarity of this drug's effects to those of

LSD and its very short duration gave DMT the reputation during the psychedelic years of the 1960s of being "the businessman's LSD." Presumably, someone could take a DMT trip during lunch and be back at the office in time for work in the afternoon.

An inhaled 30 mg dose of DMT produces physiological changes within ten seconds, with hallucinogenic effects peaking around ten to fifteen minutes later. Paranoia, anxiety, and panic also can result at this time, but most symptoms are over in about an hour.[34] A chemical found in *Bufo* toads is similar to DMT (see Drugs...in Focus, page 152).

Harmine

Among native tribes in the western Amazon region of South America, the bark of the *Banisteriopsis* vine yields the powerful drug **harmine**. A drink containing harmine, called *ayahuasca*, is frequently used by local shamans for healing rites. It is chemically similar to serotonin, like LSD and the other hallucinogens examined so far. Its psychological effects, however, are somewhat different. Unlike LSD, harmine makes the individual withdraw into a trance, and the hallucinatory images (often visions of animals and supernatural beings) are experienced within the context of a dreamlike state. Reports among shamans refer to a sense of suspension in space or flying, falling into one's body, or experiencing one's own death.[35]

Hallucinogens Related to Norepinephrine

Several types of hallucinogens have a chemical composition similar to norepinephrine. As you may recall from Chapter 4, amphetamines are also chemically similar to norepinephrine. Consequently, sometimes norepinephrine-related hallucinogens will produce amphetamine-like stimulant effects. As we will see, this is the case with MDMA but not with mescaline or DOM.

Mescaline

The hallucinogen **mescaline** is derived from the **peyote** plant, a spineless cactus with a small, greenish crown that grows above ground and a long carrot-like root. This cactus is found over a wide area, from the southwestern United States to northern regions of South America, and many communities in these regions have discovered its psychoactive properties. Given the large distances between these groups, it is remarkable that they prepare and ingest mescaline in a highly similar manner. The crowns of the cactus are cut off, sliced in small disks called buttons, dried in the sun, and then consumed. An effective dose of mescaline from peyote is 200 mg, equivalent to about five buttons. Peak response to the drug takes place thirty minutes to two hours after consumption. Mescaline is still used today as part of religious worship among many American Indians in the United States and Canada (Drugs...in Focus, page 154).

The psychological and physiological effects of mescaline are highly similar to those of LSD, though some have reported that mescaline hallucinations are more sensual, with fewer changes in mood and the sense of self. Nonetheless, double-blind studies comparing the reactions to LSD and mescaline show that subjects cannot distinguish between the two when dose levels are equivalent. While the reactions may be the same, the mescaline trip comes at a greater price, as far as physiological reactions are concerned. Peyote buttons taste extremely bitter and can cause vomiting, headaches, and, unless the stomach is empty, distressing levels of nausea.[36]

Today mescaline can be synthesized as well as obtained from the peyote cactus. The mescaline molecule resembles the chemical structure of norepinephrine but stimulates the same S_{2A} receptors as LSD and other hallucinogens that resemble serotonin. As a result, mescaline and LSD share a common brain mechanism.[37]

The peyote cactus, source of mescaline.

harmine (HAR-meen): A serotonin-related hallucinogenic drug frequently used by South American shamans in healing rituals.

mescaline (MES-kul-leen): A norepinephrine-related hallucinogenic drug. Its source is the peyote cactus.

peyote (pay-YO-tay): A species of cactus and the source for the hallucinogenic drug mescaline.

Drugs...in Focus

Present-Day Peyotism and the Native American Church

Among American Indians within the United States, the ritual use of peyote buttons, called *peyotism*, can be traced to the eighteenth century when the Mescalero Apaches (from whom the word *mescaline* was derived) adopted the custom from Mexican Indians who had been using peyote for more than three thousand years. By the late 1800s, peyotism had become widely popular among tribes from Wisconsin and Minnesota to the West Coast. It was not until the early twentieth century, however, that peyote use became incorporated into an official religious organization, the Native American Church of North America, chartered in 1918.

The beliefs of the Native American Church membership, estimated to include anywhere from 50,000 to 250,000 American Indians in the United States and Canada, combine traditional tribal customs and practices with Christian morality. To them, life is a choice between two roads that meet at a junction. The Profane Road is paved and wide, surrounded by worldly passions and temptations. The Peyote Road is a narrow and winding path, surrounded by natural, unspoiled beauty; it is also a path of sobriety (since alcohol poisons the goodness of the body), hard work, caring for one's family, and brotherly love. Only the Peyote Road leads to salvation. In their weekly ceremonies, lasting from Saturday night until Sunday afternoon, church members swallow small peyote buttons as a sacrament, similar to the ritual of taking Holy Communion, or drink peyote tea. It is considered sacrilegious to take peyote outside the ceremonies in the church.

While peyote remains classified as a Schedule I drug and therefore banned, federal law and the laws of twenty-three U.S. states have exempted the sacramental use of peyote from criminal penalties. The Religious Freedom Restoration Act of 1993 established an exemption from federal and state controlled substance laws when peyote is used for religious purposes in traditional American Indian ceremonies. In 2005, a study found that peyote use among church members does not result in impairments on tests of memory, attention, and other aspects of cognitive functioning.

Today, a handful of people are licensed by state and federal authorities to harvest peyote for religious purposes, in the brushland of south Texas near Laredo. This locale is the only place in the United States where peyote grows in the wild. As one of the harvesters has put it, "This is sacred ground to a lot of American Indian tribes. To some, the land here is very holy because it is the home to the sacred peyote."

Sources: Calabrese, Joseph D. (1997). Spiritual healing and human development in the Native American Church: Toward a cultural psychiatry of peyote. *Psychoanalytic Review, 84,* 237–255. Halpern, John H.; Sherwod, Andrea, R., Hudson, James I., Yurgelum-Tod, Deborah; and Pope, Harrison G., Jr. (2005). Psychological and cognitive effects of long-term peyote use among Native Americans. *Biological Psychiatry, 58,* 624–631. Indian religion must say no (1990, October 6). *The Economist,* pp. 25–26. Milloy, Ross E. (2002, May 7). A forbidding landscape that's Eden for peyote. *New York Times,* p. A20. Quotation on p. A20. Morgan, George (1983). Recollections of the peyote road. In Lester Grinspoon and James B. Bakalar (Eds.), *Psychedelic reflections.* New York: Human Sciences Press, pp. 91–99.

DOM

A group of synthetic hallucinogens has been developed that shares mescaline's resemblance to amphetamine but does not produce the strong stimulant effects of amphetamine. One example of these synthetic drugs, **DOM,** appeared in the 1960s and 1970s, when it was frequently combined with LSD and carried the street name of STP. The nickname supposedly was a reference to the well-known engine oil additive, while others took it to mean a "super terrific psychedelic." It is roughly eighty times more potent than mescaline, though still far weaker than LSD. At low doses of about 3 to 5 mg, DOM produces euphoria; with higher doses of 10 mg or more, severe hallucinations result, often lasting from sixteen to twenty-five hours. Though similar to LSD in many respects, DOM has the reputation of producing a far higher incidence of panic attacks, psychotic episodes, and other symptoms of a very bad trip. Cases have been reported of STP being added as an adulterant to marijuana.[38]

> **DOM:** A synthetic norepinephrine-related hallucinogenic drug, derived from amphetamine. DOM or a combination of DOM and LSD is often referred to by the street name STP.

MDMA (Ecstasy)

Another synthetic amphetamine-related hallucinogen, abbreviated **MDMA,** first appeared on the scene in the 1980s. While subject to abuse as a new designer drug, it also became known to a number of psychiatrists who used the drug as part of their therapy, believing that MDMA had a special ability to enhance empathy among their patients. In fact, some therapists at the time suggested the name *empathogens* (meaning "generating a state of empathy") to describe MDMA and related drugs. Eventually, after several years of hesitations and reversals, the Drug Enforcement Administration put MDMA permanently on the Schedule I list of controlled substances, meaning that there was no accepted medical application for the drug.[39]

Since the early 1990s, MDMA has become prominent among the new club drugs (see Chapter 1), especially popular at dance clubs and all-night "rave" parties. Widely available under names such as Ecstasy (not to be confused with the stimulant Herbal Ecstasy), E, XTC, X, Essence, Clarity, and Adam, MDMA has the reputation of having the stimulant qualities of amphetamines and the hallucinogenic qualities of mescaline.

The physical health concerns with respect to Ecstasy center on its short-term and long-term toxicity. The principal acute effect is severe hyperthermia (and heatstroke), which can be potentially lethal when Ecstasy is ingested while engaged in the physical exertion of dancing in an already overheated club environment. The dehydration associated with hyperthermia causes an elevation in blood pressure and heart rate and places a strain on kidney functioning. These problems are compounded by the highly risky practice of "Ecstasy stacking," in which multiple Ecstasy tablets are taken at once or Ecstasy is combined with LSD, alcohol, marijuana, or other drugs. Chronic effects of Ecstasy in animal studies have included significant degeneration of serotonin-using neurons in areas of the brain associated with attention, learning, and memory. In human studies, brain imaging has shown a depletion of serotonin in the brain among long-term Ecstasy users, possibly as a response to the overstimulation of serotonin-using neurons while under the effects of the drug.

Ecstasy use also has been linked to long-term cognitive impairments and emotional difficulties. Heavy and prolonged Ecstasy use can produce confusion, anxiety, sleep problems, reductions in impulse control, and declines in memory and attention. In general, women show greater behavioral effects from chronic Ecstasy use than do men.[40] The Help Line feature summarizes the major areas of MDMA toxicity.

In 2006, according to the University of Michigan surveys, approximately one out of sixteen high school seniors and one out of forty eighth graders reported having taken Ecstasy at some point in their lives. There is evidence that after a sharp rise in prevalence rates observed between 1998 and 2001, Ecstasy use among adolescents is clearly on the decline. This development is likely to be related to a greater recognition of its adverse health effects. Beginning in 2001, increasing numbers of adolescents reported Ecstasy use as representing a great risk of harm. In 2002, the number who disapproved of its use also began to rise. Together, these measures indicate that negative attitudes with respect to Ecstasy use have gained strength.[41]

Another factor has played a role in the decline of Ecstasy use since 2001. Increased scrutiny of passengers and baggage at airports in New York City and Newark, New Jersey, as a response to the September 11 attacks in 2001 has resulted in record seizures of Ecstasy pills. As a consequence, the flow of Ecstasy from abroad has slowed dramatically, reducing its availability and increasing its expense. Drug Enforcement Administration (DEA) officials have theorized that the popularity of narcotic analgesics (prescription painkillers) such as OxyContin and Vicodin (see Chapters 1 and 5) has outstripped that of Ecstasy in recent years, in part, because of their greater availability and lower expense.[42]

Hallucinogens Related to Acetylcholine

Of the acetylcholine-related hallucinogens, some enhance the neurotransmitter and some inhibit it. Some examples include *Amanita muscaria* mushrooms, atropine, scopolamine, and hyoscyamine.

Amanita muscaria

The *Amanita muscaria* mushroom, also called the fly agaric mushroom because of its ability to lure and sedate flies and other insects, grows in the upper latitudes of the

MDMA (Ecstasy): A synthetic norepinephrine-related hallucinogenic drug. Once considered useful for psychotherapeutic purposes, this drug is now known to produce significant adverse side effects, including neuronal hyperthermia, dehydration, and neurochemical changes.

Amanita muscaria (a-ma-NEE-ta mus-CAR-ee-ah): A species of mushroom containing the hallucinogenic drug ibotenic acid.

MDMA Toxicity: The Other Side of Ecstasy

- **Possible Physical Effects**
  Hyperthermia and heatstroke
  Dehydration and electrolyte depletion
  Irregular heartbeat or increased heart rate
  Kidney and liver failure
  Jaw-clenching and other forms of muscle spasms
  Long-term neurochemical changes
- **Possible Psychological Effects**
  Agitation and confusion
  Depression and anxiety
  Long-term impairments in memory recall

Note: As with other illicit drugs, adulterated versions raise significant concerns. In the case of MDMA, adulterants include dextromethorphan (a common cough suppressant) at approximately thirteen times the dose found in over-the-counter cough medications. At this dosage, dextromethorphan itself functions as a hallucinogen and inhibits sweating, further risking hyperthermia and heatstroke. More powerful hallucinogens and hyperthermic drugs have also been identified as adulterants in MDMA batches.

In 2003, the federal RAVE (Reducing American's Vulnerability to Ecstasy) Act was signed into law, making it unlawful to "knowingly open, lease, rent, use, or maintain any place, whether permanently or temporarily" for the purpose of manufacturing, distributing, or using any controlled substance." Supporters of the law view it as helping to reduce illicit drug use in dance clubs; opponents view it more as reflection of prejudice against youth culture.

Where to go for assistance:

www. nida. nih. gov/infofacts/ecstasy. html

This web site is sponsored by the National Institute on Drug Abuse, with an extensive treatment on the hazards of Ecstasy (MDMA).

Sources: Boils, Karen I. (1999). Memory impairment in abstinent MDMA ("Ecstasy") users. *Journal of the American Medical Association, 281,* 494. Chonin, Neva (2003, April 27). Congress acts out against club culture. *San Francisco Chronicle,* p. 35. Leshner, Alan I. (2002). Ecstasy abuse and control: Hearing before the Senate Subcommittee on Governmental Affairs—July 30, 2001. Statement for the record. *Journal of Psychoactive Drugs, 34,* 133–135. Schwartz, Richard H., and Miller, Norman S. (1997). MDMA (Ecstasy) and the rave: A review. *Pediatrics, 100,* 705–708. Stryker, Jeff (2001, September 25). For partygoers who can't say no, experts try to reduce the risks. *New York Times,* p. F5.

Northern Hemisphere, usually among the roots of birch trees. The mushroom has a bright red cap speckled with white dots; the dancing mushrooms in Walt Disney's film *Fantasia* were inspired by the appearance (if not the hallucinogenic effects) of this fungus (see Figure 6.1).

Amanita mushrooms are one of the world's oldest intoxicants. Many historians hypothesize that this mushroom was the basis for the mysterious and divine substance called soma that is celebrated in the *Rig-Veda*, one of Hinduism's oldest holy books, dating from 1000 B.C. It is strongly suspected that amanita mushrooms were used in Greek mystery cults and were probably the basis for the legendary "nectar of the Gods" on Mount Olympus.[43]

The effects of amanita mushrooms can be lethal if dose levels are not watched very carefully. They produce muscular twitching and spasms, vivid hallucinations, dizziness, and heightened aggressive behavior. It was briefly mentioned in Chapter 2 that Viking warriors were reputed to have ingested amanita mushrooms before sailing off to battle. The drug-induced strength and savagery of these "berserk" invaders were so widely feared that a medieval prayer was written especially for protection from their attacks: "From the intolerable fury of the Norseman, O Lord, deliver us."

Until the 1960s it was believed that the active ingredient in *Amanita muscaria* was, as the name suggests, muscarine, and that this was the drug that excited receptors sensitive to acetylcholine in the parasympathetic autonomic nervous system. Our present knowledge, however, is that the principal psychoactive agent in these mushrooms that accomplishes this effect is actually a chemical called *ibotenic acid*.

A hallucinogenic drug related to ibotenic acid, called **ibogaine,** is found in the iboga root in the western coastal region of central Africa. While higher doses of ibogaine are potentially lethal, powdered forms of the iboga root in small amounts have been used in ceremonies of the Bwiti cult among several tribal groups in Gabon and the Congo, in an effort to communicate with the spirit world and seek advice from the ancestors. Among these people, iboga root is slowly chewed and

ibogaine (IH-bo-gayn): A hallucinogenic drug originating from the West African iboga root.

the intoxication from ibotenic acid, often lasting for as long as thirty hours, is believed to allow an individual to travel down a road through a visionary landscape to the dwellings of the spirits of the dead. It is interesting that the imagery of progressing through a "trip" pervades so many experiences with hallucinogenic drugs, in both primitive and modern settings. Recently, attention has focused on the role that ibogaine may play in drug abuse treatment, specifically in cases of cocaine, opiate, alcohol, and nicotine dependence.[44]

The Hexing Drugs and Witchcraft

A number of natural plants contain chemicals that share a common feature: the ability to block the parasympathetic effects of acetylcholine in the body. The drugs with this ability, called *anticholinergic drugs,* produce specific physiological effects. The production of mucus in the nose and throat, as well as saliva in the mouth, is reduced. Body temperature is elevated, sometimes to very high fever levels. Heart rate and blood pressure go up, and the pupils dilate considerably. Psychological effects include a feeling of delirium, confusion, and generally a loss of memory for events occurring during the drugged state.[45] The amnesic property is one of the primary reasons for the minimal street appeal of these drugs.

The principal anticholinergic drugs are **atropine, scopolamine** (also called hyoscine), and **hyoscyamine.** They are found in various combinations and relative amounts in a large number of psychoactive plants. Four of the better known ones are examined here.

- Atropine is principally derived from the ***Atropa belladonna*** plant, also called deadly nightshade. Its lethal reputation is quite justified, since it is estimated that ingesting only a dozen or so berries is sufficient for death to occur. Many recipes for poisons through history have been based on this plant. At lower, more benign dose levels, plant extracts can be applied to the eyes, causing the pupils to dilate. Egyptian and Roman women used this technique to enhance their beauty or at least improve their appearance. The term "belladonna" ("beautiful lady") originates from this application. The psychological effects of atropine are generally associated with the anticholinergic effects of heart-rate acceleration and general arousal.
- The **mandrake** plant is an oddly shaped potato-like plant with a long forked root that has traditionally been imagined to resemble a human body. In ancient times, mandrake was considered to have aphrodisiac properties. According to medieval folklore, mandrake

plants supposedly shrieked when they were uprooted, understandably driving people mad.

Mandrake contains a combination of atropine, scopolamine, and hyoscyamine. Because low doses act as a depressant, mandrake has been used as a sedative-hypnotic drug to relieve anxiety and induce sleep. At higher doses, it produces bizarre hallucinations and muscular paralysis.

- **Henbane** is a strong-smelling herb, native to widespread areas of the Northern Hemisphere, with purple-veined, yellowish flowers and hairy leaves. Its English name, meaning "harmful to hens," originates from the observation that henbane seeds were toxic to chickens and other birds. The lethal possibilities for henbane potions have been described by writers since the days of the Roman Empire. Hamlet's father in Shakespeare's play was supposedly murdered with henbane poison. Lower doses of henbane, however, have been used in a more benign way, as an anesthetic and painkiller. We now know that the predominant drugs in henbane are scopolamine and hyoscyamine.
- Various species of the datura plant, containing a combination of atropine, scopolamine, and hyoscyamine, grow wild in locations throughout the world. In the United States, one particular species, ***Datura stramonium,*** is called "jimsonweed," a contraction of "Jamestown weed" (the name given to it by early American colonists). Consumption of the seeds or berries of jimsonweed produces hypnotic and hallucinogenic effects, together with disorientation, confusion, and amnesia. At high doses, jimsonweed is quite toxic. In

atropine (AT-tro-peen): An anticholinergic hallucinogenic drug derived from the *Atropa belladonna* plant.

scopolamine (scoh-POL-ah-meen): An anticholinergic hallucinogenic drug. Also called hyoscine.

hyoscyamine (HEYE-oh-SEYE-eh-meen): An anticholinergic hallucinogenic drug found in mandrake, henbane, and various species of the datura plant.

***Atropa belladonna* (a-TROH-pah BEL-ah-DON-ah):** A plant species, also called deadly nightshade, whose berries can be highly toxic. It is the principal source of atropine.

mandrake: A potato-like plant containing anticholinergic hallucinogenic drugs.

henbane: An herb containing anticholinergic hallucinogenic drugs.

***Datura stramonium* (duh-TOOR-ah strah-MOH-nee-um):** A species of the datura family of plants with hallucinogenic properties. In the United States, the plant is called jimsonweed.

recent years, there have been occasional reports of hospitalizations and even deaths among teenagers who have eaten jimsonweed seeds as an inexpensive way to get high.[46]

During medieval times, mixtures of deadly nightshade, mandrake, and henbane were responsible for the psychoactive effects of witches' potions, producing a disastrous combination of physiological and psychological effects. Satanic celebrations of the Black Mass centered on the ingestion of such brews. The atropine, in particular, produced a substantial elevation in arousal, probably leading to the feeling that the person was flying (or at least capable of it), while the hallucinogenic effects enabled the person to imagine "communing with the Devil."[47] Witches were reputed to have prepared these mixtures as

ointments and rubbed them on their bodies and on broomsticks, which they straddled. The chemicals would have been easily absorbed through the skin and the membranes of the vagina. The Halloween image of a witch flying on a broomstick has been with us ever since.

Phencyclidine (PCP)

Perhaps the most notorious of all the hallucinogens is **phencyclidine (PCP)**, commonly known as *angel dust*. The appearance of this drug from the miscellaneous group as an illicit drug in the late 1960s brought special problems to the already dangerous drug scene.

The weird combination of stimulant, depressant, and hallucinogenic effects makes PCP difficult to classify. Some textbooks treat the discussion of PCP in a chapter on hallucinogens, as is done here, whereas others include it in a chapter on stimulants because some features of PCP intoxication resemble the effect of cocaine, though ironically its medical use was originally as a depressant. A growing consensus of opinion has it that PCP, because it produces a feeling of being dissociated or cut off from one's environment, should be described as a *dissociative anesthetic hallucinogen*.[48]

History and Abuse of PCP

Technically PCP is a synthetic depressant, and it was originally introduced in 1963 as a depressant drug by the Parke-Davis pharmaceutical company, under the brand name of Sernyl. It was marketed as a promising new surgical anesthetic that had the advantage of not depressing respiration or blood pressure or causing heartbeat irregularities like other anesthetics. In addition, PCP had a higher therapeutic ratio than many other anesthetics available at that time. By 1965, however, it was withdrawn from human applications after reports that nearly half of all patients receiving PCP showed signs of delirium, disorientation, hallucinations, intense anxiety, or agitation. For a time, PCP was used for animal anesthesia, but this application ended by the late 1970s. In 1979, PCP was classified as a Schedule I drug.

PCP can be taken orally, intravenously, or by inhalation, but commonly it is smoked either alone or in

---

Quick Concept Check 6.1

Understanding Variations in Hallucinogens

Check your understanding of the psychological differences among major hallucinogens by matching the hallucinatory experience (in the left column) with the hallucinogenic drug most apt to produce such effects (in the right column).

PSYCHOLOGICAL EXPERIENCE	HALLUCINOGEN
1. "The images I saw were Mexican designs as if they were created by an Aztec artist."	DMT
	LSD
2. "As I heard the bells, I also saw the vibrations move through the air."	*Atropa belladonna*
	ibogaine
3. "The hallucinations were gone sixty minutes after they had started."	psilocybin
	mescaline
4. "As I ate the red-topped mushrooms, I felt my muscles twitch. I could see vivid hallucinations."	*Amanita muscaria*
5. "I felt as if I were flying through the air."	

Answers: 1. psilocybin   2. LSD, principally
3. DMT   4. *Amanita muscaria*   5. *Atropa belladonna*

---

phencyclidine (PCP) (fen-SIGH-klih-deen): A dissociative anesthetic hallucinogen that produces disorientation, agitation, aggressive behavior, analgesia, and amnesia. It has various street names, including angel dust.

combination with other drugs. Whatever its mode of administration, the results are extremely dangerous, with an unpredictability that far exceeds that of LSD or other hallucinogens. The symptoms may include manic excitement, depression, severe anxiety, sudden mood changes, disordered and confused thought, paranoid thoughts, and unpredictable aggression. Because PCP has analgesic properties as well, individuals taking the drug often feel invulnerable to threats against them and may be willing and able to withstand considerable pain. The mechanism behind PCP effects appears to be the blocking of a specific subtype of glutamate receptors in the brain (see Chapter 3).

Hallucinations also occur, but they are quite different from the hallucinations experienced under the influence of LSD. There are no colorful images, no intermingling of sight and sound, no mystical sense of being "one with the world." Instead, a prominent feature of PCP-induced hallucinations is the change in one's body image. As one PCP abuser has expressed it:

> The most frequent hallucination is that parts of your body are extremely large or extremely small. You can imagine yourself small enough to walk through a key hole, or you can be lying there and all of a sudden you just hallucinate that your arm is twice the length of your body.[49]

Individuals under the influence of PCP also may stagger, speak in a slurred way, and feel depersonalized or detached from people around them. A prominent feature is a prolonged visual stare, often called "doll's eyes."

The effects of PCP last from as little as a few hours to as long as two weeks, and they are followed by partial or total amnesia and dissociation from the entire experience. Considering these bizarre reactions, it is not surprising that PCP deaths occur more frequently from the behavioral consequences of the PCP experience than from its physiological effects. Suicides, accidental or intentional mutilations, drownings (sometimes in very small amounts of water), falls, and threatening behavior leading to the individual's being shot are only some of the possible consequences.[50]

Patterns of PCP Abuse

It is strange that a drug with so many adverse effects would be subject to deliberate abuse, but such is the case with PCP. Reports of PCP abuse began surfacing in 1967 among the hippie community in San Francisco, where it became known as the PeaCe Pill. Word quickly spread that PCP did not live up to its name. Inexperienced PCP abusers were suffering the same bizarre

TABLE 6.2

Street names for phencyclidine (PCP) and PCP-like drugs

PCP	jet fuel
angel dust	sherms (derived from the reaction that it hits you like a Sherman tank)
monkey dust	
peep	superkools
supergrass	cyclones
killer weed	zombie dust
ozone	ketamine
embalming fluid	special K
rocket fuel	

Note: In the illicit drug market, PCP and ketamine are frequently misrepresented and sold as mescaline, LSD, marijuana, amphetamine, or cocaine.

Source: Milburn, H. Thomas (1991). Diagnosis and management of phencyclidine intoxication. *American Family Physician, 43,* 1293.

effects as had the clinical patients earlier in the decade. By 1969, PCP had been written off as a garbage drug, and it dropped out of sight as a drug of abuse.

In the early 1970s, PCP returned under new street names and in new forms (Table 6.2). No longer a pill to be taken orally, PCP was now in powdered or liquid form. Powdered PCP could be added to parsley, mint, oregano, tobacco, or marijuana, rolled as a cigarette, and smoked.[51] Liquid PCP could be used to soak leaf mixtures of all types, including manufactured cigarettes, which could then be dried and smoked. Many new users have turned to PCP as a way to boost the effects of marijuana.

Making matters worse, as many as 120 different designer-drug variations of PCP have been developed in illicit laboratories around the country and the world. The dangers of PCP abuse, therefore, are complicated by the difficulty in knowing whether a street drug has been adulterated with PCP and what version of PCP may be present. Unfortunately, the common practice of mixing PCP with alcohol or marijuana adds to the unpredictability of the final result.[52]

Ketamine

Ketamine, a drug chemically similar to PCP, is also classified as a dissociative anesthetic hallucinogen. Like

ketamine (KET-ah-meen): A dissociative anesthetic hallucinogen related to phencyclidine (PCP).

PCP, ketamine has a mixture of stimulant and depressive properties, though its depressive effect is more extreme and does not last as long as that of PCP. Ketamine was used as an emergency surgical anesthetic on the battlefield in Vietnam as well as in standard hospital-based operations in which gaseous anesthetics could not be employed. It has also been used occasionally in short surgical procedures involving the head and neck or in the treatment of facial burns where it is not possible to use an anesthetic mask. Adverse side effects, however, have limited its therapeutic use. These problems include unpredictable and sometimes violent jerking and twitching of the body, as well as vivid and unpleasant dreams during and after surgery. During recovery, patients may experience hallucinations and feelings of disorientation. Delayed effects of ketamine, such as nightmares, have been reported to occur for weeks or longer after surgery.[53]

Ketamine abuse began to be reported in the 1980s. More recently, under the names "Special K" and "Vitamin K," it has been included among current club drugs on the scene (see Chapter 1). Its popularity has increased among college students and patrons of dance clubs and all-night "rave" parties. Like PCP, ketamine produces a dream-like intoxication, accompanied by an inability to move or feel pain. There are also experiences of dizziness, confusion, and slurred speech. As is the case with dissociative hallucinogens, ketamine produces amnesia, in that abusers frequently cannot later remember what has happened while under its influence. The primary hazard of acute ketamine ingestion is the depression of breathing. Little is known, however, of the chronic effects of extended ketamine abuse over time, except that experiences of "flashbacks" have been reported.[54] As with PCP, the effects of ketamine are associated with the blocking of specific glutamate receptors.

As with other club drugs that produce depressive effects on the central nervous system, there is the dangerous potential for ketamine to be abused as a "date-rape" drug. Women who may unwittingly take the drug can be rendered incapacitated, without the ability to recall the experience. In 1999, ketamine became classified as a Schedule III controlled substance (Drug Trafficking Update).[55]

Drug Trafficking Update
LSD, MDMA (Ecstasy), and PCP

- **Origins:** Domestic production of hallucinogens such as LSD, MDMA (Ecstasy), and PCP is very limited, even though in the case of PCP, production is relatively simple. Canada is a major production source of these products.

- **Points of Entry:** Most MDMA is now smuggled overland into the United States through U.S.-Canada points of entry, after a sharp decline in international airline distribution after 2001. Airline-based seizures, however, have increased since 2004 in northern border states, particularly at the Buffalo Niagara International Airport.

- **Traffickers:** Independent distributors, especially Caucasian males, are the primary wholesale and retail traffickers of LSD, whereas African American criminal groups and street gangs are prominent in the distribution of PCP. Wholesale distribution of MDMA, once dominated by Israeli groups prior to late 2001, has been transferred increasingly to Canada-based Asian criminal groups, though Caucasian males are the primary distributors at the retail level.

Note: Patterns of hallocinogen trafficking will be examined in more detail in Chapter 13.

Source: National Drug Intelligence Center (2006). *National Drug Threat Assessment 2007.* Washington DC: National Drug Intelligence Center, U.S. Department of Justice, pp. 21–23.

A Matter of Definition

- Hallucinogens are, by definition, drugs that produce distortions of perception and of one's sense of reality. These drugs have also been called psychedelic ("mind-expanding") drugs. In some cases, users of hallucinogens feel that they have been transported to a new reality.

- Other classes of drugs may produce hallucinations at high dose levels, but hallucinogens produce these effects at low or moderate dose levels.

Classifying Hallucinogens

- Hallucinogens can be classified in four basic groups. The first three relate to the chemical similarity between the particular drug and one of three major neurotransmitters: serotonin, norepinephrine, or acetylcholine.

- The fourth, miscellaneous group includes synthetic hallucinogens, such as phencyclidine (PCP) and ketamine, which bear little resemblance to any known neurotransmitter.

Lysergic Acid Diethylamide (LSD)

- Lysergic acid diethylamide (LSD), the best-known hallucinogenic drug, belongs to the serotonin group. It is synthetically derived from ergot, a toxic rye fungus that has been documented as being responsible for thousands of deaths over the centuries.

- Albert Hofmann synthesized LSD in 1943, and Timothy Leary led the psychedelic movement in the 1960s that popularized LSD use.

- Though the LSD experience is often unpredictable, certain features are commonly observed: colorful hallucinations, synesthesia in which sounds often appear as visions, a distortion of perceptual reality, emotional swings, a feeling of timelessness, and an illusory separation of mind from body.

- It is now known that LSD affects a subtype of brain receptors sensitive to serotonin, referred to as S_2 receptors.

- In the early 1990s, there was a resurgence in LSD abuse, particularly among young individuals, a trend that began to reverse in 1997.

Facts and Fictions about LSD

- LSD does not produce psychological or physical dependence and has only a slight chance of inducing a panic or psychotic state (providing that there is a supportive setting for the taking of LSD).

- LSD does not elevate one's level of creativity. It does not damage chromosomes (though there remains a chance of birth defects if LSD is ingested when pregnant), and a relationship between LSD abuse and violent behavior has not been established. Flashback experiences, however, are potential hazards.

Psilocybin and Other Hallucinogens Related to Serotonin

- Other hallucinogens related to serotonin are psilocybin, lysergic acid amide (LAA), dimethyltryptamine (DMT), and harmine.

Hallucinogens Related to Norepinephrine

- Mescaline is chemically related to norepinephrine, even though S_2 receptors are responsible for its hallucinogenic effects.

- Two synthetic hallucinogens, DOM and MDMA, are variations of the amphetamine molecule. MDMA (Ecstasy) is currently a popular club drug, but research studies indicate that it poses serious health risks to the user.

Hallucinogens Related to Acetylcholine

- A number of anticholinergic hallucinogens, so named because they diminish the effects of acetylcholine in the parasympathetic nervous system, have been involved in sorcery and witchcraft since the Middle Ages.

- These so-called hexing drugs contain a combination of atropine, scopolamine, and/or hyoscyamine. Sources for such drugs include the deadly nightshade plant, mandrake roots, henbane seeds, and the datura plant family.

Phencyclidine (PCP) and Ketamine

- A dangerous form of hallucinogen abuse involves phencyclidine (PCP). Originally a psychedelic street drug in the 1960s, PCP quickly developed a reputation for producing a number of adverse reactions.

- PCP reappeared in the early 1970s, in smokable forms either alone or in combination with marijuana. Extremely aggressive tendencies, as well as behaviors

drug abuse (2nd ed.). Boca Raton, FL: CRC Press, p. 269.

19. Goode, *Drugs and American society*, p. 257.

20. Ibid., p. 256.

21. Cohen, Sidney (1960). Lysergic acid diethylamide: Side effects and complications. *Journal of Nervous and Mental Diseases, 130*, 30–40. Levine, Jerome, and Ludwig, Arnold M. (1964). The LSD controversy. *Comprehensive Psychiatry, 5* (5), 314–321.

22. Wells, Brian (1974). *Psychedelic drugs: Psychological, medical, and social issues.* New York: Jason Aronson, pp. 170–188.

23. Cohen, M. M., and Marmillo, M. J. (1967). Chromosomal damage in human leukocytes induced by lysergic acid diethylamide. *Science, 155*, 1417–1419.

24. Dishotsky, Norman I.; Loughman, William D.; Mogar, Robert E.; and Lipscomb, Wendell R. (1971). LSD and genetic damage. *Science, 172*, 431–440. Grinspoon and Bakalar, *Psychedelic drugs reconsidered*, pp. 188–191.

25. Brown, *Hallucinogenic drugs*, pp. 61–64. Wells, *Psychedelic drugs*, pp. 104–109.

26. Abraham, Henry D. (1983). Visual phenomenology of the LSD flashback. *Archives of General Psychiatry, 40*, 884–889. Frosh, William A. (1969). Patterns of response to self-administration of LSD. In Roger E. Meyer (Ed.), *Adverse reactions to hallucinogenic drugs.* Washington DC: Public Health Service. Schlaadt, Richard G., and Shannon, Peter T. (1994). *Drugs: Use, misuse, and abuse.* Englewood Cliffs, NJ: Prentice Hall, p. 273.

27. Halpern, John H., and Pope, Harrison G. (1999). Do hallucinogens cause residual neuropsychological toxicity? *Drugs and Alcohol Dependence, 53*, 247–256.

28. Knudsen, Knud (1964). Homicide after treatment with lysergic acid diethylamide. *Acta Psychiatrica Scandinavica, 40* (Supplement 180), 389–395.

29. Metzner, Ralph (1998). Hallucinogenic drugs and plants in psychotherapy and shamanism. *Journal of Psychoactive Drugs, 30*, 333–341.

30. Hofmann, *LSD*, p. 112.

31. Brown, *Hallucinogenic drugs*, pp. 81–88.

32. Johnston, O'Malley, Bachman, and Schulenberg (2007a), *Monitoring the Future national results*, Table 13. Vollenweider, Franz X.; Vollenweider-Scherpenhuyzen, Margaret F. I.; Babler, Andreas; Vogel, Helen; and Hell, Daniel (1998). Psilocybin induces schizophrenia-like psychosis in humans via a serotonin-2 agonist action. *Neuroreport, 9*, 3897–3902.

33. Hofmann, *LSD*, pp. 119–127. Schultes, Richard E., and Hofmann, Albert (1979). *Plants of the gods: Origins of hallucinogenic use.* New York: McGraw-Hill, pp. 158–163.

34. Brands, Sproule, and Marshman, *Drugs and drug abuse*, pp. 512–513.

35. Frecska, Ede, White, Keith, D., and Luna, Luis E. (2003). Effects of Amazonian psychoactive beverage *ayuhuasca* on binocular rivalry: Interhemispheric switching or interhemispheric fusion? *Journal of Psychoactive Drugs, 35*, 367–374. Grinspoon and Bakalar, *Psychedelic drugs reconsidered*, pp. 14–15.

36. Ibid., pp. 20–21. Hollister, Leo E., and Sjoberg, Bernard M. (1964). Clinical syndromes and biochemical alterations following mescaline, lysergic acid diethylamide, psilocybin, and a combination of the three psychotomimetic drugs. *Comprehensive Psychiatry, 5*, 170–178.

37. Jacobs, *How hallucinogenic drugs work*, pp. 386–392.

38. Brecher, Edward, and the editors of *Consumer Reports* (1972). *Licit and illicit drugs.* Boston: Little, Brown, pp. 376–377.

39. Metzner, Hallucinogenic drugs and plants. Schmidt, C. J. (1987). Psychedelic amphetamine, methylenedioxymethamphetamine. *Journal of Pharmacology and Experimental Therapeutics, 240*, 1–7.

40. Boils, Karen I. (1999). Memory impairment in abstinent MDMA ("Ecstasy") users. *Journal of the American Medical Association, 281*, 494. Leshner, Alan I. (2002). Ecstasy abuse and control: Hearing before the Senate Subcommittee on Governmental Affairs—July 30, 2001. Statement for the record. *Journal of Psychoactive Drugs, 34*, 133–135. Kish, Stephen J.; Furukawa, Yoshiaki; Ang, Lee G.; Vorce, Shawn P.; and Kalasinsky, Kathryn S. (2000). Striatal serotonin is depleted in brain of a human MDMA (Ecstasy) user. *Neurology, 55*, 294–296. Rella, J. G., Nelson, L. S., and Hoffman, R. S. (1999). 5 years of 3,4-methylenedioxy-methamphetamine (MDMA) toxicity. *Journal of Toxicology: Clinical Toxicology, 37*, 648. Vollenweider, Franz X.; Liechti, Matthias E.; Gamma, Alex; Greer, George; and Geyer, Mark (2002). Acute psychological and neurophysiological effects of MDMA in humans. *Journal of Psychoactive Drugs, 34*, 171–184.

41. Cloud, John (2000, June 5). The lure of ecstasy. *Time*, pp. 62–68. Feuer, Alan (2000, August 6). Distilling the truth in the ecstasy buzz. *New York Times*, pp. 25, 28. Johnston, O'Malley, Bachman, and Schulenberg (2007a), *Monitoring the Future national results*, Tables 1, 7, and 10. Johnston, Lloyd D.; O'Malley, Patrick M.; Bachman, Jerald G.; and Schulenberg, John E. (2007b). *Monitoring the future: National survey results on drug use 2006. Volume II: College students and adults ages 19–45.* Bethesda, MD: National Institute on Drug Abuse, Table 2–1. Martins, Silvia, S. Mazzotti, Guido, and Chilcoat, Howard D. (2005). Trends in ecstasy use in the United States from 1995 to 2001: Comparison with marijuana users and association with other drug use. *Experimental and Clinical Psychopharmacology, 13*, 244–252.

42. Leinwand, Donna (2005, April 22–24). Post-9/11 security cuts into Ecstasy: Youths turning to prescription drugs. *USA Today*, p. 1A. Leinward, Donna (2005, April 22–24). Ecstasy's lost "its panache" among teens. *USA Today*, p. 3A.

43. Wasson, R. Gordon (1968). *Soma: Divine mushroom of immortality.* New York: Harcourt, Brace and World.

44. Cohen, Sidney (1964). *The beyond within: The LSD story.* New York: Atheneum, p. 17. Popik, Piotr, and

Glick, Stanley D. (1996). Ibogaine: A putatively anti-addictive alkaloid. *Drugs of the Future, 21,* 1109–1115. Vestag, Brian (2002). Addiction treatment strives for legitimacy. *Journal of the American Medical Association, 288,* 3096–3101.

45. Levinthal, Charles F. (1990). *Introduction to physiological psychology* (3rd ed.). Englewood Cliffs, NJ: Prentice Hall, pp. 157–158.

46. Freedman, Mitchell (1994, October 15). One teen's tale of jimsonweed. *Newsday,* p. A14. Schultes and Hofmann, *Plants of the gods,* pp. 106–111.

47. Schultes and Hofmann, *Plants of the gods,* pp. 86–91.

48. Julien, Robert M. (2001). *A primer of drug action* (9th ed.). New York: Worth, pp. 353–359.

49. James, Jennifer, and Andresen, Elena (1979). Sea-Tac and PCP. In Harvey V. Feldman, Michael H. Agar, and George M. Beschner (Eds.), *Angel dust: An ethnographic study of PCP users.* Lexington, MA: Lexington Books, p. 133.

50. Grinspoon and Bakalar, *Psychedelic drugs reconsidered,* pp. 32–33. Petersen, Robert C., and Stillman, Richard C. (1978). Phencyclidine: An overview. In Robert C. Petersen and Richard C. Stillman (Eds.), *Phencyclidine (PCP) abuse: An appraisal* (NIDA Research Monograph 21). Rockville, MD: National Institute on Drug Abuse, pp. 1–17. Robbins, *Hallucinogens,* pp. 12–14. Seeman, P., Ko, F., and Tallerico, T. (2005). Dopamine receptor contribution to the action of PCP, LSD and ketamine psychotomimetics. *Molecular Psychiatry, 10,* 877–883.

51. Zukin, Stephen, Sloboda, Zili, and Javitt, Daniel C. (1997). Phencyclidine (PCP). In Joyce H. Lowinson, Pedro Ruiz, Robert B. Millman, and John G. Langrod (Eds.), *Substance abuse: A comprehensive textbook* (3rd ed.). Baltimore, MD: Williams and Wilkins, pp. 238–246.

52. Trends in PCP-related emergency department visits (2004, January). *The DAWN Report,* pp. 1–4.

53. Brands, Sproule, and Marshman, *Drugs and drug abuse,* pp. 523–525.

54. Ibid.

55. Feds classify ketamine as controlled substance (1999, August 2). *Alcoholism and Drug Abuse Weekly,* p. 7.

chapter 7

Marijuana

Hunters and fishermen have snared the most ferocious creatures, from the tiger to the shark, in its Herculean weave. . . . Hangmen have snapped the necks of thieves and murderers with its fiber. Obstetricians have eased the pain of childbirth with its leaves. Farmers have crushed its seeds and used the oil within to light their lamps. Mourners have thrown its seeds into blazing fires and have had their sorrows transformed into blissful ecstacy by the fumes that filled the air. . . .

It is as vigorous as a weed. It is ubiquitous. It flourishes under nearly every possible climatic condition. It sprouts from the earth not meekly, not cautiously in suspense of where it is and what it may find, but defiantly, arrogantly, confident that whatever the conditions it has the stamina to survive.

—Ernest L. Abel, reviewing the many uses of the cannabis plant (hemp and marijuana) over history
Marihuana, the First Twelve Thousand Years *(1980)*

It might be fair to characterize *Cannabis sativa*, the botanical source of marijuana, as a scrawny weed with an attitude. Whether it is hot or cold, wet or dry, cannabis will grow abundantly from seeds that are unbelievably hardy and prolific. A handful of cannabis seeds, tossed on the ground and pressed in with one's foot, will usually anchor and become plants. Its roots devour whatever nutrients there are in the soil, like a vampire sucking the life blood from the earth.[1]

It is not surprising that, as a result, marijuana has managed to grow in some unorthodox places. It can be found in median strips of interstate highways or in ditches alongside country roads. The top prize for most unusual location, if the story is true and not simply an urban legend, has to go to a variety known as Manhattan Silver. Reportedly, it originated from cannabis seeds flushed down a New York sewer during a sudden police raid in the 1960s. Once the seeds hit the sewer, they produced a plant that, in the absence of light, grew silverish white leaves instead of green, hence its name.[2]

Considering its botanical origin, it is fitting that the pharmacological effects of marijuana should show something of an independent nature as well. It is not easy to place marijuana within a classification of psychoactive drugs. When we consider a category for marijuana, we are faced with an odd assortment of unconnected properties. Marijuana produces some excitatory effects, but it is not generally regarded as a stimulant. It produces some sedative effects, but a person faces no risk of slipping into a coma or dying. It produces mild analgesic effects, but it is not related chemically to opiates or opiate-like drugs. It produces hallucinations at high doses, but its structure does not resemble LSD or any other drug formally categorized as a hallucinogen. Marijuana is clearly a unique drug, in a league of its own.

Few other drugs have been so politicized in recent history as marijuana. It is frequently praised by one side or condemned by the other, on the basis of emotionally charged issues rather than an objective view of research data. The pro-marijuana faction tends to dismiss or downplay reports of potential dangers and emphasize the benefits; the antimarijuana faction tends to do the opposite, pointing out that marijuana continues to be classified as a Schedule I controlled substance, along with heroin and LSD. Marijuana often has been regarded, over the last forty years or so, not only as a drug with psychoactive

A Mexican harvester gathers his crop of *Cannabis sativa*, later to be processed into marijuana or hashish.

properties but also as a symbol of an individual's attitude toward the establishment. This makes it even more critical that we look at the effects of marijuana as dispassionately as possible.

A Matter of Terminology

Marijuana (sometimes spelled *marihuana*) is frequently referred to as a synonym for cannabis, but technically the two terms are separate. Cannabis is the botanical term for the hemp plant ***Cannabis sativa.*** With a potential height of about eighteen feet, cannabis has sturdy stalks, four-cornered in cross-section, that have been commercially valuable for thousands of years in the manufacture of rope, twine, shoes, sailcloth, and containers of all kinds. Pots made of hemp fiber discovered at archaeological sites in China date the origins of cannabis cultivation as far back as the Stone Age. It is arguably the oldest cultivated plant not used for food.[3]

Spaniards brought cannabis to the New World in 1545, and English settlers brought it to Jamestown, Virginia, in 1611, where it became a major commercial crop, along with tobacco. Like other eighteenth-century farmers in the region, George Washington grew cannabis in the fields of his estate at Mount Vernon. Entries in his diary indicate that he maintained a keen interest in cultivating better strains of cannabis, but

> ***Cannabis sativa* (CAN-uh-bus sah-TEE-vah):** A plant species, commonly called hemp, from which marijuana and hashish are obtained.

there is no reason to believe he was interested in anything more than a better-quality rope.

Marijuana is obtained not from the stalks of the cannabis plant but from its serrated leaves. The key psychoactive factor is contained in a sticky substance, or resin, that accumulates on these leaves. Depending on the growing conditions, cannabis will produce either a greater amount of resin or a greater amount of fiber. In a hot, dry climate—such as North Africa, for example—the fiber content is weak, but so much resin is produced that the plant looks as if it is covered with dew. In a cooler, more humid climate, such as North America, less resin is produced, but the fiber is stronger and more durable.[4]

As many as eighty separate chemical compounds, called **cannabinoids,** have been identified from cannabis resin. Among these, the chief psychoactive compound and the active ingredient that produces the intoxicating effects is **delta-9-tetrahydrocannabinol (THC).** The isolation and identification of THC in 1964 was a major step toward understanding the effects on the brain of marijuana and similar preparations obtained from *Cannabis sativa.*

Knowing these facts, we are now in a position to categorize various forms of cannabis products in terms of the origin within the cannabis plant and the relative THC concentration. The first and best known of these products, **marijuana,** consists of leaves and occasionally flowers of the cannabis plant that are first dried and then shredded. During the 1960s and 1970s, the typical THC concentration of street marijuana imported from Mexico was about 1 to 2 percent. More recently, higher-potency marijuana, grown in remote areas of Canada, contains a THC concentration of 6 to 8 percent and sometimes higher. Marijuana, smoked as a cigarette, is the form of cannabis most familiar to North Americans.

A more potent form of marijuana, originating in California and Hawaii, is obtained by cultivating only the unpollinated, or seedless, portion of the cannabis plant. Without pollination, the cannabis plant grows bushier, the resin content is increased, and a greater THC concentration, 8 to 15 percent, is achieved. This form is called **sinsemilla,** from the Spanish meaning "without seed."

Another cannabis product is achieved when the resin itself is scraped from cannabis leaves and then dried. It is either smoked by itself or in combination with tobacco. This form of cannabis, called **hashish,** has a THC concentration of 8 to 14 percent and is commonly available in Europe, Asia, and the Middle East. The most potent forms of cannabis are **hashish oil** and **hashish oil crystals,** produced by boiling hashish in alcohol or some other solvent, filtering out the alcohol, and leaving a residue with a THC concentration ranging from 15 to 60 percent.[5]

The Social History of Marijuana and Hashish

The first direct reference to a cannabis product as a psychoactive agent dates from 2737 B.C., in the writings of the mythical Chinese emperor Shen Nung. The focus was on its powers as a medication for rheumatism, gout, malaria, and, strangely enough, absent-mindedness. Mention was made of its intoxicating properties, but the medicinal possibilities evidently were considered more important. In India, however, its use was clearly recreational. The most popular form, in ancient times as well as in the present day, can be found in a syrupy liquid made from cannabis leaves called **bhang,** with a THC potency usually equal to that of a marijuana cigarette in the United States.[6]

The Muslim world also grew to appreciate the psychoactive potential of cannabis, encouraged by the fact that, in contrast to its stern prohibition of alcohol consumption, the Koran did not specifically ban its use. It was here in a hot, dry climate conducive to maximizing the resin content of cannabis that hashish was born, and its popularity spread quickly during the twelfth century from Persia (Iran) in the east to North Africa in the west.

cannabinoids (can-NAB-ih-noids): Any of several dozen active substances in marijuana and other cannabis products.

delta-9-tetrahydrocannabinol (THC) (DEL-tah-9-TEH-trah-HIGH-dro-CAN-a-bih-nol): The active psychoactive ingredient in marijuana and hashish.

marijuana: The most commonly available psychoactive drug originating from the cannabis plant. The THC concentration ranges from approximately 1 to 6 percent. Also spelled marihuana.

sinsemilla (SIN-sih-MEE-yah): A form of marijuana obtained from the unpollinated or seedless portion of the cannabis plant. It has a higher THC concentration than regular marijuana, as high as 15 percent.

hashish (hah-SHEESH): A drug containing the resin of cannabis flowers. The THC concentration ranges from approximately 8 to 14 percent.

hashish oil: A drug produced by boiling hashish, leaving a potent psychoactive residue. The THC concentration ranges from approximately 15 to 60 percent.

hashish oil crystals: A solid form of hashish oil.

bhang: A liquid form of marijuana popular in India.

A merchant sits outside his bhang shop in North India. Bhang ki thandai is a popular cold drink prepared with bhang combined with almonds, spices, milk, and sugar. Bhang lassi, a mixture of bhang and iced yogurt, is another popular drink. It is traditional for many Hindus to drink bhang during religious festivals, particularly in Bengal during the Kali Puja (Festival of Kali, the Mother Goddess).

Hashish in the Nineteenth Century

In Western Europe knowledge about hashish or any other cannabis product was limited until the beginning of the nineteenth century. Judging from the decree made by Pope Innocent VIII in 1484 condemning witchcraft and the use of hemp in the Black Mass, we can assume that the psychoactive properties of cannabis were known by some portions of the population. Nonetheless, there is no evidence of widespread use.

By about 1800, however, cannabis had become more widely known and the subject of a popular craze. One reason was that French soldiers who had served in Napoleon's military campaigns in Egypt brought hashish back with them to their homes in France. Another reason was a wave of romanticism that swept Europe, including an increased interest in exotic stories of the East, notably the *Arabian Nights* and the tales of Marco Polo, which contained references to hashish.

In Paris during the 1840s, a small group of prominent French artists, writers, and intellectuals formed the Club des Hachichins ("Club of the Hashish-Eaters"), where they would gather, in the words of their leader, "to talk of literature, art, and love" while consuming large quantities of hashish. The mixture consisted of a concentrated hemp paste, mixed with butter, sweeteners, and flavorings such as vanilla and cinnamon. Members included Victor Hugo, Alexandre Dumas, Charles Baudelaire, and Honoré de Balzac.

Marijuana and Hashish in the Twentieth Century

Chances are that anyone living in the United States at the beginning of the twentieth century would not have heard of marijuana, much less hashish. By 1890, cotton had replaced hemp as a major cash crop in southern states, although cannabis plants continued to grow wild along roadsides and in the fields. Some patent medicines during this era contained marijuana, but it was a small percentage compared with the number containing opium or cocaine.[7]

It was not until the 1920s that marijuana began to be a noticeable phenomenon. Some historians have related the appearance of marijuana as a recreational drug to social changes brought on by Prohibition, when it was suddenly difficult to obtain good-quality liquor at affordable prices. Its recreational use was largely restricted to jazz musicians and people in show business. "Reefer songs" became the rage of the jazz world; even the mainstream clarinetist and bandleader Benny Goodman had his popular hit "Sweet Marihuana Brown." Marijuana clubs, called tea pads, sprang up in the major cities; more than five hundred were estimated in Harlem alone, outnumbering the speakeasies where illegal alcohol was dispensed. These marijuana establishments were largely tolerated by the authorities because at that time marijuana was not illegal and patrons showed no evidence of making a nuisance of themselves or disturbing the community. Marijuana was not considered a social threat at all.[8]

The Antimarijuana Crusade

This picture started to change by the end of the 1920s and early 1930s. Even though millions of people had never heard of the plant, much less smoked it, marijuana suddenly became widely publicized as a "killer weed." The antimarijuana campaign, orchestrated by the Federal Bureau of Narcotics (FBN), was so intense that the American public quickly came to view marijuana as a pestilence singlehandedly destroying a generation of American youth (see Chapter 2).

How did this transformation occur? To understand the way in which marijuana smoking went from a localized, negligible quirk to a national social issue, we have to look at some important changes in American society that were taking place at the time.

The practice of smoking marijuana and the cultivation of cannabis plants for that purpose had been filtering slowly into the United States since 1900 as a result of the migration of Mexican immigrants. They entered the country through towns along the Mexican border and along the Gulf Coast. In Mexican communities, marijuana was, in the words of one historian, "a casual adjunct to life . . .—a relaxant, a folk remedy for headaches, a mild euphoriant cheaply obtained for two cigarettes for the dollar."[9]

It is no exaggeration to say that these immigrant communities were met with hostility and prejudice, and the smoking of an alien and foreign-sounding substance did not smooth their reception. In effect, it was a social rerun of the Chinese-opium panic of the 1870s (see Chapter 5) but with the Mexicans on the receiving end. Rumors about the violent behavioral consequences of marijuana smoking among Mexicans began to spread, largely unchallenged by objective data. In addition, economic upheavals during the Depression made it particularly convenient to vent frustrations on an immigrant group that was perceived as competing for a dwindling number of American jobs and straining an already weak economy. Antimarijuana-themed movies with provocative titles such as *Reefer Madness* and *Marihuana: Weed with Roots in Hell* were produced and distributed during the late 1930s and early 1940s with the encouragement of the FBN.

Considering the mounting hysteria against marijuana smoking and cannabis use in general during this period, it is not surprising that the Marijuana Tax Act of 1937 had little difficulty in gaining support in Congress. As with the Harrison Act of 1914, the regulation of marijuana was accomplished indirectly. The act did not ban marijuana; it merely required everyone connected with marijuana, from growers to buyers, to pay a tax. It was a deceptively simple procedure that, in effect, made it virtually impossible to comply with the law. In the absence of compliance, a person was in violation of the act and therefore subject to arrest. It was the state's responsibility to make possession of marijuana or any other product of *Cannabis sativa* illegal. Shortly after the tax act of 1937 was imposed, all of the states adopted a uniform law that did just that.

During the rest of the 1940s and 1950s, marijuana research was virtually at a standstill. The official stance of the federal government continued to be that marijuana smoking was tied to antisocial behavior. Harry Anslinger, FBN director, wrote in 1953:

> *Those who are accustomed to habitual use of the drug are said eventually to develop a delirious rage after its administration during which they are temporarily, at least, irresponsible and prone to commit violent crimes. . . . Much of the most irrational juvenile violence and killing that has written a new chapter of shame and tragedy is traceable directly to this hemp intoxication.*[10]

Over time, the "pharmacological violence" theory faded into oblivion, in the absence of any evidence to support it. In its place, however, a new concept regarding marijuana smoking was introduced by the FBN: the gateway theory. According to this idea, marijuana was purported to be dangerous because its abuse would lead to the abuse of heroin, cocaine, or other illicit drugs. This gateway hypothesis will be closely examined later in the chapter.

While marijuana research declined, penalties for involvement with it steadily increased. In certain states, the penalties were severe. Judges frequently had the option of sentencing a marijuana seller or user to life imprisonment. In Georgia, a second offense of selling marijuana to a minor could be punishable by death.

Ironically, in 1969, more than three decades after its passage, the U.S. Supreme Court ruled the 1937 Marijuana Tax Act to be unconstitutional precisely because marijuana possession was illegal. The argument was made that requiring a person to pay a tax (and that was all that the 1937 act concerned) so as to possess an illegal substance amounted to a form of self-incrimination, which would be a specific violation of the Fifth Amendment to the Constitution. It turns out that the case in question

Marijuana tax stamps were issued and valid between 1937 and 1969 when the law was overturned by the U.S. Supreme Court, though during this time stringent governmental regulations made it nearly impossible to obtain these stamps to "register" one's marijuana use. In 2007, the four stamps shown here became commercially available for collectors, at a price of $3,250.

here was brought to the high court by none other than Timothy Leary (see Portrait in Chapter 6), and the court's decision succeeded in overturning a marijuana conviction judged against him.[11]

Challenging Old Ideas about Marijuana

Prior to 1960, arrests and seizures for possession of marijuana were relatively rare and attracted little or no public attention. The social consensus was that marijuana was a drug that could be comfortably associated with, and isolated to, ethnic and racial minorities. It was relatively easy for most Americans to avoid the drug entirely. In any event, until 1960, involvement with marijuana was a deviant act, during an era when there was little tolerance for personal deviance.

By the mid-1960s, this consensus began to dissolve. Marijuana smoking suddenly was an attraction on the campuses of U.S. colleges and universities, affecting a wide cross-section of the nation. At the same time, the experimental use of drugs, particularly marijuana, by young people set the stage for a wholesale questioning of what it meant to respect authority, on an individual as well as a governmental level. We will turn to the more recent issues of medical marijuana and marijuana decriminalization later in the chapter.

Acute Effects of Marijuana

In the United States, THC is usually ingested by smoking a hand-rolled marijuana cigarette referred to as a **reefer** or, more commonly, a **joint.** Exactly how much THC is administered depends on the specific THC concentration level in the marijuana (often referred to as its quality), how deeply the smoke is inhaled into the lungs, and how long it is held in the lungs before being exhaled. In general, an experienced smoker will ingest more THC than a novice smoker by virtue of being able to inhale more deeply and hold the marijuana smoke in his or her lungs longer, for twenty-five seconds or longer, thus maximizing THC absorption into the bloodstream.

The inhalation of any drug into the lungs produces extremely rapid absorption, as noted in earlier chapters, and marijuana is no exception. In the case of THC, effects are felt within seconds. Peak levels are reached in the

reefer: A marijuana cigarette.
joint: A marijuana cigarette.

This promotional poster for the 1942 film *Devil's Harvest* depicted the supposed evils of smoking marijuana.

blood within ten minutes and start to decline shortly afterward. Behavioral and psychological effects generally last from two to four hours. At this point, low levels of THC linger for several days because they are absorbed into fatty tissue and excretion from fatty tissue is notoriously slow.[12]

One implication arising from a slow elimination rate is that the residual THC, left over from a previous administration, can intensify the effect of marijuana on a subsequent occasion. In this way, regular marijuana smokers often report a quicker and more easily obtained high, achieved with a smaller quantity of drug, than more intermittent smokers.[13]

It is also important to see the implication of slow marijuana elimination with regard to drug testing. Urine tests for possible marijuana abuse typically measure levels of THC metabolites (broken-down remnants of THC); because of the slow biotransformation of marijuana, these metabolites are detectable in the urine even when the smoker no longer feels high or shows any behavioral effects. Metabolites can remain in the body several days after smoking a single joint and several weeks later if there has been chronic marijuana smoking. Some tests are so sensitive that a positive level for marijuana can result from passive inhalation of marijuana smoke-filled air in a closed environment, even though the THC levels in these cases are substantially below levels that result from active smoking. The bottom line is that marijuana testing procedures generally are unable to indicate *when* marijuana has been smoked (if it has been smoked at all), only that exposure to marijuana has occurred (see Chapter 9).[14]

Acute Physiological Effects

Immediate physiological effects after smoking marijuana are relatively minor. It has been estimated that a human would need to ingest a dose of marijuana that was from twenty thousand to forty thousand times the effective dose before death would occur.[15] Nonetheless, there is a dose-related increase in heart rate during early stages of marijuana ingestion, up to 160 beats per minute when dose levels are high. Blood pressure either increases, decreases, or remains the same, depending primarily on whether the individual is standing, sitting, or lying down.[16] A dilation of blood vessels on the cornea resulting in bloodshot eyes peaks in about an hour after smoking a joint. Frequently there is a drying of the mouth and an urge to drink.

Other physiological reactions are inconsistent, and at least part of the inconsistency can be attributed to cultural and interpersonal influences. For example, the observation that marijuana smoking makes you feel extremely hungry and crave especially sweet things to eat (often referred to as "having the munchies") generally holds true in studies of North Americans but not for Jamaicans, who consider marijuana an appetite suppressant.

Likewise, North Americans often report enhanced sexual responses following marijuana use, whereas in India marijuana is considered a sexual depressant. These reactions, being subjective in nature, can very well be slanted in one direction or the other by the mind-set (expectations) of the marijuana smoker going into the experience. A good example is the effect on sexual responses. If you believe that marijuana turns you on sexually, the chances are that it will.

Although expectations undoubtedly play a prominent role here, we should be aware of the possibility that varying effects also may be due to differences in the THC concentration of the marijuana being smoked. In the case of sexual reactivity, studies of male marijuana smokers have shown that low-dose marijuana tends to enhance sexual desire, while high-dose

marijuana tends to depress it, even to the point of impotence. It is quite possible that the enhancement is a result of a brief rise in the male sex hormone, testosterone, and the depression a result of a rebound effect that lowers testosterone below normal levels. Typically, the THC concentration in India is higher than that in North America. As a result, we would expect different effects on sexual reactivity. The same argument could be made with respect to the differences in marijuana's effect on appetite.[17]

In 2005, approximately 242,200 drug-related emergency department (ED) visits in the DAWN statistics (see Chapter 1) involved marijuana, making it the third highest category behind cocaine and heroin. In only a small percentage of these cases, however, was marijuana the sole drug present in the patient's system at the time. In general, marijuana-related emergency department incidents have risen since the 1990s. Whether this increase is the result of more people smoking marijuana, higher THC concentration in the available marijuana, or the greater incidence of marijuana being combined with alcohol or some other drug remains uncertain.[18]

Acute Psychological and Behavioral Effects

Chapter 5 noted that a first-time heroin abuser frequently finds the experience more aversive than pleasurable. With marijuana, it is likely that a first-time smoker will feel no discernible effects at all. It takes some practice to be able to inhale deeply and keep the smoke in the lungs long enough (up to forty seconds) for a minimal level of THC, particularly in low-quality marijuana, to take effect. Novices often have to be instructed to focus on some aspect of the intoxicated state to start to feel intoxicated, but the psychological reactions, once they do occur, are fairly predictable.

The marijuana high, as the name implies, is a feeling of euphoria and well-being. Marijuana smokers typically report an increased awareness of their surroundings, as well as a sharpened sense of sight and sound. Frequently they feel that everything is suddenly very funny, and even the most innocent comments or events can set off uproarious laughter. Usually mundane ideas can seem filled with profound implications, and the individual may feel that creativity has been increased. As with LSD, however, no objective evidence shows that creativity is enhanced by marijuana. Commonly, time seems to pass more slowly while a person is under the influence of marijuana, and events appear to be elongated in duration. Finally, marijuana smokers frequently report that they feel sleepy and sometimes dreamy. The usual THC concentrations of a marijuana joint are not sufficient to be particularly sleep-inducing, though stronger cannabis preparations with higher THC can have strong sleep-inducing effects, particularly when combined with alcohol.[19]

At the same time, marijuana produces significant deficits in behavior. The major deficit is a decline in the ability to carry out tasks that involve attention and memory. Speech will be increasingly fragmented and disjointed; individuals often will forget what they, or others, have just said. The problem is that marijuana typically causes such a rush of distracting ideas to come to mind that it is difficult to concentrate on new information coming in. By virtue of a diminished focus of concentration, the performance of both short-term and long-term memory tasks is impaired. In general, these difficulties increase in magnitude as a direct function of the level of THC in the marijuana (Drugs... in Focus).[20]

It should not be surprising that complex motor tasks, such as driving a car, are also more poorly performed while a person is under the influence of marijuana. It is not necessarily a matter of reaction time; studies of marijuana smokers in automobile simulators indicate that they are as quick to respond as control subjects. The problem arises from a difficulty in attending to peripheral information and making an appropriate response while driving.[21] One researcher has put it this way:

> Marijuana-intoxicated drivers might be able to stop a car as fast as they normally could, but they may not be as quick to notice things that they should stop for. This is probably because they are attending to internal events rather than what is happening on the road.[22]

A study in 1994, conducted in Memphis, Tennessee, found that 33 percent of all reckless drivers tested positive for marijuana and 18 percent tested positive for both marijuana and cocaine. A trauma center in Maryland reported in 1995 that a positive test for marijuana was found for 32 percent of all injured automobile drivers and 39 percent of all injured motorcycle drivers. Given the slow elimination of marijuana, it is uncertain whether all of those testing positive were actually high while driving; nevertheless, the percentages of accidents are substantially higher than for the general population.[23]

An additional problem is quite serious. The decline in sensory–motor performance will persist well after the point at which the marijuana smoker no longer feels high, when there has been chronic heavy marijuana use. Significant impairments in attention and memory tasks have been demonstrated among heavy marijuana users (daily smokers) twenty-four hours after they had

Drugs... in Focus

Can You Control a Marijuana High?

Experienced marijuana smokers often report that they can turn off their high, if the motivation is sufficiently strong, and behave as if in a normal (undrugged) state. Is this really true?

Controlled laboratory studies, in which specific behaviors can be carefully measured, provide the only source for a scientific answer. In one such study, a group of marijuana smokers were instructed to minimize, as much as they could, the subjective effects of marijuana. When given a time estimation task, these subjects performed more accurately than subjects who were not

given the instructions. When given a recall task, however, the two groups were not different in their performance. All the marijuana smokers showed an impairment, regardless of efforts by some of them to resist the drug's effects.

So it appears that only some behaviors are subject to manipulation. Marijuana smokers may *feel* normal, but other aspects of their behavior remain impaired.

Source: Cappell, Howard, and Pliner, Patricia (1974). Cannabis intoxication: The role of pharmacological and psychological variables. In Loren L. Miller (Ed.), *Marijuana: Effects of human behavior.* Orlando, FL: Academic Press, pp. 233–264.

last used the drug. Therefore, we have to recognize the possibility that some important aspects of behavior can be impaired following marijuana smoking, even when an individual is not aware of it. This effect is likely due to the very slow rate with which marijuana is eliminated from the body.[24]

Acute emotional problems as a result of smoking marijuana are rare among Americans, who typically are exposed to relatively low THC concentrations, though some distortion of body image, paranoia, and anxiety may occur. It is possible that marijuana smoking among individuals predisposed toward or recovering from a psychosis may trigger psychotic behavior. Nonetheless, there is little or no support for the idea that low doses of marijuana will provoke such reactions in otherwise normal individuals.

In contrast, a substantially higher incidence of psychiatric problems arising from THC exposure has been reported in India and North Africa. In such cases, however, the THC concentrations being ingested, the frequency with which THC is ingested, and the duration of THC exposure over a lifetime are all generally greater than would be encountered in the United States.[25]

Effects of Marijuana on the Brain

Ever since THC was isolated in 1964 as the primary agent for the intoxicating properties of marijuana, the next step has been to find out specifically how THC affects the brain to produce these effects. In 1990, the mechanism was discovered. Just as with morphine, special receptors in the brain are stimulated specifically by THC. They are concentrated in areas of the brain that are important for short-term memory and motor control. Unlike morphine-sensitive receptors, however, the THC-sensitive receptors are not found in the lower portions of the brain that control breathing. As a result, no matter how high the THC concentration in the brain, there is no danger of an accidental death by asphyxiation.

Once we have identified a specific receptor for a drug, the question inevitably becomes, Why is it there? As noted in Chapter 5, when the morphine-sensitive receptor was discovered, it made sense to speculate about a natural morphine-like substance that would fit into that receptor. The same speculation surrounded the discovery of the THC-sensitive receptor until 1992, when researchers isolated a natural substance,

Quick Concept Check 7.1

Understanding the Effects of Marijuana

Check your understanding of the effects of marijuana by checking off the response (on the right) that you think is appropriate to the circumstances related to marijuana or other cannabis products (on the left).

CIRCUMSTANCE	INCREASES THE EFFECT	DECREASES THE EFFECT
1. The resin content in the cannabis is low.	_____	_____
2. You have decided to inhale more deeply.	_____	_____
3. You are smoking hashish instead of marijuana.	_____	_____
4. This is the first time you have ever smoked marijuana.	_____	_____

Answers: 1. decreases the effect 2. increases the effect 3. increases the effect 4. decreases the effect.

dubbed **anandamide,** that activates this receptor and appears to produce the same effects as THC in the brain.

The functions of anandamide and THC-sensitive receptors remain largely a mystery. One study has found that THC stimulates neurons in the nucleus accumbens in rats, the same area that is affected by a host of other psychoactive drugs, including heroin, cocaine, and nicotine. The effect, however, is much weaker than with drugs that produce strong signs of dependence. Animals will self-administer marijuana in laboratory studies and, in fact, are able to discriminate high-potency from low-potency marijuana, but their behavior is not as compulsive as that observed with heroin, cocaine, or nicotine.[26]

anandamide (a-NAN-duh-mide): A naturally occurring chemical in the brain that fits into THC-sensitive receptor sites, producing many of the same effects as marijuana.

Chronic Effects of Marijuana

Is chronic marijuana smoking harmful over a period of time? What is the extent of tolerance and dependence? Are there long-term consequences for organ systems in the body? Will marijuana lessen one's potential as a productive human being in society? Will marijuana abuse lead to the abuse of other drugs? These are questions to be considered next.

Tolerance

It is frequently reported that experienced marijuana smokers tend to become intoxicated more quickly and to a greater extent than nonexperienced smokers, when exposed to marijuana joints with equivalent THC concentrations. For many years, this observation suggested that repeated administrations of marijuana produced sensitization, or reverse tolerance (a greater sensitivity), rather than tolerance (a lesser sensitivity). If this were true, then we would have been faced with the troubling conclusion that marijuana operates in a totally opposite way to any other psychoactive drug considered so far. As it turns out, when animals or humans are studied in the laboratory, marijuana smoking shows tolerance effects that are consistent and clear-cut.

Why, then, the difference with the experience of humans outside the laboratory? One factor involves the way in which we measure the quantity of THC consumed. Reaching an effective high from marijuana requires some degree of practice. For example, novice marijuana smokers may not have mastered the breathing technique necessary to allow the minimal level of THC to enter the lungs. They may have to smoke a relatively large number of marijuana joints initially before they achieve a high. Later, when they have acquired the technique, they may need fewer joints to accomplish the same effect. In these circumstances, a calculation of the number of joints consumed does not reflect the amount of THC ingested. If you were to control the THC content entering the body, as is done in laboratory studies, you would find the predictable results of tolerance over repeated administrations.

Another factor complicating tolerance studies involves the slow elimination rate of marijuana. Regular marijuana smokers are likely to have a residual amount of THC still in the system. This buildup of THC would elevate the total quantity of THC consumed with every joint and induce a quicker high. Once again, the impression of sensitization is false; we are actually observing the enhanced effects of an accumulation of THC in the body. Once dosage levels are controlled, the results indicate a consistent pattern of tolerance rather than sensitization. In general, tolerance effects following repeated administrations of THC are greater as the dosage level of THC increases.[27]

Withdrawal and Dependence

On the basis of early studies conducted in the 1970s, it appeared that evidence of physical dependence (that is, the observation of withdrawal symptoms) following chronic administration of marijuana was limited to circumstances in which the level of THC ingestion was extreme. In one study, human volunteers were administered large doses of THC every four hours for ten to twenty days. Within twelve hours after the last administration, subjects reported physical symptoms that included hot flashes, irritability, restlessness, and insomnia. In contrast, in another study in which subjects smoked one marijuana cigarette daily for twenty-eight days, a condition closer to the typical exposure to marijuana, no withdrawal symptoms were observed.[28]

More recent studies, however, have shown that withdrawal effects can occur even with more moderate levels of THC consumed over shorter periods of time. Abstinence from smoking marijuana cigarettes with approximately 2 to 3 percent THC levels or equivalent oral doses of THC, administered four times a day over a four-day period, resulted in feelings of irritability, stomach pain, anxiety, and loss of appetite. These symptoms began within forty-eight hours and lasted at least two days.[29] Therefore, it is quite possible that daily marijuana use among chronic marijuana smokers is maintained, at least in part, because of its alleviation of withdrawal symptoms. Nonetheless, the symptoms involved here are substantially milder than those associated with the chronic use of heroin (Chapter 5) or alcohol (Chapter 11).

There is also evidence of marijuana craving, indicating a level of psychological dependence in some marijuana smokers, but it is difficult to measure the extent of these feelings or to determine whether these effects are due to circumstances in which marijuana is used in conjunction with other drugs. With marijuana smoking at the THC levels commonly encountered in the United States, there is nowhere near the degree of obsessive drug seeking and compulsive drug-taking behavior associated with alcohol, opiates, or stimulant drugs.[30]

Cardiovascular Effects

THC produces significant increases in heart rate, but there is no conclusive evidence of adverse effects in the cardiovascular functioning in young, healthy people. The reason why the emphasis is on a specific age group is that most of the studies looking at possible long-term cardiovascular effects have involved marijuana smokers under the age of thirty-five; little or no information has been compiled about older populations. For those people with preexisting disorders such as heart disease, high blood pressure, or arteriosclerosis (hardening of the arteries), it is known that the acute effects of marijuana on heart rate and blood pressure can worsen their condition.

Respiratory Effects and the Risk of Cancer

The technique of marijuana smoking involves the deep and maintained inhalation into the lungs of unfiltered smoke on a repetitive basis, probably the worst scenario for incurring chronic pulmonary problems. In addition, a marijuana joint (when compared with a tobacco cigarette) typically contains about the same levels of tars, 50 percent more hydrocarbons, and an unknown amount of possible contaminants (Table 7.1). Joints are often smoked more completely because the smoker tries to waste as little marijuana as possible.

TABLE 7.1

A comparison of the components of marijuana and tobacco smoke

COMPONENT	MARIJUANA	TOBACCO
Carbon monoxide (mg)	17.6	20.2
Carbon dioxide (mg)	57.3	65.0
Ammonia (micrograms)	228.0	178.0
Acetaldehyde (micrograms)	1,200.0	980.0
Acetone (micrograms)*	443.0	578.0
Benzene (micrograms)*	76.0	67.0
Toluene (micrograms)*	112.0	108.0
THC (tetrahydrocannabinol) (micrograms)	820.0	—
Nicotine (micrograms)	—	2,850.0
Napthalene (nanograms)	3,000.0	1,200.0

*See Chapter 8 for information about the health risks of inhaling some of these chemicals.

Source: Julien, Robert M. (2001). *A primer of drug action* (9th ed.). New York: Worth, p. 317.

Given all these factors, marijuana smoking presents several risks. One of the immediate consequences affects the process of breathing. When marijuana is inhaled initially, the passageways for air entering and leaving the lungs widen, but after chronic exposure, an opposite reaction occurs. As a result, symptoms of asthma and other breathing difficulties are increased. Overall, while the effects of a single inhalation of marijuana smoke present greater problems than a single inhalation of tobacco smoke, we need to remember that the patterns of consumption are far from comparable. All things considered, on a statistical basis, you can think of one joint as being equivalent to five cigarettes in terms of the amount of carbon monoxide intake and four cigarettes in terms of tar intake. The use of a water pipe reduces the harm somewhat, but the risks are still present. Molecular abnormalities in the respiratory tracts of heavy marijuana smokers have been identified that resemble the changes in the respiratory tracts of cigarette smokers. A recent study has shown that long-term marijuana smoking causes an obstruction of air flow in the lungs, resulting in asthma and bronchitis. The effect of a single marijuana joint is equivalent to up to five tobacco cigarettes in this regard. However, marijuana smoking does not increase the risk of developing emphysema, a chronic lung disease that is associated with tobacco smoking (see Chapter 12).

Given these risks, does smoking marijuana produce a higher incidence of cancer? There is no evidence of definitive increases in lung cancer rates among marijuana smokers, after controlling for tobacco use. In fact, no increases in risk for many types of cancer have been found as a result of marijuana use, once alcohol and cigarette use has been excluded from the analysis. But it may be too soon to decisively answer the question of cancer risk at this time. The marijuana smokers who were twenty years old in the late 1960s are just approaching the peak ages when cancers appear. Those individuals more recently exposed to higher-potency marijuana, such as those whose marijuana experience began in the 1990s, are substantially younger. Therefore, the extent to which marijuana smoking is a risk factor for cancer remains a question for the future. Fortunately, there is the possibility, as is the case with cigarette smoking (see Chapter 12), that the risk of cancer will decline after a person has stopped smoking marijuana.[31]

Effects on the Immune System

When THC is administered to animals, the immune system is suppressed, resulting in a reduction in the body's defense reactions to infection and disease. In humans, the evidence is inconclusive. Some studies indicate that THC has a suppressive effect; others indicate that no immunological changes occur at all. Because marijuana smoking has not been found to be associated with a higher incidence of any major chronic disease, we can tentatively conclude that marijuana smoking does not have a major impact on the immune system. Yet long-term epidemiological studies, in which marijuana-exposed and control populations are compared with regard to the frequency of various diseases, have not been conducted on a large-scale basis.[32]

Effects on Sexual Functioning and Reproduction

The reproductive systems of both men and women are adversely affected by marijuana smoking. In men, marijuana reduces the level of testosterone, reduces sperm count in the semen, and increases the percentage of abnormally formed sperm. In women, marijuana use results in a reduction in the level of luteinizing hormone (LH), a hormone necessary for the fertilized egg to be implanted in the uterus. As little as one marijuana joint smoked immediately following ovulation is evidently sufficient for this LH suppression to occur. Despite these hormonal changes in both males and females, however, little or no effect on fertility has been observed.[33]

The research is sparse on the question, but there does not appear to be evidence of birth defects in the off-spring of women who have smoked marijuana during their pregnancy. Studies indicate, however, a lower birth weight and shorter length among newborns, as well as a reduction in the mother's milk. It may be unfair to associate these effects specifically with marijuana smoking because other drugs, including alcohol and nicotine, are often being consumed during the same period. Even so, the best advice remains that women should avoid marijuana during pregnancy.[34]

Long-Term Cognitive Effects and the Amotivational Syndrome

Though chronic exposure to marijuana frequently has been suspected of producing some form of brain damage or long-term impairment in neural functioning, there is little or no evidence in support of this idea.[35] It

amotivational syndrome: A state of listlessness and personality change involving a generalized apathy and indifference to long-range plans.

also has been suspected that marijuana may produce more subtle neurological changes that would affect one's personality, motivation to succeed, or outlook on life.

In 1968, William McGlothin, a psychologist, and Louis West, a psychiatrist, proposed that chronic marijuana smoking among young people was responsible for a generalized sense of apathy in their lives and an indifference to any long-term plans or conventional goals. These changes were called the **amotivational syndrome.** In their words,

> Regular marijuana use may contribute to the development of more passive, inward-turning personality characteristics. For numerous middle-class students, the subtly progressive change from conforming, achievement-oriented behavior to a state of relaxed and careless drifting has followed their use of significant amounts of marijuana....Such individuals exhibit greater introversion, become totally involved with the present at the expense of future goals, and demonstrate a strong tendency toward regressive, childlike magical thinking.[36]

In effect, McGothlin and West, and probably a large number of other people in the late 1960s, were saying, "These people don't seem to care anymore and marijuana's to blame for it."

The issue of the amotivational syndrome revolves around two basic questions that need to be examined separately. The first question deals with whether such a syndrome exists in the first place, and the second deals with whether chronic abuse of marijuana is a causal factor. As to the existence of the syndrome, the evidence does suggest that students who smoke marijuana are at a disadvantage academically. Studies of high school students indicate that those who smoke marijuana on a regular basis (weekly or more frequently) earn lower grades in school (Figure 7.1), are less likely to continue on to college, are more likely to drop out, and miss more classes than those who do not smoke it.[37] In a survey of high school students graduating in the early 1980s, those who smoked marijuana on a daily basis reported several problems in their lives that are related to motivation: a loss of energy (43 percent), negative effects on relationships (39 percent), interference with work and the ability to think clearly (37 percent), less interest in other activities (37 percent), and inferior performance in school or on the job (34 percent).[38] It is likely that these percentages would be roughly the same today.

These changes are genuine, but we cannot easily establish a direct causal link between marijuana and such global problems, other than to acknowledge that the

176 ■ **Part Two   Legally Restricted Drugs in Our Society**

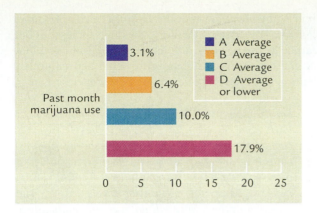

FIGURE 7.1

Percentages of past month marijuana and blunt use among students aged 12 to 17 and semester grade average.

Note: Blunts are hollowed-out cigars refilled with marijuana.

Source: Substance Abuse and Mental Health Services Administration (2007). Use of marijuana and blunts among adolescents: 2005. *The NSDUH Report*, p. 3.

presence of THC in a student's system during school hours would be reflected later in a decline in overall academic performance. More broadly speaking, we cannot exclude the possibility that marijuana smoking may be, in the words of one expert in the field, "just one behavior in a constellation of related problem behaviors and personality and familial factors" that hamper an adolescent's ability to do well in school and in life.[39] We also cannot exclude the possibility that an involvement with marijuana may closely correlate with involvement in a deviant subculture, a group of friends and associates who feel alienated from traditional values such as school achievement and a promising future (see Chapter 3). Either of these factors, in combination with the regular ingestion of marijuana, can account for the motivational changes that are observed. The point is that we cannot conclude that such life-style changes are purely pharmacological.

While it is clear that acute marijuana intoxication produces significant cognitive deficits, as evidenced by reduced scores on tasks of attentiveness and memory, the question remains whether these problems are increased or perhaps may become irreversible as a result of long-term marijuana use. Recent large and well-controlled studies have shown that cognitive deficits in heavy marijuana smokers, relative to nonusers, are observed after twelve to seventy-two hours of abstinence. In other words, the specific signs of cognitive impairment among long-term marijuana smokers may linger for as long as three days after active marijuana smoking. In one study, however, testing after twenty-eight days of abstinence revealed equivalent performance scores be-

tween nonusers and users of marijuana, even though the latter group had smoked a median of about fifteen thousand times over a period ranging from ten to thirty-three years. No correlation was seen between the test scores after twenty-eight days of abstinence and the number of episodes of marijuana use over an individual's lifetime. Therefore, it appears that problems related to attention and memory among heavy marijuana smokers can be reversed by stopping marijuana use. It is a hopeful sign in the context of drug-abuse treatment (Chapter 15).[40]

The Gateway Hypothesis

A widely publicized concern with respect to marijuana smoking deals with the relationship between marijuana use and the subsequent abuse of illicit drugs such as amphetamines, cocaine, or heroin. The contention that marijuana leads to a greater incidence of drug abuse in general is referred to as the **gateway hypothesis.** As in the consideration of the amotivational syndrome, the evidence for this hypothesis must be studied very carefully.

With respect to the gateway hypothesis, we should address three separate issues: (1) whether a fixed sequential relationship exists between the initiation of marijuana use and other forms of drug-taking behavior, (2) whether marijuana use represents a significant risk factor for future drug-taking behavior, specifically increasing the likelihood of using other illicit drugs, and (3) whether marijuana actually causes the use of other illicit drugs.

The Sequencing Question

One of the best-replicated findings in the long-term study of drug use is a developmental sequence of involvement (stages of progression) in drug-taking behavior. In the United States as well as other Western societies, use of alcohol and cigarettes precedes marijuana use, and marijuana use precedes use of other illicit drugs. As public health researcher Denise Kandel has expressed it:

> *Very few individuals who have tried cocaine and heroin have not already used marijuana; the majority have previously used alcohol or tobacco.*[41]

Nonetheless, it is important to point out that an overwhelming proportion of young marijuana smokers do

gateway hypothesis: The idea that the abuse of a specific drug will inherently lead to the abuse of other, more harmful drugs.

not go on to use other illicit drugs. As expressed in a 1999 newspaper editorial on this point, "millions of baby boomers... once did, indeed, inhale. They later went into business, not cocaine or heroin."[42]

The Association Question

From a statistical perspective, the association between marijuana use and subsequent use of other illicit drugs is not controversial. Generally speaking, marijuana smokers are several times more likely to consume illicit drugs such as cocaine and heroin during their lifetimes than are nonmarijuana smokers. Not surprisingly, the greater the frequency of marijuana smoking and the earlier an individual first engages in marijuana smoking, the greater the likelihood of his or her becoming involved with other illicit drugs in the future.

A precise determination of the magnitude of risk involved in marijuana use requires studies that take into account a range of genetic and environmental variables that might act as risk or protective factors for drug-taking behavior (see Chapter 3). A recent study set out to control for these variables by investigating a specific subpopulation of twins, one of whom reported marijuana use by the age of seventeen and the other who reported no marijuana use at all. Examining twins permitted the researchers to calculate the increased risk of future drug-taking behavior when environmental factors (in the case of fraternal twins) and both environmental and genetic factors (in the case of identical twins) were controlled. Results showed that early marijuana users were about two and one-half times more likely to use heroin later in life, four times more likely to use cocaine or other stimulants, and five times more likely to use hallucinogens. In general, they were twice as likely to become alcoholic and twice as likely to develop any form of illicit drug abuse or dependence.

The question of whether future twin studies using this approach will find the increased risk from marijuana use to be *higher than the increased risk from alcohol or tobacco use* remains unanswered. In any case, the fact that marijuana use is one of the risk factors for illicit drug use in other forms reinforces the need to develop intervention programs for marijuana users that might serve to prevent subsequent drug use, as well as prevention programs for youths to reduce the incidence of marijuana use in the first place.[43]

In the final analysis, however, the statistical relationship between marijuana smoking and other forms of drug-taking behavior merely reflects the sequential pattern of drug use among multiple-drug (polydrug) users. Essentially, drug users initiate the use of high-prevalence drugs (such as alcohol, tobacco, marijuana) earlier than they initiate the use of low-prevalence drugs (such as cocaine, heroin). This effect is not due to the drugs themselves but rather to the relative differences in prevalence rates. Numerous statistical relationships exist between other types of common and uncommon behaviors:

> *For example, most people who ride a motorcycle (a fairly rare activity) have ridden a bicycle (a fairly common activity). Indeed, the prevalence of motorcycle riding among people who have never ridden a bicycle is probably extremely low. Bicycle riding, however, does not cause motorcycle riding, and increases in the former will not lead automatically to increases in the latter.*[44]

The Causation Question

The strongest form of the gateway hypothesis relates to the possibility of a causal link between marijuana smoking and the use of other illicit drugs. With respect to the causation issue, Erich Goode, a sociologist and drug-abuse researcher, has distinguished between two schools of thought, which he calls the intrinsic argument and the sociocultural argument. The *intrinsic argument* asserts that some inherent property of marijuana exposure itself leads to physical or psychological dependence on other illicit drugs. According to this viewpoint, the pleasurable sensations of marijuana create a biological urge to consume more potent substances, through a combination of drug tolerance and drug dependence. In contrast, the *sociocultural argument* holds that the relationship exists not because of the pharmacological effects of marijuana but because of the activities, friends, and acquaintances that are associated with marijuana smoking. In other words, the sociocultural explanation asserts that those who smoke marijuana tend to have friends who not only smoke marijuana themselves but also abuse other drugs. These friends are likely to have positive attitudes toward substance abuse in general and to provide opportunities for drug experimentation.

Professionals in the drug-abuse field have concluded that if any such causal link exists, the result would be socioculturally based rather than related to the pharmacological properties of marijuana itself. The consensus is that any early exposure to psychoactive substances in general, and illicit drugs such as marijuana in particular, represents a "deviance-prone pattern of behavior" that will be reflected in a higher incidence of exposure to psychoactive drugs of many types later in life. It is interesting to note that early adolescent marijuana use among males also increases the risk in late adolescence of delinquency, having multiple sexual partners, not always using condoms during sex, perceiving drugs as not harmful, and having problems with cigarettes and alcohol. Generally speaking, marijuana smokers show a greater inclination toward risk-taking behavior and are more unconventional with regard to social norms.[45]

Patterns of Marijuana Smoking

From as early as their days in elementary school, most young Americans have had to come to terms with marijuana as a pervasive element in their lives. Just as

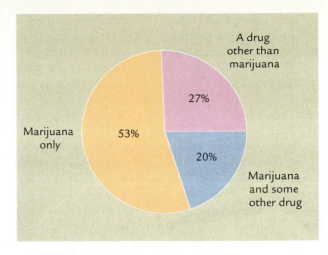

FIGURE 7.2

Types of drugs used by illicit drug users aged 12 or older in the past month in 2006.

Source: Substance Abuse and Mental Health Services Administration (2007). *Results from the 2006 National Survey on Drug Use and Health: National findings.* Rockville, MD: Office of Applied Studies, Substance Abuse and Mental Health Services Administration, p.16.

nearly all adolescents have had to make the decision whether to drink or not to drink, and whether to smoke cigarettes or not to smoke them, they also have had to decide whether to smoke or not smoke marijuana.

Marijuana is undoubtedly the dominant illicit drug in U.S. society, used by 73 percent of current illicit drug users (Figure 7.2). For about half of illicit drug users, marijuana is the *only* illicit drug being used. From the National Survey on Drug Use and Health conducted in 2006, it is estimated that an astounding 98 million Americans, about 40 percent of the U.S. population over the age of twelve, have smoked marijuana at least once during their lives. About 15 million Americans, about one out of sixteen, are estimated to have smoked marijuana within the last thirty days.

Domestic marijuana growing represents the number-one cash crop in the United States, with revenues of about $30 billion per year. Large-scale marijuana farms, financed by Mexican drug cartels, have been discovered recently in the steep Sierra Nevada foothills of Sequoia National Park in California. Almost 60 percent of the marijuana plants eradicated in California in 2002 were found on state or federal land. In addition, Canadian growers in British Columbia have developed a hydroponic technique of marijuana cultivation, in which plants are grown indoors in nutrient-rich water rather than soil. This form of cultivation allows plants to grow faster and produce larger leaves, flowers, and buds. As a result, a higher-potency marijuana, with THC levels as high as 15 to 25 percent, can be marketed.[46]

Through the University of Michigan survey we can get an idea of the prevalence rates among young people, particularly since 1992. Among high school seniors surveyed in 2006, approximately 32 percent reported having smoked marijuana in the past year, 18 percent reported having done so in the past month, and 5 percent smoked on a daily basis. Granted, these numbers are still below the peak levels reached in the late 1970s. However, they continue to be substantially higher than levels observed in 1990 and 1991. Among eighth graders, 12 percent reported smoking marijuana in the past year and 7 percent in the past month, also up substantially from the early 1990s. The current status of prevention programs, understandably under considerable pressure to reduce rates of marijuana smoking as well as involvement in other drugs among young people, will be examined in Chapter 15.[47]

Current Trends as Causes for Concern

In addition to the rise in the number of marijuana smokers among young people, there is also a change in the way marijuana use is perceived. Chapter 2 noted that until 1991, the trend in the percentage of students who thought that marijuana smoking and drug abuse in general carried significant personal risks had been steadily

upward. Survey results showed a reversal after 1991. While 58 percent of high school seniors in 2006 considered "regular marijuana smoking" harmful, this figure was down substantially from 79 percent in 1991.[48]

We also have seen a growing popular culture that reinforces the behavior of marijuana smoking as a cool thing to do. The transformation since the beginning of the 1990s has been dramatic. In 1990, marijuana smoking was not in the media spotlight and young people considered marijuana use to be "uncool." By 1993, however, the image of marijuana had changed dramatically. One student commented, "The image of the pot smoker . . . [used to be] very much of a hippie thing. Now it's completely different. There's a whole mode of dress, music, and style that didn't exist three years ago."[49]

A further concern with regard to present-day marijuana use has to do with an increased potency in the cannabis products that are available. A typical marijuana joint in the psychedelic era contained approximately 1 to 2 percent THC; the average concentration now is around 6 percent. The higher-potency form, sinsemilla, is more widely available than ever before, as is hashish. It is reasonable to assume that the adverse effects of chronic marijuana smoking, with THC concentrations approaching 15 percent in some strains of sinsemilla, will be more intense than the relatively mild symptoms associated with marijuana use in the past (Drugs . . . in Focus).

A final concern applies to any illicit street drug: the possibility for adulteration. As emphasized in earlier chapters, what you buy is not always what you get. Each year brings with it a new group of ingredients, some of them newly introduced drugs and others merely inventive creations from already available materials, ready to be combined with marijuana either to weaken its effects (and increase the profits of the seller) or to change the overall psychoactive result by some synergistic or other interactive effect (Drug Trafficking Update).

Medical Uses for Marijuana

Even though the medicinal benefits of marijuana have been noted for thousands of years, strong antimarijuana sentiment in the United States made it difficult until the 1970s to conduct an objective appraisal of its clinical applications. Early research in the effectiveness of marijuana to reduce intraocular (within the eye) pressure and dilate bronchioles in the lungs suggested uses as a possible therapy for glaucoma and asthma, respectively. However, new prescription medications have been shown to be as

The image of *Cannabis sativa* today.

effective as marijuana in the treatment of these disorders. Today the focus has turned toward the treatment of nausea and weight loss, conditions for which medications have been unsuccessful in offering significant relief.

Nausea and Weight Loss

Chemotherapy in the course of cancer treatment produces an extreme and debilitating nausea, lack of appetite, and loss of body weight, symptoms that are

Drugs . . . in Focus

Street Language for Marijuana

In the 1960s, when marijuana smoking first became widely popular, the street language was fairly simple. Marijuana was either "grass" or "pot," and a marijuana cigarette was a "joint." Here is an updated sampling of the street language, though the names (and prices) are constantly changing.

- marijuana: grass, weed, 420, skunk, boom, doobie, bud, herb, BC bud (Over the years, more than 600 slang names have been given to marijuana.)
- marijuana and alcohol: Herb and Al
- getting high on marijuana: getting lifted, booted, red, smoked out or choked out, hit the hay, poke, toke up, blast a stick, burn one, fly Mexican Airlines, mow the grass, boot the gong
- $3 bag of marijuana: a tray
- $5 "nickel" bag: a nick (usually just enough for one joint)
- $40 bag: a sandwich bag
- kinds of marijuana: chronic, chocolate tide, indigo, Hawaiian, Tropicana, Acapulco gold, Panama red

- water pipe similar to a bong: a shotgun
- joints: "blunts" (after the Phillies Blunt cigars that marijuana smokers cut open, hollow out, and fill with marijuana; other brands used, White Owls and Dutch Masters)
- hydro: hydroponic marijuana, grown in water

According to the National Survey on Drug Use and Health, more than 50 percent of marijuana users in 2005 between the ages of 12 and 17 used blunts in marijuana smoking. The popularity of blunts increased with age. Males reported more often than females to have smoked marijuana in a blunt during the past month.

Sources: Bureau of Justice Statistics Clearinghouse (1992). *Drugs, crime, and the justice system,* Washington DC: Department of Justice, pp. 24–25. Henneberger, Melinda (1994, February 6). "Pot" surges back, but it's, like, a whole new world. *New York Times,* Sect. 4, p. 18. Inciardi, James A. (2002). *The war on drugs III.* Boston, Allyn and Bacon, pp. 56–57. Use of marijuana and blunts among adolescents: 2005 (2007, March 9). *The NSDUH Report,* p. 1.

clearly counterproductive in helping an individual contend with an ongoing fight against cancer. AIDS patients suffer from similar symptoms, as do those diagnosed with the gastrointestinal ailment Crohn's disease. During these circumstances, standard antiemetic (antivomiting) drugs are frequently ineffective. The beneficial effect of marijuana, specifically THC, as an antiemetic drug is an important application of marijuana as a medical treatment.[50] This chapter's Portrait examines the present-day dilemma of turning to an illegal drug for medicinal purposes.

At the same time, the use of marijuana per se as a therapeutic agent has distinct disadvantages. First, the typical administration through smoking presents, as described earlier, a significant health risk to the lungs. Second, because marijuana is insoluble in water, suspensions in an injectable form cannot be prepared. Since 1985, however, two legal prescription drugs containing THC or a variation of it have been made available in capsule form. **Dronabinol** (brand name: Marinol) is essentially THC in a sesame oil suspension; **nabilone** (brand name: Cesamet) is a synthetic variation of THC. Both drugs have been shown to be clinically effective as antinausea treatments, though the personal reactions of patients taking these drugs vary considerably.[51]

The Medical Marijuana Controversy

While Marinol and Cesamet are presently in use, U.S. federal authorities have resisted the reclassification of marijuana itself or any other cannabis product from the Schedule I category of controlled substances (drugs that have no medical application) to the Schedule II category (which includes morphine and cocaine). Only a handful of "compassionate use" applications have been approved, and the entire program for reviewing new applications was curtailed in 1992 (see Portrait).

Despite opposition from federal authorities, advocacy for the medical application of marijuana has grown considerably. Unfortunately, the facts about medical marijuana sometimes have been lost in a thicket of politics and opposing ideologies. A case in point is the interpretation of a major report on the possibility of marijuana as a medical treatment, issued by the Institute

of Medicine, a branch of the National Academy of Sciences, in 1999. In its preface, the report began by acknowledging the problems involved:

> Although marijuana smoke delivers THC and other cannabinoids to the body, it also delivers harmful substances, including most of those found in tobacco smoke. In addition, plants contain a variable mixture of biologically-active compounds and cannot be expected to provide a precisely defined drug effect. For these reasons, this report concludes that the future of cannabinoid drugs lies not in smoked marijuana, but in chemically-defined drugs that act on the cannabinoid systems that are a natural component of human physiology.[52]

In focusing on the report's preface, the federal Office of National Drug Control Strategy has emphasized the potential health risks of marijuana smoking and the imprecision of its administration as its justification for the continued prohibition of marijuana for medical purposes. Largely ignored has been one of the report's main statements:

> Until a nonsmoked, rapid-onset cannabinoid drug delivery system becomes available, we acknowledge that there is no clear alternative for people suffering from chronic conditions that might be relieved by smoking marijuana, such as pain or AIDS wasting.[53]

In effect, the report concluded that, while not recommending smoked marijuana for long-term use, short-term use appeared to be suitable for treating specific conditions, when patients failed to respond well to traditional medications.

By 2005, eleven U.S. states (Alaska, California, Colorado, Hawaii, Maine, Maryland, Montana, Nevada, Oregon, Vermont, and Washington) had authorized marijuana smoking for the relief of pain and discomfort or the control of nausea and weight loss, when prescribed by a physician. Nonetheless, the U.S. Supreme Court in 2005 ruled that legalization of medical marijuana at the state level could not supersede federal regulations on the matter. The majority opinion upheld the power of the federal government to prohibit the possession and use of marijuana for medical purposes, even in those states that permit it.

Interestingly, the decision was based not on arguments related to the possible merits of medical marijuana as a treatment, but rather on the issue of interstate commerce. In effect, the court asserted that it was well within federal jurisdiction to "regulate purely local activities that are part of an economic 'class of activities' that

dronabinol (droh-NAB-ih-nol): A prescription drug containing delta-9-tetrahydrocannabinol (THC). Brand name is Marinol.

nabilone (NAB-ih-lone): A prescription drug containing a synthetic variation of delta-9-tetrahydrocannabinol (THC). Brand name is Cesamet.

PORTRAIT

Angel McClary Raich—The Woman Behind the *Raich v. Ashcroft* Decision

In the 2005 U.S. Supreme Court case *Raich v. Ashcroft*, the legal status of medical marijuana within the state of California was overturned in favor of arguments that federal regulations prohibiting marijuana use under any circumstances were paramount. It was a landmark decision, and the consequences with respect to marijuana as a medical treatment remain uncertain. But who was behind *Raich v. Ashcroft* in this case? Who was Raich?

Angel McClary Raich was permanently disabled in 1995. Her medical condition included an inoperable brain tumor, life-threatening wasting syndrome, chronic pain disorders, seizure disorder, nausea, and scoliosis (a painful back condition). Her physician recommended cannabis use as a medication for her symptoms. In a legal deposition submitted at the time, she described her life:

> I suffer greatly from severe chronic pain every single day. The prolonged pain and suffering from my medical condition significantly interferes with my quality of life. My treatment is complicated by the fact that I am violently allergic and have severe multiple sensitivities to almost all pharmaceutical medicines. . . . This makes it extremely difficult for doctors to effectively help me combat my diseases. Without cannabis my life would be a death sentence.[a]

Raich's primary care physician, Dr. Frank Lucido, was the one who made the recommendation of medical marijuana. He recognized that Riach was at significant risk of malnutrition and starvation as well as suffering intolerable pain. He wrote,

> Angel has no reasonable legal alternative to cannabis for the effective treatment or alleviation of her medical conditions or symptoms associated with medical conditions because she has tried essentially all other legal alternatives to cannabis and the alternatives have been ineffective or result from intolerable side effects. Angel will suffer imminent harm without access to cannabis. . . . It would be malpractice to subject the patient to further unnecessary harm. . . . Cannabis works well for Angel in a way that no other medicine has or can be expected to in order to alleviate Angel's medical conditions or symptoms associated with them.[b]

Raich became one of the fourteen "medical necessity" patients at the Oakland Cannabis Buyers' Cooperative who were represented in the court cases that led up to the Supreme Court. In 1996, California voters passed the Compassionate Use Act, legalizing marijuana for medical use within the state. After the Drug Enforcement Administration (DEA)

seized doctor-prescribed marijuana from the home of a patient, advocates of medical marijuana sued the DEA and then–U.S. Attorney General John Ashcroft in federal district court and won. Their case was upheld until the Supreme Court decision in 2005.

In November 2005, Raich filed legal papers in a federal appeals court, arguing that federal efforts and the Supreme Court decision to restrict medical marijuana violated her constitutionally guaranteed rights to take the only medication allowing her to avoid intolerable pain and death. The brief marks a new legal strategy, claiming that the concern for federal control of interstate commerce (see text) does not apply to her use of locally grown marijuana. As Raich puts it, "I just want the opportunity to be a mother to my children without having to live in constant fear that the federal government will raid my home and throw me in jail."[c]

Sources: [a]Who Is Angel McClary Raich? Angel Wings Patient Outreach, Inc. web site, *angeljustice.org.* [b]Declaration of Frank Henry Lucido, M.D., in support of the plaintiff Angel McClary Raich, October 20, 2002, U.S. District Court for the Northern District of California. [c]Ashley, Guy (2005, November 24). Woman pursues new legal strategy in medical marijuana fight. Knight Ridder/Tribune News Service.

---

have a substantial effect on interstate commerce." A restriction of medical marijuana to intrastate (within a state) commerce could not be guaranteed, and therefore federal jurisdiction took over.

While not the last word on the question, the 2005 court decision has nevertheless been a blow to advocates of medical marijuana and the movement toward its legalization at the state level. Technically, federal prosecutions can be carried out in those states where medical marijuana is legal. Whether large numbers of prosecutions will occur in the future, however, is unclear. Presently, the federal government conducts

only 1 percent of marijuana prosecutions in the United States.[54]

In contrast to the policy in the United States, Canada has officially approved the medicinal use of marijuana since 2001. It is legal for Canadian patients to grow and smoke marijuana if their symptoms have been certified by a physician as warranting this treatment. It is also permitted, under these circumstances, to request marijuana, free of charge, from government-operated cannabis farms in Manitoba. In 2005, the FDA-equivalent agency in Canada approved the prescription use of Sativex, a liquid spray derived from the cannabis plant.

More recently, the FDA has approved clinical testing of Sativex for potential sale in the United States. By providing a nonsmoking means of administration, this formulation circumvents arguments that medical marijuana smoking presents increased risks of smoking-related diseases (see Chapter 12).[55]

The Issue of Decriminalization

What, then, should public policy be toward marijuana smoking in the United States today? To deal with this question, we need first to review how public policy with respect to marijuana regulation has evolved since the 1970s. As described earlier, the dramatic emergence during the 1960s of marijuana as a major psychoactive drug initiated a slow but steady reassessment of myths that had been attached to it for decades. By 1972, the American Medical Association, the American Bar Association, William F. Buckley (a prominent conservative commentator and author), and former U.S. Secretary of State George Schultz had proposed a liberalization of laws regarding the possession of marijuana. In 1972, the National Commission on Marijuana and Drug Abuse,

decriminalization: The policy of making the possession of small amounts of a drug subject to a small fine but not criminal prosecution.

authorized by the Comprehensive Drug Abuse Prevention and Control Act of 1970, encouraged state legislators around the country to consider changes in their particular regulatory statutes related to marijuana.[56] Since that time, several states, including California, New York, Colorado, Minnesota, and North Carolina, have adopted some form of decriminalization laws with respect to the possession of marijuana in small amounts (usually less than one ounce or so). Essentially, **decriminalization** has meant that possession under these circumstances is considered a civil (noncriminal) offense, punishable by a small fine, rather than imprisonment.

The trend toward marijuana decriminalization on a state-by-state basis has largely stalled in recent years. No U.S. state has voted for decriminalization since the 1980s, and two states (Alaska and Oregon) that had previously decriminalized marijuana possession have since voted to recriminalize it. As discussed earlier, the focus of changes in legislation regarding marijuana use has been directed toward the question of its limited use as a medical application rather than decriminalization per se. Clearly, however, the era of strenuous law enforcement against marijuana smoking at low levels of usage is over. As the sociologist Erich Goode has expressed it:

For all practical purposes, the possession of [small amounts of] marijuana has become decriminalized in the United States. Since present trends are moving toward de facto legal acceptance of small-quantity marijuana possession, it will not make a great deal of difference whether this attitude is recognized by law or not. Consequently, the debate over marijuana criminalization borders on being obsolete.[57]

You may find it surprising or not surprising (depending on your personal views) that official decriminalization has not been demonstrated to result in an upturn in the incidence of marijuana smoking. Statistics drawn from states that either have or have not decriminalized show little or no difference.[58] In addition, attitude surveys conducted in California before and after the enactment of such statutes indicate that the acceptance of marijuana among college students actually declined following decriminalization.[59]

Whether or not some form of marijuana ingestion becomes officially sanctioned in the United States recently has been intertwined with the question of whether agricultural cultivation of the cannabis plant itself should be permitted for purposes other than the harvesting of marijuana. As pointed out earlier in the chapter, *Cannabis sativa* has been harvested for

thousands of years for the manufacture of hemp products rather than for its leaves. The potential economic benefit for a struggling agricultural industry in the United States has framed the argument for a reexamination of the current policy (Drugs . . . in Focus).

A DEA officer confiscates and destroys a domestic crop of *Cannabis sativa* in Kentucky. Presumably, people living downwind of this operation had been evacuated.

Drugs . . . in Focus

Hemp in America—Coming Full Circle

Faced with depressed corn and soybean prices, farmers in North Dakota and other states in the region have recently considered an interesting alternative crop: high-fiber, high-protein hemp. There is only one drawback. The U.S. government views hemp in the same category as marijuana. Since the Comprehensive Drug Abuse Prevention and Control Act of 1970, hemp has remained a Schedule I controlled substance. Hence, growing "industrial" hemp in the United States is illegal.

Pro-hemp advocates argue that the government permits manufacturers of cosmetics, clothing, paper, and foods (hemp bread being a popular example) to import hemp fiber, seed, and oil from Canada and Europe for use in their products. It is hypocritical, from their point of view, to ban its domestic cultivation. Representing the opposite side of the issue, the DEA sees hemp fields turning into marijuana fields. According to a federal official, "The pro-dope people have been pushing hemp for twenty years because they know that if they can have hemp fields,

then they can have marijuana fields. It's ... stoner logic." The retort is that industrial hemp is high in fiber, protein, vitamin E, and essential fatty acids, and because it has very low concentrations of THC, you don't get high from it.

The economic aspect of the issue weighs heavily on North Dakota farmers. There has been a rapidly emerging global market for hemp over the last decade or so, and they simply do not want to be left out. They would like to return to the days when it was legal to grow hemp in the United States. Indeed, during World War II, the government encouraged farmers to grow hemp for wartime rope and textiles. Today, the United States is the only developed nation in the world that has not established hemp as an agricultural commodity. If the current policy changes, we would be returning full circle to the colonial period of U.S. history, when hemp growers (notably George Washington himself) were dominant figures in the agricultural life of the nation.

Sources: Leinwand, Donna (2005, November 22). "Industrial" hemp support takes root. *USA Today*, p. 3A. Brown, Patricia Leigh (2006, August 28). California seeks to clear hemp of a bad name. *New York Times*, pp. A1, A13.

Summary

A Matter of Terminology

- Marijuana is one of several products of the *Cannabis sativa*, or common hemp plant, grown abundantly throughout the world.

- Various cannabis products are distinguished in terms of the content of cannabis resin and, in turn, the concentration of THC, the active psychoactive agent.

The Social History of Marijuana and Hashish

- The earliest records of marijuana come from Chinese writings nearly five thousand years ago; hashish has its origins in North Africa and Persia in the ninth or tenth centuries A.D.

- In the United States, marijuana was available in patent medicines during the late 1800s, but its popularity did not become extensive until the 1920s.

- Federal and state regulation of marijuana began in the 1930s; penalties for possessing and selling marijuana escalated during the 1940s and 1950s.

- The emergence of marijuana on American college campuses and among American youth in general during the late 1960s, however, forced a reexamination of public policy regarding this drug, leading to a more lenient approach in the 1970s.

Acute Effects of Marijuana

- Because marijuana is almost always consumed through smoking, the acute effects are rapid, but because it is absorbed into fatty tissue, its elimination is slow. It may require days or weeks in the case of extensive exposure to marijuana for THC to leave the body completely.

- Acute physiological effects include cardiac acceleration and a reddening of the eyes. Acute psychological effects, with typical dosages, include euphoria, giddiness, a perception of time elongation, and an increased hunger and sexual desire. There are impairments in attention and memory, which interfere with complex visual–motor skills such as driving an automobile.

- The acute effects of marijuana are now known to be due to the binding of THC at special receptors in the brain.

Chronic Effects of Marijuana

- Chronic marijuana use produces tolerance effects; there is no physical dependence when doses are moderate and only a mild psychological dependence.

- Carcinogenic effects are suspected because marijuana smoke contains many of the same harmful components that tobacco smoke does, and in the case of marijuana smoking inhalation is deeper and more prolonged.

The Gateway Hypothesis

- The idea that there exists an amotivational syndrome, characterized by general apathy and an indifference to long-range planning, as a result of the pharmacological effects of chronic marijuana use has been largely discredited. An alternative explanation for the behavioral changes is that chronic marijuana users are involved in a deviant subculture that is directed away from traditional values of school achievement and long-term aspirations.

- Another idea that has been related to chronic marijuana use is the gateway hypothesis, which refers to the possibility that marijuana inherently sets the stage for future patterns of drug abuse. Research studies have indicated that the use of alcohol and cigarettes precedes marijuana use, and marijuana use precedes the use of other illicit drugs. In addition, marijuana use and subsequent use of other illicit drugs are statistically correlated. However, there is little evidence that some inherent property of marijuana exposure itself leads to physical or psychological dependence on other drugs.

Patterns of Marijuana Smoking

- The current incidence of marijuana smoking among adolescents and young adults is lower than in the late 1970s, but clearly a resurgence has occurred since 1991.

- Other areas of concern are the greater potency of marijuana that is now available and the continuing potential risk of marijuana adulteration.

Medical Marijuana and Marijuana Decriminalization

- While marijuana has been useful in the treatment of glaucoma and asthma, its most effective application to date has been in the treatment of symptoms of nausea and weight loss. In 2005, the U.S. Supreme Court upheld the power of the federal government to prohibit the possession and use of marijuana for medical purposes, even in U.S. states that permit it. As a result of this decision, federal prosecutions can be carried out in these states. Whether large numbers of prosecutions will occur in the future, however, is unclear.

- Present public policy toward marijuana smoking has evolved to the point of essentially decriminalizing the possession of marijuana in small amounts.

Key Terms

amotivational syndrome, p. 176
anandamide, p. 173
bhang, p. 167
cannabinoids, p. 167

Cannabis sativa, p. 166
decriminalization, p. 184
delta-9-tetrahydrocannabinol (THC), p. 167
dronabinol (Marinol), p. 182

gateway hypothesis, p. 177
hashish, p. 167
hashish oil, p. 167
hashish oil crystals, p. 167
joint, p. 170

marijuana, p. 167
nabilone (Cesamet), p. 182
reefer, p. 170
sinsemilla, p. 167

Endnotes

1. Abel, Ernest L. (1980). *Marihuana, the first twelve thousand years.* New York: Plenum Press, p. ix.
2. Bloomquist, Edward R. (1968). *Marijuana.* Beverly Hills, CA: Glencoe Press, pp. 4–5.
3. Abel, *Marihuana*, p. 4. Palfai, Tibor, and Jankiewicz, Henry (1991). *Drugs and human behavior.* Dubuque, IA: W. C. Brown, p. 452.
4. Abel, *Marihuana*, pp. x–xi.
5. Goode, Erich (2005). *Drugs in American society* (6th ed.). New York: McGraw-Hill College, p. 234. National Drug Threat Assessment 2007. Washington DC: U.S. Department of Justice, p. 10. Office of Drug Control Policy (2002, November). *Pulse check: Marijuana report.* Washington DC: White House Office of Drug Control Policy.
6. Abel, *Marihuana*, p. 12. Bhang. Wikipedia.org. Retrieved January 4, 2007.
7. Bonnie, Richard J., and Whitebread, Charles H. (1974). *The marihuana conviction: A history of marihuana prohibition in the United States.* Charlottesville, VA: University Press of Virginia, p. 3.
8. Abel, *Marihuana*, pp. 218–222.
9. Bonnie and Whitebread, *The marihuana conviction*, p. 33.
10. Anslinger, Harry J., and Tompkins, William F. (1953). *The traffic in narcotics.* New York: Funk & Wagnalls, pp. 37–38. Cited in Inciardi, James A. (2002). *The war on drugs III.* Boston: Allyn and Bacon, p. 46.
11. Lee, Martin A., and Shlain, Bruce (1985). *Acid dreams: The complete social history of LSD.* New York: Grove Weidenfeld.
12. Julien, Robert M. (1998). *A primer of drug action* (8th ed.). New York: Freeman, pp. 327–331.
13. Ibid., pp. 330–331.
14. *Allen and Hanbury's athletic drug reference* (1992). Research Triangle Park NC: Clean Data, p. 33. Wadler, Gary I., and Hainline, Brian (1989).

Drugs and the athlete. Philadelphia: F. A. Davis, pp. 208–209.
15. Grinspoon, Lester, and Bakalar, James B. (1997). Marihuana. In Joyce H. Lowinson, Pedro Ruiz, Robert B. Millman, and John G. Langrod (Eds.), *Substance abuse: A comprehensive texbook* (3rd ed.). Baltimore, MD: Williams and Wilkins, pp. 199–206.
16. Jones, Reese T. (1980). Human effects: An overview. In Robert C. Petersen (Ed.), *Marijuana research findings: 1980* (NIDA Research Monograph 31). Rockville, MD: National Institute on Drug Abuse, p. 65.
17. Grilly, David M. (2006). *Drugs and human behavior* (5th ed.). Boston: Allyn and Bacon, p. 268.
18. Substance Abuse and Mental Health Services Administration (2007). *Drug Abuse Warning Network, 2005: National estimates of drug-related emergency department visits.* Rockville, MD: Office of Applied Studies, Substance Abuse and Mental Health Services Administration, Table 2.
19. Winger, Gail, Hofmann, Frederick G., and Woods, James H. (1992). *A handbook on drug and alcohol abuse* (3rd ed.). New York: Oxford University Press, pp. 123–125.
20. Hooker, William D., and Jones, Reese T. (1987). Increased susceptibility to memory intrusions and the Stroop interference effect during acute marijuana intoxication. *Psychopharmacology, 91,* 20–24. Ilan, Aaron B.; Gevins, A.; Coleman, M.; ElSohly, M. A.; and de Wit, H. (2005). Neurophysiological and subjective profile of marijuana with varying concentrations of cannabinoids. *Behavioural Pharmacology, 16,* 487–496.
21. Delong, Fonya L., and Levy, Bernard I. (1974). A model of attention describing the cognitive effects of marijuana. In Loren L. Miller (Ed.), *Marijuana: Effects on human behavior.* New York: Academic Press, pp. 103–117. Gieringer, Dale H. (1988). Marijuana, driving, and accident safety. *Journal of Psychoactive Drugs, 20,*

93–101. Report: Marijuana use a factor in Kentucky miner's death (2003, December). *Safety and Health*, p. 16.

22. McKim, William A. (2000). *Drugs and behavior* (4th ed.). Englewood Cliffs, NJ: Prentice Hall, p. 309.

23. Brookoff, D.; Cook, C. S.; Williams, C.; and Mann, C. S. (1994). Testing reckless drivers for cocaine and marijuana. *New England Journal of Medicine, 331,* 518–522. Kurzthaler, Ilse; Hummer, Martina; Miller, Carl; Sperner-Unterweger, Barbara; Gunther, Verena; Wechdorn, Heinrich; Battista, Hans-Juergen; and Fleischhacker, W. Wolfgang (1999). Effect of cannabis use on cognitive functions and driving ability. *Journal of Clinical Psychiatry, 60,* 395–399. Soderstrom, C. A.; Dischinger, P. D.; Kerns, T. J.; and Trifillis, A. L. (1995). Marijuana and other drug use among automobile and motorcycle drivers treated at a trauma center. *Accident Analysis and Prevention, 27,* 131–135.

24. Block, Robert I. (1997). Editorial: Does heavy marijuana use impair human cognition and brain function? *Journal of the American Medical Association, 275,* 560–561. Pope, Harrison G., Jr., and Yurgelun-Todd, Deborah (1996). The residual cognitive effects of heavy marijuana use in college students. *Journal of the American Medical Association, 275,* 521–527.

25. Winger, Hofmann, and Woods, *A handbook on drug and alcohol abuse,* pp. 118, 127–129.

26. Ameri, Angela (1999). The effects of cannabinoids on the brain. *Progress in Neurobiology, 58,* 315–348. Chait, L. D., and Burke, K. A. (1994). Preference for high- versus low-potency marijuana. *Pharmacology, Biochemistry, and Behavior, 49,* 643–647. Tanda, Gianluigi, Pontieri, Francesco E., and Di Chiara, Gaetano (1997). Cannabinoid and heroin activation of mesolimbic dopamine transmission by a common μ_1 opioid receptor mechanism. *Science, 276;* 2048–2049. Wickelgren, Ingrid (1997). Research news: Marijuana: Harder than thought? *Science, 276,* 1967–1968.

27. Abood, M., and Martin, B. (1992). Neurobiology of marijuana abuse. *Trends in Pharmacological Sciences, 13,* 201–206.

28. Frank, Ira M.; Lessin, Phyllis J.; Tyrrell, Eleanore D.; Hahn, Pierre M.; and Szara, Stephen. (1976). Acute and cumulative effects of marijuana smoking on hospitalized subjects: A 36-day study. In Monique C. Braude and Stephen Szara (Eds.), *Pharmacology of marijuana.* Vol. 2. Orlando, FL: Academic Press, pp. 673–680. Jones, Reese T., and Benowitz, Neal (1976). The 30-day trip: Clinical studies of cannabis tolerance and dependence. In Monique C. Braude and Stephen Szara (Eds.), *Pharmacology of marijuana.* Vol. 2. Orlando, FL: Academic Press, pp. 627–642.

29. Haney, Margaret; Ward, Amie S.; Comer, Sandra D.; Foltin, Richard W; and Fischman, Marian W. (1999a). Abstinence symptoms following oral THC administration in humans. *Psychopharmacology, 141,* 385–394. Haney, Margaret; Ward, Amie S.; Comer, Sandra D.; Foltin, Richard W; and Fischman, Marian W. (1999b). Abstinence symptoms following smoked marijuana in humans. *Psychopharmacology, 141,* 395–404.

30. Duffy, Anne, and Milin, Robert (1996). Case study: Withdrawal syndrome in adolescent chronic cannabis users. *Journal of the American Academy of Child and Adolescent Psychiatry, 35,* 1618–1621. Julien, Robert M. (2001). *A primer of drug action* (9th ed.). New York: Worth, pp. 320–322.

31. Earlywine, Mitch (2002). *Understanding marijuana: A new look at the scientific evidence.* New York: Oxford University Press, pp. 156–157. Julien (2001), *A primer of drug action,* pp. 316–319. Marijuana as medicine: How strong is the science? (1997, May). *Consumer Reports,* pp. 62–63. Study: Marijuana, cocaine have harmful effects on lungs (1998, September 7). *Alcoholism and Drug Abuse Weekly, 10,* p. 8. Sussman, Steve; Stacy, Alan W.; Dent, Clyde W.; Simon, Thomas R.; and Johnson, C. Anderson (1995). Marijuana use: Current issues and new research directions. *Journal of Drug Issues, 26,* 695–733.

32. Committee on Substance Abuse, American Academy of Pediatrics (1999). Marijuana: A continuing concern for pediatricians. *Pediatrics, 104,* 982–985. Hollister, Leo E. (1988). Marijuana and immunity. *Journal of Psychoactive Drugs, 20,* 3–7. Petersen, Robert C. (1984). Marijuana overview. In Meyer D. Glantz (Ed.), *Correlates and consequences of marijuana use* (Research Issues 34). Rockville MD: National Institute on Drug Abuse, p. 10.

33. Brands, Bruna, Sproule, Beth, and Marshman, Joan (Eds.). *Drugs and drug abuse: A reference text* (3rd ed.). Toronto: Addiction Research Foundation. Committee on Substance Abuse, Marijuana. Grinspoon and Bakalar, Marihuana, pp. 203–204. Male infertility: Sperm from marijuana smokers move too fast, too early (2003, November 3). *Health and Medicine Week,* pp. 459–460.

34. Grinspoon and Bakalar, Marihuana, p. 203.

35. Hollister, Leo E. (1986). Health aspects of cannabis. *Pharmacological Reviews, 38,* 1–20.

36. McGothlin, William H., and West, Louis J. (1968). The marijuana problem: An overview. *American Journal of Psychiatry, 125,* 372.

37. Goode, Erich (1999). *Drugs in American society* (5th ed.). New York: McGraw-Hill College, pp. 232–233.

38. Fox, C. Lynn, and Forbing, Shirley E. (1992). *Creating drug-free schools and communities: A comprehensive approach.* New York: HarperCollins, p. 60. Roebuck, M. Christopher, French, Michael T., and Dennis, Michael L. (2004). Adolescent marijuana use and school attendance. *Economics of Education Review, 23,* 133–141.

39. Goode (1999). *Drugs in American society,* p. 233.

40. Fried, P. A., Wilkinson, B., and Gray, R. (2005). Neurocognitive consequences of marihuana—A comparison with pre-drug performance. *Neurotoxicology and Teratology, 27,* 231–239. Pope, Harrison (2002). Cannabis,

cognition, and residual confounding. *Journal of the American Medical Association, 287*, 1172–1174. Solowij, Nadia; Stephens, Robert S.; Roffman, Roger A.; Babor, Thomas; Kadden, Ronald; Miller, Michael; Chistiansen, Kenneth; McRee, Bonnie; and Vendetti, Janice (2002). Cognitive functioning of long-term heavy cannabis users seeking treatment. *Journal of the American Medical Association, 287*, 1123–1131.

41. Kandel, Denise B. (2003). Does marijuana use cause the use of other drugs? *Journal of the American Medical Association, 289*, 482–483. Quotation on p. 482. Kandel, Denise B. (Ed.) (2002). *Stages and pathways of drug involvement: Examining the gateway hypothesis.* Cambridge, UK: Cambridge University Press.

42. Cited in Medical marijuana: Editorials debate "gateway" effect (1999, April 12). *American Health Line*, URL: http://www. ahl. com.

43. Kandel, Does marijuana use cause the use of other drugs? Lynskey, Michael T.; Hath, Andrew C.; Bucholz, Kathleen K.; Slutske, Wendy S.; Madden, Pamela A. F.; Nelson, Elliot C.; Statham, Dixie J.; and Martin, Nicholas G. (2003). The escalation of drug use in early-onset cannabis users vs co-twin controls. *Journal of the American Medical Association, 289*, 427–433. Martin, Kimberly R. (2001). Adolescent treatment programs reduce drug abuse, produce other improvements. *NIDA Notes, 16* (1), 11–12. Martin, Kimberly R. (2001). Television public service announcements decrease marijuana use in targeted teens. *NIDA Notes, 16* (1), 14.

44. Zimmer, Lynn, and Morgan, John P. (1997). *Marijuana myths, marijuana facts: A review of the scientific evidence.* New York: Lindesmith Center, p. 37.

45. Goode (1999), *Drugs in American society*, pp. 227–231.

46. Cart, Julie (2003, May 25). A national park going to pot: Marijuana farms boom in Sequoia. *Newsday*, p. A65. Pollan, M. (1995, February 13). How pot is grown. *NewYork Times Magazine*, p. 31. Substance Abuse and Mental Health Services Administration (2007). *Results from the 2006 National Survey on Drug Use and Health: National findings.* Rockville, MD: Office of Applied Studies, Substance Abuse and Mental Health Services Administration, Tables G.1, G.2, G.5, and G.6.

47. Johnston, Lloyd D.; O'Malley, Patrick M.; Bachman, Jerald G.; and Schulenberg, John E. (2007). *Monitoring the Future national results on adolescent drug use. Overview of key findings, 2006.* Bethesda, MD: National Institute on Drug Abuse.

48. Johnston, O'Malley, Bachman, and Schulenberg (2007). *Monitoring the Future national results*, Table 7.

49. Leland, John (1993, November 1). Just say maybe. *Newsweek*, pp. 50–54, quotation on p. 52.

50. Cohen, Sidney (1980). Therapeutic aspects. In Robert C. Petersen (Ed.), *Marijuana research findings: 1980* (NIDA Research Monograph 31). Rockville, MD: National Institute on Drug Abuse, pp. 199–221. Julien, *A primer of drug action* (9th ed.), pp. 322–324. Vestag, Brian (2003). Medical marijuana center opens its doors. *Journal of the American Medical Association, 290*, 877–879.

51. Plasse, Terry F.; Gorter, Robert W.; Krasnow, Steven H.; Lane, Montague; Shepard, Kirk V.; and Wadleigh, Robert G. (1991). Recent clinical experience with dronabinol. International conference on cannabis and cannabinoids, Chania, Greece. *Pharmacology, Biochemistry, and Behavior, 40*, 695–700.

52. Institute of Medicine (1999). *Marijuana as medicine: Assessing the science base.* Washington DC: National Academy Press, p. vii.

53. Inciardi, *The war on drugs III*, pp. 300–301. Institute of Medicine, *Marijuana as medicine*, p. 8.

54. Greenhouse, Linda (2005, June 7). Justices say U.S. may prohibit the use of medical marijuana. *New York Times*, pp. A1, A21. Murphy, Dean E. (2005, June 7). Drug's users say ruling won't end their efforts. *New York Times*, p. A21.

55. Bailey, Eric (2005, April 21). Canada OKs pot medicine. *Newsday*, p. A32. Rock announces medical marijuana regulation and progress report on research and domestic supply (2001, July 4). Health Canada news release.

56. National Commission on Marihuana and Drug Abuse (1972). *Marihuana: A signal of misunderstanding.* Washington DC: Government Printing Office, pp. 151–167.

57. Goode (1999). *Drugs in American society*, p. 401.

58. Earlywine. *Understanding marijuana*, pp. 223–245. Johnston, Lloyd D. (1980, January 16). Marijuana use and the effects of marijuana decriminalization. Unpublished testimony delivered at the hearings on the effects of marijuana held by the Subcommittee on Criminal Justice, Judiciary Committee, U.S. Senate, Washington DC, p. 5.

59. Dreyfuss, Robert (2005, August 11). Bush's war on pot. *Rolling Stone*, pp. 46–48. Canada ponders drug liberalization (2005, November 10). *Economist*, p. xx. Melamede, Robert J. (2005). Harm reduction—The cannabis paradox. *Harm Reduction Journal*, 2:17. O'Driscoll, Patrick (2005, November 13). Denver votes to legalize marijuana possession. *USA Today*, p. 3A. Sommer, Robert (1988). Two decades of marijuana attitudes: The more it changes, the more it is the same. *Journal of Psychoactive Drugs, 20*, 67–70.

chapter **8**

Depressants and Inhalants

"I remember," Julio says, taking quick, nervous puffs from his cigarette, "when I was a little kid, maybe eight or nine, and I used to take the garbage out for my mother, I'd always see tubes from airplane glue under the stairwell in our apartment house and in the alley out back. At first, glue just meant building models to me. But I'd see people sniffing it, under the stairwell. I was curious, and one day I tried it. It made me feel like I was in a trance. It wasn't really exciting, but I did it again and again until we moved, and in the new neighborhood people weren't into glue and I didn't see the empty tubes to remind me anymore."[1]

—A teenager relating his early experience with inhalant abuse

After you have completed this chapter, you will understand

- The acute and chronic effects of barbiturates as sedative-hypnotic drugs

- The search for the perfect nonbarbiturate sedative-hypnotic drug

- The development of benzodiazepines as antianxiety medications

- Newly developed sedative-hypnotics and antianxiety medications

- Present-day concerns about gamma-hydroxybutyrate (GHB)

- The history of psychoactive inhalants

- The acute effects and dangers of glue, solvent, or aerosol spray inhalation

- Patterns of inhalant abuse and its chronic effects

- Society's response to concerns about inhalant abuse

- The abuse of amyl nitrite and butyl nitrite

Just as cocaine, amphetamines, and other stimulants bring us up, depressants bring us down. Just as people desire to be stronger, faster, and more attuned to the world, they also desire to move apart from that world, reduce the stress and anxiety of their lives, and fall asleep more easily. We learned in Chapter 5 that the powerful effects of opiates not only relieved pain but allowed people to retreat from the world around them. In Chapter 10, we will examine the ubiquitous allure of alcohol to relax our mind and body.

In the first part of this chapter, we will focus on a group of nonopiate, nonalcoholic depressant drugs called **sedative-hypnotics,** so named because they calm us down (from the Latin verb, *sedare,* meaning "to calm or be quiet") and produce sleep (from the Greek noun, *hypnos,* meaning "sleep"). Several types of sedative-hypnotic drugs exist, ranging from drugs that were introduced more than two hundred years ago to others that have become available only recently.

A separate but related category consists of prescription drugs that provide specific relief from stress and anxiety without sedating us. These drugs have often been referred to as *tranquilizers* by virtue of their ability to make us feel peaceful or tranquil, but we will call them by their more current name, **antianxiety drugs.** Unfortunately, sedative-hypnotics and antianxiety drugs have been subject not only to legitimate medical use but to misuse and abuse as well. Many of them can be obtained through illicit sources as street drugs and are consumed for recreational purposes. The psychological problems and physical dangers associated with the misuse and abuse of these depressants are of particular concern.

This chapter also looks at a category of depressant drugs known as **inhalants,** a group of chemicals that produce breathable vapors. These chemicals do not need to be acquired in a pharmacy, a convenience store, a liquor store, or even on the street. They can be found under the sink, in kitchen or bathroom cabinets, in the basement, or in the garage. Ordinary household products frequently have the potential for giving euphoriant effects if they are sniffed or inhaled. When you consider that these substances are readily available to anyone in a family, including its youngest members, the consequences of their abuse become especially troubling. Glues, solvents, and other inhalant products will be examined as dangerous recreational drugs in our society today.

Barbiturates

In 1864, the German chemist Adolf von Baeyer combined a waste product in urine called *urea* and an apple extract called *malonic acid* to form a new chemical compound called *barbituric acid.* There are two often-told stories about how this compound got its name. One story has it that Von Baeyer had gone to a local tavern to celebrate his discovery and encountered a number of artillery officers celebrating the feast day of St. Barbara, the patron saint of explosives handlers. Inspired by their celebration, the name "barbituric acid" came to mind. The other story attributes the name to a relationship with a certain barmaid (perhaps at the same tavern) whose name was Barbara.[2]

Whichever story is true (if either is), Von Baeyer's discovery of barbituric acid set the stage for the development of a class of drugs called **barbiturates.** Barbituric acid itself has no behavioral effects, but if additional molecular groups combine with the acid, depressant effects are observed. In 1903, the first true barbiturate, diethylbarbituric acid, was created and marketed under the name Veronal. Over the next thirty years, several major barbiturate drugs were introduced: **phenobarbital** (marketed in generic form), **amobarbital** (brand name: Amytal), **pentobarbital** (brand name: Nembutal), and **secobarbital** (brand name: Seconal).

Categories of Barbiturates

Barbiturates all share a number of common features. They are relatively tasteless and odorless, and at sufficient dosages, they reliably induce sleep, although the quality of sleep is a matter that will be discussed later. Because they slow down the activity of the central nervous system (CNS), barbiturates are also useful in the treatment of epilepsy.

sedative-hypnotics: A category of depressant drugs that provide a sense of calm and sleep.

antianxiety drugs: Medications that make the user feel more peaceful or tranquil; also called tranquilizers.

inhalants: Chemicals that produce breathable vapors. They produce euphoriant and depressant effects when sniffed or inhaled.

barbiturate (bar-BIT-chur-rit): A drug within a family of depressants derived from barbituric acid and used as a sedative-hypnotic and antiepileptic medication.

phenobarbital (FEEN-oh-BAR-bih-tall): A long-acting barbiturate drug, usually marketed in generic form.

amobarbital (AY-moh-BAR-bih-tall): An intermediate-acting barbiturate drug. Brand name is Amytal.

pentobarbital (PEN-toh-BAR-bih-tall): A short-acting barbiturate drug. Brand name is Nembutal.

secobarbital (SEC-oh-BAR-bih-tall): A short-acting barbiturate drug. Brand name is Seconal.

The principal difference among them lies in how long the depressant effects will last; a rough classification of barbiturates is based upon this factor. Barbiturates are categorized as *long acting* (six or more hours), *intermediate acting* (four to six hours), or *short acting* (less than four hours).

Bear in mind, however, that these groups are relative only to one another. All other factors being equal, injectable forms of barbiturates are shorter acting than orally administered forms of the same drug, since it takes longer for the drug to be absorbed when taken by mouth and longer for it to be eliminated from the body (Chapter 1). Naturally, a higher dose of any drug lasts longer than a lower dose because it takes longer for all of the drug to be eliminated from the body (Table 8.1).

The barbiturates used in surgical anesthesia, such as thiopental (brand name: Pentothal), take effect extremely rapidly (within seconds) and last only a few minutes. For this reason, they are referred to as *ultra-short-acting barbiturates.* Because these features are undesirable to a person seeking a recreational drug, ultra-short-acting barbiturates are not commonly abused.

Acute Effects of Barbiturates

You can visualize the effects of barbiturates on the body and the mind in terms of points along a scale ranging from mild relaxation on one end to coma and death on

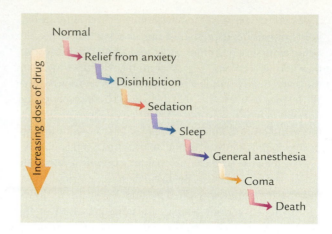

FIGURE 8.1

The downward continuum of arousal levels, as induced by depressants.

Source: Julien, Robert M. (1998). *A primer of drug action* (8th ed.). Copyright © 1998 by W. H. Freeman and Company.

the other (Figure 8.1). In this sense, barbiturate effects are the same as the effects of depressants in general. The particular point that is achieved depends upon the dose level that is taken.

At very low doses, the primary result of oral administrations of a barbiturate is relaxation and, paradoxically, a sense of euphoria. These effects derive chiefly from a disinhibition of the cerebral cortex, in which normal inhibitory influences from the cortex are reduced. These symptoms are similar to the inebriating or intoxicating effects that result from low to moderate doses of alcohol (Drugs...in Focus).

As the dose level increases, lower regions of the brain concerned with general arousal become affected. At therapeutic doses (one 100-mg capsule of secobarbital, for example), barbiturates make you feel sedated and drowsy. For this reason, patients are typically warned that barbiturates can impair the performance of driving a car or operating machinery. At higher doses, a hypnotic (sleep-inducing) effect will be achieved.

TABLE 8.1

Major barbiturates

GENERIC NAME	BRAND NAME	DURATION OF ACTION	RELATIVE POTENTIAL FOR ABUSE
phenobarbital	generic*	long	low
mephobarbital	Mebaral	long	low
butalbarbital	Pheniline Forte†	intermediate	moderate
amobarbital	Amytal	intermediate	high
secobarbital and amobarbital	Tuinal	short, intermediate	high
pentobarbital	Nembutal	short	high
secobarbital	Seconal	short	high

Note: Short-acting barbiturates begin to take effect in about fifteen minutes, intermediate-acting barbiturates in thirty minutes, and long-acting barbiturates in one hour.

*Phenobarbital is also available in combination with hyoscyamine, atropine, and scopolamine under the brand name Donnatal.

†Several brands combine butalbarbital with acetaminophen.

Sources: Henningfield, Jack E., and Ator, Nancy A. (1986). *Barbiturates: Sleeping potion or intoxicant?* New York: Chelsea House, p. 24. *Physicians' desk reference* (61st ed.) (2007). Montvale, NJ: Medical Economics Company.

Drugs . . . in Focus

Is There Any Truth Regarding "Truth Serum"?

The idea that a sedative-hypnotic drug such as amobarbital (Amytal, or "sodium amytal") may function as a "truth serum" is not at all new. It has been known for centuries that depressants can produce remarkable candor and freedom from inhibition. The oldest example is simple alcohol, whose effect on loosening the tongue has led to the Latin proverb *in vino veritas* ("in wine, there is truth").

Whether we are guaranteed truthfulness under any of these circumstances, however, is another matter entirely. Courts have ruled that expert opinion in criminal cases based *solely* on drug-assisted testimony cannot be admitted as evidence. Controlled laboratory studies have shown that individuals under the influence of Amytal, when pressed by questioners, are as likely to give convincing renditions of fabrications (outright lies) or fantasies as they are to tell the truth. So, perhaps, Amytal might be better described as a "tell anything serum."

Recently, the question of whether Amytal or other depressant drugs should be used to gain information has come up with regard to the interrogation of captured al Qaeda prisoners following the September 11, 2001, attacks. The United States has determined that such individuals are unlawful combatants, a designation that excludes them from protection under the Geneva Convention guidelines prohibiting such practices for prisoners of war. Officially, U.S. officials deny that depressant drugs are being used to gain information from captives under American jurisdiction. It is possible that this practice is in effect in other countries to which captives have been transferred.

The lack of evidence that truthful information may be gained through the use of depressant drugs has not changed, however. Nonetheless, military and intelligence experts point to the potential for gaining some relevant information that might be buried in drug-induced ramblings.

Sources: CBS News (2003, April 23). Truth serum: A possible weapon. www.cbsnews.com. Michaelis, James I. (1966). Quaere, whether 'in vino veritas': An analysis of the truth serum cases. *Issues in Criminology, 2* (2), 245–267.

Historically, the primary use of barbiturates has been in the treatment of insomnia, and they were widely recommended for this purpose from 1903, when they were first introduced, until the development of safer alternatives in the 1960s. One of the reasons why barbiturates fell from favor was that the sleep induced by these drugs turned out to be far from normal. Barbiturates tend to suppress rapid eye movement (REM) sleep, a phase of everyone's sleep that represents about 20 percent of the total sleep time each night. REM sleep is associated with dreaming and general relaxation of the body. If barbiturates are consumed over many evenings and then stopped, the CNS will attempt to catch up for the lost REM sleep by producing longer REM periods on subsequent nights. This **REM-sleep rebound** effect produces vivid and upsetting nightmares, along with a barbiturate hangover the next day, during which the user feels groggy and out of sorts. In other words, barbiturates may induce sleep, but a refreshing sleep it definitely is not.[3]

The most serious acute risks of barbiturate use involve the possibility of a lethal overdose either from taking too high a dose level of the drug alone or from taking the drug in combination with alcohol, such as when a barbiturate is taken after an evening of drinking. In these instances, sleep can all too easily slip into coma and death, since an excessive dose produces an inhibition of the respiratory control centers in the brain. The mixture of barbiturates with alcohol produces a synergistic effect (see Chapter 1) in which the combined result is greater than the sum of the effects of each drug alone.

Half of the lethal dose of secobarbital combined with ¼ the lethal dose of alcohol can kill in a synergistic double whammy. In another typical case of accidental overdose, a person takes a sleeping pill and awakens drugged and confused a few minutes later, annoyed at being aroused. The person then forgetfully takes another pill, or several, from the

REM-sleep rebound: A phenomenon associated with the withdrawal of barbiturate drugs in which the quantity of rapid eye movement (REM) sleep increases, resulting in disturbed sleep and nightmares.

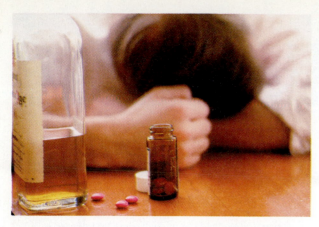

Barbiturates and alcohol have frequently been combined in attempts to commit suicide.

nightstand, and goes to sleep forever. This is called "drug automatism," a good reason not to keep medications within reach of the bed.[4]

During the period between 1973 and 1976, barbiturates were implicated in more than half of all drug-related deaths labeled as suicide by medical examiners. In fact, the suicide potential of barbiturates is the primary reason for their decline as a prescription drug.[5]

Chronic Effects of Barbiturates

The use of barbiturates as sleep medications often initiates a cycle of behavior that can lead to dependence. Even after brief use of barbiturates, anxiety may be temporarily increased during the day, and there may be an even greater degree of insomnia than before. In addition, because a barbiturate-induced sleep typically leaves a person feeling groggy the next morning, it is tempting to take a stimulant drug during the day to feel completely alert. At bedtime, the person still feels the stimulant effects and is inclined to continue taking a barbiturate to achieve any sleep at all. To make matters worse, the brain builds up a pharmacological tolerance to barbiturates quite quickly, requiring increasingly higher doses for an equivalent effect.

Withdrawal symptoms, observed when barbiturates are discontinued, indicate a strong physical dependence on the drug. A person may experience a combination of tremors (the "shakes"), nausea and vomiting, intense perspiring, general confusion, convulsions, hallucinations, high fever, and increased heart rate. Not surprisingly, considering the parallels mentioned so far with alcohol, the barbiturate withdrawal syndrome closely resembles that of withdrawal after chronic alcohol abuse.

Professionals in the treatment of drug dependence often view the effects of barbiturate withdrawal as the most distressing as well as the most dangerous type of drug withdrawal. From a medical perspective, the withdrawal process is life-threatening unless it is carried out in gradual fashion in a hospital setting. Without medical supervision, abrupt withdrawal from barbiturates carries approximately a 5 percent chance of death.[6]

Current Medical Uses of Barbiturates

Considering the problems of barbiturate use in the treatment of insomnia, it should not be surprising that the clinical use of barbiturates for this problem is essentially "obsolete."[7] Nonetheless, barbiturates continue to play an important role in the treatment of epileptic seizures. Phenobarbital and mephobarbital (two long-acting barbiturates) are prescribed to prevent convulsions. Dose levels need to be monitored carefully because the concentration must be high enough to control the development of seizures (despite the tendency for tolerance effects to occur over time) without being so high as to produce drowsiness.

Patterns of Barbiturate Abuse

There are clear indications that taking barbiturate drugs is positively reinforcing. Laboratory animals will eagerly press a lever to deliver intravenous injections of barbiturates, particularly for the short-acting types, at rates that are equal to those for cocaine.[8] When given the choice between pentobarbital and a nonbarbiturate depressant and given no knowledge as to the identity of the drugs, human drug abusers reliably select an oral dose of pentobarbital.[9]

Barbiturate abuse reached its peak in the 1950s and 1960s, later to be overshadowed by abuses of heroin, hallucinogens, nonbarbiturate depressants, amphetamines, and more recently, abuses of cocaine, crack, and various stimulants and hallucinogens (Table 8.2). The principal reason was that barbiturates became less widely available as prescription drugs. Stricter controls were placed on obtaining excessive amounts of barbiturates from pharmacies, whereas physicians, concerned with the potential of barbiturates as ways of committing suicide, became reluctant to prescribe them on a routine basis.

Despite their decline as major drugs of abuse, however, barbiturates are still being abused. The 2006 University of Michigan survey of high school seniors found that 10 percent of them had used some form of barbiturates during their lifetime, down from 17 percent in 1975, and

TABLE 8.2

Street names for various barbiturates

TYPE OF BARBITURATE	STREET NAME
pentobarbital (Nembutal)	abbotts, blockbusters, nebbies, nembies, nemmies, yellow bullets, yellow dolls, yellow jackets, yellows
amobarbital (Amytal)	blue angels, bluebirds, blue bullets, blue devils, blue dolls, blue heavens, blues
secobarbital (Seconal)	F-40s, Mexican reds, R.D.s, redbirds, red bullets, red devils, red dolls, reds, seccies, seggies, pinks
secobarbital and amobarbital (Tuinal)	Christmas trees, double trouble, gorilla pills, rainbows, tootsies, trees, tuies
barbiturates in general	downers, down, goofballs, G.B.s, goofers, idiot pills, King Kong pills, peanuts, pink ladies, sleepers, softballs, stumblers

Note: Like any other street drug, illicit barbiturate capsules often contain an unknown array of other substances, including strychnine, arsenic, laxatives, or milk sugars. Any yellow capsule may be "marketed" as Nembutal, any blue capsule as Amytal, or any red capsule as Seconal.

Source: Henningfield, Jack E., and Ator, Nancy A. (1986). *Barbiturates: Sleeping potion or intoxicant?* New York: Chelsea House, p. 82.

7 percent had taken them within the past year, down from 11 percent in 1975.[10]

Nonbarbiturate Sedative-Hypnotics

As the hazards of barbiturate use became increasingly evident, the search was on for sedative-hypnotic drugs that were not derivatives of barbituric acid and, it was hoped, had fewer undesirable side effects. One such drug, **chloral hydrate,** had been synthesized as early as 1832. As a depressant for the treatment of insomnia, it has the advantage of not producing the REM-sleep rebound effect or bringing on the typical barbiturate hangover. A major disadvantage, however, is that it can severely irritate the stomach. Like other depressants, it is also highly reactive when combined with alcohol. In the nineteenth century, a few drops of chloral hydrate in a glass of whiskey became the infamous "Mickey Finn," a concoction that left many an unsuspecting sailor unconscious and eventually "shanghaied" onto a boat for China.

The development of **methaqualone** (brand names: Quaalude, Sopor), first introduced in the United States in 1965, was a further attempt toward achieving the perfect sleeping pill. In 1972, methaqualone had become the sixth-best-selling drug for the treatment of insomnia. During the early 1970s, recreational use of methaqualone (popularly known as "ludes" or "sopors") was rapidly spreading across the country, aided by the unfounded reputation that it had aphrodisiac properties.

The problem with methaqualone was compounded by the extensive number of prescriptions written by physicians who mistakenly saw the drug as a desirable alternative to barbiturates. On the street, quantities of methaqualone were obtained from medical prescriptions or stolen from pharmacies. Methaqualone-associated deaths started to be prominent mentions in the DAWN reports of the period (see Chapter 1). In 1984, this drug's legal status changed to that of a Schedule I drug, the most restricted classification, which indicates a high potential for abuse and no medical benefits.[11] Though no longer manufactured by any pharmaceutical company, methaqualone is still available as an illicit drug. It is either manufactured in domestic underground laboratories or smuggled into the country from underground laboratories abroad.

The Development of Antianxiety Drugs

If social historians consider the 1950s "the age of anxiety," then it is appropriate that this period also would be marked by the development of drugs specifically intended to combat that anxiety. These drugs were originally called *minor tranquilizers,* to distinguish them from other drugs regarded as *major tranquilizers* and developed at about the same time to relieve symptoms of schizophrenia. This terminology is no longer used today, for we now know that the difference between the two drug categories is more than simply a matter of

chloral hydrate: A depressant drug once used for the treatment of insomnia. It is highly reactive with alcohol and can severely irritate the stomach.

methaqualone (MEH-tha-QUAY-lone): A nonbarbiturate depressant drug once used as a sedative. Brand name is Quaalude.

A person's job and other aspects of living are often sources of enormous stress and anxiety.

degree. Anxious people (or even people who are not bothered by anxiety) are not affected by drugs designed to treat schizophrenia. The current, and more logical, practice is to refer to drugs in terms of a specific action and purpose. The minor tranquilizers are now called *antianxiety drugs.*

The first antianxiety drug to be developed was **meprobamate** (brand name: Miltown), named in 1955 for a New Jersey town near the headquarters of the pharmaceutical company that first introduced it. Miltown became an immediate hit among prescription drugs, making its name a household word and essentially a synonym for tranquilizers in general.

Even though meprobamate was the first psychoactive drug in history to be marketed specifically as an antianxiety medication, most pharmacologists have identified the effects of this drug more in terms of sedation than of relief from anxiety.[12] Nonetheless, meprobamate is different from the other depressant drugs discussed so far in this chapter. The primary difference is in the way it works in the nervous system. Instead of inhibiting arousal and respiratory control centers in the brain as barbiturates do, meprobamate reduces the activity of acetylcholine at synapses where the motor nerves innervate the body's

skeletal muscles. As a result, muscle contractions are weaker and general relaxation follows.

On the positive side, the toxic dose of meprobamate is relatively high, making the possibility of suicide more remote than with alcohol, barbiturates, and other depressants. In addition, judging from the reduction in autonomic responses to stressors, there are genuine signs that people on this medication are actually less anxious.

On the negative side, motor reflexes are diminished, making driving more hazardous. People often complain of drowsiness, even at dose levels that should only be calming them down. Meprobamate also can produce both physical and psychological dependence, at slightly more than twice the normal recommended daily dose.[13] This is not a very wide margin for possible abuse, and as a result, meprobamate is classified as a Schedule IV drug, requiring limits on the number of prescription refills. Meprobamate is still prescribed occasionally for anxiety and insomnia, but by 1960 it had been far eclipsed by a different class of antianxiety drugs called *benzodiazepines.*

Benzodiazepines

The introduction of a new group of drugs, called **benzodiazepines,** was a dramatic departure from all earlier attempts to treat anxiety. On the one hand, for the first time, there now were drugs that had a *selective* effect on anxiety itself, instead of producing a generalized reduction in the body's overall level of functioning. It was their tranquilizing effects, rather than their sedative effects, that made benzodiazepines so appealing to mental health professionals. On the other hand, it is important to distinguish between the well-publicized virtues of benzodiazepines when they were first introduced in the 1960s and the data that accumulated during the 1970s as millions of people experienced these new drugs. Although certainly very useful in the treatment of anxiety and other stress-related problems, long-acting benzodiazepines are no longer recognized as the miracle drugs they were promoted to be when they first entered the market.

Medical Uses of Benzodiazepines

The first marketed benzodiazepine, **chlordiazepoxide** (brand name: Librium), was introduced in 1960, followed by **diazepam** (brand name: Valium) in 1963. Table 8.3 lists twelve of the major benzodiazepine drugs currently on the market. They are all chemically related, but their potencies and time courses vary considerably.

meprobamate (MEH-pro-BAYM-ate): A nonbarbiturate antianxiety drug and sedative. Brand name is Miltown.

benzodiazepines (BEN-zoh-dye-AZ-eh-pins): A family of antianxiety drugs. Examples are diazepam (Valium), chlordiazepoxide (Librium), and triazolam (Halcion).

chlordiazepoxide (CHLOR-dye-az-eh-POX-ide): A major benzodiazepine drug for the treatment of anxiety. Brand name is Librium.

diazepam (dye-AZ-eh-pam): A major benzodiazepine drug for the treatment of anxiety. Brand name is Valium.

TABLE 8.3

The leading benzodiazepines on the market

TRADE NAME	GENERIC NAME	ELIMINATION HALF-LIFE (in hours)
Long-acting benzodiazepines		
Valium	diazepam	20–100
Librium	chlordiazepoxide	8–100
Limbitrol	chlordiazepoxide and amitriptyline (an antidepressant)	8–100
Dalmane	flurazepam	70–160
Tranxene	clorazepate	50–100
Intermediate-acting benzodiazepines		
Ativan	lorazepam	10–24
Klonopin	clonazepam	18–50
Restoril	temazepam	8–35
ProSom	estazolam	13–35
Short-acting benzodiazepines		
Versed	midazolam	2–5
Halcion	triazolam	2–5
Xanax	alprazolam	11–18

Note: Klonopin is available in orally disintegrating wafers for panic-attack patients who need the medication in an easily administered form.

Source: Julien, Robert M. (1998). *A primer of drug action* (8th ed.). New York: Freeman, p. 99. *Physicians' desk reference* (61st ed.) (2007). Montvale, NJ: Medical Economics Company.

Valium, for example, is five to ten times stronger than Librium and takes effect about one hour sooner. The relatively quicker response from Valium is a principal factor in making it more popular than Librium.

The variations in benzodiazepine effects have led to different recommendations for their medical use. Oral administrations of the relatively long-acting benzodiazepines, in general, are recommended for relief from anxiety, with the effects beginning thirty minutes to four hours after ingestion. Besides Librium and Valium, other examples of this type include flurazepam (brand name: Dalmane) and clorazepate (brand name: Tranxene).

When a very quick effect is desired, an injectable form of diazepam is used either to reduce the symptoms of agitation that follow alcohol withdrawal (delirium tremens, or the DTs), as an anticonvulsant for epileptic patients, or as a preanesthetic drug to relax the patient just prior to surgery. In contrast, shorter-acting oral benzodiazepines are recommended for sleeping problems

because their effects begin more quickly and wear off well before morning. Examples of this type include triazolam (brand name: Halcion), alprazolam (brand name: Xanax), and temazepam (brand name: Restoril).

How effective are benzodiazepines for the treatment of anxiety? The best way to answer this question is to conduct a double-blind study (see Chapter 1) and compare a representative benzodiazepine such as Valium to a placebo control that looks like Valium but produces no physiological effects. In studies of this type, Valium is observed to be helpful for about 70 to 80 percent of people with an anxiety disorder. Approximately 25 to 30 percent of them, however, are helped by the placebo alone, so it is also evident that psychological factors play a significant role in the final outcome.[14]

Interestingly, benzodiazepines work best when the physician prescribing the medication is perceived as being warm, has a positive attitude toward use of antianxiety drugs, and believes that the patient will improve (Table 8.4).[15] The positive impact of such factors upon the outcome of treatment underscores the importance of the physician–patient relationship, along

TABLE 8.4

Factors that predict successful treatment with benzodiazepines

Physician attributes

Warmth

Liking the patient

Feeling comfortable with the patient

Believing the patient has good prospects for improvement

Patient attributes

High verbal intelligence

Compliance with the physician

Realistic treatment goals

Low verbal hostility

High level of education

High occupational status

Marital stability

Orientation and expectations prior to treatment

Realization that problems are emotional rather than physical

Expectation that drugs will be part of the treatment

Source: Rickels, Karl (1981). Benzodiazepines: Clinical use patterns. In Stephen I. Szara and Jacqueline P. Ludford (eds.), *Benzodiazepines: A review of research results 1980* (NIDA Research Monograph 33). Rockville, MD: National Institute on Drug Abuse, p. 46.

with the genuine pharmacological effects of the drugs themselves.

Acute Effects of Benzodiazepines

In general, benzodiazepines are absorbed relatively slowly into the bloodstream, so their relaxant effects last longer and are more gradual than those of barbiturates. The primary reason for these differences lies in the fact that benzodiazepines are absorbed from the small intestine rather than the stomach, as is the case with barbiturates. The relatively greater water solubility and, by implication, the relatively lower fat solubility of benzodiazepines also are factors.

The major advantage that benzodiazepines have over barbiturates is their higher level of safety. Respiratory centers in the brain are not affected by benzodiazepines, so it is rare that a person will die of respiratory failure from an accidental or intentional overdose. Even after taking fifty or sixty times the therapeutic dose, the person will still not stop breathing. It is almost always possible to arouse a person from the stupor that such a drug quantity would produce. In contrast, doses of barbiturates or nonbarbiturate sedatives that are ten to twenty times the therapeutic dose are lethal. Yet we should understand that this higher level of safety assumes that *no alcohol or other depressant drugs are being taken at the same time.*[16]

Nonetheless, despite the relative safety of Valium and other benzodiazepines, this drug family poses a number of medical risks for special populations. For elderly patients, for example, the rate of elimination of these drugs is slowed down significantly, resulting in the risk of a dangerously high buildup of benzodiazepines after several doses. In the case of a long-acting benzodiazepine such as Valium or Librium, the elimination half-life is for them as long as ten days. An elderly patient with this rate of elimination would not be essentially drug-free until two months had passed.

The continued accumulation of benzodiazepines in the elderly can produce a form of drug-induced dementia in which the patient suffers from confusion and loss of memory. Without understanding the patient's medication history, these symptoms easily can be mistaken for the onset of Alzheimer's disease. A prominent pharmacologist has remarked that his eighty-five-year-old grandmother began to experience forgetfulness and disorientation while taking Valium. "Two months after discontinuation of the drug, her dementia disappeared, and she remained lucid until her death ten years later." It is for this reason that long-acting benzodiazepines are no longer recommended for this age group, and those who are currently taking these drugs are being encouraged to switch to shorter-acting forms or alternative antianxiety therapies.[17]

Chronic Effects of Benzodiazepines

The benzodiazepines were viewed originally as having few, if any, problems relating to a tolerance effect or an acquired dependence. We now know that the *anxiety-relieving* aspects of benzodiazepines show little or no tolerance effects when the drugs are taken at prescribed dosages, but there is a tolerance to the *sedative* effects. In other words, if the drugs are taken for the purpose of relieving anxiety, there is no problem with tolerance, but if they are taken for insomnia, more of the drug may be required in later administrations to induce sleep.[18]

We also now know that physiological symptoms appear when benzodiazepines are withdrawn, an indication of benzodiazepine dependence. In the case of Valium and other long-acting benzodiazepines, the slow rate of elimination delays the appearance of withdrawal symptoms until between the third and sixth day following drug withdrawal. The first signs include an anxiety level that may be worse than the level for which the drug was originally prescribed. Later, there are symptoms of insomnia, restlessness, and agitation. In general, however, withdrawal symptoms are less severe than those observed after barbiturate withdrawal, occur only after long-term use, and are gone in one to four weeks.[19]

How Benzodiazepines Work in the Brain

The key factor in the action of benzodiazepines is the neurotransmitter gamma-aminobutyric acid (GABA), which normally exerts an inhibitory effect on the nervous system (see Chapter 3). When benzodiazepines are in the vicinity of GABA receptors, the actions of GABA are increased. The antianxiety drugs attach themselves to their own receptors on the membrane of neurons and in doing so heighten the effect of GABA. The facilitation of GABA produces a greater inhibition and a decreased activity level in the neurons involved.[20]

The receptor described here is a large protein molecule that has multiple binding locations, arranged like docking sites for different kinds of boats. As shown in Figure 8.2, the receptor consists of three binding sites: one for sedative-hypnotics (including the barbiturates), one for benzodiazepines (and alcohol), and one for GABA. When GABA attaches to its binding site, there is greater inhibition if the benzodiazepine sites are also occupied at the time by a benzodiazepine drug than if they are not occupied.[21] A successful binding of a chemical at one site facilitates the binding at the others.

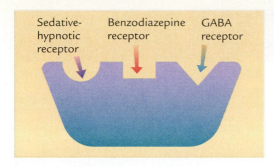

FIGURE 8.2

A simplified view fo the benzodiazepine receptor.

It is not difficult to imagine how cross-tolerance among various depressant drugs would occur. If two depressant drugs were to bind to the same receptor, the receptor would not be able to "tell the difference" between them. As far as the receptor is concerned, the effect would be the same. Evidently, sedative-hypnotics and benzodiazepines share this feature: an ability to lock into a common receptor with multiple binding locations.

Where are the receptors for benzodiazepines? They are understood to be localized primarily in the limbic system and the cerebral cortex of the brain. Receptors in the limbic system underlie the antianxiety action of benzodiazepines (the limbic system is involved with the regulation of emotionality), whereas receptors in the cortex underlie their sedative actions. Teasing apart the neuronal actions of benzodiazepines, by delineating the most relevant subtype of GABA receptor, is the key to the future development of better medications for anxiety.[22]

Patterns of Benzodiazepine Misuse and Abuse

Benzodiazepines do not present the same potential for abuse that cocaine, alcohol, or the barbiturates do, for two primary reasons. First, benzodiazepines are only weak reinforcers of behavior. When trained to press a lever for an injection of Valium, for example, laboratory animals will self-administer the drug but at far less robust levels than they would show for self-administering pentobarbital or methaqualone. Studies with normal college student volunteers show that when given the choice between a placebo and Valium and the true identity of neither choice is known, the placebo is actually preferred. For these individuals, presumably non-drug abusers and relatively anxiety free, the results show no indication of a positive Valium reaction.[23] Second, the slow onset of a benzodiazepine effect prevents the sudden "rush" feeling that is characteristic of many abused drugs such as cocaine, heroin, or amphetamines.

The foregoing is *not* to say, however, that benzodiazepines fail to be abused. It is simply that their abuse exists in the context of abusing other drugs as well, often referred to as *multiple substance abuse* or *polydrug abuse*. Alcoholics, for example, sometimes take benzodiazepines at work, in an attempt to relax and to avoid having the smell of alcohol on their breath. Heroin abusers may take benzodiazepines to augment their euphoria and reduce their anxiety when the opiate levels in their blood begin to fall. Cocaine abusers may take the drugs to soften the crashing feeling that is experienced as the cocaine starts to wear off.[24]

Therefore, the principal social problems surrounding the taking of benzodiazepine drugs, since their introduction in the 1960s, have arisen more from their *misuse* than from their *abuse* (see Chapter 1). The greatest concern during the 1970s was the enormous quantity of benzodiazepine prescriptions that were being written. In 1972, Valium ranked first (and Librium third) among the most frequently prescribed drugs of any type. At the height of their popularity in 1975, more than 100 million such prescriptions were processed around the world, with 85 million in the United States. In Western Europe and North America, it was estimated that 10 to 20 percent of adults were taking benzodiazepines on a fairly regular basis.[25]

Benzodiazepine use and misuse have since declined substantially in psychiatric practice as newer approaches to anxiety disorders have been pursued. Nonetheless, benzodiazepines remain widely prescribed drugs throughout the world, particularly for people over the age of sixty-five years, to treat problems of insomnia and anxiety. While they are useful for short-term use, unfortunate adverse side effects can arise when benzodiazepines are taken over a long period of time. The potential for cognitive impairment among elderly people and the issue of benzodiazepine dependence in general were discussed earlier in this chapter. There is also an increased risk of falls and hip fractures among the elderly owing to the disorientation that sometimes can be experienced. These possibilities are a particular problem in European countries where wine is consumed on a regular basis and, as a consequence, benzodiazepines are often combined with alcohol.[26]

In recent years, considerable publicity has focused on the social and personal concerns surrounding the abuse of a specific benzodiazepine, flunitrazepam (brand name: Rohypnol); it is not legally available in the United States but is accessible as a "club drug" through illicit channels (Help Line).

The Dangers of Rohypnol as a Date-Rape Drug

Flunitrazepam (brand name: Rohypnol) is a long-acting benzodiazepine, not unlike diazepam (Valium), except that it is approximately ten times stronger. Because of its extreme potency and the fact that it is highly synergistic with alcohol, Rohypnol is not legally available in the United States. It is, however, approved for medical use in Europe and South America, where it is marketed by Hoffmann–La Roche Pharmaceuticals as a treatment for sleep disorders and as a surgical anesthetic. The U.S. supply of Rohypnol is smuggled into the country from Mexico and South America and sold for recreational use, frequently in its original bubble packaging.

The abuse potential of Rohypnol surfaced in the mid-1990s, when the number of pills seized by the U.S. Customs Service increased by 400 percent from 1994 to 1995 alone. Increased efforts by U.S. Customs and the Drug Enforcement Administration (DEA) have drastically reduced the availability of Rohypnol in the United States, though the drug remains a matter of great concern.

Under such street names as "roofies," "rope," "wolfies," "roches," "R2," and "Mexican Valium," this drug has been promoted as an alcohol enhancer and as a strategy for getting drunk without having a blood-alcohol concentration level that would be defined as legal intoxication. Rohypnol also has been involved in numerous date-rape cases in which victims had been unknowingly slipped the drug, causing them to pass out—the ultimate vulnerable situation. The disinhibition of behavior and the subsequent memory loss of the experience are similar to an alcohol-induced blackout (see Chapter 10).

At one time, Rohypnol was odorless, colorless, and tasteless, so it could be easily combined with an alcoholic beverage without detection. Recently, in response to instances of abuse, Hoffmann–La Roche has taken steps to reformulate the drug so that it turns blue when dissolved in a clear liquid. This helps to make Rohypnol somewhat more noticeable to an unsuspecting drinker, but it is important to realize that it is difficult to notice discernible changes in beverage color under the dim illumination conditions of a typical bar. Besides, blue dye in blue tropical drinks and punches produces no color change at all.

Since 1996, U.S. federal law provides for a twenty-year sentence for the use of Rohypnol in connection with rape or other violent crime. Unfortunately, Rohypnol is an increasingly accessible illicit drug. According to one law-enforcement official in Miami, "It may be easier for teenagers to obtain flunitrazepam (Rohypnol) than alcohol." A recent study has found that a variety of benzodiazepines, all marketed by Hoffmann–La Roche, are being abused and linked to sexual assaults. Because these drugs all bear the same Roche imprint on the tablets, they are collectively known as "roches."

Rohypnol is an example of a group of present-day "club drugs" that have a dangerous potential for abuse as date-rape drugs. Other examples include MDMA or Ecstasy (see Chapter 6) and GHB (to be discussed later in this chapter).

Where to go for assistance:

www.4woman.gov/faq/rohypnol.htm

This web site is sponsored by the National Woman's Health Information Center, a service of the U.S. Department of Health and Human Services dedicated to women's health issues.

Source: Community Epidemiology Work Group (1996). *Epidemiologic trends in drug abuse,* Volume 1: *Highlights and executive summary.* Rockville, MD: National Institute on Drug Abuse, pp. 8, 64. Quotation on p. 64. Drug Enforcement Administration, U.S. Department of Justice, Washington DC, 1997. Office of National Drug Control Policy (2003, February). *ONDCP Drug Policy Clearing-house fact sheet: Rohypnol.* Washington DC: Executive Office of the President.

Nonbenzodiazepine Depressants

Just as benzodiazepines represented a great advance over barbiturates, the development of new nonbenzodiazepine drugs has provided better opportunities to treat sleep disorders and anxiety. Prominent examples of this new generation of medications are zolpidem, eszopiclone, buspirone, beta blockers, and, strangely enough, antidepressants.

Zolpidem and Eszopiclone

Zolpidem (brand name: Ambien) is not a benzodiazepine drug, but it binds to a specific subtype of GABA receptors. This is probably the reason it produces only

Drugs . . . in Focus

Ambien versus Lunesta— The Sleeping Pill War

The evidence is clear that Americans and others around the world are turning to sleep medications in dramatically increasing numbers, due in part to the heavy marketing of Ambien and its newest rival, Lunesta. Although these products offer a greater amount of safety in their treatment of sleep disorders than had been the case with barbiturates and benzodiazapines, public health officials are worried that, as an editorial in the *New York Times* in 2006 expressed it, "the pills will be overused by people who don't really need them or that doctors may reflexively prescribe pills while ignoring underlying conditions that may be responsible for sleeplessness." If this happens, widespread overuse would be a historical repeat of the 1950s (with barbiturates) and the 1970s (with benzodiazepines).

Adding fuel to the marketing fire have been reports in 2006 of bizarre behavior in some patients taking Ambien that involves dangerous driving and other behaviors while "sleepwalking." In Wisconsin between the years 1999 and 2004, for example, Ambien was in the top ten list of drugs found in the bloodstreams of 187 drivers arrested for impaired driving. Having collided into trees and engaged in erratic driving, these individuals had no memory of getting behind the wheel. In other cases, Ambien patients have found themselves in the morning engorged with food after a night of raiding the refrigerator. These effects appear to affect no more than 1 percent of Ambien users, but with more than 26 million prescriptions of Ambien filled in 2005 in the United States alone, the numbers can be substantial.

Whether marketers of Lunesta and other sleep medications in the FDA-approval pipeline will capitalize on this side effect of Ambien, or whether rival sleep medications will be shown to have similar problems, remains to be seen. The introduction of Ambien CR (a controlled-release version of Ambien) in 2005 has extended the patent protection for this formulation; otherwise the patent for the original version of Ambien would have already expired. As of 2006, Lunesta has yet to challenge the dominance of Ambien in the nonbenzodiazepine sleep medication market, but the pharmaceutical industry is extremely competitive and has been known to be highly volatile in the past. With a worldwide market for sleep medications of $4.4 billion projected in 2010, the marketing war for sleeping pills shows no sign of slowing down.

Note: Ramelton (brand name: Rozerem) was introduced as a prescription sleeping pill in 2006. Unlike Ambien and Lunesta, Rozerem works on the sleep–wake cycle mechanism in the brain.

Source: Barrett, Jennifer (updated 2006, March 16). Wakeup call. *Newsweek*, MSNBC.com. LeadDiscovery Ltd. (2005, September). The world sleep disorders market 2005–2010: A market with high growth potential. East Sussex. UK: Lead-Discovery Ltd. Saul, Stephanie (2006, March 14). To sleep, perchance to eat. Is it the pills? *New York Times*, pp. C1, C6. Saul, Stephanie (2006, March 8). Some sleeping pill users range far beyond bed. *New York Times*, pp. C1,C5. Quotation from sleeping pill wars: Editorial (2006, February 18). *New York Times*, p. A14.

---

some of the effects usually associated with benzodiazepines, with particular usefulness in the short-term treatment of insomnia. Its strong but transient sedative effects (with a half-life of about two hours) have led to the marketing of zolpidem, since its introduction in 1993, as a sedative-hypnotic rather than an antianxiety agent. Little or no muscle relaxation is experienced.

Introduced in 2004, **eszopiclone** (brand name: Lunesta, formerly known as Estorra) is also a nonbenzodiazepine drug that is prescribed for the treatment of insomnia. As a result of successful clinical trials lasting six months, the FDA has approved Lunesta for an interval of treatment that is longer than the recommended treatment with Ambien. Because its half-life of six hours is longer than that of Ambien, Lunesta has been helpful for people who have difficulty in *staying asleep* during the night as well as difficulty in *falling asleep* (Drugs . . . in Focus).[27]

zolpidem (ZOL-pih-dem): A nonbenzodiazepine sedative-hypnotic drug, first introduced in 1993, for the treatment of insomnia. Brand name is Ambien.

eszopiclone (es-ZOP-eh-clone): A nonbenzodiazepine sedative-hypnotic, first introduced in 2005, for the treatment of insomnia. Brand name is Lunesta.

Buspirone

Since 1986, a new type of antianxiety drug has been available called **buspirone** (brand name: BuSpar), with a number of remarkable features. It has been found to be equivalent to Valium in its ability to relieve anxiety. Yet, unlike the benzodiazepines in general, buspirone shows no cross-tolerance effects when combined with alcohol or other depressants and no withdrawal symptoms when discontinued after chronic use. When compared with benzodiazepines, side effects are observed less frequently and are less troublesome to the patient; approximately 9 percent report dizziness, and 7 percent report headaches. Animals do not self-administer buspirone in laboratory studies, and human volunteers indicate an absence of euphoria.

Buspirone also fails to show the impairments in motor skills that are characteristic of benzodiazepines. In other words, the relief of anxiety is attainable without the accompanying feelings and behavioral consequences of sedation. Perhaps anxiety and sedation do not necessarily have to be intertwined after all. Unlike benzodiazepines, buspirone does not affect GABA receptors in the brain but rather acts on a special subclass of serotonin receptors. Evidently, the influence of buspirone on serotonin produces the antianxiety effects.

Despite its virtues, however, buspirone has a distinct disadvantage: a very long delay before anxiety relief is felt. It may take weeks for the drug to become completely effective. While this feature makes buspirone clearly inappropriate for relieving acute anxiety conditions, patients suffering from long-term generalized anxiety disorder find it helpful as a therapeutic drug. An extra benefit of the delay in the action of buspirone is that it becomes highly undesirable as a drug of abuse. Do not expect to see news headlines in the future warning of an epidemic of buspirone abuse.[28]

Beta Blockers

The traditional medical uses of beta-adrenergic-blocking drugs, commonly known as **beta blockers,** include slowing the heart rate, relaxing pressure on the walls of blood vessels, and decreasing the force of heart contractions. The combination of a beta-blocker drug and a diuretic is a frequent treatment for the control of high blood pressure. These drugs are also prescribed for individuals facing an anxiety-producing event, such as performing on the stage or giving a speech. Examples of beta blockers include atenolol (brand name: Tenormin), metoprolol (brand name: Lopressor), and propanolol (brand name: Inderal).

Antidepressants

A recent development in the treatment of panic disorder, post-traumatic stress disorder, and social anxiety disorder has been the use of antidepressant medications—specifically, selective serotonin reuptake inhibitors (SSRIs) such as sertraline (brand name: Zoloft) and paroxetine (brand names: Paxil, Asima).[29]

A Special Alert: The Risks of GHB

Of all the much-publicized club drugs to emerge in recent years, perhaps the most notorious is the CNS depressant **gamma-hydroxybutyrate** (**GHB**). First synthesized in the 1960s, GHB is found to be produced naturally in the body in very small amounts, but no one has discovered its function. At one time, GHB was sold in health-food stores and similar establishments. It was considered to have steroid-enhancing and growth-hormone-stimulating effects, leading to interest among bodybuilders (see Chapter 9). Other promotions focused on GHB as a sedative. By 1990, however, numerous reports of GHB-related seizures and comas led the Food and Drug Administration (FDA) to remove GHB from the legitimate market. Since then, the drug has gone underground. The manufacture of GHB is currently controlled by small clandestine laboratories, guided in many instances by formulas available on the

buspirone (BYOO-spir-rone): A nonbenzodiazepine antianxiety drug, first introduced in 1986. Brand name is BuSpar.

beta blockers: Medicinal drugs that are traditionally used to treat cardiac and blood pressure disorders. They are also prescribed for individuals who suffer from "stage fright" or anxiety regarding a specific event. Examples include atenolol (brand name: Tenormin), metoprolol (brand name: Lopressor), and propanolol (brand name: Inderal).

gamma-hydroxybutyrate (GHB) (GAM-ma heye-DROX-ee-BYOO-tih-rate): A powerful depressant, often abused to induce euphoria and sedation. When slipped in an alcoholic beverage without the knowledge of the drinker, GHB has been employed as a date-rape drug.

This commercially available bar coaster is used to test for the presence of GHB in an alcoholic beverage.

Internet, and its sale is maintained by networks of illicit drug distributors.

Acute Effects

Present-day GHB abuse focuses on its ability to produce euphoria, an "out-of-body" high, with an accompanying lowering of inhibitions. Frequently, a combination of GHB and alcohol can produce a lack of consciousness in about fifteen minutes and subsequent amnesia about the experience. The notoriety of GHB as a date-rape drug stems from its being colorless, odorless, and virtually tasteless. As a result, it can be slipped easily into alcoholic beverages without the knowledge of the drinker.[30]

Protective Strategies for Women

The vulnerability of women to being drugged with GHB while consuming alcohol in a club or bar is considerable (Portrait), but a number of protective strategies can be employed to minimize the risk.

- Watch the person who pours you a drink, even if he or she is a friend or a bartender. Even better, do not drink what you cannot open or pour yourself. Avoid punch bowls and shared containers. Never accept a drink offered to you by a stranger.

- Do not leave a drink alone—not while you are dancing, using the restroom, or making a telephone call. If you have left it alone, it is better to toss the beverage.

- Appoint a designated "sober" friend to check up on you at parties, bars, clubs, and other social gatherings.

- If a friend seems extremely drunk or sick after a drink and has trouble breathing, call 911 immediately.

- If you have been slipped GHB, the drug will take effect within ten to thirty minutes. Initially, you will feel dizzy or nauseous or develop a severe headache. You can be incapacitated rapidly. This is the time when having a nondrinking friend nearby is crucial.

- If you wake up in a strange place and believe that you have been sexually assaulted while under the influence of GHB, do not urinate until you have been admitted to a hospital. There is an approximately twelve-hour window of opportunity to detect GHB through urinanalysis.

A test strip created by Drink Safe Technology is now available that can detect not only GHB but also Rohypnol and ketamine. A straw can be used to place a few drops of one's drink on the test strip. If the liquid turns blue, there is a positive result. Unfortunately, when the drink contains dairy products, an accurate detection cannot be made. Bar coasters have been developed that incorporate this particular test strip. Be aware, however, of the fact that the original and all-time leading date-rape drug is simply alcohol.[31]

PORTRAIT

Patricia White, GHB, and the "Perfect" Crime

Patricia White, a forty-seven-year-old mother of three, was at a party celebrating the birthday of her boss, Lorenzo Feal. According to testimony later given by White, as she was about to leave the party, Feal handed her a bottle of water. She took a gulp. A few hours later, White woke up in Feal's bed, naked and nauseated. She had been drugged and raped. Doctors at the emergency department of the local hospital found traces of GHB in her system, and Feal was eventually convicted of using an anesthetic substance in carrying out White's rape.

A prosecuting attorney has called GHB "ideal for predators and tough for prosecutors" because it is so easily concealed in a drink. Without toxicological evidence, it is difficult to prove that the rape victim had not given consent to sex. Perhaps GHB should really be called an "acquaintance- and date-rape drug."

In 1994, when GHB was relatively new, only 56 GHB-related emergency department "mentions" were reported through the DAWN system (see Chapter 1). By 2002, that number had grown to 3,300. Colleges and universities, as well as commercial bars, have become justifiably alarmed. The Drug Enforcement Administration (DEA) has collaborated with the Rape, Abuse, and Incest National Network (RAINN) in an effort to provide a heightened awareness of GHB and other "predatory" drugs such as Rohypnol.

Patricia White now counsels GHB rape victims and speaks out publicly about her personal story. In the case of GHB, the more you know about this drug, the safer you are.

Source: Smalley, Suzanne (2003, February 3). "The perfect crime": GHB is colorless, odorless, leaves the body within hours—and is fueling a growing number of rapes. *Newsweek*, p. 52. Substance Abuse and Mental Health Services Administration (2003). Emergency Department Trends from the Drug Abuse Warning Network, Final Estimates 1995–2002. Rockville, MD: Substance Abuse and Mental Health Services, Table 3.30.

Inhalants through History

The mind-altering effects of substances inhaled into the lungs have been known since the beginnings of recorded history. Burnt spices and aromatic gums were used in acts of worship in many parts of the ancient world; exotic perfumes were inhaled during Egyptian worship as well as in Babylonian rituals. Inhalation effects also figured prominently in the famous rites of the oracle at Delphi in ancient Greece, where trances induced by the inhaling of vapors led to mysterious utterances that were interpreted as prophecies. We know now, from archeological studies, that limestone faults underneath the temple at Delphi once caused petrochemical fumes to rise to the surface. The oracle was probably inhaling ethylene, a sweet-smelling gas that produces an out-of-body sense of euphoria.[32]

It was not until the latter part of the eighteenth century that reports about the inhalation of specific drugs began to appear. The two most prominent examples were cases involving *nitrous oxide* and *ether*. These anesthetic drugs were first used as surgical analgesics in the 1840s, but they had been synthesized decades earlier. From the very start, the word spread of recreational possibilities.

Nitrous Oxide

The British chemist Sir Humphrey Davy synthesized the gas **nitrous oxide** in 1798 at the precocious age of nineteen. He immediately observed the pleasant effects of this "laughing gas" and proceeded to give nitrous oxide parties for his literary and artistic friends. By the early 1800s, recreational use of nitrous oxide became widespread both in England and the United States as a nonalcoholic avenue to drunkenness. In the 1840s, public demonstrations were held in cities and towns, as a traveling show, by entrepreneurs eager to market the drug commercially.

It was at such an exhibition in Hartford, Connecticut, that a young dentist, Horace Wells, got the idea for using nitrous oxide as an anesthetic. One of the intoxicated participants in the demonstration had stumbled and fallen, receiving in the process a severe wound to the leg. Seeing that the man showed no evidence of pain despite his injury, Wells was sufficiently impressed to try out the anesthetic possibilities himself. The next day, he underwent a tooth extraction while under the influence of nitrous oxide. He felt no pain during the procedure,

nitrous oxide (NIGH-trus OX-ide): An analgesic gas commonly used in modern dentistry. It is also referred to as laughing gas.

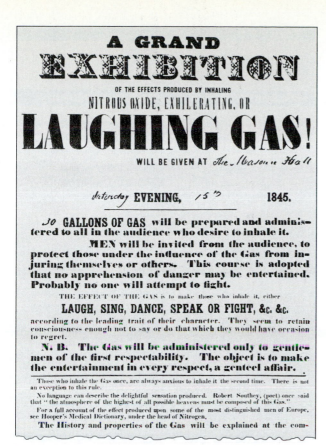

A GRAND

EXHIBITION

OF THE EFFECTS PRODUCED BY INHALING

NITROUS OXIDE, EXHILERATING, OR

LAUGHING GAS!

WILL BE GIVEN AT *The Masonic Hall*

Saturday EVENING, *15th* 1845.

50 GALLONS OF GAS will be prepared and administered to all in the audience who desire to inhale it.

MEN will be invited from the audience, to
protect those under the influence of the Gas from in-
juring themselves or others. This course is adopted
that no apprehension of danger may be entertained.
Probably no one will attempt to fight.

THE EFFECT OF THE GAS is to make those who inhale it, either

LAUGH, SING, DANCE, SPEAK OR FIGHT, &c. &c.

according to the leading trait of their character. They seem to retain
consciousness enough not to say or do that which they would have occasion
to regret.

N. B. The Gas will be administered only to gentle-
men of the first respectability. The object is to make
the entertainment in every respect, a genteel affair.

Those who inhale the Gas once, are always anxious to inhale it the second time. There is not
an exception to this rule.

No language can describe the delightful sensation produced. Robert Southey, (poet) once said
that "the atmosphere of the highest of all possible heavens must be composed of this Gas."

For a full account of the effect produced upon some of the most distinguished men of Europe,
see Hooper's Medical Dictionary, under the head of Nitrogen.

The History and properties of the Gas will be explained at the com-

Public demonstrations of nitrous oxide ("laughing gas") inhalation were popular entertainments in the first half of the nineteenth century.

and nitrous oxide has been a part of dental practice ever since, though recently its role as a routine anesthesia has become a matter of controversy.[33]

During the 1960s, nitrous oxide inhalation reappeared as a recreational drug. Tanks of compressed nitrous oxide were diverted for illicit use, and health professionals, like their counterparts one hundred years earlier, were reportedly hosting nitrous oxide parties. Small cartridges of nitrous oxide called **whippets,** generally used by restaurants to dispense whipped cream, became available through college campus "head shops" and mail-order catalogs. The customary pattern of nitrous oxide abuse was to fill a balloon from these cylinders and inhale the gas from the balloon. The result was a mild euphoric high that lasted for a few minutes and a sense of well-being that lingered for several hours. Sometimes, there would be a loss of consciousness for a few seconds and an experience of "flying." Once consciousness returned, there was the possibility of sensory distortions, nausea, or vomiting. Ordinary cans of commercial whipped cream, in which nitrous oxide is the propellant gas, currently provide easy access to this inhalant.

Nitrous oxide itself is a nontoxic gas, but its inhalation presents serious risks. As with any euphoriant drug, the recreational use of nitrous oxide can be extremely dangerous when a person is driving under its influence. In addition, if nitrous oxide is inhaled through an anesthetic mask and the mask is worn over the mouth and nose, without the combination of oxygen, the consequences can be lethal. Nitrous oxide dilutes the air that a person breathes. Unless there is a minimum of 21 percent oxygen in the mixture, reproducing the 21 percent oxygen content in the air, a lack of oxygen (called **hypoxia**) will produce suffocation or irreversible brain damage.[34]

Ether

As was true of nitrous oxide, **ether** came into use well before its anesthetic effects were appreciated by the medical profession. It was introduced by Friedrich Hoffmann at the beginning of the 1700s, under the name Anodyne, as a liquid "nerve tonic" for intestinal cramps, toothaches, and other pains. Whether it was swallowed or inhaled (it evaporated very quickly), ether also produced effects that resembled intoxication from alcohol. In fact, during the mid-1800s, when the combination of a heavy tax on alcohol and an anti-alcohol temperance campaign in England and Ireland forced people to consider alternatives to alcoholic beverages, both ether drinking and ether inhalation became quite popular. It was used for the same purpose later in the United States during the Prohibition years and in Germany during World War II when alcohol was rationed. Ether's flammability, however, made its recreational use highly dangerous.[35]

Glue, Solvent, and Aerosol Inhalation

The abuse of nitrous oxide and ether may have a relatively long history, but the more familiar reports of inhalation abuse involving glue and solvent chemicals have appeared only since the late 1950s.

whippets: Small canisters containing pressurized nitrous oxide.

hypoxia (high-POX-ee-ah): A deficiency in oxygen intake.

ether (EE-ther): An anesthetic drug, first introduced to surgical practice by William T. Morton in the 1840s. It is highly flammable.

TABLE 8.5

Common household products with abuse potential as inhalants

Gasoline

Hobby glues and cements

Paint thinners

Lacquers and enamels

Varnishes and varnish removers

Cigarette or charcoal lighter fluid

Fingernail polishes and polish remover

Stain removers, degreasers, and other dry-cleaning products

Upholstery protection spray products (e.g., Scotchgard*)

Windshield de-icers

Disinfectants

Fire extinguishing volatile chemicals

Typewriter correction fluid

Permanent felt marker ink

Aerosol hair sprays

Vegetable frying pan lubricants

Spray deodorants

Spray paints

Whipped cream propellants

Freon

Note: The above is a partial list. New products are continually being introduced.

* Scotchgard is a registered product of the 3M Corporation. In 2000, while continuing to market its well-known fabric-protection product, 3M phased out a formulation of Scotchgard that had contained perfluorooctane sulfonate (PFOS), a chemical that the U.S. Environmental Protection Agency had determined to be toxic. In late 2003, a reformulation of Scotchgard, based on a variation of PFOS considered to be safe when used as directed, was introduced.

Source: Bjorhus, Jennifer (2003, May 28). 3M looks to rebuild Scotchgard business. *Saint Paul (MN) Pioneer Press*, p. C1.

TABLE 8.6

Household products with abuse potential and their ingredients

HOUSEHOLD PRODUCT	POSSIBLE INGREDIENTS
Glues, plastic cements, and rubber cements	Acetates, acetone, benzene, hexane, methyl chloride, toluene, trichloroethylene
Cleaning solutions	Carbon tetrachloride, petroleum products, trichloroethylene
Nail polish removers	Acetone
Lighter fluids	Butane, isopropane
Paint sprays, paint thinners, and paint removers	Acetone, butylacetate, methanol, toluene, methyl chloride
Other petroleum products	Acetone, benzene, ether, gasoline, hexane, petroleum, tetraethyl lead, toluene
Typewriter correction fluid	Trichloroethylene, trichlorethane
Hair sprays	Butane, propane
Deodorants, air fresheners	Butane, propane
Whipped cream propellants	Nitrous oxide

Source: Schuckit, Marc A. (2000). *Drug and alcohol abuse: A clinical guide to diagnosis and treatment.* New York: Kluwer Academic/Plenum, p. 222. Sharp, Charles W., and Rosenberg, Neil L. (1997). Inhalants. In Joyce H. Lowinson, Pedro Ruiz, Robert B. Millman, and John G. Langrod (Eds.), *Substance abuse: A comprehensive textbook* (3rd ed.). Baltimore: Williams and Wilkins, p. 248.

Table 8.5 lists some of the common products that have been subject to abuse, including glues, paint thinners, lighter fluid, and stain removers. In addition, many aerosol products are inhalable: hair sprays, deodorants, vegetable lubricants for cooking, and spray paints. Unfortunately, new products are continually being introduced for genuinely practical uses, with little awareness of the consequences should someone inhale their ingredients on a recreational basis (Table 8.6). There are also significant problems associated with occupational exposure to solvent vapors. In a study reported in 1999, 125 pregnant women who had been exposed to solvent products at the workplace were studied over a nine-year period. There was a thirteen times greater risk of birth defects among the exposed group, relative to controls. Occupations of these women included factory workers, laboratory technicians, artists, printing industry workers, chemists, and painters.[36]

The Abuse Potential of Inhalants

Commercial glues, solvents, and aerosol sprays are prime candidates for drug abuse for a number of reasons. First, because they are inhaled into the lungs, the feeling of intoxication occurs more rapidly than with orally administered alcohol. "It's a quicker drunk," in the words of one solvent abuser.[37] The feeling is often described as a "floating euphoria," similar to the effect of alcohol but with a shorter course of intoxication. The high is over in an hour or so, and the hangover is considered less unpleasant than that following alcohol consumption. Second, the typical packaging of inhalant products makes them easy to carry around and conceal from others. Even if they are discovered, many of the products are so common that it is not difficult to invent an excuse for having them on hand.

Finally, most inhalants are easily available in hardware stores, pharmacies, and supermarkets, where they can be bought cheaply or stolen. Among some inhalant abusers, shoplifting these products from open shelves is not just routine but expected. Inhalants are even more widely available than alcohol in poor households; liquor may be in short supply but gasoline, paints, or aerosol products are usually around the house or garage.[38] All these factors contribute to the considerable potential for inhalant abuse.

Acute Effects of Glues, Solvents, and Aerosols

The fumes from commercial inhalant products fall into the general category of depressant drugs, in that the central nervous system is inhibited after they are inhaled. Brain waves, measured objectively through an electroencephalograph (EEG), slow down. Subjectively, the individual feels intoxicated within minutes after inhalation. The most immediate effects include giddiness, euphoria, dizziness, and slurred speech, lasting for fifteen to forty-five minutes. This state is followed by one to two hours of drowsiness and sometimes a loss of consciousness. Along with these effects are occasional experiences of double vision, ringing in the ears, and hallucinations.[39]

The Dangers of Inhalant Abuse

We should realize that inhalant abuse often involves concentrations of glue and solvent products that are usually fifty to a hundred times greater than the maximum allowable concentration of exposure in industry. The health of the inhalant abuser, therefore, is obviously at risk (Help line).

The dangers of inhalant abuse lie not only in the toxic effects of the inhaled compound on body organs but in the behavioral effects of the intoxication itself. Inhalant-produced feelings of euphoria include feelings of recklessness and omnipotence. There have been instances of young inhalant abusers leaping off roof tops in an effort to fly, running into traffic, lying on railroad tracks, or incurring severe lacerations when pushing their hand through a glass window that has been perceived as open. The hallucinations that are sometimes experienced carry their own personal risks. Walls may appear to be closing in, or the sky may seem to be falling. Ordinary objects may be perceived to be changing their shape, size, or color. Any one of these delusions easily can lead to impulsive and potentially destructive behavior.[40]

HELP LINE

The Signs of Possible Inhalant Abuse

- Headaches and dizziness
- Light sensitivity (from dilation of the pupils)
- Reddened, irritated eyes and rash around the mouth
- Double vision
- Ringing in the ears (tinnitus)
- Sneezing and sniffling
- Coughing and bad breath
- Nausea, vomiting, and loss of appetite
- Diarrhea
- Chest pains
- Abnormal heart rhythm (cardiac arrhythmia)

- Muscle and joint aches
- Slurred speech and unsteady muscle coordination
- Chemical odor or stains on clothing or body
- Rags, empty aerosol cans and other containers
- Plastic and paper bags found in closets and other hidden places

Where to go for assistance:

www.inhalant.org

The web site is sponsored by the National Inhalant Prevention Coalition, Austin, Texas.

Sources: Fox, C. Lynn, and Forbing, Shirley E. (1992). Creating drug-free schools and communities. New York: HarperCollins, p. 37. Schuckit, Marc A. (1995). Drug and alcohol abuse: A clinical guide to diagnosis and treatment (4th ed.). New York: Plenum Medical Book Co., p. 219.

There are also significant hazards that are related to the ways in which inhalants are administered. While solvents are sometimes inhaled from a handkerchief or from the container in which they were originally acquired ("huffing"), glues and similar vaporous compounds are often squeezed into a plastic bag and inhaled while the bag is held tightly over the nose and mouth ("bagging"). Potentially, a loss of consciousness can result in hypoxia and asphyxiation. Choking can occur if there is vomiting while the inhaler is unconscious. In an early investigation in the 1960s of nine documented deaths attributed to glue inhalation, at least six were caused specifically by a lack of oxygen.[41] Another danger lies in the inhalation of Freon, a refrigerant gas so cold that the larynx and throat can be frozen upon contact.

The toxic effects of inhalant drugs themselves depend on the specific compound, but the picture is complicated by the fact that most products subject to inhalant abuse contain a variety of compounds, and in some cases, the list of ingredients on the product label is incomplete. Therefore, often we do not know if the medical symptoms resulted from a particular chemical or its interaction with others. Nonetheless, there are specific chemicals that have known health risks. The most serious concern involves sudden-death cases, brought on by cardiac dysrhythmia, that have been reported following the inhalation of propane and butane, commonly used as a propellant for many commercial products.

Besides butane and propane, other inhalant ingredients that present specific hazards are *acetone, benezene, hexane, toluene,* and *gasoline.*

- *Acetone:* **Acetone** inhalation causes significant damage to the mucous membranes of the respiratory tract.

- *Benzene:* Prolonged exposure to **benzene** has been associated with carcinogenic (cancer-producing) disorders, specifically leukemia, as well as anemia. Benzene is generally used as a solvent in waxes, resins, lacquers, paints, and paint removers.

- *Hexane:* The inhalation of **hexane,** primarily in glues and other adhesive products, has been associated with peripheral nerve damage leading to muscular weakness and muscle atrophy. There is a latency period of a few weeks before the symptoms appear.

- *Toluene:* **Toluene** inhalation through glue sniffing has been associated with a reduction in short-term memory, anemia, and a loss of hearing, as well as dysfunctions in parts of the brain that result in difficulties in movement and coordination. Toluene also has been implicated as a principal factor in cases of lethal inhalation of spray paints and lacquers, though it is difficult to exclude the contribution of other solvents in these products.

- *Gasoline:* Concentrated vapors from gasoline can be lethal when inhaled. Medical symptoms from gasoline inhalation are also frequently attributed to gasoline additives that are mixed in the fuel. The additive **triorthocresyl phosphate (TCP),** in particular, has been associated with spastic muscle disorders and liver problems. Lead content in gasoline is generally linked to long-term CNS degeneration, but fortunately leaded gasoline is no longer commonly available in the United States. On the other hand, present-day gasoline mixtures contain large amounts of toluene, acetone, and hexane to help achieve the "anti-knock" property that lead had previously provided.[42]

acetone (ASS-eh-tone): A chemical found in nail polish removers and other products.

benzene: A carcinogenic (cancer-producing) compound found in many solvent products, representing a serious health risk when inhaled.

hexane: A dangerous compound present in many glues and adhesive products. Inhalation of these products has been associated with muscular weakness and atrophy.

toluene (TOL-yoo-ene): A compound in glues, cements, and other adhesive products. Inhalation of these products results in behavioral and neurological impairments.

triorthocresyl phosphate (TCP) (tri-OR-thoh-CREH-sil FOS-fate): A gasoline additive. Inhalation of TCP-containing gasoline has been linked to spastic muscle disorders and liver problems.

Patterns of Inhalant Abuse

Among all the psychoactive drugs, inhalants are associated most closely with the young and often the very young. For those who engage in inhalant abuse, these compounds frequently represent the first experience with a psychoactive drug, preceding even alcohol or tobacco. Overall, inhalant abuse ranks as the fourth highest incidence of drug experimentation among secondary school students, surpassed only by alcohol, tobacco, and marijuana (in that order). Most of these drug abusers, however, are younger than secondary school age; often they are between eleven and thirteen years old.

The University of Michigan survey of 2006 found that about one out of six eighth-grade students (16 percent) had used inhalants at some previous time. About 9 percent

A group of abandoned Brazilian children inhale glue from bags in Rio de Janeiro. The dazed expression is a typical sign of inhalant intoxication.

reported that they had used inhalants within the past year, and 4 percent within the past month. Inhalants are the only class of drugs for which the incidence of usage in the eighth grade significantly *exceeds* the incidence in the tenth and twelfth grades.

Evidently, awareness of this form of drug-taking activity is quite extensive in the later elementary and middle school student population. According to a recent survey, almost two-thirds of ten- to seventeen-year-olds know the meaning of "huffing" and report that they were about twelve years of age when they first knew of classmates abusing inhalants. The common knowledge of inhalant abuse in this age group and a recent decline in the proportion of eighth-grade students who believe that it is dangerous to use inhalants are two reasons that have been given for a recent upsurge in prevalence rates, relative to earlier years in the mid-1990s.[43]

In other cultures and under different circumstances, inhalant abuse affects even younger children and a wider proportion of them. In Mexico City, among street children as young as eight or nine who live without families in abandoned buildings, rates of inhalant abuse are extremely high, with 22 percent reporting some form of solvent inhalation on a daily basis. Inhalant abuse is reported to be commonplace among street children in Rio de Janeiro and other major cities in Central and South America as well as Asia (Drugs . . . in Focus).[44]

Inhalant abuse, on an experimental basis, is not restricted by social or geographic boundaries. Chronic inhalant abuse, however, is overrepresented among the poor and those youths suffering emotional challenges in their lives and seeking some form of escape. Studies of young inhalant abusers show high rates of delinquency, poor school performance, and emotional difficulties. They often come from disorganized, multiproblem homes in which the parents are actually or effectively absent or else engage themselves in abuse of alcohol or some other substance.[45] The diversity of ethnic subgroups showing high prevalence rates for inhalant abuse include such disparate groups as Latino children in a rural community in the Southwest, American Indian children on U.S. reservations, and white children in an economically disadvantaged neighborhood in Philadelphia.

Whatever the ethnic identity of the chronic inhalant abuser, a critical factor is peer influence. Most studies indicate that glue, solvent, or aerosol inhalation is generally experienced in small groups, often at the urging of friends or relatives. Young inhalant abusers tend to be more alienated than others at this age, and the feelings of alienation can be an important factor in leading a youth to others who are also alienated, thus creating a cluster of peers who engage in this form of drug-taking behavior. One survey among American Indian youth, for example, found that when friends strongly encouraged inhalant use or would not try to stop it, 84 percent of the sample reported having tried inhalants and 41 percent reported having used them recently. In contrast, when friends discouraged inhalant use or were perceived as applying strong sanctions against it, only 19 percent reported having tried inhalants and only 3 percent had used them recently.[46]

Questions about Chronic Inhalant Abuse

The long-term effects of inhalant abuse are not well documented owing to the fact that inhalant abuse frequently does not extend over more than a year or two in a person's life and may occur only sporadically. There have been reports of cases showing a tolerance to the euphoriant effects of glues and gasoline. Although it is difficult to determine the dosages that are involved with these tolerance effects, it appears that individuals exposed only to low concentrations for brief periods of time or high levels on an occasional basis do not show tolerance to the inhalants.

Inhalant dependence occurs frequently. Inhalant abusers have been reported as feeling restless, irritable, and anxious when prevented from inhaling glues, solvents, or aerosols. Physiological withdrawal symptoms are only rarely observed among inhalant abusers but are frequently observed among animals in laboratory studies, so the question of whether physical dependence exists has yet to be definitively answered.[47]

Drugs . . . in Focus

Resistol and *Resistoleros* in Latin America

In the cities of Central and South America, the street children are referred to as *resistoleros*, a name derived from their frequent habit of sniffing a commercial brand of shoemaker's glue called Resistol. Granted, many cases of inhalant abuse among the hundreds of thousands of children in Latin America do not specifically involve Resistol; nevertheless, the frequency of Resistol abuse and the fact that Resistol dominates the market in commercial solvent-based adhesives have focused attention on the company that manufactures it, the H. B. Fuller Company of St. Paul, Minnesota.

Concern for the welfare of these children also has spotlighted a thorny ethical issue: Should a corporation accept the social responsibility when widespread abuse of its product exists, either in the United States or elsewhere in the world? Testor Corporation in 1969 added a noxious ingredient to discourage abuse of its model glue; in 1994, a German chemical company marketing a Resistol rival stopped its distribution in this region. For its part, Fuller did modify the formulation of Resistol in 1992, replacing the sweet-smelling but highly toxic toluene with a slightly less toxic chemical, cyclohexane. However, it continues to sell Resistol, claiming that its legitimate uses benefit the economies of regions where it is marketed. More-over, the company has funded community programs for homeless children throughout Central America and has limited its Resistol marketing efforts to large industrial customers rather than small retailers. Unappeased, foes continue to press Fuller to discontinue the product entirely.

Note: There is no association between Resistol glue and Resistol Western Hats or any corporation-related sponsorships such as the Resistol Arena in Mesquite, Texas.

Source: Henriques, Diana B. (1995, November 26). Black mark for a "good citizen." Critics say H. B. Fuller isn't doing enough to curb glue-sniffing. *New York Times*, Section 3, pp. 1, 11.

A Gateway for Future Drug Abuse?

The young age at which inhalant abuse occurs leads to the question of whether there is a causal link between inhalant abuse and later abuse of other drugs. Without a doubt, some youths will subsequently replace inhalants with alcohol, marijuana, and other recreational drugs, but the experience of inhalants cannot be considered to lead on a pharmacological level to other drug experimentation or long-term abuse. This is how one author has put it:

> The socially and emotionally healthy juvenile casually experimenting with solvent sniffing does not bear any greater potential for heroin addiction than had he not sniffed solvents. Conversely, the disturbed youth from a broken home, who is frequently exposed to pushers, probably bears the same high risk of ultimate narcotic abuse whether or not he sniffs glue. Regardless of surrounding circumstances, however, any significant resort to intoxicating substances in childhood should be carefully noted as a potential warning of a growing emotional disturbance or as a predictor of a future drug-dependent personality.[48]

A similar "gateway argument" with respect to marijuana was reviewed in Chapter 7.

Responses of Society to Inhalant Abuse

> Sniffing gasoline or paint is a grubby, dirty, cheap way to get high. Inhalant users are, therefore, likely to be the social rejects, the emotionally disturbed, the disadvantaged minorities, the maladjusted, as well as angry and alienated. There is nothing attractive, exciting, or appealing about inhalant use or inhalant users. . . .[49]

Certainly, the concern about inhalant abuse takes a backseat to more widely publicized concerns about cocaine, methamphetamine, and heroin abuse or the recent abuse of club drugs. Despite the relatively low priority given to inhalant abuse, however, steps have been taken to reduce some of its hazards. One major approach has been to restrict the availability and sales of glues to young people, a strategy that, as you might predict, has met with mixed success. Some U.S. cities have restricted sales of plastic cement unless it is purchased with a model kit, but such legislation is largely ineffective when model kits themselves are relatively inexpensive. As with the official restriction of sales of alcohol and tobacco to minors, young people can find a way around these laws.

More direct action was taken in 1969 by the Testor Corporation, a leading manufacturer of plastic cement for models, by incorporating **oil of mustard** into the formula. This additive produces severe nasal irritation similar to the effect of horseradish while not affecting its use as a glue or the effect on the user who does not inhale it directly. Other brands of glues and adhesives, however, may not contain oil of mustard and as a result could still be available for abuse, and additives in general would not be desirable for certain products that are used for cosmetic purposes.

In an additional step taken to reduce inhalant abuse, concentrations of benzene in many household products sold in the United States have been reduced or eliminated, though it is difficult to determine the exact composition of solutions merely by inspecting the label. Standards for products manufactured and sold in foreign countries are typically far less stringent.[50]

Beyond the difficulty in identifying the toxicity of specific solvent compounds, there is the overriding general problem of the enormous variety and easy availability of solvent-containing products. As one researcher has lamented, "If sales of gold paint or paint thinner are curtailed, people may choose to use typewriter correction fluid, or shoe polish or nail polish remover, or hundreds of other items that have legitimate uses in everyday life."[51]

Ultimately, some sort of educational strategy must be coordinated that is targeted at children in the elementary grades in school and their parents at home. Different countries have differing educational approaches, ranging from nonalarmist, low-key programs to those urging absolute abstinence, and it is not clear which strategy is most effective in controlling inhalant abuse. A National Inhalants and Poisons Awareness Week is currently held each year in March to promote greater efforts to inform the public about this problem. A 2002 survey conducted by the Partnership for a Drug-Free America has shown that only a small fraction of the parents of teens who have tried inhalants are aware of that fact. On the

SNIFFING CORRECTION FLUID CAN STOP YOUR HEART.

Poster images represent a growing national effort to prevent inhalation abuse.

treatment side, special guidelines are currently being developed for a variety of inhalant-abuse populations—not only the adolescents engaging in transient inhalant abuse but also those individuals who are twenty to twenty-nine years old, have a five-year or longer history of inhalant exposure, and have sustained possible brain damage as a result.[52]

In the meantime, attention has been directed toward the abusive inhalation of two specific products, amyl nitrite and butyl nitrite, affecting a different population from the one traditionally associated with glue, solvent, or aerosol inhalants. Like nitrous oxide and ether, these nitrites have been around for some time, but their abuse has been relatively recent.

oil of mustard: An additive in Testor brand hobby-kit glues that produces nasal irritation when inhaled, thus reducing the potential for inhalant abuse.

Amyl Nitrite and Butyl Nitrite Inhalation

Amyl and butyl nitrites were first identified in the nineteenth century. When inhaled, they produce an intense vasodilation, a relaxation of smooth muscle, a fall in blood pressure, and an increase in heart rate. Since 1867, **amyl nitrite** has been used medically, on a prescription basis, in the treatment of angina pain in heart patients and as an antidote to cyanide poisoning. **Butyl nitrite** produces similar therapeutic effects but has never been used on a clinical basis.

News of the recreational potential of nitrite inhalation began to spread in the 1960s and reached a peak in the 1970s, particularly within the gay community, as it was recognized that the vasodilation of cerebral blood vessels produced a euphoric high, anal sphincter muscles were relaxed, and vasodilation of genital blood vessels enhanced sexual pleasure (Table 8.7). By 1979, more than 5 million people in the United States were using amyl or butyl nitrites more than once a week. Since then, there has been a substantial decline in their popularity. By 1986, the University of Michigan survey of young adults between nineteen and twenty-eight years of age found that only 2 percent reported having abused nitrites within the previous year, and by 1995, the percentage had declined to one-third of 1 percent.[53]

Patterns of Nitrite Inhalation Abuse

Amyl nitrite is often referred to as "poppers" or "snappers" because it is commonly available in a mesh-covered glass ampule and there is a popping sound as the ampule is broken and the vapors of the nitrite are inhaled as they are released into the air. It is quick-acting, with vasodilatory effects appearing within thirty seconds. Light-headedness, a flushing sensation, blurred vision, and euphoria last for about five minutes, followed by headache and nausea. Butyl nitrite follows a similar time course in its effects and is available in pornography shops and mail-order catalogs. Many of

> **amyl nitrite (AY-mil NIGH-trite):** An inhalant drug that relaxes smooth muscle and produces euphoria. Clinically useful in treating angina pain in cardiac patients, it is also subject to abuse.
>
> **butyl nitrite (BYOO-til NIGH-trite):** An inhalant drug, similar in its effects to amyl nitrite. It is commonly abused as it induces feelings of euphoria.

TABLE 8.7

A chronology of nitrite inhalation abuse

DATE	EVENT	DATE	EVENT
1859	Flushing of skin with amyl nitrite first described	1977	Nitrite inhalation predominant among gay men
1867	First therapeutic use of amyl nitrite for angina pain	1979	More than 5 million people estimated to have used nitrites more than once per week
1880s	Butyl nitrite studied but not used clinically		19 cases of Kaposi's sarcoma found in retrospect
1960	Amyl nitrite prescription requirement eliminated by FDA	1980	56 cases of Kaposi's sarcoma reported
1963	First reports of recreational use of nitrites	1981	Increased suspicions of a link between nitrite use and Kaposi's sarcoma
1960s	Widespread recreational use of nitrites among young adults	1985	Concerns about AIDS and HIV infection beginning to receive widespread media attention
1969	Amyl nitrite prescription requirement reinstated	1990s to present	Association between nitrite inhalation and Kaposi's sarcoma is discredited
1970	Street brands of butyl nitrite beginning to be widely available		Nitrite inhalation abuse greatly reduced among heterosexual populations
1974	Popper craze beginning		
1976	$50 million sales reported in nitrites in one U.S. city		

Source: Updated from Newell, Guy R., Spitz, Margaret R., and Wilson, Michael B. (1988). Nitrite inhalants: Historical perspective. In Harry W. Haverkos and John A. Dougherty (Eds.), *Health hazards of nitrite inhalants* (NIDA Research Monograph 83). Rockville, MD: National Institute of Drug Abuse, p. 6.

TABLE 8.8

"Brand names" for butyl nitrite

Aroma of Men	Hardware	Mama Poppers
Ban Apple Gas	Heart On	Oz
Bang	Highball	Quick Silver
Bullet	Jac Aroma	Rush
Climax	Lightning Bolt	Satan's Scent
Crypt Tonight	Liquid Increase	Thrust
Discorama	Locker Room	Toilet Water

Source: Maickel, Roger P. (1988). The fate and toxicity of butyl nitrites. In Harry W. Haverkos and John A. Dougherty (Eds.), *Health hazards of nitrite inhalants* (NIDA Research Monograph 83). Rockville, MD: National Institute on Drug Abuse, p. 16.

the various "trade names" for butyl nitrite (Table 8.8) have referred to its supposed sexual benefits as well as the fact that its vapors emit a strong odor resembling that of sweaty socks.

Cases of nitrite inhalation have also been found among both heterosexual and gay adolescents, for whom the primary attraction is a feeling of general euphoria. The University of Michigan survey began looking at

Quick Concept Check 8.2

Understanding the History of Inhalants

Check your understanding of the history of inhalant drugs by indicating whether a particular substance was used (a) first recreationally, then as an application in medicine; (b) first as an application in medicine, then recreationally; or (c) recreationally, with no known application in medicine.

1. amyl nitrite   4. toluene

2. hexane   5. ether

3. nitrous oxide   6. benzene

Answers: 1. b   2. c   3. a   4. c   5. a   6. c

prevalence rates for nitrite inhalation in 1979. In that year, approximately 11 percent of high school seniors reported having tried nitrite inhalants at least once in their lifetime. By 2003, the rate had dropped substantially to about 1 percent.[54]

Summary

Barbiturates

- Introduced in 1903 and in use until approximately 1960, the primary sedative-hypnotics (drugs that produce sedation and sleep) belonged to the barbiturate family of drugs.

- Barbiturates are typically classified by virtue of how long their depressant effects are felt, from long acting (example: phenobarbital) to intermediate acting (examples: butalbarbital and amobarbital) to short acting (examples: pentobarbital and secobarbital).

- A major disadvantage of barbiturates is the potential of a lethal overdose, particularly when combined with other depressants such as alcohol. In addition, barbiturate withdrawal symptoms are very severe and require careful medical attention.

Nonbarbiturate Sedative-Hypnotics

- Methaqualone (Quaalude) was introduced in the 1960s as an alternative to barbiturates for sedation and sleep. Unfortunately, this drug produced undesirable

side effects and became subject to widespread abuse. It is no longer available as a licit drug.

The Development of Antianxiety Drugs

- Beginning in the 1950s, a major effort was made by the pharmaceutical industry to develop a drug that would relieve anxiety (tranquilize) rather than merely depress the CNS (sedate).

- Meprobamate (Miltown) was introduced in 1955 for this purpose, though it is now understood that the effects of this drug result more from its sedative properties than its ability to relieve anxiety.

Benzodiazepines

- The introduction of benzodiazepines, specifically diazepam (Valium) and chlordiazepoxide (Librium), in the early 1960s, was a significant breakthrough in the development of antianxiety drugs. These drugs selectively affect specific receptors in the brain instead of acting as general depressants of the nervous system.

- In general, benzodiazepines are safer drugs than barbiturates, when taken alone. When taken in combination with alcohol, however, dangerous synergistic effects are observed.
- Benzodiazepines produce their effects by binding to receptors in the brain that are sensitive to the inhibitory neurotransmitter gamma aminobutyric acid (GABA).
- Social problems concerning the taking of benzodiazepine drugs during the 1970s centered on the widespread misuse of the drug. Prescriptions were written too frequently and for excessive dosages.

Nonbenzodiazepine Depressants

- Recently developed nonbenzodiazepines have provided better opportunities to treat sleep disorders and anxiety. Two examples are zolpidem and buspirone.
- Zolpidem (brand name: Ambien) and eszopiclone (Lunesta) have been useful as a sedative-hypnotic in the treatment of insomnia. They have strong but transient sedative effects and produces little or no muscle relaxation.
- Buspirone (brand name: BuSpar) has been useful as an antianxiety medication that does not cause sedation.
- Beta blockers, traditionally used to treat cardiac and blood pressure disorders, have been prescribed for individuals who are facing an anxiety-producing event, such as performing on the stage or speaking in public.
- Certain antidepressants called selective serotonin reuptake inhibitors (SSRIs) have been successful in treating a variety of anxiety disorders.

The Risks of GHB

- Gamma hydroxybutyrate (GHB) is a CNS depressant, first used by bodybuilders because of the possibility that it had growth-hormone-stimulating effects. Today, GHB is an illicit drug, available only through clandestine channels.
- As with Rohypnol, the depressant effects of GHB have made it attractive as a club drug. Its involvement as a potential date-rape drug has raised very serious concerns.

Inhalants through History

- Nitrous oxide was discovered in 1798 and became a major recreational drug in the 1880s. It is still used recreationally, but its primary application is for routine anesthesia in dentistry.
- Ether is another anesthetic drug, first introduced in the 1840s. It has also been used as a recreational drug, particularly in times when alcohol availability has been severely reduced.

Glue, Solvent, and Aerosol Inhalation

- Present-day inhalant abuse involves a wide range of commercial products: gasoline, glues and other adhesives, household cleaning compounds, aerosol sprays, and solvents of all kinds.
- These products are usually cheap, readily available, and easily concealable, and their intoxicating effects when inhaled are rapid. All these factors make inhalants prime candidates for abuse.
- The principal dangers of inhalant abuse lie in the behavioral consequences of intoxication and in the possibility of asphyxiation when inhalants are administered by an airproof bag held over the nose and mouth.
- Specific toxic substances contained in inhalant products include acetone, benzene, hexane, toluene, and gasoline.

Patterns of Inhalant Abuse

- Inhalant abuse respects no social or geographic boundaries, though prevalence rates are particularly high among poor and disadvantaged populations.
- Research studies indicate the presence of psychological dependence rather than physical dependence in inhalant abuse behavior.
- Tolerance effects are seen for chronic inhalant abusers when the inhalant concentration is high and exposure is frequent.

Responses of Society to Inhalant Abuse

- Concern about the dangers of inhalant abuse has led to restriction of the sale of model-kit glues to minors and a modification of the formulas for model-kit glue in an attempt to lessen the possibility of abuse.
- There are so many products currently on the open market that contain volatile chemicals that a universal restriction of abusable inhalants is practically impossible. Therefore, prevention efforts regarding inhalant abuse are critical elements in reducing this form of drug-taking behavior.

Amyl Nitrite and Butyl Nitrite Inhalation

- Two types of inhalants, amyl nitrite and butyl nitrite, appeared on the scene in the 1960s, reaching a peak in the late 1970s. Although they are often identified with gay men, populations of heterosexual adolescents and young adults have also engaged in this form of inhalant abuse.

acetone, p. 208
amobarbital, p. 191
amyl nitrite, p. 212
antianxiety drugs, p. 191
barbiturate, p. 191
benzene, p. 208
benzodiazepines, p. 196
beta blockers, p. 202
buspirone, p. 202

butyl nitrite, p. 212
chloral hydrate, p. 195
chlordiazepoxide, p. 196
diazepam, p. 196
ether, p. 205
eszopiclone, p. 201
gamma hydroxybutyrate
    (GHB), p. 202
hexane, p. 208

hypoxia, p. 205
inhalants, p. 191
meprobamate, p. 196
methaqualone, p. 195
nitrous oxide, p. 204
oil of mustard, p. 211
pentobarbital, p. 191
phenobarbital, p. 191
REM-sleep rebound, p. 193

secobarbital, p. 191
sedative-hypnotics, p. 191
toluene, p. 208
triorthocresyl phosphate
    (TCP), p. 208
whippets, p. 205
zolpidem, p. 201

Endnotes

1. Quotation from Silverstein, Alvin, Silverstein, Virginia, and Silverstein, Robert (1991). *The addictions handbook.* Hillside, NJ: Enslow Publishers, p. 51.

2. Palfai, Tibor, and Jankiewicz, Henry (1991). *Drugs and human behavior.* Dubuque, IA: W. C. Brown, p. 203.

3. Jacobs, Michael R., and Fehr, Kevin O'B. (1987). *Drugs and drug abuse: A reference text* (2d ed.). Toronto: Addiction Research Foundation, pp. 183–194.

4. Palfai and Jankiewicz, *Drugs and human behavior*, p. 213.

5. Jacobs and Fehr, *Drugs and drug abuse*, p. 189.

6. Kauffman, Janice F., Shaffer, Howard, and Burglass, Milton E. (1985). The biological basics: Drugs and their effects. In Thomas E. Bratter and Gary G. Forrest (Eds.), *Alcoholism and substance abuse: Strategies for clinical intervention.* New York: Free Press, pp. 107–136.

7. Sleeping pills and antianxiety drugs (1988). *The Harvard Medical School Mental Health Letter, 5* (6), 1–4.

8. Griffiths, Roland R.; Lukas, Scott E.; Bradford, L. D.; Brady, Joseph V.; and Snell, Jack D. (1981). Self-injection of barbiturates and benzodiazepines in baboons. *Psychopharmacology, 75,* 101–109.

9. Griffiths, Roland R., Bigelow, George, and Liebson, Ira (1979). Human drug self-administration: Double-blind comparison of pentobarbital, diazepam, chlorpromazine, and placebo. *Journal of Pharmacology and Experimental Therapeutics, 210,* 301–310.

10. Johnston, Lloyd D.; O'Malley, Patrick M.; Bachman, Jerald G.; and Schulenberg, John E. (2007). *Monitoring the Future national results on adolescent drug use. Overview of key findings, 2006.* Bethesda, MD: National Institute on Drug Abuse, Tables 1 and 2.

11. Carroll, Marilyn, and Gallo, Gary (1985). *Quaaludes: The quest for oblivion.* New York: Chelsea House.

12. Julien, Robert M. (2001). *A primer of drug action* (9th ed.). New York: Worth, p. 54.

13. Berger, Philip A., and Tinklenberg, Jared R. (1977). Treatment of abusers of alcohol and other addictive drugs. In Jack D. Barchas, Philip A. Berger, Roland D. Caranello, and Glen R. Elliott (Eds.), *Psychopharmacology: From theory to practice.* New York: Oxford University Press, pp. 355–385.

14. Leavitt, Fred (1982). *Drugs and behavior* (2nd ed.). New York: Wiley.

15. Rickels, Karl (1981). Benzodiazepines: Clinical use patterns. In Stephen I. Szara and Jacqueline P. Ludford (Eds.), *Benzodiazepines: A review of research results 1980* (NIDA Research Monograph 33). Rockville, MD: National Institute on Drug Abuse, pp. 43–60.

16. Substance Abuse and Mental Health Services Administration. Benzodiazepines in drug abuse-related emergency department visits: 1995–2002 (2004, April). *The Dawn Reports.* Rockville, MD: Center for Substance Abuse Treatment, Substance Abuse and Mental Health Services Administration, pp. 1–4. Lickey, Marvin E., and Gordon, Barbara (1991). *Medicine and mental illness.* New York: Freeman, p. 280. Tanaka, Einosuke (2002). Toxiological interactions between alcohol and benzodiazepines. *Journal of Toxicology—Clinical Toxicology, 40,* 69–75.

17. Julien, *A primer of drug action*, p. 161. Salzman, Carl (1999). An 87-year-old woman taking a benzodiazepine. *Journal of the American Medical Association, 281,* 1121–1125.

18. Rickels, Karl; Case, W. George; Downing, Robert W.; and Winokur, Andrew (1983). Long-term diazepam therapy and clinical outcome. *Journal of the American Medical Association, 250,* 767–771.

19. Julien, *A primer of drug action*, pp. 153–163. Longo, Lance P., and Johnson, Brian (2000). Addiction: Part I. Benzodiazepines—Side effects, abuse risk and alternatives. *American Family Physician, 61,* 2121–2128.

20. Mohler, H., and Okada, T. (1977). Benzodiazepine receptors in rat brain: Demonstration in the central nervous system. *Science, 198,* 849–851. Squires, Richard F., and Braestrup, Claus (1977). Benzodiazepine receptors in rat brain. *Nature, 266,* 732–734.

21. Lickey and Gordon, *Medicine and mental illness*, p. 291. Nelson, John, and Chouinard, Guy (1996). Benzodiazepines: Mechanisms of action and clinical indications. In Andrius Baskys and Gary Remington (Eds.). *Brain mechanisms and psychotropic drugs.* Boca Raton, FL: CRC Press, pp. 213–238.

22. Löw, Karin; Crestani, Florence; Keist, Ruth; Benke, Dietmar; Brünig, Ina; et al. (2000). Molecular and neuronal substrate for the selective attenuation of anxiety. *Science, 290,* 131–134.

23. Griffiths, Roland R., and Ator, Nancy A. (1981). Benzodiazepine self-administration in animals and humans: A comprehensive literature review. In Stephen I. Szara and Jacqueline P. Ludford (Eds.), *Benzodiazepines: A review of research results, 1980* (NIDA Research Monograph 33). Rockville, MD: National Institute on Drug Abuse, pp. 22–36.

24. Julien, Robert M. (1998). *A primer of drug action* (8th ed.). New York: Freeman, pp. 106–107.

25. Lickey and Gordon, *Medicine and mental illness,* p. 278.

26. Bakalar, Nicholas (2005, February 22). A host of anxiety drugs, begat by Valium. *New York Times,* p. F6. Lagnaouli, Rajaa; Moore, Nicholas, Dartigues, Jean François; Fourrier, Annie; and Bégaud, Bernard (2001). Benzodiazepine use and wine consumption in the French elderly. *British Journal of Clinical Pharmacology, 52,* 455–456. Pimlott, Nicholas J. G.; Hux, Janet E.; Wilson, Lynn M.; Kahan, Meldon; Li, Cindy; and Rosser, Walter W. (2003). Educating physicians to reduce benzodiazepine use by elderly patients: A randomized controlled trial. *Canadian Medical Association Journal, 168,* 835–839. Ramesh, M., and Roberts, G. (2002). Use of night-time benzodiazepines in an elderly inpatient population. *Journal of Clinical Pharmacy and Therapeutics, 27,* 93–97.

27. Gershell, Leland (2006). From the analyst's couch: Insomnia market. *Nature Reviews and Drug Discovery, 5,* 15–16.

28. Julien, *A primer of drug action* (9th ed.), pp. 169–171.

29. Julien, *A primer of drug action* (9th ed.), p. 172. Julien, Robert M. (1988). *Drugs and the body.* New York: Freeman, pp. 80–81. Kent, J. M., Coplan, J. D., and Gorman, J. M. (1998). Clinical utility of the selective serotonin reuptake inhibitors in the spectrum of anxiety. *Biological Psychiatry, 44,* 812–824.

30. Dyer, J. E. (2000). Evolving abuse of GHB in California: Bodybuilding drug to date-rape drug. *Journal of Toxicology—Clinical Toxicology, 38,* 184. Office of National Drug Control Policy (1998, October). *ONDCP Drug Policy Information Clearinghouse fact sheet: Gamma hydroxybutyrate (GHB).* Washington DC: Executive Office of the President.

31. Adams, Genetta M. (2003, January 5). A safety test for a night on the town. *Newsday,* p. D2. Information regarding bar coasters courtesy of Drink Safe Technology, Wellington, FL. Office of National Drug Control Policy, *ONDCP Drug Policy Information Clearinghouse fact sheet: Gamma hydroxybutyrate (GHB).*

32. Broad, William J. (2002, March 19). For Delphic oracle, fumes and visions. *New York Times,* pp. F1, F4. Preble, Edward, and Laury, Gabriel V. (1967). Plastic cement: The ten cent hallucinogen. *International Journal of the Addictions, 2,* 271–281.

33. Gillman, Mark A., and Lichtigfeld, Frederick J. (1997). Clinical role and mechanisms of action of analgesic nitrous oxide. *International Journal of Neuroscience, 93,* 55–62. Nagle, David R. (1968). Anesthetic addiction and drunkenness. *International Journal of the Addictions, 3,* p. 33.

34. Julien, *A primer of drug action,* pp. 121–122. Layzer, Robert B. (1985). Nitrous oxide abuse. In Edmond I. Eger (Ed.), *Nitrous oxide/N$_2$O.* New York: Elsevier, pp. 249–257. Morgan, Roberta (1988). *The emotional pharmacy.* Los Angeles: Body Press, pp. 212–213.

35. Nagle, Anesthetic addiction and drunkenness, pp. 26–30.

36. Khattak, Sohail; K-Moghtader, Guiti; McMartin, Kristen; Barrera, Maru; Kennedy, Debbie; and Koren, Gideon (1999). Pregnancy outcome following gestational exposure to organic solvents. *Journal of the American Medical Association, 281,* 1106–1109.

37. Cohen, Sidney (1977). Inhalant abuse: An overview of the problem. In Charles W. Sharp and Mary Lee Brehm (Eds.), *Review of inhalants: Euphoria to dysfunction* (NIDA Research Monograph 15). Rockville, MD: National Institute on Drug Abuse, p. 7.

38. Ibid., pp. 6–8.

39. Schuckit, Marc A. (1995). *Drug and alcohol abuse: A clinical guide to diagnosis and treatment* (4th ed.). New York: Plenum Medical Book Co., pp. 217–225. Sharp, Charles W., and Rosenberg, Neil L. (1997). Inhalants. In Joyce H. Lowinson, Pedro Ruiz, Robert B. Millman, and John G. Langrod (Eds.), *Substance abuse: A comprehensive textbook.* Baltimore: Williams and Wilkins, pp. 246–264.

40. Abramovitz, Melissa (2003, October). The dangers of inhalants. *Current Health 2,* pp. 19–21. Winger, Gail, Hofmann, Frederick G., and Woods, James H. (1992). *A handbook on drug and alcohol abuse: The biomedical aspects* (3d ed.). New York: Oxford University Press, pp. 90–91.

41. Brecher, Edward M., and the editors of *Consumer Reports* (1972). *Licit and illicit drugs.* Boston: Little, Brown, p. 331.

42. Brands, Bruna, Sproule, Beth, and Marshman, Joan (1998). *Drugs and drug abuse: A reference text.* Toronto: Addiction Research Foundation, pp. 469–471. Bruckner, James V., and Peterson, Richard G. (1977). Toxicology of aliphatic and aromatic hydrocarbons. In Charles W. Sharp and Mary L. Brehm (Eds.), *Review of inhalants: Euphoria to dysfunction* (NIDA Research Monograph 15). Rockville, MD: National Institute on Drug Abuse, pp. 124–163. Garriott, James C. (1992). Death among inhalant abusers. In Charles W. Sharp, Fred Beauvais, and Richard Spence (Eds.), *Inhalant abuse: A volatile research agenda* (NIDA Research Monograph 129). Rockville, MD: National Institute on Drug Abuse, pp. 171–193.

43. Edwards, Ruth W., and Oetting, E. R. (1995). Inhalant use in the United States. In Nicholas Kozel, Zili Sloboda, and Mario De La Rosa (Eds.), *Epidemiology of inhalant abuse: An international perspective* (NIDA Research Monograph 148). Rockville, MD: National Institute on Drug Abuse, pp. 8–28. Johnston, O'Malley, Bachman, and Schulenberg, *Monitoring the Future national results*, Tables 1 and 2. Preboth, Monica (2000, February 15). Prevalence of inhalant abuse in children. *American Family Physician*, p. 1206.

44. Howard, Matthew O.; Walker, R. Dale; Walker, Patricia S.; Cottler, Linda B.; and Compton, Wilson M. (1999). Inhalant use among urban American Indian youth. *Addiction*, 94, 83–95. Kin, Foong, and Navaratnam, Vis (1995). An overview of inhalant abuse in selected countries of Asia and the Pacific region. In Nicholas Kozel, Zili Sloboda, and Mario De La Rosa (Eds.), *Epidemiology of inhalant abuse: An international perspective* (NIDA Research Monograph 148). Rockville, MD: National Institute on Drug Abuse, pp. 29–49. Leal, Hermán; Mejía, Laura; Gómez, Lucila; and Salina de Valle, Olga (1978). Naturalistic study on the phenomenon of inhalant use in a group of children in Mexico City. In Charles W. Sharp and L. T. Carroll (Eds.), *Voluntary inhalation of industrial solvents*. Rockville, MD: National Institute on Drug Abuse, pp. 95–108. Medina-Mora, María Elena, and Berenzon, Shoshana (1995). Epidemiology of inhalant abuse in Mexico. In Nicholas Kozel, Zili Sloboda, and Mario De La Rosa (Eds.), *Epidemiology of inhalant abuse: An international perspective* (NIDA Research Monograph 148). Rockville, MD: National Institute on Drug Abuse, pp. 136–174. Surratt, Hilary L., and Inciardi, James A. (1996). Drug use, HIV risks, and prevention/intervention strategies among street youths in Rio de Janeiro, Brazil. In Clyde B. McCoy, Lisa R. Metsch, and James A. Inciardi (Eds.), *Intervening with drug-involved youth*. Thousand Oaks, MI: Sage Publications, pp. 173–190.

45. Hofmann, Frederick G. (1983), *A handbook on drug and alcohol abuse: The biomedical aspects* (2nd ed.). New York: Oxford University Press, p. 134. Howard, Matthew O., and Jenson, Jeffrey M. (1998). Inhalant use among antisocial youth: Prevalence and correlates. *Addictive Behaviors*, 24, 59–74. Mackesy-Amiti, Mary Ellen, and Fendrich, Michaeal (1999). Inhalant abuse and delinquent behavior among adolescents: A comparison of inhalant users and other drug users. *Addiction*, 94, 555–564.

46. Oetting, E. R., Edwards, Ruth W., and Beauvais, Fred (1988). Social and psychological factors underlying inhalant abuse. In Raquel A. Crider and Beatrice A. Rouse (eds.), *Epidemiology of inhalant abuse: An update* (NIDA Research Monograph 85). Rockville, MD: National Institute on Drug Abuse, pp. 172–203.

47. Hofmann, *Handbook on drug and alcohol abuse*, pp. 138– 139. Karch, *The pathology of drug abuse*, p. 432. Korman, Maurice (1977). Clinical evaluation of psychological factors. In Charles W. Sharp and Mary Lee Brehm (Eds.), *Review of inhalants: Euphoria to dysfunction* (NIDA Research Monograph 15). Rockville, MD: National Institute on Drug Abuse, pp. 30–53.

48. Hofmann, *Handbook on drug and alcohol abuse*, p. 134.

49. Oetting, Edwards, and Beauvais, Social and psychological factors, p. 197.

50. Sharp, Charles W. (1977). Approaches to the problem. In Charles W. Sharp and Mary Lee Brehm (Eds.), *Review of inhalants: Euphoria to dysfunction* (NIDA Research Monograph 15). Rockville, MD: National Institute on Drug Abuse, pp. 226–242.

51. Kerner, Karen (1988). Current topics in inhalant abuse. In Raquel A. Crider and Beatrice A. Rouse (Eds.), *Epidemiology of inhalant abuse: An update* (NIDA Research Monograph 85). Rockville, MD: National Institute on Drug Abuse, p. 20.

52. Draft of National Inhalant Prevention Coalition guidelines for inhalant abuse treatment (2003). Information courtesy of the National Inhalant Prevention Coalition, Austin, Texas. Office of National Drug Control Policy (2003, February). *Inhalants: Drug Policy Information Clearinghouse fact sheet*. Washington, DC: White House Office of National Drug Control Policy. Substance Abuse and Mental Health Services Administration (2003). *Inhalants: Substance abuse treatment advisory*. Rockville, MD: Center for Substance Abuse Treatment, Substance Abuse and Mental Health Services Administration.

53. Johnston, Lloyd D., O'Malley, Patrick M., and Bachman, Jerald D. (2001). *Monitoring the future: National survey results on drug use, 1975–2000, Vol. II: College students and young adults ages 19–40*. Bethesda, MD: National Institute on Drug Abuse, Table 5–2. Newell, Guy R., Spitz, Margaret R., and Wilson, Michael B. (1988). Nitrite inhalants: Historical perspective. In Harry W. Haverkos and John A. Dougherty (Eds.), *Health hazards of nitrite inhalants* (NIDA Research Monograph 83). Rockville, MD: National Institute on Drug Abuse, pp. 1–14.

54. Johnston, O'Malley, Bachman, and Schulenberg, *Monitoring the Future national results*, Table 1.

chapter 9

Anabolic Steroids and Drug Abuse in Sports

The public needs to be informed about the reality of steroids and how they have affected the lives of many star baseball players, including me. Have I used steroids? You bet I did. Did steroids make me a better baseball player? Of course they did. If I had it all to do over again, would I live a steroid-enriched life? Yes, I would. Do I have any regrets or qualms about relying on chemicals to help me hit a baseball so far? To be honest, no, I don't.

—*José Canseco*, Juiced *(2005)*

After you have completed this chapter, you will understand

- The history of drug abuse in sports
- How anabolic steroids work
- The health risks of steroid abuse
- Patterns of steroid abuse
- Dietary supplements marketed as ergogenic aids
- Present-day drug testing in amateur and professional athletics
- Current drug-testing techniques
- The social context of performance-enhancing drugs

In a world where running a hundredth of a second faster can mean the difference between a gold medal or a silver, where throwing a javelin a centimeter farther, hitting a baseball twenty feet farther, or lifting a kilogram more can make you either the champion or an also-ran, temptations abound. In this high-pressure world, athletes are continually on the lookout for a winning edge. The advantage formula may involve a new technique in training, a new attitude toward winning, or a special diet. Or it could involve the use of drugs. This chapter focuses on the problem of drug abuse in the world of sports—in particular, the abuse of anabolic steroids.

The use of anabolic steroids to achieve that winning edge is a problem not only among athletes who are in the public eye but also among a growing number of young people who simply want to look better by developing the musculature of their bodies. The serious dangers in such drug-taking behavior, whether the motivation lies in competitive drive or in personal vanity, are major problems that need to be examined closely. It is instructive to look first at how drugs in general have affected competitive sports over the centuries.

Drug-Taking Behavior in Sports

The first recorded athletic competition, the ancient Olympic Games in Greece, is also the place where we find the first recorded use of psychoactive drugs in sports. As early as 300 B.C., Greek athletes ate hallucinogenic mushrooms either to improve their performance in the competition or to achieve some kind of mystical connection to the gods. Later, Roman gladiators and charioteers used stimulants to sustain themselves longer in competition, even when injured by their opponents.

In the modern era, drugs continued to be a factor in athletic competitions. By the end of the nineteenth century, world-class athletes were experimenting with a variety of stimulant and depressant drugs, including cocaine, caffeine, alcohol, nitroglycerine, opiates, strychnine, and amphetamines. In 1886, while competing in a cross-country race, a Welsh cyclist died of a combination of opiates and cocaine (now referred to as a speedball), the first drug-related death ever recorded in sports. During the 1904 Olympics, U.S. marathoner Tom Hicks collapsed after winning the race and lost consciousness. When he was revived, doctors were told that he had taken a potentially lethal mixture of strychnine (a CNS stimulant when administered in low doses) and brandy.[1]

With the introduction of anabolic steroid drugs specifically patterned after the male sex hormone testosterone, a new element entered the arena of competitive sports. Here was a class of drugs that did more than alter the behavior or experience of the athlete; these drugs actually altered the structure of the athlete's body.

Anabolic steroid drugs had been studied since the 1930s as a treatment for anemia (low red blood cell count) and conditions that caused muscles to waste away. Following the end of World War II, steroid drugs were administered to people who were near death from starvation and weight loss. It quickly became apparent, however, that steroids could be useful when given to otherwise healthy individuals as well. As pharmaceutical companies began to introduce dozens of new body-building drugs based on the testosterone molecule, it was natural that information about anabolic steroids would come to the attention of athletes, as well as their coaches and trainers.[2]

What Are Anabolic Steroids?

To understand how testosterone-based steroids produce **ergogenic** (performance-enhancing) changes, we first have to recognize that testosterone itself has two primary effects on the human body. The first and most obvious effect is **androgenic** (literally, "man-producing"), in that the hormone promotes the development of male sex characteristics. As testosterone levels rise during puberty, boys acquire an enlarged larynx (resulting in a deeper voice), body hair, and an increase in body size, as well as genital changes that make them sexually mature adults. The second effect is **anabolic** (upward-changing), in that it promotes the development of protein and, as a result, an increase in muscle tissue. Muscles in men are inherently larger than muscles in women because of the anabolic action of testosterone in the male body.

Steroid drugs based on alterations in the testosterone molecule are therefore called **anabolic-androgenic steroids.** The goal, however, has been to develop drugs that emphasize the anabolic function while retaining as little of the androgenic function as possible. For that reason, they are most often called simply

ergogenic (ER-go-JEN-ik): Performance-enhancing.

androgenic (AN-droh-JEN-ik): Acting to promote masculinizing changes in the body.

anabolic (AN-ah-BALL-ik): Acting to promote protein growth and muscular development.

anabolic-androgenic steroids: Drugs that promote masculinizing changes in the body and increased muscular development.

anabolic steroids. Unfortunately, as we will see, it has not been possible to develop a testosterone-derived drug without at least some androgenic effects (Table 9.1).

It is important that anabolic steroids not be confused with **adrenocortical steroids,** drugs that are patterned after glucocorticoid hormones secreted by the adrenal glands. The major drug of this latter type is cortisone (brand name, among others: Hydrocortone injection or tablets). The molecular structure of these drugs qualifies them to belong to the steroid family, but there is no relationship to testosterone or any testosterone-like effects. Adrenocorticoidal steroids are useful in the medical treatment of tissue inflammation; in sports, they reduce the inflammation associated with muscular injuries. Their effect on muscular development can be viewed as catabolic (downward-changing), in that muscles tend to weaken as a result, so their long-term use is unlikely to be a desirable option for athletes.[3]

Anabolic Steroids at the Modern Olympic Games

By the time of the 1952 Olympic Games in Helsinki, athletes were well acquainted with ergogenic drugs. Legally available amphetamines (see Chapter 4), in particular, were commonplace, particularly in events that emphasized speed and endurance. Among events requiring strength and size, anabolic steroids were seen to be perfectly suited for gaining a competitive advantage.

It is debatable which country first used anabolic steroids. U.S. athletic officials have claimed that Soviet weight-lifting champions were using steroids in international competitions in 1954; British officials have claimed that a U.S. hammer thrower used steroids prior to 1954. Whoever has the dubious honor of being first, steroid use became the norm by the 1956 Olympic Games in Melbourne for both men and women athletes.

Steroid use was clearly out in the open during the 1968 Olympic Games in Mexico City. An estimated one-third of the entire U.S. track and field team, not

anabolic steroids: Drugs patterned after the testosterone molecule that promote masculine changes in the body and increased muscular development. The full name is anabolic-androgenic steroids.

adrenocortical steroids: A group of hormones secreted by the adrenal glands. Their anti-inflammatory action makes them useful for treating arthritis and muscular injuries.

TABLE 9.1

Anabolic steroids currently available in the United States

TYPE OF STEROID	GENERIC NAME	BRAND NAME
Oral	danazol	Danocrine
	drostanolone	Masteron
	methandrostenolone	Dianabol
	methyltestosterone	Android, Testred, Virilon
	oxyandrolone	Oxandrin
	oxymetholone	Android-50, Anadrol
	stanozolol	Winstrol V
	boldanone undecylenate	Equipoise, Equi-Gan, Equidren
	norbolethone	(never marketed)
Intramuscular injection	nandrolone decanoate	Deca-Durabolin IM
	nandrolone phenprionate	Durabolin IM
	testosterone cyprionate	Virilon IM
	testosterone enantrate	Delatestryl IM
Transdermal patch	testosterone	Androderm transdermal system, Testoderm transdermal system

Note: Anabolic steroids are Schedule III controlled substances. As such, they are considered illicit drugs under federal guidelines when not obtained with a medical prescription and restricted to medical use along with other Schedule III controlled substances. Several "brand names" marketed for performance-enhancing purposes are combinations of various forms of steroids.

Sources: National Institute on Drug Abuse (2000, April). Anabolic steroids. *Community drug alert bulletin.* Bethesda, MD: National Institute on Drug Abuse. *Physicians' desk reference* (61st ed.) (2007). Montvale, NJ: Medical Economics Company. Shipley, Amy (2003, March 23). Drug testers have designs on new steroid. *Washington Post,* p. D1.

merely the strength-event and field-event competitors but the sprinters and middle-distance runners as well, were using anabolic steroids. The controversy did not concern the appropriateness or morality of taking steroids, only which particular steroids worked best.

Strength-event athletes were taking at least two to five times the therapeutic recommendations (based on the original intent of replacing body protein). The following year, an editor of *Track and Field News* dubbed anabolic steroids "the breakfast of champions." In 1971, one U.S. weight lifter commented to a reporter in reference to his Soviet rival,

> Last year the only difference between me and him was I couldn't afford his drug bill. Now I can. When I hit Munich [in 1972] I'll weigh in at about 340, or maybe 350. Then we'll see which is better, his steroids or mine.[4]

In the meantime, the masculine features of many female athletes from eastern European countries in the 1960s and 1970s, not to mention the number of Olympic records that were suddenly broken, made it reasonable to ask whether they were either men disguised as women or genetic "mistakes." Questions about the unusually deep voices of East German women swimmers prompted their coach, at one point, to respond: "We came here to swim, not to sing."

From information that has come to light since then, we now know that the effects were chiefly due to large doses of steroids. Until the late 1980s, the East German government was conducting a scientific program specifically to develop new steroid formulations that would benefit their national athletes and, at the same time, be undetectable by standard screening procedures. In 2000,

Russian pentathlon champion Nadezhda Tkachenko was one of several world-class female athletes in the 1970s who later tested positive for anabolic steroids.

When cleanup workers found blood-transfusion equipment in a house that had been rented by the Austrian Nordic cross-country ski team at the Salt Lake City Olympics in 2002, the Austrian federation claimed the equipment had been used for ultraviolet radiation treatment of athletes' blood to prevent colds and flu. The International Olympic Committee did not "buy" their explanation. Two nonmedalist Austrian skiers were judged disqualified and their performance scores stricken from the official record.

the principal physician in the East German Swimming Federation at the time when these steroids were being administered was convicted on charges that from 1975 to 1985 the program caused bodily harm to more than four dozen young female swimmers.[5]

The 2000 Olympic Games in Sydney, Australia, instituted the strictest drug-testing procedures to date for all competing athletes, including a new screening for EPO, a drug that enhances endurance by increasing red blood cells. For the first time, a specific phrase was inserted into the Olympic Oath, recited by all athletes at the beginning of the games: "... committing ourselves to a sport without doping and without drugs." Unfortunately, accusations of illegal performance-enhancing drug use and expulsions of athletes continued to plague the 2004 Summer Olympic Games in Athens as well as the 2006 Winter Olympic Games in Turin, as they had in previous ones since the 1950s.

In 2003, for the first time, a comprehensive anti-drug code was adopted for international sport competitions, covering all Olympic sports, the national federations that govern them in their respective countries, and all of their athletes. Professional leagues in the United States participating in the Olympic Games and other international competitions, such as the National Basketball Association and National Hockey League, are subject to the code. More than 70 nations have signed the agreement, after two years of hearings and negotiations under the sponsorship of the World Anti-Doping Agency, setting a standard list of banned drugs, systems for testing for them, and penalties for violators. Even though an international drug code is now in place, drug-related scandals continue to be reported (Drugs...in Focus).[6]

Anabolic Steroids in Professional and Collegiate Sports

The wholesale use of anabolic steroids in international athletics in the 1950s soon filtered down to sports closer to home. Beginning in the early 1960s, trainers in the National Football League began to administer anabolic steroids to their players. By the 1970s and 1980s, virtually all the NFL teams were familiar with these drugs. Estimates of how many players were on anabolic steroids varied from 50 to 90 percent. We will never know precisely the full extent of the practice, except to say that it was certainly substantial.

Several professional football players remarked at the time that their steroid use had begun while they were playing on collegiate teams, and indeed, football players in several colleges and universities during the 1980s were implicated in steroid use. Football players were not alone in this regard. Use of anabolic steroids had found its way into other collegiate and even high school sports of all kinds, including track and field, baseball, basketball, gymnastics, lacrosse, swimming, volleyball, wrestling, and tennis. It is fair to say that until the late 1980s,

Drugs...in Focus

Disqualified by DNA?

Since the 1964 Winter Olympic Games in Innsbruck, Finland's gold-medalist cross-country skier Eero Mantyranta had been rumored to be using performance-enhancing drugs in competition, though he never failed a drug test. Decades later, DNA technology has made it possible for Mantyranta to be exonerated of any suspicion of wrongdoing. It turns out that Mantyranta had a naturally occurring genetic mutation that produced increased levels of erythropoietin (EPO), a hormone that regulates red blood cells in the body. Since 2000, synthetic forms of EPO have been among the many steroid and nonsteroid drugs screened in the Olympic Games. In the drug testing administered in today's competitions, Mantyranta would have failed the test and would have been required to submit his DNA to prove himself innocent of "blood doping."

Advancement in gene therapy techniques may in the future lead to all sorts of ergogenic mischief. It is conceivable that we might be able to alter the EPO gene so as to increase the number of red blood cells carrying oxygen to muscles, the vascular endothelial growth factor (VEGF) gene so as to increase the number of blood vessels, or the short form of the angiotensin-converting enzyme (ACE) gene so as to increase the performance of "fast-twitch" muscles necessary for sudden bursts of speed. On the one hand, increasing EPO levels might help people who are anemic, increasing VEGF levels might help people with clogged arteries and other circulatory diseases, and increasing ACE levels might help people suffering from chronic fatigue. On the other hand, for healthy athletes, the procedure would be, in effect, "gene doping."

Perhaps, as investigations of the human genome continue, it may become possible to specify sets of naturally occurring gene mutations that result in unusually high levels of athletic prowess. Would the identification of these mutations in future world champions justify a potential disqualification by virtue of their DNA? Today, the burden of proof is on officials to establish that an athlete is guilty of using a banned ergogenic substance. In the future, the burden of proof might be on the athlete to establish his or her innocence. How would athletes prove that their DNA had not been intentionally modified? Some interesting questions to ponder.

Sources: Begley, Sharon (2002, February 18). Science of speed. *Newsweek*, pp. 56–58. Cooke, Robert (2002, June 18). Fixed genes, fixed games? *Newsday*, pp. D1, D5. Pincock, Stephen (2005). Gene doping. *Lancet, 366*, 518–519. Sokolove, Michael (2004, January 18). The lab animal: Elite atheletes always have and always will pursue every competitive advantage—health and the law be damned. Is genetic manipulation next? *New York Times Magazine*, pp. 28–33. Sweeney, H. Lee (2004, July). Gene doping. *Scientific American*, pp. 37–43.

when screening procedures became commonplace, there was no sport, professional or amateur, for which the use of anabolic steroids was not an accepted element in athletic training.[7]

A Watershed Year in the History of Anabolic Steroids

Two events in 1988 made that year a turning point in the history of anabolic steroids in sports. Magazine articles and news accounts had been exposing their widespread use. In September 1988 at the Seoul Olympic Games, the Canadian sprinter Ben Johnson won the gold medal in the men's 100-meter dash in the world-record-breaking time of 9.79 seconds, only to be denied his achievement shortly afterward when it was determined that he had tested positive for anabolic steroids. Stunned, the world suddenly had to confront the pervasiveness of the practice as well as its consequences once and for all.

At about the same time, a major study published in the *Journal of the American Medical Association* reported the outcome of the first nationwide survey on use of anabolic steroids among adolescent boys in the United States. The survey found that approximately 7 percent of all high school seniors were using or had used anabolic steroids. More than 77 percent of the users were white and middle class; more than 52 percent had parents who were college graduates; nearly 50 percent had started using steroids before they were fifteen years old. More than 47 percent said that their motivation was to improve their athletic performance, but almost 27 percent said that the motivation was completely outside the realm of organized sports: They simply wanted to look better.[8]

Steroid Abuse and Baseball

Record-breaking home-run performances in the late 1990s and early 2000s raised suspicions that these achievements in baseball may not have been solely due to athletic prowess but rather to some pharmacological assistance. Yet, until recently, major league baseball stood apart from other professional sports in the United States and sports organizations around the world that had set up regulatory policies regarding steroid abuse and the use of other performance-enhancing drugs. In 2004, a prominent track coach, two executives of a nutritional supplements laboratory in California, and Barry Bonds's personal trainer were indicted on charges of illegally distributing steroids and other

Fans expressed their opinion on steroid use at Major League Baseball's All-Star Game in 2002. Between 5 and 7 percent of MLB players tested positive for anabolic steroids as a result of randomized screening conducted during spring training in 2003. Steroid testing began in earnest in 2005.

performance-enhancing drugs to dozens of professional athletes in baseball and other sports. More recently, a New York Mets clubhouse assistant pleaded guilty to having supplied performance-enhancing drugs to dozens of current and former MLB players and their associates beginning in 1995 until 2005, and subsequently laundering the proceeds from these transactions.

With intense pressure from public opinion as well as governmental officials, major league baseball (MLB) players agreed in early 2005 to a policy of steroid testing that was more in line with those of the National Football League and the National Basketball Association. In late 2005, MLB penalties for steroid use were stiffened (Drugs... in Focus). Testing for amphetamine use, previously omitted from consideration in the earlier agreement, was added with its own set of penalties for violation. Unfortunately, recent revelations indicate that drug testing in MLB has failed to eliminate the use of performance-enhancing drugs.[9]

The Hazards of Anabolic Steroids

One of the problems that complicates any look at the adverse effects of steroid abuse is that the dosage levels vary over an enormous range. Further, since nonmedical steroid use is illegal, it is virtually impossible to know the exact dosage levels or even the exact combinations of steroids a particular individual may be taking. It is estimated that a "typical" body builder on anabolic steroids may be taking in a minimum of three to ten

Drugs . . . in Focus

Suspension Penalties for Steroid Use in American Professional Sports

The 2005 agreement on regulations against steroid use in major league baseball (MLB) included a ban on "all substances regarded now, or in the future, by the federal government as steroids" as well as human growth hormone and steroid precursor hormones such as androstendione. Suspension penalties for positive-test infractions under these new regulations are shown in comparison to previous MLB regulations and those of other U.S. and international athletic organizations.

	First	Second	POSITIVE TEST Third	Fourth	Fifth
Major League Baseball					
Pre-2005	counseling	15 days	25 days	50 days	1 year
Late 2005	50 games	100 games	lifetime suspension, with right of reinstatement after two years		
Minor League Baseball	15 days	30 days	60 days	1 year	lifetime
National Football League	4 games	6 games	1 year	1 year	1 year
National Basketball Association	5 games	10 games	25 games	25 games	25 games
National Hockey League			—no testing for steroids—		
World Anti-Doping Association (Olympic sports)	2 years	lifetime			

Source: Curry, Jack (2006, November 16). Baseball lacks stiffer penalties for steroid use. *New York Times,* pp. A1, D2. NFL will ban amphetamines as enhancers (2006, June 28). *Newsday,* p. A53.

---

times the therapeutic doses recommended for the medical use of these drugs, but in some cases, the estimates have gone as high as a hundred to a thousand times the recommended therapeutic dose.[10]

Effects on Hormonal Systems

At these huge dosages, anabolic steroids are literally flooding into the body, upsetting the delicate balance of hormones and other chemicals that are normally controlled by testosterone. The primary effect in men is for the testes gland to react to the newly increased testosterone levels in the blood by producing *less* testos-

> **gynecomastia (GUY-neh-coh-MAST-ee-ah):** An enlargement of the breasts.
> **priapism (PRY-ah-pih-zem):** A condition marked by persistent and frequently painful penile erections.

terone on its own. In other words, the gland is getting the incorrect message that its services are no longer needed. As a result, the testicles shrink, and a lower sperm count leads to sterility, reversible for most men but irreversible in a small number of cases. Paradoxically, the male breasts enlarge (a condition called **gynecomastia**) because steroids break down eventually into estradiol, the female sex hormone. Other related consequences include frequent, sustained, and often painful penile erections (a condition called **priapism**) and an enlargement of the prostate gland. Severe acne, particularly on the shoulders and back, results from an increase in the secretions of the sebaceous glands in the skin. Other testosterone-related effects include two changes in hair growth patterns: increased facial hair growth and accelerated balding on the top of the head.

Some athletes attempt to counter these undesirable hormonal effects by combining anabolic steroids with human chorionic gonadotropin (HCG), a hormone that

Anabolic steroids produce massive development of musculature, a prized asset in competitive body building.

TABLE 9.2

Reported side effects of anabolic steroids in
ten women

EFFECT	NUMBER REPORTING THE EFFECT	REVERSIBLE AFTER END OF USE
Lower voice	10	no
Increased facial hair	9	no
Enlarged clitoris	8	no
Increased aggressiveness	8	yes
Increased appetite	8	unknown
Decreased body fat	8	unknown
Diminished or stopped menstruation	7	yes
Increased sexual drive	6	yes
Increased acne	6	yes
Decreased breast size	5	unknown
Increased body hair	5	no
Increased loss of scalp hair	2	no

Note: The ten women were all weight-trained athletes.

Sources: Strauss, Richard H., and Yesalis, Charles E. (1993).
Additional effects of anabolic steroids in women. In Charles E.
Yesalis (Ed.), *Anabolic steroids in sport and exercise.* Champaign,
IL: Human Kinetics Publishers, pp. 151–160. Strauss, Richard H.,
Ligget, M. T., and Lanese R. R. (1985). Anabolic steroid use and
perceived effects in ten weight-trained women athletes. *Journal
of the American Medical Association, 253,* 2871–2873.

ordinarily stimulates the testes to secrete testosterone. In
theory, this strategy can work, but the dosages have to be
carefully controlled, something that self-medicating athletes are unlikely to do. Repeated HCG treatments actually can have the opposite effect from the one that is
intended, making matters worse rather than better. In
addition, HCG itself has its own adverse effects, including headaches, mood swings, depression, and retention
of fluids.[11]

Among women taking anabolic steroids, the dramatically increased levels of testosterone in bodies that
normally have only trace amounts produce major physiological changes, only some of which return to normal
when steroids are withdrawn. Table 9.2 lists the major
reversible and irreversible effects among women.

Effects on Other Systems of the Body

Given the fact that the liver is the primary means for
clearing drugs from the body (see Chapter 1), it is not
surprising that large doses of anabolic steroids should
take their toll on this particular organ. The principal
result is a greatly increased risk of developing liver
tumors. The type of liver tumors frequently seen in these
circumstances are benign (noncancerous) blood-filled
cysts, with the potential for causing liver failure. In addition, a rupture in these cysts can produce abdominal
bleeding, requiring life-saving emergency treatment.
Fortunately, these liver abnormalities are reversible
when steroids are withdrawn from use.[12]

There is evidence from animal studies that
increased steroid levels in the body can produce high
blood pressure and high cholesterol levels, as well as
heart abnormalities. Whether cardiovascular effects

present a problem for steroid abusers, however, is not
well established, and the often publicized cardiovascular risks associated with anabolic steroids may be exaggerated. It is extremely difficult to determine whether
the small number of documented cases of heart-disease-
related deaths among steroid abusers have been specifically linked to chronic intake of steroid drugs.[13]

Psychological Problems

Stories abound of mood swings and increased aggressiveness, often referred to by athletes as "roid rage," when
taking anabolic steroids. Numerous anecdotal reports
force us to consider the possibility that real psychological
changes are going on.[14] As an example, this is how one
sportswriter recalled the unusual behavior of the professional football player Lyle Alzado during the 1980s:

*I was covering the Los Angeles Raiders when Alzado,
who had played previously with the Denver Broncos*

and Cleveland Browns, joined [the team] in 1982. In 1984, I was talking to one of his teammates across the Raiders' dressing room, when Alzado, with no provocation, picked up his gray metal stool and threw it in my direction, shouting something about "reporters in the locker room." Shaken, I asked several players who knew him best what was bugging him. They said Alzado probably just had a steroid injection and to stay out of his way. Good advice.[15]

Beyond the well-publicized anecdotal reports, however, more rigorous laboratory investigations into the relationship between anabolic steroid use and psychological problems are required to provide a better understanding of the phenomenon. In a recent double-blind study, a group of male volunteers were randomly administered intramuscular injections of testosterone cyprionate or a placebo over a period of twenty-five weeks. All of them were screened for current or prior psychological problems. One subgroup was engaged in weight training but had no prior history of steroid use. A second subgroup had no training experience and had not used steroids. A third group reported a history of steroid use but had refrained from any use for a minimum of three months prior to the beginning of the study.

The results showed that, on average, testosterone significantly increased manic behavior and feelings of aggressiveness, but the individual reactions were quite variable. Only eight of the fifty men in the study showed any mood changes at all. Two of them showed marked symptoms. One of these men experienced an aggressive outburst at work and, on one occasion, reacted to being cut off in traffic by following the person in his car for several miles. The other man developed extreme euphoria and reported a decreased need for sleep. Six other study participants showed more moderate changes. One man in this category found himself wanting to beat up his opponent in a college sports competition, even though he had never had such aggressive feelings before in the course of a game. All of the other participants in the study showed minimal or no effects, and in no case was there an incident of actual violent behavior. Neither previous steroid use nor regular weight training was associated with the symptoms observed in the men responding to testosterone.

Because the study used a double-blind design, neither the experimenters nor the men being studied knew whether they were being injected with testosterone or a placebo (see Chapter 1); half the men started with the active drug condition, and half started with the placebo condition. Therefore, we can eliminate the possible influences of expectations and preconceptions about

Quick Concept Check 9.1

Understanding the Effects of Anabolic Steroids

Check your understanding of the effects of anabolic steroids by identifying whether the following conditions can be attributed to steroid use.

1. severe acne on the lower extremities of the body
2. increased aggressiveness and mood swings
3. premature balding in men
4. increased development of the testicles
5. enlarged breasts (gynecomastia) among women
6. accelerated growth in adolescents around the time of puberty

Answers: 1. no 2. yes 3. yes 4. no 5. no 6. no

what different behaviors and experiences might result from anabolic steroids to explain the study findings.

On the basis of this information, mood changes and aggressiveness as a result of an elevation in testosterone levels appears to be a genuine effect, though the reactions of people taking anabolic steroids are far from uniform. Extrapolating from the available research literature on this issue, it has been estimated that somewhere between 2 and 20 percent of men will develop mood-related psychological problems from anabolic steroid use. However, it is important to realize that experimental studies of this type may underestimate the extent of the phenomenon in the real world. In the study reported here, the maximum dosage of testosterone was 600 mg per week. In actual practice, steroid abusers often take drugs that boost testosterone to as much as 1,000 to 1,500 mg per week, levels that far exceed those that can be safely studied in the laboratory. As a consequence, the percentage of individuals developing significant mood changes and behavioral problems is likely to be much higher, and the changes and problems themselves can be expected to be substantially greater.[16]

Special Problems for Adolescents

During puberty, a particularly crucial process among boys is growth of the long bones of the body, which results in an increase in height. Anabolic steroids suppress growth hormones; as a result, muscular development is enhanced

Steve T. isn't his real name. But his story is not only real but undoubtedly a recognizable one to young men in nearly every American community where the importance of personal appearance has managed to outweigh physical risks and criminal prosecution.

Steve was not an aspiring athlete or competitive bodybuilder. The drug-testing program at his school would not have affected him in any way. He was simply a sixteen-year-old suburban teenager, short of stature and self-confidence and convinced that muscles would make the difference. "I wanted people to notice me," he said. In particular, he wanted the girls to notice him.

It began with hours pumping weights at home and poring over muscle web sites on the Internet. One day, he asked for a "shortcut" at a gym he had joined. Soon, he was injecting $150 doses of testosterone on a regular basis. In the meantime, Steve packed on twenty pounds of muscle and finally got all the attention he had always craved from his friends and from girls. He could now bench-press 180 pounds with ease and curl 100 pounds "For a little guy, I was really putting it up," he said. He ignored the acne that spread across his back.

Steve was also getting careless. Afraid to keep his steroids at home, he would take them to school. When they were discovered, school officials notified the police and Steve was arrested for possession of a controlled substance. While charges were reduced to a misdemeanor offense, the real punishment came later when a family physician noted a low sperm count. His mother was convinced that Steve's growth had been stunted. "I was scared," he said. "I kept saying to myself: 'I don't belong here [in this predicament]. I'm not a bad kid.'"

Steve canceled his gym membership and set his sights on turning his life around. Working out was no longer so important to him. Currently, he has a girlfriend and claims that he is off steroids. His parents still worry.

Source: Bruchey, Samuel (2004, December 19). Steroids in the suburbs. *Newsday,* pp. A3, A48–A49.

but overall body growth is stunted. Among girls, testosterone-related drugs delay the onset of puberty, making the body shorter, lighter, and more "girl-like" while enhancing the user's overall strength. On a psychological level, feelings of euphoria and aggression that adolescents experience while using anabolic steroids can be replaced by lethargy, loss of confidence, and depression when these drugs are discontinued (Portrait).[17]

Patterns of Anabolic Steroid Abuse

In 1990, as a response to the increasing awareness of the abuse of anabolic steroids both in and out of competitive sports, Congress passed the Anabolic Steroids Control Act, reclassifying anabolic steroids as Schedule III controlled substances, on a par with codeine preparations and barbiturates. Jurisdiction was transferred from the Food and Drug Administration (FDA) to the Drug Enforcement Administration (DEA). As a result of this legislation, pharmacies are permitted to fill anabolic-steroid prescriptions up to a maximum of five times, but penalties for violating the law can result in a five-year prison term and a $250,000 fine for illegal nonmedical sales and a one-year term and a $1,000 fine for nonmedical possession.

Penalties are doubled for repeated offenses or for selling these drugs to minors (see Chapter 13). States are permitted to draft their own laws regarding the definition of anabolic steroids and set sentencing guidelines for steroid offenders. While most states follow the federally mandated Schedule III classification, New York lists steroids in Schedule II, and Alaska does not schedule them at all. In some states, possession of small quantities of steroids is regarded as a misdemeanor; other states regard it as a felony. In most but not all states, first-time offenses do not result in imprisonment, unless there are aggravating circumstances such as possession of large quantities or evidence of intent to sell or distribute the drugs.[18]

Despite the regulations now in effect, steroid abuse today remains a major problem. Steroid distribution has become an enormous black-market enterprise. With their use commonly referred to as being "on the juice," these drugs are channeled principally through people associated with body-building gyms and through Internet web sites that frequently change the identity of a company's location in an effort to stay one step ahead of the law. Some Internet-based suppliers include a warning on their web sites, "Due to their profound effects and potencies, it is recommended to seek the guidance of a physician prior to use," to protect themselves from liability, though no customer would voluntarily divulge his or her steroid abuse, much less seek medical guidance.

It is estimated that the illicit anabolic steroid market is valued at between $300 million to $400 million each year, with the drugs smuggled into the United States from Europe, Canada, and Mexico. In 2006, the University of Michigan survey reported that 2 percent of eighth-grade boys and 2 percent of tenth-grade boys and 3 percent of high school seniors had used anabolic steroids in their lifetime.[19]

The Potential for Steroid Dependence

While some anabolic steroids can be taken orally and others through intramuscular injections, abusers often administer a combination of both types in a practice called *stacking*. Hard-core abusers may take a combination of three to five different pills and injectables simultaneously, or they may consume any steroid that is available ("shot-gunning"), with the total exceeding a dozen. In addition to the complications that result from so many different types of steroids being taken at the same time, multiple injections into the buttocks or thighs, with 1.5-inch needles (called "darts" or "points"), are painful and inevitably leave scars. If these needles are shared, as they frequently are, the risk of hepatitis or HIV contamination is significant.

Steroid abusers often engage in a practice called *cycling*, in which steroids are taken for periods lasting

> **muscle dysmorphia (dis-MORF-ee-ah):** The perception of one's own body as small and weak and one's musculature as inadequately developed, despite evidence to the contrary. Also known as megorexia the condition of muscle dysmorphia is a form of body dysmorphic disorder.

from four to eighteen weeks, each separated by an "off" period of abstention. Unfortunately, when the drugs are withdrawn, the newly developed muscles tend to "shrink up," throwing the abuser into a panic that his or her body is losing the gains that have been achieved. In addition, abstention from steroids can lead to signs of depression, sleep problems, lack of appetite, and general moodiness. All these effects encourage a return to steroids, frequently in even larger doses, and a craving for the euphoria that the person felt while taking them.

A variation of the cycling pattern is the practice of *pyramiding*. An individual starts with low doses of steroids, gradually increases the doses over several weeks prior to an athletic competition, then tapers off entirely before the competition itself in an attempt to escape detection during drug testing. However, pyramiding leads to the same problems during withdrawal and abstention as cycling, except that the symptoms occur during the competition itself.

A major problem associated with steroid abuse is the potential for an individual to believe that his or her physique will forever be imperfect. In a kind of "reverse anorexia" that has been called **muscle dysmorphia,** some body builders continue to see their bodies as weak and small when they look at themselves in the mirror despite their greatly enhanced physical development. Peer pressure at the gyms and clubs is a factor in never being satisfied with the size of one's muscles, but it is becoming apparent that societal pressures play a role as well. In the case of males, it is interesting to examine the evolution of the design of G.I. Joe action figures over the years, from the original toy introduced in 1964 to the incarnation introduced in 1998 (Figure 9.1). Just as the

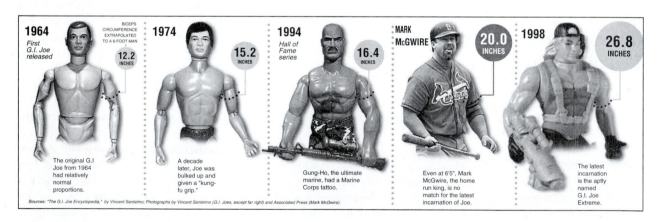

1964 First G.I. Joe released — BICEPS CIRCUMFERENCE EXTRAPOLATED TO A 6-FOOT MAN — 12.2 INCHES — The original G.I Joe from 1964 had relatively normal proportions.

1974 — 15.2 INCHES — A decade later, Joe was bulked up and given a "kung-fu grip."

1994 Hall of Fame series — 16.4 INCHES — Gung-Ho, the ultimate marine, had a Marine Corps tattoo.

MARK McGWIRE — 20.0 INCHES — Even at 6'5", Mark McGwire, the home run king, is no match for the latest incarnation of Joe.

1998 — 26.8 INCHES — The latest incarnation is the aptly named G.I. Joe Extreme.

Sources: "The G.I. Joe Encyclopedia," by Vincent Santeimo; Photographs by Vincent Santeimo (G.I. Joes, except far right) and Associated Press (Mark McGwire).

FIGURE 9.1

The muscular development of the G.I. Joe action figure has increased dramatically since its introduction in 1964. The estimated bicep circumference for a six-foot man, based on dimensions of the action figure, more than doubled from 1964 to 1998.

Source: As G.I. Joe bulks up, concern for the 98-pound weakling (1999, May 30). *New York Times,* p. D2.

Barbie doll has been criticized as setting an impossible ideal for the female body among girls, male-oriented action figures can be criticized on the same basis for boys.[20]

It has been estimated that between 13 and 18 percent of those who have taken steroids show signs of physical and psychological dependence, in that they are unable to control or cut down on them, take more steroids than they intended, develop a tolerance to them, or take them to relieve or avoid undesirable withdrawal symptoms (Help Line).[21]

In light of the potential for steroid dependence and the adverse effects of acute steroid use, prevention programs have been instituted to address the problems of steroid abuse, particularly among adolescents. The most prominent example, developed by Linn Goldberg at Oregon Health Sciences University at Portland, is called the Adolescents Training and Learning to Avoid Steroids (ATLAS) program. Young athletes, team coaches, and team captains receive instruction on both sides of the issue—the desirable effects as well as the adverse effects of steroid use. This approach is taken because a failure to acknowledge potential benefits reduces the credibility of the intervention.

Evaluations of the ATLAS program have shown that program participants, relative to a control group, were better informed about proper exercise, had a better understanding of the harmful effects of steroids, developed a more negative attitude toward others who used steroids, and were more likely to engage in healthier eating habits. They also showed a 53 percent reduction in new use of anabolic steroids after one year as well as a 63 percent reduction in the intention to use these drugs in the future.[22]

Counterfeit Steroids and the Placebo Effect

As with many illicit drugs, some products marketed to look like anabolic steroids are not the real thing. The problem here is that athletes are notoriously superstitious and easily leave themselves open to placebo effects. On the one hand, in the case of anabolic steroids, the effects on muscle development are usually so dramatic that it is difficult to mistake the response as simply a result of a placebo effect. On the other hand, several other forms of ergogenic drugs have far more subtle effects, and psychological factors can

---

HELP LINE

The Symptoms of Steroid Abuse

For Both Sexes

1. Rapid increases in strength and/or size beyond what you would expect in a relatively short time. Putting on ten to twenty pounds of solid muscle within a period of a few weeks or so should be a major warning.
2. Involvement in activities in which steroid abuse is known to be condoned or encouraged
3. Sudden increases in appetite and preoccupation with changes in one's physical condition
4. Recent appearance of acne, particularly on the upper back, shoulders, and arms
5. Premature male-pattern baldness, including a rapidly receding hairline or loss of hair from the top rear of the head
6. A puffy appearance in the face as if the individual is retaining water
7. An increase in moodiness or unusual shifts in mood
8. A reddening of the face, neck, and upper chest, appearing as if one is constantly flushed
9. A yellowing of the skin or the whites of the eyes, stemming from a disturbance in liver function

For Men

1. An enlargement of the breasts, often accompanied by protruding nipples
2. An increase in sexual interest and a tendency to display that interest more aggressively

For Women

1. A lowering of the vocal range
2. Smaller or flatter breasts (see Table 9.2)

Where to go for assistance:
    www. nida. nih. gov/ Infofacts/ Steroids. html
The National Institute on Drug Abuse sponsors a vast array of web sites related to drug use and abuse. This web site on steroid abuse includes a comprehensive list of potential adverse effects of anabolic steroids.

Source: Wright, James E., and Cowart, Virginia S. (1990). Anabolic steroids: Altered states. Carmel, IN: Benchmark Press, pp. 71–91.

end up playing a greater role. Consider the clever strategy a baseball trainer claims to have used for the St. Louis Cardinals in the 1960s:

> In 1964, I devised a yellow RBI pill, a red shutout pill, and a potent green hitting pill. Virtually every player on the team took them, and some wouldn't go out on the field until they took my pills. They worked so well that we won the pennant. We used them again in 1967 and 1968 and also won the pennant. They worked because I never told them that the pills were placebos.[23]

Frequently, a bogus drug can achieve enormous popularity simply by word of mouth. A former steroid "customer" relates the following story:

> Bolasterone. It swept the country. They made millions. Millions, those California guys. All it was, was vegetable oil, a little bit of testosterone, and liquid aspirin. And they called it Bolasterone. And they hyped it up so much. It was selling for $250 to $275 a bottle. You would do anything to get this stuff. [They said] "Mr. Olympia used it! Secretly." I tell you, Madison Avenue could not have come up with a better campaign to sell this stuff.... If you had a bottle of it, I mean you could sell it for anything.... [It was hyped] through the grapevine. Underground. The network was incredible. From gym to gym to gym.... They'll say, "Did you see M.? He put on 15 pounds in a week." "What the hell is he using?" "Don't say anything. He's using Bolasterone!" "Wow. What the hell is it? Can you get it?" "Yeah, I can."[24]

Nonsteroid Hormones and Ergogenic Supplements

Certainly anabolic steroids have dominated the ergogenic drug scene, but other products have been promoted as having ergogenic properties. They include human growth hormone, androstendione, and creatine.

> **human growth hormone (hGH):** A naturally occurring hormone promoting growth, particularly in the long bones of the body.
>
> **acromegaly (A-kroh-MEG-ah-lee):** A condition resulting in structural abnormalities of the head, hands, and feet, as well as damage to internal organs.

Human Growth Hormone

One illicit alternative, **human growth hormone (hGH)**, has become increasingly popular, according to experts in this field, because it is more widely available and cheaper than in previous years, in contrast to the ever more costly illicit steroids. Those who take this pituitary hormone, however, face the increased risk of developing a significant side effect called **acromegaly**, a condition resulting in a coarse and misshapen head, enlarged hands and feet, and damage to various internal organs.

Prior to 1985, hGH was obtained from the pituitary glands of human cadavers, but now genetically engineered hGH (brand names: Protropin and Humatrope) is available, approved by the FDA for the treatment of rare cases of stunted growth. While the distribution of these drugs is controlled by their manufacturers as carefully as possible, supplies manage to get diverted for illicit use. Because hGH has a very short half-life, no screening procedure has yet been developed to detect it, so long as the individual abstains from it immediately prior to the test.

HGH has been shown to increase lean body mass and decrease fat tissue in men over sixty years of age. However, no controlled studies are available for assessing the ergogenic potential of hGH for younger populations, much less for athletes.[25]

Dietary Supplements as Ergogenic Aids

As recently as ten to twenty years ago, fitness-oriented young people might have taken only basic vitamins and minerals to help them build muscle mass or improve cardiovascular performance. Today, the fitness market is inundated with a growing number of dietary supplement products with presumed ergogenic properties, with sales of about $1.9 billion each year in the United States. They are sold under short, appealing names like Adenergy and Lean Stack alongside impressive before-and-after photographs or under long, pseudoscientific names like Vaso XP Xtreme Vasodilator and Xenadrine-NRG that are accompanied by complex molecular diagrams.

> A product called Aftermath, for example, boasts that it can help "swell your muscles to grotesque size" and eliminate the change of "dooming yourself to girly-man status." Xpand Nitric Oxide Reactor, a drink mix that comes in tropical berry and piña colada flavors, offers bodybuilders "the most unbelievable muscular and vascular pumps you have ever experienced."[26]

Because dietary supplements are not classified by the FDA as drugs (see Chapter 1), they can be marketed and sold without a prescription. Moreover, except in rare instances, there is no regulatory authority over their safety or effectiveness.

A prominent example of a dietary supplement used for ergogenic purposes is **androstenedione.** Technically speaking, androstenedione is not an anabolic steroid because it is not based on the specific structure of testosterone itself. Nonetheless, it is testosterone-related because it is a naturally occurring metabolic precursor to testosterone. In other words, the body converts androstenedione to testosterone due to the action of specific enzymes in the liver. At the recommended daily dose of 300 mg, androstenedione has been found to increase testosterone levels by an average of 34 percent above normal. Despite the increase in testosterone, however, no change in body composition or strength is observed when compared to placebo controls. There is no evidence that androstenedione promotes muscle protein synthesis at these dosage levels.[27]

Androstenedione rose to prominence in the late 1990s when it became public that St. Louis Cardinals baseball player Mark McGwire had been taking the supplement during his phenomenal 1998 hitting season (seventy home runs, far eclipsing the previous record). A storm of controversy ensued, with some commentators suggesting that McGwire's record be disallowed because of his androstenedione use. While banned by the National Football League and other professional and amateur sports organizations, androstenedione is not banned in major league baseball, and as such, McGwire's use was not illegal.

In 1999, McGwire discontinued taking the supplement, basing his decision largely on his concern about his effect as a role model on young people. Interestingly, his 1999 hitting record diminished only slightly, still reaching the third-highest total home runs in professional baseball history at that time. However, the publicity surrounding McGwire's use of androstenedione and its easy availability were blamed for a 30 percent increase among eighth-grade boys and a 75 percent increase among tenth-grade boys in the use of anabolic steroids from 1998 to 2000. In 2005, the FDA banned the over-the-counter sale of androstenedione (Andro) and other testosterone precursors.[28]

Another dietary supplement marketed as an ergogenic agent is **creatine** (brand names Creatine Fuel, Muscle Power, and many others), a nonprotein amino acid synthesized in the kidney, liver, and pancreas from L-arginine, glycine, and L-methionine. Ingestion of creatine has been found to enhance the retention of water by muscle cells, causing them to expand in size. One hypothesis is that water retention might stimulate protein synthesis and increase muscle mass as a result, but there is no evidence

from controlled studies that this is the case. Although creatine appears to enhance performance in repetitive bouts of high-intensity cycling, the weight gain experienced by creatine users makes it undesirable for runners or swimmers.

Short-term use of creatine has been found to produce muscle cramping, and its long-term adverse effects have not been fully explored. In 2006, one-seventh of all twelfth-grade boys and one-eighth of all tenth-grade boys in the United States had used creatine in the previous twelve months, a very high prevalence rate given the marginal ergogenic advantage and the present uncertainty about possible adverse health consequences.[29]

Current Drug-Testing Procedures and Policies

Since the mid-1960s, organizers of major athletic competitions have attempted to develop effective screening procedures to prevent the use of ergogenic drugs from resulting in one competitor having an unfair advantage over another. Needless to say, these procedures have neither proved perfect nor served as an effective deterrent for drug use among athletes. We are used to hearing about championship events accompanied by reports of an athlete disqualified from competing or denied the honor of winning because he or she tested positive for a particular banned substance. Ironically, the present status of drug testing as a fact of life in modern sports has brought with it a new form of contest, pitting the skill and ingenuity of the laboratory scientist whose job it is to detect the presence of ergogenic drugs against the skill and ingenuity of the athlete in devising ways to use them without detection (Drugs . . . in Focus).[30]

This section looks at drug-testing techniques designed to detect not only performance-enhancing drugs that are relevant to sports but also a wider range of illicit drugs, such as heroin, cocaine, and marijuana. Within some sports organizations, such as the National Collegiate Athletic Association (NCAA), drug tests are conducted not only for the presence of ergogenic drugs but also for the presence of drugs that have no particular ergogenic benefits. In the case of marijuana, for example, the proper description for

androstenedione (AN-dro-steen-DYE-own): A dietary supplement, acting as a metabolic precursor to testosterone and used as an ergogenic agent.

creatine (CREE-ah-teen): A dietary supplement available for ergogenic uses.

Drugs...in Focus

THG and the War on Performance-Enhancing Drugs

In June 2003, Donald H. Catlin, director of the Olympic drug-testing laboratory at the University of California at Los Angeles, received an unexpected package. According to an attached note written by a track coach who wished to remain anonymous, the test tube inside the package contained the residue of an undetectable anabolic steroid from a used syringe. Catlin had suspected for several years that designer-type steroids were being used by both amateur and professional athletes, but these drugs had remained undetected by standard testing procedures. Within three months, the drug in question had been identified as tetrahydrogestrinone (THG), which has a chemical structure resembling steroids such as gestrinole, used as a therapy for gynecological problems, and trenbolone, used by ranchers to increase the beef content of cattle.

THG had been undetectable because the substance would ordinarily disintegrate during standard drug screening. When Catlin's laboratory succeeded in stabilizing THG, its "chemical fingerprint" became obvious. By September, a test for THG was developed and ready to be used to screen 550 refrigerated urine samples obtained from athletes at the U.S. track and field championships held three months earlier, as well as samples forwarded from international track and field competitions. As a result, two U.S. track and field champions, 1,500-meter runner Regina Jacobs and shotputter Kevin Troth, tested positive for THG, as did other athletes in the United States and the United Kingdom.

Indictments were issued in 2004 to two executives of the nutritional supplement laboratory in California where THG was made, as well as to the personal trainer of San Francisco Giants star Barry Bonds and a prominent track-and-field coach. They were charged with illegally distributing steroids and other performance-enhancing drugs to dozens of professional athletes in football, baseball, and track and field. Whether athletes testing positive for THG eventually will be disqualified remains to be determined, as is the question of how widely used THG might be in the present-day sports world. The scope of THG use is expected to become clearer in the future as international sports federations undertake retrospective tests from frozen urine samples collected during championship events that occurred in the past few years.

Despite the negative publicity of the THG scandal, some view these developments in a positive light. According to Gary I. Wadler, an expert on the subject of drug testing in sports, "There is no question that this is a real blow to the integrity of sport, but there's a silver lining to the black cloud." Wadler has noted that the United States Anti-Doping Association quickly shared the THG data with the World Anti-Doping Agency (WADA), which then distributed the findings to sports organizations throughout the world.

To some, increased public attention to the problems of performance-enhancing drugs might help to make doping in sports as socially unacceptable as drinking and driving. Others, however, view the THG scandal from a darker perspective—as simply a small victory in an unending game of pharmacological "cat and mouse."

Sources: Ashley, Steven (2004, February). Doping by design. Scientific American, pp. 22–23. Curry, Jack (2004, February 13). Four indicted in a steroid scheme that involves top pro athletes. New York Times, pp. A1, D3. Kondro, Wayne (2003). Athletes' "designer steroid" leads to widening scandal. The Lancet, 362, 1466. Longman, Jere, and Drape, Joe (2003, November 2). Decoding a steroid: Hunches, sweat, and vindication. New York Times, pp. 1, 26. Schnirring, Lisa (2003). Experts see silver lining in THG scandal. Physician and Sportsmedicine, 31, 16–17. Quotation on page 16.

its effects with regard to athletic competitions might be *ergolytic* ("performance-reducing"). The policy is defended on the premise that athletes have the potential for exposure to illicit substances, and no collegiate athlete should be permitted to compete while engaging in illegal activity.

Techniques for Drug Testing

Present-day drug-testing procedures begin with a urine sample from the individual in question. The advantages lie in the ease and noninvasiveness of collecting urine, the ease with which urine can be analyzed for specific factors, and the fact that drugs or their metabolites (by-products) are usually very stable in frozen urine. Therefore, it is possible to provide long-term storage of positive samples, in the event that the results are disputed. The disadvantages are that many perceive urine collection to be a humiliating experience, a dehydrated athlete immediately after competing may find it difficult to urinate, and there may be ways to tamper with the urine sample prior to testing.

The two major urinanalysis methods are the **enzyme immunoassay (EIA)** technique and a procedure combining **gas chromatography and mass spectrometry (GC/MS).** In both methods, the collected urine is divided into two samples prior to being sent off to the laboratory so that if the analysis of one sample yields a positive outcome, the analysis can be repeated on the other sample. This reanalysis procedure is usually required if an individual appeals the original test result.[31]

With the EIA method, a separate test must be run on each particular drug that is being screened. First, at an earlier time, the substance to be tested for (THC or cocaine, for example) has been injected into an animal, eliciting specific immunological antibodies to that substance. The antibodies are then purified into a testing substrate. The combination of the collected urine and the testing substrate will yield a specific reaction if the urine contains the banned substance. A popular commercial testing kit for screening major controlled substances (opiates, amphetamines, cocaine, benzodiazepines, and marijuana), called **EMIT (enzyme multiplied immunoassay technique),** has been marketed by Syva Laboratories, a subsidiary of Syntex Corporation in Palo Alto, California, since the early 1970s. This kit is relatively inexpensive and can be used to screen large numbers of urine samples. It is so widely available that its trademark name, EMIT, is often used to mean any form of EIA method.

With the GC/MS method, the urine is first vaporized and combined with an inert gas and then passed over a number of chemically treated columns. Through the process of gas chromatography, technicians are able to identify the presence of a banned substance by the different colorations that are left on the columns. After this has been done, the gas is then ionized (converted into an electrically active form) and sent through an electric current and magnetic field that separates out each of the different ions (electrically charged particles) in the gas. Through the process of mass spectrometry, a particular "fingerprint," or "signature," of each chemical substance can be detected and measured. The GC/MS technique is regarded as more definitive than the EIA technique, but it is considerably more expensive and time-consuming. It is also the only testing procedure adequate to screen for anabolic steroids.[32]

Until recently, the predominant means for drug testing has been through urinanalysis. Since the late 1990s, however, increasing interest has been directed toward oral fluid testing. In this procedure, a collection pad is placed between the lower cheek and gum for two to five minutes. The collection pad is then sealed and later analyzed by EIA. Sensitivity and specificity of the results (see the next section) are comparable with those obtained through

National concern about drug abuse in all its forms has caused us to consider an increased level of drug testing in our society. Here is an editorial cartoonist's comment on the extent to which this policy might be applied.
© Tribune Media Services, Inc. All Rights Reserved. Reprinted with permission.

urinanalysis. As with positive urinanalysis tests, confirmation of positive oral fluid results is made by GC/MS.

Currently available FDA-approved drug-testing systems using oral fluid samples can now provide test results in approximately fifteen minutes. The advantages over traditional urinanalysis are obvious. Analyses of samples are accomplished on-site rather than having to send samples to laboratories for analysis. Specimen collection can be performed face-to-face (literally) with the donor, with little risk of sample substitution, dilution, or adulteration. Embarrassment on the part of the donor is eliminated as well as privacy concerns.[33]

Sensitivity and Specificity

As you might imagine, the two principal questions surrounding drug-testing methods are (1) how much of the banned substance needs to be in the body fluid before it is picked up as a positive test (the sensitivity of the test) and (2) whether it is possible to yield a false-positive result in which the test comes out positive but the body fluid is in actuality "clean" (the specificity of the test). In this regard, the GC/MS test is more sensitive and specific than the EIA test.

enzyme immunoassay (EIA): One of the two major drug-testing techniques for detecting banned substances or drugs.

gas chromatography/mass spectrometry (GC/MS): A drug-testing technique based on the combination of gas chromatography and mass spectrometry.

EMIT (enzyme multiplied immunoassay technique): A commercial testing kit for screening major controlled substances, based on enzyme immunoassay analysis.

Frequently, the GC/MS analysis is performed as a confirmation of a positive EIA test. Nonetheless, false positives can occur even with the GC/MS test. Eating a poppy seed roll prior to drug testing or taking quinolone antibiotic medications such as ofloxacin (brand name: Floxin) and ciprofloxacin (brand name: Cipro), for example, has resulted in false-positive indications of opiate use. Therapeutic levels of ibuprofen (brand names: Advil, Motrin, and Nuprin, among others) have resulted in false-positive indications of marijuana smoking. In addition, the passive inhalation of marijuana smoke can leave sufficient levels of THC metabolites to result in false-positive indications of marijuana smoking, though the density of smoke that needs to be present for this to happen makes it unlikely that individuals would be completely unaware that they were being exposed to marijuana.[34]

Masking Drugs and Chemical Manipulations

Two specific tactics have been employed to disguise the prior use of anabolic steroids so that the outcome of a drug test becomes, in effect, a false negative; both are now relatively obsolete. The first strategy was to take the antigout drug probenecid (brand name: Benemid). Available since 1987, it does mask the presence of anabolic steroids, but it

is now on the list of banned substances for competitive athletes and is easily detected by GC/MS techniques. The second strategy was to increase the level of epitestosterone in the body. The standard procedure for determining the present or prior use of anabolic steroids is to calculate the ratio of testosterone against the level of epitestosterone, a naturally occurring hormone that is usually stable at relatively low levels in the body. International athletic organizations now use a ratio of 4:1 (formerly 6:1) or higher as the standard for indicating steroid use. If epitestosterone is artificially elevated, the ratio can be manipulated downward so as to indicate a false-negative result in drug testing. However, suspiciously high levels of epitestosterone can now be detected by GC/MS techniques, so this form of manipulation is no longer successful.[35]

Pinpointing the Time of Drug Use

It is important to remember that a positive result in a drug test indicates merely that the test has detected a minimal level of a drug or its metabolite. It is difficult to determine when that drug was introduced into the body or how long the drug-taking behavior continued. In the case of urinalysis testing, the time it takes for the body to get rid of the metabolites of a particular drug varies considerably, from a few hours to a few weeks (Table 9.3).

TABLE 9.3

Detection periods for various drugs in urinanalysis tests

DRUG	DETECTION PERIOD	DRUG	DETECTION PERIOD
alcohol	1/2 to 1 day	opiates and opiate-like drugs	
amphetamines and derivatives	1–7 days	Dilaudid	2–4 days
barbiturates		Darvon	6–48 hours
amobarbital, pentobarbital	2–4 days	heroin or morphine	2–4 days
phenobarbital	up to 30 days	methadone	2–3 days
secobarbital	2–4 days	phencyclidine (PCP)	
benzodiazepines	up to 30 days	casual use	2–7 days
cocaine		chronic, heavy use	several months
occasional use	6–12 hours	Quaalude	2–4 days
repeated use	up to 48 hours	anabolic steroids	
marijuana (THC)		fat-soluble injectables	6–8 months
casual use up to 4 joints per week	5–7 days	water-soluble oral types	3–6 weeks
daily use	10–15 days	over-the-counter cold medications containing ephedrine derivatives as decongestants	48–72 hours
chronic, heavy use	1–2 months		

Sources: Allen and Hanbury's athletic drug reference (1994). Durham, NC: Clean Data, p. 19. Inaba, Darryl S., and Cohen, William E. (1989). Uppers, downers, all arounders. Ashland, OR: Cinemed, p. 206.

In the case of oral-fluid drug testing, the window of detection may be different, depending on the drug being screened. Opiates and cocaine are detected within two to three days of ingestion; THC in marijuana is detected within a period ranging from one hour after ingestion to fourteen hours later. Because THC metabolites are excreted into the urine for several days or in some cases for several weeks, oral-fluid testing for marijuana is better suited for determining when marijuana has been last used. In effect, the "window of detection" is more narrow. If the interval between use and testing has been longer than fourteen hours or so but shorter than a few days, urinanalysis would pick up a positive result, while oral-fluid testing would not.[36]

Owing to the expense of randomized drug-testing programs, not every institution can afford the costs. Large corporations may be able to budget for potentially thousands of tests for preemployment screening purposes, but relatively few colleges and considerably fewer high schools may be able to establish the level of funding needed to test their respective student populations. Even if the costs were lower, the question still remains as to whether illicit drug-taking behavior would be reduced in the long run as a result. Interestingly, recent evidence indicates that the prospect of randomized drug testing in schools fails to act as a deterrent among students. University of Michigan researchers found virtually identical rates of illicit drug use in schools that had drug-testing programs and schools that did not.[37]

It is also worth considering the following fact regarding abusers of steroids and related ergogenic drugs: Individuals who are no longer students in a public institution or participants in an organized athletic program do not need to fear a positive drug test because they will never be required to undergo any form of drug testing, random or otherwise

The Social Context of Performance-Enhancing Drugs

Anabolic steroids and other ergogenic agents are quite different from many of the abused drugs covered in previous chapters in that they affect the way we look and

The pressure to be number one exists in all areas of athletic competition. Temptations to secure a competitive edge, however, extends to the corporate world and academia as well. A growing acceptance of stimulants as "brain steroids" (Chapter 4) reflects our modern-day culture.

how we compare to others rather than the way we feel. Charles E. Yesalis, one of the leading experts in steroid abuse, has put it this way:

> If you were stranded on a desert island, you might use cocaine if it were available, but nobody would use steroids. On a desert island, nobody cares what you look like and there is nothing to win. We are the ones who have made the determination that appearance and winning are all important. We're telling kids in our society that sports is more than a game. Until we change those signals, for the most part, we might as well tell people to get used to drug use.[38]

The future of the fight against anabolic steroid abuse is, in part, staked to whether we can change the winner-take-all mentality of our culture. Unfortunately, there seems to be little cause for optimism. Numerous surveys taken among young athletes and nonathletes alike indicate that the social signals are crystal clear and they are more than willing to take up the challenge, despite the risks. They have typically been asked variations on the following question: "If you had a magic drug that was so fantastic that if you took it once you would win every competition you would enter, from the Olympic decathlon to Mr. Universe, for the next five years, but it had one minor drawback—it would kill you five years after you took it—would you still take the drug?" More than half of those polled answered "yes" to this question.[39]

There seems to be a more general sense of competition that goes beyond dreams of athletic performance. It is apparent that an idealized body image is part of today's standard for a sense of sexuality and social acceptance. This standard might not be news at all to women, but it is a fairly recent development in men. The temptations of steroid use as a way of accelerating the effects of weight training are increasing in our culture. One high school senior has said, "The majority now are guys that don't do it for sports. They do it for girls. For the look." Another senior has remarked on a different kind of lifter in weight rooms and gyms: the vanity bodybuilder (see Portrait on page 227). As he expressed it, "We notice a lot of kids now; they just want this certain type of body—with the abs and the ripped chest—and they want it quick."[40] Exercise physiologist David Pearson has remarked on the social pressures involved:

> The teenage years are the skinniest and most awkward, and the idea of being the skinniest kid in the locker room is absolutely terrifying to a teenage boy.[41]

Internet web sites deliver mixed messages, promoting anabolic steroids as well as steroid precursors such as androstenedione with the promise "You'll get huge!" while saying on the labels of their products that people younger than age eighteen should not take them.

Summary

Drug-Taking Behavior in Sports

- The use of ergogenic (performance-enhancing) drugs in athletic competition has a long history, dating from the original Olympic Games in ancient Greece.
- In the modern era, the principal type of ergogenic drugs has been anabolic steroids. These synthetic drugs are all based on variations of the testosterone molecule.
- Since the late 1980s, anabolic steroids have been popular with body builders as well as competitive athletes. This latter group typically takes steroids in enormous quantities and administers them in a largely unsupervised fashion.

The Hazards of Anabolic Steroids

- The hazards of steroid use include liver tumors, mood swings, and increased aggressiveness.
- For men, the effects include lower sperm count, enlargement of the breasts, atrophy of the testicles, baldness, and severe acne. For women, masculinizing changes occur, only some of which are reversible if steroids are withdrawn.

Patterns of Anabolic Steroid Abuse

- Since 1990, possession and sales of anabolic steroids have been illegal without specific medical prescriptions. These drugs are now distributed through illicit black-market channels.

- It is estimated that about one out of eight individuals taking large doses of steroids develops both physical and psychological dependence.

Nonsteroid Hormones and Ergogenic Supplements

- Human growth hormone (hGH) is a nonsteroid hormone that has been used for ergogenic purposes.
- Two dietary supplements, androstenedione and creatine, have been prominent recently as ergogenic aids.

Current Drug-Testing Procedures and Policies

- Drug-testing procedures, chiefly for those in organized athletics, have become increasingly sophisticated in their ability to detect the presence of banned substances.
- Two major techniques, based either on urine or on oral-fluid samples, are enzyme immunoassay (EIA) and a combination of gas chromatography and mass spectrometry (GC/MS).
- The ultimate goal of drug-testing procedures is to make it impossible to yield either a false-negative or false-positive result.

Endnotes

1. Dolan, Edward F. (1986). *Drugs in sports* (rev. ed.). New York: Franklin Watts, pp. 17–18. Meer, Jeff (1987). *Drugs and sports*. New York: Chelsea House, p. 21. Wadler, Gary I., and Hainline, Brian (1989). *Drugs and the athlete*. Philadelphia: F. A. Davis, pp. 3–17.

2. Meer, *Drugs and sports*, pp. 61–75. Taylor, William N. (1991). *Macho medicine: The history of the anabolic steroid epidemic*. Jefferson, NC: McFarland and Co., pp. 3–16.

3. Bhasin, Shalender; Storer, Thomas W.; Berman, Nancy; Callegari, Carlos; Clevenger, Brenda; Phillips, Jeffrey; Bunnel, Thomas J.; Tricker, Ray; Shirazi, Aida; and Casaburi, Richard (1996). The effects of supraphysiologic doses of testosterone on muscle size and strength in normal men. *New England Journal of Medicine, 335*, 1–7. Lombardo, John (1993). The efficacy and mechanisms of action of anabolic steroids. In Charles E. Yesalis (Ed.), *Anabolic steroids in sport and exercise*. Champaign, IL: Human Kinetics Publishers, p. 100.

4. Scott, Jack (1971, October 17). It's not how you play the game, but what pill you take. *New York Times Magazine*, p. 41.

5. Catlin, Don H., and Murray, Thomas H. (1996). Performance-enhancing drugs, fair competition, and Olympic sport. *Journal of the American Medical Association, 276*, 231–237. Longman, Jere (2004, January 26). East German steroids' toll: "They killed Heidi." *New York Times*, pp. D1, D8. Maimon, Alan (2000, February 6). Doping's sad toll: One athlete's tale from East Germany. *New York Times*, pp. A1, A6. Yesalis, Charles E., Courson, Stephen P., and Wright, James (1993). History of anabolic steroid use in sport and exercise. In Charles E. Yesalis (Ed.), *Anabolic steroids in sport and exercise*. Champaign, IL: Human Kinetics Publishers, pp. 1–33.

6. Dobie, Michael (2004, August 30). Good job, Athens, and good night. *Newsday*, p. A61. Litsky, Frank (2003, March 6). International drug code is adopted. *New York Times*, p. D5. Longman, Jere (2003, October 24). Steroid is reportedly found in top runner's urine test. *New York Times*, p. D2. Starr, Mark (2003, November 3). Blowing the whistle on drugs: A raid on a California laboratory threatens to blemish America's athletes—again. *Newsweek*, pp. 60–61. Vecsey, George (2002, March 1). More curious material in skiing's closet. *New York Times*, pp. D1, D4.

7. Schmidt, Michael S. (2007, March 1). Steelers deny players received doctor's drugs. *New York Times*, p. D7.

W.W.F.'s McMahon indicted (1993, November 19). *New York Times*, p. B12. Yesalis, Courson, and Wright, History of anabolic steroid use, pp. 40–42.

8. Buckley, William E.; Yesalis, Charles E.; Friedl, Karl E.; Anderson, William A.; Streit, Andrea L.; and Wright, James E. (1988). Estimated prevalence of anabolic steroid use among male high school seniors. *Journal of the American Medical Association, 260,* 3441–3445. Dolphin, Ric (1989, March 13). The steroid scandal. *Maclean's,* pp. 36–39.

9. Curry, Jack (2006, June 8). A new front in baseball's drug war. Player's testimony points to holes in testing policy. *New York Times,* pp. D1, D5. Curry, Jack (2005, November 16). Baseball backs stiffer penalties for steroid use. *New York Times,* pp. A1, D2. Fainaru-Wada, Mark, and Williams, Lance (2006). *Game of shadows: Barry Bonds, Balco and the steroids scandal that rocked professional sports.* New York: Gotham Books. Longman, Jere (2005, May 18). Steroid-assisted fastballs? Pitchers face new spotlight. *New York Times,* pp. A1, D3. Macur, Juliet (2007, April 29). Records show steriod inquiry is continuing. *New York Times,* Section 8, pp. 1, 6.

10. Brower, Kirk J.; Catlin, Donald H.; Blow, Frederic C.; Eliopulos, George A.; and Bereford, T. P. (1991). Clinical assessment and urine testing for anabolic-androgenic steroid abuse and dependence. *American Journal of Drug and Alcohol Abuse, 17,* 161–172. Council on Scientific Affairs (1990). Medical and nonmedical uses of anabolic-androgenic steroids. *Journal of the American Medical Association, 264,* 2923–2927.

11. Friedl, Karl E. (1993). Effects of anabolic steroids on physical health. In Charles E. Yesalis (Ed.), *Anabolic steroids in sport and exercise.* Champaign, IL: Human Kinetics Publishers, pp. 107–150. Galloway, Gantt P. (1997). Anabolic-androgenic steroids. In Joyce H. Lowinson; Pedro Ruiz; Robert B. Millman; and John G. Langrod (Eds.). *Substance abuse: A comprehensive textbook* (3rd ed.). Baltimore: Williams and Wilkins, pp. 308–318.

12. Friedl, *Effects of anabolic steroids,* pp. 121–131.

13. Ibid., pp. 116–121. Karch, Steven B. (2002). *The pathology of drug abuse* (3rd ed.). Boca Raton, FL: CRC Press, pp. 490–491. Scharhag, Jürgen, Urhausen, Axel, and Kindermann, Wilfried (2003). Anabolic steroid-induced echocardiographic characteristics of professional football players. *Journal of the American College of Cardiology, 42,* 588.

14. Su, Tung-Ping; Pagliaro, Michael; Schmidt, Peter J.; Pickar, David; Wolkowitz, Owen; and Rubinow, David R. (1993). Neuropsychiatric effects of anabolic steroids in male normal volunteers. *Journal of the American Medical Association, 269,* 2760–2764.

15. Greenberg, Alan (1991, June 29). Alzado has a serious message to kids about steroids—Don't use them. *Hartford (CT) Courant,* cited in Jim Ferstle (1993), Evolution and politics of drug testing. In Charles E. Yesalis (Ed.), *Anabolic steroids,* p. 276.

16. Pope, Harrison G., Jr., Kouri, Elena M., and Hudson, James I. (2000). Effects of supraphysiologic doses of testosterone on mood and aggressiveness in normal men: A randomized controlled trial. *Archives of General Psychiatry, 57,* 133–140. Stocker, Steven (2000). Study provides additional evidence that high steroid doses elicit psychiatric symptoms in some men. *NIDA Notes, 15* (4), pp. 8–9. Trenton, Adam J., and Currier, Glenn W. (2005). Behavioural manifestations of anabolic steroid use. *CNS Drugs, 19,* 571–595.

17. Adler, Jerry (2004, December 20). Toxic strength. *Newsweek,* pp. 45–52. Bahrke, Michael S. (1993). Psychological effects of endogenous testosterone and anabolic-androgenic steroids. In Charles E. Yesalis (Ed.), *Anabolic steroids in sport and exercise.* Champaign, IL: Human Kinetics Publishers, pp. 161–192. Doff, Wilson (2005, March 10). After a young athlete's suicide, steroids called the culprit. *New York Times,* pp. A1, D8. Estrada, Manuel, Varshney, Anurag, and Ehrlich, Barbara E. (2006). Elevated testosterone induces apoptosis in neuronal cells. *Journal of Biological Chemistry, 281,* 25492–25501. Longman, Jere (2003, November 26). An athlete's dangerous experiment: Using steroids enhanced his physique, but he died trying to stop. *New York Times,* pp. D1, D4.

18. National Institute on Drug Abuse (2000, April). Anabolic steroids. *Research report series.* Bethesda, MD: National Institute on Drug Abuse. Collins, Rick (2003, January 5). Federal and state steroid laws. Posted on the web site of Collins, McDonald, and Gann, P. C., Attorneys-at-law, Nassau County and New York, NY, www. steroidlaw. com.

19. DEA leads largest steroid bust in history (2005, December 15). Drug Enforcement Administration, U.S. Department of Justice. Johnston, Lloyd D.; O'Malley, Patrick M.; Bachman, Jerald G.; and Schulenberg, John E. (2007a). *Monitoring the Future national results on adolescent drug use. Overview of key findings, 2006.* Bethesda, MD: National Institute on Drug Abuse, Table 1.

20. Pope, Harrison G.; Gruber, Amanda J.; Choi, Priscilla; Olivardia, Roberto; and Phillips, Katherine A. (1997). Muscle dysmorphia: An underrecognized form of body dysmorphic disorder. *Psychosomatics, 38,* 548–557. Wroblewska, Anna-M. (1997). Androgenic-anabolic steroids and body dysmorphia in young men. *Journal of Psychosomatic Research, 42,* 225–234.

21. Bahrke, Michael S., Yesalis, Charles E., and Brower, Kirk J. (1998). Anabolic-androgenic steroid abuse and performance-enhancing drugs among adolescents. *Sport Psychiatry, 7,* 821–838. Beel, Andrea, Maycock, Bruce, and McLean, Neil (1998). Current perspectives on anabolic steroids. *Drug and Alcohol Review, 17,* 87–103. Karch, *The pathology of drug abuse.* Kashkin, Kenneth B., and Kleber, Herbert D. (1989). Hooked on hormones? An anabolic steroid addiction hypothesis. *Journal of the American Medical Association, 262,* 3166–3169. Schrof, Joanne M. (1992, June 1). Pumped up. *U.S. News and World Report,* pp. 55–63.

22. Goldberg, Linn; Mackinnon, David P.; Elliot, Diane L.; Moe, Esther L.; Clarke, Greg; and Cheong, JeeWon (2000). The Adolescents Training and Learning to Avoid Steroids program. *Archives of Pediatrics and Adolescent Medicine, 154,* 332–338. Moe, Esther L.; Goldberg, Linn D.; MacKinnon, David P.; and Cheong, JeeWon (1999). Reducing drug use and promoting healthy behaviors among athletes: The ATLAS program. *Medical Science Sports Exercise, 31* (5), S122.

23. Quotation by Bob Bauman (1992). In Bob Goldman and Ronald Klatz, *Death in the locker room II: Drugs and sports.* Chicago: Elite Sports Medicine Publications, pp. 10–11.

24. Goldstein, Paul J. (1990). Anabolic steroids: An ethnographic approach. In Geraline C. Lin and Lynda Erinoff (Eds.), *Anabolic steroid abuse* (NIDA Research Monograph 102). Rockville, MD: National Institute on Drug Abuse, p. 84.

25. Catlin, Don; Wright, Jim; Pope, Harrison; and Liggett, Mariah (1993). Assessing the threat of anabolic steroids: Sportsmedicine update. *The Physician and Sportsmedicine, 21,* 37–44. Juhn, Mark S. (2003). Popular sports supplements and ergogenic aids. *Sports Medicine, 33,* 921–939. Wadler and Hainline, *Drugs and the athlete,* pp. 70–74.

26. Tuller, David (2005, January 18). For sale: "muscles" in a bottle. *New York Times,* pp. F5, F10. Quotation on p. F5.

27. Androstenedione (2001). *PDR for nutritional supplements* (1st ed.). Montvale NJ: Medical Economics, pp. 26–28. Juhn, Popular sports supplements. Leder, Benjamin Z.; Longcope, Christopher; Catlin, Don H.; Ahrens, Brian; and Schoenfeld, Joel S. (2000). Oral androstenedione administration and serum testosterone concentrations in young men. *Journal of the American Medical Association, 283,* 779–782.

28. FDA bans andro sales (2004, March 12). *Newsday,* p. A38. Johnston, O'Malley, Bachman, and Schulenberg (2007a), Table 1. Mravic, Mark (2000, February 21). Ban it, bud. *Sports Illustrated,* pp. 24, 26.

29. Creatine (2001). *PDR for nutritional supplements* (1st ed.). Montvale, NJ: Medical Economics, pp. 114–117. Gower, Timothy (1999, February 17). Safety and the search for muscle in a bottle. *New York Times,* p. 14. Freeman, Mike (2003, October 21). Scientist fears athletes are using unsafe drugs: Discovery of an undetected steroid confirms suspicions. *New York Times,* p. D2. Johnston, Lloyd D.; O'Malley, Patrick M.; Bachman, Jerald G.; and Schulenberg, John E. (2007b). *Monitoring the Future national survey results on drug use, 1975–2006, Volume I: Secondary school students 2006.* Bethesda, MD: National Institute on Drug Abuse, Tables 10–5b and 10–5c. Juhn, Popular sports supplements.

30. Hamilton, Martha McNeil (2003, February 23). Beating drug screening builds cottage industry. Evaders change faster than testing technology. *Houston Chronicle,* p. 2.

31. Wadler and Hainline, *Drugs and the athlete,* pp. 201–202.

32. Meer, *Drugs and sports,* pp. 92–95.

33. Alternate specimen testing policies may be set soon (2005, September). *Occupational Health and Safety,* p. 26. Cone, Edward J.; Presley, Lance; Lehrer, Michael; Seiter, William; Smith, Melissa; Kardos, Keith W.; Fritch, Dean; Salamone, Sal; and Niedbala, R. Sam (2002). Oral fluid testing for drugs of abuse: Positive prevalence rates by Intercept immunoassay screening and GC-MS confirmation and suggested cutoff concentrations. *Journal of Analytical Toxicology, 26,* 540–546.

34. *Allen and Hanbury's athletic drug reference* (1994). Durham NC: Clean Data, pp. 65–66. Baden, Lindsey R.; Horowitz, Gary; Jacoby, Helen; and Eliopoulos, George M. (2001). Quinolones and false-positive urine screening for opiates by immunoassay technology. *Journal of the American Medical Association, 286,* 3115–3119. Struempler, Richard E. (1987, May/June). Excretion of codeine and morphine following ingestion of poppy seeds. *Journal of Analytical Toxicology, 11,* 97–99. Wadler and Hainline, *Drugs and the athlete,* pp. 208–209.

35. Catlin, Wright, Pope, and Liggett, Assessing the threat, p. 39.

36. Rosenberg, Ronald (2000, October 12). Citgo to use Avitar drug tests, Job applicants to undergo new saliva-based exam. *Boston Globe,* p. C3.

37. Yamaguchi, Ryoko, Johnston, Lloyd D., and O'Malley, Patrick M. (2003). Relationship between student illicit drug use and school drug-testing policies. *Journal of School Health, 73,* 159–164.

38. Quotation of Charles E. Yesalis. In Wright and Cowart, *Anabolic steriods,* p. 196. Schwerin, Michael J.; Corcoran, Kevin J.; Fisher, Leslee; Patterson, David; Askew, Waide; Orlich, Tracy; and Shanks, Scott (1996). Social physique anxiety, body esteem, and social anxiety in bodybuilders and self-reported anabolic steroid users. *Addictive Behaviors, 21,* 1–8.

39. Goldman, Bob, and Klatz, Ronald (1992). *Death in the locker room II: Drugs and sports.* Chicago: Elite Sports Medicine Publications, pp. 23–24.

40. Egan, Timothy (2002, November 22). Body-conscious boys adopt athlete's taste for steroids. *New York Times,* pp. A1, A24. Quotations on p. A24. Kolata, Gina; Longman, Jere; Weiner, Tim; and Egan, Timothy (2002, December 2). With no answers on risks, steroid users still say "yes." *New York Times,* pp. A1, A19. Pope, Harrison G., Jr., Phillips, Katherine A., and Olivardia, Roberto (2002). *The Adonis complex: How to identify, treat, and prevent body obsession in men and boys.* New York: Simon and Schuster.

41. Kilgannon, Corey (2001, May 27). Strong Island: More youngsters seek great physiques, and risky ways to get them. *New York Times,* Section 14 (Long Island), pp. 1, 9. Quotation on p. 9. Kolata, Gina (2002, December 2). With no answers on risks, steroid users still say "yes." *New York Times,* pp. A1, A10. Morgan, Richard (2002). The men in the mirror. *Chronicle of Higher Education, 49,* A53–A54.

PART THREE

Legal Drugs in Our Society

chapter **10**

Alcohol: Social Beverage/Social Drug

I was invited to address a convention of high school teachers on the topic of drug abuse. When I arrived at the convention center to give my talk, I was escorted to a special suite, where I was encouraged to join the executive committee in a round of drug taking—the drug was a special high-proof single-malt whiskey. Later, the irony of the situation had its full impact. As I stepped to the podium under the influence of a psychoactive drug (the whiskey), I looked out through the haze of cigarette smoke at an audience of educators who had invited me to speak to them because they were concerned about the unhealthy impact of drugs on their students. The welcoming applause gradually gave way to the melodic tinkling of ice cubes in liquor glasses, and I began. They did not like what I had to say.

—*John P.J. Pinel*, Biopsychology *(2003)*

After you have completed this chapter, you will understand

- How alcoholic beverages are produced
- Alcohol use through history
- Patterns of alcohol consumption
- The pharmacology of alcohol
- Acute physiological and behavioral effects of alcohol
- Alcohol and health benefits
- Strategies for responsible alcohol consumption

Pinel's experience in this opening vignette sums up the central problem facing American society in its dealings with alcohol use and abuse: the frequent failure to acknowledge that alcohol is indeed a psychoactive drug.[1] You may have heard someone remark, "He drinks a little too much, but at least he's not doing drugs." To many people, an alcoholic beverage is simply a social beverage; in actuality, it is a social drug.

We can see this problem reflected in a number of ways. College courses that cover drug abuse and its effect on society, perhaps the one you are taking right now, are often entitled "Drugs and Alcohol." Would you personally have expected to cover the effects of alcohol in a course simply entitled "Drugs" in your college catalog? If you answer no, then alcohol had better stay in the course title.

Even the U.S. federal government perpetuates the distinction, with separate agencies for alcohol abuse (the National Institute on Alcohol Abuse and Alcoholism, NIAAA) and the abuse of other drugs (the National Institute on Drug Abuse, NIDA). This bureaucratic partitioning admittedly has historic roots, and there may be valid reasons to continue the division from a management or budgetary point of view, but it has inadvertently reinforced an unfortunate and inaccurate notion that alcohol is somehow a substance that stands apart from other drugs of potential abuse. Fortunately, the phrase "alcohol and other drug abuse," often shortened to "AOD abuse," has become increasingly popular as a way of conveying the idea that problems of substance abuse can come from many sources.

To recognize the special status of alcohol as a psychoactive drug in our society, two chapters are devoted to alcohol-related issues. This chapter considers alcohol as a drug, with a unique history and tradition and its own

set of acute risks. The next chapter turns to an examination of alcohol's chronic effects, specifically the potential problems of alcohol abuse and alcoholism. We begin by considering the nature of alcohol itself.

What Makes an Alcoholic Beverage?

Creating **ethyl alcohol,** through a process known as **fermentation,** is a remarkably easy thing to do. Almost every culture in the world, at one time or another, has stumbled on the basic procedure. All you need is organic material with a sugar content (honey, grapes, berries, molasses, rye, apples, corn, sugar cane, rice, pumpkins, to name some examples) left undisturbed in a warm container for a time, and nature does the work. Microscopic yeast cells, floating through the air, land on this material and literally consume the sugar in it so that, for every one sugar molecule consumed, two molecules of alcohol and two molecules of carbon dioxide are left behind as waste. The carbon dioxide bubbles out, and what remains is an alcoholic beverage, less sweet than the substance that began it all but with a new, noticeable kick. Basic fermentation results in an alcohol content of between 12 and 14 percent, best exemplified by standard grape wine.

The process of fermenting starchy grains such as barley to produce beer, called **brewing**, is somewhat more complicated. The barley first needs to be soaked in water until it sprouts, producing an enzyme that is capable of breaking down the starch into sugar. It is then slowly dried, the sprouts are removed, and the remainder (now called **barley malt**) is crushed into a powder. The barley malt is combined with water, corn, and rice to form a mixture called a **mash.** The water activates the enzyme so that the starches convert into sugars. The addition of yeast to the mash starts the fermentation process and produces an alcohol content of approximately 4.5 percent. The dried blossoms of the hop plant, called *hops*, are then added to the brew for the characteristic pungent flavoring and aroma.

Relying on fermentation alone gives a potentially maximal concentration of alcohol of about 15 to 16 percent. The reason for this limit is that an alcohol content above this level starts to kill the yeast and, in doing so, stops the fermentation process. To obtain a higher alcoholic content, another process, called **distillation,** must occur.

Distillation involves heating a container of some fermented mixture until it boils. Because alcohol has a lower boiling temperature than water, the vapor produced has a higher alcohol-to-water ratio than the original mixture. This alcohol-laden vapor is then drawn off

ethyl alcohol: The product of fermentation of natural sugars. It is generally referred to simply as *alcohol,* though several types of nonethyl alcohol exist.

fermentation: The process of converting natural sugars into ethyl alcohol by the action of yeasts.

brewing: The process of producing beer from barley grain.

barley malt: Barley after it has been soaked in water, sprouts have grown, sprouts have been removed, and the mixture has been dried and crushed to a powder.

mash: Fermented barley malt, following liquification and combination with yeasts.

distillation: A process by which fermented liquid is boiled and then cooled so that the condensed product contains a higher alcoholic concentration than before.

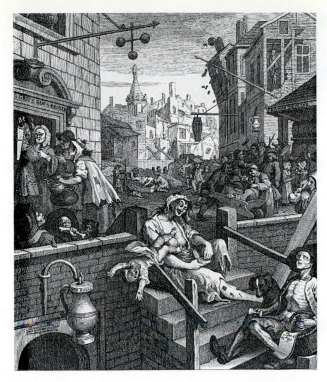

The social chaos of "Gin Lane" in London, as interpreted in this satirical engraving by William Hogarth (1697–1764).

into a special coiled apparatus (often referred to as a *still*), cooled until it condenses back to a liquid, and poured drop by drop into a second container. This new liquid, referred to as **distilled spirits** or simply *liquor*, has an alcohol content considerably higher than 15 percent, generally in the neighborhood of 40 to 50 percent.

It is possible through further distillations to achieve an alcohol content of up to 95 percent. At this point, however, the alcohol content of distilled spirits is not commonly described by percentage but rather by the designation "proof." Any proof is twice the percentage of alcohol: An 80-proof whiskey contains 40 percent alcohol; a 190-proof vodka contains 95 percent alcohol.

The three basic forms of alcoholic beverages are wine, beer, and distilled spirits. Table 10.1 shows the sources of some well-known examples.

Alcohol Use through History

Historians point out that fermented honey, called *mead*, was probably the original alcoholic beverage, dating from approximately 8000 B.C. Beer, requiring more effort than simple fermentation, came on the scene much later, with the Egyptians establishing the first official brewery about 3700 B.C. At that time, beer was quite different from the

watery forms we know today. It was more similar to a bread than a beverage, and the process of producing it was closer to baking than to brewing.[2]

Evidence of the development of wine comes from references to its sale in the Code of Hammurabi, King of Babylonia, recorded about 1700 B.C Wine-making itself, however, appears to have begun more than three thousand years before that. Excavations of an ancient village in modern-day Iran have revealed the remains of wine-stained pottery dating back to as early as 5400 B.C.[3]

The first documented distillation of alcohol was the conversion of wine into brandy during the Middle Ages, at a medical school in Salerno, Italy. The emphasis at first was on its medicinal applications rather than the level of intoxication that could be achieved with it. The new beverage became known in Latin as **aqua vitae** ("the water of life"). People quickly caught on to its inebriating possibilities, and brandy became the primary distilled liquor in Europe until the middle of the seventeenth century. At that time the Dutch perfected the process of distilling liquor and flavoring it with juniper berries. A new alcoholic beverage was born: gin.

The enormous popularity of gin throughout Europe marked a crucial point in the history of alcohol's effect on European society. Because it was easily produced, cheaper than brandy, and faster-acting than wine, gin became attractive as an alcoholic beverage to all levels of society, particularly the poorer classes of people. By the mid-1700s, alcohol abuse was being condemned as a major societal problem, and concerns about drunkenness had become a public issue.

Although gin affected life in many parts of Europe, it was in English cities that the gin epidemic became a genuine crisis. By 1750, gin consumption in England had grown to twenty-two times the level in 1685, and the social devastation was obvious. In London, infant mortality rose during this period, with only one of four baptized babies between 1730 and 1749 surviving to the age of five, despite the fact that mortality rates were falling in the countryside. In one section of the city, as many as one in five houses was a gin shop.

Consumption of other distilled spirits, such as rum and whiskey, added to the overall problem, but gin was undoubtedly the prime culprit. The epidemic of gin drinking in England during the first half of the eighteenth century illustrates how destructive the introduction of a

distilled spirits: The liquid product of distillation, also known as *liquor*.

aqua vitae (AH-kwa VEYE-tee): A brandy, the first distilled liquor in recorded history.

TABLE 10.1

Prominent alcoholic beverages and their sources

BEVERAGE	SOURCE
Wines	
Red table wine	Fermented red grapes with skins
White table wine	Fermented skinless grapes
Champagne	White wine bottled before yeast is gone so that remaining carbon dioxide produces a carbonated effect
Sparkling wine	Red wine prepared like champagne or with carbonation added
Fortified wines	Wines whose alcohol content is raised or fortified to 20% by the addition of brandy (see below)—for example, sherry, port, Marsala, and Madeira
Wine-like variations	
Hard cider	Fermented apples
Sake	Fermented rice
Beers	Types of beer vary depending on brewing procedures.
Draft beer	Contains 3–6% alcohol
Lager beer	Contains 3–6% alcohol
Ale	Contains 3–6% alcohol
Malt liquor	Contains up to 8% alcohol
Distilled spirits	
Brandy	Distilled from grape wine, cherries, peaches, or other fruits
Liqueur or cordial	Brandy or gin, flavored with blackberry, cherry, chocolate, peppermint, licorice, etc. Alcohol content ranges from 20% to 55%
Rum	Distilled from the syrup of sugar cane or from molasses
Scotch whiskey	Distilled from fermented corn and barley malt
Rye whiskey	Distilled from rye and barley malt
Blended whiskey	A mixture of two or more types of whiskey
Bourbon whiskey	Distilled primarily from fermented corn
Gin	Distilled from either barley, potato, corn, wheat, or rye, and flavored with juniper berries
Vodka	Approximately 95% pure alcohol, distilled from grains or potatoes and diluted by mixing with water
Tequila	Distilled from the fermented juice of the maguey plant
Aquavit or akvavit	Distilled from grains or potatoes, flavored with caraway seeds
Grain neutral spirits	Approximately 95% pure alcohol, used either for medicinal purposes or diluted and mixed in less-concentrated distilled spirits

Source: Adapted from Becker, Charles E., Roe, Robert L., and Scott, Robert A. (1979). *Alcohol as a drug: A curriculum on pharmacology, neurology, and toxicology.* Huntington, NY: Robert Krieger Publishing, pp. 10–12.

potent and easily available psychoactive drug into an urban society already suffering from social dislocation and instability can be. The consequences in many ways mirrored the introduction of crack cocaine into the ghettos of the United States during the 1980s.[4]

Alcohol in Early U.S. History

Judging from the records of Pilgrims aboard the *Mayflower* in 1620, alcohol played a pivotal role in the earliest days of settling the American colonies. William Bradford, historian of the *Mayflower* voyage and later governor of Plymouth Colony in Massachusetts, wrote that in looking for a place to land, they had decided not to "take time for further search or consideration, our victuals [supplies] being much spent, especially our Beere." Evidently, the Pilgrims arrived at Plymouth Rock not only with a passion for freedom but also with a considerable thirst.[5]

To be fair, however, we need to understand that these English settlers, like other travelers at that time, had little choice but to take along alcoholic beverages. Water would have spoiled easily during the sea voyage. Besides, the Pilgrims were not against alcohol per se, merely against the drunken behavior that resulted from its excessive use.

General approval of the moderate use of alcohol was a fact of American life well into the nineteenth century. It is not surprising, therefore, that the social focus for communities in colonial America was the tavern. Not only did taverns serve as public dispensers of alcoholic beverages, but they also served as centers for local business dealings and town politics. Mail was delivered there; travelers could stay the night; elections were held there. As an institution, the tavern was as highly regarded, and as regularly attended, as the local church.[6]

By today's standards, it is difficult to imagine the extent of alcohol consumption during the early decades of American history. In 1830, the average per capita intake was an immoderate five drinks a day, roughly four times the level of consumption today. It was common to take "whiskey breaks" at 11 A.M. and 4 P.M. each day (except Sunday), much as we take coffee breaks today. As far as types of liquor were concerned, rum was the favorite in New England and along the North Atlantic coast, but elsewhere whiskey was king. George Washington himself went into the whiskey business at Mount Vernon in 1797, eventually establishing the largest whiskey distillery of his time.[7]

The Rise of Temperance in the United States

In or about 1830, alcohol consumption in the United States started to decrease. This decline coincided with the growing influence of a **temperance movement** among religious leaders, physicians, and social reformers across the nation. Temperance goals originally focused on the moderation, not necessarily the prohibition, of alcohol consumption in society and drew attention to the long-term consequences of chronic alcohol abuse. The distinction between temperate use and total prohibition, however, began to blur over the years. The shift from temperance to prohibition, from 1830 through the beginning of the twentieth century, will be examined in the next chapter.

Patterns of Alcohol Consumption Today

It has been theorized that the earliest systems of agriculture in human history were born of the desire to secure a dependable supply of beer.[8] If this is so, then alcohol,

commercialization, and economics have been linked from the very beginning. Today, of course, alcohol is not merely a big business, but an enormous business. Americans spend about $116 billion on the purchase of alcoholic beverages each year, and the alcohol industry spends about $1.4 billion advertising its products. More than one-third of this advertising budget is typically devoted to television commercials for beer.[9]

Overall Patterns of Alcohol Consumption

How much do Americans actually drink? Estimates of the current annual per capita consumption of pure alcohol in the United States vary between 1.3 gallons (4.9 liters), according to alcohol industry statistics, and 2.4 gallons (9.1 liters), according to World Health Organization statistics. If we take the lower estimate, the per capita consumption amounts to about one-half of an ounce of alcohol per day; if we take the higher estimate, the daily consumption rises to a bit more than three-fourths of an ounce per day. Owing to the difficulty of obtaining this kind of information and the varying standards upon which information is based, it is fair to say that the true value is probably somewhere in the middle.[10]

How many alcoholic drinks do these estimated daily amounts add up to? To answer this question, it is important first to consider the amount of pure alcohol that is contained in each of four basic types of

The stainless steel tanks of the world's largest wine maker, the Ernest and Julio Gallo Winery, are located in Modesto, California. More than 440 million gallons of wine were produced by E. & J. Gallo in 2007.

temperance movement: The social movement in the United States, beginning in the nineteenth century, that advocated the renunciation of alcohol consumption.

Drugs . . . in Focus

What Is a Standard Drink?

A standard drink is any drink that contains about 14 grams of pure alcohol (about 0.5 fluid ounce). These are some standard drink equivalents.

12 oz of beer or wine cooler	8–9 oz of malt liquor 8.5 oz shown in a 12 oz glass that, if full, would hold about 1.5 standard drinks of malt liquor	5 oz of table wine*	3–4 oz of fortified wine (such as sherry or port) 3.5 oz shown	2–3 oz of cordial, liqueur, or aperitif 2.5 oz shown	1.5 oz of brandy (a single jigger)	1.5 oz of spirits (a single jigger of 80-proof gin, vodka, whiskey, etc.) Shown straight and in a highball glass with ice to show level before adding mixer †
12 oz	8.5 oz	5 oz	3.5 oz	2.5 oz	1.5 oz	1.5 oz

Many people do not know what counts as a standard drink, and thus are unaware of how many standard drinks are held in the containers in which these drinks are often sold. Some examples:

■ For beer, the approximate number of standard drinks in
- 12 oz = 1
- 16 oz = 1.3
- 22 oz = 2
- 40 oz = 3.3

■ For malt liquor, the approximate number of standard drinks in
- 12 oz = 1.5
- 16 oz = 2
- 22 oz = 2.5
- 40 oz = 4.5

■ For table wine, the approximate number of standard drinks in
- a standard 750 mL (25 oz) bottle = 5

■ For 80-proof spirits, or "hard liquor," the approximate number of standard drinks in
- a mixed drink = 1 or more†
- a pint (16 oz) = 11
- a fifth (25 oz) = 17
- 1.75 L (59 oz) = 39

*In recent years it has been common for wines to contain an alcohol concentration of 16 percent. In these instances, 5 ounces of wine would be equivalent to 0.80 ounces of alcohol, which is 33 percent higher than when a 12 percent wine is considered. Another way of thinking about this is that for a drink of wine with 16 percent alcohol concentration to be equivalent to a 12-ounce can of beer or a typical shot of liquor, the quantity of wine consumed should be reduced to approximately 4 ounces. In this chapter, however, we will retain the concept of 5 ounces of wine as representing a standard drink, since it is traditional that alcohol equivalencies are calculated on this basis.

† It can be difficult to estimate the number of standard drinks served in a single mixed drink made with hard liquor. Depending on factors such as the type of spirits and the recipe, one mixed drink can contain from one to three or more standard drinks.

Source: National Institute on Alcohol Abuse and Alcoholism (2005). Helping patients who drink too much: A clinician's guide. Bethesda, MD: National Institute on Alcohol Abuse and Alcoholism, p. 12.

alcoholic beverages. Drugs . . . in Focus on page 246 shows that a single half-ounce of alcohol is approximately equivalent to any of the following:

- One 5-ounce glass of wine
- One 12-ounce bottle or can of beer
- One 12-ounce bottle of wine cooler
- One shot (1.5 ounce size) of 80-proof liquor

All these quantities are approximately equal to about one-half ounce in terms of pure alcohol, and they are often referred to as "standard drinks."

Based on these equivalencies, the average alcohol consumption in the United States can be approximated as between 1 and 1.5 "standard drinks" per day. Bear in mind, however, that a "standard drink" may not be the drink you consume and, therefore, is not necessarily the appropriate unit to use when computing your own personal level of alcohol consumption. Draft beer, for example, is typically dispensed in large glasses that exceed 12 ounces in capacity. A mixed drink in a bar might contain a quantity of liquor that exceeds a standard amount, if the bartender is particularly generous. In either of these circumstances, an

Drugs . . . in Focus

Visualizing the Disparity of Alcohol Consumption in the United States

To appreciate the uneven pattern of alcohol consumption in the population, try the following demonstration:

Assemble ten people and ten bottles of beer (preferably empty).

Separate three people who hold nothing. They represent the 30 percent of the population that does not drink alcohol at all.

Separate five people; together they hold two bottles. They represent the 50 percent of the population that drinks 20 percent of the total alcohol supply.

Separate the ninth person; this person holds two bottles. This individual represents the 10 percent of the population that drinks another 20 percent of the total alcohol supply.

Separate the tenth person; this person holds a six-pack of bottles. This individual represents the 10 percent of the population that drinks 60 percent of the total alcohol supply.

The Moral of the Story

Twenty percent of the entire population (the ninth and tenth persons in this demonstration) drinks 80 percent of the total alcohol consumed in the United States each year. Of those who drink some alcohol, two-sevenths (roughly 30 percent) of them drink 80 percent of the total alcohol consumed each year, while five-sevenths (roughly 70 percent) of them drink the remaining 20 percent. These figures correspond to those expressed in the text.

Source: Kinney, G. Jean (2006). *Loosening the grip: A handbook of alcohol information,* 8th ed. New York: McGraw-Hill, p. 30.

A Tale of 10 Beers and 10 People

3 drink none

5 share 2 beers

1 drinks 2

1 drinks 6

individual can be misled into believing that an "average" amount is being consumed (in terms of drinks) when, in fact, the quantity of alcohol being consumed is considerably larger.

Another consideration when looking at statistics based on population averages is the obvious fact that not everyone is "average." There is an enormous disparity in terms of how much alcohol each person actually consumes during a given year. Some people drink no alcohol at all, whereas others drink heavily. *In fact, 80 percent of the total amount of alcohol consumed in the United States each year is consumed by only the 30 percent of Americans who drink and only 20 percent of the population in general.* Drugs . . . in Focus on page 247 provides a demonstration that illustrates the pattern of alcohol consumption in the United States today.

Looking at the types of alcohol consumed in the United States, beer consumption represents 88 percent of the overall alcoholic beverage market and a disproportionate share of heavy alcohol drinking. When five or more 12-ounce beers are consumed in a day, there is a stronger association with alcohol-related problems than when there are comparable consumption levels of wine or liquor. We can conclude that beer is the most problematic form of alcohol consumption in the United States today.[11]

Trends in Alcohol Consumption since the Late 1970s

Overall, alcohol consumption levels among Americans steadily declined each year from the late 1970s through the mid-1990s and has remained roughly stable since then. Because a large part of the decline was tied to a growing attention to weight, health, and fitness, the industry responded with the introduction of lighter wines, with fewer calories and a reduced alcohol content, as well as a popular line of wine coolers (wine mixed with sugar and fruit juice), roughly equal in alcoholic content to regular beer. In addition to lighter beers, which have a roughly equivalent alcoholic content but fewer calories, there has been a growing market for "ice beer," created by a brewing method in which temperatures just slightly below freezing temporarily allow small ice crystals to form. Generally speaking, ice beers have a slightly higher alcohol content (in the 5.0 to 6.5 percent range) because the ice (nonalcoholic) crystals are removed prior to the final stages of filtration.

In general, alcohol drinking preferences among Americans have shifted over recent years from beer to wine. In 2005, 41 percent of drinkers in the United States reported that they drank beer most often, whereas 33 percent reported that they usually drank wine. Beer had been reported to be preferable over wine by an almost two-to-one ratio in 1992.[12]

The Demographics of Alcohol Consumption

Preferences for particular types of alcoholic beverages are influenced by a host of factors, including age, gender, education, and income. In general, among individuals in the United States who drink alcoholic beverages, women are twice as likely as men not to prefer beer, three times as likely as men to prefer wine, and somewhat more likely than men to prefer liquor. The preference for wine and liquor over beer increases as people get older.

Increased years of education are also associated with an increased preference for wine over beer and liquor. The same is true with income levels, except that the change in preference for liquor is less clear. Individuals earning more than $50,000 prefer wine and beer to liquor, and those earning less than $20,000 prefer beer to liquor and wine. In general, the relationship between personal income and overall alcohol consumption is a curvilinear one: Abstainers and heavy drinkers both earn less than moderate drinkers.[13]

In general, college students consume a large amount of alcohol, though it appears that the establishment of twenty-one as a mandated legal drinking age in all states has delayed the occurrence of *peak* consumption levels to the junior or senior year. Nonetheless, the prevalence of moderate alcohol consumption in college, assessed by those having a drink in the last thirty days, rises substantially from levels encountered in high school.

Binge drinking among college students and other young adults is a common social ritual as well as a continuing social concern.

Drugs . . . in Focus

When Is a Binge Not a Binge?

Since the first survey conducted by the Harvard School of Public Health on alcohol consumption among college students in 1993 (see Table 10.2), the term "binge drinking" has become synonymous in the public mind with the behavior of drinking alcohol with the intention of getting drunk. It is commonly defined in the case of men as having consumed five or more alcoholic drinks on a single occasion (typically within a two-hour interval) or four drinks or more in the case of women. This definition has been referred to as the "5/4 criterion."

Recently, however, some clinicians and researchers in the alcohol abuse field have objected to this term as misleading. While acknowledging that consuming a series of alcoholic drinks on a single occasion should be considered a form of risky behavior that brings with it a host of adverse consequences, they contend that the concept of a "binge" should be restricted to an extended bout of drinking or other substance use (often operationalized as lasting at least two days) in which the person neglects other activities so as to drink or use other psychoactive substances. Indeed, this is the traditional sense of the word.

The *Journal of Studies on Alcohol* presently requires that authors of all submitted manuscripts refrain from the term "binge" unless it refers to an extended period of intoxication, prolonged use, and a giving up of usual activities. Any behavior defined by the 5/4 criterion, as expressed in guidelines for authors of articles in this journal, should be referred to as "heavy episodic drinking" or "heavy episodic use." Other researchers in the field refer to the alcohol-related behavior commonly reported among college students as "episodic high-risk drinking." It may not be nearly as catchy a phrase as "binge drinking," and it is

certainly less convenient for writers of newspaper headlines, but this term is nevertheless more accurate as a description of the phenomenon. Proponents of this terminology argue that the alcohol consumption pattern of behavior among college students is (1) typically restricted to going out and getting drunk one night on a weekend, from once a week to once a month or less often, (2) cyclical in nature, with the highest frequency occurring early in a semester, though it peaks following exam times, home football weekends, and during spring breaks, and (3) strongly determined by living in a college environment, in that it ends for practically all students when they graduate from college and move on.

In the meantime, the 5/4 criterion for binge drinking has the public health community divided. While the Centers for Disease Control and Prevention in Atlanta will continue to define the term "binge drinking" in the 5/4 manner for the foreseeable future, the National Institute on Alcohol Abuse and Alcoholism (NIAAA), the leading federal agency for research on alcohol abuse prevention and treatment, will not. The best advice when perusing the alcohol literature might be to examine carefully the way in which "binge drinking" is defined in a particular article.

Sources: Brower, Aaron M. (2002). Are college student alcoholics? *Journal of American College Health, 50,* 253–255. DeJong, William (2003). Definitions of binge drinking. *Journal of the American Medical Association, 289,* 1635. Naimi, Tim; Brewer, Bob; Mokdad, Ali; Denny, Clark; Serdula, Mary; and Marks, Jim (2003). In reply: Definitions of binge drinking. *Journal of the American Medical Association, 289,* 1636. Wechsler, Henry, and Kuo, Meichun (2000). College students define binge drinking and estimate its prevalence: Results of a national survey. *Journal of American College Health, 49,* 57–64.

Among young adults, *binge drinking*—defined for men as having five or more alcoholic drinks and for women as having four or more alcoholic drinks in a row (Drugs . . . in Focus)—rises sharply from age eighteen, peaks at ages twenty-one to twenty-two, then steadily declines over the next ten years. The prevalence of daily drinking also rises from levels encountered in high school but remains relatively stable through age thirty-two.

Table 10.2 shows the results of a 2001 survey of the drinking habits of nearly 11,000 college students at 119 U.S. campuses, the fourth survey in a series that began in 1993. Overall, 44 percent of students reported having engaged in binge drinking during the two weeks prior to

the administration of the survey—41 percent of the women and 49 percent of the men. About one in five students abstained from alcohol in 2001, whereas one in four was a frequent binge drinker. Not surprisingly, students who drank alcohol at some time over the past year frequently reported alcohol-related problems while at college. These problems included missing a class, doing something they regretted, forgetting where they were or what they did while intoxicated, arguing with friends, and failing to practice safe sex. While the percentages of binge drinkers in 2001 remained approximately the same as those reported in 1993, the percentage who reported alcohol-related problems increased.

The survey also reported that a large number of *nondrinkers* (defined as either abstainers or nonbinge drinkers) were adversely affected by binge drinking patterns of behavior on their campus. These situations, called secondhand effects (because the individuals themselves were not intoxicated but were affected by those who were), are analogous to the problems of secondhand smoking, which will be examined in Chapter 12.

In general, an estimated 500,000 full-time four-year college students (drinkers and nondrinkers) were unintentionally injured and more than 1,400 were killed while under the influence of alcohol, principally due to motor vehicle accidents. In addition, more than 600,000 were unintentionally assaulted by another student who had been drinking, and 400,000 reported having unprotected sex as a result of being intoxicated.[14]

Looking at the early years of teenage drinking, we find that alcohol use has been extensive by the eighth grade. In fact, among young people who report some alcohol consumption between the ages of twelve and twenty, the average age when drinking began is fourteen years. In the 2006 University of Michigan survey, 41 percent of eighth graders reported that they had consumed alcohol and 20 percent reported that they had been drunk sometime in their lives. Fortunately, these figures are

TABLE 10.2

Alcohol-related problems and secondary effects among college students, 2001

Alcohol-related problems among college students who drank alcohol

PROBLEM	PERCENTAGE REPORTING AN OCCURRENCE DURING THE PAST 30 DAYS	SIGNIFICANT INCREASE/ DECREASE SINCE 1993
Missed a class	29.5	Increase
Got behind in schoolwork	21.6	Increase
Did something I regretted	35.0	Increase
Forgot where I was or what I did	26.8	Increase
Argued with friends	22.9	Increase
Engaged in unplanned sex	21.3	Increase
Had unprotected sex	21.3	Increase
Had five or more alcohol-related problems	20.3	Increase

Secondary effects of binge drinking on nonbinge drinkers, 2001

PROBLEM	PERCENTAGE REPORTING INCIDENT	SIGNIFICANT INCREASE/ DECREASE SINCE 1993
Been insulted or humiliated	29.2	No change
Had a serious argument or quarrel	19.0	No change
Been pushed, hit, or assaulted	8.7	No change
Had to take care of drunken student	15.2	No change
Experienced an unwanted sexual advance	18.9	Increase
Been a victim of sexual assault or date rape (women only)	1.0	Decrease

Note: Drinking alcohol refers to consumption within the past year. Binge drinking is defined as having consumed five or more alcoholic drinks on one occasion (in the case of men) and four or more alcoholic drinks on one occasion (in the case of women).

Source: Wechsler, Henry; Lee, Jae Eun; Kuo, Meichun; Seibring, Mark; Nelson, Toben F.; and Lee, Hang (2002). Trends in college binge drinking during a period of increased prevention efforts: Findings from four Harvard School of Public Health College Alcohol Study Surveys: 1993–2001. *Journal of American College Health, 50,* 203–217. Reprinted with permission of the Helen Dwight Reid Educational Foundation. Published by Heldref Publications, 1319 Eighteenth St., NW, Washington DC 20036–1802. Copyright © 2002.

down significantly from those found in earlier surveys. However, approximately one out of nine students at this age reported consuming more than five drinks on a single occasion in the previous two weeks, a pattern of behavior that is only slightly down from that reported in 1991.

A recent concern related to the issue of teenage drinking has been raised as a response to the introduction of new malt liquor products called Spykes. These drinks are sold in sweet flavor varieties like chocolate, mango, and melon and are marketed in 2-ounce bottles resembling beauty products. Costing less than a dollar each, Spykes have an alcohol content of approximately 12 percent. They are advertised as shots to be drunk alone or added to beer. The addition to beer is particularly troublesome, as many young people refrain from drinking excessive amounts of beer because they do not like its taste.[15]

The Pharmacology of Alcohol

Alcohol is a very small molecule, in liquid form, that is moderately soluble in fat and highly soluble in water—all characteristics that make it easily absorbed through the gastrointestinal tract once it is ingested, without needing any digestion. About 20 percent of it is absorbed into the bloodstream directly from the stomach, whereas the remaining 80 percent is absorbed from the upper portion of the small intestine.

On entering the stomach, alcohol acts initially as an irritant, increasing the flow of hydrochloric acid and pepsin, chemicals that aid digestion. Therefore, in small amounts, alcohol can help digest a meal. In large amounts, however, alcohol will irritate the stomach lining. This is a concern for those already having stomach problems; preexisting ulcers are worsened by drinking alcohol, and heavy alcohol drinking can produce ulcers.

The irritating effect on the stomach explains why the alcohol proceeds on to the small intestine more quickly if alcohol concentrations are high. The stomach is simply trying to get rid of its irritant. Over time, the chronic consumption of alcohol can produce an inflammation of the stomach (gastritis) or the pancreas (pancreatitis).

Because the small intestine assumes the lion's share of the responsibilities and acts extremely rapidly (more rapidly than the stomach), the rate of total alcohol absorption is based largely on the condition of the stomach when the alcohol arrives and the time required for the stomach to empty its contents into the small intestine. If the stomach is empty, an intoxicating effect

(the "buzz") will be felt very quickly. If the stomach is full, absorption will be delayed as the alcohol is retained by the stomach along with the food being digested, and the passage of alcohol into the small intestine will slow down.

Besides the condition of the stomach, there are other factors related to the alcohol itself and the behavior of the drinker that influence the rate of alcohol absorption. The principal factor is the concentration of alcohol in the beverage being ingested. An ounce of 80-proof (40 percent) alcohol will be felt more quickly than an ounce of wine containing 12 percent alcohol, and of course the level of alcohol in the blood will be higher as well. Also, if the alcoholic beverage is carbonated, as are champagne and other sparkling wines, the stomach will empty its contents faster and effects will be felt sooner. Finally, if the alcohol enters the body at a rapid pace, such as when drinks are consumed in quick succession, the level of alcohol in the blood will be higher because the liver cannot eliminate it at a fast enough pace. All other factors being equal, a bigger person requires a larger quantity of alcohol to have equivalent levels accumulating in the blood, simply because there are more body fluids to absorb the alcohol, thus diluting the overall effect.[16]

The Breakdown and Elimination of Alcohol

Its solubility in water helps alcohol to be distributed to all bodily tissues, with those tissues having greater water content receiving a relatively greater proportion of alcohol. The excretion of alcohol is accomplished in two basic ways. About 5 percent will be eliminated by the lungs through exhalation, causing the characteristic "alcohol breath" of heavy drinkers. Breathalyzers, designed to test for alcohol concentrations in the body and used frequently by law-enforcement officials to test for drunkenness, work on this principle. The remaining 95 percent will be eliminated in the urine, after the alcohol has been biotransformed into carbon dioxide and water.[17]

The solubility of alcohol in fat facilitates its passage across the blood-brain barrier (see Chapter 1). As a result, approximately 90 percent of the alcohol in the blood reaches the brain almost immediately. Unfortunately, alcohol passes the blood-placental barrier with equal ease, so alcohol intake by women during pregnancy affects the developing fetus. As a result, fetal alcohol levels are essentially identical to those of the mother who is drinking.[18] This important matter will be discussed in the next chapter, when we consider a type of mental and physical retardation called *fetal alcohol syndrome.*

The body recognizes alcohol as a visitor with no real biological purpose. It contains calories but no vitamins, minerals, or other components that have any nutritional value. Therefore, the primary reaction is for the body to break it down for eventual removal, through a process called **oxidation.** This biotransformation process consists of two basic steps. First, an enzyme, **alcohol dehydrogenase,** breaks down alcohol into **acetaldehyde.** This enzyme is present in the stomach, where about 20 percent of alcohol is broken down prior to absorption into the bloodstream, and in the liver, where the remaining 80 percent is broken down from accumulations in the blood. Second, another enzyme, **acetaldehyde dehydrogenase,** breaks down acetaldehyde in the liver into **acetic acid.** From there, further oxidation results in oxygen, carbon dioxide, and calories of energy.

The entire process is determined by the speed with which alcohol dehydrogenase does its work, and for a given individual, it works at a constant rate, no matter how much alcohol needs to be broken down. Imagine a bank at which only one teller window stays open, no matter how long the line of customers grows, and you will understand the limitations under which the body is operating.

The specific rate of oxidation is approximately 100 milligrams of alcohol per hour per kilogram of body weight. To put this in perspective, 8 grams of alcohol will be broken down in an hour if you weigh 176 pounds (80 kilograms), and 5 grams of alcohol will be broken down in an hour if you weigh 110 pounds (50 kilograms). Certain conditions and circumstances, however, can alter this basic biotransformation rate (Drugs . . . in Focus).

In terms of alcoholic beverages, the oxidation rate for adults in general is approximately one-third to one-half ounce of pure alcohol an hour. If you sipped (not gulped) slightly less than the contents of one 12-ounce bottle of beer, 5-ounce glass of wine, or any equivalent portion of alcohol (see Drugs . . . in Focus, page 246) very slowly over an hour's time, the enzymes in the stomach and liver would keep up, and you would not feel intoxicated. Naturally, if you consume larger amounts of alcohol at faster rates of consumption, all bets are off.[19]

It is no secret that alcohol consumption is conducive to the accumulation of body fat, most noticeably in the form of the notorious beer belly. It turns out that alcohol does not have significant effects on the biotransformation of dietary carbohydrates and proteins, so a drinking individual who consumes a healthy diet does not have to worry about getting enough nutrients. Alcohol does, however, reduce the breakdown of fat, so dietary fat has a greater chance of being stored rather than expended. Over time, the accumulation of fat in the liver is particularly serious because it eventually interferes with normal liver function. This condition will be examined in the next chapter as one of the major adverse effects of chronic alcohol consumption on the body.[20]

Measuring Alcohol in the Blood

Alcohol levels in the blood, like levels of any drug, vary considerably not only by virtue of how much is ingested and how long ago but also as a result of differences in an individual's body size and relative proportions of body fat. Consequently, we have to consider a specific ratio referred to as the **blood-alcohol concentration (BAC)** when assessing physiological and psychological effects (an alternative term is blood-alcohol level [BAL]).

The BAC refers to the number of grams of alcohol in the blood relative to 100 milliliters of blood, expressed as a percentage. For example, 0.1 gram (100 mg) of alcohol in 100 milliliters of blood is represented by a BAC of 0.10 percent. Table 10.3 shows the BAC levels that can be estimated from one's body weight, number of standard drinks consumed, and hours elapsed since starting the first drink. From these figures, BAC levels typically are considered in terms of three broad categories of behavior: caution (0.01 to 0.05 percent), driving impaired (0.05 to 0.08 percent), and legally drunk (in nearly all U.S. states, 0.08 percent and higher). In effect, you need to compute the accumulated BAC levels for your body weight after having a specific number of drinks, and then subtract 0.015 percent BAC for each hour since the drinking occurred.[21]

oxidation: A chemical process in alcohol metabolism.

alcohol dehydrogenase (AL-co-haul DEE-high-DRAW-juh-nays): An enzyme in the stomach and liver that converts alcohol into acetaldehyde.

acetaldehyde (ASS-ee-TAL-duh-hide): A by-product of alcohol metabolism, produced through the action of alcohol dehydrogenase.

acetaldehyde dehydrogenase (ASS-ee-TAL-duh-hide DEE-hide-DRAW-juh-nays): An enzyme in the liver that converts acetaldehyde to acetic acid in alcohol metabolism.

acetic acid (a-SEE-tik ASS-id): A by-product of alcohol metabolism, produced through the action of acetaldehyde dehydrogenase.

blood-alcohol concentration (BAC): The number of grams of alcohol in the blood relative to 100 milliliters of blood, expressed as a percentage.

Drugs . . . in Focus

Gender, Race, and Medication: Factors in Alcohol Metabolism

Since enzymes play such a critical role in alcohol breakdown, it is important to consider factors that alter the levels of these enzymes. As mentioned in Chapter 1, two of the factors involve gender and ethnicity. In general, women have about 60 percent less alcohol dehydrogenase in the stomach than men; thus their oxidation of alcohol is relatively slower, even when different body weights have been taken into account.

In addition, about 50 percent of all people of Asian descent have a genetically imposed lower level of acetaldehyde dehydrogenase in the liver. As a consequence, acetaldehyde builds up, causing nausea, itching, facial flushing, and cardiac acceleration. The combination of these symptoms, often referred to as *fast flushing*, makes alcohol consumption very unpleasant for many Asians.

It would be reasonable to expect then that those who experienced fast-flushing would drink less alcohol than those who do not. A study of Japanese Americans indicates that this is true when you look at a large community sample. For Japanese American college students who have to contend with peer pressure to drink, however, the relationship between the physiological response and the quantity of alcohol consumed is not nearly as strong. For them, environmental factors encourage alcohol consumption, despite their genetically determined predisposition to get sick. In a similar way, the social life of Japanese businessmen has promoted alcohol consumption, though many get sick as a result. A journalist describes the dilemma in present-day Japan in this way:

> *Perhaps in no other nation is drinking so extensively and tightly woven in business. Drinking after work is not only an extension of the company, it is virtually a requirement.*

Refuse the boss's offer to go out drinking, and your standing in the firm begins to slide.

Medications also can influence alcohol breakdown by altering levels of alcohol dehydrogenase in the stomach. Aspirin, for example, when taken on a full stomach, reduces enzyme levels by one-half, causing more alcohol to accumulate in the blood. Among women, aspirin has a greater inhibiting effect than among men, so it is possible that enzyme levels may be reduced to nearly zero if a woman is taking aspirin prior to drinking alcoholic beverages. Gastric ulcer medications also inhibit alcohol dehydrogenase and thus increase the physiological impact of alcohol. Any combination of these factors appears to produce additive effects. (See Table 10.4 on page 247 for other examples of alcohol–medication interactions.)

Sources: Frezza, Mario; DiPadova, Carlo; Pozzato, Gabrielle; Terpin, Maddalena; Baraona, Enrique; and Lieber, Charles S. (1990). High blood alcohol levels in women: The role of decreased gastric alcohol dehydrogenase activity and first-pass metabolism. *New England Journal of Medicine, 322,* 95–99. Gibbons, Boyd (1992, February). Alcohol: The legal drug. *National Geographic Magazine, 181,* p. 27. Goodman, Deborah (1992, January–February). NIMH grantee finds drug responses differ among ethnic groups. *ADAMHA News,* pp. 5, 15. Nakawatase, Tomoko V., Yamamoto, Joe, and Sasao, Toshiaki (1993). The association between fast-flushing response and alcohol use among Japanese Americans. *Journal of Studies on Alcohol, 54,* 48–53. Roine, Risto; Gentry, Thomas; Hernandez-Muñoz, Rolando; Baraona, Enrique; and Lieber, Charles S. (1990). Aspirin increases blood alcohol concentrations in humans after ingestion of ethanol. *Journal of the American Medical Association, 264,* 2406–2408.

Effects of Alcohol on the Brain

Alcohol is clearly a CNS depressant drug, though it is often misidentified as a stimulant. The reason for this confusion is that alcohol, at low doses, first releases the cerebral cortex from its inhibitory control over subcortical systems in the brain, a kind of double-negative effect. In other words, alcohol is depressing an area of the brain that normally would be an inhibitor, and the result is the illusion of stimulation. The impairment in judgment and thinking (the classic features of being drunk) stems from a loosening of social inhibitions that allow us to be relatively civil and well behaved.

As the BAC level increases, more widespread areas of the brain are affected until an inhibition of the respiratory centers in the medulla becomes a distinct possibility. As with other depressant drugs, acute alcoholic poisoning produces death by asphyxiation. The LD50 level (the lethal dose for 50 percent of the population) for alcohol, at which death is likely to occur, is approximately

TABLE 10.3

When are you drunk? Calculating your blood-alcohol concentration (BAC) level

STANDARD DRINKS

WEIGHT (POUNDS)	1	2	3	4	5	6	7	8	9	10
100	.029	.058	.088	.117	.146	.175	.204	.233	.262	.290
120	.024	.048	.073	.097	.121	.145	.170	.194	.219	.243
140	.021	.042	.063	.083	.104	.125	.146	.166	.187	.208
160	.019	.037	.055	.073	.091	.109	.128	.146	.164	.182
180	.017	.033	.049	.065	.081	.097	.113	.130	.146	.162
200	.015	.029	.044	.058	.073	.087	.102	.117	.131	.146
220	.014	.027	.040	.053	.067	.080	.093	.106	.119	.133
240	.012	.024	.037	.048	.061	.073	.085	.097	.109	.122

CAUTION   DRIVING IMPAIRED   LEGALLY DRUNK

Alcohol is "burned up" by your body at .015% per hour, as follows:

Hours since starting first drink	1	2	3	4	5	6
Percent alcohol burned up	.015	.030	.045	.060	.075	.090

To calculate your BAC level correctly, you must consider the number of standard drinks you have consumed, your body weight, and how much time has passed since the first drink. Note that a BAC level of .10% or higher has been, until recently, the standard for drunk driving in most U.S. states. Nearly all U.S. states have now adopted the .08% standard.

Source: Updated from *A primer of drug action,* 8th ed., by Robert M. Julien, M.D. © 2001 Worth Publishers. Used with permission.

0.50 percent. Remember, however, the nature of the LD50 curve (see Chapter 1); deaths can occur at lower concentrations and fail to occur at higher ones.[22]

The effect of alcohol at the neuronal level is less well understood, but the picture is starting to emerge. At present, the leading candidate for a mechanism is the GABA receptor in the brain. This receptor contains three locations: one sensitive specifically to the neurotransmitter GABA, one sensitive to barbiturates, and one sensitive to a type of antianxiety medication (Chapter 8). The last location is also sensitive to alcohol, and the research suggests that alcohol acts at this site, making it more difficult for the neuron to be stimulated.[23]

More worrisome than alcohol's depressive effects on the brain, however, is its ability to set up a pattern of psychological dependence (see Chapter 1). Since the late 1980s, evidence has accumulated that the reinforcing action of alcohol is a result of its influence on dopamine-releasing neurons in the nucleus accumbens of the brain. The fact that alcohol shares this effect with other abused drugs, including heroin, cocaine, and nicotine, suggests the possibility that treatments for one form of drug abuse might also be useful for others. Chapter 11 will describe the recent research concerning the use of naltrexone, an opiate antagonist, in the treatment of alcohol abuse.[24]

Acute Physiological Effects

Alcohol can produce a number of immediate physiological effects; they will be examined here. The physiological effects resulting from *chronic* alcohol consumption will be covered in the next chapter.

Toxic Reactions

We need to consider potentially life-threatening situations associated with alcohol as seriously as we would those with any other depressant drug. In general, the therapeutic index for alcohol, as measured by the LD50/ED50 ratio (see Chapter 1), is approximately 6. Because this figure is not very high, caution is strongly advised; the risks in being the "big winner" in a drinking contest should be weighed very carefully. On the one hand, to achieve a lethal BAC level of 0.50 percent, a 165-pound man needs to have consumed approximately twenty-three drinks over a four-hour period.[25] On the other hand, consuming ten drinks in one hour, a drinking schedule that achieves a BAC level of 0.35 percent, puts a person in extremely dangerous territory. We need to remember that LD50 is the *average* level for a lethal effect; there is no way to predict where a particular person might be located on the normal curve!

Fortunately, two mechanisms are designed to protect us to a certain degree. First, alcohol acts as a gastric irritant so that frequently the drinker will feel nauseous and vomit. Second, the drinker may simply pass out, and the risk potential from further drinking becomes irrelevant. Nonetheless, there are residual dangers in becoming unconscious; vomiting while in this state can prevent breathing, and so death can occur from asphyxiation (Help Line).

Heat Loss and the Saint Bernard Myth

Alcohol is a peripheral dilator, which means that blood vessels near the skin surface enlarge, leading to overall warmth and redness. This effect is most likely the basis for the myth that alcohol can keep you warm in freezing weather. In actuality, however, alcohol produces a greater heat loss than would be the case without it. In studies conducted of exercising men and women following consumption of alcohol, exaggerated heat loss was significantly greater in men than in women.[26] So if you are marooned in the snow and you see an approaching Saint Bernard with a cask of brandy strapped to its neck, politely refuse the offer. It will not help and could very well do you harm. (But feel free to hug the dog!)

Diuretic Effects

As concentration levels rise in the blood, alcohol begins to inhibit the **antidiuretic hormone (ADH),** a hormone that normally would act to reabsorb water in the kidneys prior to elimination in the urine. As a result, urine is more diluted and, because large amounts of liquid are typically being consumed at the time, more copious. Once blood alcohol concentrations have peaked, however, the reverse occurs. Water is now retained in a

> **antidiuretic hormone (ADH):** A hormone that acts to reabsorb water in the kidneys prior to excretion from the body.

HELP LINE

Emergency Signs and Procedures in Acute Alcohol Intoxication

Emergency Signs

- Stupor or unconsciousness
- Cool or damp skin
- Weak, rapid pulse (more than 100 beats per minute)
- Shallow and irregular breathing rate, averaging around one every three or four seconds
- Pale or bluish skin

Note: Among African Americans, color changes will be apparent in the fingernail beds, mucous membranes inside the mouth, or underneath the eyelids.

Emergency Procedures

- Seek medical help immediately.
- Drinker should lie on his or her side, with the head slightly lower than the rest of the body. This will prevent blockage of the airway and possible asphyxiation if the drinker starts to vomit.
- If drinker is put to bed, maintain some system of monitoring until he or she regains consciousness.

Note: There is no evidence that home remedies for "sobering up," such as cold showers, strong coffee, forced activity, or induction of vomiting, have any effect in reducing the level of intoxication. The only factors that help are the passage of time, rest, and perhaps an analgesic if there is a headache.

> **Where to go for assistance:**
> www.postgradmed.com/issues/2002/12_02/yost1.htm
> This web site is adapted from Yost, David A. (2002). Acute care for alcohol intoxication: Be prepared to consider clinical dilemmas. *Postgraduate Medicine Online.*

Source: Victor, Maurice (1976). Treatment of alcohol intoxication and the withdrawal syndrome: A critical analysis of the use of drugs and other forms of therapy. In Peter G. Bourne (Ed.), *Acute drug abuse emergencies: A treatment manual.* New York: Academic Press, pp. 197–228.

condition called **antidiuresis**, resulting in swollen fingers, hands, and feet. This effect is more pronounced if salty foods (peanuts or pretzels, for example) have been eaten along with the alcohol.

The inhibition of ADH during the drinking of alcoholic beverages can be a serious concern, particularly following vigorous exercise when the body is already suffering from a loss of water and fluid levels are low. Therefore, the advice to the marathoner, whose body may lose more than a gallon of water over the course of a warm three-hour run, is not to celebrate the end of the race with a beer but with nonintoxicating liquids such as Gatorade or similar mineral-rich drinks.[27]

Cardiovascular Effects

Long-term, excessive consumption of alcohol increases the risk of heart disease, elevated blood pressure, and stroke. These chronic effects will be examined more closely in Chapter 11. In addition, when alcohol consumption continues for at least two days in an extended bout of drinking (the more extreme definition of binge drinking), the acute effects can be severe. In these cases, there is an increased likelihood of cardiac arrhythmia, owing to the lowered threshold for ventricular fibrillation and the scarring of heart muscle. Cardiovascular deaths reported by emergency departments in hospitals around the world that peak in frequency on Mondays and during weekends have been attributed, at least in part, to increased cardiovascular risk within this subpopulation of heavy drinkers.[28]

Effects on Sleep

It might seem tempting to induce sleep with a relaxing "nightcap," but in fact the resulting sleep patterns are adversely affected. Alcohol reduces the duration of a phase of sleep called rapid eye movement (REM) sleep (Chapter 8). Depending on the dose, REM sleep can be either partially or completely suppressed during the night. When alcohol is withdrawn, REM sleep rebounds and represents a higher percentage of total sleep time than before alcohol consumption began. As a result, individuals sleep poorly and experience nightmares.[29]

Effects on Pregnancy

The consumption of alcohol during pregnancy, even in moderation, greatly increases the risk of retardation in the development of the fetus, and a reduction in the incidence of this behavior has been a major public health objective since 1995. Unfortunately, surveys of pregnant women reporting in 1999 a consumption of five or more alcoholic drinks on a single occasion or seven or more drinks per week did not decline from the numbers reported in 1995. However, those women reporting total abstinence during their pregnancy increased from 84 to 87 percent. National public health goals for the United States in 2010 include increasing this percentage to 94 percent.[30]

Interactions with Other Drugs

A very serious concern is the complex interaction of alcohol with many drugs. As noted in Chapter 1, the DAWN reports of emergency department admissions and deaths show an extremely high incidence of medical crises arising from the combination of alcohol not only with prescribed medications but also with virtually all the illicit drugs on the street. Opiates and opiate-like drugs, marijuana, and many prescription medicines interact with alcohol such that the resulting combination produces effects that are either the sum of the parts or greater than the sum of the parts. In other cases, the ingestion of medications with alcohol significantly lessens the medication's benefits. Anticoagulants, anticonvulsants, and monoamine oxidase inhibitors (used as an antidepressant medication) fit into this second category. Table 10.4 shows a partial listing of major therapeutic drugs that interact with alcohol with undesirable, if not dangerous, outcomes. The complete list is so lengthy that it is fair to say that, whenever any medication is taken, the individual should inquire about possible interactions with alcohol.

Hangovers

About four to twelve hours after heavy consumption of alcohol, usually the next day, unpleasant symptoms of headache, nausea, fatigue, and thirst may occur, collectively known as the *hangover*. At least one such experience has been reported by 40 percent of all men and 27 percent of all women over the age of eighteen.[31] Why these symptoms occur is not at all clear. The probable explanations at present focus on individual aspects of a hangover, though it is likely that several factors contribute to the total phenomenon.

antidiuresis: A condition resulting from excessive reabsorption of water in the kidneys.

TABLE 10.4

A partial listing of possible drug-alcohol interactions

GENERIC DRUG (BRAND NAME OR TYPE)	CONDITION BEING TREATED	EFFECT OF INTERACTION
chloral hydrate (Noctec)	Insomnia	Excessive sedation that can be fatal; irregular heartbeat; flushing
glutethimide (Doriden)	Insomnia	Excessive sedation; reduced driving and machine-operating skills
antihypertensives (Apresoline, Diuril)	High blood pressure	Exaggeration of blood pressure–lowering effect; dizziness on rising
diuretics (Aldactone)	High blood pressure	Exaggeration of blood pressure–lowering effect; dizziness on rising
antibiotics (penicillin)	Bacterial infections	Reduced therapeutic effectiveness
nitroglycerin (Nitro-bid)	Angina pain	Severe decrease in blood pressure; intense flushing; headache; dizziness on rising
warfarin (Coumadin)	Blood clot	Decreased anti-blood-clotting effect, easy bruising
insulin	Diabetes	Excessive low blood sugar; nausea; flushing
disulfiram (Antabuse)	Alcoholic drinking	Intense flushing; severe headache; vomiting; heart palpitations; could be fatal
methotrexate	Various cancers	Increased risk of liver damage
phenytoin (Dilantin)	Epileptic seizures	Reduced drug effectiveness in preventing seizures; drowsiness
prednisone (Deltasone)	Inflammatory conditions (arthritis, bursitis)	Stomach irritation
various antihistamines	Nasal congestion	Excessive sedation that could be fatal
acetaminophen (Tylenol)	Pain	Increased risk of liver damage

Sources: National Institute on Alcohol Abuse and Alcoholism (1995, January). Alcohol alert: Alcohol–medication interactions. No. 27, PH355. Bethesda, MD: National Institute on Alcohol Abuse and Alcoholism. Office of Substance Abuse Prevention (1988). *The fact is . . . It's dangerous to drink alcohol while taking certain medications.* Rockville, MD: National Institute on Drug Abuse. Parker, Christy (1985). *Simple facts about combinations with other drugs.* Phoenix, AZ: Do It Now Foundation.

One factor, beyond the simple fact of drinking too much, is the type of alcohol that has been consumed. Among distilled spirits, for example, vodka has a lower probability of inducing hangovers than whiskey. A possible reason is the relatively lower amount of **congeners**. These are substances in alcoholic beverages, including trace amounts of nonethyl alcohol, oils, and other organic matter, that are by-products of the fermentation and distillation processes and give the drinks their distinctive smell, taste, and color. A common congener is the tannin found in red wines. Although no harm is caused by congeners in minute concentrations, they are still toxic substances and, most likely, contribute to hangover symptoms.[32]

Other possible factors include traces of nonoxidized acetaldehyde in the blood, residual irritation in the stomach, and a low blood sugar level rebounding from the high levels induced by the previous ingestion of alcohol. The feeling of swollenness from the antidiuresis, discussed earlier, may contribute to the headache pain. The thirst may be due to the dehydration that occurred the night before.

Numerous "remedies" for a hangover have been concocted over the centuries, but it appears that the best treatment consists of rest, an analgesic medication for the headache, and the passage of time. Since the hangover can be considered basically as a collection of symptoms of withdrawal from alcohol, some people have taken to the remedy of consuming more alcohol, a strategy known as "the hair of the dog that bit you." This approach can relieve the symptoms, but it merely delays the inevitable consequences and leads to further alcohol use. Recently, herbal products have been marketed as hangover remedies or even preventives, but their effectiveness remains untested. As a spokesman for a major alcohol abuse treatment center has put it, "The best advice I can give in regard to 'hangover teas and pills' would be to avoid the need for them."[33]

congeners (KON-jen-ers): Nonethyl alcohols, oils, and other organic substances found in trace amounts in some distilled spirits.

Acute Behavioral Effects

The consumption of alcoholic beverages is so pervasive in the world that it seems almost unnecessary to comment on how it feels to be intoxicated by alcohol. The behavioral effects of consuming alcohol in more than very moderate quantities range from the relatively harmless effects of exhilaration and excitement, talkativeness, slurred speech, and irritability to behaviors that have the potential for causing great harm: uncoordinated movement, drowsiness, sensorimotor difficulties, and stupor.[34] Some of the prominent behavioral problems associated with acute alcohol intoxication will be examined in this section.

Every community has its tragic stories of preventable deaths due to drunk driving. Alcohol is also recognized as a major factor in more than 800 boating fatalities in the United States each year.

Blackouts

A **blackout** is an inability to remember events that occurred during the period of intoxication, even though the individual was conscious at the time. For example, a drinker having too much to drink at a party drives home, parks the car on a nearby street, and goes to bed. The next morning, he or she has no memory of having driven home and cannot locate the car. Owing to the possibility of blackouts, drinkers can be easily misled into thinking that because they can understand some information given to them during drinking, they will remember it later. The risk of blackouts is greatest when alcohol is consumed very quickly, forcing the BAC to rise rapidly. In a recent e-mail survey of college students to learn more about their experiences with blackouts, approximately half of those who had ever consumed alcohol reported having experienced a blackout at some point in their lives and 40 percent reported having had at least one experience in the twelve months prior to the survey.[35]

Driving Skills

There is no question that alcohol consumption significantly impairs the ability to drive or deal with automobile traffic, particularly among young people. In 2006, of the 42,600 traffic fatalities that occurred in the United States, approximately 15,100 of them (about 35 percent) were alcohol-related. To put this statistic in better perspective, there were approximately forty-one alcohol-related fatalities every day during that year.

blackout: Amnesia concerning events occurring during the period of alcoholic intoxication, even though consciousness had been maintained at that time.

These circumstances involved drivers who had a BAC of 0.08 percent or higher, the minimum standard for legal intoxication in all U.S. states, as of 2005.

It is important to recognize that a BAC level of 0.08 percent does not have to be reached to cause impairment in driving. It has been estimated that the risk of a single-vehicle fatal crash escalates rapidly as alcohol consumption increases. Relative to drivers who have not consumed any alcohol at all, those with BAC levels between 0.02 and 0.04 percent have a 40 percent greater risk. When BAC levels are between 0.05 and 0.09 percent, the risk is 11 times greater; when BAC levels are between 0.10 and 0.14 percent, the risk is 48 times greater; when BAC levels are above 0.15 percent, the risk is 380 times greater. Therefore, it is quite possible for an accident to occur even though the driver is not officially "driving while intoxicated" (DWI).[36]

All these statistics could be viewed as correlational and not necessarily proof of a causal relationship between alcohol and automobile accidents, were it not for the data from laboratory-based experiments showing a clear deterioration of sensorimotor skills following the ingestion of alcohol. Reaction times are significantly prolonged, the coordination necessary to steer a car steadily is hampered, and the ability to stay awake when fatigued is impaired following BAC levels as low as 0.03 percent.[37]

More important, however, is a major decline in the ability to be aware of peripheral events and stimuli. One researcher in this area expresses the deficit in this way:

The overwhelming majority of accidents involving alcohol are not accidents in which tracking is the prime error. Contrary to what most people think, it isn't that people are weaving down the road, which is a sign of very high blood alcohol levels; it's that they have failed to see something. They go through a red light, they fail to see a pedestrian or a motorcyclist, they fail to see that the road is curving. Their perceptual and attentive mechanisms are affected very early, after just one drink. These are the things that are the prime causes of accidents.[38]

Unfortunately, it is the weaving behavior, or other extreme examples of driving impairments, that most often signals the police to stop a car for a possible DWI violation; other impairments frequently go unnoticed until it is too late. Figure 10.1 illustrates a recent technology designed to monitor alcohol consumption of repeated DWI offenders on an on-going basis, as a deterrent against future DWI offenses.

Increasing the minimum age for alcoholic consumption from eighteen to twenty-one, now mandated throughout the United States, has had a major impact on the likelihood of accident fatalities among young people. During the early 1980s, when changes in the minimum age were taking place state by state, it was possible to anticipate the improvements that could be made. On average, fatal nighttime accidents involving eighteen- and nineteen-year-old drivers decreased 13 percent between 1975 and 1984 in twenty-six states that raised the minimum drinking age during that interval. A decrease of 16 percent in nighttime accidents in Michigan following the change in the drinking law was maintained six years later.[39]

With the minimum age now set at twenty-one years and the minimum BAC level for intoxication lowered to 0.08 percent, there is reason to be cautiously optimistic. According to estimates made by the National Highway Traffic Safety Administration, the reduction of the minimum BAC level to 0.08 percent has saved five hundred lives each year on the nation's highways. In 1998, a nationwide minimum level of intoxication for drivers younger than twenty-one years of age was set at a BAC

(a)

(b)

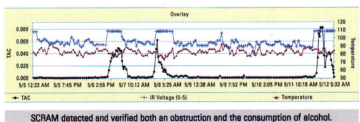

Verifiable four-day drinking event.

SCRAM detected and verified both an obstruction and the consumption of alcohol.

(c)

FIGURE 10.1

Recent technologies, such as the Secure Continuous Remote Alcohol Monitoring (SCRAM), have been developed to monitor alcohol consumption of DWI offenders on probation by measuring BAC levels in the perspiration of the skin. An 8-ounce sensor device is strapped to the ankle. A transmitter in the ankle bracelet (a) sends BAC information to a remote computer (b) that produces an ongoing record of alcohol consumption (c).

Source: Alcohol Monitoring Systems, Inc. Givens, Ann (2006, August 25). Braced against DWI. *Newsday*, p. A3.

In 1980, Candace Lightner's thirteen-year-old daughter, Cari, was killed by a hit-and-run intoxicated driver in California. The driver had been out of jail on bail for only two days, a consequence of another hit-and-run drunk driving crash, and he had three previous drunk driving arrests and two previous convictions. He was allowed to plea bargain to vehicular manslaughter. Although the sentence was to serve two years in prison, the judge allowed him to serve time in a work camp and later a halfway house.

It was appalling to Lightner that drunk drivers, similar to the one who had killed her daughter, were receiving such lenient treatment, with many of them never going to jail for a single day. Lightner quit her job and started an organization that has become a household name: Mothers Against Drunk Driving (MADD).

Since then, MADD has campaigned for stricter laws against drunk driving, and most of the present DWI legislation around the country is a result of its intense efforts. In addition, MADD acts as a voice for victims of drunk-driving injuries and the families of those who have been killed. From a single act of courage, despite enormous grief, Lightner has spawned an organization that boasts more than 3 million members in the United States, with groups in virtually every state and more than four hundred local chapters.

More recently, MADD has set for itself the goal of reducing the number of all traffic fatalities associated with alcohol drinking. In 2005, the percentage was 39 (down from 45 in 1992). These are some of the group's proposals for change:

1. More effective enforcement of the minimum-drinking-age law.
2. A "0.00 percent BAC" criterion for drivers under twenty-one, making it illegal to drive with *any* measurable level of blood alcohol in any state. In 1998, the criterion of 0.02 percent was set nationwide for drivers under twenty-one years of age.
3. Driver's license suspensions for underage persons convicted of purchasing or possession of alcoholic beverages.
4. Alcohol-free zones for youth gatherings.
5. Criminal sanctions against adults who provide or allow alcoholic beverages at events for underage participants.
6. Mandatory alcohol and drug testing for all drivers in all traffic crashes resulting in fatalities or serious bodily injury.
7. Sobriety checkpoints to detect and apprehend alcohol-impaired drivers and as a visible deterrent to drinking and driving.

Source: Information courtesy of Mothers Against Drunk Driving, Dallas, Texas, 2006. Interview with Candace Lightner.

---

level of 0.02 percent. Prior to 1998, averaging across fourteen years during which thirty U.S. individual states had adopted their own reduced minimum BAC levels for youths, the frequency with which high school seniors reported having driven after drinking any alcohol declined by 19 percent and the frequency with which they reported having driven after drinking five drinks or more declined by 23 percent. In addition, educational programs in schools and communities emphasizing the advantage of "designated drivers" as well as public education and lobbying groups such as Mothers Against Drunk Driving (MADD) and Students Against Drunk Driving (SADD) have had positive effects (see Portrait).[40]

Even so, much work remains to be done. The United States presently has one of the most lenient standards for driving while intoxicated among nations in the world (Table 10.5). The number of alcohol-related accidents, particularly among male drivers, whose involvement

TABLE 10.5

Blood alcohol concentration at which drivers in different nations are legally drunk.

BAC	0.00+	0.02	0.03	0.05	0.08
COUNTRY	Czech Republic, Slovakia Hungary	Norway, Poland, Sweden	Japan, China	Argentina, Australia, Costa Rica, Denmark, Finland France, Italy, Germany, Greece, Netherlands, Peru, Russia, South Africa, Spain, Thailand	Brazil, Britain, Canada, Chile, Ecuador, Ireland, Jamaica, New Zealand, Singapore, United States

Sources: Valenti, John (2005, July 13). U.S. lags others in DWI toughness. *Newsday,* p. A15.

exceeds that of female drivers by a factor of more than 2:1, is far too high. Meanwhile, the drinking-and-driving phenomenon is widespread throughout the population. In 2006, approximately 31 million people over the age of twelve (about 12 percent of the U.S. population) reported drinking and driving during the past year, with the peak age being between twenty-one and twenty-five.[41]

Alcohol, Violence, and Aggression

It is difficult to avoid sweeping generalizations when confronted with statistics about alcohol and violent behavior both in the United States and in other countries. In a major study conducted in a community in northwestern Ontario, Canada, reported in 1991, more than 50 percent of the most recent occasions of physical violence were found to be preceded by alcohol use on the part of the assailant and/or the victims themselves.[42] Other studies show from 50 to 60 percent of all

murders being committed when the killer had been drinking. About 40 percent of all acts of male sexual aggression against adult women and from 60 to 70 percent of male-instigated domestic violence occur when the offender has been drunk; more than 60 percent of all acts of child molestation involve drunkenness.[43]

Researchers have advanced several theories to account for the linkage between alcohol intoxication and violent behavior. The traditional *disinhibition theory* holds that alcohol on a pharmacological level impairs normal cortical mechanisms responsible for inhibiting the expression of innate or suppressed aggressive inclinations. Another viewpoint, referred to as the *cognitive-expectation theory*, holds that learned beliefs or expectations about alcohol's effects can facilitate aggressive behaviors. This second theory implies that violence is induced by virtue of the act of drinking combined with one's personal view of how a person is "supposed to respond" rather than by the pharmacological effects of alcohol itself (Drugs . . . in Focus).[44]

Drugs . . . in Focus

Alcohol, Security, and Spectator Sports

The National Basketball Association (NBA) issued in 2005 a new set of security guidelines for all thirty teams, including a Fan Code of Conduct specifying that "guests will enjoy the basketball experience free from disruptive behavior, including foul or abusive language or obscene gestures." In the words of NBA Commissioner David Stern, "We look at this as an opportunity to remind people that coming to an arena is an opportunity to share an experience of rooting a home team on to victory and booing the opposition, but not doing it in an antisocial way that goes against our civil society."

Acknowledging the connection between disruptive behavior and alcohol, the NBA now bans alcohol sales during the fourth quarter of every game and imposes a 24-ounce limit on the size of alcoholic drinks sold in an arena, with a maximum of two alcoholic drinks per customer. It is presently unclear how the two-drink limit has been enforced.

Increased security measures and restrictions on alcohol sales came about after basketball players and fans brawled in the stands and on the court at the end of a game in November 2004 between the Indiana Pacers and Detroit Pistons. Indiana's Ron Artest went into the seats

after being hit by a full cup of beer that had been tossed by a spectator. As a result of the melee, considered to be one of the most violent episodes in NBA history, Artest was suspended for the rest of the 2004–2005 season and other players were given suspensions of as many as thirty games. All told, ten players and fans were charged with fighting.

Alcohol consumption has also come under scrutiny during college and professional football games, where binge drinking at tailgating parties and after-game celebrations frequently results in property damage and sometimes leads to injuries or deaths. At the University of Virginia, a tradition that began in the 1980s has seniors individually drinking a fifth of liquor by kickoff time at the final game of the football season (the so-called "Fourth-Year Fifth"). This practice has been associated with the deaths of eighteen students between 1990 and 2002. A university organization, Fourth-years Acting Responsibly (FAR), has been set up to increase awareness of this problem and reduce alcohol-related incidents.

Sources: Eskenazi, Gerald (2005, December 21). For Patriots and Jets, a sobering experience. *New York Times,* p. D3. Football, tailgating parties, and alcohol safety (2005, October 1). *The NCADI Reporter.* Bethesda, MD: National Clearinghouse for Drug Information. NBA issuing sterner security, beer guidelines. *USA Today.com,* accessed May 8, 2005.

Expectations about the consequences of drug-taking behavior or of any behavior at all, as noted in Chapter 1, are studied experimentally through the placebo research design. In the case of the cognitive-expectation theory, it is necessary to use a variation of this design, called the **balanced placebo design**. Subjects are randomly divided into four groups. Two groups are given an alcoholic drink, with one group being told that they are ingesting alcohol and the other that they are ingesting a nonalcohol substitute that tastes and smells like alcohol. Two other groups are given the nonalcohol substitute, with one group being told that they are ingesting this substitute and the other that they are ingesting alcohol.

Studies using the balanced placebo design have shown clearly that beliefs (mind-sets) concerning the effects of drinking are more influential in determining a subject's behavior than the more direct physiological effects of the alcohol. In other words, *what they are told they are consuming is more important than what they consume.* Unfortunately, for a true test of the cognitive-expectation theory, a balanced placebo design cannot be used with BAC levels above 0.035 percent because subjects are no longer fooled by the deception with larger quantities, and most alcohol-associated acts of violence occur with BAC levels at least six times higher.[45]

Sex and Sexual Desire

If they were asked, most people would say that alcohol has an enhancing or aphrodisiac effect on sexual desire and performance. The actual effect of alcohol, however, is more complex than these commonly held beliefs express. In fact, it is because of these beliefs that people are frequently more susceptible to the expectations of what alcohol *should* do for them than they are to the actual physiological effects of alcohol.

To examine the complex relationship between alcohol and sex, we need to turn again to studies using the balanced placebo design. The general results from such studies are quite different for men and women. Among men, those who expected to be receiving low levels of alcohol had greater penile responses, reported greater subjective arousal, and spent more time watching erotic pictures, *regardless of whether they did indeed receive alcohol.* When alcohol concentrations rise to levels that

reflect genuine intoxication, however, the pharmacological actions outweigh the expectations, and the overall effect is definitely inhibitory. Men who are drunk have less sexual desire and a decreased capacity to perform sexually.

In contrast, expectations among women play a lesser role. They are more inclined to react to the pharmacological properties of alcohol itself, but the direction of their response depends on whether we are talking about subjective or physiological measures. For women receiving increasing alcohol concentrations, measures of subjective arousal increase, but measures of vaginal arousal decrease. Ironically, the pattern of their responses mirrors Shakespeare's quotation in *Macbeth* that alcohol "provokes the desire, but it takes away from the performance," a comment originally intended to reflect only the male point of view.[46]

Alcohol and Health Benefits

The documented health benefits of moderate levels of alcohol consumption over the last thirty years of research have presented a major dilemma among medical and public health professionals. The crux of the dilemma is that moderate amounts of alcohol can possibly save your life, while immoderate amounts can possibly destroy it. As one writer has expressed it, "Alcohol has become the sharpest double-edged sword in medicine."

It started as an observation that did not seem to make sense. Epidemiological studies of French and other European populations who consumed large amounts of butter, cheese, liver, and other animal fats—a diet associated with elevated cholesterol and an elevated risk for coronary failure—found that these populations had a remarkably low incidence of coronary heart disease. The answer seemed to be that relatively more alcohol was consumed along with their dietary food. The "French paradox" was resolved when later research showed that alcohol increases high-density lipoprotein (HDL) cholesterol (the so-called good cholesterol) levels in the blood, with HDL acting as a protective mechanism against a possible restriction of blood flow through arteries. The greatest benefit was seen in those individuals who had high concentrations of low-density lipoprotein (LDL) cholesterol (the so-called bad cholesterol) and therefore had the greatest risk for coronary heart disease. It was estimated that consumption of approximately 8 ounces of wine (a bit less than two standard drinks) per day resulted in a 25 percent reduction in the risk of coronary heart disease.[47]

---

balanced placebo design: An experimental design that can separate psychological effects (due to subjective expectations) and physiological effects (due to the pharmacology of the drug).

Moderate alcohol intake reduces the risk of diabetes mellitus, reduces the risk of stroke, and reduces the risk of dementia (possibly by reducing the incidence of mini-strokes or by boosting concentrations of vitamin B_6, which is essential for the formation of essential brain chemicals).[48]

Of course, the key to the health benefits of alcohol consumption lies in its moderation. Moderate drinking has been defined as taking no more than one drink per day for women and no more than two drinks per day for men. The newest (2000) Dietary Guidelines for Americans, released by the U.S. Department of Agriculture and the U.S. Department of Health and Human Services, acknowledge the effect of alcohol on reducing the risk of coronary heart disease but limits the recommendation of moderate drinking to men over age forty-five and women over age fifty-five, a subpopulation that carries an elevated risk for the disease.

Despite the weight of evidence tilting toward the potential health benefits of alcohol, the medical field remains divided on the question of whether to encourage patients who do not drink alcohol to start at a moderate level of consumption. In some cases, moderate intake is not advisable. Even one drink per day slightly increases the risk for breast cancer in women, and in no circumstances should alcohol be consumed during pregnancy.

Some public health researchers are concerned that an endorsement of moderate alcohol drinking may open up a range of possible risks, in effect giving alcohol a kind of "halo effect" that might be confusing to the public. In any case, public opinion remains unconvinced that moderate alcohol consumption has health benefits. About three-fourths (73 percent) of American adults believe that it is either bad for one's health or makes no difference one way or another, a perception that has remained unchanged since this survey question was first asked in 2001.[49]

Frequently, the focus is on wine consumption, and particularly red wine consumption, but the accumulated research findings indicate that beneficial health effects can result from the consumption of *any* type of alcoholic beverage, whether it is beer, wine, or liquor. And the benefits extend beyond coronary heart disease.

Strategies for Responsible Social Drinking

The various negative acute effects of alcohol on physiological responses and behavior have been considered. Yet it is necessary to remember that there are very large numbers of people who drink alcoholic beverages and avoid the adverse effects that have been detailed here. An overwhelming proportion of the population, for example, drink on occasion and have never engaged in any violent or aggressive acts. They drink in moderate

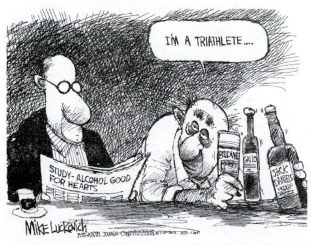

A modern-day medical dilemma: health benefits of moderate alcohol consumption versus the potential for alcohol abuse. (By permission of Mike Luckovich and Creators Syndicate, Inc.)

amounts, according to the federal guidelines for diet and nutrition. In addition, they avoid situations (such as driving) in which alcohol consumption would impair their performance and endanger their lives. The issue of responsible drinking is an important one; it may not be easy for us to accomplish but, fortunately, guidelines exist that make it easier.[50] Help Line features some strategies to reduce the problems associated with alcoholic intake.

At the same time, however, we must remember that, regardless of how it is consumed, alcohol remains a drug with a significant potential for dependence. It is not difficult to get hooked. As it has been said, people may plan to get drunk, but no one plans to be an alcoholic. The problems surrounding chronic alcohol abuse and alcoholism will be examined in the next chapter.

HELP LINE

Guidelines for Responsible Social Drinking

- **Know how much you are drinking.** Measure your drinks. Beer is often premeasured (unless you are drinking draft beer from a keg), but wine and liquor drinks frequently are not. Learn what a 5-ounce quantity of wine or a 1½-ounce shot of liquor looks like, and use these measures to guide your drinking.

- **Choose beer or wine over liquor.** Beer especially will make you feel fuller more quickly, with a smaller intake of alcohol. But be careful. A 12-ounce beer is equivalent in alcohol content to a 5-ounce glass of wine or a 1-shot drink of liquor.

- **Drink slowly.** One drink an hour stays relatively even with your body's metabolism of the alcohol you consume. Sipping your drinks is a good strategy for slowing down your consumption. If you are a man, you'll look cool; if you are a woman, you'll look refined.

- **Don't cluster your drinking.** If you are going to have seven drinks during a week, don't drink them all on the weekend.

- **Eat something substantial while you are drinking.** Protein is an excellent accompaniment to alcohol. Avoid salty foods because they will make you thirstier and more inclined to have another drink.

- **Drink only when you are already relaxed.** Chronic alcohol abuse occurs more easily when alcohol is viewed as a way to relax. If you have a problem, seek some nondrug alternative.

- **When you drink, savor the experience.** If you focus on the quality of what you drink rather than the quantity you are drinking, you will avoid drinking too much.

- **Never drink alone.** Drinking cannot be dealt with as an answer to social isolation. Besides, having people around you provides the means for someone to look out for you.

- **Beware of unfamiliar drinks.** Some drinks, such as zombies and other fruit and rum drinks, are deceptively high in kinds of alcohol that are not easily detected by taste.

- **Never drive a car after having had a drink.** Driving impairment begins after very low quantities of alcohol consumption.

- **Be a good host or hostess.** If you are serving alcohol at a party, do not make drinking the focus of activity. Do not refill your guests' glasses. Discourage intoxication and do not condone drunkenness. Provide transportation options for those who drink at your party. Present nonalcoholic beverages as prominently as alcoholic ones. Prior to the end of the party, stop serving alcohol and offer coffee or other warm nonalcoholic beverages and a substantial snack, providing an interval of nondrinking time before people leave.

- **Support organizations that encourage responsible drinking.** If you are on a college campus, get involved with the local chapter of BACCHUS (Boost Alcohol Consciousness Concerning the Health of University Students). If there is no chapter, start one.

Where to go for assistance:

www.indiana.edu/~engs/hints/holiday.html

This web site on sensible, moderate, and responsible alcohol consumption and party hosting is adapted from Engs, R. C. (1987). *Alcohol and other drugs: Self-responsibility.* Bloomington, IN: Tichenor Publishing.

Sources: Gross, Leonard (1983). *How much is too much? The effects of social drinking.* New York: Random House, pp. 149–152. Hanson, David J., and Engs, Ruth C. (1994). Drinking behavior: Taking personal responsibility. In Peter J. Venturelli (Ed.), *Drug use in America: Social, cultural, and political perspectives.* Boston: Jones and Bartlett, pp. 175–181. *Managing alcohol in your life.* Mansfield, MA: Steele Publishing and Consulting.

Summary

What Makes an Alcoholic Beverage?

- Drinkable alcohol is obtained from the fermentation of sugar in some natural products such as grapes, apples, honey, or molasses. The result is some form of wine.

- Beer is obtained from barley, after the starch has first been converted into sugar and then fermented along with other grains and hops, and aged.

- To obtain very strong alcoholic beverages, it is necessary to boil the fermented liquid and condense it later by cooling. This process, called distillation, results in alcohol concentrations of up to 95 percent, and the products are known as distilled spirits or liquors.

Alcohol Use through History

- The history of alcohol use dates back many thousands of years; the process of fermentation is very simple and its discovery was probably accidental.

- Distillation techniques were perfected during the Middle Ages, with brandy being the first distilled spirit. In later centuries, gin gained popularity in Europe, as did whiskey in the United States.

Patterns of Alcohol Consumption Today

- The demographics of alcohol consumption reveal a large disparity in the drinking habits of the population. About a third do not drink at all, and only about 30 percent of those who drink account for 80 percent of all the alcoholic beverages consumed in the United States.

- Peak alcohol consumption occurs at ages twenty-one to twenty-two.

The Pharmacology of Alcohol

- Alcohol is a very small molecule, easily soluble in both water and fat. Its absorption into the bloodstream is extremely rapid. The breakdown of alcohol is handled by two special enzymes in the stomach and liver.

- The rate of alcohol biodegradation is constant, so alcohol can only leave the body at a specific pace, despite the quantity taken in.

- The effective level of alcohol in the body is measured by the blood-alcohol concentration (BAC) level, which adjusts for differences in body weight and the time since ingestion of the last alcoholic beverage.

Effects of Alcohol on the Brain

- Although alcohol affects several neurotransmitters in the brain, it is presently agreed that the principal effect is the stimulation of the GABA receptor.

- Generally, the neural effect of alcohol proceeds downward, beginning with an inhibition of the cerebral cortex, then lower brain regions. Inhibition of respiratory systems in the medulla, usually accomplished at BAC levels in the neighborhood of 0.50 percent, results in asphyxiation and death.

Acute Physiological Effects

- Alcohol at very high levels produces life-threatening consequences and at moderate levels produces a loss of body heat, increased excretion of water, an increase in heart rate and constriction of coronary arteries, disturbed patterns of sleep, and serious interactions with other drugs.

Acute Behavioral Effects

- On a behavioral level, serious adverse effects include blackouts, significant impairment in sensorimotor skills such as driving an automobile, and an increased potential for aggressive or violent acts.

- The relationship between alcohol consumption and sexual desire and performance is a complex one, with differences being observed for men and women.

Alcohol and Health Benefits

- The accumulated evidence of medical research has indicated that there is a reduced risk for coronary heart disease and stroke with moderate consumption levels of alcohol. Possible health benefits may also include a reduction of risk for diabetes and dementia.

- Moderate alcohol consumption has been defined as no more than one drink per day for women and no more than two drinks per day for men. There should be zero tolerance for alcohol consumption among pregnant women.

Strategies for Responsible Social Drinking

- Despite the potential for alcohol consumption to produce adverse effects, most people can drink alcohol in a responsible way that avoids these harmful consequences. However, the risk of alcohol dependence is always present.

Key Terms

acetaldehyde, p. 252
acetaldehyde
    dehydrogenase, p. 252
acetic acid, p. 252
alcohol dehydrogenase,
    p. 252
antidiuresis, p. 256

antidiuretic hormone
    (ADH), p. 255
aqua vitae, p. 243
balanced placebo design,
    p. 262
barley malt, p. 242
blackout, p. 258

blood-alcohol concentration
    (BAC), p. 252
brewing, p. 242
congeners, p. 257
distillation, p. 242
distilled spirits, p. 243
ethyl alcohol, p. 242

fermentation, p. 242
mash, p. 242
oxidation, p. 252
temperance movement,
    p. 245

Endnotes

1. Pinel, John P. J. (2003). *Biopsychology* (5th ed.). Boston: Allyn and Bacon, p. 381.
2. Gibbons, Boyd (1992, February). Alcohol: The legal drug. *National Geographic Magazine*, pp. 2–35. Roueché, Berton (1963). Alcohol in human culture. In Salvatore P. Lucia (Ed.), *Alcohol and civilization.* New York: McGraw-Hill, pp. 167–182. Vallee, Bert L. (1998, June). Alcohol in the western world. *Scientific American*, pp. 80–85.
3. McGovern, Patrick E.; Glusker, Donald L.; Exner, Lawrence J.; and Voigt, Mary M. (1996). Neolithic resinated wine. *Nature, 381*, 480–481.
4. Sournia, Jean-Charles (1990). *A history of alcoholism.* Cambridge, MA: Basil Blackwell, pp. 14–50. U.S. Department of Health, Education, and Welfare (1978). *Perspectives on the history of psychoactive substance use*, pp. 67–75.
5. Grimes, William (1993). *Straight up or on the rocks: A cultural history of American drink.* New York: Simon and Schuster, p. 36. Musto, David F. (1996, April). Alcohol in American history. *Scientific American*, pp. 78–83.
6. Lender, Mark E., and Martin, James K. (1982). *Drinking in America: A history.* New York: Free Press, pp. 13–14.
7. First in war, peace—and hooch, by George! (2000, December 7). *Newsday*, p. A86. Grimes, *Straight up*, p. 51.
8. Gibbons, Alcohol, p. 7.
9. Garfield, Craig F., Chung, Paul J., and Rathouz, Paul J. (2003). Alcohol advertising in magazines and adolescent readership. *Journal of the American Medical Association, 289*, 2424–2429. Hanson, Glen R., and Li, Ting-Kai (2003). Public health implications of excessive alcohol consumption. *Journal of the American Medical Association, 289*, 1031–1032. US top five beer companies ranked by prime-time network television advertising outlays in dollars with the top three network TV programs ranked by beer ad expenditures. *Adweek* (2003, April 21), p. SR14.
10. Statistics on 1998 consumption from Holleran, Joan (1999, May). Drinking up: U.S. alcoholic beverage consumption in gallons per capita by type (beer, wine, distilled spirits) in 1993 and 1998. *Beverage Industry*, pp.

17–21. Statistics on 2000 consumption from World Health Statistical Information System (2003). *Alcohol: A global overview.* Geneva: World Health Organization, Table 2.
11. Center for Science in the Public Interest (2003, December 16). Press release: "Alcohol facts" label proposed for beer, wine, and liquor. Center for Science in the Public Interest, Washington DC. Rogers, John D., and Greenfield, Thomas K. (1999). Beer drinking accounts for most of the hazardous alcohol consumption reported in the United States. *Journal of Studies on Alcohol, 60*, 732–739.
12. The Gallup Organization (2006, July 9). Alcohol and drinking. Gallup Organization, Princeton, NJ.
13. Dawson, Deborah A., Grant, Bridget F., and Chou, Patricia S. (1995). Gender differences in alcohol intake. In Walter A. Hunt and Sam Zakhari (Eds.), *Stress, gender, and alcohol-seeking behavior* (NIAAA Research Monograph 29). Bethesda, MD: National Institute on Alcohol Abuse and Alcoholism, pp. 1–21. Heien, Dale (1996). The relationship between alcohol consumption and earnings. *Journal of Studies on Alcohol, 57*, 536–542.
14. Denizet-Lewis, Benoit (2005, January 5). Band of brothers. *New York Times Magazine*, pp. 32–33, 52, 73–74. Hingson, Ralph W.; Heeren, Timothy; Zakocs, Ronda C.; and Kopstein, Andrea (2002). Age of first intoxication, heavy drinking, driving after drinking and risk of unintentional injury among U.S. college students. *Journal of Studies on Alcohol, 63*, 136–144. Wechsler, Henry; Lee, Jae Eun; Kuo, Meichun; Seibring, Mark; Nelson, Toben F.; and Lee, Hang (2002). Trends in college binge drinking during a period of increased prevention efforts: Findings from four Harvard School of Public Health College Alcohol Study Surveys: 1993–2001. *Journal of American College Health, 50*, 203–217. Who's drinking? More than half of underage college students (2006, November/December). *SAMHSA News*, p. 9. Zernike, Kate (2005, March 15). A 21st-birthday drinking game can be a deadly rite of passage. *New York Times*, pp. A1, A13.
15. Foster, Susan E.; Vaughan, Roger D.; Foster, William H.; and Califano, Joseph A. (2003). Alcohol consumption and expenditures for underage drinking and adult excessive drinking. *Journal of the American Medical Association, 289*,

989–995. Johnston, Lloyd D.; O'Malley, Patrick M.; Bachman, Jerald G.; and Schulenberg, John E. (2007). *Monitoring the Future national results on adolescent drug use. Overview of key findings, 2006.* Bethesda, MD: National Institute on Drug Abuse, Tables 1 and 4. Radnofsky, Louise (2007, April 6). Outrage flows over Spykes. *Newsday,* p. A17.

16. U.S. Department of Health and Human Services (1990). *Alcohol and health.* (The Seventh Special Report to the U.S. Congress). Rockville, MD: National Institute on Alcohol Abuse and Alcoholism.

17. Dubowski, Kurt M. (1991). *The technology of breath-alcohol analysis.* Rockville, MD: National Institute on Alcohol Abuse and Alcoholism.

18. Julien, Robert M. (2000). *A primer of drug action* (9th ed.). New York: Worth, p. 95.

19. National Institute on Alcohol Abuse and Alcoholism (1997, January). Alcohol alert: Alcohol metabolism. No. 35, PH371. Bethesda, MD: National Institute on Alcohol Abuse and Alcoholism. Friedman, Nancy (1985, August–September). Anatomy of a drink. *Campus Voice,* pp. 61–63. Julien, *A primer of drug action,* pp. 91–97.

20. Suter, Paolo M., Schutz, Yves, and Jequier, Eric (1992). The effect of ethanol on fat storage in healthy subjects. *New England Journal of Medicine, 326,* 983–987.

21. Hawks, Richard L., and Chiang, C. Nora (1986). Examples of specific drug assays. In Richard L. Hawks and C. Nora Chiang (Eds.), *Urine testing for drugs of abuse* (NIDA Research Monograph 73). Rockville, MD: National Institute on Drug Abuse, p. 103. Julien, *A primer of drug action,* pp. 91–97.

22. Levinthal, Charles F. (1990). *Introduction to physiological psychology* (3rd ed.). Englewood Cliffs, NJ: Prentice Hall, pp. 181–184.

23. U.S. Department of Health and Human Services (1994). *Alcohol and health.* (The Eighth Special Report to the U.S. Congress). Bethesda, MD: National Institute on Alcohol Abuse and Alcoholism, pp. 4–6, 4–7.

24. Koob, G. F.; Rassnick, S.; Heinrichs, S.; and Weiss, F. (1994). Alcohol, the reward system and dependence. In B. Jansson, H. Jörnvall, U. Rydberg, L. Terenius, and B. L. Vallee (Eds.), *Toward a molecular basis of alcohol use and abuse.* Basel: Birkhäuser-Verlag, pp. 103–114. Schuckit, Marc A. (1994, August). Naltrexone and the treatment of alcoholism. *Drug Abuse and Alcoholism Newsletter,* San Diego, CA: Vista Hill Foundation.

25. Grilly, David M. (2006). *Drugs and human behavior* (5th ed.). Boston: Allyn and Bacon, p. 144.

26. Luks, Allan, and Barbato, Joseph (1989). *You are what you drink.* New York: Villiard, p. 44.

27. Ibid., pp. 42–43.

28. Chenet, Laurent, and Britton, Annie (2001). Weekend binge drinking may be linked to Monday peaks in cardiovascular deaths. *British Medical Journal, 322,* 998.

29. National Institute on Alcohol Abuse and Alcoholism (1998, July). Alcohol alert: Alcohol and sleep. No. 41. Bethesda, MD: National Institute on Alcohol Abuse and Alcoholism.

30. Morbidity and Mortality Weekly Report (2002). Alcohol use among women of childbearing age—United States, 1991–1999. *Journal of the American Medical Association, 287,* 2069–2071.

31. Schuckit, Marc A. (1989). *Drug and alcohol abuse: A clinical guide to diagnosis and treatment* (3rd ed.). New York: Plenum, p. 62.

32. Wiese, Jeffrey G., Shlipak, Michael G., and Browner, Warren S. (2000). The alcohol hangover. *Annals of Internal Medicine, 232,* 897–902.

33. Wotapka, Dawn (2003, May 20). Effects of hangover remedy still dim. *Newsday,* p. A39. Quotation by Ames Sweet of the National Council on Alcoholism and Drug Dependence, New York.

34. Victor, Maurice (1976). Treatment of alcohol intoxication and the withdrawal syndrome: A critical analysis of the use of drugs and other forms of therapy. In Peter G. Bourne (Ed.), *Acute drug emergencies: A treatment manual.* New York: Academic Press, p. 199.

35. Luks and Barbato, *You are what you drink,* pp. 52–53. White, Aaron M., Jamieson-Drake, David W., and Swartzwelder, H. Scott (2002). Prevalence and correlates of alcohol-induced blackouts among college students: Results of an e-mail survey. *Journal of American College Health, 51,* 117–131.

36. Alcohol-related traffic deaths over last decade increase in a third of states (2004, January). *NCADD Report.* Silver Springs, MD: National Commission Against Drunk Driving, p. 1. National Highway Traffic Safety Administration (2007, July). 2006 traffic safety annual assessment—A preview.

37. National Institute on Alcohol Abuse and Alcoholism (1994, July). Alcohol alert: Alcohol-related impairment. No. 25, PH351. Bethesda, MD: National Institute on Alcohol Abuse and Alcoholism.

38. Gross, Leonard (1983). *How much is too much: The effects of social drinking.* New York: Random House, p. 29. Quotation of Dr. Herbert Moskowitz.

39. Fortini, Mary-Ellen (1995). Youth, alcohol, and automobiles: Attitudes and behaviors. In Ronald R. Watson (Ed.), *Alcohol, cocaine, and accidents.* Totowa, NJ: Humana Press, pp. 25–39. National Institute on Alcohol Abuse and Alcoholism (2003, April). Alcohol Alert: Underage drinking: A major public health challenge, No. 59. Bethesda, MD: National Institute on Alcohol Abuse and Alcoholism. U.S. Department of Health and Human Services (1990). *Alcohol and health,* pp. 216–217. Wald, Matthew L. (2006, November 20). A new strategy to discourage driving drunk. *New York Times,* pp. A1, A20.

40. National Institute on Alcohol Abuse and Alcoholism (2001, April). Alcohol alert: Alcohol and transportation safety. No. 52. Bethesda, MD: National Institute on Alcohol Abuse and Alcoholism. Wagenaar, Alexander C., O'Malley, Patrick M., and LaFond, Colette (2001). Lowered legal blood alcohol limits for young drivers: Effects on drinking, driving, and driving-after-drinking behaviors in 30 states. *American Journal of Public Health, 91,* 801–803. Williams, Allan F. (2006). Alcohol-impaired

driving and its consequences in the United States. *Journal of Safety Research, 37,* 123–138.

41. Hingson, Ralph; Heeren, Timothy; Zakocs, Ronda; Winter, Michael; and Wechsler, Henry (2003). Age of first intoxication, heavy drinking, driving after drinking and risk of unintentional injury among U.S. college students. *Journal of Studies on Alcohol, 64,* 23–31. Liu, Simin; Siegel, Paul Z.; Brewer, Robert D.; Mokdad, Ali H.; Sleet, David A.; and Sardula, Mary (1997). Prevalence of alcohol-impaired driving: Results from a national self-reported survey of health behaviors. *Journal of the American Medical Association, 277,* 122–125. National Highway Traffic Administration (1999, March). The relationship of alcohol safety laws to drinking drivers in fatal crashes. Washington DC: U.S. Department of Transportation. Substance Abuse and Mental Health Services Administration (2007). *Results from the 2006 National Survey on Drug Use and Health: National Findings.* Rockville, MD: Office of Applied Studies, Substance Abuse and Mental Health Services Administration, page 37 and Figures 3.5 and 3.6.

42. Pernanen, Kai (1991). *Alcohol in human violence.* New York: Guilford Press, pp. 192–193. Haggård-Grann, Ulrika; Hallqvist, Johan; Långström, Niklas; and Möller, Jette (2006). The role of alcohol and drugs in triggering criminal violence: A case-crossover study. *Addiction, 101,* 100–108.

43. Collins, James J., and Messerschmidt, Pamela M. (1993). Epidemiology of alcohol-related violence. *Alcohol Health and Research World, 17,* 93–100. Goode, Erich (2005). *Drugs in American society* (6th ed.). New York: McGraw-Hill, pp. 340–343. National Institute on Alcohol Abuse and Alcoholism (1997, October). Alcohol alert: Alcohol, violence, and aggression. No. 38. Bethesda, MD: National Institute on Alcohol Abuse and Alcoholism.

44. Giancola, Peter R. (2002). Alcohol-related aggression in men and women: The influence of dispositional aggressivity. *Journal of Studies on Alcohol, 63,* 696–708. Norris, Jeanette; David, Kelly Cue; George, William H.; Martell, Joel; and Heiman, Julia R. (2002). Alcohol's direct and indirect effects on men's self-reported sexual aggression likelihood. *Journal of Studies on Alcohol, 63,* 688–695. Parrott, Dominic, and Zeichner, Amos (2002). Effects of alcohol and trait anger on physical aggression in men. *Journal of Studies on Alcohol, 63,* 196–204.

45. Pernanen, Kai (1993). Research approaches in the study of alcohol-related violence. *Alcohol Health and Research World, 17,* 101–107. Taylor, Stuart P. (1993). Experimental investigation of alcohol-induced aggression in humans. *Alcohol Health and Research World, 17,* 108–112.

46. Abel, Ernest L. (1985). *Psychoactive drugs and sex.* New York: Plenum Press, pp. 19–54. Cooper, M. Lynne (2006). Does drinking promote risky sexual behavior? A complex answer to a simple question. *Current Directions in Psychological Science, 15,* 19–23. George, William H., and Norris, Jeanette (1993). Alcohol, disinhibition, sexual arousal, and deviant sexual behavior. *Alcohol Health and Research World, 17,* 133–138. Testa, Maria, Vanzile-Tamsen, Carol, and Livingston, Jennifer A. (2004). The role of victim and perpetrator intoxication on sexual assault outcomes. *Journal of Studies on Alcohol, 65,* 320–329.

47. Rimm, Eric B. (2000). Moderate alcohol intake and lower risk of coronary heart disease: Meta-analysis of effects on lipids and haemostatic factors. *Journal of the American Medical Association, 283,* 1269. Zuger, Abigail (2002, December 31). The case for drinking (all together now: in moderation). *New York Times,* pp. F1, F6. Quotation on p. F1.

48. Howard, Andrea A., Arnsten, Julia H., and Gourevitch, Marc N. (2004). Effect of alcohol consumption on diabetes mellitus: A systematic review. *Annals of Internal Medicine, 140,* 211–219. Mukamal, Kenneth J.; Conigrave, Katherine M.; Mittleman, Murray A.; Carmargo, Carlos A., Jr.; Stampfer, Meir J.; Willett, Walter C.; and Rimm, Eric B. (2003). Roles of drinking pattern and type of alcohol consumed in coronary heart disease in men. *New England Journal of Medicine, 348,* 109–118. Mukamal, Kenneth J.; Kuller, Lewis H.; Longstreth, W. T.; Mittleman, Murray A; and Siscovick, David S. (2003). Prospective study of alcohol consumption and risk of dementia in older adults. *Journal of the American Medical Association, 289,* 1405–1413. Reynold, Kristi; Lewis, L. Brian; Nolen, John David L.; Kinney, Gregory L.; Sathya, Bhavani; and He, Jiang (2003). Alcohol consumption and risk of stroke: A meta-analysis. *Journal of the American Medical Association, 289,* 579–588. Wade, Nicholas (2006, November 17). Red wine ingredient increases endurance, study shows. *New York Times,* p. A20.

49. Alcohol Policies Project, Center for Science in the Public Interest (2000). Victory for public health: New U.S. guidelines on alcohol consumption drop positive spin on drinking. Washington DC: Center for Science in the Public Interest. The Gallup Organization (2005, July 22). Fewer young adults drinking to excess. Gallup Organization, Princeton, NJ. Goldberg, Ira (2003). To drink or not to drink. *New England Journal of Medicine, 348,* 163–164. Klatsky, Arthur (2003, February). Drink to your health? *Scientific American,* pp. 75–81.

50. Darby, William, and Heinz, Agnes (1991, January). *The responsible use of alcohol: Defining the parameters of moderation.* New York: American Council on Science and Health, pp. 1–26. Hanson, David J., and Engs, Ruth C. (1994). Drinking behavior: Taking personal responsibility. In Peter J. Venturelli (Ed.), *Drug use in America: Social, cultural, and political perspectives.* Boston: Jones and Bartlett, pp. 175–181.

chapter 11

Chronic Alcohol Abuse and Alcoholism

When you live in an alcoholic family, you sometimes lie in bed and dream. You dream that your parents are going to quit drinking, that you are going to get closer to them. You are going to have a better life. . . . You picture your parents beginning to care for themselves and for you. You imagine it being beautiful. Your home is clean and organized. Instead of abusing you, or being nice to you just to get rid of you, your parents are helping you with your homework.

—*Teens talk about alcohol and alcoholism (1987)*

After you have completed this chapter, you will understand

- Problems surrounding the definition of alcoholism

- The social history of regulating alcohol use

- Chronic effects of alcohol

- Social patterns of chronic alcohol abuse

- Special problems among the elderly

- Family dynamics in alcoholism

- Genetic and environmental influences in alcoholism

- Approaches to treatment for alcoholism

- Alcoholism in the workplace

Chronic abuse of alcohol has been called the hidden addiction. There is no need to get out on the street and find a dealer; for many people, it is remarkably easy to conceal their problem (at least in the beginning) from family and friends. Alcohol consumption is so tightly woven into the fabric of U.S. social life that it may be difficult to catch on that an individual is drinking too much too often. All too frequently, chronic abuse of alcohol has been treated as a genteel affair, rarely with the same degree of concern as that associated with the chronic abuse of other drugs. Yet from a pharmacological point of view, it is the same, and we have to realize that fact. This chapter will deal with the very serious consequences of this condition on more than 18 million people in the United States and on American society at large.

Alcoholism: Stereotypes, Definitions, and Criteria

Close your eyes and try to imagine an alcoholic. It is possible that you are forming an image of someone, probably male, who is down on his heels, perhaps dirty and disheveled, with a bottle of cheap wine in his hands, living from day to day in a state of deteriorating health, with no one caring about him except a social worker or police officer or, inevitably, the medical examiner. You would be imagining less than 5 percent of all alcoholics; more than 95 percent of them look quite different. In fact, the demographics of alcoholism include every possible category. Alcoholics can be fourteen years old or eighty-four, male or female, professional or blue-collar, urbanite, suburbanite, or rural resident in any community large or small.

What aspects of their behavior tie them all together, allowing us to describe their condition with a single label? Because of the wide diversity of alcoholics, no one has come up with one encompassing definition of alcoholism. Instead, we are left with a set of criteria, basically a collection of signs, symptoms, and behaviors that help us make the diagnosis. A single individual may not fulfill all of these criteria, but if he or she fulfills enough of them, we decide that the standard has been met.

The criteria adopted here focus on four basic life problems that are tied to the consumption of alcohol: (1) problems associated with a preoccupation with drinking, (2) emotional problems, (3) vocational, social, and family problems, and (4) problems associated with physical health.[1] Notice that these criteria make no mention of the cause or causes of alcoholism, only its behavioral, social, and physical consequences. In short, we are recognizing that **alcoholism** is a complex phenomenon with psychological-behavioral components (criteria 1 and 2), social components (criterion 3), and a physical component (criterion 4).

Problems Associated with a Preoccupation with Drinking

The dominant characteristic of alcoholics is their preoccupation with the act of drinking and their incorporation of drinking into their everyday lives. An alcoholic may need a drink prior to a social occasion to feel "fortified." With increasing frequency, such a person sees alcohol as a way of dealing with stress and anxiety. Drinking itself becomes a routine, no longer a social affair. The habit of taking a few drinks on a daily basis on arriving home from work is an example of **symptomatic drinking,** in which alcohol is viewed specifically as a way of relieving tension. Also increasing are incidences of unintentional states of severe intoxication and blackouts of events surrounding the time of drinking, a condition quite different from "passing out" from a high BAC level. One such occurrence may not be a particularly critical sign, but recurrences definitely are.[2]

Traditionally, alcoholism is associated with consumption of a large quantity of alcohol. This sounds pretty obvious and it is true of most alcoholics, but we still have to be careful about overgeneralizing. There are significant differences in the way alcoholics consume their alcohol. Not all of them drink alone or begin every day with a drink. Many of them drink on a daily basis, but others are spree or binge alcoholics who might become grossly intoxicated on occasion and totally abstain from drinking the rest of the time.[3]

Another feature often attributed to alcoholics is the loss of control over their drinking. The alcoholic typically craves a drink and frequently engages in compulsive behavior related to alcohol. There may be a stockpiling of liquor, taking a drink or two before going to a party, or feeling uncomfortable unless alcohol is present. The alcoholic may be sneaking drinks or having drinks that others do not know about, such as surreptitiously having an extra drink or two in the kitchen out of the sight of the party guests.[4] Particularly when the alcoholic is trying to abstain from or reduce the quantity of

---

alcoholism: A condition in which the consumption of alcohol has produced major psychological, physical, social, or occupational problems.

symptomatic drinking: A pattern of alcohol consumption aimed at reducing stress and anxiety.

The typical alcoholic American

Doctor, age 54

Farmer, age 35

Unemployed, age 40

College student, age 19

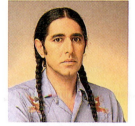
Counselor, age 38

Retired editor, age 86

Dancer, age 22

Police officer, age 46

Military officer, age 31

Student, age 14

Executive, age 50

Taxi driver, age 61

Homemaker, age 43

Bricklayer, age 29

Computer programmer, age 25

Lawyer, age 52

There's no such thing as typical. We have all kinds.
10 million Americans are alcoholic.
It's our number one drug problem.

Alcoholism affects such a diverse group of people that it is virtually impossible to make generalizations about the typical profile of an alcoholic. Here are sixteen examples of individuals to whom the term "alcoholic" may not have been immediately applied.

alcohol consumed, his or her thoughts become focused on the possibility of drinking or ways to rationalize it.[5]

Yet professionals disagree whether all alcoholics are necessarily out of control with respect to alcohol. As discussed later in the chapter, this controversy has major implications for choosing the treatment approach in cases of alcohol abuse. If it is true that even a small amount of alcohol will propel a recovering alcoholic back to alcohol abuse, then a primary focus of treatment should be on no drinking at all, better known as absolute **abstinence.** If it is not true, then there is the possibility of controlled drinking without the fear of "falling off the wagon." The well-known alcohol treatment program Alcoholics Anonymous, for example, functions under the premise that an alcoholic must never drink again, even in minute quantities, if recovery is to be long lasting.

Emotional Problems

Given that alcohol is a depressant drug on the central nervous system, it should not be surprising that chronic alcohol intake produces depressive symptoms. Serious depressions and thoughts of suicide frequently occur in the midst of heavy drinking. However, only about 15 percent of individuals who meet the criteria for alcohol dependence have experienced major depression either before the onset of their alcoholic condition or during extended periods of abstinence. Therefore, it is reasonable to conclude that the depressive symptoms are alcohol-induced. Alcoholics are no more likely than others in the general population to have suffered an episode of major depression.[6]

Vocational, Social, and Family Problems

No one questions the potential problems that chronic alcohol abuse can bring to the maintenance of a job or career, social relationships, and a stable family life. These three areas frequently intertwine, and trouble in one usually exacerbates the others. A job loss puts stress on marital and family relationships, just as marital and family difficulties put stress on occupational performance.

Numerous clinical studies support the idea of increased domestic instability in the lives of alcoholics, but the true extent of these problems is difficult to assess. Family violence, for example, is frequently examined through cases seen in treatment or social service programs. As a result, these agencies may interpret the domestic behavior of a father not known to have a drinking problem differently from that of a father with a history of alcoholism. A man who drinks heavily and abuses his children may be more likely to be "counted" as an alcoholic than a nonabusive father who consumes just as much alcohol. It is much easier to assess the likelihood of domestic violence or decline in job performance due to acute intoxication than it is to evaluate the influence of chronic abuse of alcohol. Even so, there is no doubt that the cumulative effects of alcoholism on family dynamics are devastating.[7]

Physical Problems

There is also no question that chronic alcohol consumption has a destructive effect on the body. Not surprisingly, a principal site of damage is the brain. Neuroimaging procedures, such as CT and MRI scans, reveal a consistent link between heavy drinking and physical shrinkage of brain matter, particularly in the cerebral cortex, cerebellum, and regions associated with memory and other cognitive functions. These neurological changes are observed even in the absence of other alcohol-related medical conditions such as chronic liver disease.[8]

Hiding the Problems: Denial and Enabling

The major life problems that serve as rough criteria for determining the condition of alcoholism are often not recognized by alcoholics themselves because of their tendency to deny that their drinking has any influence on their lives or the lives of people around them. When in denial, the alcoholic can be extremely sensitive to any mention of problems associated with drinking. A hangover the next day, for example, is seldom discussed because it would draw attention to the fact that drinking has occurred.[9]

Denial also can be manifest among the people around the alcoholic. Members of an alcoholic's family, for example, may try to function as if life were normal. Through their excuse making and efforts to undo or cover up the frequent physical and psychological damage the alcoholic causes, they inadvertently prevent the alcoholic from seeking treatment or delay that treatment until the alcoholism is more severe. These people are referred to as **enablers** because they enable the alcoholic to function as an alcoholic as opposed to a sober person. Both processes of denial and enabling present major

abstinence: The avoidance of some consumable item or behavior.

enablers: Individuals whose behavior consciously or unconsciously encourages another person's continuation in a pattern of alcohol or other drug abuse.

A Self-Administered Short Michigan Alcoholism Screening Test (SMAST)

The Michigan Alcoholism Screening Test (MAST), twenty-four questions to be answered in ten to fifteen minutes, is designed as a structured interview instrument to detect alcoholism. A shorter thirteen-question version (SMAST), shown here, has approximately the same level of reliability and validity. Score one point for each response that matches the one in parentheses. According to the authors of the test, a total score of 0 or 1 indicates a nonalcoholic, 2 a possible alcoholic, and 3 or more an alcoholic. A more recent screening instrument for pregnant women, the TWEAK, appears later in this chapter.

1. Do you feel you are a normal drinker? (By normal we mean you drink less than or as much as most other people.) (NO)
2. Does your wife, husband, a parent, or other near relative ever worry or complain about your drinking? (YES)
3. Do you ever feel guilty about your drinking? (YES)
4. Do friends or relatives think you are a normal drinker? (NO)
5. Are you able to stop drinking when you want to? (NO)
6. Have you ever attended a meeting of Alcoholics Anonymous? (YES)

7. Has drinking ever created problems between you and your wife, husband, a parent, or other near relative? (YES)
8. Have you ever gotten into trouble at work because of drinking? (YES)
9. Have you ever neglected your obligations, your family, or your work for two or more days in a row because you were drinking? (YES)
10. Have you ever gone to anyone for help about your drinking? (YES)
11. Have you ever been in a hospital because of drinking? (YES)
12. Have you ever been arrested for drunken driving, driving while intoxicated, or driving under the influence of alcoholic beverages? (YES)
13. Have you ever been arrested, even for a few hours, because of other drunken behavior? (YES)

> **Where to go for assistance:**
>
> www.projectmainstream.net/projectmainstream.asp?cid=915
>
> This web site is sponsored by Project Mainstream (Improving Substance Abuse Education for Health Professionals), Providence, Rhode Island.

Source: Selzer, Melvin L., Vinokur, Amiram, and van Rooijen, Louis (1975). A self-administered Short Michigan Alcoholism Screening Test (SMAST). *Journal of Studies on Alcohol, 36,* 117–126.

difficulties not only in establishing problem-oriented criteria for diagnosing alcoholism but also in carrying out necessary interventions. Denial and enabling are clearly relevant processes in the area of alcoholism, but it is not difficult to see that they present problems with regard to *any* form of drug abuse (see Chapter 15).

Help Line provides a useful self-survey for determining the signs of potential alcoholism. You may want to try it out on yourself and people that you know.

Alcohol Abuse and Alcohol Dependence: The Professional's View

As you can see, the criteria commonly employed in determining the presence of alcoholism are at times quite murky, and often there are nearly as many counter examples to each of the criteria as there are examples.

The American Psychiatric Association, through its Diagnostic and Statistical Manual, fourth edition (DSM-IV), has attempted to put together as many common features as possible and has established two basic syndromes. It is important to understand these technical definitions, because professionals in the field of alcoholism commonly use the DSM-IV either in their research or in clinical practice.[10]

The first syndrome, referred to as **alcohol abuse,** is characterized as either (1) the continued use of alcohol for at least one month despite the knowledge of having a persistent or recurring physical problem or some difficulty in social or occupational functioning, or (2) the recurring use of alcohol in situations (such as driving) when alcohol consumption is physically hazardous.

> **alcohol abuse:** A syndrome characterized primarily by the continued use of alcohol despite the drinker's knowledge of having a persistent physical problem or some social or occupational difficulty.

The second syndrome, referred to as **alcohol dependence,** is characterized as alcohol abuse that involves any three of the following seven situations:

- Consuming alcohol in amounts or over a longer period than the person intends

- A persistent desire, or one or more unsuccessful attempts, to cut down or control drinking

- A great deal of time spent drinking or recovering from the effects of drinking

- Alcohol consumption continuing despite knowledge that drinking either causes or exacerbates recurrent physical or psychological problems

alcohol dependence: A syndrome in which alcohol abuse involves a variety of significant physical, psychological, social, and behavioral problems.

- Important social, occupational, or recreational activities given up or reduced because of alcohol

- Marked tolerance or the need to drink more than before to achieve previous levels of intoxication

- Symptoms of alcohol withdrawal or the consumption of alcohol to relieve or avoid withdrawal symptoms

Obviously, individuals fitting the second definition are considered more greatly impaired than those fitting the first. That distinction also was true with regard to the more general criteria for substance abuse and substance dependence (see Chapter 1). Approximately 8.5 percent of U.S. adults, about one in twelve, are either alcohol abusers or alcohol dependent according to the DSM-IV standards.

As you might expect, the highest percentages of "heavy drinkers" are found among people eighteen to twenty-five years old. The "heavy drinker" category is defined as having consumed five or more alcoholic drinks on the same occasion on at least five different days within the previous month. The incidence within the eighteen to twenty-five age range has been estimated to be about 15 percent, with a peak incidence of 20 percent at age twenty-one.[11]

The Social History of Regulating Alcohol Use

In the late 1700s, prominent physicians, writers, and scientists began to consider the long-term adverse effects of alcohol consumption and tried to formulate some kind of social reform to mitigate them. The goal at that time was to reduce the consumption of distilled spirits (liquor) only. It was a temperate attitude toward drinking (hence the phrase "temperance movement") rather than an insistence on the total prohibition of alcohol.

In the United States, where the temperance movement was to be stronger than anywhere else, its most influential spokesman was Benjamin Rush, a physician, Revolutionary War hero, and signer of the Declaration of Independence. In his 1785 pamphlet, *An Inquiry into the Effects of Ardent Spirits on the Human Mind and Body,* Rush vividly described the range of mental and physical dangers associated with alcohol abuse:

> *Strong liquor is more destructive than the sword. The destruction of war is periodic, whereas alcohol exerts its influence upon human life at all times and in all seasons. . . . A nation corrupted by alcohol can never be free.*[12]

Even though this 1874 engraving shows a temperance crusader in full battle regalia, relatively few temperance activists resorted to physical violence.

Rush's efforts did not have a major impact on the drinking habits of American society during his lifetime. As described in Chapter 10, alcohol consumption in the United States at that time was enormous and continued to rise until about 1830. Rush's words, however, served as an inspiration to political and religious groups around the country who saw alcohol abuse in social and moral terms. In their view, drunkenness led to poverty, a disorderly society, and civil disobedience. In short, it was unpatriotic at best and subversive at worst. When we hear the phrase "demon rum," we have to recognize that many Americans during the nineteenth century took the phrase quite literally. Liquor was demonized as a direct source of evil in the world. The idea, like any other form of scapegoating, spread like wildfire. In 1831, the American Temperance Society reported that nearly 2 million Americans had renounced strong liquor and that more than eight hundred local societies had been established. By the 1850s, twelve U.S. states and two Canadian provinces had introduced legislation forbidding the sale of "alcoholic" (distilled) drink.

Whether or not they were justified in doing so, temperance groups took credit for a drastic change that was occurring in the levels of alcohol consumption in the United States. From 1830 to 1850, consumption of all types of alcohol plummeted from an annual per capita level of roughly 7 gallons to roughly 2 gallons, approximately today's consumption level (see Chapter 10). It is quite possible that this decline encouraged the temperance movement to formulate its ultimate goal, a prohibition of alcohol consumption in any form.

The Road to National Prohibition

A major development in the temperance movement was the formation in 1873 of a women's organization called the Woman's Christian Temperance Union (WCTU). Almost from the beginning, its primary target was a highly visible fixture of late-nineteenth-century American life: the saloon. These establishments were now vilified as the source of all the troubles alcohol could bring. It is not difficult to imagine how the saloon would have been seen as a significant threat to American women in general.

> Bars appeared to invite family catastrophe. They introduced children to drunkenness and vice and drove husbands to alcoholism; they also caused squandering of wages, wife beating, and child abuse; and, with the patron's inhibitions lowered through drink, the saloon led many men into the arms of prostitutes (and not incidentally, contributed to the alarming spread of syphilis).[13]

No wonder the WCTU hated the saloon, and no saloon in the country was safe from their "pray-in" demonstrations, vocal opposition, and in some cases violent interventions. Their influence eventually extended into every aspect of American culture. The WCTU and other anti-alcohol forces, such as the newly formed Anti-Saloon League and National Prohibition Party, were soon electing congressional candidates who pledged to enact national legislation banning alcohol consumption throughout the land.

The Beginning and Ending of a "Noble Experiment"

In December 1917, Congress passed a resolution "prohibiting the manufacture, sale, transportation, or importation of intoxicating liquors," the simple wording that would form the basis for the Eighteenth Amendment to the U.S. Constitution. (Notice that it did not forbid purchase or use of alcohol.) The Volstead Act of 1919 set up the enforcement procedures. By the end of the year, the necessary thirty-six states had ratified the amendment, and Prohibition took effect in January 1920.

Despite its lofty aims, Prohibition was doomed to failure. In the countryside, operators of illegal stills (called "moonshiners" because they worked largely at night) continued their production despite the efforts of an occasional half-hearted raid by Treasury agents (known as "revenooers"). The major cities became centers of open defiance. Liquor, having been smuggled into the country, flowed abundantly as saloons turned into speakeasies and operated in violation of the law.

The early years of Prohibition did, however, show positive effects in the area of public health. Alcohol-related deaths, cirrhosis of the liver, mental disorders, and alcohol-related crime declined in 1920 and 1921, but in a few years, the figures began to creep up again, and the level of criminal activity associated with illegal drinking was clearly intolerable.[14] By the end of the decade, for the vast majority of Americans, it had become obvious that the experiment was not working.

In 1933, President Franklin D. Roosevelt, having run on a platform to repeal the Volstead Act, signed the necessary legislation that became the Twenty-first Amendment; ratification was swift. Alcohol was restored as a legal commodity and its regulation was returned once more to local authorities. Since that time, state prohibition laws have gradually been repealed, with Mississippi in 1966 being the last state to do so.

Present-Day Regulation by Taxation

One immediate benefit of repealing Prohibition was the return of federal revenue from taxes on alcohol. Indeed, the impact on a struggling national economy hard hit by the Depression had been one of the arguments advanced by the repeal movement. In 1933 alone, such excise taxes brought in $500 million, which was used to finance social programs. The concept of collecting taxes on the basis of alcohol consumption dates back to the very beginning of the United States as a nation. In 1794, the newly formed U.S. Congress passed a law requiring an excise tax on the sale of whiskey. After a short-lived Whiskey Rebellion in which President Washington had to order federal militia to subdue Appalachian farmers who had refused to pay the new tax, the practice of taxing alcohol was accepted and has continued to the present day as a way of raising tax money.

Taxes on alcohol sales have been an indirect mechanism for regulating the consumption of alcohol by increasing its price, not unlike taxes on tobacco products (see Chapter 12). More than $8 billion each year is collected from federal excise taxes on alcohol. Total annual revenues exceed $18 billion, when additional excise taxes imposed by all U.S. states and some local communities are included. Today, alcoholic beverages are one of the most heavily taxed consumer products. Approximately 42 percent of the retail price of an average bottle of distilled spirits, for example, is earmarked for federal, state, or local taxes.[15]

Should the price of alcohol be used to affect the pattern of consumption? As noted in Chapter 10, alcohol consumption rates have declined over the last decade or so, in part as a result of changing attitudes toward personal health and dieting. The alcohol beverage industry is quick to blame the governmental taxes for decreasing their retail sales and often observes that because of reduced sales, the net income to the government actually ends up less than before the tax increase. Those in favor of these taxes argue that the nation's taxation policy with regard to alcohol and other legal psychoactive drugs (such as nicotine) that have negative consequences on society is an appropriate option of government.

It has been proposed that alcohol taxes be set high enough to begin to offset the total societal costs resulting from alcohol abuse. This approach would place a type of "user fee" on the consumption of alcohol. However, there is the possibility that raising alcohol prices by additional taxation might lead to the development of a black market for alcohol purchases, little change in alcohol consumption, and a net decline in tax revenues.[16]

Physiological Effects of Chronic Alcohol Use

This section will deal with what we know about the consequences of long-term (chronic) consumption of alcohol on the body over and above the acute effects that were discussed in the last chapter.

Tolerance and Withdrawal

As with other CNS depressants, alcohol consumption over a period of time will result in a tolerance effect. On a metabolic level, alcohol dehydrogenase activity during tolerance becomes higher in the stomach and liver, allowing the alcohol to leave the body somewhat faster; on a neural level, the brain is less responsive to alcohol's depressive effects.[17] Therefore, if alcohol consumption remains steady, the individual feels less of an effect.

As a result of tolerance and the tendency to compensate for it in terms of drinking a greater quantity, the chronic alcohol abuser is subject to increased physical risks. There are serious behavioral risks as well; for example, an alcohol-tolerant drinker may consider driving with a BAC level that exceeds the standard for drunk driving, thinking that he or she is not intoxicated and hence not impaired. A person's driving ability, under these circumstances, will be substantially overestimated.

An alcohol-dependent person's abrupt withdrawal from alcohol can result in a range of serious physical symptoms beginning from six to forty-eight hours after the last drink, but estimates vary as to how many people are typically affected. Among hospitalized patients, only 5 percent appear to show withdrawal symptoms, whereas other studies of alcoholics using outpatient facilities have estimated the percentage to be as high as 18. Although the exact incidence may be somewhat unclear, there is less disagreement as to what takes place. Physical withdrawal effects are classified in two clusters of symptoms.

The first cluster, called the **alcohol withdrawal syndrome,** is the more common of the two. It begins with insomnia, vivid dreaming, and a severe hangover; these discomforts are followed by tremors (the "shakes"), sweating, mild agitation, anxiety (the "jitters"), nausea, and vomiting, as well as increased heart rate and blood pressure. In some patients, there are also brief tonic-clonic (grand mal) seizures, as the nervous system rebounds from the chronic depression induced by alcohol. The alcohol withdrawal syndrome usually reaches a peak from twenty-four to thirty-six hours after the last drink and is over after forty-eight hours.

The second cluster, called **delirium tremens (DTs),** is much more dangerous and is fortunately less common. The symptoms include extreme disorientation and confusion, profuse sweating, fever, and disturbing nightmares. Typically, there are also periods of frightening hallucinations, when the individual might experience seeing snakes or insects on the walls, ceiling, or his or her skin. These effects generally reach a peak three to four days after the last drink. During this time, there is the possibility of life-threatening events such as heart failure, dehydration, or suicide, so it is critical for the individual to be hospitalized and under medical supervision at all times. The current medical practice for treating individuals undergoing withdrawal is to administer antianxiety medication (see Chapter 8) to relieve the symptoms. After the withdrawal period has ended, the dose levels of the medication are gradually reduced and discontinued.[18]

Liver Disease

Chronic consumption of alcohol produces three forms of liver disease. The first of these is a **fatty liver,** resulting from an abnormal concentration of fatty deposits inside liver cells. Normally, the liver breaks down fats adequately, but when alcohol is in the body the liver breaks down the alcohol at the expense of fats. As a result, fats accumulate and ultimately interfere with the functioning of the liver. The condition is fortunately reversible, if the drinker abstains. The accumulated fats are gradually metabolized, and the liver returns to normal.

The second condition is **alcoholic hepatitis,** an inflammation of liver tissue causing fever, jaundice (a yellowing of the skin), and abdominal pain, resulting at least in part from a lower functioning level of the immune system. It is also reversible with abstinence, though some residual scarring may remain.

The third and most serious liver condition is **alcoholic cirrhosis,** characterized by the progressive development of scar tissue that chokes off blood vessels in the liver and destroys liver cells by interfering with the cell's utilization of oxygen. At an early stage, the liver is enlarged from the accumulation of fats, but at later stages it is shrunken as liver cells begin to degenerate (Figure 11.1). Though abstinence helps to prevent further liver degeneration when cirrhosis is diagnosed, the condition is not reversible except by liver transplantation surgery.

Prior to the 1970s, alcoholic cirrhosis was attributed to nutritional deficiencies that are often associated with an alcoholic's diet. We know now that, although nutritional problems play a role, alcohol itself is toxic to the liver. After a pattern of heavy alcohol consumption of

alcohol withdrawal syndrome: The more common of two general reactions to the cessation of alcohol consumption in an alcoholic. It is characterized by physiological discomfort, seizures, and sleep disturbances.

delirium tremens (DTs): The less common of two general reactions to the cessation of drinking in an alcoholic. It is characterized by extreme disorientation and confusion, fever, hallucinations, and other symptoms.

fatty liver: A condition in which fat deposits accumulate in the liver as a result of chronic alcohol abuse.

alcoholic hepatitis (AL-co-HAUL-ik hep-ah-TIE-tus): A disease involving inflammation of the liver as a result of chronic alcohol abuse.

alcoholic cirrhosis (AL-co-HAUL-ik seer-OH-sis): A disease involving scarring and deterioration of liver cells as a result of chronic alcohol abuse.

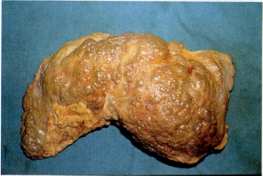

The dramatic difference between a healthy liver (top) and a cirrhotic liver (bottom).

many years, it is possible to develop cirrhosis, even when nutrition is adequate. A major cause of liver cell damage is the toxic accumulation of free radicals, molecule fragments that are by-products of acetaldehyde (Chapter 10).

Cirrhosis is ranked as the ninth leading cause of death in the United States, affecting approximately 30,000 each year. Most deaths occur in people forty to sixty-five years old. Daily drinkers are at a higher risk of developing cirrhosis than binge drinkers, though this risk may be the result of the relatively larger quantity of alcohol consumed over a long period of time. Generally, patients showing liver damage have been drinking for ten to twenty years. Only 10 to 20 percent of all heavy drinkers develop cirrhosis, however, in contrast to 90 to 100 percent who show evidence of either fatty liver or hepatitis. There may be a genetic predisposition for cirrhosis that puts a subgroup of alcoholics at increased risk.[19]

> **alcoholic dementia (AL-co-HAUL-ik dih-MEN-chee-ah):** A condition in which chronic alcohol abuse produces cognitive deficits such as difficulties in problem solving and memory.

Cardiovascular Problems

About one in every four alcoholics develops cardiovascular problems owing to the chronic consumption of alcohol. The effects include inflammation and enlargement of the heart muscle, poor blood circulation to the heart, irregular heart contractions, fatty accumulations in the heart and arteries, high blood pressure, and stroke.[20]

Cancer

Chronic alcohol abuse is associated with the increased risk of several types of cancers—in particular, cancers of the pharynx and larynx. Nearly 50 percent of all such cancers are associated with heavy drinking. If alcohol abusers also smoke cigarettes, the increased risk is even more dramatic. An increased risk of liver cancer is also linked to chronic alcoholic abuse, whether or not cirrhosis is also present. In addition, an association has been made between alcohol consumption and breast cancer in women. There is either a weaker association or no association at all with cancers of the stomach, colon, pancreas, or rectum.

Alcohol is not technically considered a carcinogen (a direct producer of cancer), so why the risks are increased in certain cancer types is at present unknown. It is possible that the increased risk is a combined result of alcohol enhancing the carcinogenic effects of other chemicals and, as is true with the development of hepatitis, depressing the immune system. With a reduced immune response, the alcoholic may have a lowered resistance to the development of cancerous tumors.[21]

Dementia and Wernicke-Korsakoff Syndrome

Chronic alcohol consumption can produce longer-lasting deficits in the way an individual solves problems, remembers information, and organizes facts about his or her identity and surroundings. These cognitive deficits are commonly referred to collectively as **alcoholic dementia** and are associated with structural changes in brain tissue. Specifically, there is an enlargement of brain ventricles (the interior fluid-filled spaces within the brain), a widening of fissures separating sections of cerebral cortex, and a loss of acetylcholine-sensitive receptors. The combination of these effects results in a net decrease in brain mass. CT and MRI scans, two imaging techniques that reveal the structural features of the brain, show that the degree of enlargement of the ventricles correlates with a decline in overall intelligence, verbal learning and retention, and short-term memory, particularly for middle-aged and elderly alcoholics.

Some 50 to 75 percent of all detoxified alcoholics and nearly 20 percent of all individuals admitted to state mental hospitals show signs of alcohol-related dementia. Through abstinence, it is possible to reverse some of the cognitive deficits and even some of the abnormalities in the brain, depending on the age of the alcoholic when treatment begins. As you might suspect, younger alcoholics respond better than older ones.[22]

A more severe form of cognitive impairment related to chronic alcohol consumption is a two-stage disease referred to as **Wernicke-Korsakoff syndrome.** In the first stage, called *Wernicke's encephalopathy* or simply *Wernicke's disease,* the patient shows confusion and disorientation, abnormal eye movements, and difficulties in movement and body coordination. These neurological problems arise from a deficiency in Vitamin B_1 (**thiamine**), a necessary nutrient for glucose to be consumed by neurons in the brain. Extreme alcoholics may go days or weeks at a time eating practically nothing and receiving calories exclusively from drinking alcoholic beverages.

As a result of thiamine deficiency, large numbers of neurons die in areas of the brain specifically concerned with thinking and movement. About 15 percent of patients with Wernicke's disease, however, respond favorably to large amounts of thiamine supplements in combination with abstinence from alcohol, restoring their previous level of orientation, eye movements, and coordination.

Many Wernicke's disease patients, whether or not they recover from confusion and motor impairments, also display a severe form of chronic amnesia and general apathy called *Korsakoff's psychosis.* Specifically, such patients cannot remember information that has just been presented to them and have only a patchy memory for distant events that occurred prior to their alcoholic state. They frequently attempt, through a behavior called **confabulation,** to compensate for their gaps in memory by telling elaborate stories of imagined past events, as if trying to fool others into thinking that they remember more than they actually do.

Thiamine deficiency is linked to Korsakoff's psychosis as well. About 20 percent of patients completely recover and 60 percent partially recover their memory after being treated with thiamine supplements. Yet the remaining 20 percent, generally the most severely impaired patients and those with the longest history of alcohol consumption, show little or no improvement and require chronic institutionalization.[23]

Fetal Alcohol Syndrome

The disorders just reviewed generally have been associated with consumption of large quantities of alcohol over a long period of time. In the case of the adverse effects of alcohol during pregnancy on unborn children, we are dealing with a unique situation. First of all, we need to recognize the extreme susceptibility of a developing fetus to conditions in the mother's bloodstream. In short, if the mother takes a drink, the fetus takes one, too. And to make matters worse, the fetus does not have sufficient levels of alcohol dehydrogenase to break down the alcohol properly; thus the alcohol stays in the fetus's system longer than in the mother's. In addition, the presence of alcohol coincides with a period of time in prenatal development when critical processes are occurring that are essential for the development of a healthy, alert child.

Although it has long been suspected that alcohol abuse among pregnant women might present serious risks to the fetus, a specific syndrome was not established until 1973, when Kenneth L. Jones and David W. Smith described a cluster of characteristic features in children of

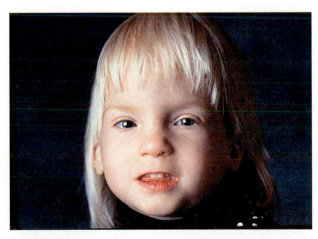

The face of a child with fetal alcohol syndrome, showing the wide-set eyes and other features that are characteristic of this condition.

Wernicke-Korsakoff syndrome (VERN-ih-kee KOR-sa-kof SIN-drohm): A condition resulting from chronic alcohol consumption, characterized by disorientation, cognitive deficits, amnesia, and motor difficulty.

thiamine (THY-ah-meen or THY-ah-min): Vitamin B_1.

confabulation: The tendency to make up elaborate past histories to cover the fact that long-term memory has been impaired.

alcoholic mothers that is now referred to as **fetal alcohol syndrome (FAS)**.[24] Their studies, and research conducted since then, have shown clearly that alcohol is **teratogenic**; that is, it produces specific birth defects in offspring by disrupting fetal development during pregnancy, even when differences in prenatal nutrition have been accounted for. Later in life, FAS children show deficits in short-term memory, problem solving, and attentiveness.

Present-day diagnoses of FAS are made on the basis of three groups of observations: (1) prenatal or post-natal growth retardation in which the baby's weight or length is below the 10th percentile, (2) evidence of CNS abnormalities or mental retardation, and (3) a characteristic skull and facial appearance that includes a smaller-than-normal head; small, wide-set eyes; drooping eyelids; a flattening of the vertical groove between the mouth and nose; a thin upper lip; and a short, upturned nose. If only some of these characteristics are observed, the condition is referred to as possible **fetal alcohol effect (FAE)**.

The incidence of FAS is approximately 0.5 to 3 cases per thousand live births in the general U.S. population, but the rates vary greatly within that population. Incidence is generally higher among Native Americans within the United States.[25]

We do not know at present how alcohol causes FAS or FAE, except that the greatest risk is in the first trimester of pregnancy, especially the third week of gestation when craniofacial formation and brain growth are prominent developmental milestones. Concentrated periods of drinking during this time appear to be very damaging to the fetus. For example, if two mothers consumed a similar overall quantity of alcohol during their pregnancies, but Mother A consumed one drink on each of seven days in a week and Mother B consumed all seven drinks on two weekend evenings, then Mother B would have incurred a far greater risk to her child than Mother A (Help Line).[26]

Although not all alcoholic mothers will give birth to babies with FAS or FAE, the research findings are clear: Risks are greatly increased when excessive drinking is taking place. Although an occasional drink may have minimal effects, no one has determined a "safe" level of drinking during pregnancy that would make this behavior risk-free. The objective of prevention, therefore, is to educate women to the dangers of drinking at any level and to encourage complete abstinence from alcohol (as well as other psychoactive drugs) during pregnancy. Since 1989, all containers of alcoholic beverages must contain two warning messages, one of which is that "according to the Surgeon General, women should not drink alcoholic beverages during pregnancy because of the risk of birth defects."

Fortunately, the public is aware of the problem and the number of women who consume alcohol during pregnancy has declined over the last twenty-five years. In some instances, it has been possible to reduce prenatal exposure to alcohol through broad social change. For example, in 1978, a change in social policy among members of a Southwestern Plains American Indian tribe, shifting the distribution of mineral-rights income toward social programs on the reservation, resulted in the prevalence rate for FAS decreasing from fourteen per thousand live births to none at all. A combined prevalence rate of FAS and FAE decreased from twenty-seven per thousand live births to five. The potential influence of sociocultural factors in altering alcohol consumption patterns needs to be examined closely in all high-risk populations.[27]

The bad news, however, is that the rates of alcohol consumption among several other high-risk populations in the United States, such as pregnant smokers, unmarried women, women under the age of twenty-five, and women with the fewest years of education, have remained relatively unchanged despite the fact that about 90 percent of women are aware of the potential harm. Twenty percent of pregnant women nationwide continue to consume alcohol, with the percentage rising to 37 percent among smokers. Until these statistics improve, FAS and FAE will continue to be the third leading cause of mental retardation not only in the United States but in the entire Western world, exceeded only by Down syndrome and spina bifida. The fact that the development of alcohol-related fetal defects is entirely preventable makes the incidence of these conditions all the more tragic.[28]

Social Patterns of Chronic Alcohol Abuse

When we consider the range of direct and indirect costs to society that result from chronic abuse of alcohol, the price we pay is enormous. These costs include the expense of treatment for alcoholism and of medical intervention for alcohol-related diseases, lost productivity from absenteeism and decreases in worker performance, treatment

fetal alcohol syndrome (FAS): A serious condition involving mental retardation and facial-cranial malformations in the offspring of an alcoholic mother.

teratogenic (TER-ah-tuh-JEN-ik): Capable of producing specific birth defects.

fetal alcohol effect (FAE): A cognitive deficiency in the offspring of an alcoholic mother. It is regarded as less serious than fetal alcohol syndrome.

The TWEAK Alcoholism Screening Instrument for Pregnant Women

One of the difficulties in getting information about possible alcoholic behavior is the tendency for the individual to deny that alcohol abuse is going on. It is especially important to find out whether pregnant women are engaging in this behavior. The following is a brief screening questionnaire, called the TWEAK, that provides personal information about drinking problems, without asking about them in a direct fashion. There are five basic questions (one question for each letter in the acronym TWEAK), with the first question presented in two alternative forms. The choice of whether to ask Question 1a or 1b is left to the health professional collecting the information.

1a. How many drinks does it take before you begin to feel the first effects of alcohol? (T—it asks about tolerance in terms of an initial state of intoxication)

1b. How many drinks does it take before the alcohol makes you fall asleep or pass out? Or, if you never drink until you pass out, what is the largest number of drinks you have? (T—it asks about tolerance in terms of an extreme level of intoxication)

2. Have your friends or relatives worried or complained about your drinking in the past year? (W—it asks about the extent of worry about one's drinking)

3. Do you sometimes take a drink in the morning when you first get up? (E—it refers to an "eye opener")

4. Are there times when you drink and afterward you can't remember what you did or said? (A—it refers to amnesia or a blackout episode)

5. Do you sometimes feel the need to cut down on your drinking? (K—it refers to the need to cut down on the level of alcohol consumption)

Three drinks or more is considered a positive answer to Question 1a; five drinks or more is considered a positive answer to Question 1b. Positive answers count for two points in Questions 1 and 2, and one point each for Questions 3, 4, and 5. A score of 3 or more, out of a maximum of 7, is interpreted as an indication of a possible alcohol problem.

Researchers have found that TWEAK scores can accurately identify up to 77 percent of women who are problem drinkers (an indication of the sensitivity of the questionnaire) and up to 93 percent of women who are not (an indication of the specificity of the questionnaire). Other short surveys are available, but they do not differentiate the two groups as well as the TWEAK. Using this instrument is a major step toward preventing FAS by identifying those women whose drinking during pregnancy will have potentially adverse effects on the developing fetus.

> **Where to go for assistance:**
>
> www. marchofdimes. com/ pnhec/ 159 530, asp
>
> This web site is sponsored by the March of Dimes, a leading organization for the prevention of birth defects.

Sources: Bradley, Katharine A.; Boyd-Wickizer, Jodie; Powell, Suzanne H.; and Burman, Marcia L. (1998). Alcohol screening questionnaires in women: A critical review. *Journal of the American Medical Association, 280,* 166–171. Chan, W. K.; Pristach, E. A.; Welte, J. W.; and Russell, M. (1993). Use of the TWEAK test in screening for heavy drinking in three populations. *Alcoholism: Clinical and Experimental Research, 17,* 1188–1192. Copyright 1993 by Williams and Wilkins. Reprinted with permission. National Institute on Alcohol Abuse and Alcoholism (2002, April). Alcohol alert: Screening for alcohol problems—an update. No. 56. Rockville, MD: National Institute on Alcohol Abuse and Alcoholism.

for alcohol-related injuries, and the lost value of future earnings of individuals who die prematurely because of alcoholism. The total costs in the United States are estimated to be close to $200 billion annually, even without taking into consideration the incalculable costs of human suffering that are involved in the estimated 125,000 alcohol-related deaths each year.[29]

The Demographics of Alcoholism

As mentioned earlier, alcoholics can be found in every age, gender, racial, ethnic, and religious group, and in all socioeconomic levels and geographic regions of the country. Nonetheless, large differences in prevalence exist within these categories. For example, men outnumber women in the incidence of alcoholism by about six to one, with men tending to be steadier from day to day in their consumption of alcohol and women tending to abstain from drinking for lengths of time and to binge once they start drinking again. Overall, women are more vulnerable to alcohol-related organ damage. Whether this higher risk is a result of differences in the pattern of drinking or in differences in the way alcohol is processed in a woman's body is at present unknown.[30]

Figure 11.2 shows a state-by-state analysis of alcohol problems as measured by alcohol consumption level.[31] Some of the other demographic differences have been examined in Chapter 10.

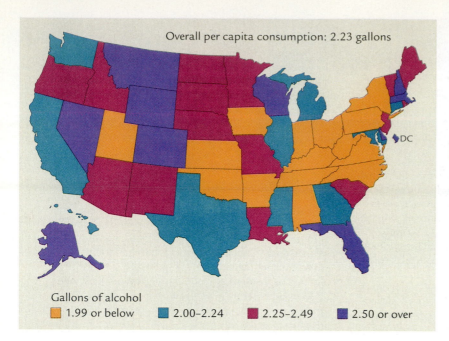

Overall per capita consumption: 2.23 gallons

Gallons of alcohol
■ 1.99 or below ■ 2.00–2.24 ■ 2.25–2.49 ■ 2.50 or over

FIGURE 11.2

Annual per capita alcohol consumption in gallons for the U.S. population fourteen years and older by state.

Source: Lakins, Nekisha E., Williams, Gerald D., and Yi, Hsiao-ye (2006, August). *Surveillance report #78: Apparent per capita alcohol consumption: National, state, and regional trends, 1977–2004.* Bethesda, MD: National Institute on Alcohol Abuse and Alcoholism, Division of Epidemiology and Prevention Research.

Alcohol Abuse among the Elderly

There is a widely held belief that alcohol abuse is not much of a problem with the elderly. Unfortunately, that is a myth. On the basis of careful studies addressing the problem of chronic alcohol abuse among the elderly, it has been estimated that between 2 and 10 percent of the elderly population have alcohol problems, with the proportion rising to nearly 50 percent among those residing in nursing homes. An analysis of Medicare records has indicated that more people over the age of sixty-five are hospitalized each year for alcohol-related problems than for heart attacks.[32]

One of the reasons for the underreporting of this problem is that we typically use the quantity of alcohol consumed as a primary index of alcoholism, and alcohol consumption does indeed decline with age. Yet, because of the changes in alcohol biotransformation over a lifetime, three drinks consumed at age sixty can be equivalent in their effects to four times as many drinks for someone at age twenty. In addition, the indications of social and occupational problems, traditionally part of the criteria for alcoholism, are often irrelevant for an elderly drinker. There would be no incidence of drunk driving if the person is no longer driving, no job supervisor to notice a decline in work performance, and frequently no spouse to complain of social difficulties. Finally, the occurrence of blackouts or symptoms of Wernicke-Korsakoff syndrome may be misdiagnosed

simply as an indication of senility or the onset of Alzheimer's disease.

A number of problems particularly affect the elderly who chronically abuse alcohol. One problem is the risk of the alcohol interacting with the many medications that the elderly typically take. Another is the risk of complications for already existing medical conditions, such as gastrointestinal bleeding, hypertension and cardiac arrhythmias, osteoporosis, depression, and cognitive impairment–related disorders.

There is growing recognition that treatment programs for alcoholism ought to be tailored to the special needs of the elderly; frequently the traditional treatment programs that benefit much younger individuals do not work well with older people. Many seniors were brought up in an era when highly negative attitudes toward drinking prevailed, so if they are drinking themselves, they feel stigmatized and resist treatment. On a brighter note, however, it has been found that, when treatment programs are designed specifically with the elderly in mind, older alcoholics will often respond well to treatment.[33]

The Family Dynamics of Alcoholism: A Systems Approach

Alcoholism, like any form of drug abuse, is an especially traumatizing experience for the families involved. For every one person who has a problem with alcohol, there are, on average, at least four others who are directly affected on a day-to-day basis. It is therefore important to examine some of these effects on particular family members. Since the 1950s, a **systems approach** has advocated looking at how the alcoholic and other members of the family interact.[34] We discussed one of these aspects earlier in the chapter in connection with the adverse effects of enabling behavior on the alcoholic. Another important aspect related to an alcoholic's family is the possibility of codependency.

Beginning in the early 1980s, the concept of **codependency** has gained widespread attention as a way of understanding people who live on a day-to-day basis with an alcoholic or any individual with a drug dependence. Definitions vary but most identify four essential features. In members of the family of an alcoholic, therapists have observed (1) an overinvolvement with the alcoholic, (2) obsessive attempts to control the alcoholic's behavior, (3) a strong reliance upon external sources of self-worth, through the approval of others, and (4) an attempt to make personal sacrifices in an effort to improve the alcoholic's condition.[35]

In the mind of a codependent, it is not considered OK to have one's own feelings, not OK to have problems of one's own, and not OK to enjoy oneself. If people in a relationship with a codependent act badly, the codependent believes that he or she is responsible for their behavior. Because codependency is considered to be a learned pattern of thinking rather than an innate trait, the goal of therapy is to teach the codependent person to detach himself or herself from the alcoholic and begin to meet his or her needs rather than to be controlled by the value judgments of others.[36]

Some professionals, however, question the validity of the codependency concept. They argue that by labeling a person a codependent, the therapist is promoting feelings of helplessness or victimization in these individuals that might not have existed before. Indeed, the idea of codependency might diminish the person's incentive to begin efforts to take control over his or her life by reinforcing the feeling that he or she is "doomed to suffer." Critics also point out that actual patterns of codependency may not be specific to particular individuals but rather are common to practically everyone. Codependency simply may reflect the problems of living in modern society, only now we have found language to explain our own failures by blaming other people.[37]

Children of an Alcoholic Parent or Parents

Considering the immense impact that our parents have in our lives, it is understandable that an alcoholic family will have distinct negative consequences on the psychological development of the children in that family. As a result, **children of alcoholics (COAs)** have a higher statistical risk of becoming alcoholics than do children of nonalcoholics. Whether this increased risk is genetically or environmentally based is a complex issue that will be reviewed in the next section.

An equally important and independent risk factor, however, may be the specific behavioral and physiological reactions a person has to alcohol itself. Men who at age twenty have a relatively low response to alcohol, in that they need to drink more than other people to feel intoxicated, carry a higher risk of becoming alcoholic by the time they are thirty, regardless of their pattern of drinking at an earlier age and regardless of their parents' drinking. Sons of alcoholics having a low response to alcohol have a 60 percent chance of becoming alcoholics, compared with a 42 percent chance for sons of alcoholics in general. Sons of nonalcoholics having a low response to alcohol have a 22 percent chance of becoming alcoholics, compared with an 8 to 9 percent chance for sons of nonalcoholics in general.

The combination of these two risk factors—family history and a low response to alcohol—is obviously the worst scenario for a development of alcoholism, at least in males. Nonetheless, we should remember that a large proportion of people still *do not* become alcoholics, even with both risk factors present. The question of what protective factors may contribute to the resilience of high-risk individuals with regard to alcoholism is a major subject of current research.[38]

The Genetics of Alcoholism

For centuries, alcoholism has appeared to run in families. Today, this casual observation has led to a specific question: To what extent is alcoholism genetically determined (through the genes of the parents) and to what extent is it environmentally determined (through

systems approach: A way of understanding a phenomenon in terms of complex interacting relationships among individuals, family, friends, and community.

codependency: A concept that individuals who live with a person having an alcohol (or other drug) dependence suffer themselves from difficulties of self-image and social independence.

children of alcoholics (COAs): Individuals who grew up in a family with either one or two alcoholic parents.

the living conditions in which the offspring have been brought up)? One approach is to examine the inheritance pattern in a family tree. It is impossible, however, to tease out the separate genetic (nature) and environmental (nurture) factors from information of this kind.

For more precise answers, one option is to turn to cases of adoption in which children can be compared with either their biological or adoptive parents. In 1981, an extensive research study in Sweden looked at the adoption records of approximately three thousand children who had alcoholic biological parents but lived with nonalcoholic adoptive parents. The results showed that a larger percentage of these children become alcoholics than would be seen in the general population. The greater incidence was present even when the children had been raised by their adoptive parents immediately after being born, indicating that a strong genetic component was operating.

There were, however, two subgroups among those children who eventually became alcoholics. One subgroup, called *Type 1 alcoholics,* developed problem drinking later in life and generally functioned well in society. In addition to a genetic predisposition toward alcoholism, there was for this subgroup a strong environmental factor as well. Whether the child was placed in a middle-class or poor adoptive family influenced the final outcome. A second subgroup, called *Type 2 alcoholics,* developed alcoholism earlier in life and had significant antisocial patterns of behavior. A strong genetic component was operating in this subgroup, and because the socioeconomic status of the adoptive family made no difference in the outcome, we can conclude that environmental factors played a negligible role. Table 11.1 gives a more complete picture of the characteristics associated with Type 1 and Type 2 alcoholics.[39]

The study of twins is another source of information about the genetic and environmental influences in alcoholism. Probably the most important piece of data is the **concordance rate** for alcoholism in pairs of identical twins—that is, how likely one member of a pair is to be alcoholic if the other one is. The concordance rate has been found to be only 58 percent. If genetics were the whole story in determining the incidence of alcoholism, the concordance rate would have been 100 percent.

TABLE 11.1

Two types of alcoholics

CHARACTERISTICS	TYPE 1	TYPE 2
Usual age at onset	(late onset) after 25	(early onset) before 25
Inability to abstain	infrequent	frequent
Fights and arrests when drinking	infrequent	frequent
Psychological dependence (loss of control)	infrequent	frequent
Guilt and fear about alcoholism	frequent	infrequent
Novelty-seeking personality	low	high
Tendency to use alcohol to escape negative feelings	high	low
Tendency to use alcohol to achieve positive feelings	low	high
Gender	male and female	male only
Extent of genetic influences	moderate	high
Extent of environmental influences	high	low
Serotonin abnormalities in the brain	absent	present

Source: Updated from Cloninger, C. Robert (1987). Neurogenetic adaptive mechanisms in alcoholism. *Science, 236,* 410–416.

If we look closely at the type of alcoholic involved and whether the alcoholic is male or female, the data from twin studies are similar to those found in the adoption research. For example, the concordance rate for identical twins has been found to be significantly higher than the concordance rate for fraternal twins when one member of the pair is a male alcoholic whose drinking problems started in adolescence (in other words, a Type 2 alcoholic). For female and male alcoholics whose drinking problems started after adolescence (the Type 1 subgroup), a comparison of concordance rates shows that genetic factors played a lesser role.[40]

As exploration of the human genome continues, it is increasingly clear that no single gene for alcoholism or alcohol-related traits will be found. Instead, the most likely scenario is that several different genes interact with environmental factors, placing some individuals at a significantly higher risk for alcohol dependence.[41]

The Concept of Alcoholism as a Disease

In contrast to the days when alcoholism was considered a moral failure or worse, the majority opinion today is that alcoholism is best characterized as a disease and that the alcoholic should be treated rather than punished. This viewpoint has evolved over the years, originating from the writings of E. M. Jellinek in the late 1940s. Jellinek proposed that alcohol dependence progressed through a natural sequence of stages, much as a physical illness develops.[42] In more recent interpretations, the disease concept has moved away from the idea that all alcoholics follow a common path (many of Jellinek's ideas have not been confirmed) to a more general focus on the biological factors that might differentiate alcoholics from nonalcoholics. In addition, the disease concept has led to the idea that the alcoholics are fundamentally out of control and that abstinence is the only answer to their recovery.[43]

Since 1957, the American Medical Association has defined alcoholism as a disease, and numerous other health organizations have adopted a similar position. As reasonable as this position might sound, the disease concept has created something of a dilemma among professionals concerned with the treatment of alcohol abuse. It places the burden on physicians to deal with the alcoholic through medical interventions, and unfortunately the medical profession is frequently ill equipped to help. A study in 2000, for example, found that 94 percent of a group of primary care physicians failed to make a correct diagnosis of early-stage alcohol abuse when presented with symptoms typical of this condition. Only a small percentage, approximately one out of five, considered themselves "very prepared" to diagnose alcoholism in the first place.[44]

Approaches to Treatment for Alcoholism

Alcoholism, as should be clear at this point, is a study in diversity, and it makes sense that there might be some advantage in matching alcoholics with certain characteristics to specific forms of treatment. One treatment program might be best suited for one subgroup, another for another subgroup. As reasonable as this hypothesis sounds, however, a major study begun in the late 1980s and completed in 1997 has shown little or no benefit in patient–treatment matching. Apparently, no one treatment approach is overwhelmingly superior to others.[45] In this section, we will examine forms of alcoholism treatment as classified into two broad areas: biological interventions, which involve medications, and psychosocial interventions, such as Alcoholics Anonymous and other self-help programs.

Biologically Based Treatments

The use of **disulfiram** (brand name: Antabuse) is based on the idea that if a drug induces an aversive reaction in alcoholics when alcohol is consumed, then consumption will be avoided and the problems of alcoholism will be reduced. Disulfiram, taken orally as a pill once each day, inhibits alcohol dehydrogenase, allowing acetaldehyde to build up in the bloodstream. As a result, individuals who consume alcohol in combination with disulfiram experience a flushing of the face, rapid heart rate and palpitations, nausea, and vomiting. These effects occur not only by consuming alcoholic beverages but by ingesting alcohol in other forms such as mouthwashes, cough mixtures, and even by the absorption of aftershave lotions and shampoos through the skin.

Clearly the symptoms caused by a combination of disulfiram and alcohol can be a powerful short-term deterrent to alcoholic drinking, but the question is whether this kind of aversion therapy is an effective treatment over the long run. Careful studies in which disulfiram has been administered to large numbers of alcoholics indicate that it is not effective when it is the sole treatment. One major problem is that alcoholics must take the drug regularly every day, and because disulfiram does nothing to reduce the alcoholic's craving for alcohol, compliance rates are low.

The consensus among professionals in this field is that disulfiram can be useful in a subgroup of higher-functioning alcoholics with exceptionally high motivation to quit drinking; for others, disulfiram can be useful as a transitional treatment until other support programs are in place. In the future, a transdermal patch for the slow absorption of disulfiram through the skin, such as the ones currently available for nicotine, may be feasible. Physicians and drug counselors could ensure compliance by checking the continued presence of the patch on the alcoholic's skin, particularly if the patch were designed so that the user could not repeatedly remove and reapply it.[46]

A more direct approach to treatment than aversion therapy is to reduce the actual craving for alcohol on a physiological level. As noted in Chapter 10, evidence suggests that alcohol dependence is related to neural activity

> **disulfiram (dye-SULL-fih-ram):** A medication that causes severe physical reactions and discomfort when combined with alcohol. Brand name is Antabuse.

in the same dopamine-releasing receptors in the nucleus accumbens that have been implicated in heroin craving as well as craving for cocaine and nicotine. Based upon the association with heroin dependence, it makes sense that opiate receptor antagonists in this region of the brain, such as **naltrexone** (brand name: ReVia) and **nalmefene** (brand name: Revex), should be useful in alcohol-dependence treatment. Another drug related to GABA activity, **acamprosate** (brand name: Campral), was FDA-approved in 2004. The question of which combination of medications, along with behavioral counseling, might prove most effective as a treatment program is presently under investigation. Recently, it has been found that alcohol craving during treatment is a stronger predictor of subsequent drinking (and a failure of alcoholism treatment) than drinking behavior itself prior to treatment.

An alternative approach has focused on the role of serotonin levels in the brains of alcoholics. Since early-onset (Type 2) alcoholism differs from late-onset (Type 1) alcoholism owing to its association with serotonin abnormalities in the brain (see Table 11.1), a drug that reduces serotonin levels such as **ondansetron** (brand name: Zofran), typically used as an antinausea medication, should be beneficial in treating this subgroup. A recent study has confirmed this prediction. Among Type 2 alcoholics, Zofran significantly reduced their drinking behavior and provided a longer period of abstinence.[47]

Alcoholics Anonymous

The best-known treatment program for alcoholism is **Alcoholics Anonymous (AA)**. Founded in 1935, this organization has been conceived basically as a fellowship of alcoholics who wish to rid themselves of their problem drinking by helping one another maintain sobriety. The philosophy of AA is expressed in the famous Twelve Steps (Table 11.2). Members must have acknowledged that they were "powerless over alcohol" and that their lives became

naltrexone (nal-TREX-ohn): A long-lasting opiate antagonist for the treatment of alcoholism. Brand name is ReVia.

nalmefene (nal-MEH-feen): A long-lasting opiate antagonist for the treatment of alcoholism. Brand name is Revex.

acamprosate (A-cam-PRO-sate): A GABA-related drug for the treatment of alcoholism. Brand name is Campral.

ondansetron (on-DANS-eh-tron): A serotonin-related drug for the treatment of alcoholism. Brand name is Zofran.

Alcoholics Anonymous (AA): A worldwide organization devoted to the treatment of alcoholism through self-help groups and adherence to its principles.

An anonymous group of men and women at a typical Alcoholics Anonymous meeting.

TABLE 11.2

The famous Twelve Steps of Alcoholics Anonymous

1. We admitted we were powerless over alcohol—that our lives had become unmanageable.

2. Came to believe that a Power greater than ourselves could restore us to sanity.

3. Made a decision to turn our will and our lives over to the care of God *as we understood Him.*

4. Made a searching and fearless moral inventory of ourselves.

5. Admitted to God, to ourselves, and to another human being the exact nature of our wrongs.

6. Were entirely ready to have God remove all these defects of character.

7. Humbly asked Him to remove our shortcomings.

8. Made a list of all persons we had harmed and became willing to make amends to them all.

9. Made direct amends to such people wherever possible, except when to do so would injure them or others.

10. Continued to take moral inventory and when we were wrong, promptly admitted it.

11. Sought through prayer and meditation to improve our conscious contact with God *as we understood Him,* praying only for knowledge of His will for us and the power to carry that out.

12. Having had a spiritual awakening as a result of these steps, we tried to carry this message to alcoholics, and to practice these principles in all our affairs.

Source: The Twelve Steps are reprinted and adapted with permission of Alcoholics Anonymous World Services, Inc. Permission to reprint this material does not mean that AA has reviewed or approved the contents of this publication, nor that AA agrees with the views expressed herein. AA is a program of recovery from alcoholism *only.* Use of Twelve Steps in connection with programs and activities that are patterned after AA, but that address other problems, does not imply otherwise.

unmanageable, and to have turned their will and their lives over "to the care of God *as we understood Him.*" As the steps indicate, there is a strong spiritual component to the AA program, though the organization vigorously denies that any religious doctrine prevails (Portrait).

AA functions as a type of group therapy with each member oriented toward a common goal: the maintenance of abstinence from alcohol despite a powerful and continuing craving for it. All meetings are completely anonymous (only first names are used in all communications), and the proceedings are dominated by members recounting their personal struggles with alcohol, their efforts to stop drinking, and their support for fellow alcoholics in their own struggles. New members are encouraged to pair up with a sponsor, typically a more experienced AA member who has successfully completed the Twelve Steps and can serve as a personal source of support on a day-to-day basis. According to AA, no alcoholic is ever cured, only recovered, and the process of recovery continues throughout that person's life. Alcoholism, in its view, is a disease, and relapse from sobriety can occur at any moment (Drugs . . . in Focus).

AA has grown to more than 100,000 groups around the world and more than 2 million members, though it is difficult to get a precise count because the organization is deliberately structured very loosely. Perhaps more important than its size is the powerful impact it has made not only on the way we deal with alcoholism but also on the way we consider treatment for any compulsive behavior. Over the years, the twelve-step program has become a generic concept, as the precepts and philosophy of AA have been widely imitated. We now have Al-Anon for the spouses and family of alcoholics going through the AA program and Alateen as a specialized AA program for teenage alcoholics, as well as Gamblers Anonymous, Nicotine Anonymous, Narcotics or Cocaine Anonymous, and Overeaters Anonymous.

PORTRAIT

Bill W. and Dr. Bob—Founders of Alcoholics Anonymous

The backgrounds of William Griffith Wilson (above photo) and Dr. Robert Smith, when they met in the spring of 1935, could not have been more different, but they shared an important common problem. They were both alcoholics, and their lives had come apart because of it. Wilson had gone from being a successful businessman, whose investments on Wall Street during the 1920s had made him rich, to a penniless failure after losing his entire fortune in the 1929 crash. Whether rich or poor, he had been a drunk, but his poverty made the condition worse. In 1934 Wilson was admitted to Towns Hospital in New York City and agreed to subject himself to the "belladonna cure," a treatment based on his receiving morphine and the powerful hallucinogen belladonna. Under the influence of this combination of drugs, Wilson experienced "his spiritual awakening." He later wrote,

In the wake of my spiritual experience there came a vision of a society of alcoholics. If each sufferer were to carry the news of the scientific hopelessness of alcoholism to each new prospect, he might be able to lay every newcomer wide open to a transforming spiritual experience.

For several months following his new-found mission in life, Wilson sought out drunks to "work on." On a trip to Akron, Ohio, where he was seeking a new job, he was introduced by mutual friends to a proctologist and surgeon named Dr. Robert Smith. Smith's alcoholism had wrecked a distinguished medical career, and in 1935, he was in severe financial straits. Wilson's determination combined with Smith's desperation led to their taking on the task of keeping each other sober and helping others do the same. On June 10, 1935 (the official date of the founding of Alcoholics Anonymous), Smith took his last drink. By 1939, Wilson had completed the writing of the Twelve Steps and an extended explanation of the AA philosophy, known today as the Big Book. Wilson and Smith had discovered that they were most successful in keeping alcoholics abstinent when they attended meetings on a regular basis and were assured of complete privacy and anonymity. Wilson became Bill W., and Smith became Dr. Bob.

It was not until the 1940s that AA started to be nationally known. The *Saturday Evening Post*, one of the leading magazines of the day, gave them their first real publicity break, publishing an article about the organization that generated an avalanche of responses and a dramatic increase in membership. During this time, a prayer was composed that would eventually be repeated millions of times in AA meetings throughout the world: "God grant me the serenity to accept the things I cannot change, the courage to change the things I can, and the wisdom to know the difference."

Sources: Alcoholics Anonymous comes of age: A brief history of AA (1959). New York: Alcoholics Anonymous World Services. Alibrandi, Lucinda A. (1982). The fellowship of Alcoholics Anonymous. In E. Mansell Pattison and Edward Kaufman (Eds.), The encyclopedic handbook of alcoholism. New York: Gardner Press, p. 979. Cheever, Susan (2004). My name is Bill. New York: Simon and Schuster.

Drugs . . . in Focus

Is Controlled Drinking Possible for Alcoholics?

One of the most intensely debated questions in the field of alcoholism treatment has been whether it is possible for alcoholics to achieve a level of "controlled drinking" without falling back into a state of alcohol dependence.

On one side are well-entrenched organizations such as Alcoholics Anonymous (AA) and the National Institute on Alcohol Abuse and Alcoholism, as well as many other organizations that assert that alcoholism is an irreversible disease, that abstinence is the only answer, and that even the slightest level of alcohol consumption will trigger a cascade of problems that the alcoholic is constitutionally incapable of handling.

On the other side are groups, represented in greater numbers in Canada and Europe than in the United States, asserting that uncontrolled drinking is a reversible behavioral disorder and that for many alcoholics the promotion of total abstinence as a treatment goal is a serious obstacle to their success in rehabilitation. The organization Moderation Management (MM) is an example of this type of therapeutic approach.

Some of the early controlled-drinking studies had enough methodological flaws that the abstinence-only group were justified in denouncing them. But later research, using carefully randomized assignment of alcoholic subjects to either an abstinence-oriented treatment or a controlled-drinking one, has shown that long-term results are comparable for either group. This is not to say that the prospects are wonderful for either of them; the odds are still higher *against* long-term recovery from alcoholism than *for* it, no matter what the treatment. But it does appear that controlled drinking can occur.

How many alcoholics can manage to achieve a continued level of nonproblem drinking? Percentages vary from 2 to 10 to 15, though the lower figure is probably more accurate for those individuals with severe alcoholic difficulties. Perhaps a more important point is that no one knows how to predict whether an alcohol abuser will be one of that small number of successful controlled drinkers. Obviously, most alcoholics are convinced that they will be the lucky ones. How does an alcoholism-treatment counselor handle this? A prominent expert offers one strategy:

My own perspective is that there is little sense in losing a client by a standoff on this issue. . . . It has been my clinical experience that an unsuccessful trial at "controlled drinking" may be a more persuasive confrontation of the need for abstinence than any amount of argumentation between therapist and client.

Sources: Goode, Erich (1999). *Drugs in American society* (5th ed.). Boston: McGraw-Hill College, p. 194. Hester, Reid K., and Miller, William R. (1989). Self-control training. In Reid K. Hester and William R. Miller (Eds.), *Handbook of alcoholism treatment approaches*. New York: Pergamon Press, pp. 141–149. Miller, William R. (1989). Increasing motivation for change. In Reid K. Hester and William R. Miller (Eds.), *Handbook of alcoholism treatment approaches*. New York: Pergamon Press, pp. 67–80. Quotation on p. 77. Sobell, Mark B., and Sobell, Linda C. (1978). *Behavioral treatment of alcohol problems: Individualized therapy and controlled drinking*. New York: Plenum.

Despite its stature as an approach to treatment, however, there are relatively few scientific appraisals of the overall effectiveness of AA. One of the principal problems is the anonymity that is guaranteed to all members, making it difficult to conduct well-controlled follow-up studies on how well AA members are doing. Nonetheless, AA is widely regarded in the field of alcohol rehabilitation as a beneficial self-help approach, particularly when it is combined with other treatments such as individual counseling and medical interventions.[48] It has been pointed out that AA employs four factors that are widely shown to be effective in preventing relapse in alcohol dependence: (1) the imposition of external supervision, (2) the substitution of dependence on a group activity rather than drug-taking behavior, (3) the development of caring relationships, and (4) a heightened sense of spirituality.[49] Drugs . . . in Focus on page 289 examines the success of AA from a sociological perspective.

SMART Recovery

In contrast to AA, the self-help program **SMART Recovery** assumes that people do not need to believe they are

> **SMART Recovery:** An alcoholism and other drug-abuse treatment program emphasizing a nonspiritual philosophy and a greater sense of personal control in the abuser. SMART stands for "Self-Management And Recovery Training."

Drugs . . . in Focus

The Sociology of Alcoholics Anonymous

Alcoholics Anonymous (AA) is arguably the most successful treatment program in history. Here is a selection of excerpts from a major analysis by Mariana Valverde and Kimberly White-Mair into the sociological aspects of AA that, in their judgment, have led to this accomplishment:

- Practice-driven rather than theory-driven activity

  AA does have some theories; for instance, members almost universally believe that "once an alcoholic, always an alcoholic." Nevertheless, it is a fundamentally pragmatic organization, and its basis of unity is not a set of beliefs but rather a set of practices: the twelve steps and the twelve traditions, plus the organisational practices that have evolved in group meetings over the years. (p. 394)

  Activity is the key term here: AA, although driven by beliefs and dogmas to an extent perhaps not recognized by most of its members, is nevertheless an anti-intellectual, and particularly anti-scientific, organization. (p. 399)

- A fellowship, not a movement

  AA describes itself not as a movement but as "a fellowship," and it positively refuses to engage in political and social change, to lobby for or against legislation, or to participate in the public arena in any way. . . . The explicit refusal of a public image, unusual in the context of American philanthropic or spiritual organizations, is best explained, we argue, as a reaction to the old temperance movement. (p. 395)

  If AA had set itself squarely against the liquor industry, it probably would have melted into oblivion, given the historical defeat of the temperance movement and the rise in the post–World War II period of a culture of consumerism. (p. 396)

- Beyond outward sobriety to inner peace

  The ultimate goal of AA is not the already ambitious one of helping people stop drinking: it is the even more ambitious one of helping people achieve inner peace. . . . Sobriety is thus more than the absence of drinking: it is difficult to define but is nevertheless a positively existing state. (pp. 397–398)

- Gaining power through powerlessness

  . . . AA indirectly subverts the neoliberal discourse of personal entrepreneurship and perpetual improvement. . . . AA members are perpetually in recovery, always working on

their souls, but they do not imagine they will ever re-make themselves from scratch. (p. 401)

- Telling one's story without confessing your sins

  AA is one of the many movements in today's world that relies heavily on autobiographical narratives. First-person accounts of movement from alcoholism to sobriety form a large part of the Big Book, and open group meeting have at least one or two autobiographical segments. . . . In group meetings, the key feature distinguishing "telling one's story" from confession is that the people listening do not either interpret or judge the speaker. (p. 403)

- Appealing to "my" Higher power, not necessarily "your" Higher Power

  In meetings, people talk not about "the" Higher Power but rather about "my" Higher Power—as in the phrase heard at a meeting, "my Higher Power must have a sense of humour. . . ." The proliferation of individualized higher powers would suggest that today's AA members believe in guardian angels without believing in a God that guarantees the truth of angels. . . . (p. 405)

- Building a life on a twenty-four-hour cycle

  One is the custom of celebrating months or years of sobriety with commemorative tokens, a round of applause, and sometimes even a party—a technique that rewards long-term abstinence. But the other technique, embodied in the "one day at a time" slogan, counteracts the tendency of "oldtimers" to feel superior. Although long-term abstention is prized, AA members sometimes say that the person with the longest sobriety is "whoever woke up the earliest that morning." (p. 406)

- Anonymity at all costs

  . . . Anonymity is perhaps less essential now to protect the individual—in some circles, being a recovering alcoholic is no longer stigmatized, and may even bring some cachet—but rather that the group does not succumb to the temptation of money, fame, and power that have crippled other organizations. [An AA member writes]: "Anonymity keeps us focused on principles rather than personalities. There are no 'stars' in AA. . . . External anonymity is thus clearly linked to one of AA's key traditions, namely the refusal to own property." (pp. 401–402)

Source: Valverde, Mariana, and White-Mair, Kimberly (1999). "One day at a time" and other slogans for everyday life: The ethical practices of Alcoholics Anonymous. *Sociology, 33,* 393–410.

"powerless over alcohol" or submit to "a Power greater than ourselves" (excerpts taken from the Twelve Steps) to recover from alcoholism. Instead, the dominant philosophy is that individuals have the power themselves to overcome anything, including drinking. The strategy is based on Rational Emotive Behavior Therapy (REBT), developed by the psychologist Albert Ellis, which emphasizes rooting out irrational thoughts, emotions, and beliefs that prevent the achievement of personal goals.

Another major difference is that SMART Recovery insists on professional involvement in its program, with a professional adviser (often a clinical psychologist) assisting members in learning the fundamentals of REBT. No reference is made to God or a higher power; the objective is "NHP (no higher power) sobriety." The goal is that within a year and a half members will be able to maintain sobriety without going to meetings. In contrast, AA members are encouraged to continue going to meetings for the rest of their lives.

Since 1990, there has been increased interest in secular (nonreligious) approaches to self-help alcoholism treatment such as that practiced by SMART Recovery. Other examples include Men for Sobriety (MFS), Women for Sobriety (WFS), Moderation Management (MM), and Secular Organization for Sobriety (SOS). Nonetheless, recent research has indicated that alcoholics benefit from participation in AA programs, regardless of their religious beliefs.[50]

Alcoholism in the Workplace

Considering the adverse impact of alcoholism on worker productivity, it makes sense that corporations, hospitals, the armed services, and many other large organizations should profit by the existence of workplace programs for employees needing help. Two major programs address this problem. The first are employer-sponsored **employee assistance programs (EAPs)** and the second are union-supported **member assistance programs (MAPs)**.

Whereas EAPs have been created as a way of increasing the productivity of the organization, MAPs are oriented toward enhancing the welfare of the individual worker. In either case, the major thrust of workplace interventions has been to change the culture of drinking both within the workplace and outside it. For example, problems can arise when employees tend to drink heavily in order to conform to workplace drinking norms. Within a heavy drinking culture, employees are more likely to use alcohol to cope with stress and feelings of alienation in their personal lives. Workplace EAPs and MAPs will be examined in Chapter 15 in the larger context of alcohol and other drug abuse prevention and treatment.[51]

Quick Concept Check 11.2

Understanding Alcoholics Anonymous

Check your understanding of the principles and philosophy of Alcoholics Anonymous by checking off whether the following statements would be ascribed to by Alcoholics Anonymous.

1. I have always had the power to control my drinking. ☐ yes ☐ no

2. I must put myself in the hands of a Higher Power if I am to be sober for the rest of my life. ☐ yes ☐ no

3. It is possible to be cured of alcoholism. ☐ yes ☐ no

4. I am capable of having a drink once in a great while without slipping back into alcoholism. ☐ yes ☐ no

5. The more meetings I attend, the better chance I have of remaining sober. ☐ yes ☐ no

Answers: 1. no 2. yes 3. no 4. no 5. yes

employee assistance programs (EAPs): Corporate or institutional programs for workers or employees to help them with alcohol or other drug-abuse problems.

member assistance programs (MAPs): Institutional programs for workers or employees to help them with alcohol or other drug-abuse problems, set up by established unions within the organization and tailored for union members.

Alcoholism: Stereotypes, Definitions, and Criteria

- Alcoholism is a multidimensional condition that is typically defined in terms of four major criteria: (1) problems associated with a preoccupation with drinking, (2) emotional problems, (3) vocational, social, and family problems, and (4) physical problems. Not all criteria have to be met, however, for alcoholism to be diagnosed.

Alcohol Abuse and Alcohol Dependence

- According to health professionals, alcohol abuse is defined in terms of (1) persistent physical, social, or occupational problems that have become associated with alcohol use and (2) recurring use of alcohol in physically hazardous situations. Alcohol dependence is defined in terms of uncontrolled alcohol intake, unsuccessful efforts to reduce alcohol use, life problems, and alcohol tolerance and withdrawal.

- It is estimated that approximately 8.5 percent of U.S. adults can be classified as either alcohol abusers or as alcohol dependent.

The Social History of Regulating Alcohol Use

- An appreciation of the adverse consequences of chronic alcohol abuse started in the late 1700s and took root in the United States as a temperance movement. This movement addressed its concerns primarily toward the drinking of distilled spirits.

- The differentiation among forms of alcohol drinking became blurred during the nineteenth century, as temperance advocates began to promote a total ban on alcohol consumption. National Prohibition was the law in the United States from 1920 to 1933.

- Since the end of Prohibition, government regulation has been carried out chiefly through education and the taxation of alcohol.

Physiological Effects of Chronic Alcohol Use

- Physical effects of alcoholism include tolerance and withdrawal, liver disease, cardiovascular disease, cancer, and neurological disorders such as Wernicke-Korsakoff syndrome.

- A particular concern is the development of fetal alcohol syndrome (FAS) in the offspring of alcoholic mothers.

Social Patterns of Chronic Alcohol Abuse

- Alcoholics can be found in every age, gender, racial, ethnic, and religious group and in all socioeconomic and geographic categories. Nonetheless, men outnumber women in the incidence of alcoholism by about six to one, though women are more vulnerable to alcohol-related organ damage. The elderly tend to be an underreported group with respect to alcoholism.

- A systems approach to alcoholism examines the complex interacting relationships among individuals, family, friends, and community. The concept of codependency has helped shed light on the specific effects of alcoholism on spouses and other family members. The children of alcoholics (COAs) carry an increased risk of becoming alcoholic as a result of a vulnerability toward alcoholism that is genetically or environmentally based, or both.

The Genetics of Alcoholism

- Studies of adoptions and twins have provided information about the relative influences of genetics and environment on the development of alcoholism.

- A distinction has been made between a male or female alcoholic with drinking problems occurring late in life (Type 1) and a male alcoholic with drinking problems occurring in adolescence (Type 2). The latter subgroup appears to have a greater genetic component in the inheritance pattern.

The Concept of Alcoholism as a Disease

- The majority position with respect to alcoholism is that it should be considered a disease and that alcoholics should be treated rather than punished. Since 1957, the American Medical Association has supported this idea.

- Unfortunately, recent surveys of primary-care physicians indicate that the medical profession is frequently ill prepared to diagnose alcoholism or supervise effective treatment.

Approaches to Treatment for Alcoholism

- Approaches include biologically based treatments and psychosocial treatments such as the self-help programs of Alcoholics Anonymous (AA).

- Objections to certain aspects of the AA philosophy have promoted the growth of other self-help organizations, such as Moderation Management (MM) and SMART Recovery.

- Corporations and other large organizations have instituted employee assistance programs (EAPs) and unions have instituted member assistance programs (MAPs) to help workers with problems of alcohol abuse or other forms of drug abuse.

Endnotes

1. Goodwin, Donald W., and Gabrielli, William F. (1997). Alcohol: Clinical aspects. In Joyce H. Lowinson, Pedro Ruiz, Robert B. Millman, and John G. Langrod (Eds.), *Substance abuse: A comprehensive textbook*. Baltimore: Williams and Wilkins, pp. 142–148. Julien, Robert M. (2001). *A primer of drug action* (9th ed.). New York: Worth, pp. 108–110.

2. Hoff, Ebbe Curtis (1974). *Alcoholism: The hidden addiction*. New York: Seabury Press, pp. 75–88.

3. Hofmann, Frederick G. (1983). *A handbook on drug and alcohol abuse* (2nd ed.). New York: Oxford University Press, p. 99.

4. Hoff, *Alcoholism*, pp. 78–79.

5. Drobes, David J., and Thomas, Suzanne E. (1999). Assessing craving for alcohol. *Alcohol Research and Health, 23*, 179–186. Ludwig, Arnold M. (1988). *Understanding the alcoholic's mind: The nature of craving and how to control it*. New York: Oxford University Press.

6. Conner, Kenneth R.; Yue, Li; Meldrum, Sean; Duberstein, Paul R.; and Conwell, Y. (2003). The role of drinking in suicidal ideation: Analysis of Project MATCH data. *Journal of Studies on Alcohol, 64*, 402–408. Schuckit, Marc A. (2000). *Drug and alcohol abuse: A clinical guide to diagnostic and treatment* (5th ed.). New York: Kluver Academic/Plenum, pp. 54–97.

7. Maiden, R. Paul (1997). Alcohol dependence and domestic violence: Incidence and treatment implications. *Alcohol Treatment Quarterly, 15*, 31–50. U.S. Department of Health and Human Services (1990). *Alcohol and health* (Seventh Special Report to the U.S. Congress). Rockville, MD: National Institute on Alcohol Abuse and Alcoholism, p. 174.

8. Hofmann, *Handbook on drug and alcohol abuse*, pp. 98–99. National Institute on Alcohol Abuse and Alcoholism (2000, April). Alcohol Alert: Imaging and alcoholism: A window on the brain. No. 47. Rockville, MD: National Institute on Alcohol Abuse and Alcoholism.

9. Fishbein, Diana H., and Pease, Susan E. (1996). *The dynamics of drug abuse*. Needham Heights, MA: Allyn and Bacon, pp. 122–124.

10. American Psychiatric Association (2000). *Diagnostic and statistical manual of mental disorders* (4th ed.). *Text Revision*. Washington DC: American Psychiatric Association, pp. 213–214.

11. Grant, Bridget F.; Stinson, Frederick S.; Dawson, Deborah A.; Chou, S. Patricia; Dufour, Mary C.; Compton, Wilson; Pickering, Roger P.; and Kaplan, Kenneth (2004). Prevalence and co-occurrence of substance use disorders and independent mood and anxiety disorders. *Archives of General Psychiatry, 61*, 807–816. National Institute on Alcohol Abuse and Alcoholism (1995, October). Alcohol Alert: Diagnostic criteria for alcohol abuse and dependence. No. 30. Bethesda, MD: National Institute on Alcohol Abuse and Alcoholism.

12. Quoted in Sournia, Jean-Charles (1990). *A history of alcoholism*. Cambridge, MA: Basil Blackwell, p. 29.

13. Lender, Mark E., and Martin, James R. (1982). *Drinking in America: A history*. New York: Free Press, p. 107.

14. Blocker, Jack S. (2006, February). Did Prohibition really work? Alcohol prohibition as a public health innovation. *American Journal of Public Health*, pp. 233–243. Lerner, Michael A. (2007). *Dry Manhattan: Prohibition in New York City*. Cambridge, MA: Harvard University Press. Sournia, *History of alcoholism*, p. 122.

15. *Standard and Poor's Industry Surveys* (2003, January 23). Alcoholic beverages and tobacco, p. 19. U.S. Department of Health and Human Services (2000). *Alcohol and health* (Tenth Special Report to the U.S. Congress). Rockville, MD: National Institute on Alcohol Abuse and Alcoholism, p. 370. *Standard and Poor's Industry Surveys* (1997, January 23). Alcoholic beverages and tobacco, p. 15. *Standard and Poor's Industry Surveys* (1997, September 11). Alcoholic beverages and tobacco, p. 16.

16. U.S. Department of Health and Human Services (2000). *Alcohol and health*, pp. 341–354.

17. Schuckit, *Drug and alcohol abuse,* pp. 79–80.

18. Sellers, Edward M., and Kalant, Harold (1982). Alcohol withdrawal and delirium tremens. In E. Mansell Pattison and Edward Kaufman (Eds.), *Encyclopedic handbook of alcoholism.* New York: Gardner Press, pp. 147–166.

19. Lieber, Charles S. (2001). Alcohol and hepatitis C. *Alcohol Research and Health, 25,* 245–254. National Institute on Alcohol Abuse and Alcoholism (1998, October). Alcohol Alert: Alcohol and the liver: Research update. No. 42. Rockville, MD: National Institute on Alcohol Abuse and Alcoholism.

20. Brands, Bruna, Sproule, Beth, and Marshman, Joan (Eds.) (1998). *Drugs and drug abuse: A reference text* (3rd ed.). Toronto: Addiction Research Foundation, p. 271. Mukamal, Kenneth J.; Tolstrup, Janne S.; Friberg, Jens; Friberg, Jens; and Gronbaek, Morton (2005). Alcohol consumption and risk of atrial fibrillation in men and women. *Circulation, 112,* 1736–1742.

21. Bagnardi, Vincenzo, Blangliardo, Marta, and LaVecchia, Carlo (2001). Alcohol consumption and the risk of cancer. A meta-analysis. *Alcohol Research and Health, 25,* 263–270. Smith-Warner, Stephanie A.; Spiegelman, Donna; Shiaw-Shyuan, Yuan; Van den Brandt, Piet A.; Folsom, Aaron R.; Goldbohm, Alexandra; Graham, Saxon; Holmberg, Lars; Howe, Geoffrey R.; et al. (1998). Alcohol and breast cancer in women: A pooled analysis of cohort studies. *Journal of the American Medical Association, 279,* 535–540.

22. National Institute on Alcohol Abuse and Alcoholism (2001, July). Alcohol Alert: Cognitive impairment and recovery from alcoholism. No. 53. Rockville, MD: National Institute on Alcohol Abuse and Alcoholism. U.S. Department of Health and Human Services (1990). *Alcohol and health,* pp. 123–124.

23. McEvoy, Joseph P. (1982). The chronic neuropsychiatric disorders associated with alcoholism. In E. Mansell Pattison and Edward Kaufman (Eds.), *Encyclopedic handbook of alcoholism.* New York: Gardner Press, pp. 167–179.

24. Golden, Janet (2005). *Message in a bottle: The making of fetal alcohol syndrome.* Cambridge, MA: Harvard University Press. Jones, Kenneth L., and Smith, David W. (1973). Recognition of the fetal alcohol syndrome in early infancy. *Lancet, 2,* 999–1001. Sokol, Robert J., Delaney-Black, Virginia, and Nordstrom, Beth (2003). Fetal alcohol spectrum disorder. *Journal of the American Medical Association, 290,* 2996–2999.

25. Ma, Grace X.; Toubbeh, Jamil; Cline, Janette; and Chisholm, Anita (1998). Fetal alcohol syndrome among Native American adolescents: A model prevention program. *Journal of Primary Prevention, 19,* 43–55. Morbidity and Mortality Weekly Report (2002). Fetal alcohol syndrome—Alaska, Arizona, Colorado, and New York, 1995–1997. *Journal of the American Medical Association, 288,* 38–40. U.S. Department of Health and Human Services (2000). *Alcohol and health,* pp. 283–299.

26. National Institute on Alcohol Abuse and Alcoholism (2000, December). Alcohol Alert: Fetal alcohol exposure and the brain. No. 13. Bethesda, MD: National Institute on Alcohol Abuse and Alcoholism. U.S. Department of Health and Human Services (2000). *Alcohol and health,* pp. 300–322.

27. May, Philip A. (1991). Fetal alcohol effects among North American Indians. *Alcohol Health and Research World, 15,* 239–248. National Institute on Alcohol Abuse and Alcoholism (2004, July). Alcohol Alert: Alcohol—An important women's health issue. Bethesda, MD: National Institute on Alcohol Abuse and Alcoholism. U.S. Department of Health and Human Services (2000). *Alcohol and health,* pp. 323–336.

28. Alcohol alert: Fetal alcohol exposure. Carroll, Linda (2003, November 4). Alcohol's toll on fetuses: Even worse than thought. *New York Times,* pp. F1, F6. Ebrahim, Shahul H.; Diekman, Shane T.; Floyd, R. Louise; and Decoufle, Pierre (1999). Comparison of binge drinking among pregnant and nonpregnant women, United States, 1991–1995. *American Journal of Obstetrics and Gynecology, 180,* 1–7. Floyd, R. Louise; O'Connor, Mary J.; Sokol, Robert J.; Bertrand, Jacquelyn; and Cordero, José F. (2005). Recognition and prevention of fetal alcohol syndrome. *Obstetrics and Gynecology, 106,* 1059–1064.

29. U.S. Department of Health and Human Services (2000). *Alcohol and health,* pp. 364–372.

30. Cloninger, C. Robert (1987). Neurogenetic adaptive mechanisms in alcoholism. *Science, 236,* 410–416. National Institute on Alcohol Abuse and Alcoholism (1999, December). Alcohol Alert: Are women more vulnerable to alcohol's effects? No. 46. Rockville, MD: National Institute on Alcohol Abuse and Alcoholism.

31. Nephew, T. M.; Williams, G. D.; Hoy, A. K.; Stinson, F. S.; Sanchez, L. L.; and Dufour, M. C. (2003, August). *Surveillance report #62: Apparent per capita alcohol consumption: National, state, and regional trends, 1977–2000.* Bethesda, MD: National Institute on Alcohol Abuse and Alcoholism.

32. Maletta, Gabe J. (1982). Alcoholism and the aged. In E. Mansell Pattison and Edward Kaufman (Eds.), *Encyclopedic handbook of alcoholism.* New York: Gardner Press, pp. 779–791.

33. Brody, Jane E. (2002, April 2). Hidden plague of alcohol abuse by the elderly. *New York Times,* p. F7. Fleming, Michael F.; Manwell, Linda, B.; Barry, Kristen L.; Adams, Wendy; and Stauffacher, Ellyn A. (1999). Brief physician advice for alcohol problems in older adults: A randomized community-based trial. *Journal of Family Practice, 48,* 378–384. Graham, Kathryn; Della Clarke, Christine B.; Carver, Virginia; Dolinki, Louise; Smythe, Cynthia; Harrison, Susan; Marshman, Joan; and Brett, Pamela (1996). Addictive behaviors in older adults. *Addictive Behaviors, 21,* 331–348. Substance Abuse and Mental Health Services Administration (2007, January/February). Treatment for older adults: What works best? *SAMHSA News,* pp. 1–5.

34. DiNitto, Diana M., and McNeece, C. Aaron (1994). *Chemical dependency: A systems approach*. Englewood Cliffs, NJ: Prentice-Hall, pp. 214–239.

35. Doweiko, Harold E. (1993). *Concepts of chemical dependency* (2nd ed.). Pacific Grove, CA: Brooks-Cole, p. 265.

36. Whitfield, Charles L. (1997). Co-dependence, addictions, and related disorders. In Lowinson et al. (Eds.), *Substance abuse: A comprehensive textbook* (3rd ed.). Baltimore: Williams and Wilkins, pp. 672–683.

37. Doweiko, *Concepts of chemical dependency*, pp. 269–271, 282–284.

38. Erblich, Joel, and Earleywine, Mitchell (1999). Children of alcoholics exhibit attenuated cognitive impairment during an ethanol challenge. *Alcoholism: Clinical and Experimental Research, 23*, 476–482. Hussong, Andrea M., Curran, Patrick J., and Chassin, Laurie (1998). Pathways of risk for accelerated heavy alcohol use among adolescent children of alcoholic parents. *Journal of Abnormal Child Psychology, 26*, 453–466.

39. Cloninger, Neurogenetic adaptive mechanisms. Cloninger, C. Robert, Gohman, M., and Sigvardsson, S. (1981). Inheritance of alcohol abuse: Cross fostering analysis of adopted men. *Archives of General Psychiatry, 38*, 861–868.

40. McGue, Matt, Pickens, Roy W., and Svikis, Dace S. (1992). Sex and age effects on the inheritance of alcohol problems: A twin study. *Journal of Abnormal Psychology, 101*, 3–17.

41. Dick, Danielle M., and Foroud, Tatiana (2002). Genetic strategies to detect genes involved in alcoholism and alcohol-related traits. *Alcohol Research and Health, 26*, 172–180. Edenberg, Howard J. (2002). The Collaborative Study on the Genetics of Alcoholism: An update. *Alcohol Research and Health, 26*, 214–218. National Institute on Alcohol Abuse and Alcoholism (2003, July). Alcohol Alert: The genetics of alcoholism. No. 60. Rockville, MD: National Institute on Alcohol Abuse and Alcoholism.

42. Jellinek, E. M. (1952). Phases of alcohol addiction. *Quarterly Journal of Studies in Alcohol, 13*, 672. Jellinek, E. M. (1960). *The disease concept of alcoholism*. New Haven, CT: Hillhouse Press. Vaillant, George E. (1995). *The natural history of alcoholism revisited*. Cambridge, MA: Harvard University Press.

43. George, William H., and Marlatt, G. Alan. (1983). Alcoholism: The evolution of a behavioral perspective. In Marc Galanter (Ed.), *Recent developments in alcoholism*. Vol. 1. New York: Plenum, pp. 105–138.

44. Fingarette, Herbert. (1988, November/December). Alcoholism: The mythical disease. *Utne Reader, 30*, 66. Maltzman, Irving (1994). Why alcoholism is a disease. *Journal of Psychoactive Drugs, 26*, 13–31. National Center on Addiction and Substance Abuse at Columbia University (2000, May). *Missed opportunity: National survey of primary care physicians and patients on substance abuse*. New York: National Center on Addiction and Substance Abuse at Columbia University.

45. Fuller, Richard K., and Hiller-Sturmhöfel, Susanne (1999). Alcoholism treatment in the United States. *Alcohol Research and Health, 23*, 69–77.

46. Banys, Peter (1988). The clinical use of disulfiram (Antabuse): A review. *Journal of Psychoactive Drugs, 20*, 243–261.

47. Flannery, B. A.; Poole, S. A.; Gallop, R. J.; and Volpicelli, J. R. (2003). Alcohol craving predicts drinking during treatment: An analysis of three assessment instruments. *Journal of Studies on Alcohol, 64*, 120–126. National Institute on Alcohol Abuse and Alcoholism (2001, October). Alcohol Alert: Craving research: Implications for treatment. No. 54. Rockville, MD: National Institute on Alcohol Abuse and Alcoholism. National Institute on Alcohol Abuse and Alcoholism (2004, April). Alcohol Alert: Neuroscience research and therapeutic targets. No. 61. Rockville, MD: National Institute on Alcohol Abuse and Alcoholism. Scott, Lesley J.; Figgitt, David P.; Keam, Susan J.; and Waugh, John (2005). Acamprosate: A review of its use in the maintenance of abstinence in patients with alcohol dependence. *CNS Drugs, 19*, 445–464.

48. Hopson, Ronald E., and Beaird-Spiller, Bethany (1995). Why AA works: A psychological analysis of the addictive experience and the efficacy of Alcoholics Anonymous. *Alcoholism Treatment Quarterly, 12*, 1–17. Morgenstern, Jon; Bux, Donald; LaBouvie, Erich; Blanchard, Kimberly A.; and Morgan, Thomas J. (2002). Examining mechanisms of action in a 12-step treatment: The role of 12-step cognitions. *Journal of Studies on Alcohol, 63*, 665–672.

49. Forcehimes, Alyssa A. (2004). *De Profundis*: Spiritual transformations in Alcoholics Anonymous. *Journal of Clinical Psychology/In Session, 60*, 503–517. How effective is Alcoholics Anonymous? (2003, December). *Harvard Medical Letter*, p. 7. Vaillant, George E. (2005). Alcoholics Anonymous: Cult or cure? *Australian and New Zealand Journal of Psychiatry, 39*, 431–436.

50. Ellis, Albert, and Velten, Emmett (1992). *When AA doesn't work for you: Rational steps to quitting alcohol*. Fort Lee, NJ: Barricade Press. Horvath, Arthur T. (1997). Alternative support groups. In Lowinson et al. (Eds.), *Substance abuse: A comprehensive textbook*. Baltimore: Williams and Wilkins, pp. 390–396. Kaskutas, Lee A. (1996). A road less traveled: Choosing the "Women for Sobriety" program. *Journal of Drug Issues, 26*, 77–94. Schmidt, Eric (1996). Rational recovery: Finding an alternative for addiction treatment. *Alcoholism Treatment Quarterly, 14*, 47–57. SMART Recovery (2004). *SMART Recovery handbook*. Mentor, OH: SMART Recovery®. Winzelberg, Andrew, and Humphreys, Keith (1999). Should patients' religiosity influence clinicians' referral to 12-step self-help groups? Evidence from a study of 3,018 male substance abuse patients. *Journal of Consulting and Clinical Psychology, 67*, 790–794.

51. Ames, Genevieve M., Grube, Joel W., and Moore, Roland S. (1997). The relationship of drinking and hangovers to workplace problems: An empirical study. *Journal of Studies on Alcohol*, 58, 37–47. Bacharch, Samuel B. (2007, March 15). Battling addiction: The workplace matters. Courtesy of the Smithers Institute for Alcohol-Related Workplace Studies at Cornell University, Ithaca, New York. Blum, Terry C., Roman, Paul M., and Martin, Jack K. (1993). Alcohol consumption and work performance. *Journal of Studies on Alcohol*, *54*, 61–70. U.S. Department of Health and Human Services. *Alcohol and health*, pp. 252–254. National Institute on Alcohol Abuse and Alcoholism (1999, July). Alcohol Alert: Alcohol and the workplace. No. 44. Rockville, MD: National Institute on Alcohol Abuse and Alcoholism. Smith, Deborah (2001, June). Impairment on the job. *Monitor on Psychology*, pp. 52–53.

chapter 12

Nicotine and Tobacco

Mark Twain is supposed to have said that quitting smoking was the easiest thing he ever did and that he should know because he had done it a thousand times. Well, I should know too. It seems that I've tried to quit a million times. I realize it's not good for me; I'm no fool. But you have to know that when I wake up in the morning, all I can think about is that first cigarette. Without it, my day doesn't begin.

I'm willing to suffer the indignity and inconvenience of standing out there in the rain and the cold, not to mention the disapproving glances of a lot of my friends, to have a cigarette. It's so hard to stop.

—Anonymous

After you have completed this chapter, you will understand

- The story of tobacco through history
- The present-day tobacco industry
- The main culprits: carbon monoxide, tar, and nicotine
- Nicotine as a stimulant drug
- Nicotine and smoking dependence
- Adverse health consequences from smoking
- Patterns of tobacco use in the United States
- Global issues in the control of tobacco use
- Strategies for people who want to stop smoking

In some ways, our attitudes toward tobacco have not changed. Many people still find tobacco smoke and the behavior of smoking as personally objectionable as they did in the sixteenth century when tobacco was first introduced to the Western world, and, judging from the opening quotation, people today have as much difficulty quitting as they did in Mark Twain's time.

In other ways, however, the times have definitely changed. For almost fifty years, until the middle 1960s, lighting up and smoking a cigarette was an unquestionable sign of sophistication. There was little or no public awareness that physical harm would come of it. It was an era before surgeon general's reports, National Smoke-out Days, no-smoking sections in restaurants, and (since May 2007) smoke-free restaurants in twenty U.S. states.

Today, it is no longer a matter of debate that tobacco smoking is a major health hazard, not only to the person doing the smoking but also to society at large. These concerns are based not on public attitudes that can vacillate over time but on solid scientific fact. It is also no longer a matter of debate that the main psychoactive ingredient in tobacco, nicotine, is a major dependence-producing drug.

Yet we need to recognize that tobacco products are legally sanctioned commodities with an economic significance, both to the United States and to the world, that cannot be ignored. How did we arrive at this paradoxical point, and what lies ahead? This chapter will explore what we now know about the effects of tobacco smoking and other forms of tobacco consumption, the impact these behaviors have had on U.S. society, and the ways in which society has dealt with the issue of tobacco over the years. It also will consider current approaches toward helping people who choose to stop smoking.

Tobacco Use through History

Shortly after setting foot on the small Caribbean island of San Salvador on October 12, 1492, Christopher Columbus received from the inhabitants a welcoming gift of large, green, sweet-smelling tobacco leaves. Never having seen tobacco before, Columbus did not know what to make of this curious offering, except to observe in his journal that the leaves were greatly prized by the "Indians." In the first week of November, two members of the expedition ventured to the shores of Cuba, searching at Columbus's insistence for the great khan of Cathay (China). They found no evidence of the khan but did return with reports of natives who

apparently were "drinking smoke." They rolled up tobacco leaves in dried corn leaves or stuffed them into hollow reeds, lit them with fire, and then inhaled the smoke through the nose and mouth. It was a totally bizarre scene to these European observers; one interpretation was that the natives were perfuming themselves in some exotic ritual.

Before long, Columbus's men tried "tobacco drinking" themselves. One sailor in particular, Rodrigo de Jerez, became quite fond of the practice. He was, in fact, history's first documented European smoker, though he lived to regret it. When Rodrigo returned to Spain, he volunteered to demonstrate the newfound custom to his neighbors, who instead of being impressed thought that anyone who could emit smoke from the nose and mouth without burning had to be possessed by the Devil. A parish priest turned Rodrigo over to the Inquisition, which sentenced him to imprisonment for witchcraft. He spent several years in jail, presumably without a supply of tobacco. Rodrigo therefore also may be remembered as the first European smoker to quit cold turkey.[1]

In 1560, the year historians mark as the year tobacco was officially introduced to Europe, a Spanish physician brought some tobacco plants back from the New World and presented them to King Philip II of Spain. Meanwhile, in England, both Sir Francis Drake on his return from his voyage around the world and Sir Walter Raleigh on his return from the new colony of Virginia championed the use of tobacco. Suddenly, the practice of smoking tobacco through long, elaborate pipes became a fashionable pastime among the aristocracy.

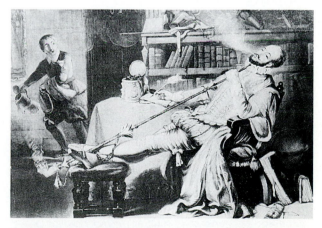

Sir Walter Raleigh (1552–1618) relaxes with a long smoking pipe as his servant rushes in to extinguish the fire with a pail of beer.

Not everyone was enthusiastic about this new fad of smoking. Predating a modern-day surgeon general's report by more than 350 years, King James I of England wrote in 1604, "A Counter-blaste to Tobacco," a lengthy treatise condemning tobacco use. Referring to tobacco as a "stinking weede," he characterized smoking as "a custom loathsome to the eye, hateful to the nose, harmful to the brain, [and] dangerous to the lung." In the first recorded comment on its potential for causing dependence, the king observed that "he that taketh tobacco saith he cannot leave it, it doth bewitch him."

Politics, Economics, and Tobacco

Elsewhere in the world, during the early seventeenth century, the condemnation of tobacco became extreme. In Russia, conservatives in power saw tobacco as a dangerous "Western" influence on the purity of Russian culture and established penalties for smoking that included whipping, mutilation, exile to Siberia, and death. Turkey, Japan, and China tried similar tactics, but, not surprisingly, tobacco use continued to spread.[2]

By the end of the seventeenth century even the fiercest opponents of tobacco had to concede that it was here to stay. A sultan of Turkey in 1648 became a smoker himself, and naturally, penalties for tobacco use vanished overnight; Czar Peter the Great in 1689 pledged to open up Russia to the West, and tobacco suddenly became a welcome symbol of modernism; Japan and China stopped trying to enforce a prohibition that citizens obviously did not want. Even England's James I put aside his personal dislike for tobacco and quickly recognized the attractive prospect of sizable revenue from taxes imposed on this popular new commodity.[3]

Snuffing and Chewing

One form of tobacco use observed by the early Spanish explorers was the practice of grinding a mixture of tobacco into a fine powder (**snuff**), placing or sniffing a pinch of it into the nose, and exhaling it with a sneeze. By the 1700s, this custom, called **snuffing,** overtook smoking as the dominant form of tobacco use. Among French aristocrats, both men and women, expensive snuffs, perfumed with exotic scents and carried in jeweled and enameled boxes, became part of the daily routine at the court in France and then in the rest of Europe. There were snuffs for the morning, snuffs for the afternoon, and snuffs for after dinner; some were designed for the ladies, the aged, novices, and the advanced. Sneezing was considered to clear the head of "superfluous humours," invigorate the brain, and brighten the eyes. In an era when bad smells were constant features of daily living, snuffing brought some degree of relief, not to mention a very effective way of sending nicotine to the brain (see Chapter 1).

Because of their dominance in the rapidly expanding tobacco market, the English colonies in America, particularly Virginia, prospered greatly. England enjoyed a profitable tobacco trade, but you might say that its development of colonial tobacco growing eventually backfired. In 1777, when Benjamin Franklin was sent as an envoy to France to gain support against the British in the American War for Independence, a key factor in his success was an offer to deliver prime Virginia tobacco in return for French money. The French agreed, and the rest is history. Had it not been for American tobacco, there might not have been a United States of America at all.[4]

In the United States, snuffing was soon replaced by a more rough-and-ready method for using tobacco: chewing. The practice was not totally new; early Spanish explorers had found the natives chewing tobacco as well as smoking it from the earliest days of their conquest, though North American tribes preferred smoking exclusively. Chewing tobacco had the advantage of freeing the hands for work, and its low cost made it a democratic custom befitting a vigorous new nation in the nineteenth century.

However, the need to spit out tobacco juices on a regular basis raised the tobacco habit to unimaginable heights of gross behavior. It was enough to make the objections to smoke and of possible fire fade into insignificance; now the problem was a matter of public health. Tobacco spitting became a major factor behind the spread of infectious diseases such as tuberculosis. Adding to this unsavory picture was the likelihood that a man's accuracy in targeting the nearest spittoon was inevitably compromised by his level of alcohol consumption, which was setting all-time records during this period (see Chapter 10). Charles Dickens, on his travels through the United States, commented in 1842 that the demise of the once-handsome carpet in the U.S. Senate chamber was personally depressing:

Washington may be called the head-quarters of tobacco-tinctured saliva. . . . In all the public places

---

snuff: A quantity of finely shredded or powdered tobacco. Modern forms of snuff are available in either dry or moist forms.

snuffing: The ingestion of snuff either by inhalation or absorption through tissue in the nose.

---

of America, this filthy custom is recognized. In the courts of law, the judge has his spittoon, the crier his, the witness his, and the prisoner his, while the jury-men and spectators are provided for.[5]

A present-day baseball dugout seems, by comparison, to be a model of decorum. The growth in the popularity of smokeless (chewing) tobacco since the 1970s will be examined in a later section.

Cigars and Cigarettes

By the time of the American Civil War, the fashion in tobacco use began to shift once more, as its overall popularity continued to soar. Although the plug of tobacco suitable for chewing was still a major seller and would remain so until the early twentieth century, two new trends developed, particularly in the growing industrial cities.

The first trend was the popularity of smoking **cigars** (commonly known as "seegars"), tight rolls of dried tobacco leaves. New innovations in curing (drying) tobacco leaves had produced a milder and lighter-quality leaf that was more suitable for smoking than the older forms that had been around since the colonial period. North Carolina, with its ideal soil for cultivating this type of tobacco, began to dominate as the tobacco-growing center of the United States; it continues to do so today. With the advent of cigars, tobacco consumers could combine the feeling of chewing (since the cigar remained in the mouth for a relatively long period of time) and the effects of ingesting tobacco smoke. Pioneers heading west could indulge in foot-long cigars called "stogies," named after the Conestoga wagons that they rode during the long and tedious journey.

The second trend was the introduction of **cigarettes,** rolls of shredded tobacco wrapped in paper. They had become popular among British soldiers returning from the Crimean War in 1856, who had adopted the practice from the Turks, who were their allies in the conflict. All of Europe took to cigarettes immediately, but the United States proved a harder sell. Part of the problem was the opposition of a well-entrenched U.S. cigar industry, which did not look kindly on an upstart competitor. Cigar makers did not discourage the circulation of rumors that the cigarette paper wrapping was actually soaked in arsenic or white lead, that cigarette factory workers were urinating on the tobacco to give it an extra "bite," or that Egyptian brands were mixed with crushed camel dung.[6]

An even greater marketing problem than unsubstantiated rumors, however, was the effeminate image of cigarette smoking itself. A cigarette was looked upon as a dainty, sissy version of the he-man cigar; cigars were fat, long, and dark, whereas cigarettes were slender, short, and light. Well into the beginning of the twentieth century, this attitude persisted. This is what John L. Sullivan, champion boxer and self-appointed defender of American masculinity, thought of cigarettes in 1904:

> *Who smokes 'em? Dudes and college stiffs—fellows who'd be wiped out by a single jab or a quick undercut. It isn't natural to smoke cigarettes. An American ought to smoke cigars. . . . It's the Dutchmen, Italians, Russians, Turks, and Egyptians who smoke cigarettes and they're no good anyhow.*[7]

The public image of the cigarette eventually would change dramatically; until then, cigarette manufacturers had to rely instead on a powerful marketing advantage: low cost. In 1881, James Bonsack patented a cigarette making machine that transformed the tobacco industry. Instead of producing at most 300 cigarettes an hour by hand, three machine operators could now turn out 200 a minute, or roughly 120,000 cigarettes a day. This is a snail's pace compared to the present state-of-the-art machines capable of producing 10,000 cigarettes a minute, but in those days, the Bonsack machine was viewed as an industrial miracle. Cigarette prices by the end of the 1800s were as cheap as twenty for a nickel.[8]

Tobacco in the Twentieth Century

At the beginning of the twentieth century, Americans could choose from a variety of ways to satisfy their hunger for tobacco. Cigars and pipes were still the dominant form of tobacco use. Plugs of chewing tobacco were still enjoyed by many, and spittoons were still in evidence, but with the new emphasis on social manners and crackdowns by public health officials concerned with major epidemics of infectious diseases, their days were numbered in the big cities. Chewing remained popular, however, in rural towns of America, and present-day sales are concentrated in these regions.

The future seemed to favor the cigarette for two basic reasons. First, a growing number of women began to challenge the idea of masculine domination, and smoking tobacco was one of the privileges of men that

cigars: Tightly rolled quantities of dried tobacco leaves.

cigarettes: Rolls of shredded tobacco wrapped in paper, today usually fitted at the mouth end with a filter.

Cigarette advertisements once drew on an association with glamorous women, Hollywood celebrities, and baseball players.

women now wanted to share. Not that women smoking was met with immediate acceptance; in one famous case in 1904, a New York City woman was arrested for smoking in public. Nonetheless, as smoking among women became more common, the mild-tasting, easy-to-hold cigarette was the perfect option for them. By the 1920s, advertising slogans such as "Reach for a Lucky instead of a sweet" (a clever effort to portray cigarette smoking as a weight-control aid) as well as endorsements by glamorous celebrities were being designed specifically for the women's market.

A second factor was World War I, during which time cigarettes were a logical form of tobacco to take along to war. Times of tension have always been times of increased tobacco use. When the war was over, the cigarette was, in the words of one historian, "enshrined forever as the weary soldier's relief, the worried man's support, and the relaxing man's companion."[9]

Cigarettes really came into their own in the 1920s, with the introduction of heavily advertised brand names and intense competition among American tobacco companies. Some of the major brand names introduced during this period were Camel, Chesterfield, Lucky Strike, Philip Morris, and Old Gold. Cigarette sales in

the United States increased from $45 billion in 1920 to $80 billion in 1925 and $180 billion by 1940.[10]

Health Concerns and Smoking Behavior

A combination of promotion through mass-media advertising and the implied endorsement of smoking by glamorous people in the entertainment industry and sports celebrities enabled the tobacco industry, now dominated by cigarettes, to increase its volume of sales from the 1940s to the 1980s by a steady 9 billion cigarettes each year. The peak in domestic sales was reached in 1981, when approximately 640 billion were sold. Owing to the increase in population, however, per capita consumption in the United States had peaked in 1963 at approximately 4,300 cigarettes per year (roughly twelve cigarettes per day).

Beginning in 1964, per capita consumption began a steady decline, with the present level at approximately 2,100 cigarettes per year (roughly six cigarettes per day). The year of the turnaround in per capita consumption is significant because it coincided with the U.S. surgeon general's first report on smoking and health. For the first time, the federal government asserted publicly what had been suspected for decades: that tobacco smoking was linked to cancer and other serious diseases.

From the standpoint of tobacco use in America, the surgeon general's report had three major effects. First, in the month or so immediately after the report was released, there was a dramatic dip (approximately 25 percent) in per capita consumption levels. Although succeeding months in 1964 showed a bounce upward, most likely reflecting the fact that many people who tried to quit had only temporary success, the long-term trend in U.S. tobacco consumption from that point on would never be upward again.

As evidence of health risks accumulated, restrictions on public consumption were instituted. In 1971, all television advertising for tobacco was banned, and in 1984, a rotating series of warning labels (already on all packages of tobacco products since 1966) was required on all print advertisements and outdoor billboards.[11]

A second major effect was the change in the types of cigarettes smoked by the average smoker. In the 1950s, more and more cigarette smokers chose to smoke filtered as distinct from unfiltered cigarettes, in an effort to ingest less of the toxins in tobacco. By the 1990s, about 95 percent of all smokers were using filtered brands.[12]

Unfortunately, the dominance of filtered cigarettes has not lessened the health consequences of smoking, only created the illusion of having done so. One problem is that when filtered cigarettes were introduced, the industry changed the formulation of the cigarette tobacco, substituting a stronger blend of tobacco with an increased tar content. Tar, as will be shown, represents a major factor in smokers' health problems, but it is also the primary source of a cigarette's flavor.

In short, a higher-tar blend of tobacco was used to satisfy the consumer, even though it essentially counteracted the point of using a filter in the first place or even made matters worse. As a result of a stronger "filter blend" formula in the cigarette, **sidestream smoke**, the smoke directly inhaled by a nonsmoker from a burning cigarette, ends up more toxic when originating from a filtered cigarette than it is from an unfiltered one. In principle, a cigarette filter should allow a flow of air through small holes in the filter itself. Because a smoker typically holds the cigarette with the fingers covering these holes, however, little or no filtering is accomplished.

From the standpoint of profits, filtered cigarettes were a boon to the tobacco industry. Filters were only paper and therefore cost considerably less than filling

the same space with tobacco. One prominent brand went one step further in the 1960s by advertising its recessed filter as "a neat, clean, quarter inch away," giving the further illusion of filtering away impurities but actually only creating air space.[13]

A third consequence was a direct response to the assertion by the surgeon general that tar and nicotine were specifically responsible for increased health risks from smoking. New cigarette brands were introduced that were low in tar and nicotine (T/N), and the Federal Trade Commission began to issue a listing of tar and nicotine levels in major commercial brands.

As later surgeon general's reports have indicated, however, smokers can essentially cancel out the benefits of switching to low T/N brands by varying the manner in which they smoke a low T/N cigarette. Smokers take more puffs, inhale more deeply, and smoke more of the cigarette when it has a lower T/N level so as to maintain the same amount of nicotine (the same number of nicotine "hits"). Moreover, a greater number of low T/N cigarettes have to be smoked in order to satisfy the smoker's needs. In 2003, Philip Morris announced that the designation of "lowered tar and nicotine" on packages of Marlboro Lights cigarettes would be dropped. Its decision was in response to a 2001 National Cancer Institute report that found no health benefits from smoking low T/N cigarettes instead of regular ones.

In 2006, an analysis of nicotine content in major brands of cigarettes revealed that levels had risen from 1998 to 2004 by approximately 10 percent. Of 179 brands tested, 168 brands were rated high in nicotine, including 59 brands that the manufactureres had labeled "light," 14 brands labeled as "ultra-light," and three of the most popular brands (Marlboro, Newport, and Camel). The nicotine level of Kool cigarettes, a popular menthol brand, had increased by 20 percent (Drugs . . . in Focus).[14]

Tobacco Today: An Industry on the Defensive

The tobacco industry in the United States, since the early 1990s, has faced continuing challenges from federal governmental agencies, as well as individuals and groups who have sued tobacco companies for damages resulting from

sidestream smoke: Tobacco smoke that is inhaled by nonsmokers from the burning cigarettes of nearby smokers. Also referred to as environmental tobacco smoke.

Drugs...in Focus

African Americans, Smoking, and Mentholated Cigarettes

It has long been puzzling that African Americans tend to smoke fewer cigarettes than white smokers but carry a higher risk of tobacco-related disorders such as lung cancer and heart disease. One factor that has been used as an explanation is the relatively slower rate of nicotine metabolism among African Americans following cigarette smoking (Chapter 1). African Americans may be taking in and retaining relatively more nicotine per cigarette and, as a result, may not need to smoke as many cigarettes per day to take in an equivalent dose of nicotine.

A recent study indicates that there may be more to the story. The menthol in certain brands of cigarettes, much preferred over nonmentholated brands by African Americans (just the reverse of preference patterns among white smokers), allows smokers to take in more smoke and possibly hold it in longer. The addition of menthol, in effect, cancels any benefit of choosing a "light" or "ultralight" brand to smoke. Relative to other smokers, African Americans who smoked menthol cigarettes had higher levels in their saliva of a specific nicotine by-product that indicates that they were ingesting a greater amount of toxins inherent in tobacco products.

The growing evidence of the effect of menthol content in cigarettes on smoking behavior and the implications with regard to smoking cessation have led to calls for tobacco companies to report how much menthol is contained in various cigarette brands, as they now do for levels of nicotine and tars. A particular concern is that, according to a recent study, 69 percent of menthol smokers are still smoking after fifteen years, compared to 54 percent of nonmenthol smokers.

Sources: Celebucki, Carolyn C.; Wayne, Geoffrey, F.; Connolly, Gregory N.; Pankow, James F.; and Chang, Elsa I. (2005). Characterization of measured menthol in 48 U.S. cigarette sub-brands. *Nicotine and Tobacco Research, 7,* 523–531. Mustonen, Tanu K.; Spencer, Stacie M.; Hoskinson, Randall A.; Sachs, David P.L.; and Garvey, Arthur J. (2005). The influence of gender, race, and menthol content on tobacco exposure measures. *Nicotine and Tobacco Research, 7,* 581–590. Pletcher, Mark J.; Hulley, Benjamin J.; Houston, Thomas; Kiefe, Catarina; Benowitz, Neal; and Sidney, Stephen (2006). Menthol cigarettes, smoking cessation, atherosclerosis, and pulmonary function. *Archives of Internal Medicine, 166,* 1915–1922.

---

their ingestion of tobacco products. As a result, at the beginning of the new millennium, the legal and economic status of the tobacco industry has been altered significantly. In 1993, the U.S. Environmental Protection Agency (EPA) announced its conclusion from available research that **environmental tobacco smoke (ETS)**, the sidestream smoke in the air that is inhaled by nonsmokers as a result of tobacco smoking, causes lung cancer. Since then, most U.S. states, cities, and communities have enacted laws mandating smoke-free environments in all public and private workplaces, unless ventilated smoking rooms have been provided. It is now typical for restaurants, hotels, and other commercial spaces to be at least partially smoke-free. In 1994, congressional hearings were held on allegations that during the 1970s tobacco companies had suppressed research data obtained in their own

research laboratories regarding the hazards of cigarette smoking. The Philip Morris company has since issued a statement, formally admitting that "there is overwhelming

In 1994, tobacco industry executives testified before a congressional committee in defense of cigarette smoking and other tobacco use. In 1999, the Philip Morris company formally reversed its earlier position that smoking was not addictive.

environmental tobacco smoke (ETS): Tobacco smoke in the atmosphere as a result of burning cigarettes; also called sidestream or secondary smoke.

medical and scientific consensus that cigarette smoking causes cancer, heart disease, emphysema, and other serious diseases" and that "cigarette smoking is addictive, as that term is most commonly used today." This stance represents a complete reversal of the industry's 1994 congressional testimony regarding tobacco use.

The Tobacco Settlement

In 1998, the major American tobacco corporations entered into an agreement with all fifty U.S. states to resolve claims that the states should be compensated for the costs of treating people with smoking-related illnesses. Under the terms of the settlement, the tobacco industry agreed to pay the states approximately $246 billion in annual installments until 2023. The tobacco industry also agreed to refrain from marketing tobacco products to those under eighteen and pay $24 million annually over ten years for a research foundation dedicated toward finding ways to reduce smoking among youths. In contrast to earlier proposed settlements, however, tobacco corporations under this agreement would not be penalized if levels of underage smoking did not decline over that period of time. In addition, the settlement did not prevent individuals or groups of individuals from suing tobacco corporations in separate actions.

Whether the 1998 tobacco settlement has had a specific impact on cigarette smoking among young people is difficult to determine. As will be discussed later in this chapter, there has been a substantial decline since 1998 in smoking levels among secondary school students, particularly eighth graders, and the prospects are encouraging that the same will eventually be observed among college students and young adults between the ages of nineteen and twenty-eight as these adolescents become older.

On the one hand, this decline appears to have occurred despite the paucity of tobacco-prevention programs at the state level and the continuance of cigarette advertising in youth-oriented magazines. By and large, the compensation funds awarded to the states have been used to keep taxes down or pay off debt—not to support tobacco-prevention programs. A recent analysis has shown that as the amount of settlement funds that a particular state invested, on a per capita basis, in tobacco use prevention among youths increases, the prevalence rate of cigarette consumption among youths in that state decreases. It has been estimated that if the minimum amount of money recommended by the Centers for Disease Control and Prevention had been spent for this purpose between 1991 and 2000, the prevalence rate for

this age group would have been between 3 and 14 percent lower than current levels.[15]

On the other hand, tobacco companies have increased their cigarette prices to help finance their settlement costs and several U.S. states have substantially increased their excise taxes on tobacco products, making cigarette purchases more difficult for an age group with relatively little money to spend. Recent proposals in several U.S. states to increase excise taxes substantially (Figure 12.1), if enacted, have the potential of making the financial burden still greater. In addition, the settlement has financed an increase in antismoking television advertisements on a national level as well as the removal of specific youth-oriented advertising images such as Joe Camel. All of these factors may have played a role in the recent decline in smoking among teenagers.[16]

Tobacco Regulation and Economics

Some have argued that an effective way to reduce the rate of smoking is to make smoking more expensive. Why not increase cigarette taxes, the logic goes, when cigarette smoking contributes so substantially to major disease? The prospect of reducing cigarette sales by increasing cigarette taxation is supported by data from U.S. states and other countries where tobacco excise taxes have been

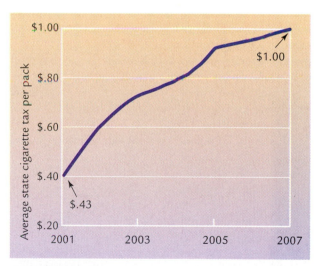

FIGURE 12.1

State taxes on cigarettes rose, on average, about 130 percent from 2001 to 2007. Currently, Rhode Island has the highest state tax on cigarettes—$2.46 per pack.

Sources: Campaign for Tobacco-Free Kids, Washington DC. Wolf, Richard (2007, February 27). States consider tobacco tax hikes: Health coverage would expand. *USA Today,* pp. 1A, 4A.

Cigarette Purchases on the Internet

The economic difference can be dramatic. A carton of Marlboro Full Flavor Kings ordered online from a web site in Paducah, Kentucky, might cost approximately $35, including shipping. No state sales tax is charged, and the state excise tax amounts to 3 cents per pack. In New York City, the same carton would cost $30 in city and state taxes alone. The significance of the price difference has produced a rapidly expanding industry that has seen annual online cigarette sales jump in a single year from $1.2 billion in 2002 to $2.2 billion in 2003.

The Internet as a smoker's haven may soon be extinct. Several states have passed laws barring both online and mail-order sales of cigarettes, in an attempt to protect the economic interests of both traditional merchants and the states themselves. Most web sites have no mechanism by which one can verify that the purchaser meets the minimum age to buy cigarettes in the first place. In California,

online retailers are now required to verify the age of the customer by matching names, addresses, and dates of birth to government records. If a tobacco retailer does not collect California excise tax at the time of a California resident's purchase, the outside surface of the shipping container must include a notification that the state has been informed of the sale and that the customer is responsible for reporting such purchases on his or her tax returns. In most other states, however, no age-verification regulations are presently in place. Therefore, regulation of Internet cigarette sales is viewed as a significant step toward the reduction of underage smoking.

Sources: Phan, Monty (2003, June 19). Law smokes out online cigarette sales. *Newsday*, A46. Ribisi, Kurt M., Williams, Rebecca S., and Kim, Annice E. (2003). Internet sales of cigarettes to minors. *Journal of the American Medical Association, 290*, 1356–1359. Tedeschi, Bob (2003, February 24). E-commerce report: Pressure grows from states to restrict and tax a smoker's haven—the Internet. *New York Times*, p. C7.

increased. As a rule of thumb, for every 10 percent increase in the retail price of cigarettes, consumption has fallen by 2 to 3 percent among adult smokers and by 6 to 7 percent among youth smokers. Recently, largely as a result of dramatically higher state and local taxes, increased cigarette prices have caused even die-hard smokers to enroll in smoking-cessation programs, on the basis of economic considerations alone (Drugs . . . in Focus).

It should be noted that policy decisions regarding smoking in the United States concern tobacco products sold only within the United States. As will be discussed later in this chapter, many other nations have substantially higher prevalence rates for cigarette smoking, and their governments have taken far fewer steps toward instituting policies to reduce smoking behavior. For American tobacco corporations, an expanding global marketplace for American cigarettes has given them the opportunity for an increase in profits from foreign sales that has largely compensated for the finan-

cial losses from a decline in domestic sales. Moreover, in a larger sense, cigarette sales abroad represent a major component of overall U.S. foreign trade. In recent years, U.S. exports of tobacco products have exceeded imports by billions of dollars, creating a significant trade surplus. Therefore, the U.S. trade deficit (defined as an excess of imports over exports) would be worse than it is today were it not for the export of tobacco products to other nations.[17]

What's in Tobacco?

When a smoker inhales from a lit cigarette, the temperature at the tip rises to approximately 1,700 degrees Fahrenheit (926 degrees Centigrade), as oxygen is drawn through the tobacco, paper, and other additives. This is the reason for the bright glow as a smoker inhales from a cigarette. At this intense heat, more than four thousand separate compounds are oxidized and released through cigarette smoke. The smoker inhales the result as **mainstream smoke,** usually screened through the cigarette filter and cigarette paper. As mentioned earlier,

mainstream smoke: The smoke inhaled directly from cigarettes or other tobacco products.

the sidestream smoke that is released from the burning cigarette tip itself is unfiltered, and because it is a product of a slightly less intense burning process occurring between puffs, more unburned particles are contained in the smoke.

In general, we can speak of two components in tobacco smoke. The **particulate phase,** consisting of small particles (one micrometer or larger in diameter) suspended in the smoke, includes water droplets, nicotine, and a collection of compounds that will be referred to collectively as **tar.** The particles in tar constitute the primary source of carcinogenic compounds in tobacco. The second component is the **gaseous phase,** consisting of gas compounds in the smoke, including carbon dioxide, carbon monoxide, ammonia, hydrogen cyanide, acetaldehyde, and acetone. Among these gases, carbon monoxide is clearly the most toxic.

This diverse collection of physiologically active toxins is quite unique to tobacco. One way of putting it is that the fifty thousand to seventy thousand puffs per year that a one-pack-a-day cigarette smoker takes in amounts to a level of pollution far beyond even the most polluted urban environment anywhere in the world.[18] The following discussion will focus on three of the most important compounds in tobacco smoke: carbon monoxide, tar, and nicotine.

Carbon Monoxide

As most people know, **carbon monoxide** is an odorless, colorless, tasteless, but extraordinarily toxic gas. It is formed when tobacco burns because the oxidation process is incomplete. In that sense, burning tobacco is similar to an inefficient engine, like a car in need of a tune-up. The danger in carbon monoxide is that it easily attaches itself to hemoglobin, the protein inside red blood cells, occupying those portions of the hemoglobin molecule normally reserved for the transport of oxygen from the lungs to the rest of the body. Carbon monoxide has about a two hundred times greater affinity for hemoglobin than does oxygen, so oxygen does not have much of a chance. Carbon monoxide is also more resistant to detaching itself from hemoglobin, so there is an accumulation of carbon monoxide over time.

The ultimate result of carbon monoxide is a subtle but effective asphyxiation of the body from a lack of oxygen. Generally, people who smoke a pack a day accumulate levels of carbon monoxide in the blood of 25 to 35 parts per million blood components (ppm), with levels of 100 ppm for short periods of time while actually smoking. Of course, greater use of tobacco produces proportionally higher levels of carbon monoxide. Carbon monoxide is the primary culprit in producing cardiovascular disease among smokers, as well as in causing deficiencies in physiological functioning and behavior.[19]

Tar

The quantity of tar in a cigarette varies from levels of 12 to 16 mg per cigarette to less than 6 mg. It also should be noted that the last third of each cigarette contains 50 percent of the total tar, making the final few puffs far more hazardous than the first ones.

The major problem with tar lies in its sticky quality, not unlike that of the material used in paving roads, which allows it to adhere to cells in the lungs and the airways leading to them. Normally, specialized cells with small, hairlike attachments called **cilia** are capable of removing contaminants in the air that might impede the breathing process. These cilia literally sweep the unwanted particles upward to the throat, in a process called the **ciliary escalator,** where they are typically swallowed, digested, and finally excreted from the body through the gastrointestinal system. Components in tar alter the coordination of these cilia so that they can no longer function effectively. The accumulation of sticky tar on the surface of the cells along the pulmonary system permits carcinogenic compounds that normally would have been eliminated to settle on the tissue. As will be discussed later, the resulting cellular changes produce lung cancer, and similar carcinogenic effects in other tissues of the body produce cancer in other organs.[20]

Nicotine

Nicotine is a toxic, dependence-producing psychoactive drug found exclusively in tobacco. It is an oily compound

---

particulate phase: Those components of smoke that consist of particles.

tar: A sticky material found in the particulate phase of tobacco smoke and other pollutants in the air.

gaseous phase: The portion of tobacco smoke that consists of gases.

carbon monoxide: An extremely toxic gas that prevents blood cells from carrying oxygen from the lungs to the rest of the body.

cilia: Small hair cells.

ciliary escalator: The process of pushing back foreign particles that might interfere with breathing upward from the air passages into the throat, where they can be swallowed and excreted through the gastrointestinal tract.

nicotine: The prime psychoactive drug in tobacco products.

varying in hue from colorless to brown. A few drops of pure nicotine, about 60 mg, on the tongue would quickly kill a healthy adult, and it is commonly used as a major ingredient in insecticides and pesticides of all kinds. Cigarettes, however, contain from 0.5 to 2.0 mg of nicotine (depending on the brand), with about 20 percent being actually inhaled and reaching the bloodstream. This means that 2 to 8 mg of nicotine is ingested per day for a pack-a-day smoker, and 4 to 16 mg of nicotine for a smoker of two packs a day.[21]

Inhaled nicotine from smoking is absorbed extremely rapidly and easily passes through the blood-brain barrier, as well as through the blood-placental barrier in pregnant women, in a few seconds. The entire effect is over in a matter of minutes. By the time a cigarette butt is extinguished, nicotine levels in the blood have peaked, and its breakdown and excretion from the body are well underway. The elimination half-life of nicotine is approximately two to three hours.

The speed of nicotine absorption ordinarily would be much slower if it were not for the presence of ammonia as an additive in the tobacco blend. The combination of nicotine and ammonia changes the naturally acidic nicotine into an alkalinic free-base form that more easily passes from body tissues into the bloodstream. As a result, ammonia increases the availability of nicotine in the blood, much as the addition of alkaline materials like baking soda converts cocaine into crack cocaine (see Chapter 4). The information that ammonia had been introduced into the manufacture of cigarette tobacco during the 1970s, in an apparent effort to increase the "kick" of nicotine, came to light in 1995 and was confirmed by tobacco company documents released in 1998.[22]

The primary effect of nicotine is to stimulate CNS receptors that are sensitive to acetylcholine (see Chapter 3). These receptors are called *nicotinic receptors* because they are excited by nicotine. One of the effects of activating them is the release of adrenalin, which increases blood pressure and heart rate. Another effect is to inhibit activity in the gastrointestinal system. At the same time, however, as most smokers will tell you, a cigarette is a relaxing factor in their lives. Part of this reaction may be due to an effect on the brain that promotes a greater level of clear thinking and concentration; another part may relate to the fact that nicotine, at moderate doses, serves to reduce muscle tone so that muscular tightness is decreased. Research has shown that cigarette smoking helps to sustain performance on monotonous tasks and to improve short-term memory. We can assume that it is the nicotine in cigarettes and other tobacco products that is responsible because nicotine tablets have comparable behavioral effects.[23]

The Dependence Potential of Nicotine

Historically, the dependence potential of nicotine has been demonstrated at times in which the usual availability of tobacco has suddenly been curtailed. In Germany following the end of World War II, for example, cigarettes were rationed to two packs a month for men and one pack a month for women. This "cigarette famine" produced dramatic effects on the behavior of German civilians. Smokers bartered their food rations for cigarettes, even under the extreme circumstances of chronic hunger and poor nutrition. Cigarette butts were picked from the dirt in the streets by people who admitted that they were personally disgusted by their desperation. Some women turned to prostitution to obtain cigarettes, whereas alcoholics of both sexes testified that it was easier to abstain from drinking alcohol than it was to abstain from smoking.[24]

It is now known that nicotine stimulates the release of dopamine in the nucleus accumbens, the same area of the brain responsible for the reinforcing properties of opiates, cocaine, and alcohol.[25] In addition, several behavioral factors combine with this physiological effect to increase the likelihood that a strong dependence will be created. One of these factors is the speed with which smoked nicotine reaches the brain. The delivery time has been estimated as five to eight seconds. A second factor is the wide variety of circumstances and settings surrounding the act of smoking that later come to serve as learned rewards. A smoker may find, for example, that the first cigarette with a cup of coffee in the morning (a source of another psychoactive drug, caffeine) is strongly reinforcing. These events parallel the release of dopamine in the brain (Chapter 3). As a major researcher in this area has expressed it,

> Smoking . . . comes to be rewarded by the enjoyment of oral, manual, and respiratory manipulations involved in the process of lighting, puffing, and handling cigarettes, the pleasure and relaxation associated with using alcohol, finishing a good meal, . . . and the perceived diminution of unpleasant affective [emotional] states of anxiety, tension, boredom, or fatigue. . . . No other substance can provide so many kinds of rewards, is so readily and cheaply available, and can be used in so many settings and situations.[26]

A third factor is the sheer number of times the smoker experiences a dose of nicotine. When you consider that a smoker takes from one to two hundred puffs each day from the twenty cigarettes that represent a pack-a-day pattern of smoking, you realize that smoking is a highly practiced, overlearned behavior.[27]

The Titration Hypothesis of Nicotine Dependence

There is considerable evidence that smokers adjust their smoking behavior to obtain a stable dose of nicotine from whatever cigarettes they are smoking, an idea called the **titration hypothesis.** When exposed to cigarettes of decreasing nicotine content, smokers will smoke a greater number of them to compensate and will increase the volume of each puff. When they inhale more puffs per cigarette, a greater interval of time will elapse before they light up another one. If they are given nicotine gum to chew, the intensity of their smoking behavior will decline, even though they have not been told whether the gum contains nicotine or is a placebo. All these studies indicate that experienced smokers arrive at a consistent "style" of smoking that provides their bodies with a relatively constant level of nicotine.[28]

Tolerance and Withdrawal

First-time smokers often react to a cigarette with a mixture of nausea, dizziness, or vomiting. These effects typically disappear as tolerance develops in the nicotinic receptors in the brain. Other physiological effects, such as increases in heart rate, tremors, and changes in skin temperature, show weaker tolerance effects or none at all. The strongest dependence-related effect of cigarette smoking can be seen in the symptoms of withdrawal that follow the discontinuation of smoking. Within about six hours after the last cigarette, a smoker's heart rate and blood pressure will decrease. Over the next twenty-four hours, common symptoms will include headache, an inability to concentrate, irritability, drowsiness, and fatigue, as well as insomnia and other sleep disturbances. Most striking of all are the strong feelings of craving for a cigarette. Ex-smokers can attest to cravings that slowly diminish but nonetheless linger on for months and, in some cases, for years.[29]

Nicotine dependence is clearly the central factor in the continuation of smoking behaviors. The level of dependence is significant, even when compared with dependence levels of illicit drugs available on the street. In a study of people who smoked and were also in some form of drug-abuse treatment, 74 percent judged the difficulty of quitting smoking to be at least as great as the difficulty in stopping their drug of choice. One in three considered it "much harder" to quit smoking.[30]

Health Consequences of Tobacco Use

The adverse health consequences of tobacco use can be classified in three broad categories: cardiovascular disease, respiratory disease, and cancer. In addition,

titration hypothesis: The idea that smokers will adjust their smoking of cigarettes so as to maintain a steady input of nicotine into the body.

there are special health difficulties that smoking can bring to women and hazards from using smokeless tobacco. An enormous literature on the adverse effects of tobacco use has grown steadily since the original surgeon general's report in 1964, though by that time more than thirty thousand research studies had been conducted on the question.

Beyond all the research reports are the sheer numbers of people who are affected. In the United States alone, of the estimated half-million deaths each year that are attributed to substance abuse of one kind or another, approximately 430,000 are specifically tied to cigarette smoking. This figure is higher than the total number of American casualties during World War II (Drugs . . . in Focus). The public health community considers these deaths to be premature deaths because they are entirely preventable; these people would have been alive if their behaviors had been different.

The numbers are simple, and staggering: Smoking-related deaths account for at least one out of every five deaths in the United States every year, nearly 1,200 deaths each day. A person's life is shortened by fourteen minutes every time a cigarette is smoked. Smoking two packs a day for twenty years reduces one's lifespan by approximately eight years.

An estimated 8.6 million persons in the United States have serious illnesses that are attributable to cigarette smoking. Unlike alcohol, which presents no significant health hazards when consumed in moderation, tobacco is a dangerous product *when used as intended* (Figure 12.2).[31]

Cardiovascular Disease

Cardiovascular disease includes a number of specific conditions. Some of these diseases are **coronary heart disease (CHD)**, in which damage to the heart is incurred due to the restriction of blood flow through narrowed or blocked coronary arteries; **arteriosclerosis**, in which the walls of arteries harden and lose their elasticity; **atherosclerosis**, in which fatty deposits inside

coronary heart disease (CHD): Disease that damages the heart as a result of a restriction of blood flow through coronary arteries.

arteriosclerosis (ar-TEER-ee-oh-scluh-ROH-sis): A disease in which blood flow is restricted because the walls of arteries harden and lose their elasticity.

atherosclerosis (ATH-er-oh-scluh-ROH-sis): A disease in which blood flow is restricted because of the buildup of fatty deposits inside arteries.

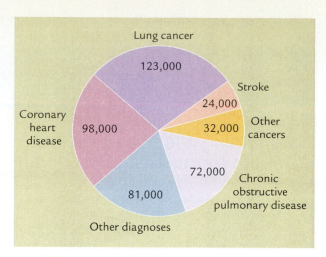

FIGURE 12.2

The distribution of approximately 430,000 U.S. deaths attributed each year to cigarette smoking.

Source: Centers for Disease Control and Prevention (1999, March 3). *Morbidity and Mortality Weekly Report.* Atlanta: Centers for Disease Control and Prevention.

arteries impede blood flow; and ischemic stroke, in which interruption or reduction in blood flow causes damage to the brain. In all these diseases, cigarette smoking increases the risk dramatically.

We know now that smoking is responsible for approximately 30 percent of all CHD deaths. The risk of CHD doubles if you smoke and quadruples if you smoke heavily. On average, smoking also raises the risk of a sudden death (such as from a fatal heart attack) by two to four times, with the degree of risk increasing as a direct function of how many cigarettes are smoked per day. To put it even more boldly, it has been estimated that unless smoking patterns change dramatically in the future, about 10 percent of all Americans now alive may die prematurely from some form of heart disease as a result of their smoking behavior. Yet, strangely enough, a recent study has shown that only 29 percent of current smokers and only 39 percent of heavy smokers believe that they have a higher-than-average risk of a heart attack.[32]

These statistics are strengthened by the understanding we have of how cigarette smoking actually produces these dangerous cardiovascular conditions. The major villains are nicotine and carbon monoxide.

Nicotine, as a stimulant drug, increases the contraction of heart muscle and elevates heart rate. At the same time, nicotine causes a constriction of blood vessels, leading to a rise in blood pressure, and also increases *platelet adhesiveness* in the blood. As a result of a greater adhesiveness, platelets clump together and increase the risk of developing a blood clot. If a clot forms within coronary arteries, a heart attack can occur; a clot traveling into the blood vessels of the brain can produce a stroke. Finally, nicotine increases the body's serum cholesterol and fatty deposits, leading to the development of atherosclerosis.

While nicotine is doing its dirty work, carbon monoxide makes matters worse. A lack of oxygen puts further strain on the ability of the heart to function under already trying circumstances.[33]

Respiratory Diseases

The general term **chronic obstructive pulmonary disease (COPD)** refers to several conditions in which breathing is impaired because of some abnormality in the air passages either leading to or within the lungs. In the United States, 80 to 90 percent of all such cases are the result of cigarette smoking. With the exception of a rare genetic defect, cigarette smoking is the only established cause for clinically significant COPD.

Two examples of COPD are **chronic bronchitis,** in which excess mucus builds up in air passages, leading to an inflammation of bronchial tissue, and **emphysema,** in which air sacs in the lungs are abnormally enlarged and the air sac walls either become inelastic or rupture, leading to extreme difficulty in inhaling oxygen and exhaling carbon dioxide. In the case of advanced emphysema, more than 80 percent of a patient's energy is required merely to breathe. Either disease or a combination of the two causes more than seventy thousand deaths each year, and many additional thousands are forced to lead increasingly debilitating lives, gasping and struggling each day to breathe:

> Many of [the thousands of people with COPD] are attached to oxygen tanks, imprisoned at home or in the hospital because they are too weak to breathe on their own. Often their friends or family members will pound on their backs, temporarily freeing the lungs of the yellow mucus that impedes their breathing every day.[34]

Pulmonary damage, however, is not limited to adults who have been smoking for many years. Cigarette smoking is also associated with airway obstruction and slower growth of lung function in younger populations. Adolescents who smoke five or more cigarettes a day are 40 percent more likely to develop asthma and 30 percent more likely to have symptoms of wheezing but not asthma than those who do not smoke. Girls show a greater loss of pulmonary function than boys in the smoking group, even though boys report that they smoke more cigarettes.[35]

Lung Cancer

At the beginning of the twentieth century, lung cancer was a rare disease. Its steady increase in the United States as well as the rest of the world since then has occurred in direct proportion to the growing prevalence of cigarette smoking and other tobacco use. Today, nearly 90 percent of the more than approximately 213,000 new cases of lung cancer in the United States in 2007 have been determined by the American Cancer Society to be due to smoking. While there has been a steady decline in deaths due to lung cancer among American males since 1990, there remains an approximately 35 percent greater mortality rate among African American males due to smoking relative to white males. In general, males who are currently smoking incur a risk of lung cancer that is about twenty-two times higher than the risk for nonsmokers.

Another important change has occurred over the years with respect to the incidence of lung cancer among women. Lung cancer was once considered a "man's disease." More recently, however, increasing numbers of women have contracted lung cancer as a result of their increased level of cigarette smoking. The age-adjusted mortality rate for women is still about one-half that for men, but the decline in mortality rates seen among men since 1990 has yet to be realized among women. Since 1988, lung cancer has exceeded breast cancer as the leading cause of cancer deaths among women (Figure 12.3). In general, females who are currently smoking incur a risk of lung cancer that is about twelve times higher than that for nonsmokers.

These facts about lung cancer become even more tragic when you consider that the overall five-year survival rate after initial diagnosis of lung cancer (for all stages of cancer combined) is only 15 percent. Lung cancer patients have an approximately 50 percent chance of living five years when the disease is still

chronic obstructive pulmonary disease (COPD): A group of diseases characterized by impaired breathing due to an abnormality in the air passages.

chronic bronchitis: A respiratory disease involving inflammation of bronchial tissue following a buildup of excess mucus in air passages.

emphysema (EM-fuh-SEE-mah): An enlargement of air sacs in the lungs and abnormalities in the air sac walls, causing great difficulty in breathing.

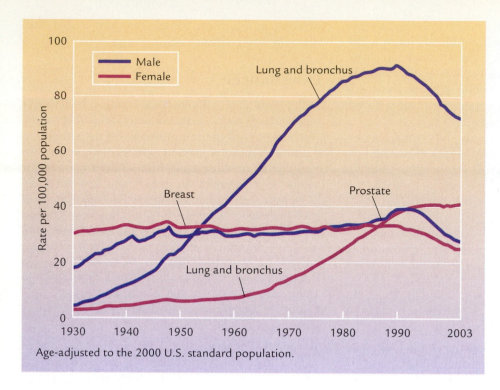

localized at the time of diagnosis, but only 15 percent of lung cancers are diagnosed at this early stage.

As discussed earlier in the chapter, the exposure to tar in cigarette smoke disrupts the necessary action of ciliary cells in the bronchial tubes leading to the lungs. Without their protective function, the lungs are open to attack. Several carcinogenic compounds in the smoke can now enter the lungs and stimulate the formation of cancerous growths, **carcinomas**, in lung tissue. One of these compounds, *benzopyrene*, has been found to cause genetic mutations in cells that are identical to the mutations observed in patients who have developed carcinomas in their lungs. This finding is important because it establishes a causal link between a specific ingredient in tobacco smoke and human cases of cancer.[36]

carcinomas (CAR-sih-NOH-mas): Cancerous Tumors or Growths.

leukoplakia (LOO-koh-PLAY-kee-ah): Small white spots inside the mouth and nasal cavity, indicating precancerous tissue.

erythroplakia (eh-RITH-ro-PLAY-kee-ah): Small red spots inside the mouth and nasal cavity, indicating precancerous tissue.

nitrosamines (nih-TRAW-seh-meens): A group of carcinogenic compounds found in tobacco.

Other Cancers

Certainly lung cancer is the best-known and most common example of smoking-related cancers; unfortunately, other organs are affected in a similar way. In the United States, approximately 30 percent of cancer deaths *of all types* have been linked to smoking. It has been estimated that smokers increase their risk by as much as twenty-seven times for cancer of the larynx, thirteen times for mouth or lip cancer, two to three times for bladder cancer, two times for pancreatic cancer, and five times for cancers of the kidney or uterine cervix (Portrait).[37]

Despite a widespread belief to the contrary, using smokeless tobacco, in the form of chewing tobacco or snuff, does not prevent the user from incurring an increased risk of cancer. Continuing contact with tobacco in the mouth has been shown to produce precancerous cell changes, as revealed by **leukoplakia** (white spots) and **erythroplakia** (red spots) inside the mouth and nasal cavity. Even though smokeless tobacco obviously avoids the problems associated with tobacco smoke, it does not prevent the user from being exposed to carcinogens, specifically a class of compounds called **nitrosamines** that are present in all tobacco products. As a result of federal legislation enacted in 1986, all forms of smokeless tobacco must contain, on the package, a set of specific warnings that these products may cause mouth cancer as well as gum disease and tooth loss (Help Line).

Probably the best-known photograph of Sigmund Freud, founder of psychoanalysis and one-time proponent of cocaine use (see Chapter 4), shows him with a cigar in hand. Given that Freud typically smoked twenty cigars each day, it is not surprising that he did not set it aside merely to have his picture taken. But there is a story behind this photograph, a lesson about the power of smoking over the will to stop and the tragic health consequences when the will succumbs.

In 1923, at the age of sixty-seven, Freud noted sores on his palate and jaw that failed to heal, a sign of oral cancer. Surgery was indicated and fortunately proved successful in removing the cancerous tissue. This would be only the first of thirty-three surgical operations on the jaw and oral cavity that Freud was to endure for the remaining sixteen years of his life. As the leukoplakia and finally genuine carcinomas returned to his mouth, he was repeatedly warned by specialists that his practice of smoking cigars was the root of his problems and that he must stop. Despite these warnings, Freud kept on smoking.

Freud tried very hard to stop; indeed, sometimes he would not smoke for a few weeks at a time. In addition to his problems with cancer, he suffered from chest pains called "tobacco angina." In 1936, the angina became acutely painful and as his biographer, Ernest Jones, has noted, "It was evidently exacerbated by nicotine, since it was relieved as soon as he stopped smoking."

By this time, Freud's jaw had been entirely removed and an artificial jaw substituted in its place. He was almost constantly in pain, often could not speak, and sometimes could not eat or swallow. Despite the agony, Freud still smoked a steady stream of cigars until he finally died at the age of eighty-three.

Here was a man whom many consider to be one of the intellectual giants of the twentieth century. Yet the giant was a slave to his cigars.

Source. Brecher, Ruth; Brecher, Edward; Herzog, Arthur; Goodman, Walter; Walker, Gerald; and the Editors of *Consumer Reports* (1963). *The Consumer Union's report on smoking and the public interest.* Mount Vernon, NY: Consumer Union, pp. 91–95.

To reinforce the idea that dangers are still present in smokeless tobacco, one of these warnings reads: "This product is not a safe alternative to cigarette smoking."

Special Health Concerns for Women

There are significant health risks to a developing fetus and to the newborn when the mother smokes during pregnancy. Added to these concerns is the toxic interaction of tobacco smoke with birth control pills. Women who smoke have a more than three times greater risk of dying from stroke due to brain hemorrhaging and an almost two times greater risk of dying from a heart attack. If they are using birth control pills as well, the risk increases to twenty-two times and twenty times, respectively. While there has been a

HELP LINE

Signs of Trouble from Smokeless Tobacco

- Lumps in the jaw or neck area
- Color changes or lumps inside the lips
- White, smooth, or scaly patches in the mouth or on the neck, lips, or tongue
- A red spot or sore on the lips or gums or inside the mouth that does not heal in two weeks
- Repeated bleeding in the mouth
- Difficulty or abnormality in speaking or swallowing

Any of these signs should be reported to a physician as soon as possible. In the meantime, and in the future, use of smokeless tobacco should be discontinued.

Where to go for assistance:

www.quitnet.com

This web site is sponsored by the Department of Public Health, Boston University.

Source: Payne, Wayne A., and Hahn, Dale B. (1992). *Understanding your health.* St. Louis: Mosby Year Book, p. 278.

decline in smoking in recent years among pregnant women, it has been attributed more to an overall decline in smoking among women of childbearing age than to an increase in the rate of smoking cessation during pregnancy.[38]

The Hazards of Environmental Smoke

In the early days of development of methods for detecting the effects of nicotine in the bloodstream, scientists were puzzled to find traces of a nicotine metabolite in nonsmokers. They suspected at first that there was some flaw in their analysis but later had to conclude that their measurements were indeed accurate. Nonsmokers testing positive had shared car rides or workplaces with smokers shortly before their tests. Today, a large body of evidence indicates not only the presence of tobacco smoke compounds in the bodies of nonsmokers but also the adverse consequences that such "involuntary smoking" can provoke. In other words, environmental tobacco smoke is a significant health hazard even to people who are not actively smoking.

Approximately 85 percent of the smoke in an average room where people are smoking cigarettes is generated by sidestream smoke, and about three-fourths of the nicotine originating from these cigarettes ends up in the atmosphere. In some cases, the carcinogens released in ETS are so potent that they are dangerous even in their diluted state. For example, N-nitrosamine (an example of a group of carcinogens mentioned earlier in connection with smokeless tobacco) is so much more concentrated in sidestream smoke than in mainstream smoke that nonsmokers will end up inhaling as much of it after one hour in a very smoky room as will a smoker after inhaling mainstream smoke from ten to fifteen cigarettes.[39]

The U.S. surgeon general's report on involuntary exposure to tobacco smoke in 2006 confirmed previous data and extended its conclusions to the following:

- For nonsmoking adults, exposure to environmental smoke raises the risk of heart disease by 25 to 30 percent in both men and women. The risk of lung cancer is increased by 20 to 30 percent among nonsmokers who live with a smoker.

- Environmental smoke is a cause of sudden infant death syndrome (SIDS), accounting for 430 deaths per year in the United States. The risk is higher for children whose mothers were exposed to tobacco smoke during pregnancy and for children exposed during infancy.

- Among children of parents who smoke in the home, there is an increased risk of lower respiratory illnesses such as bronchitis, middle ear disease, wheezing, and childhood asthma.

It is estimated that environmental smoke exposure accounts for 46,000 premature deaths from heart disease and 3,000 premature deaths from cancer among adults in the United States each year. Although the proportion of nonsmokers has declined substantially as a result of publicity about the hazards of ETS and extensive smoking bans and restrictions (see Drugs . . . in Focus), more than 126 million Americans remain subject to exposure at some time in their lives.[40]

Patterns of Smoking Behavior and Use of Smokeless Tobacco

In 1965, about 40 percent of all American teenagers and adults smoked cigarettes, and it is estimated that more than 50 percent did in the 1940s. In 2006, however, according to the National Survey on Drug Use and Health, approximately 25 percent of people aged twelve or older smoked a cigarette within the past month, qualifying as regular smokers. Though this percentage is significantly less than it had been, we are still considering a very large number of people. Extrapolating to the U.S.

Drugs . . . in Focus

Smoking in Movies and Movie Ratings

Concerns about the influence of the media on young people with respect to various forms of drug-taking behavior have recently turned to the issue of cigarette smoking in movies. In May 2007, the Motion Picture Association of America (MPAA) announced a significant change in its movie rating system. Previously, the portrayal of teenage smoking in a movie, along with sexual situations, violence, and adult language, would be a factor in deciding whether a movie merited an R rating (which requires those under 17 to be accompanied by a parent or adult guardian). Now, the Film Ratings Board would consider *any* portrayal of smoking in a movie, not just teenage smoking, in their rating decision, unless smoking was central to the movie's historical content. Depictions that glamorized smoking or movies that featured pervasive smoking could receive a higher rating than PG-13, according to the new standards. The MPAA made the following statement:

> *Clearly, smoking is increasingly an unacceptable behavior in our society. There is broad awareness of smoking as a unique public health concern due to nicotine's highly*

addictive nature, and no parent wants their child to take up the habit. The appropriate response of the rating system is to give more information to parents on this issue.

Media reporters quickly came up with "WARNING: Smoking may be hazardous to your movie rating."

Antismoking organizations, however, were not entirely satisfied with the MPAA announcement. According to the Campaign for Tobacco-Free Kids, the new policy fell short "of the real change needed to reduce youth exposure to smoking in the movies." They pointed out that the Film Ratings Board would only "consider smoking" in their decisions. "Meaningful, objective standards that produce measurable reductions in smoking in the movies" had not been established. Whether the new MPAA policy reduces the incidence of smoking in future movies remains to be seen.

Sources: Cieply, Michael (2007, May 11). Puffing away that PG rating: Smoking to join sex and violence in determining ratings for movies. *New York Times*, pp. C1, C4. Press release. Motional Picture Association of America, Hollywood, California. May 10, 2007. Press release. Campaign for Tobacco-Free Kids, Washington DC. May 10, 2007.

---

population, a 25 percent prevalence rate corresponds to approximately 62 million Americans. American Indians and Alaska natives are more likely to smoke than any other group in the United States, with 42 percent of adults defined as smokers. For individuals reporting two or more races, the prevalence decreases to 34 percent. In contrast, individuals of Asian descent are the least likely to smoke, with 16 percent admitting to have smoked a cigarette in the past month.

A steady decline in the percentage of American smokers stopped around 1991, and the prevalence rate has declined only slightly since then. Among college students, thirty-day prevalence rates had been increasing from 1990 to 1999, but now they have started to slowly decline. In 2006, about 19 percent of college students had smoked cigarettes within the previous month, six points below the national average. This figure is not likely to decrease in the next few years as the current plateau in smoking among secondary students noted in the 2006 University of Michigan survey becomes evident as these youths enter college. These projections are based on the

finding that about 15 percent of tenth graders in 2006 and 22 percent of high school seniors reported cigarette smoking within the previous month. It is unlikely that many tenth and twelfth graders will begin smoking past this point in their lives.[41]

The Youngest Smokers

In the University of Michigan survey, approximately 25 percent of eighth graders reported that they had tried cigarettes in their lifetime and about 9 percent reported smoking at least once in the previous month in 2006. These figures are down substantially from the 49 and 21 percent figures, respectively, found in 1996. Approximately 4 percent of eighth graders smoked on a daily basis in 2006, and less than 2 percent had smoked at least a half a pack a day, once again down substantially from 10 and 4 percent, respectively, in 1996.

The peak years for starting to smoke were reported in the survey to be in the sixth and seventh grade, but a significant number of eighth graders who were regular

Cigarette smoking among minors is a continuing social problem.

cigarettes per day and 60 percent reported that such behavior would present "great risk" of harming themselves physically or otherwise.[43]

Interestingly, adolescent attitudes toward the *social* aspects of smoking have become more negative as well. About half of tenth and twelfth graders agree with the statement "I strongly dislike being near people who are smoking." Between 75 and 80 percent of them prefer to date nonsmokers. About two out of three view smoking as a behavior that reflects poor judgment on the part of those who smoke. This continuing disinclination toward dating smokers over recent years has been observed equally among males and females. As Lloyd D. Johnston of the University of Michigan observed in 2002:

> *It now appears that taking up smoking makes a youngster less attractive to the great majority of the opposite sex, just the opposite of what cigarette advertising has been promising all these years. I think this is something that teens need to know, because it may be the most compelling argument for why they should abstain from smoking or, for that matter, quit if they have already started.*[44]

smokers said that they had started earlier. About 15 percent have reported that they had begun prior to the sixth grade; in fact, about 9 percent have reported that they had started prior to the fifth grade. In general, it has been estimated that between 80 and 90 percent of regular smokers began to smoke by the age of eighteen.[42]

Attitudes toward Smoking among Young People

Adolescent attitudes toward cigarette smoking have changed dramatically during the early years of the twenty-first century. In general, young people in middle and high school have become less accepting of cigarette smoking. About 86 percent of eighth graders, for example, reported in 2006 their disapproval of someone smoking a pack of

In 1997, the FDA established eighteen as the national minimum age at which tobacco products could be purchased and required vendors to verify the ages of purchasers up to the age of twenty-seven as a means for reducing the access of young people to tobacco. In some U.S. states, efforts are under way to raise the minimum age for tobacco purchases to nineteen or twenty-one. This change would prevent high school seniors from buying cigarettes for their younger friends.

A goal of 80 percent compliance on the part of tobacco vendors, a standard set in federal regulations

The nine-year Joe Camel advertising campaign ended in 1997 as opposition mounted against tobacco promotions targeting youth. Here is a parody from the early 1990s of the Camel campaign through the eyes of Garry Trudeau, creator of *Doonesbury*.

DOONESBURY © 1992 G. B. Trudeau. Reprinted with permission of UNIVERSAL PRESS SYNDICATE. All rights reserved.

on underage smoking, has apparently been successful. Compliance rates nationwide, based on retailer violation reports received in 2003, increased to about 87 percent, which is substantially higher than the 60 percent rate reported in 1996. However, about 58 percent of eighth graders said in 2006 that cigarettes were fairly easy or very easy to get. This percentage was significantly lower than percentages reported in the 1990s, but it still reflected relatively easy access. Proposed upward adjustments in the minimum age for tobacco purchases are intended to reduce this discrepancy.[45]

Use of Smokeless Tobacco

Smokeless tobacco is ingested, as the name implies, by absorption through the membranes of the mouth rather than by inhalation of smoke into the lungs (Table 12.1). The two most common forms are the traditional loose-leaf chewing tobacco (brand names include Red Man and Beech Nut) and moist, more finely shredded tobacco called **moist snuff** or simply snuff (brand names include Copenhagen and Skoal).

TABLE 12.1

Forms of smokeless tobacco

TYPE	DESCRIPTION
Chewing	
Loose-leaf	Made of cigar-leaf tobacco, sold in small packages, heavily flavored or plain
Fine-cut	Similar to loose-leaf but more finely cut so that it resembles snuff
Plug	Leaf tobacco pressed into flat cakes and sweetened with molasses, licorice, maple sugar, or honey
Twist	Made of stemmed leaves twisted into small rolls and then folded

(Chewing tobacco is not really chewed but rather held in the mouth between the cheek and lower jaw.)

Snuff
Dry, moist, sweetened, flavored, salted, scented

(A pinch of snuff, called a *quid*, is typically tucked between the gum and the lower lip. Moist varieties are currently the most popular.)

Source: Adapted from Popescu, Cathy (1992). The health hazards of smokeless tobacco. In Kristine Napier (Ed.), *Issues in tobacco.* New York: American Council on Science and Health, pp. 11–12.

Snuff, by the way, is no longer sniffed into the nose, as in the eighteenth century, but rather placed inside the cheek or alongside the gum inside the lower lip. Some varieties of snuff are available in a small absorbent-paper sack (like a tea bag) so that the tobacco particles do not get stuck in the teeth. The practice is called "dipping."

In the national sample responding to the University of Michigan survey, about 4 percent of eighth graders, 6 percent of tenth graders, and 6 percent of high school seniors in 2006 had used smokeless tobacco within the previous thirty days. In general, smokeless tobacco use among teens is down substantially from the peak levels reported in the mid-1990s. More so than with respect to cigarette smoking, major demographic differences exist in the prevalence of smokeless tobacco use. Prevalence rates are higher for males than for females, higher for young people in the southern and North Central regions of the United States than for those in the Northeast or West, and higher for white students than for African American and Latino students. The greatest concentration of smokeless tobacco use is reported in nonmetropolitan areas of the nation.[46]

Currently, the form of smokeless tobacco showing the most consistent gains in recent sales is moist snuff, with some brands sold in cherry or wintergreen flavors. As with cigarette tobacco, variations in the alkalinity of different brands of moist snuff allow for different percentages of the nicotine in the tobacco to be absorbed through the membranes of the mouth. Thus, snuff users typically start with brands that release relatively low levels of nicotine, then "graduate" to more potent brands. The most potent brand on the current market, Copenhagen, is also the best-selling snuff in the United States.[47]

Despite continuing warnings that smokeless tobacco presents great risk to one's health, its popularity continues. As stated earlier, while smokeless tobacco presents no immediate danger to the lungs, there are substantial adverse effects on other organs of the body. At the very least, regular use of smokeless tobacco increases the risk of gum disease, damage to tooth enamel, and eventually the loss of teeth. More seriously, the direct contact of the tobacco with membranes of the mouth allows carcinogenic nitrosamines to cause tissue changes that can lead to oral cancer. Delay in the treatment of oral cancer increases the likelihood of the cancer spreading to the

moist snuff: Damp, finely shredded tobacco, placed inside the cheek or alongside the gum inside the lower lip.

Madonna's cigar smoking on the *David Letterman* show reflected the glamorization of cigars in the 1990s.

Cigars

For a brief time in the 1990s, there was a resurgence in the popularity of cigars, spurred on by images of media stars, both male and female, who had taken up cigar smoking as the tobacco use of choice.

By the end of the decade, however, the cigar-smoking craze had "gone up in smoke." While part of the problem related to changing market conditions for imported cigars, a major contributing factor was the increasing recognition that cigars could not be regarded as a safe alternative to cigarettes.[49] Cigar smoke is more alkaline than cigarette smoke, so the nicotine content in cigars can be absorbed directly through tissues lining the mouth rather than requiring inhalation into the lungs. In addition, due to the tar content, the risk of lung cancer is five times higher for those who smoke cigars, eight times higher for those smoking three or more cigars a day, and eleven times higher for those inhaling the smoke of cigars, relative to nonsmokers. Regular cigar smokers have a doubled risk, relative to nonsmokers, for cancers of the mouth, throat, and esophagus; they also incur a 45 percent higher risk of COPD and a 27 percent higher risk of coronary heart disease (see Portrait on page 311). Major cigar manufacturers have now agreed to place warning labels on their products,

jaw, pharynx, and neck. When swallowed, saliva containing nitrosamines can produce stomach and urinary tract cancer. All the negative consequences of ingesting nicotine during tobacco smoking are also present in the use of smokeless tobacco.[48]

Drugs . . . in Focus

Introducing Light and Luscious Camel No. 9

Camel No. 9 cigarettes are sold in hot-pink fuchsia and minty-green packages, designed to evoke associations with the popular women's fragrance Chanel No. 19 and perhaps with the song "Love Potion No. 9," "dressing to the nines," or even "being on cloud nine." The logo on the pack describes the cigarettes as "light and luscious," and flowers surround the packs in magazine advertisements. Whether in mentholated or nonmetholated forms (the tobacco blend itself is identical to that of "regular" Camels), the new branding is an effort to widen the male-oriented Camel image, so as to compete with rival brands like Marlboro and Newport, for which a larger portion of the customers are women.

Anti-tobacco advocates have criticized the move as a way of increasing the rates of tobacco-related diseases among women. They cite statistics that show that more women are now dying of lung cancer than breast cancer

and have increased concern about the effect that cigarette smoking among women has on heart disease, emphysema, and other disorders. In its defense, R. J. Reynolds Tobacco, makers of Camel cigarettes, argue that "what we're about is giving adult smokers a choice with products we believe are more appealing than existing products."

An editorial in the *New York Times* has expressed the following opinion:

> No doubt Reynolds will fall back on the tobacco company mantra: it's not trying to woo new smokers to a dangerous product; it's just trying to convert existing ones to its brand. But we all know that the tobacco business will wither away unless it finds new smokers to replace those who quit or die.

What do you think?

Sources: Don't fall for hot pink Camels (2007, February 19). *New York Times*, p. A14. Elliott, Stuart (2007, February 15). A new Camel brand is dressed to the nines. *New York Times*, p. C9. Quotation of the Reynolds Tobacco Company on p. C9.

alerting consumers to the risk of mouth and throat cancer, lung cancer and heart disease, and hazards to fertility and unborn children.[50]

Flavored Cigarettes and Other Developments in Tobacco Use

A recent phenomenon in tobacco use is the increasing presence of flavored cigarettes. Hand-rolled cigarettes from India, flavored with cinnamon, orange, strawberry, or chocolate, called *bidis* (pronounced BEE-dees), and clove-flavored cigarettes from Indonesia, called *kreteks* (pronounced KRAY-teks) have become popular among teenagers. In the University of Michigan survey regarding smoking bidis or kreteks in the past year, the prevalence rates for high school seniors in 2006 were 2 percent and 6 percent, respectively. These figures are substantially lower than those for regular cigarettes, but significant health concerns remain. Bidis and kreteks are unfiltered, contain higher nicotine and tar concentrations than traditional American brands, and require more vigorous puffing, thus pulling a greater amount of smoke into the lungs.[51]

Since 1999, flavored American-brand cigarettes have also become available. Kool cigarettes are marketed in Caribbean Chill, Midnight Berry, Mocha Taboo, and Mintrique varieties. Flavored versions of Camel cigarettes known as Exotic Camel Blends include Crema, Dark Mint, Mandarin Mint, and Bayou Blast (the latter marketed nationwide as a tie-in with Mardi Gras). Health professionals have criticized these new products as ways to appeal to young nonsmokers, an assertion that the tobacco industry denies.[52]

Another development is the recent introduction by R. J. Reynolds Tobacco of a new brand of Camel cigarettes, oriented toward female smokers, called "Camel No. 9" (Drugs...in Focus).

Tobacco Use around the World

Since the seventeenth century, the practice of tobacco smoking has spread throughout the world, but until the 1980s the behavior itself had been largely independent of American tobacco corporations. Today, the picture has changed dramatically. Between 1985 and 1991 alone, U.S. cigarette exports increased 200 percent. During this brief period, cigarette exports to Japan increased by more than 700 percent and those to South Korea increased by more than 1,200 percent. Since the late 1990s, American-made cigarettes have moved into significant markets in Eastern Europe and Russia, where smoking prevalence rates (Figure 12.4) are substantially

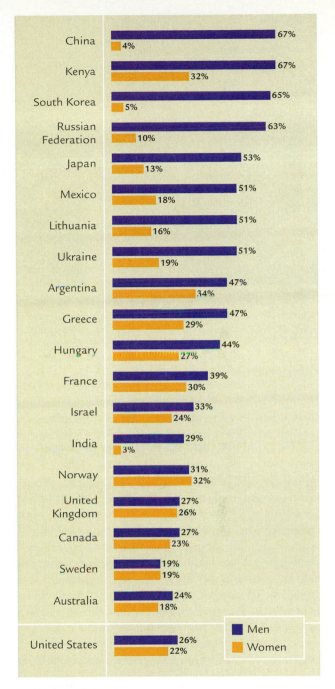

FIGURE 12.4

Smoking rates for men and women over fifteen years old in selected countries.

Note: Percentages for the United States differ slightly from data in the National Household Survey on Drug Use and Health, due to differences in criteria and age range.

Source: Mackay, Judith, and Eriksen, Michael (2003). *The tobacco atlas.* Geneva, Switzerland: World Health Organization, Table A.

A young student enjoys a cigarette with friends before class outside his school in Perm, Russia. There are regulations against smoking in public places, but they are routinely ignored and rarely enforced. Smoking-related illnesses are among the reasons for the life expectancy rate for men in Russia to have dropped to fifty-nine years.

higher than those in the United States. Presently, U.S. tobacco exports total more than $6 billion each year.

Unfortunately, the prevalence rate of smoking in many foreign countries far exceeds that of the United States, coupled with substantially less public concern for the consequences of smoking on health. In Japan, for example, 53 percent of all adult men smoke cigarettes. No-smoking sections in restaurants and offices are uncommon; approximately half a million outdoor vending machines allow minors to purchase cigarettes easily, though officially such sales are illegal; and there is little or no governmental opposition to smoking in general. The Japanese currently enjoy the longest life expectancy in the world, but health officials are concerned that this status is certain to change over the next twenty years. Deaths from lung, tracheal, and bronchial cancer among the Japanese have risen dramatically since 1980, and there is little indication that this trend will moderate in the future.[53]

Perhaps nowhere in the world is the impact of cigarette smoking on public health more evident than in present-day China. Because of its huge population, an estimated 300 to 340 million Chinese smokers, out of a population of 900 million adults, account for 30 percent of the world's total consumption of tobacco. Approximately 67 percent of all Chinese men smoke regularly. One million Chinese die each year from tobacco-related illnesses and, unless smoking patterns change, 3 million are expected to die by 2050.

Clearly, tobacco use is a global public health concern. According to the World Health Organization (WHO), 47 percent of men and 12 percent of women *worldwide* are smokers; an estimated 4.9 million people *worldwide* died in 2003 of tobacco-related illnesses, with the figure projected to increase to approximately 10 million by 2030. In recognition of the enormous health crisis that exists in the present and the calamity that looms in the future, a Framework Convention on Tobacco Control was unanimously adopted in May 2003 by the World Health Assembly at the WHO headquarters in Geneva, setting objectives for tobacco-use prevention and tobacco advertisements. Ratification by the 192 member nations, however, has been slow and uncertain. Many of them are benefiting from and in some cases are dependent upon tax revenues from tobacco sales; some countries receive direct profits from state-owned tobacco corporations within their borders.[54]

Quitting Smoking: The Good News and the Bad

Given the grim story of all the documented health risks associated with tobacco, it is at least reassuring to know that if a smoker does succeed in quitting, some of the damage can be undone. Here are the benefits:

- Within eight hours—Carbon monoxide levels in the blood drop to normal.
- Within twenty-four hours—Chances of a heart attack decrease.
- Within two weeks to three months—Circulation improves. Lung function increases by up to 30 percent.
- Within one to nine months—Coughing, sinus congestion, fatigue, and shortness of breath decrease. Cilia regain normal function in the lungs, increasing ability to handle mucus, clean the lungs, and reduce infection.
- Within one year—Excess risk of coronary heart disease is half that of a smoker's.
- Within five to ten years—Risk of stroke is reduced to that of a nonsmoker's.
- Within ten years—Lung cancer death rate is about half that of a continuing smoker's.
- Within fifteen years—Risk of coronary heart disease is equal to that of a nonsmoker's.[55]

The Bad News: How Hard It Is to Quit

The advantages of quitting are real and most people are aware of them, but the fact remains that, in the words of the surgeon general's report in 1988, "The pharmacologic and behavioral processes that determine tobacco addiction are similar to those that determine addiction to drugs such as heroin and cocaine."[56] It may be easy to quit smoking for a short while but it is very difficult to avoid a relapse, as any former or present smoker will tell you.

About one-third of all smokers in the United States try to quit each year, the vast majority of them without any treatment, but only about 3 percent succeed with their initial attempt. Nonetheless, about half of all smokers do eventually manage to achieve long-term abstinence from the nicotine in tobacco products, but only after multiple attempts at quitting. Research studies on smoking cessation indicate that there are no gender differences with regard to the likelihood that a person will quit smoking for one to four years, though men are more likely than women to have been abstinent for five years or more. The fact that a higher level of smoking is consistently related to a lower level of education and family income makes it vital that smoking-cessation programs be available to those who ordinarily would not be able to afford them.[57]

The options available to smokers who want to quit are numerous. In addition to behaviorally oriented social support groups (Smokers Anonymous, SmokeEnders, Smoke-Stoppers), counseling either in person or through telephone "quitlines," hypnosis, acupuncture, and specific prescription drugs can help reduce the withdrawal symptoms and feelings of nicotine craving. One example is a sustained-release form of the antidepressant drug bupropion. Originally marketed as a treatment for depression under the name Wellbutrin, it was approved by the FDA in 1997 for use as an aid for smoking cessation and renamed Zyban when marketed for this purpose. Doctors recommend taking Zyban daily for a week prior to the last cigarette to allow drug levels to build up in the bloodstream and buffer the loss of nicotine when smoking stops. About 44 percent of individuals taking Zyban have refrained from smoking after seven weeks, and 23 percent remain smoke-free after one year, roughly twice the percentage of those who receive a placebo. Since 1999, the costs of all prescription medications and quit-smoking programs have been tax-deductible as medical expenses.[58]

In 2006, a twice-daily tablet called Chantix became available in the United States as a nicotine-free stop-smoking medication. Clinical trials of Chantix have shown that the rate of abstinence from tobacco is 22 percent, compared to 16 percent among those taking Zyban. Forty-four percent of long-time, one-pack-per-day smokers quit after a twelve-week treatment with Chantix, compared to 30 percent among Zyban patients. Successful long-term abstinence may require multiple treatments. As a spokesperson for the American Cancer Society remarked, "It's not going to be a revolution; it's going to be a substantial step forward."[59]

Nicotine Gums, Patches, Sprays, and Inhalers

The long-term goal in quitting smoking is to withdraw from dependence-producing nicotine altogether and to be totally free of any hazard associated with tobacco. In the meantime, however, it is possible to employ an alternate route of ingestion for nicotine that avoids inhaling carbon monoxide and tar into the lungs. Chewing gum containing nicotine (brand name: Nicorette), available since the early 1970s as a prescription drug, is now marketed on a nonprescription basis. Transdermal nicotine patches are marketed on a nonprescription basis as well. Prescription nicotine-substitute options include a nasal spray (brand name: Nicotrol NS) and an oral inhalation system (brand name: Nicotrol Inhaler) in which nicotine is inhaled from a cartridge through a plastic mouthpiece, and lozenges (brand name: Commit). With any of these nicotine substitute approaches, behavioral counseling is advised while nicotine levels are gradually reduced. Behavioral counseling greatly increases the smoker's chance of becoming an ex-smoker (Help Line).[60]

The Role of Physicians in Smoking Cessation

Owing to the fact that tobacco use is the leading cause of preventable death in the United States, it is becoming clear that physicians must play a critical role in addressing the issue of tobacco use in their patients as part of an intervention to help them quit smoking. Suggestions for a greater role of the physician in this regard have been dubbed the "Five A's":

- *Ask about tobacco use.* Identify and document tobacco-use status for every patient at every visit.
- *Advise to quit.* In a clear, strong, and personalized manner, urge every tobacco user to quit.
- *Assess willingness to make a cessation attempt.* Is the tobacco user willing to make a cessation attempt at this time?

Ten Tips on How to Succeed When Trying to Quit Smoking

- Choose a quit date and stick to it.
- Remember that you are dependent, physiologically and psychologically, on nicotine and that the first few days without cigarettes will be the hardest.
- Change the habits that are associated with smoking. If you have had a cigarette with your morning coffee, drink orange juice instead.
- Tell all the people you know that you are quitting and ask for their support.
- Drink lots of water and brush your teeth frequently to rid yourself of the taste of tobacco.
- Never carry matches or a lighter with you. Put away your ashtrays or fill them with something else.
- Spend time with people who don't smoke.
- Keep a supply of sugarless gum, celery sticks, or hard candy on hand to use as a cigarette substitute.

- If you have an uncontrollable urge to light up, take ten deep breaths instead. Hold the last breath, then exhale slowly, and tell yourself you have just had a cigarette.
- Think about all the money you are saving by not buying cigarettes. A simple calculation will convince you that the amount saved in five years from just a moderate level of smoking (say half a pack a day) can be more than $5,000.

Where to go for assistance:

www. cdc. gov/ tobacco/ data_statistics/ Factsheets/ smokeless_tobacco. htm

This web site is sponsored by the Centers for Disease Control and Prevention, U.S. Department of Health and Human Services, Atlanta, Georgia.

Source: Updated from American Cancer Society (1986).
Breaking free. Atlanta: American Cancer Society, p. 9.

- *Assist in cessation attempt.* For the patient willing to make a cessation attempt, use counseling and pharmacotherapy to help him or her quit.
- *Arrange follow-up.* Schedule follow-up contact, preferably within the first week after the cessation date.[61]

A Final Word on Quitting

It should be emphasized, however, that approximately 90 percent of all smokers who quit do so on their own, without any professional or outside help, simply by quitting cold turkey and deciding to forgo all cigarettes in the future, despite the withdrawal symptoms that will persist for several days and the craving that can continue for months afterward.[62]

It is when these efforts have failed that alternative approaches need to be considered. Health professionals emphasize that if one treatment strategy does not work out, the smoker should try another. The long-term consequences of failure are just too great.

Part of California's antismoking campaign, this billboard focuses on the dangers of environmental tobacco smoke. Researchers have found that an approach based on the potential decline in social attractiveness reduces the desire among adolescents to start smoking. In 2005, state health officials announced that smoking rates among adolescents and adults in California had declined sharply since the inception of the anti-tobacco campaign in 1990.

The best option, of course, is never to start in the first place, which brings us back to the teenage years, when virtually all adult smokers pick up the habit. The challenge at the beginning of the twenty-first century will be to maintain the communication of effective messages that prevent the initiation of cigarette smoking as well as other forms of tobacco use by young people (see Chapter 15). While we have a way to go in this respect, present indications are that we are heading in the right direction.[63]

Summary

Tobacco Use through History

- Tobacco use originated among the original inhabitants of North and South America, and its introduction to Europe and the rest of the world dates from the first voyage of Columbus. Europeans used tobacco initially in the form of pipe smoking and later in the form of snuff.

- In the nineteenth-century United States, the most popular form was tobacco chewing and later cigar smoking. It was not until the late nineteenth century and early twentieth century that cigarette smoking became popular.

Health Concerns and Smoking Behavior

- The 1964 surgeon general's report, the first official statement on the connection between smoking and adverse health consequences, produced a general reversal in the previously climbing per capita consumption of cigarettes.

- Since 1964, the surgeon general's reports have solidified the position that nicotine is a clearly addicting component of tobacco and that tobacco use, whether in a smoked or smokeless form, causes significant health risks.

- Since 1964, there has been increased use of filtered, low-tar, and low-nicotine cigarettes.

Tobacco Today: An Industry on the Defensive

- Since the early 1990s, most U.S. states, cities, and communities have enacted laws mandating smoke-free environments in all public and private workplaces. It is now typical for restaurants, hotels, and other commercial spaces to be partially, if not totally, smoke-free.

- Additional pressure on the tobacco industry has come from proposals to increase the federal excise tax on tobacco products.

- Increased public pressure since the mid-1990s has resulted in a greatly limited marketing approach for tobacco products, particularly with respect to sales to young people.

- In 1998, the major American tobacco corporations entered into a $246 billion settlement agreement with all fifty U.S. states to resolve claims that the states should be compensated for the costs of treating people with smoking-related illnesses.

What's in Tobacco?

- The principal ingredients consumed during the smoking of tobacco are nicotine, tar, and carbon monoxide.

- The smoker inhales smoke in the form of mainstream smoke (through the cigarette itself) and sidestream smoke (released from the cigarette tip into the air).

The Dependence Potential of Nicotine

- Nicotine ingestion produces both tolerance effects and physical withdrawal symptoms. A prominent feature of nicotine withdrawal is the strong feeling of craving for a return to tobacco use.

- Smokers typically adjust their smoking behavior to obtain a stable dose of nicotine.

Health Consequences of Tobacco Use

- Tobacco smoking produces an increased risk of cardiovascular disease such as coronary heart disease and stroke, lung cancer and other forms of cancer, and respiratory diseases such as chronic bronchitis and emphysema.

- In addition to the hazards to the smoker through the inhalation of mainstream smoke, there are hazards to the developing fetus when the mother is smoking and hazards to nonsmokers who inhale sidestream smoke (environmental tobacco smoke).

Patterns of Smoking Behavior and Use of Smokeless Tobacco

- In 2006, the prevalence rate for smoking in the United States was approximately 25 percent.

- The peak years for starting to smoke are in the sixth and seventh grades of school.

- A disturbingly high percentage of students think that cigarette smoking does not present "great risk" to their health, despite well-publicized information regarding adverse affects.

- A steady increase in the prevalence of smoking among secondary school students during the 1990s has recently been reversed. There is a growing social disapproval of cigarette smoking in general among this population. As these young people get older, the prevalence rates for cigarette smoking among college students and young adults are likely to decline.

- A global trend of unabated smoking rates in Asia, Eastern Europe, Russia, and elsewhere threatens the future health of huge populations of people worldwide.

Quitting Smoking: The Good News and the Bad

- Research has clearly shown that when people quit smoking, many health risks diminish rapidly. Unfortunately, nicotine dependence is very strong, and it is difficult to quit smoking. Nonetheless, a wide range of smoking cessation treatments are available, and about 50 percent of smokers eventually succeed in quitting on a permanent basis.

- Present-day approaches toward smoking cessation include behavioral treatment programs, hypnosis, acupuncture, and prescription drugs to reduce withdrawal symptoms and craving, as well as a variety of nicotine substitutes.

Key Terms

arteriosclerosis, p. 308
atherosclerosis, p. 308
carbon monoxide, p. 305
carcinomas, p. 310
chronic bronchitis, p. 309
chronic obstructive
    pulmonary disease
    (COPD), p. 309

cigarettes, p. 299
cigars, p. 299
cilia, p. 305
ciliary escalator,
    p. 305
coronary heart disease
    (CHD), p. 308
emphysema, p. 309

environmental tobacco
    smoke (ETS), p. 302
erythroplakia, p. 310
gaseous phase, p. 305
leukoplakia, p. 310
mainstream smoke, p. 304
moist snuff, p. 315
nicotine, p. 305

nitrosamines, p. 310
particulate phase, p. 305
sidestream smoke, p. 301
snuff, p. 298
snuffing, p. 298
tar, p. 305
titration hypothesis,
    p. 307

Endnotes

1. Brooks, Jerome E. (1952). *The mighty leaf: Tobacco through the centuries.* Boston: Little, Brown, pp. 11–14. Fairholt, Frederick W. (1859). *Tobacco: Its history and associations.* London: Chapman and Hill, p. 13.

2. Brooks, *The mighty leaf*, pp. 74–80. White, Jason M. (1991). *Drug dependence.* Englewood Cliffs, NJ: Prentice Hall, pp. 32–33.

3. Austin, Gregory A. (1978). *Perspectives on the history of psychoactive substance use.* Rockville, MD: National Institute on Drug Abuse, pp. 1–12.

4. Brooks, *The mighty leaf*, p. 181. Lehman Brothers (1955). *About tobacco.* New York: Lehman Brothers, pp. 18–20.

5. Quotation from Dickens, Charles (1842). *American notes.* Cited in Brooks, *The mighty leaf*, pp. 215–216.

6. Kluger, Richard (1996). *Ashes to ashes: America's hundred-year cigarette war, the public health, and the "unabashed" triumph of Philip Morris.* New York: Knopf, p. 14. Tate, Cassandra (1989). In the 1800s, antismoking was a burning issue. *Smithsonian, 20*(4), 111.

7. Quotation originally in Bain, John, and Werner, Carl (1905). *Cigarettes in fact and fancy.* Boston: H. M. Caldwell. Cited in Brooks, *The mighty leaf*, p. 259.

8. Kluger, *Ashes to ashes*, pp. 16–26. Lehman Brothers, *About tobacco*, pp. 24–27. Slade, John (1992). The

tobacco epidemic: Lessons from history. *Journal of Psychoactive Drugs, 24,* 99–109.

9. Lehman Brothers, *About tobacco*, p. 30.

10. Ibid., p. 31.

11. U.S. Department of Health and Human Services (1991). *Strategies to control tobacco use in the United States: A blueprint for public health action in the 1990s* (NIH Smoking and Tobacco Control Monograph No. 1). Bethesda, MD: National Cancer Institute.

12. Federal Trade Commission Report to Congress (1992). Pursuant to the Federal Cigarette Labeling and Advertising Act, p. 31.

13. Short, J. Gordon (1990, fall). The golden leaf. *Priorities,* p. 10.

14. Nicotine in cigarettes increases significantly since 1998: DPH Report (2006, August 26). Department of Public Health, Commonwealth of Massachusetts, Boston, MA. Gerstein, Dean R., and Levison, Peter K. (Eds.) (1982). *Reduced tar and nicotine cigarettes: Smoking behavior and health.* Washington DC: National Academy Press. Mann, Charles K. (1975). *Tobacco: The ants and the elephants.* Salt Lake City, UT: Olympus Publishing, pp. 91–109. Study: Low-tar cigarettes don't cut risks. (2004, January 9). *Newsday,* p. A28.

15. Ochs, Ridgely (2000, December 28). An ounce of prevention? Little money from suit used to halt tobacco. *Newsday*, pp. A6, A62–A63. Tauras, John A.; Chaloupka, Frank J.; Farrelly, Matthew C.; Giovino, Gary A.; Wakefield, Melanie; Johnson, Lloyd D.; O'Malley, Patrick M.; Kloska, Deborah D.; and Pechacek, Terry F. (2005). State tobacco control spending and youth smoking. *American Journal of Public Health*, 95, 338–344.

16. Johnston, Lloyd D.; O'Malley, Patrick M.; Bachman, Jerald G.; and Schulenberg, John E. (2007). *Monitoring the Future national results on adolescent drug use: Overview of key findings, 2006.* Bethesda, MD: National Institute on Drug Abuse, Tables 1 and 2.

17. Alcoholic beverages and tobacco (1997, September 11). *Standard and Poor's Industry Surveys*, p. 10. Lok, Corie (2002, August 5). Hitting teen smokers where it hurts: In the wallet. *Newsweek*, p. 47. Wilgoren, Jodi (2002, July 17). Facing new costs, some smokers say "enough." *New York Times*, p. A14.

18. Payne, Wayne A., and Hahn, Dale B. (1992). *Understanding your health.* St. Louis: Mosby Year Book, p. 270.

19. Schlaadt, Richard G. (1992). *Tobacco and health.* Guilford, CT: Dushkin Publishing, p. 41.

20. Gahagan, Dolly D. (1987). *Switch down and quit: What the cigarette companies don't want you to know about smoking.* Berkeley, CA: Ten Speed Press, p. 44. Payne and Hahn, *Understanding your health*, pp. 273–275.

21. Jacobs, Michael R., and Fehr, Kevin O'B. (1987). *Drugs and drug abuse: A reference text* (2nd ed.). Toronto: Addiction Research Foundation, pp. 417–425. Julien, Robert M. (2001). *A primer of drug action* (9th ed.). New York: Worth, p. 229.

22. Meier, Barry (1998, February 23). Cigarette maker manipulated nicotine, its records suggest. *New York Times*, pp. A1, A15. Pankow, J. F.; Mader, B. T.; Isabelle, L. M.; Luo, W. T.; Pavlick, A.; and Liang, C. K. (1997). Conversion of nicotine and tobacco smoke to its volatile and available free-base form through the action of gaseous ammonia. *Environmental Science & Technology*, 31, 2428–2433.

23. Julien, *A primer of drug action*, p. 231. Phillips, Sarah, and Fox, Pauline (1998). An investigation into the effects of nicotine gum on short-term memory. *Psychopharmacology*, 140, 429–433. Schuckit, Marc A. (2000). *Drug and alcohol abuse: A clinical guide to diagnosis and treatment* (5th ed.). New York: Kluwer Academic/Plenum, pp. 262–264. Zhang, Hui, and Sulzer, David (2004). Frequency-dependent modulation of dopamine released by nicotine. *Nature Neuroscience*, 7, 581–582.

24. Brecher, Edward M., and the editors of *Consumer Reports* (1972). *Licit and illicit drugs.* Boston: Little, Brown, pp. 220–228.

25. Pontieri, Francesco E.; Tanda, Gianluigi; Orzi, Francesco; and DiChiara, Gaetano (1996). Effects of nicotine on the nucleus accumbens and similarity to those of addictive drugs. *Science*, 382, 255–257. Risso, Francesca; Parodi, Monica; Grilli, Massimo; Molfino, Francesca; Raiteri, Maurizio; and Marchi, Mario (2004). Chronic nicotine causes functional upregulation of ionotropic glutamate receptors medicating hippocampal noradrenaline and stratal dopamine release. *Neurochemistry International*, 44, 293–301.

26. Lichtenstein, Edward, and Brown, Richard A. (1980). Smoking cessation methods: Review and recommendations. In William R. Miller (Ed.), *The addictive behaviors: Treatment of alcoholism, drug abuse, smoking, and obesity.* New York: Pergamon Press, pp. 169–206. Quotation on p. 173.

27. Ibid., pp. 172–173.

28. Herning, Ronald I., Jones, Reese T., and Fischman, Patricio (1985). The titration hypothesis revisited: Nicotine gum reduces smoking intensity. In John Grabowski and Sharon M. Hall (Eds.), *Pharmacological adjuncts in smoking cessation* (NIDA Research Monograph 53). Rockville MD: National Institute on Drug Abuse, pp. 27–41. Jarvik, Murray E. (1979). Biological influences on cigarette smoking. In Norman A. Krasnegor (Ed.), *The behavioral aspects of smoking* (NIDA Research Monograph 26). Rockville, MD: National Institute on Drug Abuse, pp. 7–45.

29. Jarvik, Biological influences, pp. 25–29. Schuckit, *Drugs and alcohol abuse*, pp. 264–265.

30. Koslowski, Lynn T.; Wilkinson, Adrian; Skinner, Wayne; Kent, Carl; Franklin, Tom; and Pope, Marilyn. (1989). Comparing tobacco cigarette dependence with other drug dependencies. *Journal of the American Medical Association*, 261, 898–901.

31. Centers for Disease Control and Prevention (2003). Cigarette smoking-attributable morbidity—United States, 2000. *Morbidity and Mortality Weekly Report*, 52, 842–844. Centers for Disease Control and Prevention (2002). Annual smoking attributable mortality, years of potential life lost and economic costs—United States, 1995–1999. *Morbidity and Mortality Weekly Report*, 51, 300–303. Centers for Disease Control and Prevention (1997, May 23). *Fact sheet: Facts about cigarette mortality.* Atlanta, GA: Office of Communication, Centers for Disease Control and Prevention. Julien, *A primer of drug action*, p. 236. Roper, W. L. (1991). Making smoking prevention a reality. *Journal of the American Medical Association*, 266, 3188–3189.

32. Ayanian, John Z., and Cleary, Paul D. (1999). Perceived risks of heart disease and cancer among cigarette smokers. *Journal of the American Medical Association*, 281, 1019–1021. Howard, George; Wagenknecht, Lynne E.; Burke, Gregory L.; Diez-Roux, Ana; Evans, Gregory W.; McGovern, Paul; Nieto, Javier; and Tell, Grethe S. (1998). Cigarette smoking and progression of atherosclerosis. *Journal of the American Medical Association*, 279, 119–124. U.S. Department of Health and Human Services, Public Health Service, Office of Smoking and Health (1983). *The health consequences of smoking: Cardiovascular disease* (A report of the surgeon general) Rockville, MD: U.S. Public Health Service, pp. 63–156.

33. Payne and Hahn, *Understanding your health*, pp. 272–273.

34. Schlaadt, *Tobacco and health*, p. 52.

35. Gold, Diane R.; Wang, Xiaobin; Wypij, David; Speizer, Frank E.; Ware, James H.; and Dockery, Douglas W. (1996). Effects of cigarette smoking on lung function in adolescent boys and girls. *New England Journal of Medicine, 335*, 931–937. U.S. Department of Health and Human Services, Public Health Service, Office of Smoking and Health (1984). *The health consequences of smoking: Chronic obstructive lung disease* (A report of the surgeon general). Rockville, MD: U.S. Public Health Service, pp. 329–360.

36. American Cancer Society (2007). *Cancer facts and figures 2007.* Atlanta GA: American Cancer Society, pp. 2–3, 13–14. Denissenko, Mikhail F.; Pao, Annie; Tang, Moon-Shong; and Pfeifer, Gerd P. (1996). Preferential formation of benzopyrene adducts at lung cancer mutational hotspots in *P53. Science, 274,* 430–432.

37. Schuckit, *Drug and alcohol abuse,* p. 264.

38. Ebrahim, Shahul H.; Floyd, R. Louise; Merritt II, Robert K; Decoufle, Pierre; and Holtzman, David (2000). Trends in pregnancy-related smoking rates in the United States, 1987–1996. *Journal of the American Medical Association, 283,* 361–366. Li, Yu-Fen; Langholz, Bryan; Salam, Muhammad T.; and Gilliland, Frank D. (2005). Maternal and grandmaternal smoking patterns are associated with early childhood asthma. *Chest, 127,* 1232–1241. U.S. Department of Health and Human Services, Public Health Service, Office of Smoking and Health (1980). *The health consequences of smoking for women* (A report of the surgeon general). Rockville, MD: U.S. Public Health Service, pp. 98–101.

39. Davis, Ronald M. (1998). Exposure to environmental tobacco smoke: Identifying and protecting those at risk. *Journal of the American Medical Association, 280,* 1947–1949. Ginzel, K. H. (1992). The ill-effects of second hand smoke. In Kristine Napier (Ed.), *Issues in tobacco.* New York: American Council on Science and Health, pp. 6–7.

40. Aligne, C. Andrew; Moss, Mark E.; Auinger, Peggy; and Weitzman, Michael (2003). Association of pediatric dental caries with passive smoking. *Journal of the American Medical Association, 289,* 1258–1264. Fielding, Jonathan E., and Phenow, Kenneth J. (1989). *Health effects of involuntary smoking.* Atlanta, GA: American Cancer Society. Kawachi, Ichiro; Colditz, Graham A.; Speizer, Frank E.; Manson, JoAnn E.; Stampfer, Meir J.; Willett, Walter C.; and Hennekens, Charles H. (1997). A prospective study of passive smoking and coronary heart disease. *Circulation, 95,* 2374–2379. Nafstad, Per; Fugelseth, Drude; Qvigstad, Erik; Zahlsen, Kolbjørn; Magnus, Per, and Lindenmann, Rolf (1998). Nicotine concentration in the hair of nonsmoking mothers and size of offspring. *American Journal of Public Health, 88,* 120–124. U.S. Department of Health and Human Services, Public Health Service, Office of Smoking and Health (2006). *The health consequences of involuntary exposure to tobacco smoke* (A report of the surgeon general). Rockville, MD: U.S. Public Health Service.

41. Johnston, Lloyd D.; O' Malley, Patrick M.; Bachman, Jerald G.; and Schulenberg, John E. (2007a). *Monitoring the Future: National survey results on drug use, 1975–2006. Volume I. Secondary school students.* Bethesda, MD: National Institute on Drug Abuse, Table 2-3. Johnston, Lloyd M.; O'Malley, Patrick M.; Bachman, Gerald G.; and Schulenberg, John E. (2007b). *Monitoring the Future: National survey results on drug use, 1975–2006. Volume II. College students and adults ages 19–45, 2006.* Bethesda, MD: National Institute on Drug Abuse, Table 2–3. Substance Abuse and Mental Health Administration (2007). *Results from the 2006 National Survey on Drug Use and Health: National findings.* Rockville, MD: Office of Applied Studies, Substance Abuse and Mental Health Administration, pp. 41–48. Survey: Smoking highest among Indians (2004, January 30). Reuters News Service, Washington, DC. Wechsler, Henry, Rigotti, Nancy A., and Gledhill-Hoyt, Jeana (1998). Increased levels of cigarette use among college students: A cause for national concern. *Journal of the American Medical Association, 280,* 1673–1678.

42. Centers for Disease Control and Prevention (2003). Tobacco use among middle and high school students—New Hampshire, 1995–2001. *Morbidity and Mortality Weekly Report, 52,* 7–9. Johnston, O'Malley, Bachman, and Schulenberg (2007a), *Monitoring the Future,* Vol. I, Tables 2.1, 2.3, 2.4, and 6.1.

43. Johnston, O'Malley, Bachman, and Schulenberg (2007a), *Monitoring the Future,* Vol. I, Tables 8-1 and 8-4.

44. Johnston, Lloyd D., O'Malley, Patrick M., and Bachman, Jerald G. (2002, December 16). Teen smoking declines sharply in 2002, more than offsetting large increases in the early 1990s. University of Michigan News and Information Service, Ann Arbor, pp. 4–5. Quotation on page 4.

45. Johnston, O'Malley, Bachman, and Schulenberg (2007a), *Monitoring the Future,* Vol. I, Table 9-6. Emmons, Karen M.; Wechsler, Henry; Dowdall, George; and Abraham, Melissa (1998). Predictors of smoking among U.S. college students. *American Journal of Public Health, 88,* 104–107. Pearson, Dave C.; Song, Lin; Valdez, Roger B., and Angulo, Antoinette S. (2007). Youth tobacco sales in a metropolitan country: Factors associated with compliance. *American Journal of Preventive Medicine, 33,* 91–97. Retailers cut cigarette sales to youth (2005, January/February). *SAMHSA News,* p. 10. Ribisi, Kurt M., Williams, Rebecca S., and Kim, Annice E. (2003). Internet sales of cigarettes to minors. *Journal of the American Medical Association, 290,* 1356–1359. Rigotti, Nancy A.; DiFranza, Joseph R.; Chang, YuChiao; Tisdale, Thelma; Kemp, Becky; and Singer, Daniel E. (1997). The effect of enforcing tobacco-sales laws on adolescents' access to tobacco and smoking behavior. *New England Journal of Medicine, 337,* 1044–1057.

46. Johnston, O'Malley, Bachman, and Schulenberg (2007), *Monitoring the Future,* Vol. I, Tables 2-3, D-97, D-98, and D-99.

47. Freedman, Alix M. How a tobacco giant doctors snuff brands to boost their "kick." (1994, October 26). *Wall Street Journal*, pp. A1, A14.

48. U.S. Department of Health and Human Services, Public Health Service, Office of Smoking and Health (1986). *The health consequences of smokeless tobacco* (A report of the advisory committee to the surgeon general). Rockville MD: Public Health Service.

49. Hamilton, Kendall (1997, July 21). Blowing smoke. *Newsweek*, pp. 54–60.

50. Ackerman, Elise (1999, November 29). The cigar boom goes up in smoke. *Newsweek*, p. 55. Baker, Frank, et al. (2000). Health risks associated with cigar smoking. *Journal of the American Medical Association*, 284, 735–740. Substance Abuse and Mental Health Administration (2001, December 21). *The NHSDA report: Cigar use*. Rockville, MD: Office of Applied Studies, Substance Abuse and Mental Health Administration.

51. Johnson, O'Malley, Bachman, and Schulenberg (2007a), *Monitoring the Future*, Vol. I, Table 2-2. Small Indian cigarettes light up teen smokers (1999, May 11). *Newsday*, p. A49. Watson, Clifford H.; Polzin, Gregory, M.; Calafat, Antonia M.; and Ashley, David, L. (2003). Determination of tar, nicotine, and carbon monoxide yields in the smoke of bidi cigarettes. *Nicotine and Tobacco Research*, 5, 747–753.

52. Ives, Nat (2004, March 9). Flavored Kool cigarettes are attracting criticism. *New York Times*, p. C11.

53. American Cancer Society. *Cancer facts and figures 1993*, p. 22. Sterngold, James (1993, October 17). When smoking is a patriotic duty. *New York Times*, Sect. 3, pp. 1, 6. Strom, Stephanie (2001, June 13). Japan and tobacco revenue: Leader faces difficult choice. *New York Times*, pp. A1, A14. Tagliabue, John (2005, September 8). The ash may finally be falling from the Gauloise. *New York Times*, p. A4. Watts, Jonathan (1999). Smoking, sake, and suicide: Japan plans a healthier future. *The Lancet*, 354, p. 843. Winter, Greg (2001, August 24). Enticing Third World youth. *New York Times*, pp. C1, C4.

54. Ezzati, Majid, and Lopez, Alan D. (2003). Estimates of global mortality attributable to smoking in 2000. *Lancet*, 362, 847–852. Reeves, Hope (2000, November 5). Blowing smoke: What's one little worldwide anti-smoking treaty compared to the force of 1.1 billion nicotine-craving cigarette fiends? *New York Times Magazine*, p. 26. Rosenthal, Elisabeth, and Altman, Lawrence K. (1998, November 30). China, a land of heavy smokers, looks into abyss of fatal illness. *New York Times*, pp. A1, A16. Tyler, Patrick E. (1996, March 16). In heavy smoking, grim portent for China. *New York Times*, pp. 1, 5. World Health Organization, Geneva, Switzerland.

55. American Cancer Society, Atlanta. Cited in *The world almanac and book of facts 2000* (1999). Mahwah, NJ: Primedia Reference, p. 733.

56. U.S. Department of Health and Human Services, Public Health Service, Office of Smoking and Health (1988). *The health consequences of smoking: Nicotine addiction* (A report of the surgeon general). Rockville, MD: Public Health Service, p. 9.

57. American Legacy Foundation (2003). Fact sheet: Quitting Smoking. Washington DC: American Legacy Foundation. Ehrich, Beverly, and Emmons, Karen M. (1994). Addressing the needs of smokers in the 1990s. *The Behavior Therapist*, 17 (6), 119–122. Schuckit, *Drug and alcohol abuse*, p. 267. U.S. Department of Health and Human Services, Public Health Service, Office of Smoking and Health (1990). *The health benefits of smoking cessation* (A report of the surgeon general). Atlanta, GA: Office of Smoking and Health, pp. 610–611.

58. Ahluwalia, Jasjit S.; Harris, Kari Jo; Catley, Delwyn; Okuyemi, Kolawole S.; and Mayo, Matthew S. (2002). Sustain-release bupropion for smoking cessation in African Americans: A randomized controlled trial. *Journal of the American Medical Association*, 288, 468–474. Benowitz, Neal L. (1997). Treating tobacco addiction—Nicotine or no nicotine? *New England Journal of Medicine*, 337, 1230–1231. Jain, Anjali (2003). Treating nicotine addiction. *British Medical Journal*, 327, 1394–1395. Smoking treatments deductible (1999, June 11). *Newsday*, p. A66. Zickler, Patrick (2003). Genetic variation may increase nicotine craving and smoking relapse. *NIDA Notes*, 18(3), 1, 6.

59. High hopes for new stop-smoking pill (2006, May 12). *Newsday*, p. A36.

60. Franzon, Mikael, Gustavsson, Gunnar, and Korberly, Barbara H. (2002). Effectiveness of over-the-counter nicotine replacement therapy. *Journal of the American Medical Association*, 288, 3108–3110. Mathias, Robert (2001). Nicotine patch helps smokeless tobacco users quit, but maintaining abstinence may require additional treatment. *NIDA Notes*, 16(1), 8–9. Shiffman, Saul, Dresler, Carolyn M., and Rohay, Jeffrey M. (2004). Successful treatment with a nicotine lozenge of smokers with prior failure in pharmacological therapy. *Addiction*, 99, 83–92.

61. Fiore, Michael C., Hatsukami, Dorothy K., and Baker, Timothy, B. (2002). Effective tobacco dependence treatment. *Journal of the American Medical Association*, 288, 1768–1771. Spangler, John G.; George, Geeta; Foley, Kristie Long; and Crandall, Sonia J. (2002). Tobacco intervention training: Current efforts and gaps in U.S. medical schools. *Journal of the American Medical Association*, 288, 1102–1109.

62. Schuckit, *Drug and alcohol abuse*, pp. 268–269.

63. Goldman, Lisa K., and Glantz, Stanton A. (1999). Evaluation of antismoking advertising campaigns. *Journal of the American Medical Association*, 279, 772–777. Raising kids who don't smoke (2003), created by Philip Morris USA Youth Smoking Prevention. Story, Louise (2007, January 2). Kicking an addiction, with real people. *New York Times*, p. C7.

PART FOUR

Drug Abuse and Drug Policy

chapter 13

Drugs and Crime

In the last couple of years we have found a large number of marijuana plots in the Chattahoochee National Forest. Growers are planting their marijuana in this area to escape forfeiture laws. So I came up with this idea that I never thought would work but I figured was worth a try. I typed a letter and left it at one of the larger plots we found in the national forest. The letter said, "You have been caught by the Lumpkin County Sheriff's Office. We have had you under constant surveillance. If you do not turn yourself in by calling the following number, your penalties for growing marijuana will be doubled."

I couldn't believe it, but it actually worked. I had had one grower call me and turn himself in. He claimed that he was only growing marijuana for personal use. I didn't even have to pick him up. He drove to the sheriff's office and turned himself in. Incredible but true!

—*A sheriff's deputy from Lumpkin County, Georgia*

For law enforcement officers and other criminal justice professionals who contend with drugs and crime on a daily basis, the drugs–crime connection is all too real and an inarguable fact of contemporary society. As stated in a 1989 training manual sponsored by the International Association of Chiefs of Police, "If there is a reduction in the number of people who abuse drugs in your community, there will be a reduction in the commission of certain types of crime in your community." For the general public, the news headlines reporting acts of social violence linking the world of illicit drugs and the impact of those acts on our society are relentless. Although crime rates have declined significantly in recent years, we remember past decades in which the social fabric of America was being torn apart—innocent children killed in the crossfire of rival drug gangs, thousands of crimes against individuals and property to pay for a continuing pattern of drug abuse, terrorization of whole communities by drug dealers. In general, illicit drugs and crime are seen as being bound together in a web of greed and callous disregard for human life. As is the case with many issues that appear so simple at first glance, however, the relationship between drugs and crime is complex. As we advance into the twenty-first century, the key factor in untangling this relationship is to map out an agenda for research to be done on this question. In 2001 an effort was made in this regard in a major conference sponsored by two federal agencies, the National Institute of Justice and the National Institute on Drug Abuse. This chapter will concern itself with the facts and still-unanswered questions about drugs and crime in our society.[1]

Crimes that involve illicit drugs can be placed into two general categories: (1) drug-defined offenses and (2) drug-related offenses. **Drug-defined offenses** are violations of laws prohibiting the possession, use, distribution, or manufacture of illegal drugs. The possession of cocaine, the cultivation of marijuana, and the sale of methamphetamine are all examples of drug-defined offenses. Today, more inmates are serving time for drug-defined offenses than for any other type of criminal offense, and even though rates of illicit drug use in America have declined since 1979, the number of

inmates serving time for drug-defined offenses has increased by more than 25 percent. The increase in incarceration rates of drug offenders has been generated by an intensified effort to step up drug-law enforcement and the prosecution and punishment of drug offenders. In addition, since the mid-1980s, state and federal legislatures have enacted a wider range of criminal laws with respect to the selling and possession of illicit drugs, and judges have imposed longer prison sentences for drug offenders.

Drug-related offenses are offenses in which a drug's pharmacological effects contribute to an offender committing a crime or an offender commits a crime to gain money to purchase drugs. An important source of drug-related crime is the violence that occurs with drug dealing. Violence can often result from disputes over territory between rival drug dealers, punishment for defrauding a buyer, retaliation toward police informants, or acts committed to enforce discipline. Drug use, the drug business, and the violence connected with both are all aspects of a life-style that increases one's risk of becoming a victim or perpetrator of drug-related violence. As we will see, it is the character of the drug-use life-style that underlies the complex relationship between drugs, crime, and violence. We will look at the present-day problems of international and domestic trafficking of illicit drugs and money laundering later in this chapter.

Understanding Drug Use and Crime

Empirical studies of the relationship between alcohol and drug use and the commission of crime are unanimous in their findings: Drug use and crime are strongly correlated. It is virtually impossible to find a study that has failed to find a relationship between these two behaviors. Individuals who drink alcohol and/or use drugs are significantly more likely to commit crimes than are individuals who neither drink nor use drugs.

Historically, the general linkage between drug use and crime has been explored through three major explanatory models: Enslavement, predisposition, and intensification. The enslavement model, also referred to as the "medical model," asserts that individuals become forced into a life of crime and drug abuse, either from social situations such as poverty or from personal circumstances such as a mental defect. The predisposition model, also referred to as the "criminal model," asserts that drug abusers are far from law-abiding

drug-defined offense: Violation of laws that prohibit the possession, use, distribution, and manufacture of illegal drugs.

drug-related offense: Offense in which a drug contributes to the commission of a crime, either by virtue of the drug's pharmacological effects or the economic need to secure the drug itself.

citizens in the first place and that they have already been involved in criminal activity prior to initial drug use. A predisposition toward criminal activity is increased by the fact that criminals exist in social subcultures in which drug use is readily accepted and encouraged. The intensification model, essentially a combination of the previous perspectives, asserts that drug use tends to perpetuate a life of crime. In the words of one prominent researcher, "Drug use freezes its devotees into patterns of criminality that are more acute, dynamic, unremitting, and enduring than those of other [non-drug-using] offenders." In short, criminal careers already are in existence, but they are intensified by drug involvement. The intensification model is able to account for two basic facts in the drug–crime research literature: (1) criminal careers typically begin prior to drug use and (2) criminal activity declines substantially during times of drug abstinence.[2]

Collecting the Statistics

Figure 13.1 shows the result of the Arrestee Drug Abuse Monitoring (ADAM) Program conducted by the U.S. Department of Justice, in which individuals arrested for a serious offense are tested for various drugs through urinanalysis. ADAM statistics show that a high percentage of arrestees test positive for illicit drugs, regardless of the specific offense. In thirty-nine cities studied in the program, urinalysis revealed 67 percent of adult male arrestees having recently used at least one of five drugs: cocaine, marijuana, heroin, methamphetamine, or PCP. Marijuana was the most commonly used drug, with the incidence ranging from 31 to 55 percent. The second most commonly used drug was cocaine (between 3 and 51 percent) and methamphetamine showed the greatest variation by geographical region (between 0 percent in the eastern U.S. cities and 38 percent in some areas of the West). ADAM statistics confirm that there is a strong correlation between criminal behavior and drug use.[3]

Studies conducted by the Federal Bureau of Justice Statistics show that jail and prison inmates in the United States have much higher rates of drug use than individuals in the general population. More than 80 percent of inmates interviewed in prisons and jails stated that they had used drugs on at least one occasion, and about 70 percent used drugs on a regular basis at some point in their lives. In a survey of inmates in state and federal correctional facilities, more than half reported the use of alcohol or drugs while committing their offense, and 17 percent of state inmates and 18 percent of federal inmates said that they committed their current offense to obtain money for drugs. The percentage of prison

Percentage Testing Positive for Any of Five Drugs	Percentage Testing Positive				
0 20 40 60 80 100	Methamphetamine	Cocaine	Heroin	Marijuana	Multiple Drugs
Birmingham, AL — 66	1	34	8	45	20
Cleveland, OH — 75	0	39	5	49	25
Denver, CO — 66	5	38	7	42	23
Minneapolis, MN — 65	3	28	6	48	65
New York, NY — 70	0	36	15	43	22
Phoenix, AZ — 74	38	23	4	41	28
Portland, OR — 72	25	30	15	38	30
San Diego, CA — 67	36	10	5	41	24
San Jose, CA — 63	37	13	3	35	25
Tulsa, OK — 70	17	20	5	52	24

FIGURE 13.1

Prevalence of illicit drug use among male adult arrestees in ten selected U.S. cities in 2003. Percentages for cocaine, heroin, and multiple drugs, and any of five drugs are generally much higher among adults than juveniles; percentages for marijuana are generally higher among juveniles than adults.

Source: National Institute of Justice (2005). *Drug and alcohol use and related matters among arrestees 2003.* Washington DC: Arrestee Drug Abuse Monitoring Program, Department of Justice, Tables 3, 5, 6, 7, and 8.

inmates who reported they were under the influence of drugs at the time of their offense varied across the major offense categories. Drug offenders, burglars, and robbers were the most likely to report having been under the influence of drugs, while prison inmates convicted of homicide, assault, and public-order offenses were among those least likely to report being under the influence of drugs.[4]

Undoubtedly, a wide range of violent acts and crimes are associated with some form of alcohol or illicit drug use, but we have to be careful in the conclusions we draw from the statistics. Do drugs actually *cause* violent behavior and crime? If they do, which drugs have a greater responsibility than others? The idea that drug use and criminal behavior are strongly correlated forms the basis of a large proportion of laws regulating and prohibiting drug use.

Nonetheless, correlation does not imply causation. Although drug users are more likely than nonusers to commit crimes, drug users cannot be classified as a homogeneous group. Some drug users do not commit crimes other than the possession and sale of illicit drugs. Other drug users commit crimes to buy illicit drugs, whereas for others drug use and crime are both part of an overall deviant life-style. It will be useful to break down the question of the relationship between drugs and crime into three specific theoretical positions: (1) drug use causes crime, (2) crime causes drug use, and (3) both drug use and crime share common causes.

Drug Use Causes Crime

Throughout the history of the United States, it has been commonly believed that drug use "causes" criminal behavior. As discussed in Chapter 2, the legal prohibition of a particular drug often has been associated with society's fear of a given drug's effect on a threatening minority group. Some of these fears include the belief that cocaine would cause southern blacks to rape white women, opium would facilitate sexual contact between Chinese and white Americans, and marijuana would incite violence among Hispanics/Latinos. Explanations for how drug use may cause crime generally fall into two broad categories commonly referred to as "pharmacological" and "economic" explanations.

pharmacological violence: Violent acts committed while under the influence of a particular psychoactive substance, with the implication that the drug itself caused the violence to occur.

Pharmacological violence refers to the effect of a drug having a direct influence on an offender committing a crime. The implication is that a specific drug caused violent or criminal behavior while the drug was actually present in the individual's system. Although the statistics show that a large proportion of people have some drug in their system at the time of arrest, it is difficult to say whether the offense was committed as a result of the influence of that drug. The main criticism of pharmacological explanations stems from the fact that the detection period in a standard urinanalysis drug test can range from a matter of days to two months in the case of marijuana (see Table 9.3). Therefore, testing positive for a drug at the time of arrest for a crime indicates only that the individual *might* have become violent while under the influence of the drug, if indeed that drug has the potential for creating an acute violence-producing effect in the first place.

In some instances, the physiological nature of the drug itself makes the possibility of a pharmacological explanation for interpersonal violence quite unlikely. Marijuana, for example, makes the user more lethargic than active, in effect quite mellow in circumstances in which there may be some interpersonal conflict. Heroin produces a passive state of mind that reduces the inclination toward violent behavior. In fact, as rates of heroin abuse rise, the incidence of crimes against individuals (as opposed to crimes against property) declines.[5]

Psychoactive stimulants such as amphetamines and cocaine or the hallucinogen PCP (known as "angel dust"), however, produce an on-edge frame of mind and a social paranoia that can lead to violent behavior, although there is no current physiological evidence that these drugs specifically stimulate violent behavior. Yet we need to be careful in interpreting studies linking violence with stimulant drug abuse.[6] For example, in a study conducted at an Atlanta medical center, more than half of all patients being treated for acute cocaine intoxication were reported to be aggressive, agitated, and paranoid just prior to and at the time of hospital admission. It is impossible to determine whether these patients were mentally unstable prior to their taking cocaine. People who have long-standing psychological problems may be overrepresented in any population of cocaine abusers.[7]

Crack cocaine has the dubious reputation of making the crack smoker irritable, suspicious, and inclined to lash out at another person at the slightest provocation, but whether these effects are due to being under the influence of the drug is unclear. Tendencies toward violence are observed during time of *crack withdrawal* as well as crack intoxication.

Of all the psychoactive drugs that we could consider, the one with the most definitive and widely reported links to violent behavior toward individuals is alcohol. In this case, the violence is clearly pharmacological, because the effects of being drunk from the ingestion of alcohol are apparent almost immediately (see Chapter 10). On a domestic level, males involved in spousal abuse commonly report having been drinking or having been drunk during the times that abuse has occurred. Moreover, violent crime outside the home is strongly related to alcohol intoxication. The more violent the crime, the greater is the probability that the perpetrator of the crime was drunk while committing it. Studies show that a majority of all homicides and almost a majority of all sexually aggressive acts (rapes and attempted rapes) are committed while the offender is drunk. From a victim's perspective, alcohol intoxication on the part of the offender accounts for about 20 percent of occasions in which *a violent act of any kind* has been committed, whereas other drugs or drugs in combination with alcohol intoxication appear to be involved in fewer instances (Figure 13.2).[8]

Economic explanations of the drug–crime link suggest that drug use may cause users to commit crimes to obtain money to buy drugs to support their habit. This is referred to as **economically compulsive crime.** Several studies show economically compulsive crime to be a major component of the link between drugs and crime.

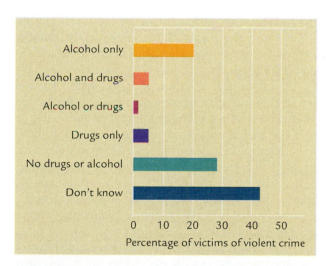

FIGURE 13.2

Victim's perception of the use of alcohol and drugs by the violent offender.

Source: Bureau of Justice Statistics (2006, June). *Criminal victimization in the United States, 2004.* Washington, DC: U.S. Department of Justice, Table 32.

A 1990 study of crack cocaine users, for example, showed that 59 percent participated in 6,669 robberies over a twelve-month period, averaging thirty-one robberies per individual, or roughly one every twelve days. Yet, while most of these robberies were carried out to buy drugs, we cannot assume that they all involved the classic picture of break-ins and holdups. A large percentage involved the theft of drugs from drug dealers or other users or themselves being victims of a drug robbery.[9] Nonetheless, a large proportion of the crimes committed to obtain drug money involved violent acts directed against individuals within the community. Particular targets included storekeepers, children, and the elderly.

When robbery is the means for financing drug abuse, the extent of this crime has been shown to be closely related to "market conditions" at the time. When heroin prices are high, for example, the level of property crime goes up; when heroin prices are low, the crime level goes down. In other words, heroin abusers apparently steal to maintain a stable consumption of heroin. Therefore, the deliberate elevation of drug prices that occurs as a result of reducing the supply not only fails to reduce the incidence of abuse but also tends to increase the incidence of criminal behavior among drug abusers.[10]

The type of crime a drug user commits is typically related to gender. Males are more likely to commit crimes against persons, property, or drug laws, whereas females are more likely to commit crimes against the public order, such as prostitution. One study, for example, found that 64 percent of female crack users exchanged sex for money to buy drugs and that 24 percent reported trading sex for drugs.[11] In "crack houses," women and young girls often bartered sex for crack cocaine. Many of these women remained in the crack houses for extended periods of time, providing sexual favors to multiple customers in order to acquire a continuous supply of the drug.[12]

Crime Causes Drug Use

The drug–crime connection also can be explained from the standpoint that *crime causes drug use.* In this view, persons who are predisposed to commit crimes also use drugs. Drugs may be used before an offense to bolster courage or afterward to celebrate success. Thieves and rapists, for example, may use alcohol and stimulants to

economically compulsive crime: Criminal act committed by a drug abuser to obtain money to buy drugs.

give them energy and increase their confidence. Prostitutes may turn to alcohol and drugs as a method of coping with the stresses of their way of life. It is also common for successful criminals or "gangsters" to keep large stores of illicit drugs to show off their wealth and success. In these cases, drug use does not necessarily cause crime but is part of an overall criminal life-style.

The viewpoint that crime causes drug use is further supported by the fact that longitudinal studies (studies conducted over a period of time) have found that initial involvement in criminal activity begins *prior* to experimentation with drugs for many users. Several studies of drug users in Miami, conducted during the 1970s and 1990s, found that the only drug use that preceded the first crime they committed was the use of alcohol and marijuana. Use of more expensive drugs, such as heroin and cocaine, usually did not begin until two to four years after their first crime.[13] A survey of inmates in Michigan, California, and Texas prisons found that only 20 percent of those who used drugs reported that their drug use began prior to their first crime, and more than 52 percent reported that they began using drugs and committing crimes at about the same time.[14] The National Youth Survey Family Study conducted by the University of Colorado, which followed 1,700 youths over a ten-year period, also supported the idea that initial involvement in criminal activity often preceded drug use. Their first criminal offense preceded their first alcohol use in 63 percent of cases, and their first criminal offense preceded their first marijuana use in 93 percent of cases.[15]

Drug Use and Crime Share Common Causes

A third explanation of the relationship between drug use and crime is the view that both drug use and crime share a common cause. According to this perspective, drug use and crime do not cause one or the other but are both aspects of a overall deviant life-style or culture. In other words, social risk factors lead to deviant behavior, and deviant behavior includes both drug abuse and criminal behavior.

interactional circumstances: The idea that there may not be a direct relationship between drug use and crime but rather an indirect relationship.

systemic violence: Violent acts that arise from the traditionally aggressive patterns of behavior occurring within a network of illicit drug trafficking and distribution.

Frequently, for example, individuals with the greatest chance of abusing drugs have such socioeconomic disadvantages as a low level of education, a broken family, little or no social supervision, and low social status that also produce a greater chance of criminal behavior.[16] In this case, there may not be a direct relationship between drug use and crime but rather an indirect relationship that has been called by the U.S. Department of Justice **interactional circumstances.**[17] While the effects of marijuana may not directly motivate a user to commit crime, both marijuana use and crime may be common characteristics of an overall deviant life-style. In short, the type of person who is a heavy drug user also could be the type of person who is likely to have short-term goals supported by illegal activities and is more likely to be exposed to situations and persons that encourage criminal behavior.[18]

A study of 559 males in Philadelphia, for example, found that 96 percent of those who used marijuana said that they "never" or "almost never" felt an urge to hurt someone while under the influence of the drug. An overwhelming majority of the respondents said that marijuana made them feel more peaceful and passive than before its use.[19] On the other hand, the Philadelphia study did find that individuals who used marijuana were significantly more likely than nonusers to have committed multiple criminal offenses. The results of this study show that marijuana use on its own may not cause crime per se, but the drug may be part of the life-style of people who commit crime. The relationship may be due to the fact that the same types of people who are most likely to commit crime—young males of lower socioeconomic status—are also the same types of people who are most likely to use drugs.[20]

A substantial number of drug users become involved in drug distribution as their drug-using careers progress and hence become part of a criminal subculture that uses violence to maintain control over its "business." Researchers refer to the term **systemic violence** as violence that arises from the activities of drug dealing. Systemic violence can result from such situations as territorial disputes, the consequences of selling inferior grades of illicit drugs, and fraudulent handling of funds from drug sales (Figure 13.3).

The prominence of systemic violence in crack cocaine abuse during the mid-1980s was particularly striking. Studies show that as the involvement of a youth in crack distribution increased, the more likely it was that the person would become involved in criminal violence. In addition, the most violent drug users often were the most respected role models for young people. Sociologists have observed that in many communities

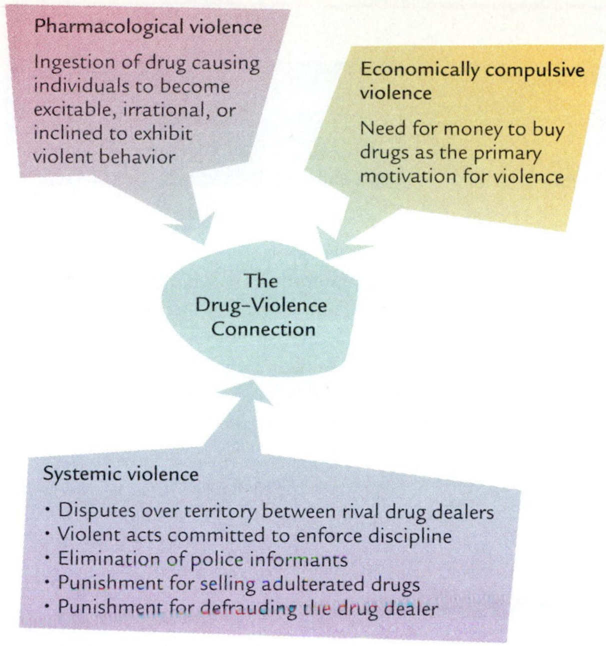

Pharmacological violence

Ingestion of drug causing individuals to become excitable, irrational, or inclined to exhibit violent behavior

Economically compulsive violence

Need for money to buy drugs as the primary motivation for violence

The Drug-Violence Connection

Systemic violence

- Disputes over territory between rival drug dealers
- Violent acts committed to enforce discipline
- Elimination of police informants
- Punishment for selling adulterated drugs
- Punishment for defrauding the drug dealer

FIGURE 13.3

The tripartite model of drugs and violence, showing the importance of distinguishing three major types of drug-related violence.

Source: Goldstein, Paul (1985, Fall). The drug-violence nexus: A tripartite framework. *Journal of Drug Issues*, 493–506.

adolescents feel the need to prove that they can be brutal to avoid being harassed by their peers. The pressure to be an accepted member of such a community may be more responsible for a drug abuser's committing frequent violent acts than the effects of the drugs themselves or even the need for money to buy drugs.

As the street sale of crack cocaine declined in the 1990s, there was an accompanying decline in homicide rates and violent crime in areas where crack sales had been dominant. Community policing procedures focused on breaking up drug gangs and large street-level drug markets, thereby changing the pattern of drug buying and selling.[21] An expert in the area of criminal justice put it this way:

> The reconfiguration of drug markets in the mid-1990s appreciably reduced the level of neighborhood violence. As distribution retired indoors, turf battles were eliminated, and because organizers of the drug business hired a few trusted friends rather than easily replaceable workers, there was less conflict between them. Distributors were robbed by users less frequently because they were more protected selling indoors to known customers.[22]

We can conclude from studies of the nature of the drug–crime relationship that it is not possible to explain drug use and crime in terms of a simple overall cause-and-effect relationship. A heroin addict from a low socioeconomic neighborhood preparing to commit a robbery against a rival dealer may ingest alcohol or stimulants to give himself the courage to commit the crime. In the case of a prostitute, there are circumstances under which drug use precedes prostitution, circumstances under which prostitution precedes drug use, and circumstances under which initiation into both drug use and prostitution occur at about the same time (Drugs . . . in Focus).[23]

Drugs . . . in Focus

From HeroinGen and CrackGen to BluntGen—The Rise and Fall of Drugs and Violence

From a sociological point of view, the impact of drug use on violent crime over the last forty years or so can be examined in terms of the dominant drug of abuse at a particular time. Sociologists Bruce D. Johnson, Andrew Golub, and Eloise Dunlap have divided the drug scene in inner-city New York City into three distinct eras, each defined by a specific drug subculture and set of shared social norms. Each subculture has been guided by a set of expected behaviors that have dictated what subculture participants must do, what they must refrain from doing, and what the consequences are for non-compliance. An agreed-upon set of norms defining their conduct allows participants to function as if on "automatic pilot."

The HeroinGen

According to their analysis, the period 1960–1973 was the era of heroin injection and a subculture of heroin-abusing participants (the heroin-injection generation, or HeroinGen for short). In the peak year of 1968, the HeroinGen members were between fifteen and twenty-five years old. Quite often, they had grown up in a subculture of alcohol abuse, with their parents being heavy alcohol consumers. In mid-adolescence, HeroinGen members were turned on to marijuana, but by 1964–1965, heroin had hit the New York streets in a major way. The promise was that heroin would give them a better high than marijuana or alcohol, and a process of introduction into heroin use began. A dominant feature of the subculture was the act of robbery. The conduct norms for HeroinGen members were clear:

> Locate ordinary citizens who are apt to carry a lot of cash. Try to identify persons leaving banks on paydays. Target working-class and pink-collar workers who typically cash their payroll checks. Hold up businesses with other robbers. . . . Don't attempt to rob someone when stoned on alcohol or heroin.

Handguns were rarely carried or used; instead, knives and blunt instruments were the weapons of choice.

The CrackGen

Crack cocaine became available around 1984 in New York City and other metropolitan communities. Subculture members, born between 1955 and 1969, came of age during the height of the cocaine/crack era (1985–1989). For these individuals, called the Crack Generation or CrackGen, conduct norms were quite different from those of the HeroinGen. Crack use was carried out in intensive binges. Hyperactivity, rapid cycling between euphoria and dysphoria, and paranoia dominated their behavior.

Sales of crack became so profitable that the entire illicit drug industry revolved around it. Vicious competition between crack dealers ensued. The key factor was "keeping the money and product straight." At this point, handguns became commonplace. There were 218 recorded drug-related homicides in New York in 1988 alone, as well as other forms of systemic violence.

> Other violent acts, such as assaulting a subordinate or shooting him in the kneecap, were mostly unrecorded in official statistics. However, the number of crippled young men wheeling themselves around the inner-city provides ample testament to this brutality.

The BluntGen

By the 1990s, remaining members of the CrackGen were in their thirties and increasingly isolated as they continued their compulsive drug-taking behavior. In their place were members of the Marijuana/Blunt subculture (BluntGen, for short). Born in the 1970s, the BluntGen smoked marijuana as a cigar. They would combine funds in a peer group to buy marijuana, occasionally committing a crime to get money for their purchases. They saw no need for handguns.

Evidence shows that members of the BluntGen viewed the ravages of the lives of HeroinGen and CrackGen members as a reason to limit their pursuit of drug-taking behavior to the use of marijuana and alcohol. The subculture of assault and disregard for human life had been transformed into a subculture of "stay safe, stay alive." Rates of violence and non-drug-related criminality, relative to that of an earlier era, declined sharply. Conduct norms of the BluntGen even impacted on alcohol abuse in a positive way. Here is a description of current drug use among BluntGen members:

> A typical blunt-using episode will involve two or three peers in their twenties sharing a half ounce of marijuana and two or three quarts of malt beer over two to five hours. While passing the marijuana blunt around, each person will also sip beer or malt liquor so that everyone enjoys a modest high while talking and listening to rap music. The conduct norms discourage rapid ingestion of alcohol and displays of drunken comportment. . . . If one consistently and rapidly consumes large quantities of alcohol, acts drunk, or is violent toward others, that person will be sanctioned and, if necessary, excluded from the blunt-sharing group at future times.

Source: Johnson, Bruce D., Golub, Andrew, and Dunlap, Eloise (2006). The rise and decline of hard drugs, drug markets, and violence in inner-city New York. In Alfred Blumstein and Joel Wallman (Eds.), *The crime drop in America*. New York: Cambridge University Press, pp. 164–206. Quotations on pages 173, 178, 180, and 186.

The Social Structure of the Illicit Drug Trade

According to the U.S. Office of National Drug Control Policy, Americans spend about $66 billion annually on heroin, cocaine, methamphetamine, marijuana, and other illicit drugs. Drug trafficking and distribution is an international operation of enormous magnitude.

As with other businesses, the illicit drug business can be divided into various "stages" of production and distribution that include (1) cultivation and manufacturing, (2) importation, (3) wholesale distribution, and (4) retail distribution. For many drugs, such as cocaine and heroin, peasant farmers living in remote locations in Third World countries carry out the actual cultivation and manufacturing of drugs. Growers then sell the drugs to importers or drug traffickers who smuggle large quantities of drugs into the United States and other worldwide markets. Once inside the United States, large quantities of drugs are sold to wholesalers who often keep the drugs in a "stash house." Some major wholesalers may supply entire regions of the country. Wholesalers then sell smaller quantities of the drugs to lower-level retail sellers or street dealers, often in adulterated forms.

In the trafficking of cocaine, for example, the first level of the process involves the cocaine farmers in Colombia, Bolivia, and Peru who cultivate the cocaine and process the coca into coca paste. Once the coca paste has been produced, it is bought by midlevel producers who make cocaine hydrochloride, or powdered cocaine, from the paste. Traffickers then buy the cocaine from the midlevel producers and smuggle the drug into the destination countries. To increase profits, wholesalers and retail-level dealers often "cut" or mix their drugs with other substances. Cocaine sold on the street frequently is cut or diluted with such substances as baking soda, various sugars such as lactose, and Novacaine.[24]

Drug dealers at the retail level generally follow two types of drug distribution models: (1) the freelance model and (2) the business model.[25] As we will see, the first model can evolve into the second model, as the character of drug dealing matures from an informal style of interaction to a more formal one.

Independent individuals working together without a previously established relationship characterize the **freelance model** of retail drug distribution. These dealers and buyers are not part of any large-scale drug organization. It is a "cash only" business, in that the buyer must pay for the drugs at the time of purchase. Both wholesalers and retailers usually do not "front" the drugs, and the price of a drug is negotiated at the time of the buy. Dealers may have many different buyers, some of whom they never see again after a given transaction is completed. If transactions occur successfully, dealers and buyers may negotiate similar arrangements on a more regular basis, but there is no expectation that they will cooperate in the future.

The freelance model typically is associated with the street sale of marijuana and hallucinogens such as LSD and MDMA. Marijuana sellers are more likely to operate independently than as part of an organized operation, and marijuana often is sold through acquaintance or referral networks. LSD and MDMA are sold principally at concerts, nightclubs, and raves, where sellers and buyers do not know each other, providing a level of anonymity combined with a sense of being part of a common subculture.

In the early years of crack cocaine abuse, from 1984 to 1987, the freelance model dominated as the means by which crack was sold and distributed. The principal drug dealer was a "juggler" who would buy a supply of ten to twenty vials of crack and sell them at a standard retail price, approximately twice the initial cost. When the supply was sold, the juggler would "re-up" by obtaining a new supply that would then be sold. Through several cycles, a freelance seller could make up to fifty deals a day. Since most of these freelancers used their product themselves, however, the quantity of sales did not produce substantial incomes. Fewer than one out of ten dealers during this period had lengthy drug-dealing careers.[26]

The **business model** of street dealing is organized as a "business" in a hierarchical fashion with numerous individuals occupying a range of roles. At the center of the business model is the crew boss who receives a supply of drugs from the wholesaler. Drugs are "fronted" at each level of the organization. The wholesaler fronts the drugs to the crew boss, who then divides the drugs and fronts them to street dealers often called "runners." Runners most often are young (aged fourteen to twenty-three) males recruited from inner-city neighborhoods. Each crew boss may have as many as 20 runners working under his direction. Runners are assigned to work at a particular street location, sell only at a given price, and then hand

freelance model: A model of retail drug distribution in which dealers and buyers transact their business with relative anonymity, outside of the structure of a large-scale drug organization.

business model: A model of retail drug distribution in which drug transactions are conducted within a hierarchically structured organization.

over all of the money to the crew boss. As the drugs are sold, the money flows up the chain, from runners, to crew boss, and back to the wholesaler. Prices are agreed upon before the drugs are fronted. At the end of the day, each runner is paid in money or drugs for his or her work. To avoid rip-offs and robberies, each crew is guarded by an armed lieutenant who supervises several street sellers.

Crack dealing organizations located in many urban neighborhoods best exemplify the business model of street dealing. In contrast to the freelance dealer, business-model dealers and crew bosses who managed to limit their personal use of crack would soon make more than one thousand dollars per day. Competition among crack dealers would necessitate "protectors," whose worth was often measured by their violent inclinations and ability to instill fear in others. Thus, the subculture of crack abuse became dominated by an environment of systemic violence.[27]

The Trafficking of Cocaine

Cocaine is derived from the leaves of the coca shrub, grown in the high-altitude rain forests and fields that run along the slopes of the Andes in South America (see Chapter 4). Until recently, virtually all the world's coca was cultivated in Bolivia and Peru, but the success of crop eradication has resulted in a decline in coca production in these countries. Today, most of the world's coca cultivation and cocaine production takes place in Colombia (Table 13.1), located in the northwestern part of South America, with coasts on both the Pacific Ocean and the Caribbean. This location enables traffickers to smuggle cocaine to the United States by a variety of routes. Traditionally, cocaine has been smuggled through the Caribbean by air and sea. Shipments of

Traffickers often use "go-fast boats" or speedboats to smuggle cocaine into the United States.

cocaine often move from Colombia to Puerto Rico, the Bahamas, or the Dominican Republic, where it is repackaged for shipment to south Florida.

Smuggling techniques used to transfer their drugs to U.S. markets include small commercial fishing vessels that "hug" or keep close to the coasts of eastern Caribbean islands, allowing them to blend in with other vessel traffic and minimizing the opportunity for detection. Waterproof bundles of cocaine are air-dropped to waiting boat crews, who then deliver the cocaine to shore in speedboats. Multi-ton shipments of cocaine also are smuggled through the port of Miami by being concealed in the compartments of large commercial cargo vessels.[28]

Until the early 1970s, Cuban-organized crime groups controlled the importation of cocaine from Colombia into the United States. When Fidel Castro established a communist government in 1959, many Cubans involved in organized criminal activities fled to the United States. Later, some of these same Cubans became part of an exiled Cuban army that was trained by the U.S. Central Intelligence Agency (CIA) in an effort to remove Castro from power. After this force's failed Bay of Pigs military operation in 1961, many of the American-trained Cuban guerrilla fighters had no lawful source of income. Some began to enter the drug trade by smuggling cocaine from Colombia to the United States and then setting up distribution networks in Miami, New York, and Chicago. During the 1970s, Colombian producers and traffickers of cocaine came to believe that there was no reason for the Cubans to keep most of the profits from the cocaine trade while they did most of the work. Colombian cocaine producers sent in groups of "enforcers," young men from crime-ridden, low-income Colombian cities, to execute the Cubans. By the mid-1970s, control of the cocaine industry was in the hands of Colombians, and any

TABLE 13.1

Andean region cocaine production (metric tons)

	PERU	BOLIVIA	COLOMBIA
2001	160	60	700
2002	175	60	585
2003	155	60	460
2004	145	65	430
2005	165	70	545

Source: National Drug Intelligence Center (2006).
National Drug Threat Assessment 2007. Washington, DC:
U.S. Department of Justice, Table 1.

Cubans remaining in the cocaine business had become subordinate to the Colombians.[29]

For the next two decades, two of the most powerful criminal organizations in history controlled the production and distribution of cocaine: the **Medellin and Cali drug cartels** (named after cities in Colombia that were their home bases). In the mid-1970s, most of the cocaine that was brought into the United States was smuggled in hidden suitcases. As demand for cocaine in the United States exceeded supplies, several criminal entrepreneurs, one of whom was Pablo Escobar (see Portrait), formed an alliance and realized that they could fly small airplanes loaded with cocaine into the United States, thus avoiding the need for countless suitcase trips. Known as the Medellin Cartel, this drug trafficking alliance led by Escobar had great success, reinvesting some of its huge profits into more sophisticated cocaine labs, better airplanes, and even an island in the Bahamas where their planes could refuel.

The cartel was structured in what can be characterized as an onion-like layering of organizational power, with kingpins at the center directing operations and groups of self-contained cells managed by a small number of cartel managers. Each cell specialized in a different aspect of the drug business, such as production, distribution, smuggling, or money laundering. If police arrested members of one cell, a second or third cell would step up operations to make up for loss of profits, and members of each of cell rarely were connected directly with any of the leaders of the cartel. Pablo Escobar and the other leaders of the Medellin Cartel often used violence to solve any problems they may have had with law enforcement or the Colombian government and were considered to be responsible for the murder of hundreds of government officials, police, prosecutors, judges, journalists, and innocent bystanders. The flamboyant life-style of the Medellin Cartel's leaders and their extreme use of violence made them a primary target for both Colombian and U.S. law enforcement. By the early 1990s, the leaders of the cartel either had been gunned down by police or had turned themselves over to authorities in exchange for lenient prison sentences.

While law-enforcement anti-drug efforts focused on the high-profile Medellin Cartel for several years, the less flashy Cali Cartel operated without much law-enforcement interference. The members of the Cali Cartel were more subtle in their operations than their Medellin counterparts, relying on bribes over violence, conducting their business in a discreet and business-like manner, and reinvesting much of their profits from the illicit drug trade into legitimate businesses. The Cali Cartel relied heavily on political bribes for protection. Former President of Colombia, Ernesto Samper, and hundreds of Colombian congressmen and senators were accused of accepting campaign financing from the cartel. During the 1980s, while the Medellin Cartel controlled the drug market in south Florida, the Cali Cartel controlled the distribution of cocaine in New York. The Cali Cartel also expanded its market to Europe and Asia, forming alliances with other organized-crime groups such as the Japanese Yakuza. Cali smuggling techniques also differed greatly from those of the Medellin Cartel. Members of the Medellin Cartel relied on small airplanes and speedboats, whereas the Cali Cartel smuggled most of its shipments in large cargo ships, hiding the drugs in all types of legitimate cargo, from cement blocks to bars of chocolate. The Cali Cartel outlasted the Medellin Cartel until 1995, when its leaders eventually were tracked down and arrested.[30]

The arrest of the top leaders of the Medellin and Cali drug cartels in the 1990s has led to a decentralization of the cocaine trade in which smaller independent Bolivian, Peruvian, Colombian, and Mexican organizations have taken control of production and trafficking. New traffickers now realize that large organizations are more vulnerable to U.S. prosecution and are forming smaller, more controllable groups.

Marxist guerrilla groups in Colombia also have taken a more active role in the Colombian drug trade. Colombia has always had a history of antigovernment revolutionary groups with links to cocaine trafficking. In November 1985, the Medellin Cartel is believed to have hired members of the guerilla group M-19 to storm Colombia's Palace of Justice, murder eleven Supreme Court Justices, and destroy the extradition case files of Medellin Cartel members. Colombian drug cartels also have hired guerrilla groups to protect the coca fields and cocaine labs, as well as trafficking routes in remote areas of Colombia, in exchange for large amounts of money.

One of the largest guerilla forces in Colombia, the Revolutionary Armed Forces of Colombia (FARC), presently controls an area of Colombia exceeding 42,000 square kilometers (the approximate size of Kentucky), from which they arrange kidnappings, carry out executions, and sponsor coca plantations. In the late 1990s, several producers of cocaine shifted their crops to this area, experimenting with coca plants to produce a stronger coca leaf with a higher cocaine yield. Recently, FARC has taken control of coca crops and boosted its income to more than $600 million a year, making it

Medellin and Cali drug cartels: Two major Colombian drug cartels that controlled much of the illicit drug distribution in South America from the mid-1970s to the mid-1990s.

Pablo Escobar—Formerly Known as the Colombian King of Cocaine

Pablo Escobar was one of the most powerful, profitable, and violent organized crime bosses in history. Escobar began his career as a small-time criminal in the slums and back roads outside Medellin, Colombia. At age twenty-six, Escobar was arrested for possession of thirty-nine pounds of cocaine, his first and only drug bust. Escobar was never tried for the crime. The arresting officer was mysteriously murdered, and nine judges refused to hear the case because of death threats. With the help of two other South American criminal entrepreneurs, Jorge Luis Ochoa Vasquez and Carlos Lehder Rivas, Escobar formed a cocaine trafficking alliance that later became known as the Medellin Cartel. The Medellin Cartel followed the model of a large corporation; it was vertically integrated and controlled virtually all aspects of the cocaine business from manufacturing and smuggling to wholesale distribution of cocaine in the United States. The organization transported coca and coca paste from Peru and Bolivia to Colombia, where it was converted into cocaine hydrochloride powder. The cartel used small airplanes to fly loads of the product to a privately owned island in the Bahamas and then smuggled the cocaine into the United States by speedboat.

In an attempt to give himself a more legitimate image, Escobar became involved in politics, and in 1982, he was elected to the Colombian Congress, giving him immunity from arrest. Escobar's career in politics only lasted a short time, and he soon realized that he could gain more power in Colombia through violence and bribes than politics. By 1984, Escobar controlled over 80 percent of the Colombian drug trade. It was estimated that Escobar was making over $2.75 billion a year, earning him a place on the *Forbes* magazine list of the wealthiest people in the world. Escobar owned several luxury estates, one of which was a seven-thousand-acre, $63 million ranch that included his own private zoo with giraffes, camels, and kangaroos. Escobar often tried to project himself as "a man of the people," and he was loved by many of the poor in Colombia, gaining a reputation as a Robin Hood type of figure. Escobar built housing for the poor, schools, hospitals, and even a soccer stadium, all of which earned him favorable media coverage.

Escobar used violence and assassination to keep his cocaine flowing and to terrorize his enemies. The result was a country that resembled an armed camp, where police officers, judges, public officials, and journalists were in constant fear of being assassinated. Public bombings and drive-by shootings were common, and Escobar was believed to be behind the murder of three presidential candidates, a Colombian attorney general, more than 200 judges, 100 police officers, and dozens of journalists. Pablo Escobar also was believed to be responsible for the bombing of a Colombian jetliner, causing the death of 107 persons. In 1990, Escobar offered a bounty of $4,000 for each police officer killed in Colombia. In the following month, 42 city police officers were murdered.

In response to the reign of terror waged by the Medellin Cartel, the Colombian government offered drug traffickers immunity from extradition to the United States if they turned themselves in. In turn, the traffickers would server shorter prisons terms in Colombia. In 1991, at the age of forty-one, Pablo Escobar surrendered to authorities with the agreement that he would be placed in a specially built prison. The prison was a converted mountaintop ranch, built by Escobar himself, containing many amenities, such as a bar and a discotheque. Escobar still managed to oversee his cocaine empire from the prison, and many of his top lieutenants were allowed to visit him. After Escobar tortured and murdered one of his men in prison, the Colombian government attempted to move Escobar to a more secure prison. Escobar, however, was tipped off by one of the guards, and he and a number of his men escaped.

In one the most famous manhunts in history, Escobar managed to elude a search team comprised of an elite Colombian police commando squad, members of the U.S. Central Intelligence Agency (CIA), and agents of the Drug Enforcement Administration (DEA) for over a year. Escobar moved secretly among his friends and supporters, sometimes disguising himself as a woman and hiding in secret rooms carved out between walls and under stairs. His closeness to his family, however, proved to be Escobar's weakness. After he telephoned his family on December 1993 to tell them that he was fine, his call was traced by agents of the DEA. The trace led the team to a two-story house in Medellin. As he ran up to the rooftop in an attempt to escape, Escobar was hit with a barrage of bullets, leaving him dead on the roof.

Within months of Escobar's death, the Cali Cartel, a long-standing rival to the Medellin Cartel, had taken over the cocaine business in Colombia. The newfound dominance of the cartel, however, was soon to end. Cali Cartel leaders were arrested in Colombia in 1997 and later extradited to the United States. In September 2006, a plea agreement included a judgment of forfeiture in the amount of $2.1 billion to be levied against Cali Cartel narcotic-related assets as well as businesses around the world. Today, cocaine trafficking is controlled by more than 300 "mini-cartels" in the Andean region.

Sources: Brooke, James. (1990, June 7). In the capital of cocaine, savagery is the habit. *New York Times*, p. 4. Drug Enforcement Administration (2006, September 26). Cali cartel leaders plead guilty to drug and money laundering conspiracy charges. News release. Washington, DC: U.S. Department of Justice. Fedarko, Kevin (1993, December 13). Escobar's dead end. *Time*, p. 46. Lyman, Michael D., and Potter, Gary W. (2000). *Organized crime*. Upper Saddle River, NJ: Prentice Hall. Watson, Russel, and Katel, Peter. (1993, December 13). Death on the spot: The end of a drug king. *Newsweek*, pp. 18–21.

possibly the richest insurgent group in history. Without any large drug cartels to contend with, guerilla groups such as FARC are no longer mere passive profiteers of the cocaine trade; they are now active participants in the processing and distribution of cocaine.[31]

During the 1980s and early 1990s, the United States began to place immense pressure on drug trafficking organizations operating in the Caribbean and south Florida. As a response, traffickers in Colombia formed alliances with Mexican trafficking groups in order to transport cocaine across the southwestern border of the United States. With the disruption of the Cali and Medellin drug cartels, Mexican groups such as the Amando Carrillo-Fuentes Organization and the

Drugs . . . in Focus

The Arellano-Félix Organization—A Family Affair

For the past two decades, the Arellano-Félix Organization (AFO) has been one of the most lucrative and violent Mexican drug cartels, supplying over 40 percent of the cocaine that enters the United States. Based in Tijuana, the AFO is responsible for the importation and distribution of multi-ton quantities of cocaine, marijuana, heroin, and methamphetamine into the United States. The cartel also controls one of the largest land ports of entry in the world, the San Diego–Tijuana border crossing. If a drug trafficker wants to bring drugs across this border, he has to pay a tax to the AFO to do so. If the tax is not paid, the trafficker is usually later found dead. The cartel maintains a well-equipped and well-trained security force and often uses San Diego and Tijuana street gangs as assassins and enforcers.

The AFO has corrupted countless public officials, army generals, and top police officers. Witness statements indicate that the organization is paying as much as $1 million every week to federal, state, and local officials in Mexico to ensure that they will not interfere with the group's drug trafficking activities. The cartel also has been responsible for the murder of several Mexican law-enforcement officials, lawyers, journalists, and a U.S. DEA agent. The killings often are brutal and frequently involve long hours of torture. When special prosecutor for the Mexican attorney general's drug unit Jose "Pepe" Patino Moreno was caught by the AFO, for example, his death was reported to involve hours of torture that eventually led to the crushing of his skull.

Drug trafficking within the AFO is a family affair. Seven brothers and four sisters inherited the cartel in 1989 after the first "boss" of the family, Miguel Angel Félix Gallardo, was arrested for his involvement in the murder of DEA Agent Enrique "Kiki" Camarena. For over thirteen years, the two top leaders of the AFO, brothers Ramon and Benjamin Arellano-Félix, were untouchable by law enforcement. Ramon was the more violent of the two brothers, acting as the AFO's chief enforcer, killing numerous rivals and informants. On September 11, 1997, he was added to the FBI's "10 Most Wanted List." In February

Benjamin Arellano-Félix (left) and Ramon Arellano-Félix.

2004, Ramon went to Mazatlán, Mexico, during its annual carnival to kill a rival drug trafficker. While Ramon and his crew cruised the beach strip looking for the rival, police stopped their van, and a gun battle broke out leaving one officer and Ramon dead. A month later, Benjamin Arellano-Félix was arrested at his home in Puebla, Mexico.

With the capture of a third brother, Francisco Javier Arellano-Félix, and his extradition to the United States in 2007, the Arellano-Félix organization era in Mexican drug trafficking is considered to be essentially over. Benjamin Arellano-Félix has reportedly continued to issue orders, but his influence is greatly diminished. Control of Mexicali, an important drug corridor about 120 miles east of Tijuana, has been surrendered. Whether these developments, however, signal a significant change in the battle against drug trafficking in Mexico remains to be seen.

Sources: Amos, Deborah. (2004, June 1). Kingpins fall, but drugs keep coming. ABCNews.com. Constantine, Thomas A. (1998, February 26). *DEA congressional testimony: International organized crime syndicates and their impact on the United States.* Washington, DC: Drug Enforcement Administration. Hoffman, Allison (2006, August 18). Suspected Mexican druglord pleads not guilty. *BostonGlobe*, p. A3.

A Mexican federal agent crawls through a hidden U.S.–Mexico border tunnel, presumably used to transport drugs from Mexico to the United States.

were a significant force in international organized crime, beyond their former role as mere middlemen in the cocaine transportation business.

Current intelligence reports from the Drug Enforcement Administration (DEA) indicate that approximately 72 percent of the cocaine available in the United States is smuggled across the U.S.–Mexico border. Typically, cocaine shipments from South America are moved overland or by air to staging sites in northern Mexico. The cocaine is then broken down into smaller loads for smuggling across the U.S.–Mexico border. Large loads of cocaine generally are smuggled across the border in land vehicles, such as semi trucks, where it is often concealed in shipments of fruits and vegetables. Cocaine is also carried in small, concealed kilogram quantities across the border by couriers known as "mules," who enter the United States either legally through ports of entry or illegally through undesignated points along the border. Once the loads of cocaine arrive in the United States, they are taken to established safe houses where workers watch over the cocaine and prepare it for distribution across the United States (Figure 13.4).

Arellano-Felix Organization began to consolidate their power and soon dominated drug trafficking along the U.S.–Mexico border and in many American cities (Drugs . . . in Focus). Until 2007, these organizations

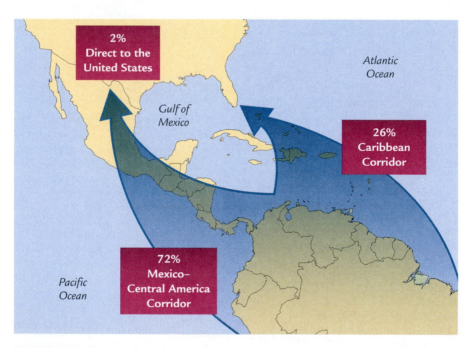

FIGURE 13.4

The flow of cocaine into the United States. Several Central American countries function as the "trans-shipment corridor" from Colombia to Mexico.

Sources: Office of Drug Control Policy (2002, March). *Annual assessment of cocaine movement.* Washington, DC: Office of National Drug Control Policy. Bureau of International Narcotics and Law Enforcement Affairs (2007, March). *2007 International narcotics control strategy report. Volume 1: Drug and chemical control.* Washington, DC: U.S. Department of State, pp. 147–149, 154–166, 173–179.

While distributors of cocaine within the United States traditionally have been Colombian nationals, the DEA recently has come upon evidence that Mexican trafficking organizations are also involved directly in cocaine distribution. One of the principal motivations for this change is an extradition law enacted by the Colombian National Assembly in 1997 that allows Colombians involved in international drug trafficking to be tried in the United States, where they face the prospect of lengthy prison sentences. After this act went into effect, Colombians attempted to distance themselves from overt drug trafficking acts in the United States as much as possible, minimizing U.S. law enforcement's ability to gather sufficient evidence to support extradition requests.[32]

On the street level, cocaine typically is distributed as a white crystalline powder or as an off-white chunky material that is sold by the gram. The price of a gram of cocaine ranges from $85 to $275 depending on demand, availability, and purity. The street purity of cocaine is usually less than 70 percent because it is commonly "cut" or diluted with a variety of substances.

As discussed in Chapter 4, most users begin ingesting cocaine by snorting or inhaling cocaine powder through the nose, where it is absorbed into the bloodstream through the nasal tissues. Once dependence has been established, users may attempt to save money and get the most out of their cocaine supplies by using a needle to inject the drug directly into the bloodstream. In that case, the cocaine is usually mixed with water and injected via a syringe. Unlike heroin, cocaine is extremely soluble in water and does not have to be heated in water before being injected.

Intravenous drug users who inject a mixture of cocaine and heroin known as a **speedball** generally "cook" both drugs together in water on a spoon by lighting a match under the spoon. Speedballers report that the combined effect is the quick rush or "flash" of cocaine combined with the more mellowing effect of heroin. The heroin "smoothes out" the stimulant effect of cocaine by reducing nervousness and excitability and softening the "crash" after an extended cocaine binge. "Speedballing" can be one of the most dangerous drug combinations because both cocaine and heroin can reduce respiratory activity and produce a lapse of breathing leading to death.[33]

Although use of the inexpensive, smokable form of cocaine referred to as crack cocaine, or simply crack, has declined over the past decade, the drug continues to be distributed and used in most major cities within the United States. Typically, cocaine powder is converted into crack cocaine by secondary wholesalers or street dealers within the United States and sold in small pieces or rocks, packaged in small vials or film canisters. The price of a rock generally ranges from $10 to $20.

Street gangs currently dominate the retail market for crack nationwide. Jamaican criminal gangs, known as **Jamaican posses,** distribute large quantities of crack throughout the United States, their name being taken on the basis of their fondness for American western films. One of the most violent and most established of the posses is the Shower Posse, which is believed to have gotten its name from its willingness to shower its enemies with bullets. Jamaican posses often purchase cocaine from Colombians, make large amounts of crack from the powdered cocaine, and then sell the crack through crack houses. While crack houses often are located in low-income apartments or houses, they can be sophisticated operations. Jamaican-operated crack houses employ extensive defensive tactics, such as well-armed guards and specially constructed barricades and booby traps. Jamaicans also commonly use lookouts to warn of impending police raids, and houses usually are equipped with secret hiding places or hidden emergency exit routes.[34]

The Trafficking of Heroin

As discussed in Chapter 5, the origin of heroin is opium, produced from the opium poppy, a plant that lives only one season and must be replanted every year. It is native to the Mediterranean region of the world, but it grows well in any warm and moist climate. The poppy is usually planted in late summer or fall and takes approximately three months to mature to its normal height of three to four feet. The mature plant has a long tubular stem with a seedpod at the end, from which flower petals grow. Once the plant reaches its maximum growth, the flower petals begin to drop off, leaving behind only the seedpod. Opium harvesters then go through the poppy fields and slit the seedpod with a special knifelike instrument. A milky fluid (raw opium) oozes from the slit in the seedpod and is allowed to "bleed" overnight. When the white gummy sap is exposed to air, it turns to dark brown. The next day the harvesters go back through the poppy fields and collect the dried opium from the seedpods.

speedball: A combination of injected cocaine and heroin.

Jamaican posses: Criminal street gangs from Jamaica, dominant in the retail market for crack cocaine in the United States.

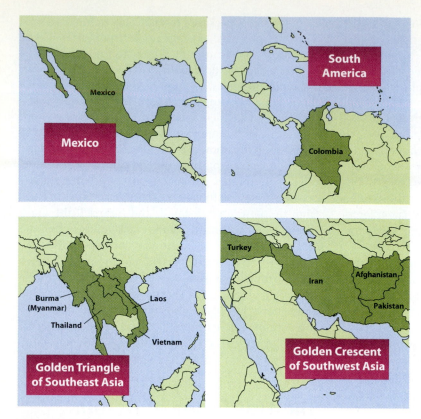

FIGURE 13.5

Primary sources of heroin.

Source: National Drug Intelligence Center (2004). *National drug threat assessment.* Washington, DC: U.S. Department of Justice.

Heroin is produced from morphine, the active ingredient in raw opium. The production of heroin is a complex and sometimes dangerous process that involves bonding the morphine molecules with acetic acid. The mixture usually produces a fluffy white powder that can be injected with a syringe and hypodermic needle. There are currently four major sources of heroin: (1) the Golden Triangle, (2) the Golden Crescent, (3) Mexico, and (4) South America (Figure 13.5).

A major source of heroin was once the so-called **Golden Triangle** of Southeast Asia, comprising the

> **Golden Triangle:** A once-dominant opium-producing region of Southeast Asia, now eclipsed by opium-producing nations of the Golden Crescent.
>
> **China White:** A street name for heroin from the Golden Triangle or, alternatively, a name for the synthetic opiate, fentanyl.
>
> **triads and tongs:** Ethnic Chinese and non-Chinese Asian groups, functioning as principal transporters of Southeast Asian heroin to North America.

countries of Thailand, Burma (Myanmar), Laos, and Vietnam. Heroin from the Golden Triangle was usually sold as a white or off-white powder and sometimes was called **China White** on the street. Southeast Asian heroin was smuggled into the United States primarily via containerized maritime cargo from such locations as Taiwan and Hong Kong and often was concealed among legitimate commodities in these shipping containers. The cargo shipments traveled to major ports of entry along the West Coast of the United States and western Canada, where they were transported eastward to cities such as Chicago and Detroit.

Ethnic Chinese and Asian groups known as **triads and tongs,** secret Chinese criminal organizations tracing their history back as far as the seventeenth century, were the primary transporters of Southeast Asian heroin to North America. Chinese triads migrated to Hong Kong and Taiwan when Communists took control of mainland China in 1949. After the People's Republic of China assumed control of Hong Kong in 1997, the triads expanded their criminal operations to the United States and Europe. The term "triad" was based on the triangular symbol on the organizations' flags and banners that represented the three essential elements of heaven, earth, and man. They were extremely hierarchical, secretive, and closed criminal fraternities, maintaining highly ritualized initiation ceremonies that instilled a strong sense of loyalty in their members. They operated their criminal enterprises in the United States with the help of American-based tong gangs.

Chinese tongs were started in the 1800s to protect Chinese immigrants and railroad workers from bands of racist white hoodlums. While Chinese triads controlled the production and smuggling of Southeast Asian heroin, Chinese tongs and street gangs were responsible for the wholesale distribution and street sale of heroin. In 2003, in an operation named "City Lights," law-enforcement agents from the DEA and Hong Kong joined together to dismantle a Chinese criminal organization led by a group known as the "Four Untouchables." This organization had cells operating in New York, North Carolina, and Florida and was responsible for smuggling more than $100 million worth of Southeast Asian heroin into the United States each year.[35]

TABLE 13.2

Afghanistan opium and heroin production (metric tons)

	1999	2000	2001	2002	2003	2004	2005
Opium Production	2,861	3,656	74	1,278	2,865	Unavailable	Unavailable
Heroin Production	218	365	7	150	337	582	526

Note: Assuming an approximate 10 to 1 yield of grown opium to manufactured heroin, 2004 and 2005 opium production figures can be estimated at 5,800 and 5,300 metric tons, respectively.

Sources: National Drug Intelligence Center (2005, February). *National drug threat assessment 2005 summary report.* Washington, DC: U.S. Department of Justice, Table 8. Tandy, Karen P. (2004, February 26). *DEA congressional testimony: Afghanistan: Law enforcement interdiction efforts in transshipment countries to stem the flow of heroin.* Washington, DC: Drug Enforcement Administration.

Currently, the single largest source of heroin is the **Golden Crescent** of Pakistan, Afghanistan, Turkey, and Iran. Afghanistan alone is responsible for approximately 92 percent of the world's supply of heroin.

Heroin from Afghanistan helped to finance Osama bin Laden and Taliban's terrorist activities for years. Bin Laden allegedly would take a cut of the drug trade money in exchange for protecting smugglers and laundering their profits. In 2000, Afghanistan accounted for more than 70 percent of the world's supply of heroin, producing an estimated 365 metric tons of heroin. In 2001, the Taliban banned the cultivation of the opium poppy for religious reasons, which caused opium production to plummet to 74 metric tons. U.S. officials believe that the ban was most likely an attempt by the Taliban to raise the price of opium, which had fallen significantly owing to the abundant supply produced in 2000. After the fall of the Taliban in 2002, Afghan growers resumed opium cultivation, and production increased to 2,865 metric tons (Table 13.2). Although the Karzai government in Afghanistan also has banned the cultivation of opium poppies, three decades of civil war and unrest have left the criminal justice system in disarray, and it is therefore difficult for the Afghan government to enforce the ban. There is concern that large heroin cartels may form in Afghanistan, much like the cocaine cartels in Colombia. With such a weak central government, these drug trafficking organizations could develop into a primary power base within Afghanistan. Europe is the primary destination for Afghan heroin, with relatively little Afghan heroin reaching the United States. A number of European criminal organizations, including Russian and Sicilian mafia groups, distribute Afghan heroin to markets in Europe and Asia.[36]

A third major source of heroin is Mexico. Mexican heroin is often crudely processed with many impurities. Therefore, it is usually black or brown in color and is

An Afghan drug police chief shows confiscated hashish (in his right hand) and heroin folded into pieces of paper (in his left hand), among other drugs on his desk, in central Kandahar, Afghanistan.

called *black tar* or "Tootsie Roll" on the street. Although Mexico cultivates only 2 percent of the world's opium, Mexico's opium production is significant because virtually all the Mexican opium that is converted into heroin is

Golden Crescent: A major opium-producing region of Southwest Asia, comprising Pakistan, Afghanistan, Turkey, Iran, and former regions of the Soviet Union.

destined for the United States. Despite Mexico's extensive eradication campaign, the production of Mexican heroin has been relatively stable over the past several years, and recent intelligence reports indicate that the price of Mexican heroin has decreased while the purity has increased.

Most of the opium in Mexico is grown by small, independent farmers (known as *campesinos*) who have the equipment necessary to cultivate opium poppies on a relatively small scale. *Campesinos* are often contracted or recruited by an individual trafficker or trafficking organization. Traffickers, in turn, pay a prearranged price for the opium crop, the equipment used in harvesting, and food for the farmer's family. A middleman or opium broker then collects the opium gum and transports it to a clandestine laboratory to be processed into heroin. One of the most powerful of the Mexican heroin trafficking organizations is the Herrera family, which has been involved in drug trafficking since the mid-1950s. The organization is comprised of multiple families, all of which are related to the Herrera family through either blood or marriage. Although the patriarch of the Herrera family, Jaime Herrera-Nevarez, was arrested in Guadalajara, Mexico, in 1987, members of the Herrera family continue to be active in the Mexican heroin trade.[37]

Mexican heroin is smuggled into the United States primarily overland across the Mexico–U.S. border via private and commercial vehicles that have been equipped with hidden compartments. Packages containing large amounts of Mexican heroin are usually wrapped in clear plastic or cellophane and duct tape. Smaller quantities of Mexican heroin often are carried across the border by illegal aliens or migrant workers who hide the drugs in backpacks, in the soles of their shoes, or on their bodies. The primary market for heroin produced in Mexico is Los Angeles. From Los Angeles, Mexican heroin is transported in private vehicles to markets in the Southwest and West Central regions of the United States. Over the last few years, the distribution patterns of Mexican heroin have expanded beyond the southwestern and western states. Mexican heroin has increased in popularity in large midwestern cities such as Chicago and has been found in several cities with large Hispanic/Latino communities such as Atlanta and Dallas.[38]

South America is the fourth major producer of opium and heroin. By global standards, Colombia produces relatively little heroin (less than 5 percent of the world's total estimated production). However, most of the heroin used in the United States is produced in Colombia. During the 1980s and 1990s, Southeast and Southwest Asian heroin dominated the U.S. market. As the demand for cocaine in the United States began to decline in the 1990s, Colombians began cultivating opium poppies high in the Andes Mountains.

Today, the DEA estimates that up to 80 percent of all heroin in the United States is produced in South America. There are no dominant "heroin kingpins" in Colombia. Instead, peasant farmers and small independent Colombian trafficking groups currently dominate the South American heroin trade. Many of these heroin traffickers work under the protection of revolutionary guerilla groups in Colombia, such as the Revolutionary Armed Forces of Colombia (FARC) and the National Liberation Army (ELN), which charge a tax to opium framers and heroin traffickers in the areas they control. It is estimated that groups such as FARC derive roughly 70 percent of their operating revenues from heroin trafficking.[39]

South American heroin typically is transported from Colombia to the United States by couriers aboard commercial flights from one of the Colombian airports to international airports in Miami, Atlanta, or New York. Couriers often swallow small pellets of heroin that have been placed in condoms or balloons or wrapped in latex from surgical gloves. Couriers also conceal heroin in body cavities, tape it to their bodies, or conceal it in their clothing or shoes. They smuggle larger quantities of heroin into the United States by transporting the drug in suitcases filled with clothing in which the heroin has been sewn into the seams or clothing that has been soaked with liquid heroin. Increasingly, Colombian heroin traffickers are recruiting Mexican couriers to transport South American heroin through Mexico into the United States. South American heroin is smuggled across the Mexico–U.S. border via Mexican couriers using overland routes and via private or commercial vehicles crossing at border checkpoints.

Within the United States, ethnic Dominican criminal groups currently play a significant role in retail-level distribution of South American heroin. Colombian wholesalers of heroin usually deal directly with Dominican trafficking groups that dominate retail heroin markets in northeastern cities such as New York, Boston, and Philadelphia. Traditionally, heroin abusers themselves have been responsible for selling heroin at the retail level. Seven grams of heroin may be bought, for example, from a wholesaler, three grams kept for personal use, and four grams then sold at a profit on the street. Street gangs and ethnic criminal groups that once dealt only in South American cocaine are engaging in a practice that has come to be called **double-breasted dealing,** in which both cocaine and heroin are distributed together. As the number of cocaine abusers continues to decline

double-breasted dealing: A practice of distributing cocaine and heroin within the same drug organization.

(see Chapter 4), street gangs and other criminal groups are evidently attempting to maintain a substantial share of the drug market by selling heroin.[40]

On the street, heroin is sold in deflated balloons or wrapped in tin foil as a twenty bag ($20) or a hit ($30) or by the gram ($300). Heroin often is cut or diluted with such substances as caffeine, various sugars such as lactose, and depressants such as methaqualone or phenobarbital. South American heroin is usually brownish red in color and is not "cut" or diluted with as many as ingredients as is heroin from the Golden Triangle or the Golden Crescent. South American heroin passes through fewer hands from production to street sale than heroin produced in Asia.

It is common for South American heroin to be 60 or 80 percent pure. Because of its high purity, South American heroin is often referred to as **Red Rum** ("murder" spelled backward) on the street. With purity at such a high level, South American heroin can be snorted or smoked ("chasing the dragon") rather than injected intravenously ("mainlined"). A new technique of administering South American heroin has become known as "shabanging." This method involves dissolving heroin into a liquid, drawing it up into a syringe, and squirting it into the nasal passages. The membranes of the nose absorb the liquid in the same manner as a nasal spray. It is seen among many new young users of heroin as a "partying" activity rather than as an alternative method of administration among established users.[41]

The Trafficking of Marijuana

The overall demand for marijuana in the United States remains at a high level, and both law-enforcement and public health agencies identify marijuana as the most commonly used illicit drug in the nation.[42] Mexico is currently the major foreign source for marijuana smuggled into the United States. Most of the marijuana, whether grown in Mexico or transported through Mexico from other locations such as Colombia, is smuggled across the Southwest border.

Over the past decade, the U.S. government has increased the detection and monitoring of air traffic at the Mexican border. As a result, most of the marijuana that enters the United States through this route is smuggled by land. Drug trafficking organizations operating from Mexico employ a wide variety of methods for smuggling marijuana, such as concealing the drug in false vehicle compartments located in doors, fuel tanks, seats, or tires. Marijuana often is hidden in tractor-trailer trucks among shipments of legitimate agriculture products, such as fruits and vegetables. Smaller quantities of marijuana can be smuggled across the border by horse, raft, and backpack. Once the marijuana is smuggled successfully across the border, traffickers consolidate the shipments at central sites or "safe houses" in cities such as Tucson and Houston. From these distribution sites, marijuana is transported to cities throughout the United States.[43]

In addition to traffickers operating in Mexico and Colombia, a number of groups from Jamaica and the Bahamas smuggle marijuana to the southeastern United States. Shipments of marijuana originating in Colombia or Jamaica are typically first transported by boat or plane to remote islands in the Bahamas. These shipments are then distributed to the United States by sea in commercial fishing trawlers, pleasure craft, or cargo ships. Containers of choice are often refrigerated cargo compartments because marijuana can be concealed within or under materials, and such compartments are usually difficult for custom agents to search. Traditionally, the largest seizures of marijuana have been made in commercial maritime vessels in Miami. Recently, however, traffickers have begun to bypass U.S. Customs security points in south Florida by shifting their cargo to small cities located farther north, such as Charleston, South Carolina. Marijuana also may be packed in waterproof containers, flown from the Bahamas to the East Coast in small aircraft, and airdropped to secluded sites or lakes in Florida or Georgia. Most of the marijuana smuggled through points of entry along the eastern seaboard is distributed in drug markets located exclusively in the eastern part of the United States.[44]

Recently, there has been an enormous growth in the Canadian marijuana trade. Canadian growers in British Columbia have begun to use sophisticated hydroponic cultivation techniques to produce a potent form of marijuana that has come to be known as **BC Bud** or "skunk weed." Hydroponic cultivation refers to a technique in which marijuana plants are grown in nutrient-rich water rather than soil. In soil, young plants spread their roots wide and have access to water and nutrients. In hydroponic cultivation, the water and nutrients are readily supplied to the plant so that the plant will grow just enough roots to keep its stem immobile and be able to absorb the supplied food and water. Plants therefore

Red Rum: "Murder" spelled backward, referring to high-purity South American heroin.

BC Bud: British Columbia–grown marijuana, produced under hydroponic (water-based) cultivation methods.

Lamps cast a yellowish glow over hydroponic cannabis plants in a recently seized marijuana cultivation laboratory.

bia chapter of the Hell's Angels is reportedly one of the most profitable organizations of its kind in the world. According to DEA officials, BC Bud has reached as far south as Atlanta.[45]

The production of domestically cultivated or "home grown" marijuana has increased within the United States in the last several years. Domestic marijuana cultivation exists throughout the United States and ranges from a few plants grown for personal use to thousands of plants cultivated by organized criminal groups. Domestic growers most frequently plant marijuana in remote areas, often camouflaging it in surrounding vegetation. Major outdoor cannabis cultivation takes place in such states as California, Hawaii, Washington, Oregon, and the Appalachian region of Kentucky and Tennessee. Approximately 80 percent of all outdoor cultivated plants eradicated by law enforcement have originated from these six states (Figure 13.6). The mountainous rural landscape in these regions offers numerous hollows and other secluded areas where growers can cultivate their crop in relative isolation from public view.

Domestic marijuana producers usually reflect the demographic makeup of the area in which the

can grow faster and grow larger leaves, flowers, and buds. BC Bud has been found to have a THC content ranging from 15 to 25 percent, more potent than commonly available hashish (Chapter 7).

Most of the hydroponic labs in Canada are operated by Vietnamese criminal groups or by associates of the Hell's Angels motorcycle gang. The British Colum-

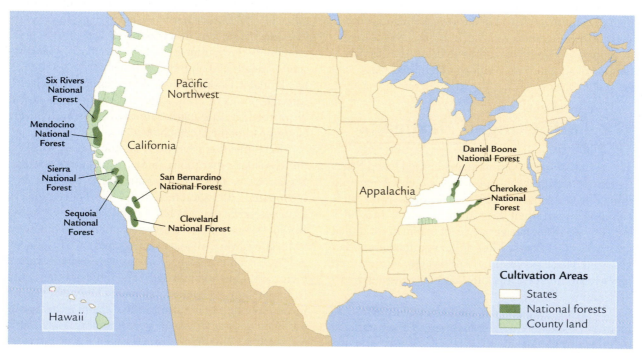

FIGURE 13.6

Approximately 3.9 million outdoor plants and 271,000 indoor plants were seized by the Drug Enforcement Administration in 2005. The map shows the major outdoor areas of marijuana cultivation.

Source: National Drug Intelligence Center (2006, October). *National drug threat assessment 2007.* Washington, DC: U.S. Department of Justice, Table 4.

marijuana is cultivated. In the Appalachian region of Kentucky and Tennessee, for example, marijuana producers are often long-time residents of the area, white males between the ages of thirty-five and fifty, with a high school education who live in rural areas. Most of these marijuana producers are not marijuana users and are often well-respected community members with no previous arrest records. Many of these individuals acknowledge that growing marijuana is morally and legally wrong but grow it because of economic hardship and often feel that they have no better option. Families in this region have a history of making "extra money" by being involved in bootlegging and moonshining (see Chapter 10), and marijuana cultivation has become an extension of this traditional involvement in the black market. The tight kinship networks of these small rural communities provide a culture of safety and protection for marijuana growers. Residents of Appalachia do not want their "kin" to be arrested and therefore often remain silent to protect those involved in the marijuana industry.[46]

In response to the increase in domestically grown marijuana, law-enforcement agencies have come to rely on the use of Blackhawk helicopters to carry out clandestine monitoring of marijuana plots from the air. Growers have countered by covering the plots with camouflage netting or by tying the stems and branches of marijuana plants to small stakes on the ground. This type of cultivation technique produces what has become known as **spider marijuana** because the plant branches out along the ground like the legs of a spider. Out of fear of civil forfeiture, growers also have begun cultivating plants on governmental lands, such as national forests and national parks. Some domestic marijuana traffickers have taken to cultivating their crop indoors using hydroponics. Law enforcement has responded by equipping helicopters with heat-detecting devices to identify unusual sources of light or by checking for unusually high power bills of suspected growers. In several southern states, growers have countered by setting up hydroponic plots in chicken houses, which often rely on intense light and heat sources.

While Mexican drug trafficking organizations control the wholesale distribution of most of the foreign-produced marijuana in the United States, their influence becomes diluted at lower levels, where street-level dealers of marijuana typically reflect the demographic makeup of their local area. Marijuana is usually packaged for street sale by being placed in a clear plastic sandwich bag, which is then rolled up and taped. Marijuana is often sold on the street as a "dime bag"

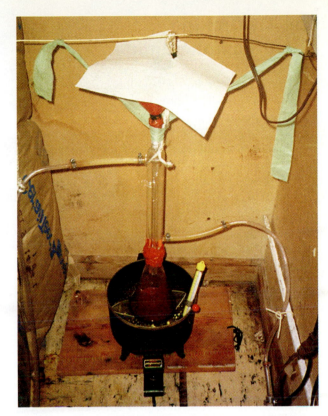

In a makeshift but sophisticated "meth factory," a combination of ephedrine, hydrochloric acid, and red phosphorus (shown as red liquid in the picture) is heated in a flask placed in an electric pot. Rubber tubes attached to each side of the glass condenser circulate cold water to reduce the escape of toxic fumes.

(sold for $10 to $30) or a "quarter bag," which is one-quarter of an ounce (sold for $40 to $60), and by the ounce (sold for $110 to $130). At the street level, new dangerous marijuana mixtures have appeared in several communities across the United States. In these cases, marijuana is being mixed with other illicit drugs, such as PCP, cocaine, and opium. These mixtures are often smoked in "blunts"—oversized joints constructed from commercial cigars that are gutted and refilled. In the Southwest, the practice of smoking cocaine-laced blunts is common. In Chicago, marijuana cigarettes laced with PCP and crack are called "ozones" and usually sell for $15 a cigarette. Marijuana also may be laced with various insecticides and sold on the street as "wac," or else it is soaked in formaldehyde, a preparation known as "wet" or "fry."[47]

> **spider marijuana:** A type of marijuana grown in such a way that the cannibis plant branches out along the ground like the legs of a spider.

The Trafficking of Methamphetamine

During the early 1990s, methamphetamine reemerged as a popular recreational drug in the United States after a previous period of popularity in the 1960s and 1970s. Methamphetamine's chemical structure is similar to that of amphetamine, but it has a more pronounced effect on the central nervous system. It is a white, odorless, bitter-tasting crystalline powder and is commonly referred to as "speed," "meth," and "crank." The drug is usually snorted or injected intravenously and typically is sold for $50 to $150 a gram. While methamphetamine traditionally has been popular among white lower-class males (giving the drug the name "redneck cocaine"), its use has increased recently among college and high school students, especially those involved in the club scene or participating in rave parties, where the drug is used alongside a variety of other drugs.

As discussed in Chapter 4, methamphetamine is made easily in clandestine laboratories with relatively inexpensive over-the-counter ingredients. There are two primary methods of producing clandestine methamphetamine. The first method uses ephedrine or pseudoephedrine as the precursor, and the second method uses phenyl-2-propanone (commonly called the "P2P method"). The ephedrine method is preferred over the P2P method because it is simpler, ephedrine is easier to obtain than phenyl-2-propanone, and it produces a more potent form of methamphetamine. To produce methamphetamine using the ephedrine method, ephedrine is combined with hydrochloric acid and red phosphorus and heated at various stages. The mixture is strained through a bed sheet or pillowcase to remove the red phosphorus. Sodium hydroxide is added, and the mixture is cooled in ice to prevent a volatile reaction. After the mixture is cooled, it is placed in a bucket or drum with Coleman fuel. As the Coleman fuel extracts the methamphetamine from the mixture, the drug floats to the top of the liquid, is scraped off the top, and dries into a white crystalline powder.

Throughout the 1970s and 1980s, the production and trafficking of methamphetamine were controlled by motorcycle gangs such as Hell's Angels and the Pagans. Today, methamphetamine is still called "crank" because many outlaw motorcyclists hid the drug in the crankshafts of their motorcycles. Over the last ten years or so, ethnic Mexican drug trafficking organizations based in Mexico and California have begun to take control of the production and distribution of methamphetamine. In the mid-1990s, these Mexican organizations began operating large-scale "superlabs" capable of producing as much as ten pounds of methamphetamine in a twenty-four-hour period. The entry of ethnic Mexican trafficking organizations into the drug trade has resulted in a significant increase in the supply of high-purity, low-cost methamphetamine that usually enters the United States by being transported across the Mexican border in concealed compartments of passenger vehicles.

Smaller independent "mom and pop" laboratories also supply methamphetamine to users in the United States. These independent "cooks" operate clandestine laboratories and often obtain the ingredients necessary for manufacture from retail and convenience stores. A growing number of Internet sites have provided access to methamphetamine "recipes," resulting in a dramatic increase in the number of these laboratories throughout the United States. The number of domestic clandestine methamphetamine laboratories seized by the DEA increased from 263 in 1994 to 1,815 in 2000, a 590 percent increase (Figure 13.7). State and local police agencies seized almost 8,000 clandestine laboratories in the United States during 2001 alone.[48]

The peak year for methamphetamine laboratory seizures was in 2003 and 2004, when approximately 10,000 seizures were made in each of those years. Since 2004, however, forty-four states have restricted retail sales of ephedrine and pseudoephedrine products, and the prevalence of small methamphetamine laboratories has decreased substantially. The federal Combat Methamphetamine Epidemic Act, passed in 2005, provided the basis for nationwide regulations and law enforcement initiatives. In 2006, approximately 2,000 seizures were made. In the meantime, the focus of enforcement has been on "superlab" operations in rural areas of California, operated by Mexican criminal groups, which import methamphetamine from Mexico.[49]

As with marijuana, Appalachian families in Georgia, North Carolina, and Kentucky who were once involved in moonshining and bootlegging are now producing batches of methamphetamine. The mountainous regions of Appalachia are perfect for small-time meth cookers who often set up their labs in trailers or mobile homes located in secluded heavily forested areas. Cooks typically dispose of highly toxic wastes of meth production by dumping the material into a nearby lake, pond, or stream.

Labs can be detected through a urine-like smell that results from the cooking process; however, other signs of meth labs include destruction of plant life in the surrounding area from the disposal of by-products of meth cooking, a large number of ice bags used in the cooling process, thirty- or fifty-five-gallon drums, and

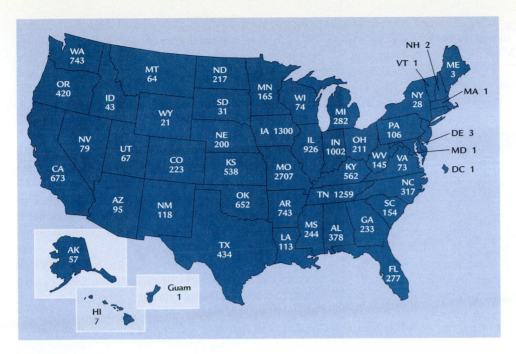

FIGURE 13.7

Geographic distribution of all methamphetamine clandestine laboratory incidents (including labs, dumpsites, chemicals/glass/equipment), 2004.

Source: National Clandestine Laboratory Database, 2004.

large ventilation fans positioned toward the inside of a mobile home.

Police officers sometimes refer to meth labs as "chemical time bombs" because of the presence of highly flammable and toxic chemicals used in the production of methamphetamine. Explosions at meth labs are very common, and fires or explosions occur every year at a number of meth lab sites, leading to their discovery and the death of those making the drug. Meth lab operators, often called "cooks," are also beginning to place mechanical or chemical booby traps in and around the sites of their labs; as a result, an officer may inadvertently come into contact with such booby traps when responding to a domestic call or when serving a search warrant.

The by-products of the methamphetamine manufacturing process are extremely hazardous chemical wastes that contaminate glassware, equipment, and the structure in which the lab is located. The hazardous chemical wastes are also commonly disposed of by dumping into nearby lakes, streams, and sewage systems, posing a serious threat to the environment. For every pound of methamphetamine produced, about five pounds of highly toxic waste are generated. When law enforcement seizes a meth lab, the cleanup costs often exceed $100,000. Even with careful cleanup procedures, many sites of meth labs will never be fit for human occupancy again. The chemicals and fumes that permeate the walls, carpets, plaster, and wood of the site, as well as the surrounding soil, are known to cause cancer, short-term and permanent brain damage, and immune and respiratory system problems.

The Trafficking of Hallucinogens

Lysergic acid diethylamide (LSD) is a clear or white, odorless crystalline material that is soluble in water (see Chapter 6). The drug is usually dissolved in a solvent for application onto paper, commonly referred to as blotter paper or blotter acid. Blotter acid consists of sheets of paper soaked or sprayed with LSD and decorated with a variety of colorful designs and symbols. A sheet of paper LSD blotter may contain hundreds of small, perforated, one-quarter-inch squares, with each square representing one individual dose. The price of one dosage unit of LSD ranges from $2 to $10 depending on demand and the potency of the drug. LSD also may be found in tablet form (microdots), in thin squares of gelatin ("window panes"), or in a dissolved liquid form, which is often kept in an eyedrop container or glass vial. Eyedroppers allow users to disperse hundreds of doses of LSD at large parties or concerts by dropping the drug on users' tongues. Because LSD degrades quickly when exposed to heat, light, and air, users may keep doses of LSD in a freezer or refrigerator, where it is either wrapped in tin foil or kept in plastic film containers.

LSD is commonly produced from lysergic acid, which, in turn, is made from **ergotamine tartrate,** a substance that is derived from the ergot fungus. Since ergotamine tartrate is not readily available in the United States and is regulated under the Chemical Diversion and Trafficking Act, most of the production of LSD is believed to come from sources located abroad, such as Europe and Mexico. Nearly all the LSD that is produced in the United States originates from a small number of laboratories operating in northern California since the 1960s.

Only a small amount of ergotamine tartrate is required to produce a large number of dosage units of LSD. For example, twenty-five kilograms can produce five kilograms of pure LSD crystal, and only one kilogram of crystal LSD can yield approximately ten million dosage units of LSD. It takes as long as three days to produce one to four ounces of crystal LSD. As a result, it is believed that most LSD is not produced in large quantities but rather in a series of small batches. Once crystal LSD is produced, it can be mixed with binding agents, such as spray-dried skim milk, for producing tablets, or it is dissolved and diluted in a solvent for application onto paper or other materials. Decorated sheets of paper are usually dipped into a shallow pan containing crystal LSD dissolved in methanol, ethanol, or another solvent and then are laid out or hung to dry. Once the sheets of paper are dry, they are perforated and ready for distribution.

After production, LSD usually is distributed to traffickers and users in two ways. The primary method of transportation is by mail, using overnight delivery services. LSD is frequently concealed in greeting cards, cassette tapes, plastic film containers, or articles of clothing that are mailed to a post office box established by the recipient. The post office box is usually listed under a fictitious name or business, and no return address is

typically provided on the package or envelope. Rock concerts also have been a traditional means of distributing LSD. Throughout the 1970s and 1980s, traffickers used concerts of the rock band The Grateful Dead as a network to distribute and sell both large and small quantities of LSD.[50]

The use of MDMA, commonly referred to as Ecstasy, XTC, X, Bean(s), or Adam on the street, is often referred to as **rolling.** Before using MDMA, a user may say, "I'm going to roll tonight," or after a person has used the drug, he or she may say, "I rolled last night." MDMA is taken orally, usually in the form of a pill or tablet. In most cases, approximately one-third of a pill or tablet is pure MDMA; the rest is a "filler," such as baking powder. Prices range from $20 to $30 per dosage unit, although prices as high as $50 per dosage unit have been reported. MDMA manufacturers commonly press brand names, symbols, or logos onto their pills to use as a marketing tool and to distinguish their product from that of competitors. Among the more popular logos are the Rolex symbol, Pink Panther, butterfly, lightning bolt, and the four-leaf clover.

Most of the MDMA in the United States has been produced in clandestine laboratories operating in Europe, primarily in the Netherlands and to a lesser extent in Belgium and Eastern European countries. In recent years, Israeli criminal organizations, some with associations with Russian organized-crime syndicates, have forged relationships with Western European traffickers and gained control over MDMA distribution in the United States. Prior to the tightening of security at international airports, Israeli and Russian criminal groups operating in Europe were able to recruit couriers who transported MDMA from Europe to the United States on commercial flights and then delivered the drug to a wholesaler at a location near the airport.[51]

Phencyclidine (PCP) is a synthetic drug first used as an anesthetic (see Chapter 6). Today, all the PCP encountered for sale on the street in the United States has been produced in clandestine laboratories. While chemicals needed to manufacture PCP are readily available and inexpensive, and the drug is not particularly difficult to make, it does require many complicated steps and some of those steps can be quite dangerous. Occasionally, individuals making PCP in their bathroom, kitchen, or basement are killed from the inhalation of poisonous fumes produced when the drug is being manufactured. Most of the production and distribution of PCP in the United States are controlled primarily by African American criminal groups and street gangs in California.

ergotamine tartrate: A substance derived from ergot fungus that has infected rye and other grains.

rolling: A slang term for the use of MDMA (Ecstasy).

PCP typically is produced in a liquid form that is sprayed or sprinkled onto leafy material such as tobacco, marijuana, mint, oregano, or parsley and rolled into a cigarette or joint. One PCP joint purchased on the street usually costs from $15 to $25. Mexican drug trafficking organizations operating in the United States also produce PCP and distribute wholesale quantities to Hispanic/Latino street gangs. Mexican organizations typically produce PCP in powder or crystal form, whereas the liquid typically is produced by African American organizations. PCP has a variety of street names including angel dust, rocket fuel, killer weed, embalming fluid, ozone, or Sherman (because the drug supposedly "hits you like a Sherman tank").[52]

Ketamine is a drug that is chemically similar to PCP but produces less confusion, irrationality, and violence. Since ketamine is currently marketed as a general anesthetic for veterinary use, most of the ketamine sold on the street is stolen from supplies kept in veterinary facilities. In veterinary clinics, ketamine is found in a liquid form for injection, but ketamine sellers prefer to market the drug in a powdered form and often crystallize it themselves. When ketamine liquid is evaporated, a white crystalline powder is left behind, somewhat duller in color and more powdery than cocaine. Ketamine powder can be snorted, smoked (sprinkled on tobacco or marijuana), or ingested by being dropped into a drink.

Often referred to as K or **Special K** on the street, ketamine is similar to PCP in that it produces a mixture of stimulant and depressive effects. A small quantity of powdered ketamine (approximately 0.2 gram) is often called a "bump" and costs about $20. Bumps are usually stored in small plastic bags or folded in paper or tin foil. Users usually inhale a bump of ketamine every 5 to 10 minutes until the desired state is reached. Low doses of ketamine may produce feelings of intoxication and an experience called "K-land," described as a mellow, colorful "wonder world." Higher doses of ketamine may result in an effect referred to as "K-hole," described as an "out of body" or "near death" experience. Use of ketamine also may produce delirium, amnesia, depression, long-term memory and cognitive difficulties, and fatal respiratory problems. Ketamine was placed on Schedule III of the Controlled Substance Act in 1999.[53]

Money Laundering

Because practically every transaction in the illicit drug business is conducted in cash, a conspicuously large

Quick Concept Check 13.2

Understanding Drug Trafficking

Check your understanding of drug trafficking by matching the statement on the left with the correct answer on the right. *Note:* Some of the answers may be used more than once.

1. Source country of most of the foreign-produced marijuana in the United States.

2. Most of the heroin used in the United States comes from this country.

3. Most of the cocaine used in the United States comes from this country.

4. One of the countries within the Golden Crescent

5. One of the countries in the Golden Triangle.

6. Most of the foreign-produced methamphetamine in the United States comes from this country.

7. Most of the LSD used in the United States is produced in this country.

8. Most of MDMA used in the United States is produced in clandestine laboratories operating in this country.

9. Primary source of PCP.

10. Source of BC Bud.

a. Afghanistan
b. Thailand
c. The Netherlands
d. United States
e. Mexico
f. Colombia
g. Canada

Answers: 1. e 2. f 3. f 4. a 5. b 6. e 7. d 8. c 9. d 10. g

number of small bills can render drug traffickers vulnerable to law enforcement interdiction. Drug traffickers cannot simply deposit their profits into a local bank. The

Special K: A street name for ketamine.

Bank Secrecy Act of 1970 requires that financial institutions in the United States report cash transactions of $10,000 or more to the Internal Revenue Service (IRS), and these institutions must identify the depositors and the sources of the money. Drug traffickers, therefore, must rely on a variety of money-laundering methods to convert bulk amounts of drug profits into legitimate revenue. **Money laundering** refers to the process where illegal sources of income are disguised to make them appear legitimate. Money laundering conceals the illegal sources of money and gives the money a legitimate history.

One of the simplest methods of money laundering is called "smurfing," by which a number of persons, or "smurfs," deposit random amounts of less than $10,000 into variously named accounts at many different banks. Using twenty smurfs, for example, each depositing $9,000 in cash, a trafficker could launder as much as $180,000 in less than an hour and circumvent the regulations of the Bank Secrecy Act. After the money is deposited, it can be withdrawn by the trafficker to purchase money orders in U.S. funds, which are sent out of the country to purchase more drugs or for safekeeping. It can be a quite successful technique, except for the fact that traffickers have to give each of their smurfs a cut of their profits. Therefore, smurfing is not the most profitable method of money laundering.

A second technique of money laundering is for traffickers to ship the money abroad and deposit it in banks located in countries that have few, if any, money laundering regulations. Commonly called "offshore banks," unregulated banks in the Caribbean nations that were formerly British colonies, such as the Cayman Islands, have become favorite laundering havens. With the seventh largest deposit base in the world, the Cayman Islands have 550 banks, only seventeen of which have a physical presence and operate without any requirement to report transactions. Typically, these offshore banking havens have very strict policies with regard to nondisclosure, effectively shielding foreign investors from investigations and prosecutions from their home countries.[54]

The principal difficulty in using offshore banks as a money laundering method is getting the money from the United States into the foreign country in which the money is to be laundered. U.S. law requires that any person taking $10,000 or more out of the country must disclose this information in writing. If this information is not disclosed to a customs agent and the money is found, it will be confiscated. In many instances, the same methods used to smuggle illicit drugs *into* the United States are used to smuggle bulk shipments of money *out of* the United States. Colombian traffickers, for example, move large shipments of cash through air cargo or commercial cargo freighters, and Mexican traffickers often use tractor trailers and cars with hidden compartments to carry large quantities of U.S. currency across the border. Once the money is smuggled abroad and deposited in offshore banks, drug traffickers make extensive use of electronic payments and wire transfers to transfer millions of dollars instantly to different bank accounts around the world. The rapid movement of funds between accounts in different jurisdictions increases the complexity of investigating and tracing the source of funds.

One of the oldest methods of money laundering is for drug traffickers to operate a cash-based retail service business such as laundromats, car washes, vending-machine routes, video rentals, or bars and restaurants, mixing the illegal and legal cash and reporting the total as the earnings of the cover business. In fact, the term "money laundering" is said to originate from Mafia ownership of laundromats in the United States during Prohibition. Bootleggers needed to show a legitimate source for their monies, and laundromats were chosen because they were cash businesses that could be bought easily. Later, in the 1970s, the Mafia used pizza parlors to launder money made from the sale of heroin. Acquiring a legitimate business to launder money provides drug traffickers with a reportable income for tax purposes, and the businesses themselves help drug traffickers to cultivate a respectable public image with the community.

Alternative methods of money laundering include bribing employees of financial institutions, acquiring financial institutions, arranging business loans, using real estate transactions, and disguising the money as casino winnings. The globalization of financial markets through the growth of international trade and the expansion of international corporations has provided more opportunities for the conversion of illegal proceeds into what appear to be legitimate funds. It is important to note that the success of a drug trafficking organization is based not only on its ability to produce, distribute, and sell drugs but also on its ability to launder the money made from the illicit drug business (Drugs . . . in Focus).[55]

money laundering: The process where illegal sources of income are concealed or disguised to make the sources appear legitimate.

Drugs . . . in Focus

A Forty-Year Chronology of Drug Interdiction

Since the late 1960s, when the "war on drugs" was officially declared, a number of significant events have occurred in the area of illicit drug seizures and interceptions in the United States. Here are some of the highlights:

- **1969:** In September, Operational Intercept forces the essential closure of the U.S.–Mexico border. Customs Department personnel examine every vehicle crossing the border from Mexico in a three-minute inspection. The two-week operation brings economic havoc on both sides of the border. As a result, Mexico agrees to fight the marijuana trade more aggressively, but there is little long-term impact on the smuggling of marijuana into the United States.

- **1972:** The French Connection is severed. A joint U.S.–French initiate carries out successful busts of Marseilles-based heroin organization, controlled by Corsican and U.S. criminal groups.

- **1973:** The Drug Enforcement Administration is established as a "super agency" to handle all aspects of illicit drug traffic and distribution.

- **1979:** Carlos Lehder, a key member of the Medellin Cartel, initiates a new method of cocaine smuggling, when he purchases Norman's Cay in the Bahamas as a refueling stopover for small planes transporting cocaine from Colombia and to the United States. A Bahamian crackdown on Lehder's operation in 1982 causes Lehder to flee the island, though operations continue for another year.

- **1984:** DEA and Colombian police discover Transquilandia, a cocaine-processing laboratory controlled by the Medellin Cartel, located deep in the Colombian jungle. In a coordinated bust operation, fourteen laboratory complexes are destroyed, as well as seven airplanes and 13.8 metric tons of cocaine. Conservative estimates of the assets seized or destroyed are set at $1.2 billion.

- **1984:** DEA and Mexican officials raid a large marijuana cultivation and processing complex in the Chihuahua desert, in what is termed the "Bust of the Century." Seven thousand workers are arrested, and 5,000 to 10,000 tons of high-grade marijuana worth $2.5 billion are found and destroyed.

- **1989:** The assassination of Colombian presidential candidate Luis Carlos Galán near Bogota escalates the battle between the Colombian government and cocaine cartels. Bombing and murders will continue until 1991.

- **1998:** Operation Casablanca leads to the indictment of three Mexican and four Venezuelan banks, as well as the arrest of 167 individuals in the largest money-laundering probe in U.S. history.

- **1999:** Operation Millennium results in the arrests of thirty-one major drug traffickers in Mexico, Colombia, and Ecuador.

- **2002:** Two commandants of the Autodefensas Unidas de Colombia (AUC) are arrested in an elaborate cocaine-for-arms deal. Paramilitary weapons worth $25 million were to be purchased by the group. Colombian officials claim that the AUC is responsible for 804 assassinations, 203 kidnappings, and 75 massacres with 507 victims, as well as their involvement with cocaine trafficking and distribution.

- **2005:** Operation Cali Exchange results in twenty-four indictments, eighteen arrests, and the seizure of more than $7 million, more than 2,000 kilograms of cocaine, and more than 500 pounds of marijuana in a raid on a major drug-trafficking and money-laundering organization operating in the United States, as well as Panama, Colombia, the Dominican Republic, Brazil, and the Bahamas.

- **2007:** Newly elected Mexican President Felipe Calderón moves quickly to crack down on drug cartels within Mexico. Thousands of federal police officers and soldiers are sent into major cities such as Tijuana, Acapulco, and Morella, where drug-smuggling operations are dominant.

Sources: Frontline—Public Broadcasting Service (2000). Thirty years of Americas's drug war: A chronology. In Huggins, Laura E. (Ed.), *Drug war deadlock: The policy battle continues.* Stanford, CA: Hoover Institute Press, Stanford University. Information courtesy of the Drug Enforcement Administration, U.S. Department of Justice, Washington, DC. McKinley, James C. (2007, January 27). Mexico's latest war on drug gangs is off to a rapid start. *New York Times,* p. A10.

Summary

Understanding Drug Use and Crime

- Empirical studies on the relationship between alcohol and drug use and the commission of crime are unanimous in their findings: Crime and drug use are strongly correlated. Individuals who drink alcohol and/or use drugs are significantly more likely to commit crimes than are individuals who neither drink nor use illegal drugs. Jail and prison inmates in the United States have much higher rates of drug use relative to the general population. The principal question is whether drug use and criminal behavior have a cause-and-effect relationship.

- Pharmacological explanations suggest that the effects of a drug contribute to an offender committing a crime. The drug causes violent or criminal behavior while the drug is actually present in the individual's system. While there is an overall association between the taking of illicit drugs and crime, a careful analysis indicates that the drug with the closest connection to social violence is alcohol. In contrast, heroin and marijuana typically cause the user to be less inclined toward violence rather than more so. Economic explanations of the drug–crime link suggest that drug use may cause users to commit crimes to obtain money to buy drugs to support drug-taking behavior financially. Criminal activity of this type is referred to as economically compulsive crime. Several studies show that economically compulsive crime is a major component of the link between drugs and crime.

- The drug–crime connection also can be explained from the standpoint that crime causes drug use. In this view, persons who are predisposed to commit crime also take drugs. Drugs may be used before committing an offense to bolster courage or afterward to celebrate success. The viewpoint that crime causes drug use is further supported by longitudinal studies (studies conducted over a period of time) finding that initial involvement in criminal activity occurs prior to the experimentation with drugs for most users.

- A third way of explaining the relationship between drug use and crime is the view that both drug use and crime share a common cause. According to this perspective, drug use and crime do not cause one or the other but are both aspects of a deviant life-style or culture. The same types of individuals who are most likely to commit crime are also the same types who are most likely to use drugs.

The Social Structure of the Illicit Drug Trade

- The illicit drug business can be divided into various "stages" of production and distribution that include (1) cultivation and manufacturing, (2) importation, (3) wholesale distribution, and (4) retail distribution. In this sense, the illicit drug business is no different from that of a foreign or domestic commodity on the legitimate market.

- At the retail level, drug dealers follow either the freelance model in which dealers and buyers transact their business with relative anonymity or the business model in which drug transactions are conducted within a hierarchically structured organization.

The Trafficking of Cocaine

- Today, most of the world's coca cultivation and cocaine production take place in Colombia, South America. The arrest of the top leaders of the Colombian Medellin and Cali drug cartels in the 1990s has led to a decentralization of the cocaine trade in which smaller independent organizations currently have taken control of the production and trafficking of cocaine.

- Mexican criminal organizations are currently responsible for smuggling the majority of cocaine that is imported into the United States.

- Street gangs such as the Crips and Bloods and criminal ethnic gangs currently dominate the retail market for crack nationwide. Jamaican criminal gangs, known as Jamaican posses, distribute large quantities of crack cocaine throughout the United States, often purchased from Colombian sources.

The Trafficking of Heroin

- There are currently four major sources of heroin: (1) the Golden Triangle, (2) the Golden Crescent, (3) Mexico, and (4) South America.

- The Golden Triangle of Southeast Asia was once the world's largest source of heroin. It included such countries as Thailand, Burma (Myanmar), Laos, and Vietnam. Ethnic Chinese and Asian criminal groups known as triads and tongs were the primary heroin transporters to North America.

- Currently, the largest source for the world's supply of heroin is the Golden Crescent of Pakistan, Afghanistan, Turkey, and Iran. Heroin from Afghanistan helped finance Osama bin Laden and the Taliban's terrorist activities prior to 2002.

- A third major source of heroin is Mexico. Since Mexican heroin is often crudely processed with many impurities, it is typically black or brown in color and is referred to as "black tar" or "Tootsie Roll" on the street.

- Most of the heroin supply in the United States originates in Colombia. South American heroin is typically transported from Colombia to the United States by couriers aboard commercial flights from Colombia to international airports in Miami, Atlanta, or New York. Couriers often swallow small pellets of heroin that have been placed in condoms or balloons or wrapped in latex from surgical gloves.

The Trafficking of Marijuana

- Mexico is currently the major foreign source for marijuana imported into the United States. Marijuana is often smuggled across the border in tractor-trailer trucks, where it is hidden in shipments of legitimate agriculture products, such as fruits and vegetables.

- Recently, there has been an enormous growth in the Canadian marijuana trade. Canadian growers in British Columbia have used sophisticated hydroponic cultivation techniques to produce a potent form of marijuana that has come to be commonly known as "BC Bud" or "skunk weed."

- The production of domestically cultivated or "home grown" marijuana has increased within the United States in the last several years. Major outdoor cannabis cultivation takes place in such states as California, Hawaii, Washington, Oregon, and the Appalachian region of Kentucky and Tennessee. Approximately 80 percent of all outdoor cultivated plants recently eradicated by law enforcement have originated in these six states.

The Trafficking of Methamphetamine

- Since the mid-1990s, ethnic Mexican drug trafficking organizations based in Mexico and California have begun to take control of the production and distribution of methamphetamine. These Mexican organizations operate large-scale "superlabs" capable of producing in excess of ten pounds of methamphetamine in a twenty-four-hour period.

- Smaller independent "mom and pop" laboratories also supply methamphetamine to users in the United States. These independent operations consist of clandestine laboratories, and they often obtain the ingredients necessary for manufacture from retail and convenience stores.

The Trafficking of Hallucinogens

- Nearly all the LSD available in the United States is being manufactured by a small number of laboratories that have been operating in Northern California since the 1960s.

- Most of MDMA in the United States originates from operations in Europe, primarily in the Netherlands and to a lesser extent in Belgium and Eastern European countries. In recent years, Israeli criminal organizations, some with associations with Russian organized-crime syndicates, have forged relationships with Western European traffickers to gain control over a significant share of the MDMA market.

- Most of the production and distribution of PCP in the United States is controlled by African American criminal groups and street gangs in California. These groups produce PCP in a liquid form that is sprayed or sprinkled onto leafy material such as tobacco, marijuana, mint, oregano, or parsley and rolled into a cigarette or joint.

- Ketamine is chemically similar to PCP but produces less confusion, irrationality, and violence. Most of the ketamine sold on the street is stolen from stores kept in veterinary facilities, since ketamine is available legitimately as an animal anesthetic.

Money Laundering

- To escape the attention of law enforcement agencies, the enormous amount of income gained from "cash only" drug distribution and sales must be converted into legitimate revenue in a process called money laundering.

- One method of money laundering, called "smurfing," is to enlist a number of individuals to deposit random amounts of less than $10,000 into accounts at many different banks. A second method is to ship the money abroad and deposit it into banks located in countries with few, if any, banking regulations. A third method is to operate cash-based retail service businesses that serve as "fronts" for illegal drug distribution activities.

Key Terms

Endnotes

1. International Association of Chiefs of Police (1989). *Reducing crime by reducing drug abuse: A manual of police chiefs and sheriffs.* Gaithersburg, MD: International Association of Chiefs of Police. Quotation on p. 5. Office of Justice Programs (2003). *Toward a drugs and crime research agenda for the 21st century.* Washington, DC: National Institute of Justice, U.S. Department of Justice.

2. Anglin, M. Douglas, and Speckart, George (1988). Narcotics use and crime: A multisample, multimethod analysis. *Criminology, 26,* 197–233. Ball, John C., Shaffer, John W., and Nurco, David N. (1983). The day-to-day criminality of heroin addicts in Baltimore: A study in the continuity of offense rates. *Drug and Alcohol Dependence, 12,* 119–142. Chaiken, Marcia R., and Chaiken, Jan M. (1982). *Varieties of criminal behavior.* Santa Monica, CA: RAND. Farabee, David, Joshi, Vandana, and Anglin, M. Douglas (2001). Addiction careers and criminal specialization. *Crime and Delinquency, 47,* 196–220. Goode, Erich (2005). *Drugs in American society* (6th ed.). New York: McGraw-Hill, pp. 332–334. Inciardi, James A. (1992). *The war on drugs II: The continuing epic of heroin, cocaine, crack, AIDS, and public policy.* Mountain View, CA: Mayfield. Quotation on p. 158.

3. National Institute of Justice (2005). *Drug and alcohol use and related matters among arrestees 2003.* Washington, DC: Arrestee Drug Abuse Monitoring Program, U.S. Department of Justice, Tables 3, 5, 6, 7, and 8.

4. Bureau of Justice Statistics (2006, October). *Drug use and dependence, state and federal prisoners, 2004.* Washington, DC: U.S. Department of Justice.

5. De La Rosa, Mario, Lambert, Elizabeth Y., and Gropper, Bernard (1990). Introduction: Exploring the substance abuse-violence connection. In *Drugs and violence: Causes, correlates, and consequences* (NIDA Research Monograph 103). Rockville, MD: National Institute on Drug Abuse, pp. 1–7.

6. Roth, Jeffrey A. (1994, February). *Psychoactive substances and violence: Research brief.* Washington, DC: National Institute of Justice.

7. Gold, Mark S. (1991). *The good news about drugs and alcohol: Curing, treating and preventing substance abuse in the new age of biopsychiatry.* New York: Villard Books.

8. Bureau of Justice Statistics (2006, June). *Criminal victimization in the United States, 2004, statistical tables.* Washington, DC: U.S. Department of Justice, Table 32. Bushman, Brad J. (1993, October). Human aggression while under the influence of alcohol and other drugs: An integrative research review. *Current Directions in Psychological Science.* pp. 148–152. Collins, James J., and Messerschmidt, Pamela M. (1993). Epidemiology of alcohol-related violence. *Alcohol Health and Research World, 17,* 93–100. Goode, Erich (2005), *Drugs in American society,* pp. 329–350. Pernanen, Kai (1991). *Alcohol in human violence.* New York: Guilford Press, pp. 192–193.

9. Inciardi, James A. (1990). The crack–violence connection within a population of hard-core adolescent offenders. In Marion De La Rosa, Elizabeth Y. Lambert, and Bernard Gropper (Eds.), *Drugs and violence: Causes, correlates, and consequences* (NIDA Research Monograph 103). Rockville, MD: National Institute on Drug Abuse, pp. 92–111.

10. Silverman, Lester P., and Spruill, Nancy L. (1977). Urban crime and the price of heroin. *Journal of Urban Economics, 4,* 80–103.

11. McCoy, Virginia H.; Inciardi, James A.; Metsch, Lisa R.; Pottieger, Anne.; and Saum, Christine A. (1995). Women, crack and crime: Gender comparisons of criminal activity among crack cocaine users. *Contemporary Drug Problems. 22* (3), 435–452.

12. Inciardi, J. A. (1995). Crack, crack house sex, and HIV risk. *Archives of Sexual Behavior, 24,* 249–269.

13. Inciardi, James A. (1979). Heroin use and street crime. *Crime and Delinquency, 25,* pp. 335–346. Inciardi, James A., and McBride, David C. (1976). Considerations in the definitions of criminality for the assessment of the relationship between drug use and crime. In Research Triangle Institute (Ed.). *Crime and drugs,* pp. 123–137. Springfield, VA: National Technical Information Service.

Inciardi, James A., and Pottieger, Anne E. (1994). Crack-cocaine and street crime. *Journal of Drug Issues, 24,* pp. 273–292. Inciardi, James A., Horowitz, Robert, and Pottieger, Anne E. (1993). *Street kids, street drugs, street crime.* Belmont, CA: Wadsworth.

14. Chaiken and Chaiken, Marcia R. (1982). *Varieties of criminal behavior.*

15. Elliot, Delbert S., Huizinga, David, and Menard, Scott (1989). *Multiple problem youth: Delinquency, substance use and mental health problems.* New York: Springer-Verlag.

16. Harris, Jonathan (1991). *Drugged America.* New York: Four Winds Press, p. 112.

17. Bureau of Justice Statistics (1992). *Drugs, crime, and the justice system: A national report from the Bureau of justice statistics.* Washington, DC: U.S. Department of Justice.

18. White, Jason (1991). *Drug dependence.* Englewood Cliffs, NJ: Prentice Hall, p. 200.

19. Goode, Erich (1972). Excerpts from marijuana use and crime. In National Commission of Marijuana and Drug Abuse, *Marijuana: A signal of misunderstanding,* Appendix, Vol. 1. Washington, DC: U.S. Government Printing Office, pp. 447–453.

20. Goode, Erich. (2005). *Drugs in American society* (6th ed.). New York: McGraw-Hill, pp. 329–350.

21. Berger, Gilda (1989). *Violence and drugs.* New York: Franklin Watts, p. 16. Blumstein, Alfred, and Rosenfeld, Richard (1998, October). Assessing the recent ups and downs in U.S. homicide rates. *National Institute of Justice Journal,* pp. 9–11. Curtis, Richard (1998, October). The improbable transformation of inner-city neighborhoods: Crime, violence, drugs, and youths in the 1990s. *National Institute of Justice Journal,* pp. 16–17.

22. Harris, *Drugged America,* p. 117.

23. Goldstein, Paul J. (1979). *Prostitution and drugs.* Lexington, MA: Lexington Books. Goldstein, Paul J. (1985, Fall). The drugs/violence nexus: A triparite conceptual framework. *Journal of Drug Issues,* 493–506.

24. Paterline, Brent (2003). *Drug identification and investigation for law enforcement.* Temecula, CA: Staggs Publishing, p. 2.

25. Alder, P. (1985). *Wheeling and dealing.* New York: Colombia University Press. Hamid, Ansely. (1990). The political economy of crack-related violence. *Contemporary Drug Problems* 17(1), 31–78. Johnson, Bruce D., Hamid, Ansely, and Sanabria, Harry (1992). Emerging models of crack distribution. In Thomas Mieczkowski (Ed.). *Drugs, crime and social policy: Research, issues, and concerns.* Boston: Allyn and Bacon. Moore, M. (1976). *Buy and bust.* Lexington, MA: D.C. Heath. Preble, E., and Casey, J. (1969). Taking care of business: The heroin user's life on the streets. *International Journal of Addictions,* 4, 1–24.

26. Johnson, Bruce D., Golub, Andrew, and Dunlap, Eloise (2006). The rise and decline of hard drugs, drug markets, and violence in inner-city New York. In Alfred Blumstein and Joel Wallman (Eds.), *The crime drop in America.* New York: Cambridge University Press, pp. 164–206. Office of National Drug Control Policy (2004, January). *Pulse check: Trends in drug abuse, drug markets and chronic users in 25 of America's largest cities.* Washington, DC: Office of National Drug Control Policy.

27. Drug Enforcement Administration (2001, September). *Drug trafficking in the United States.* Washington, DC: Department of Justice. Johnson, Golub, and Dunlap (2006). The rise and decline of hard drugs, pp. 164–206. Office of National Drug Control Policy (2002, April). *Pulse check: Trends in drug abuse.* Office of National Drug Control Policy (2004, January). *Pulse check: Trends in drug abuse.* Vannostrand, Lise-Marie, and Tewksbury, Richard (1999). The motives and mechanics of operating an illegal drug enterprise. *Deviant Behavior, 20,* 57–83.

28. Drug Enforcement Administration (2003). *Drug trafficking in the United States.* Washington, DC: U.S. Department of Justice.

29. Abadinsky, Howard (1993). *Drug abuse* (2nd ed.). Chicago: Nelson-Hall Publishers.

30. Constantine, Thomas A. (1998). *DEA congressional testimony: International organized crime syndicates and their impact on the United States.* Washington, DC: Drug Enforcement Administration.

31. Marshall, Donnie R. (2001). *DEA congressional testimony: Plan Colombia.* Washington, DC: Drug Enforcement Administration. Pardo, Rafael. (2000). Colombia's two-front war. *Foreign Affairs,* 79, 4–15.

32. Drug Enforcement Administration (2003). *Drug trafficking in the United States.* Washington, DC: Department of Justice.

33. Paterline, *Drug identification and investigation for law enforcement.*

34. Kenney, Dennis J., and Finckenauer, James O. (1995). *Organized crime in America.* Belmont, CA: Wadsworth Publishing Company. Lyman, Michael D., and Potter, Gary W. (2003). *Organized crime.* (3rd ed.). Upper Saddle River, NJ: Prentice Hall.

35. DEA Press Release (2003, May 16). *Massive heroin-smuggling organization dismantled.* Washington, DC: DEA Office of Public Affairs. Drug Enforcement Administration (2002, August). *Drug intelligence brief: Anatomy of a Southeast Asian heroin conspiracy.* Washington, DC: Drug Enforcement Administration.

36. Moreau, Roy, and Yousafzai, Sami (2006, January 9). A harvest of treachery. *Newsweek,* pp. 32–35. Mulrine, Anna (2007, July 9). The drug trade's collateral damage. *Newsweek,* p. 33. Rohde, David (2007, August 26). Taliban push poppy production to a record again. *New York Times,* p. 3. Tandy, Karen P. (2004, February 26). *DEA Congressional testimony: Afghanistan: Law enforcement interdiction efforts in transshipment countries to stem the flow of heroin.* Washington, DC: Drug Enforcement Administration.

37. Drug Enforcement Administration (2001). *Intelligence report: The Mexican heroin trade.* Washington, DC: Drug Enforcement Administration. Noriega, Roger F. (2007, August 16). It's our drug war, too. How America and Mexico can defeat the cartels. *Washington Post*, p. A15.

38. National Drug Intelligence Center. 2004. *National drug threat assessment.* Washington, DC: U.S. Department of Justice.

39. Drug Enforcement Administration (2002, December). *Drug intelligence brief: Increase in Mexican couriers transporting Colombian heroin to Mexico.* Washington, DC: Drug Enforcement Administration. Guevara, Rogelio (2002, December 12). *DEA congressional testimony: Colombian heroin trafficking.* Washington DC: Drug Enforcement Administration.

40. Jacobs, Bruce A. (1999). Crack to heroin? Drug markets in transition. *British Journal of Criminology*, 39(4), 555–574. Office of National Drug Control Policy (1998, summer). *Pulse check: Trends in drug abuse.* Washington, DC: Office of National Drug Control Policy.

41. National Drug Intelligence Center (2004, summer). *National drug threat assessment.* Washington, DC: U.S. Department of Justice. Office of National Drug Control Policy (1998). *Pulse check: Trends in drug abuse.* Washington, DC: Office of National Drug Control Policy. Office of National Drug Control Policy (2004, January). *Pulse check: Trends in drug abuse.* Washington, DC: Office of National Drug Control Policy.

42. Substance Abuse and Mental Health Services Administration (2007). *Results from the 2005 national survey on drug use and health: National findings.* Washington, DC: National Institute on Drug Abuse.

43. Drug Enforcement Administration (2001, September). *Drug trafficking in the United States.* Washington, DC: Department of Justice. Office of National Drug Control Policy (2002). *Pulse check: Trends in drug abuse, marijuana section.* Washington, DC: Office of National Drug Control Policy.

44. National Drug Intelligence Center (2004). *National drug threat assessment 2004.* Washington, DC: U.S. Department of Justice

45. Drug Enforcement Administration (2000, December). *Intelligence brief: BC bud.* Washington, DC: U.S. Department of Justice.

46. Hafley, Sandra R., and Tewksbury, Richard (1996). Reefer madness in bluegrass country: Community structure and roles in the rural Kentucky marijuana industry. *Journal of Crime and Justice*, 19(1), 75–92. National Drug Intelligence Center. (2004). *National drug threat assessment 2004.* Washington, DC: U.S. Department of Justice.

47. Elwood, William N. (1998). *"Fry": A study of adolescent use of embalming fluid with marijuana and tobacco.* Dallas, TX: Texas Commission on Alcohol and Drug Abuse. National Institute on Drug Abuse (2001, October). *Infofacts: Marijuana.* Washington, DC: National Institute on Drug Abuse.

48. Drug Enforcement Administration (2001, September). *Drug trafficking in the United States.* Washington, DC: Department of Justice. Hargraves, Gary (2000), Clandestine drug labs: Chemical time bombs. *FBI Law Enforcement Bulletin*, 69. Jonsson, Patrick (2003, March 21). Modern-day moonshine: Appalachia's new cottage industry: Meth. *Christian Science Monitor*, pp. 80–83.

49. Drug Enforcement Administration (2006, March). *National Drug Threat Assessement 2007.* Washington, DC: U.S. Department of Justice, p. 12.

50. National Institute on Drug Abuse (2003, January). *Infofacts: LSD.* Washington, DC: National Institute on Drug Abuse.

51. Drug Enforcement Administration (2001, September). *Club drugs: An update.* Washington, DC: U.S. Department of Justice.

52. Drug Enforcement Administration. (2003, May). *Drug intelligence brief: PCP: The threat remains.* Washington, DC: U.S. Department of Justice.

53. National Drug Intelligence Center. (2004). *National drug threat assessment 2004.* Washington, DC: U.S. Department of Justice. Drug Enforcement Administration (2001, September). *Club drugs: An update.* Washington, DC: U.S. Department of Justice.

54. Mark, Clayton. (1995, September). Where the world's crooks go to do their dirty laundry. *Christian Science Monitor*, p. 1.

55. Motivans, Mark. (2003, July). *Money laundering offenders, 1994–2001.* Washington, DC: U.S. Department of Justice. Office of National Drug Control Policy (2002, January). *ONCP fact sheet: International money laundering and asset forfeiture.* Washington, DC: Office of National Drug Control Policy. Wankel, Harold D. (1996, February 28). *DEA congressional testimony: Money laundering by drug trafficking organizations.* Washington, DC: U.S. Department of Justice.

chapter 14

Drugs and the Criminal Justice System

If I pull someone over for a traffic offense and they are act-ing really nervous, I usually ask if I can search their vehicle. Even though they may have drugs in their vehicle, most people still consent to the search. If they refuse to consent, then I usually call for a drug dog. When it arrives, the dog smells around the outside of the vehicle. If the dog hits on drugs, we have probable cause to conduct a search of the entire vehicle. You would not believe all the places I have found drugs. People have hidden drugs in their tires and inside hidden compartments in their dashboard, and one guy even hid cocaine in a false leg that he was wearing.

—*A sheriff's deputy from Gwinnett County, Georgia*

After you have completed this chapter, you will understand

● Attempts to control the production and/or cultivation of illicit drugs in foreign countries

● The role of law enforcement in drug interdiction

● Different types of street-level drug operations

● The process of asset forfeiture

● The consequences of mandatory minimum sentencing policies

● Drug courts as an alternative to standard sentencing

The criminal justice system in the United States plays a major role in our society's response to drug abuse. Essentially, it attempts to reduce the availability of illicit drugs to the general public and penalize the producers, distributors, and users of illicit drugs. This chapter will examine the principal strategies devised to accomplish these goals, including programs aimed at crop eradication, the control of precursor chemicals, efforts at interdiction of illicit drugs at our borders, the use of undercover operations, the use of asset forfeiture, punishments for those possessing or trafficking in illicit drugs, and the establishment of drug courts.

Law enforcement has always been, and remains, the predominant method of waging the "war on drugs" at the federal, state, and local levels. Of the billions of dollars spent, most of the money is spent on drug-law enforcement (Table 14.1). The goal of drug-law enforcement is to control the supply of illegal drugs by interrupting the source, transit, and distribution of drugs. Therefore, it is useful to examine drug-law enforcement in terms of four major activities: (1) source control, (2) interdiction, (3) street-level enforcement, and (4) the correctional system.

Source Control

Source control involves activities aimed at limiting the cultivation and production of illicit drugs in foreign countries. These activities include crop eradication, control of precursor chemicals, and the U.S. certification process.

One of the first major U.S.-led source control efforts occurred in the early 1970s in Turkey, where 80 percent of the heroin used in the United States at the time originated from opium poppies grown there. The opium was shipped to southern French port cities, where it was converted to heroin and then later smuggled into the United States—the "French Connection." In an attempt to reduce the amount of heroin coming into the United States, the United States and France offered Turkey $35 million to ban opium production and to help Turkish farmers develop new cash crops. Initially, this action did lead to a shortage of heroin on American streets in 1973. The decline in heroin production, however, did not last long. In 1974, Mexico became a primary source of opium

source control: Law enforcement actions that reduce or eliminate the cultivation and production of illicit drugs in foreign countries.

crop eradication: Programs in which opium poppies, coca plants, and marijuana plants are destroyed in their countries of origin, prior to transport overseas.

TABLE 14.1

U.S. federal drug control budget (in billions)—fiscal year 2008

Drug treatment (with research)	3.043
Drug prevention (with research)	1.575
Domestic law enforcement	3.652
International law enforcement	1.399
Interdiction	3.292
Total drug control budget	12.961

Source: Office of National Drug Control Policy (February, 2007). National drug control strategy: FY 2008 budget summary. Washington, DC: Office of National Drug Control Policy.

production, and in response, the U.S. government began to finance opium eradication programs in Mexico.[1] By the mid-1990s, U.S. officials estimated that 65 percent of heroin smuggled into America was produced from opium poppies cultivated in Colombia. Since then, the dominance of Colombian heroin trafficking has increased to even higher levels (Chapter 13).[2]

Crop Eradication

In the 1980s, the United States adopted a "king pin" strategy, designed to apprehend the top members of the world's largest drug organizations, with some success. By the late 1990s, most of the top leaders of the two largest drug cartels in Colombia, the Medellin and Cali, had been arrested. As a consequence, the drug trade in Latin America began to fragment into a number of smaller organizations with no clear leadership structure (Chapter 13).

A second strategy was developed to combat the new decentralized trafficking organizations through crop eradication. **Crop eradication** programs promoted the destruction of opium poppies, coca plants, and marijuana plants in their countries of origin. Eradication programs were driven by the premise that decreasing coca and poppy production would make cocaine and heroin more expensive and thus would decrease use. Crops were eradicated both manually and with herbicides. Herbicides were either sprayed or dropped from the air as pellets that melted into the soil when it would rain, and these methods continue today. From 1998 to 2002, the aerial spraying of coca and poppies in Colombia increased from less than 60,000 hectares (148,000 acres) to more than 120,000 hectares (296,000 acres).[3]

Many environmental groups believe that eradication programs have led to significant ecological damage.

The primary problem is that when an area is sprayed with a herbicide, growers simply move into another area, clear the land, and plant more coca or poppy plants. In South America, deforestation of the rain forest and severe erosion in mountainous areas have occurred. Proponents of crop eradication, on the other hand, claim that coca production is more harmful to the environment than crop eradication. Multiple harvests of coca on steep mountain slopes can accelerate soil erosion, and improper use of dangerous chemical fertilizers causes water contamination. In addition, the processing of coca leaves into cocaine paste involves a series of toxic chemicals that causes further environmental pollution.[4]

Crop eradication also has been criticized for disrupting the local economy of many rural regions in Latin America and creating tensions between peasant farmers and local governments. For many poor families in South America, the cultivation of coca and poppies is their only source of significant income. In 1996, for example, more than 50,000 peasants from several remote areas in southern Colombia converged on larger towns to protest the fumigation of their fields of coca and poppies. The demonstrators burned vehicles and tried to block local airstrips to disrupt the local economy. In confrontations with armed forces, two peasants were killed and several others were injured. To put a halt to the revolt, the Colombian army had to blow up the few roads leading to the main towns to obstruct the way of the demonstrators. Many of the farmers whose crops were destroyed simply moved deeper into the jungle and started cultivating coca in more inaccessible areas.[5]

To avoid a similar revolt, the Peruvian government in 2002 launched a financial plan, backed by the United States, to provide money for peasant farmers who voluntarily got rid of their coca crops. No soldiers or police were assigned to take part in the eradication effort. Their absence was intended to avoid conflict between the government and the approximately 400,000 families that subsisted directly or indirectly through coca production. Families received $150 in Peruvian currency for every hectare (2.47 acres) of destroyed coca. The Peruvian government also attempted to promote alternative crops for the farmers, such as corn, banana trees, and rubber. Even the peasants who have received money, however, have found it difficult to stop growing coca because no alternative crop is as lucrative. Unlike the wealthy Colombian drug traffickers, coca growers in South America live a life of poverty. The money that coca brings is vital to their existence.[6]

Whether or not crop eradication has been successful depends on whom one asks. On the one hand, according to many Third-World governments, eradication has been

Coca plants are destroyed in a crop eradication program in Colombia. These efforts are financed, in large part, by the U.S. Department of State through the Andean Counterdrug Initiative.

successful. The Bolivian government, for example, has claimed that the amount of land used for growing coca decreased from 127,000 hectares (314,000 acres) in 1997 to about 5,000 hectares (12,000 acres) in 2002 as a result of eradication programs.[7] On the other hand, empirical studies of both crop eradication and crop substitution programs have found that these programs have had little impact on the production of cocaine and opium. The available evidence has shown that at the global level, there rarely has been more than a 10 percent decrease of any one type of illicit crop in any given year.

Even when there is a reduction in the cultivation of a crop, such as coca or poppies, in one part of the world, there is often an increase in the cultivation in another part of the world. Crop eradication programs in Peru and Bolivia, for example, have led to an increase in coca production in Colombia. This is often called the "push down, pop up phenomenon" or the "balloon effect." Nonetheless, the U.S. government continues to endorse aerial spraying of coca and poppies as a strategy for disrupting the production of cocaine and heroin.[8]

Monitoring Precursor Chemicals

The monitoring and control of **precursor chemicals** and other substances used in the manufacture of illicit drugs is also a significant method of attacking illicit drug production before the drugs enter the market. With the exception of cannabis (see Chapter 7), every illicit drug requires an alteration of the natural product by specific chemicals before it reaches its final consumable form. Most of these chemicals are produced by legitimate companies, then diverted by illegitimate chemical companies or by criminal organizations.

Drug Enforcement Administration (DEA) agents regularly monitor and track large shipments of precursor chemicals. In one program called "Operation Purple," to reduce the illicit manufacture of cocaine in South America, the DEA monitors and tracks shipments of potassium permanganate, the chemical oxidizer of choice for cocaine production.[9] The DEA also commonly monitors shipments of acetic anhydride, the most commonly used chemical agent in heroin processing, and pseudoephedrine, the primary precursor chemical used in the production of methamphetamine. There is also an attempt to assist other countries in their monitoring and control of precursor chemicals, but many nations lack the capacity to determine whether the import or export of precursor chemicals is related to illicit drug production or to legitimate needs. The problem is complicated by the fact that precursor chemicals are often transshipped through third-party countries in an attempt to disguise their purpose or destination.

Certification

A third method by which the United States attempts to control the production of illicit drugs in foreign countries is through a certification process. Enacted by Congress in

Chemicals used in the manufacture of illicit drugs are sometimes hidden in ordinary chemical drums.

1986, **certification** is a process in which the U.S. government evaluates the cooperation of foreign countries in counter-drug efforts. Each March, the president is required to compile a list of countries that have been determined to be major illicit producing and/or drug transit countries. Countries on this list are then divided into three categories: (1) those that are fully compliant with U.S. counter-drug efforts ("certified"), (2) those not compliant with U.S. efforts ("decertified"), and (3) those that are noncompliant but certified based on vital U.S. national interests. If a country is decertified, U.S. law requires that all foreign aid be withheld until the president determines whether the country should be certified. In addition, U.S. representatives to multinational banks such as the World Bank and the International Monetary Fund are required to vote against any loans or grants to a decertified country.[10]

Many Latin American countries, however, feel that the certification concept is hypocritical. A prominent Venezuelan government official has spoken of the bitterness that many Latin Americans feel toward the certification policy: "How does the country which figures as the principal market for narcotics get off certifying the efforts of other nations in this area?" Critics in Latin American argue that it is, after all, U.S. citizens who make the choice to buy drugs, and it is the responsibility of the United States to curb that demand, not Latin American countries.[11]

Interdiction

The second aspect of drug-law enforcement is **interdiction**—that is, the attempt to prevent drugs from being smuggled across the U.S. border by deny-

precursor chemicals: Substances required for the production of illicit drugs. Examples are acetic anhydride and pseudoephedrine for the production of methamphetamine.

certification: The process by which the United States has the option of withholding foreign aid to a country if that country is judged to be noncompliant with U.S. counter-drug efforts, by virtue of its participation in major illicit drug production and/or trafficking.

interdiction: Efforts to prevent illicit drugs from being transported across the U.S. border.

ing drug smugglers the use of air, land, and maritime routes. Over the years, drug agents have witnessed a variety of unusual, if not bizarre, drug smuggling methods. Shipments of cocaine have been fashioned into plastic statues of the Virgin Mary, packed in hollow plaster shells shaped and painted to resemble yams, implanted in a man's thigh, and hidden beneath a shipment of iced fish fillets. Law enforcement officers in Florida once intercepted a shipment of boa constrictors from Colombia with their intestines stuffed with condoms full of cocaine. In 1994, federal agents at Kennedy Airport in New York noticed an emaciated and ailing sheepdog on a flight from Bogota, Colombia. Suspicious of the cargo, X-rays and surgery revealed that five pounds of cocaine in ten rubber balloons had been surgically implanted in the dog's abdomen. New York Police Department

detectives later arrested a twenty-two-year-old man from New Jersey after he came to claim the animal. The dog survived the surgery to remove the condoms and was taken to the Canine Enforcement Training Center in Front Royal, Virginia, where its handlers named it "Cokie."[12]

With tightened security after September 11, 2001, it has become difficult for drug traffickers to use air cargo as a method of smuggling drugs into the United States. In response, traffickers in South America have resorted to using women from Colombia and Peru to act as drug "mules." The female mules sometimes swallow as many as fifty condoms filled with cocaine or heroin and then board a flight on a commercial airline. They are often given a topical anesthetic to deaden the throat before they ingest the condoms and then are told to use laxatives to help them "retrieve" the condoms after reaching their destination. Unfortunately, these condoms sometimes break and leak into the stomach, causing a drug overdose and death. Most of these "mules" are desperate for money and enter the business willingly. There are, however, an increasing number of women who are forced into the drug trade. The traffickers will kidnap a woman's children or other family members and threaten to kill the hostages unless the woman successfully smuggles drugs into the United States.[13] Table 14.2 lists recent DEA drug seizures for cocaine, heroin, marijuana, methamphetamine, and hallucinogens.

Changes in airport security also have caused traffickers to scale back their smuggling of drugs through airports and redirect their drug shipments over the nation's highways. Most of this smuggling occurs at the U.S.–Mexican border, where drug traffickers use various types of vehicles to conceal their contraband, ranging from cars, commercial trucks, and tractor trailers to minivans. These vehicles are fitted with hidden compartments, known as "traps," where the drugs are concealed. In some cases, complex sequences of dashboard buttons and switches are required to provide access to concealed compartments in and/or under seats, in both the center and overhead consoles, or behind air-conditioning vents. In the spring of 2002, U.S. Customs agents discovered a new method of concealment at the southwest border in Arizona. More than fourteen pounds of marijuana were found in a hidden compartment located in the dash of a minivan. The packages of marijuana were wrapped in cotton and placed in a sealed rectangular mold made of a honey and wax mixture. The marijuana escaped detection by drug-detecting dogs.[14]

A police officer collects heroin capsules after displaying them during a news conference in Panama in 2004. A police operation uncovered some fifteen kilograms of heroin, one of the largest confiscations in Panama, from a group of five Colombians.

TABLE 14.2

Drug Seizures by the Drug Enforcement Administration, 2000–2006

DRUG	2000	2002	2004	2006
Cocaine (in kilograms)	58,674	63,640	117,854	69,826
Heroin (in kilograms)	546	710	672	805
Marijuana (in kilograms)	331,964	238,024	265,813	322,438
Methamphetamine (in kilograms)	1,771	1,353	1,659	1,711
Hallucinogens (in dosage units)	29,307,427	11,661,157	2,261,706	4,606,277

Note: One kilogram equals 2.2 pounds.

Source: Drug Enforcement Administration (2007). The System to Retrieve Information on Drug Evidence (STRIDE) Program. Washington, DC: Drug Enforcement Administration, U.S. Department of Justice.

Federal Agencies Involved in Interdiction

The primary federal agencies involved in drug interdiction include the DEA, the U.S. Customs and Border Protection Agency, the U.S. Coast Guard, and the U.S. military. Of these agencies, only the DEA has drug-law enforcement as its only responsibility. Employing more than 4,000 officers with the authority to make arrests and carry firearms, the DEA investigates major drug-law violators, enforces regulations governing the manufacture and dispensing of controlled substances, and performs various other functions to prevent and control drug trafficking. DEA agents also work overseas, where they engage in undercover operations in foreign countries, work in coop-

eration with foreign governments to apprehend major drug traffickers, help to train foreign law enforcement officials, and collect intelligence about general trends in drug trafficking, drug production (illicit farming operations and laboratories), and criminal organizations operating in the illicit drug trade.[15]

The U.S. Customs and Border Protection Agency, operating under the Department of Homeland Security, is responsible for curtailing the flow of illicit drugs across America's borders. More than 7,500 customs inspectors screen incoming travelers, conveyances, and cargo at more than 300 ports of entry across the United States, often working with drug-detection dogs. The Customs and Border Protection Agency also employs a number of special agents who are responsible for conducting investigations into drug smuggling and money laundering schemes. The agency maintains several specialized branches as well. The Marine Branch, for example, is responsible for interdicting drugs in nearshore waters by stopping and searching incoming vessels that behave suspiciously, especially small boats with large engines commonly referred to as "go-fast boats." The Air Branch is responsible for interdicting suspicious aircraft, such as small low-flying aircraft operating at night. Once a suspicious aircraft has been detected, it is normally tracked and forced down by high-speed chase planes and then searched. Customs inspectors are not hampered by constitutional protections that typically limit the power of other law enforcement agencies; they can search a person, vehicle, or container at ports of entry or near to a U.S. shoreline without probable cause.

The U.S. Coast Guard is the lead federal agency for maritime drug interdiction and shares responsibility for air interdiction with the U.S. Customs and Border Protection Agency. The Coast Guard is a key player in combating the flow of illegal drugs to the United States by denying

An X-ray view of a truck stopped at the Mexico–U.S. border with concealed packages filled with drugs (shown with arrow).

Members of the U.S. Coast Guard law enforcement team gather in Miami around more than 5,000 pounds of cocaine seized from a Honduran fishing boat off the coast of Colombia. The drugs were discovered hidden in compartments within the fuel tank, and eight Colombians were arrested. The 110-foot boat was later towed to Miami and confiscated.

The U.S. military supports the drug interdiction efforts of many federal and state drug enforcement agencies by providing air and ground observation and reconnaissance, environmental assessments, intelligence analysts and linguists, and transportation and engineering support. Military training teams also teach civilian law enforcement officers such skills as combat lifesaving, surveillance techniques, and advanced and tactical military operations that can be used in counter-drug operations. Military personnel can support counter-drug efforts, but they cannot search or arrest drug traffickers. Law enforcement agencies and the military both benefit from this relationship. Police are able to use military resources, and service members are able to practice their military skills in real-world situations.

The U.S. military is also active in drug interdiction by working with foreign militaries and law enforcement agencies in many drug-producing countries. It provides intelligence, strategic planning, and training for anti-drug operations in several Latin American countries, such as Colombia, Mexico, Peru, and Bolivia. A key element of the military's anti-drug program in Latin America is its Tactical Analysis Teams (TATs), made up of a small number of U.S. Special Forces and military intelligence personnel. These teams gather intelligence and plan operations that are carried out by host nations and DEA agents.

Critics have claimed that there are a number of problems inherent in the use of TATs. First, TATs are aiding and training troops of foreign militaries that have documented records of human rights violations without insisting on fundamental reforms in those countries. A second problem with the use of TATs is that, in some cases, U.S. military personnel actually may be training future drug traffickers. In several Latin American countries, such as Bolivia, most of the American-trained army personnel are required to serve only one year in the military. Upon release from the service, some of these soldiers work for the drug traffickers, who pay substantial salaries, or become drug traffickers themselves, after having learned skills useful in avoiding drug interdiction by legitimate authorities.[17]

The Posse Comitatus Act of 1878 forbids the military to be used as a law enforcement agency within the borders of the United States. The law was designed originally to bar federal troops from policing southern states after the Civil War and to protect Americans against abuses by their own military by dictating that federal troops could not enter private land or dwellings and could not detain or search civilians. In 1988, Congress expanded the National Guard's role in drug interdiction and allowed the guard to be actively involved in drug-law enforcement.

smugglers the use of maritime routes in the "transit zone," a six-million-square-mile area including the Caribbean, the Gulf of Mexico, and the Eastern Pacific. Coast Guard ships can stop and board any maritime vessel operating within a twelve-mile radius of U.S. shoreline. Drug interdictions by the Coast Guard account for about 50 percent of all government seizures of cocaine each year, and Coast Guard seizures in 2006 had an estimated value of $3.1 billion. The U.S. Coast Guard also organizes maritime interdiction efforts with other foreign countries. Coast Guard cooperation with the Mexican Navy in 2002, for example, was instrumental in seizing over thirty thousand pounds of cocaine destined for American towns and cities. Like Customs inspectors, Coast Guard personnel do not have to establish probable cause before boarding and searching a vessel at sea.[16]

How does the National Guard circumvent the Posse Comitatus Act? The key to National Guard involvement in drug operations is the word "federal" in the language of Posse Comitatus Act. Since 1912, the National Guard has had a two-tier mission to serve both the state and federal governments. Guard units involved in anti-drug operations typically work for the state government under the supervision of a state governor. Therefore, while the soldiers' salary and other benefits are paid by the federal government, it is argued that they are not bound by the Posse Comitatus Act. Critics claim that the National Guard is a federal agency and that when the guard is involved in drug-law enforcement operations, it is violating federal law.[18]

Profiling and Drug-Law Enforcement

Over the years, drug-law enforcement agents have often developed "drug courier profiles" to help them identify potential drug smugglers. In *United States v. Sokolow* (1989), the U.S. Supreme Court ruled that drug courier profiles at airports could be used as a legitimate law-enforcement tool, the Fourth Amendment to the U.S. Constitution notwithstanding. In this case, Andrew Sokolow, a young African American male dressed in a black jumpsuit with gold jewelry, purchased two airline tickets in Miami with $1,200 in cash. Sokolow flew from Honolulu to Miami, planning to return to Hawaii forty-eight hours later. He also was traveling under a false name, did not check any luggage, and appeared very nervous. Drug agents stopped him at the Honolulu airport and used a drug-sniffing dog, which led them to 1,063 grams of cocaine in his carry-on luggage. Chief Justice William H. Reinquist stated, "While a trip from Honolulu to Miami, standing alone, is not a cause for any sort of suspicion, here there was more: Surely few residents of Honolulu travel from that city for twenty hours to spend forty-eight hours in Miami during the month of July." In a seven-to-two decision, the Court ruled that the drug courier profile could provide a "reasonable basis" for officials to suspect that a person is transporting drugs (Drugs . . . in Focus).[19]

The most significant criticism of drug courier profiling is that some law enforcement officers have created their own profiles based solely on race, ethnicity, or

racial profiling: A practice of arresting or detaining an individual for possible drug violations, based on race, ethnicity, or national origin rather than on the individual's behavior.

national origin rather than on the behavior of an individual, a practice that has become known as **racial profiling.** In the late 1990s, racial profiling became a major topic of controversy. National and local media reports often proclaimed that racial profiling was a significant social problem, and national surveys confirmed that most Americans agreed. In a 1999 Gallup Poll, more than half the Americans polled believed that police actively engaged in the practice of racial profiling, and 81 percent said that they disapproved of the practice. When responses to survey questions were broken down by race, 56 percent of whites and 77 percent of African Americans believed that racial profiling was a pervasive problem.[20]

One of the most common complaints about racial profiling was the claim that police were stopping vehicles simply because the race of the driver did not appear to "match" the type of automobile he or she was driving. In a widely cited case, Dr. Elmo Randolph, a forty-two-year-old African American dentist, was stopped more than fifty times over an eight-year span while driving his BMW car to his office near Newark. New Jersey state troopers, believing that Dr. Randolph was "driving the wrong car," would pull Dr. Randolph over, check his license, and ask him if he had any drugs or weapons in his car. Randolph claims that he did not drive at excessive speeds and that he had never been issued a ticket.[21]

The experience of Dr. Randolph and other minority drivers in New Jersey led the New Jersey State Police in 1999 to conduct a study on the race and ethnicity of persons stopped by state troopers. They found that New Jersey state troopers had indeed engaged in racial profiling along the New Jersey Turnpike. Although individuals of color comprised 13.5 percent of the New Jersey Turnpike population, they represented 41 percent of those stopped on the turnpike and 77 percent of those searched. Studies in other U.S. states also have found that police regularly engage in racial profiling.[22]

Police officers who defend racial profiling often believe that African Americans, Latinos, Asians, and other minorities are more likely to carry drugs than their white counterparts. Several studies, however, suggest that African Americans and Latinos are no more likely than whites to be in the possession of illicit drugs. One study of motorists on an interstate highway in Maryland found that 28 percent of African American drivers and passengers who were searched were found with contraband compared with 29 percent of white drivers.[23] In New York in 1988 and 1989, 13 percent of whites were arrested for possessing illicit drugs

Drugs . . . in Focus

Drug Smuggler Profiles

Profile for Commercial Airline Smuggling

1. Arriving from an identified source country
2. Traveling alone
3. Traveling by an unusual itinerary, such as a rapid turnaround time
4. Carrying little luggage or a large-quantity suitcase.
5. Purchasing airline tickets with cash
6. Displaying unusual nervousness
7. Passenger tries to avoid questioning
8. Passenger makes contradictory statements during questioning

Profile for Automobile Smuggling

1. Unusually wide tires
2. Rear of vehicle visibly weighted down
3. Welding marks along edges of vehicle
4. Accumulation of trash inside vehicle that suggests long stretches without stopping
5. Lack of vehicle registration
6. Spare tire in back seat
7. Driver displaying unusual nervousness
8. Signs of drug use
9. Conflicting or inconsistent stories concerning destination among the driver and passengers

Profile for Maritime Smuggling

1. No fishing gear or nets visible on fishing vessel
2. Crew does not wave back to passing law enforcement vessel or aircraft
3. Erratic course change when sighted by law enforcement vessel or aircraft
4. Not sailing in usual shipping lanes or fishing grounds
5. Hatches padlocked and extra fuel drums on deck
6. Vessel does not use running lights at night
7. Vessel does not respond to radio contact or claims radio trouble
8. Vessel does not fly nationality flag

Profile for Small Aircraft Smuggling

1. Aircraft landing or flying after dark
2. Propellers, undersurface, and lower sides of aircraft pitted or scratched with grass stains or dirt from landing on grass fields or dirt roads
3. Aircraft parked far from airport offices or in a remote part of the airfield
4. Van, truck, or motor home camper parked near aircraft
5. Factory-installed long-range fuel tanks
6. Aircraft windows covered by curtains, tape, or other material
7. Pilot or passengers reluctant to leave aircraft unattended when refueling or ground servicing
8. Pilots or passengers showing large amounts of cash when paying for fuel or parts
9. Pilots or passengers reluctant to discuss points of origin or point of destination
10. Removal of passenger seats inside the aircraft

Profile for Postal Package Smuggling

1. Heavily taped packages
2. Packages that smell of masking agents such as coffee or perfume
3. False return addresses or zip codes
4. Packages originating from a source country
5. Packages sent from person to person
6. Packages with handwritten labels

Sources: Langan, Mark T. (1996). Profiling postal packages, *FBI Law Enforcement Bulletin, 65* (2.3), pp. 17–21. Macdonald, John M., and Kennedy, Jerry (1983). *Criminal investigation of drug offenses: The narc's manual.* Springfield, IL: Charles C. Thomas. *United States v. Sokolow,* 490 U.S. 1 (1989).

compared with 11 percent of African Americans and 11 percent of Latinos.[24] A study of drug interdiction at major U.S. airports, found that African Americans (6 percent) and Latinos (3 percent) were less likely to possess illicit contraband than whites (7 percent). In 2003, President George W. Bush banned racial and ethnic profiling at all federal agencies with law enforcement powers under a Justice Department directive. The only exception applies to investigations involving terrorism and national security.[25]

Street-Level Drug-Law Enforcement

As the third aspect of drug-law enforcement, street-level drug-law enforcement is the responsibility of federal agencies, state agencies, or local sheriff's and police departments. Increasingly, these different agencies are joining forces and working together to form multijurisdictional drug task forces. Most of these task forces are coalitions of five or more local and state agencies that work closely with federal law enforcement agencies. Multijurisdictional task forces allow agencies at different levels of government to share funds, personnel, and intelligence and allow drug agents to track drug traffickers across many different jurisdictions. Nationwide, an estimated 21 percent of local police departments and 40 percent of sheriffs' offices have had one or more officers assigned full time to a drug task force.[26] Four drug-law enforcement operations used by police departments to apprehend drug offenders are (1) the reverse sting, (2) the controlled buy, (3) the undercover buy, and (4) the "knock and talk."

The **reverse sting** is a drug-law enforcement operation in which undercover agents pose as drug dealers and sell a controlled substance or imitation version of a controlled substance to buyers. Community policing programs have made reverse stings popular because such operations can be used as a method of "cleaning up" a neighborhood. The reverse sting operation also makes money for law enforcement because asset forfeiture laws allow agencies to keep at least part of the proceeds made in these operations. The reverse sting has been criticized on the grounds that such operations attack only the demand side of the drug problem. Drug abusers are arrested, but the drug dealers or drug traffickers are not.

Undercover operations frequently involve the use of an informant. In the **controlled buy** operation, an undercover informant buys the drug under the supervision of the police. The informant may be a paid informant or a person who has been convinced by agents to "roll over" on other traffickers because they themselves have been charged with the possession or trafficking of an illicit drug. In the latter case, criminal charges against the informant may be either reduced or dropped for their participation in the operation. After agents have gained confidence in the informant, the informant is allowed to set up a controlled buy. Before the informant enters the dwelling in which the buy is to take place, he or she is usually searched to ensure that there are no drugs on his or her person before conducting the buy. After the buy has been made, the informant is again searched and asked to turn over the drugs bought in the transaction. To protect the identity of the informant, arrests are usually not made at the time of the buy. Warrants are obtained and later executed within ten days.

There are two types of **undercover buy** operations: (1) the buy-bust and (2) the buy-walk. During a buy-bust operation, an undercover agent makes a buy, and immediately thereafter, the seller is arrested for the drug sale. During a buy-bust, an undercover agent sets up a drug deal for a specified time and location. A cover team monitors the transaction via surveillance equipment, which is either hidden on the agent or in the room. After a "bust signal" is given by the undercover agent, a cover team rapidly moves in to make the arrest. Generally, the undercover agent is also "arrested" to protect his or her identity.

In a buy-walk operation, an undercover agent buys drugs but does not arrest the dealer at the time of the deal. The drug deal is used to obtain a warrant for the dealer that is served at a later time. The advantage of this operation is that it protects the identity of the undercover agent while at the same time ensuring his or her immediate safety during the time of the operation. Buy-walk operations are often used when a drug deal takes place at the residence of a drug dealer and officer safety is a concern.

The **knock and talk** is an operation that is used when officials receive information that an individual is dealing drugs but do not have probable cause to seek a search warrant. In this case, agents arrive at a suspect's residence, knock on the door, identify themselves as police officers, and ask permission to enter the residence. Once inside, agents ask the suspect if any one in the residence is producing or dealing drugs. After the suspect responds to the allegations, agents ask for permission to search the residence for illicit drugs.

The element of surprise obviously is an important factor in the success of the knock and talk. If there has been no prior warning, suspects do not expect law enforcement officers to knock on their door and confront them with an allegation. To "confuse" suspects,

---

reverse sting: A law-enforcement operation in which an undercover agent posing as a drug dealer sells a controlled substance, or an imitation of it, to a buyer.

controlled buy: A law-enforcement operation in which an undercover informant buys an illicit drug under the supervision of the police.

undercover buy: A law-enforcement operation in which an undercover law-enforcement agent buys an illicit drug in order to arrest the drug seller. The two types are the buy-bust and the buy-walk.

knock and talk: A law-enforcement operation in which agents ask for permission to search a residence for illicit drugs after asking the suspect whether any one in the residence has been engaged in drug production or dealing.

agents often make misleading allegations. To find evidence against a marijuana dealer, agents may state that they believe the suspect is producing methamphetamine at his residence. Knowing that such charges are ridiculous, even though they are dealing in marijuana, suspects usually allow a **consent search**. Agents state that approximately 75 to 85 percent of drug dealers waive their constitutional right to privacy and consent to a search. When later asked why they consent to such a search, dealers often state, "I thought I would have been in worse trouble if I didn't let you search" or "I didn't know I had the right to refuse." Once evidence of illicit drug trafficking is found, agents typically make an arrest or return with a **search warrant**.

Asset Forfeiture

Asset forfeiture is the process by which the government seizes cash, cars, homes, and other property that it claims are the result of criminal activity. Forfeiture is particularly useful in drug-law enforcement because it reduces the financial incentive to reap the often enormous profits involved in drug trafficking and disrupts a drug trafficking organization by seizing any vehicles, boats, planes, or property used to transport or produce illicit drugs. As shown in Table 14.3, the DEA made 17,362 domestic seizures of nondrug property, valued at approxi-

TABLE 14.3

DEA asset seizures in 2004

TYPE OF ASSET	NUMBER OF SEIZURES	VALUE
Cash	8,913	$324,240,827
Weapons	878	289,666
Real property	582	106,388,307
Vehicles	4,895	70,026,695
Vessels	94	3,917,839
Aircraft	39	12,293,970
Other	1,961	28,240,021
Total	17,362	645,397,325

Note: Total assets seized in 2005 and 2006 have values of $496,000,000 and $507,000,000, respectively.

Source: Drug Enforcement Administration (2005). DOJ Computerized Asset Tracking System, calendar year 2004. Washington, DC: Drug Enforcement Administration, U.S. Department of Justice. Updated information courtesy of the Drug Enforcement Administration, 2007.

Quick Concept Check 14.1

Understanding Drug-Law Enforcement Operations

Check your understanding of drug-law enforcement operations by matching the descriptions on the left with the types of operations on the right.

1. An undercover informant makes a drug buy under the supervision of the police.

2. Undercover agents pose as drug dealers and sell a controlled substance or imitation controlled substance to buyers.

3. A police officer, posing as a drug abuser, buys illicit drugs from a suspected drug dealer. The dealer is later arrested for drug trafficking.

4. Agents arrive at a suspect's residence, identify themselves as police officers, and ask permission to enter the residence.

5. Colombian drug control officials spray herbicides on fields of coca.

6. Drug smugglers are apprehended outside Miami and their "go-fast" boat is confiscated by authorities.

a. the knock and talk
b. the undercover buy
c. the controlled buy
d. the reverse sting
e. interdiction and asset forfeiture
f. crop eradication

Answers: 1. c   2. d   3. b   4. a   5. f   6. e

consent search: A procedure in which law-enforcement agents ask and receive permission from a suspect to inspect a residence or vehicle for illicit drugs.

search warrant: A court-ordered document providing law-enforcement agents the right to search a residence or vehicle for illicit drugs.

asset forfeiture: A process used in drug-law enforcement in which cash, automobiles, homes, and other property are seized if these items have been acquired or used as a result of criminal activity.

mately $645 million in 2004 as a result of drug investigations.[27]

There are two types of forfeitures: criminal (*in personam*) forfeitures and civil (*in rem*) forfeitures. The distinction between criminal and civil forfeitures is based upon whether the penalty involves a person or a thing. Criminal forfeitures are primarily against a specific person and result after a conviction for a crime to which the forfeited property is related. This can occur upon showing during the course of sentencing or plea-bargaining that the property is contraband (illegally obtained through the profit of a crime). Such criminal forfeitures are subject to all the constitutional and statutory procedural safeguards available under criminal law, and the forfeiture case and the criminal case are both tried together. Forfeiture must be included in the indictment of the defendant, which means that the grand jury must find a basis for the forfeiture, as well as punishment for the criminal offense itself.

Civil forfeitures, on the other hand, are *in rem* actions based upon the unlawful use of property irrespective of its owner's culpability. Traditionally, civil forfeiture has operated on the premise that the property itself is the guilty party, and the fact that the forfeiture of the property affects an individual's property rights is not considered. With civil forfeiture, the offender does not need to be convicted or even charged with a crime because it is contended that the property "itself" is guilty. The property owner's guilt or innocence is therefore irrelevant, and civil forfeiture proceedings can be pursued independently or in lieu of a criminal trial.

Forfeitures have existed for thousands of years and are traceable to biblical and pre-Judeo-Christian times. Early English law recognized a kind of forfeiture known as "deodand," which required forfeiture of the instrument of a person's death. The principle was based on the legal fiction that the instrument causing death was deemed "guilty property" capable of doing further harm. For example, if a domesticated animal killed a person, it would be forfeited, usually to the King, whether or not its owner was responsible. The original purpose for creating this legal fiction was to satisfy the superstition that a dead person would not lie in tranquility unless the "evil property" was confiscated and viewed by the deceased's kin as the object of their retribution. The King often used forfeiture to enhance royal revenues, and this corrupt practice led to the statutory abolishment of deodand in England in 1846.[28]

Throughout history, forfeiture laws have arisen primarily during perceived crises. The Confiscation Act of 1862, passed during the Civil War, authorized the use of *in rem* civil procedures against southern rebels and their sympathizers who possessed property in the North. The law stated that the properties seized were to be used for supporting the Union cause in waging its war. It was a response to a Confederate law that confiscated the southern properties belonging to supporters of the Union. It was not until the late twentieth century that civil forfeiture was "rediscovered" to address a pressing social concern: the war on drugs. The primary justification for extending forfeiture into the realm of drugs was one of deterrence. Legislators believed that imprisonment of drug traffickers often was treated as a mere cost of business, and therefore, forfeiture could be used to attempt to reduce the profits of drug transactions and topple drug trafficking organizations.

The 1970 Comprehensive Drug Abuse Prevention and Control Act provided, in part, for the forfeiture of property used in connection with controlled substances. In 1978, the law was expanded to include all profits from drug trafficking and all assets purchased with drug profits as items subject to forfeiture. The scope of the statue was further amended in 1984 to include all property that was used, or intended to be used, in a drug offense, and every drug offense, from simple possession to mass distribution, could trigger forfeiture. In recent years, civil asset forfeiture has become the weapon of choice in combatting drug abuse in America.

Police officials argue that civil forfeiture allows them to combat drug crime by attacking the economic viability of drug trafficking organizations while at the same time raising money for future law enforcement operations. Critics argue that forfeiture laws distort law enforcement priorities. In many states, local, state and federal agencies have pooled personnel and resources to form multiagency drug task forces. Many of these task forces finance themselves, at least in part, through asset forfeiture. By allowing such agencies to rely on asset forfeiture as a source of revenue, critics claim, the law enforcement priorities are shifted from efforts toward crime control to "funding raids" (see Portrait).

While it is claimed that forfeiture promotes ordinary law enforcement business while at the same time raising money, 80 percent of seizures are unaccompanied by any criminal prosecution.[29] This may stem from the fact that, for many law enforcement agencies, civil forfeiture creates a temptation to depart from legitimate law enforcement goals in order to maximize funding. Some police departments now prefer to arrest drug buyers rather than drug sellers by employing a "reverse sting." The chief attraction of which is the confiscation of a buyer's cash rather than a seller's drugs.

Supporters of forfeiture claim that the lack of criminal prosecutions in such a large number of

Policing for Profit—The Death of Donald Scott

On October 2, 1992, a task force composed of Los Angeles County sheriff's deputies, DEA agents, and U.S. Park Service officers executed a search warrant on California millionaire Donald Scott's 250-acre estate. The search warrant was based on information from an informant that marijuana was being grown on Scott's land.

The task force arrived at Scott's house around 9:00 A.M. and broke down the door. Scott's wife claimed that the deputies pushed her from the kitchen into the living room, and then she screamed, "Don't shoot me. Don't kill me." The noise awakened Donald Scott from his sleep, and he came down the stairs holding a .38 caliber snub-nosed revolver over his head. When he pointed it in the direction of the deputies, they shot and killed him. When Scott's wife ran to the body, drug agents "hustled her out of the house." Recorded phone conversations also show that while Scott lay dead or dying in a pool of blood, police used his phone to make calls and answered a call from one of Scott's neighbors, telling the neighbor that Scott was "busy." A search of

Scott's ranch did not find one trace of marijuana or any other illicit drug.

The Ventura County District Attorney's Office concluded that the Sheriff's Department was motivated, at least in part, by a desire to seize and forfeit Scott's land for the government. Deputies and DEA agents knew that Scott's estate was an extremely valuable piece of real estate, and most of the proceeds from the sale of the property would go to the Sheriff's Department. In fact, sheriff's deputies had several documents on their desk that estimated the amount of money the department could get for the sale of Scott's land.

The investigation also showed that the search warrant that was used in the drug raid was not supported by probable cause. The District Attorney's office recommended that, in the future, when preparing search warrant affidavits, law enforcement officers should not compromise their objectivity based upon forfeiture concerns. Regardless of whether a given search warrant may result in the forfeiture of valuable property, officers should ensure that there is adequate probable cause.

Not surprisingly, Scott's death gen-

erated several lawsuits. Scott's widow and four of his children filed a $100 million wrongful death suit against the county and the federal government. After eight years, attorneys for Los Angeles County and the federal government finally agreed to award the family $5 million in return for dropping the wrongful death lawsuit.

The Sheriff's Department still maintains that its deputies did nothing wrong and the sheriff himself sued Ventura County's District Attorney for slander and defamation. A state appeals court declared that the district attorney was within his First Amendment rights when he criticized the Sheriff's Department. The court ordered the sheriff to pay the district attorney $50,000 in legal fees. The sheriff declared bankruptcy, and no payments were ever made.

Sources: Bradbury, Michael D. (1993). Report on the death of Donald Scott. Office of the District Attorney, Ventura, CA, March 30, 1993. Ciotti, Paul (2000). Ranch-coveting officials settle for killing owner, WorldNetDaily.com, January 23, 2000.

forfeiture cases is simply an indication that police and prosecuting attorneys are using the process as a bargaining chip in plea-bargaining negotiations. Defendants may be given the choice of not fighting the civil forfeiture procedure in exchange for avoiding criminal prosecution. This type of arrangement would benefit both the prosecutor and the prosecuted. The government would be able to "punish" defendants in legally weak cases that involve inadmissible or insufficient evidence, and the defendant would escape the monetary and social costs of a criminal conviction. Advocates of forfeiture also argue that forfeiture is an effective tool because it deters criminal activity, saves taxpayers' money by allowing law enforcement to self-fund many of their operations, and increases police officer morale.[30]

Drugs and the Correctional System

Most inmates in U.S. prisons and jails are serving time for drug-law violations (Table 14.4). From 1995 to 2001, the number of drug offenders in state prisons increased by 15 percent, and as shown in Figure 14.1, the number of drug offenders serving time in federal prisons increased from 16 percent in 1970 to 54 percent in 2007. This surge in incarceration rates of drug offenders has been generated by an intensified effort to step up drug-law enforcement as well as the prosecution and punishment of drug offenders. In 1987, drug arrests were 7 percent of the total of all arrests reported to the FBI; by 2002, drug arrests had risen to 11 percent of all

TABLE 14.4

Inmates serving time in federal prison by type of offense

Offense	Number	Percentage
Drug offense	96,139	53.5%
Weapons, explosives, arson	25,590	14.2%
Immigration violation	19,358	10.8%
Robbery	9,607	5.3%
Extortion, fraud, bribery	7,678	4.3%
Burglary, larceny, property offense	6,831	3.8%
Homicide, aggravated assault, kidnapping	5,557	3.1%
Sex offense	4,281	2.3%
Banking and insurance, counterfeiting, embezzlement	1,018	0.6%
Violations related to courts and corrections	747	0.4%
Continuing criminal enterprise	576	0.3%
National security violation	98	0.1%
Miscellaneous	2,170	1.2%

Source: Federal Bureau of Prisons (2007, February). *Quick facts about the bureau of prisons.* Washington, DC: Federal Bureau of Prisons, U.S. Department of Justice.

mandatory minimum sentencing: A policy that requires a judge to impose a fixed minimal term in prison for individuals convicted of certain crimes, regardless of the individual's role in the crime or other mitigating circumstances.

arrests. Arrest rates for drug-related violations have continued to increase at a time when drug use has been declining in the United States (see Chapter 2).

State and federal authorities also have enacted a greater number of criminal laws with respect to the selling and possession of illicit drugs, and judges have imposed lengthier prison sentences for drug offenders. At the same time, little attempt has been made to deal with drug dependence among inmates. Inmates who are alcohol and drug abusers are likely to repeat their criminal behavior, be arrested on future occasions, and receive even lengthier sentences as repeat offenders. The result has been a dramatic rise in the nation's prison population since the 1980s.[31]

Mandatory Minimum Sentencing

No other legislative policy has contributed more to the increase in the number of drug offenders in U.S. prisons than the policy of mandatory minimum sentencing. Essentially, **mandatory minimum sentencing** requires that a judge impose a fixed minimal term in prison for individuals convicted of certain crimes, regardless of the individual's role in the crime or other mitigating circumstances. Guidelines for sentences are based on the type of drug, the weight of a drug, and the number of prior convictions, and offenders are required to serve their entire sentence without parole. Under current federal law, for example, anyone convicted of selling 500 grams of powder cocaine receives a minimum prison sentence of five years. A judge can issue a sentence shorter than the mandatory

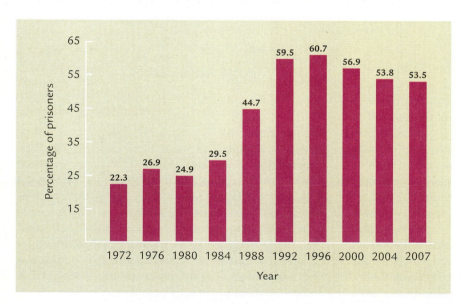

FIGURE 14.1

Percentage of prisoners who are drug offenders in federal prison from 1972 to 2007.

Source: Federal Bureau of Prisons (2007, March). *Quick facts about the bureau of prisons.* Washington, DC: Federal Bureau of Prisons, U.S. Department of Justice.

minimum only if the defendant provides "substantial assistance" or cooperation in the prosecution of another offender. This means that if the defendant implicates someone else in a crime (rightly or wrongly), he or she can possibly escape a mandatory sentence. Even then, however, the prosecutor, not the judge, has the power to decide whether this "assistance" is valuable enough to warrant a reduction in sentence.

Proponents of mandatory sentencing believe that the policy is an effective deterrent to drug use and drug trafficking because it enhances awareness of the consequences of breaking the law and keeps drug offenders off the streets. Supporters of tough sentences for drug crimes claim that the "drug epidemic" has had a devastating effect on many communities, and the law needs to protect these vulnerable communities by keeping drug offenders in prison. Mandatory sentences also make the task of judges easier by allowing each offender to be sentenced equally under the law. Judges no longer have to weigh conflicting evidence in the course of deciding how much time a convicted offender would spend in jail or prison. In addition, mandatory sentences aid prosecutors and police because such lengthy sentences tend to persuade lower-level drug dealers to testify against upper-level ones.

Critics of mandatory sentences maintain that such sentences are one of the principal reasons that the U.S. prison population has quadrupled since 1980. Over two million people are now in prison in the United States, placing the United States as the leading nation in terms of the percentage of incarcerated citizens. Mandatory minimum sentencing has, according to critics, filled our prisons with minor players, such as drug abusers, rather than major drug traffickers. The cost of building and maintaining a prison system to hold drug offenders sentenced under mandatory minimums has skyrocketed, with the federal government's annual prison budget now exceeding $1 billion and the annual prison budgets of U.S. states such as New York and Texas also exceeding $1 billion. Critics claim that as federal and state governments continue to spend billions of dollars on prisons, they have neglected other social needs, such as drug-abuse prevention and education. Several U.S. states now have faster-growing prison budgets than drug-abuse education budgets, a trend that is particularly disturbing given that spending more money on treatment, education, and other social programs actually could reduce the number of persons who abuse drugs.[32]

The court system in the United States is greatly burdened with the large number of cases that involve drug-law violations. The establishment of drug courts is an effort to help ease this burden.

In the last several years, there has been a movement to overturn or modify mandatory sentencing laws and focus on other methods to reduce the number of drug abusers in the United States. Families Against Mandatory Minimums (FAMM), founded in 1991, and a growing number of other organizations, such as the U.S. Sentencing Commission, the American Psychological Association, the National Association of Criminal Defense Lawyers, and the American Bar Association, have endorsed and promoted the end of mandatory sentencing (Drugs . . . in Focus).

Since 1993, at least six U.S. states have repealed or reformed their mandatory sentencing laws. In Michigan, possession with intent to deliver more than 650 grams of heroin or cocaine once carried a mandatory life sentence with no chance of parole. This law now has been changed to twenty years to life, with the possibility of parole after fifteen years. Other U.S. states are beginning a policy shift from punishment to treatment for drug offenders. California recently passed a law that imposes treatment rather than imprisonment for many first-time drug possession offenses. A drug conviction is then removed from the offender's record if he or she completes a treatment program. Arizona has established a similar program where individuals convicted of drug possession are placed on probation and assigned to drug treatment rather than prison. As prison overcrowding increases, policymakers will need to consider whether mandatory minimum sentences are the best means of achieving drug control objectives, and if so, at what cost.[33]

Drugs . . . in Focus

Penalties for Crack versus Penalties for Cocaine: A Racial Disparity?

Under the 1986 Anti-Drug Abuse Act, the penalties for possession of crack (the smokable form of cocaine) are much more severe than those for possession of cocaine itself (the powder form), though the effects of both drugs are very similar. A mandatory minimum prison sentence of five years is imposed upon conviction of possessing more than 500 grams of powder forms of cocaine, whereas the possession of as little as 5 grams of crack can result in the same penalty. In 1988, the federal penalty for possession of more than 5 grams of cocaine powder was set at a minimum of one year imprisonment; the penalty for possessing an equivalent amount of crack was set at a minimum of five years.

This disparity, according to critics of this policy, has resulted in far more African Americans in prison for five years or more than white drug offenders. Why? Statistics show that whites are more likely to snort or inject cocaine, whereas African Americans are more likely to smoke cocaine in its cheaper crack form. The differential effects of drug-law enforcement for the two forms of cocaine are reflected in a drug offense inmate population that is currently divided along racial lines. On the one hand, 90 percent of crack cocaine convictions involve African Americans; on the other, nearly two-thirds of powder cocaine abusers in the United States are white. Moreover, it is more common for offenses relating to the possession of powder cocaine to be prosecuted under state regulations, under which mandatory minimum sentences frequently do not apply.

Recently, federal officials have recommended a smaller gap between the two circumstances. One proposal is to raise the five-year sentence threshold in crack cocaine cases from 5 grams to somewhere between 25 and 75 grams and lower the threshold for powder cocaine cases from 500 grams down to somewhere between 125 and 375 grams. The gap would still remain, but the disparity would be far less than is presently in force.

Sources: Hatsukami, Dorothy K., and Fischman, Marian W. (1996). Crack cocaine and cocaine hydrochloride: Are the differences myth or reality? *Journal of the American Medical Association, 276,* 1580–1588. Wren, Christopher S. (1997, July 22). Reno and top drug official urge smaller gap in cocaine sentences. *The New York Times,* pp. A1, A12.

Drug Courts

Drug courts are specialized courts designed to handle adult, nonviolent offenders with substance abuse problems, incorporating an intensely supervised drug treatment program as an alternative to standard sentencing. Several of the characteristics of drug courts include early identification and placement of eligible participants, drug treatment with clearly defined rules and goals, a nonadversarial approach, a monitoring of abstinence, judicial involvement and interaction with the participants, and a team approach in which judges, defense attorneys, prosecutors, probation officers, and treatment counselors coordinate their efforts. Those offenders who complete the program successfully may have their charges dropped or sentences revoked, whereas unsuccessful participants are returned to the regular court system and face possible imprisonment. Since the first drug court began operation in Florida in 1989, more than 1,600 drug courts have come into operation across the United States.[34]

The first step in the drug court program begins with defense attorneys, probation officers, or prosecutors referring a potential candidate to the drug court itself. A probation officer then screens candidates for eligibility. Candidates must be judged (using a screening instrument) to be serious drug abusers, cannot be on parole, and cannot have a prior serious or violent felony conviction. When he or she agrees to enter the program, the candidate waives his or her right to a jury and agrees to enter a treatment program for a year, during which he or she is subject to random drug tests. Participants are supervised by a probation officer to ensure that they adhere to program rules.

Numerous studies have shown that drug court programs are successful. First of all, they decrease the

drug courts: Specialized court systems that handle adult, nonviolent offenders of drug laws, incorporating a supervised drug treatment program as an alternative to standard criminal sentencing.

rate of criminal recidivism (repeated arrests). In a sample of 17,000 drug court graduates nationwide within one year of graduating from the program, only 16 percent had been rearrested and charged with a felony offense, approximately one-third the level observed in drug offenders not participating in a drug court. Second, they are cost effective. Approximately $250 million in incarceration costs are saved each year in New York State alone by diverting 18,000 non-violent drug offenders into treatment. Third, drug courts increase the length of time an individual remains in treatment. The coercive power of the criminal justice system with respect to getting into treatment and staying in treatment is dramatic. Ordinarily, between 40 percent and 80 percent of drug abusers drop out of treatment within ninety days, and between 80 percent and 90 percent drop out within twelve months. In sharp contrast, more than two-thirds of drug-court participants complete a treatment program lasting a year or more. The benefits of drug court programs have been demonstrated in nonurban as well as urban communities (Figure 14.2).[35]

Clearly, the drug court movement represents a shift away from a criminal justice policy oriented toward punishing drug users to a policy that focuses on treatment and recovery. Several U.S. states have begun to develop driving under intoxication (DUI) courts, whereas other U.S. states are expanding the drug treatment programs within their correctional facilities.

According to experts in the field of drug-abuse treatment, the mandated treatment approach in drug-court programs is more likely to result in a successful outcome than in circumstances in which the decision to go into treatment is made on a voluntary basis. One man in a Boston drug court expressed his feelings in this way:

Drug court at first was just getting in the way of my using. But I think without drug court, I probably would never have went to Gaven House, got me a program, got me in line for getting sober. I didn't want to be here, but at the same time now that it's almost over, I'm kind of grateful for it, because I probably would not have stopped or even wanted to. You know? So I'm grateful for drug court.[36]

Since the early 1990s, a number of problem-solving court programs have been created to foster treatment for other psychosocial difficulties. Mental-health courts, for example, provide a means for mentally ill defendants who have committed nonviolent criminal offenses to receive psychiatric evaluation and treatment. Other programs address problems of domestic violence (Drugs . . . in Focus).[37]

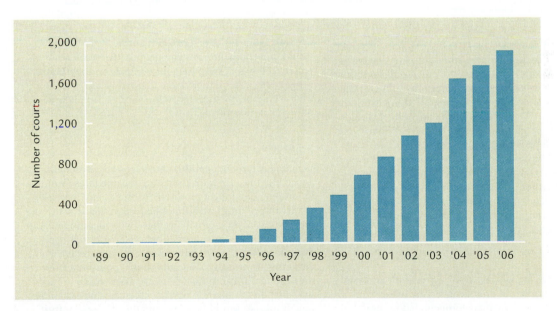

FIGURE 14.2

The growth in the number of drug courts nationwide, 1989–2006.

Source: National Drug Court Institute, National Association of Drug Court Professionals, Alexandria, VA.

Drugs . . . in Focus

A Simulated Debate: Should We Legalize Drugs?

The following discussion of viewpoints represents the opinions of people on both sides of the controversial issue of the legalization of drugs. Read them with an open mind. Don't think you have to come up with the final answer, nor should you necessarily agree with the argument you heard last. Many of the ideas in this discussion come from the sources listed.

Point

Legalization would get the problem under some degree of control. The "war on drugs" does nothing but increase the price of illicit drugs to what the market will bear, and it subsidizes the drug dealers and drug kingpins around the world. If we legalize drugs, we can take the profit out of the drug business because legalization would bring the price down dramatically. We could regulate drug sales, as we do now with nicotine and alcohol, by setting up centers that would be licensed to sell cocaine and heroin, as well as sterile syringes, while any drug sales to minors would remain a criminal offense. Regulations would also ensure that drugs maintained standards of purity; the health risks of drug contamination would be drastically reduced.

Counterpoint

Legalization is fundamentally immoral. How can we allow people to run to the nearest store and destroy their lives? Don't we as a society have a responsibility for the health and welfare of people in general? If the drugs (pure or impure) were available, the only effect would be to increase the number of drug abusers. When Britain allowed physicians to prescribe heroin to "registered" addicts, the number of heroin addicts rose fivefold (or more according to some informal estimates), and there were then cases of medical abuse as well as drug abuse. A few unscrupulous doctors were prescribing heroin in enormous amounts, and a new drug culture was created.

Point

How moral is the situation now? We have whole communities living at the mercy of drug dealers. Any increase in drug users would be more than compensated for by the gains of freedom from such people. Even if the sale of crack were kept illegal, conceding that this drug is highly dangerous to society, we would have an 80 percent reduction in the black market for drugs, a substantial gain for the welfare of society. We can't guarantee that our inner cities would no longer be places of hopelessness and despair, but at least we would not have the systemic violence associated with the drug world. Besides, with all the money saved from programs set up to prevent people from getting hold of illicit drugs, we could increase the funding for drug treatment programs for all the drug abusers who want them and for research into ways of understanding the nature of drug dependence.

Counterpoint

No doubt, many drug abusers seek out treatment and want to break their drug dependence. Perhaps there may be some individuals who seek treatment under legalization because there would no longer be a social stigma associated with drug abuse, but many drug abusers have little or no long-term commitment toward drug treatment. In the present situation, the illegality of their behavior allows us to compel them to seek and stay in treatment, as well as monitor their abstinence by periodic drug testing. How could we do this when the drug was legal? Besides, how would we approach the education of young people if drugs were legal? We could not tell them that cocaine would give them cancer or emphysema, as we warn them of the dangers of nicotine, only that it would prevent them from being a productive member of society and would have long-term effects on their brains. If the adults around them were allowed to use cocaine, what would be the message to the young? Simply wait until you're twenty-one?

Point

We already have educational programs about alcohol abuse; the message for heroin and cocaine abuse would be similar. The loss of productivity due to any increased availability of drugs would not be as significant as the present loss of productivity we have with alcohol and cigarettes. With the tax revenues obtained from selling drugs legally, we could have money for more extensive anti-drug advertising. We could send a comprehensive message to our youth that there are alternatives to their lives that do not include psychoactive substances. In the meantime, we would be removing the "forbidden fruit" factor in drug-taking behavior. Drugs wouldn't be a big deal.

Counterpoint

Arguing that people take drugs because drugs are forbidden or hard to get ignores their basic psychological allure. If you lowered the price of a very expensive sports car, would you have fewer people wanting to buy one? Of course not. People would want a fast car because they like fast cars, just as people will still want to get high on drugs. Legalizing present drugs would only encourage the development of more dangerous drugs in the future. Look at what happened with crack. Cocaine was bad enough but crack appeared on the scene, making the situation far worse.

Point

It can be argued that crack was marketed because standard cocaine powder was too expensive for people in the inner cities. If cocaine had been legally available, crack might not ever have been created because the market would not have been there. Even with crack remaining illegal under a legalization plan, there is at least the possibility that the appeal of crack would decline. The trend has been lately that illegal drugs are getting stronger, while legal drugs (alcoholic beverages and cigarettes) are getting weaker as people become more health-conscious. Legalization might make presently illicit drugs weaker in strength, as public opinion turns against them. The main problem we face is that spending 60 percent of a multibillion-dollar drug-law-enforcement program on the "supply" side of the question, and only 40 percent on reducing the demand for drugs is not working. If one source of drugs is controlled, another source takes its place. The link between drugs and crime is a direct result of the illegality of drugs. It's not the individuals with drug dependence that are destroying the country; it's the drug dealers. Right now, the criminals are in charge. We have to change that. Only legalization would take away their profits, and refocus our law-enforcement efforts on other crimes that continue to undermine our society.

Counterpoint

The frustration is understandable, but let's not jump into something merely because we're frustrated. We can allocate more funds for treatment without making drugs legal. We can increase funds for scientific research without making drugs legal. We need a more balanced program, not an entirely new one. Polls do not indicate general support for drug legalization. Between 60 percent and 80 percent of the U.S. public supports continued prohibition of drugs. Most citizens appear to recognize that legalization would make a bad situation worse, not better.

Critical Thinking Questions for Further Debate

1. Is it valid in this debate to make a distinction between "hard drugs" such as heroin and cocaine and "soft drugs" such as marijuana and hallucinogens?
2. What is your prediction of what would happen if all our drug-abuse-prevention efforts were focused exclusively on the Harm Reduction approach?

Sources: Dennis, Richard J. (1990, November). The economics of legalizing drugs. *The Atlantic,* 126–132. Goldstein, Avram (2001). *Addiction: From biology to drug policy* (2nd ed.). New York: Oxford University Press. Goode, Erich (1997). *Between politics and reason: The drug legalization debate.* New York: St. Martin's Press. Gray, James P. (2001). *Why our drug laws have failed and what we can do about it.* Philadelphia: Temple University Press. Kleiman, Mark A. R. (2001, May/June). Science and drug abuse control policy. *Society,* 7–12. Levinthal, Charles F. (2003). *Point/counterpoint: Opposing perspectives on issues of drug policy.* Boston: Allyn and Bacon, Chapter 1. U.S. Department of Justice, Drug Enforcement Administration. *Speaking out against drug legalization.* http://www .usj.gov. Wilson, James Q. (1990, February). Against the legalization of drugs. *Commentary,* 21–28.

Summary

- Of the billions of dollars spent annually on the "war on drugs," the greatest proportion of the money is spent on drug-law enforcement
- There are four general levels of present-day drug-law enforcement: (1) source control, (2) interdiction, (3) street-level enforcement, and (4) the correctional system.

Source Control

- Source control involves actions focusing on reducing the cultivation and production of illicit drugs in foreign countries.
- Crop eradication programs involve the destruction of opium poppies, coca plants, and marijuana plants in their countries of origin. Crops are eradicated both

manually and with herbicides. Critics point out that these programs are responsible for causing environmental damage and disrupting the local economy of many rural regions in Latin America.

- Agents of the U.S. Drug Enforcement Administration (DEA) regularly monitor and track large shipments of precursor chemicals to prevent them from reaching the producers of illicit drugs.
- "Certification" is a process by which the U.S. government evaluates the cooperation of foreign countries in counter-drug efforts.

Interdiction

- Interdiction efforts attempt to prevent drugs from being smuggled across the U.S. border by denying drug smugglers the use of air, land, and maritime routes. The primary agencies involved in drug interdiction include the DEA, the U.S. Customs and Border Protection Agency, the U.S. Coast Guard, and the United States military. The DEA is the only federal agency that has drug-law enforcement as its only responsibility.
- Over the years, drug-law enforcement agents have developed "drug courier profiles" to help in the identification of potential drug smugglers. Police officers have been criticized for developing profiles based solely on race, a practice known as racial profiling.

Street-Level Drug-Law Enforcement

- The reverse sting is a drug-law enforcement operation in which undercover agents pose as drug dealers and sell a controlled substance or imitation version of a controlled substance to buyers.
- The controlled buy is an operation in which an undercover informant makes a drug buy under the supervision of the police

- Undercover buy operations involve an undercover agent making a drug buy. The seller may be arrested immediately after the deal, or the drug deal may be used to obtain a search warrant to be served at a later time. The "knock and talk" occurs when agents arrive at a suspect's residence and ask permission to conduct a consent search of the residence.
- Asset forfeiture is the process by which the government seizes cash, cars, homes, and other property that it claims has been involved in or associated with criminal activity.
- Criminal forfeitures result after a conviction for a crime to which the forfeited property is related. Civil forfeitures are based upon the unlawful use of property, irrespective of its owner's culpability. With civil forfeiture, the offender does not need to be convicted or even charged with a crime, since the contention is that the property "itself" is guilty.
- Critics argue that forfeiture laws distort law enforcement priorities from crime control to "funding raids."

Drugs and the Correctional System

- Inmates serving time for drug-law violations currently dominate prison populations in the United States.
- Mandatory minimum sentencing requires that a judge impose a fixed minimal length of imprisonment for individuals convicted of certain crimes, regardless of a person's role in the crime or other mitigating factors. This policy has generated a significant increase in the incarceration rates of drug offenders.
- Drug courts are specialized courts designed to handle adult, nonviolent offenders with substance abuse problems. They involve an intensely supervised drug treatment program as an alternative to standard sentencing.

Key Terms

asset forfeiture, p. 369	crop eradication, p. 360	mandatory minimum sentencing, p. 372	reverse sting, p. 368
certification, p. 362	drug courts, p. 374		search warrant, p. 369
consent search, p. 369	interdiction, p. 362	precursor chemicals, p. 362	source control, p. 360
controlled buy, p. 368	knock and talk, p. 362	racial profiling, p. 366	undercover buy, p. 368

Endnotes

1. Marshall, Elliot (1971, July 27). Cold turkey: Heroin: The source supply. *New Republic, 165*(4), 23–25.
2. National Narcotics Intelligence Consumers Committee (1996). *The supply of illicit drugs to the United States,* Washington, DC: National Narcotics Intelligence Consumers Committee.
3. Office of National Drug Control Policy (2003, February). *National drug control strategy update 2003.* Washington DC: Office of National Drug Control Policy.
4. Vargas, Ricardo (2002). The anti-drug policy, aerial spraying of illicit crops and their social, environmental and political impacts on Colombia. *Journal of Drug Issues, 32,* 11–61.

5. Matheson, Mary (1996, August 12). Colombian leader tries to please U.S. on drugs, but ignites peasant revolt. *Christian Science Monitor, 88,* 7–8.

6. Lama-Tierramrica, Abraham (2002, November 18). Peru: Cash for farmers who destroy their coca crops. *Global Information Network,* p. 1

7. Office of National Drug Control Policy. *National drug control strategy update 2003.*

8. Farrell, Graham (1998). A global empirical review of drug crop eradication and United Nations crop substitution and alternative development strategies. *Journal of Drug Issues, 28,* 395–437.

9. Office of National Drug Control Policy (1999). *ONCP fact sheet: Efforts to control precursor chemicals.* Washington DC: Office of National Drug Control Policy.

10. U.S. Department of State (2003, January 31). *The certification process: Fact sheet released by the Bureau of International Narcotics and Law Enforcement Affaires.* Washington DC: U.S. Department of State.

11. Twentieth General Assembly of the Organization of American States (1999). Guatemala City: Guatemala.

12. Miller, D. W. (1994, December 19). Canine carrier. *U.S. News and World Report, 117,* 14.

13. McCleland, Susan (2003, July 28). Drug mules. *Maclean's, 116,* 25–31.

14. Drug Enforcement Administration (2003). *Drug intelligence brief: Common vehicle concealment methods.* Washington DC: Drug Enforcement Administration.

15. Office of National Drug Control Policy (2003, March). *Drug data summary fact sheet.* Washington DC: Office of National Drug Control Policy.

16. Office of National Drug Control Policy (2002, September 5). *ONDCP fact sheet: Interdiction operations.* Washington DC: Office of National Drug Control Policy. Information Courtesy of U.S. Coast Guard.

17. Peters, Katherine M. (2003, April). Troops on the beat. *Government Executive, 35,* 56. Zirnite, Peter (1998, April). The militarization of the drug war. *Current History, 97,* 166–186.

18. Vaughn, Ed (1992, December). National Guard involvement in the drug war. *Justicia, the Newsletter of the Judicial Process Commission,* p. 1.

19. *United States v. Sokolow* (1989). 490 U.S. 1.

20. Gallup Poll Organization (1999, December 9). *Gallup poll organization poll release: Racial profiling is seen as widespread, particularly among young black men.* Princeton, NJ: Gallup Poll Organization.

21. Hosenball, Mark (1999, May 17). It is not the act of a few bad apples: Lawsuit shines the spotlight on allegations of racial profiling by New Jersey state troopers. *Newsweek,* pp. 34–35.

22. Verniero, Peter, and Zoubek, Paul (1999, April 20). *New Jersey Attorney General's interim report of the state police review team regarding allegations of racial profiling.* Trenton, NJ: Office of the New Jersey Attorney General.

23. Lamberth, John (1999, April 16). Driving while black: A statistician proves that prejudice still rules the road. *Washington Post,* p. C1.

24. New York Attorney General (1999, December 1). *New York City Police, "stop and frisk" practices: A report to the people of New York from the Office of the Attorney General.* New York: New York Office of the Attorney General.

25. U.S. Customs Service (1998). *Personal searches of air passengers results: Positive and negative.* Washington DC: U.S. Customs Service.

26. Bureau of Justice Statistics (2003, January). *Sheriff's offices 2000.* Washington DC: Bureau of Justice Statistics, U.S. Department of Justice.

27. Drug Enforcement Administration (2005). *DOJ computerized asset program.* Washington DC: Drug Enforcement Administration, U.S. Department of Justice.

28. Finkelstein J. (1973). The goring ox: Some historical perspectives on deodands, forfeitures, wrongful death and the Western notion of sovereignty. *Temple Law Quarterly, 46,* 169–290.

29. Maguire, Kathleen, and Pastore, Anne L. (Eds.) (1995). *Sourcebook of criminal justice statistics 1994.* Washington DC: Bureau of Justice Statistics, U.S. Department of Justice.

30. Hawkins, C. W., Jr., and Payne, T. E. (1999). Civil forfeiture in law enforcement: An effective tool or cash register justice? In J. D. Sewall (Ed.), *Controversial issues in policing.* Boston: Allyn and Bacon, pp. 23–34.

31. Bureau of Justice Statistics (1998). *Sourcebook of criminal justice statistics, 1997.* Washington DC: Bureau of Justice Statistics, U.S. Department of Justice. Bureau of Justice Statistics (2003, July). *Prisoners in 2002.* Washington DC: Bureau of Justice Statistics, U.S. Department of Justice.

32. Donohue, John J., III, and Siegelman, Peter (1998). Allocating resources among prisons and social programs in the battle against crime. *Journal of Legal Studies, 27,* 30–43. Horowitz, Heather, Sung, Hung-En, and Foster, Susan E. (2006, January–February). The role of substance abuse in U.S. juvenile justice systems and populations. *Corrections Compendium,* pp. 1–4, 24–26.

33. Harrison, Blake (2001, July/August). Rethinking drug policy. *State Legislatures, 27,* 53–61.

34. General Accounting Office (2002). *Drug courts: Better DOJ data collection and evaluation efforts needed to measure impact of drug court programs.* Washington DC: General Accounting Office. Office of National Drug Control Policy (2005, February). The President's National Drug Control Strategy. Washington DC: Office of National Drug Control Policy.

35. Gottfredson, D.C., Najaka, S. S., and Kearley, B. (2003). Effectiveness of drug treatment courts: Evidence from a randomized trial. *Criminology and Public Policy, 2,* 401–426. Huddleston, C. West,

Freeman-Wilson, Karen, and Boone, Donna L. (2004, May). *Painting the current picture: A national report card on drug courts and other problem-solving court programs in the United States.* Alexandria, VA: National Drug Court Institute. National Institute of Justice (2006, June). *Drug courts: The second decade.* Washington DC: National Institute of Justice, U.S. Department of Justice.

36. Galloway, Alyson L., and Drapela, Laurie A. (2006). Are effective drug courts an urban phenomenon? Considering their impact on recidivism among a nonmetropolitan adult sample in Washington State. *International Journal of Offender Therapy and Comparative Criminology, 50,* 280–293. Goldkamp, John S. (2001). Do drug courts work? Getting inside the drug court black box. *Journal of Drug Issues, 31,* 27–73. Huddleston, C. West; Freeman-Wilson, Karen; Marlowe, Douglas B.; and Russell, Aaron (2005, May). *Painting the current picture: A national report card on drug courts and other problem-solving court programs in the United States.* Alexandria, VA: National Drug Court Institute. Meyer, William G., and Ritter, William A. (2001). Drug courts work. *Federal Sentencing Reporter, 14,* 179–186. Quotation from Home Box Office (2007, March). Mandated Treatment. www.hbo.com/addiction.

37. Huddleston et al. (2005). *Painting the current picture.*

chapter 15

Drug Policy: Prevention, Education, and Treatment

I would lie about everything, and I lied to everybody. I was so good at it because it was so easy to do. My parents were in major denial, and I played off of that. What is all that drug stuff in my room? Oh, I'm just holding it for a friend. It would get me so angry that the lies worked so well with them. They would never call me on anything.

It became a way of life. But after a while I got sick and tired of all the lying. And I started to think about the possibility that I might be dead at an early age. Half of my friends are now dead; the other half are in jail. That's why I'm here to get help. I had to change somehow. It really just came down to that.

—A seventeen-year-old recovering drug abuser, explaining why he came to Daytop Village

Consider for a moment the goal of preventing the misuse and abuse of psychoactive drugs in our society. Everyone is obviously in favor of prevention; no one questions that the personal damage and social havoc wrought by the sale, distribution, and consumption of illicit drugs are devastating. As political leaders continually remind us, we have to "do something" if this monster is to be slain. At the same time, we are appalled by the magnitude of preventable disease and death associated with *licit* drugs such as alcohol and nicotine. It is imperative that we reduce the risks to our health and the health of our families and friends.

Yet, as unanimous as we may be in the necessity for some prevention strategy, the issues are terribly complex and the answers have been elusive. It has been a great challenge to create social programs that have a significant and long-lasting positive impact on an individual's inclination to use drugs. In the final chapter we turn to an examination of drug-abuse prevention in our society and strategies that have been devised to treat drug-related problems.

Levels of Intervention in Drug-Abuse Prevention

Traditionally, efforts to prevent the abuse of drugs have been divided into three levels of intervention: primary, secondary, and tertiary. Each intervention has its own target population and goals.

In **primary prevention**, efforts are directed to those who have not had any experience with drugs or those who have been only minimally exposed. The objective is to prevent drug abuse from starting in the first place, "nipping the problem in the bud" so to speak. Targets in primary prevention programs are most frequently elementary school or middle school youths, and intervention usually occurs within a school-based curriculum or specific educational program. For example, a primary prevention program would include teaching peer-refusal skills that

> **primary prevention:** A type of intervention in which the goal is to forestall the onset of drug use by an individual who has had little or no previous exposure to drugs.
>
> **secondary prevention:** A type of intervention in which the goal is to reduce the extent of drug use in individuals who have already had some exposure to drugs.
>
> **tertiary (TER-shee-eh-ree) prevention:** A type of intervention in which the goal is to prevent relapse in an individual following recovery in a drug-treatment program.

students can use when they are offered marijuana, alcohol, or cigarettes (that is, ways to say no).

In **secondary prevention**, the target population has already had some experience with drugs. The objective is to limit the extent of drug abuse (reducing it, if possible), prevent the spread of drug abuse to substances beyond the drugs already encountered, and teach strategies for the responsible use of alcohol. Ordinarily, those receiving secondary-prevention efforts are older than those involved in primary-prevention programs. High school students who are identified as alcohol or other drug users may participate in a program that emphasizes social alternatives to drug-taking behavior. College students may focus on the skills necessary to restrict their behavior to the moderate use of alcohol, the dangers of combining drinking and driving, and the signs of chronic alcohol abuse.

In **tertiary prevention**, the objective is to ensure that an individual who has entered treatment for some form of drug-abuse problem stays drug-free, without reverting to former patterns of drug-taking behavior. Successful prevention of relapse is the ultimate indication that the treatment has taken hold.[1]

Whether we are addressing issues of primary or secondary prevention, however, we must remain fully aware that the entire range of drug-taking behaviors needs to be considered. This range encompasses not only illicit drug use but also the drinking of alcohol, the inappropriate use of medications, and the consumption of tobacco products. As a consequence, it will be useful in this chapter to adopt a somewhat awkward but necessary phrase *alcohol, tobacco, and other drug (ATOD) prevention* to describe our society's response in this regard. As we will see, a conspicuous target behavior within the overall mission of prevention and education in recent years has been tobacco use among young people.

ATOD Prevention: Strategic Priorities, Goals, and Resilience

The U.S. federal agency specifically charged with the prevention of alcohol, tobacco, and other drug abuse is the Center for Substance Abuse Prevention (CSAP). According to CSAP guidelines, ATOD prevention is accomplished through two major efforts. The first is the promotion of constructive life-styles and norms that discourage ATOD use. The second is the development of social and physical environments that facilitate ATOD-free life-styles.

You may recall from Chapter 3 that two groups of factors play a major role in predicting the extent of ATOD use in a particular individual—risk factors that increase the likelihood of ATOD use and protective factors that decrease it. You can think of the two components of prevention in those terms. On one hand, it is a matter of minimizing the impact of risk factors in an individual's life. On the other hand, it is a matter of maximizing the impact of protective factors. The number of "developmental assets" (see Chapter 3) increases the chances that ATOD prevention and education efforts will be successful.

Resilience and Primary Prevention Efforts

Successful primary prevention programs are built around the central idea that an individual is less inclined to engage in ATOD use if the protective factors in his or her life are enhanced and the risk factors are diminished. Only then can a young person be resilient

enough to overcome the temptations of alcohol, tobacco, and other drugs. **Resilience**, defined as the inclination to resist the effect of risk factors through the action of protective factors, can be a make-or-break element in his or her social development. Social and personal skills, as well as other aspects of successful primary prevention efforts, enhance the "buffering effect" of protective factors with respect to ATOD use and other forms of deviant behavior. To be most effective, it is necessary to incorporate aspects of a young person's environment beyond the school itself in the fight against ATOD use. In a later section we will turn to primary prevention efforts that involve the community at large.[2]

National Drug-Control Strategy Priorities

The overall national policy for the control of drug use in the United States is coordinated by the White House Office of National Drug Control Policy (ONDCP). Three priorities have been set as components of a national strategy.[3]

- *Priority I—Stopping drug use before it starts.* Primary prevention programs, to be reviewed in this chapter, are essentially the first line of defense against drug-abuse problems among young people. The key characteristic of effective programs is their basis on research ("research based" programs). That is, the outcome measures of individuals who have participated in the program are directly compared with those of individuals who have not participated in the program (the control group). If drug use among eighth graders has declined as a result of a prevention program, for example, but this decline is not greater than a decline among eighth graders in the control group, then the prevention program is essentially ineffective. As we will see, effective school-based prevention programs do exist, but the overall effectiveness is enhanced when there is a combination of education and community action.

- *Priority II—Healing America's drug users.* The concept of tertiary prevention programs, accomplished through intervention and drug-abuse treatment, was discussed earlier. As with primary prevention programs, treatment programs are judged effective based on the comparison of program outcome measures

> **resilience:** The inclination to resist the negative impact of risk factors in a person's life through the positive impact of protective factors.

(the period of time during which individuals remain drug-free, for example) to measures for individuals in appropriate control groups. In 2003, a new federal "voucher program" was instituted for people in need of treatment for services that could be obtained in a variety of contexts, including emergency departments in hospitals, health clinics, the criminal justice system, schools, or the faith community. In addition, drug court programs were expanded to provide treatment, mandatory drug testing, and vigorous aftercare services to help sustain drug-abuse recovery.

- *Priority III—Disrupting the market.* Attacking the economic basis of the drug trade, from the cultivation of raw materials for illicit drugs and drug trafficking on domestic and international levels to the sale of illicit drugs at the local level, form the "supply side" approach to the drug-abuse problem. Chapter 13 specifically addressed attempts to reduce the influx and distribution of illicit drugs. Chapters 10 and 12 addressed efforts to reduce the sale of alcohol and tobacco to individuals below legally defined age limits.

The Public Health Model of ATOD Prevention

It is important to recognize that an ATOD-free life constitutes a major element in a healthy life and, in turn, a healthy society. Figure 15.1 shows dramatically how ATOD-taking behaviors impact upon the nation's health in general. As you can see, one-half of all preventable deaths in the United States are accounted for by the abuse of either alcohol products (9 percent), tobacco products (39 percent), or illicit drugs (2 percent). Each year, more than 500,000 deaths are attributed to these three circumstances.[4]

It is not surprising that in 1992, when the U.S. Public Health Service established its long-range health-promoting goals in a program called Healthy People 2000, a major component was devoted to ATOD use among young people aged twelve to twenty-five years.[5] According to its projections, by the year 2000, using baseline figures from the period 1987–1991, the United States should have achieved the following goals:

- Increased by at least one year the average age of first use of alcohol, tobacco, and marijuana.

- Reduced alcohol, marijuana, and cocaine use, measured by past thirty-day use, by 50 percent and tobacco use among young people by 53 percent.

- Increased the percentage of young people who perceive social disapproval in the heavy use of alcohol, occasional use of marijuana, trying cocaine once or twice, or smoking one or more packs of cigarettes per day to 70, 85, 95, and 95 percent, respectively.

- Reduced the percentage who have engaged in recent heavy alcohol drinking by 15 percent among high school seniors and 23 percent among college students.

- Increased the percentage of high school seniors who associate a risk of physical or psychological harm with heavy use of alcohol, trying cocaine once or twice, or regular use of marijuana, or smoking one or more packs of cigarettes per day to 70, 80, 90, and 95 percent, respectively.

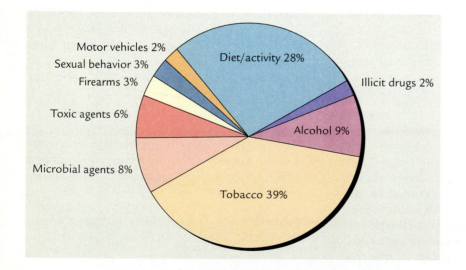

FIGURE 15.1

The relative incidence of deaths associated with ATOD use annually in the United States.

Source: Center for Substance Abuse Prevention, Substance Abuse and Mental Health Services Administration.

- Reduced the percentage of male high school seniors who use anabolic steroids to 3 percent.
- Reduced alcohol-related motor vehicle deaths by 44 percent, cirrhosis-related deaths by 35 percent, and drug-abuse-related hospital emergency room visits by 20 percent.

Unfortunately, by 2000, most of these goals were not met. In fact, in the areas of teenage ATOD prevalence rates, we had actually lost ground. Despite the failures of Healthy People 2000 (or perhaps because of it), a new program called Healthy People 2010 was enacted, with a new set of target goals.[6]

A set of shorter-range goals were established using the 2001 Monitoring the Future survey for youths and the 2002 National Survey on Drug Use and Health for adults as baselines:

- *Two-year goals.* A 10 percent reduction in current use of illicit drugs by eighth, tenth, and twelfth graders; a 10 percent reduction in current use of illicit drugs by adults age eighteen or older
- *Five-year goals.* A 25 percent reduction in current use of illicit drugs by eighth, tenth, and twelfth graders; a 25 percent reduction in current use of illicit drugs by adults age eighteen or older

While these goals were ambitious, forecasters had the advantage of projecting from a point in time in which illicit drug use had peaked and signs of a downward trend had already begun (see Chapter 2). Use of alcohol and tobacco products, although illegal for youths, was not measured in these projected goals, though they obviously represent a major component of healthy behavior.[7]

Lessons from the Past: Prevention Approaches That Have Failed

When deciding how to solve a problem, it always helps to look at what has *not* worked in the past. That way, we can avoid wasting time, effort, and money on nonsolutions. In the general opinion of health professionals and researchers, the following efforts have been largely unsuccessful with regard to primary prevention when positioned as the major thrust of a particular program. Nonetheless, some of these approaches have been incorporated successfully as one of several components within an overall effective package.

Reducing the Availability of Drugs

It is reasonable to expect that the problems of illicit drug abuse would diminish if the availability of these drugs were reduced or eliminated altogether. This is essentially the "supply/availability" argument in drug prevention, and you will recall that Priority III of the National Drug Control Strategy concerned the reduction of the manufacture and distribution of illicit drugs into and within the United States. As noted in Chapter 14, a huge amount of governmental resources is spent on reducing the supply or availability of these substances.

According to the economic principle of supply and demand, however, a decline in supply or availability works to produce an increase in value and an increase in demand. If one accepts the first viewpoint, then reductions in supply or availability should help prevent drug-taking behavior; if one accepts the second viewpoint, then such reductions should exacerbate the situation. Which theoretical viewpoint is operating with respect to illicit drugs (or with respect to alcohol, tobacco, and other licit drugs) is a point of controversy among health professionals both inside and outside the government.

Given the fact that the United States has adopted the policy of reducing the supply or availability of illicit drugs as part of an overall national strategy, how successful have we been? Have we been able, for example, to reduce the production of illicit drugs around the world and their influx into the United States? Unfortunately, drug cultivation (such as the harvesting of opium, coca leaves, and marijuana) and the exportation of processed illicit drugs from their points of origin are so deeply entrenched in many regions of the world and the resourcefulness of drug producers is so great that our global efforts have been frustratingly inadequate. As was pointed out in Chapter 14, a production crackdown in one region merely serves to create a marketing vacuum that another region quickly fills. Moreover, efforts to control international drug smuggling have been embarrassingly unsuccessful despite well-publicized drug busts, arrests, and seizures. It is estimated that only a small fraction of illicit drugs is interdicted at U.S. borders.[8]

With respect to alcohol, a strategy of reduced availability has been implemented on a nationwide basis since 1984 for a specific age group by prohibiting alcohol to young people under the age of twenty-one (see Chapter 10). Prior to this time, some states had adopted this policy while neighboring states had not, allowing for comparisons in alcohol consumption rates and the incidence of alcohol-related automobile accidents. In one study, the percentage of teenage, nighttime, single-vehicle accident fatalities in Massachusetts was found to have declined in

1979 (the year the legal drinking age in that state was raised to twenty-one) to a significantly greater degree than in New York, which at that time still had a minimum drinking age of eighteen. That was the good news.

The bad news was that levels of alcohol consumption in this age range stayed the same. Therefore, although one particular consequence of immoderate alcohol use (drunk driving) was reduced as a secondary prevention intervention, the prevalence of alcohol use itself as a result of a primary prevention intervention was unaffected. As we are all aware, underage drinking still is widespread; minors still find opportunities to drink and to drink in excess. The fact that minimum-age requirements have only a limited effect on drinking among minors reinforces the complexity of dealing with primary prevention, whether we are considering licit or illicit drugs (Drugs . . . in Focus).[9]

Punitive Measures

In the last chapter, the question of deterrence was raised with respect to the preventive role of law enforcement and judicial policies toward drug offenders. The expectation from such policies is that an individual would be less inclined to use and abuse illicit drugs for fear of being arrested, prosecuted, convicted, and incarcerated. The available statistics show that this deterrent factor has failed to take hold. The enticements of many psychoactive drugs are extremely powerful, and the imposition of harsh penalties frequently has been delayed or inconsistent. Mandatory minimum sentencing laws have resulted in a clogged judicial system and vastly overcrowded prisons without any noticeable dent in the trafficking in or consumption of illicit drugs. Although the enforcement of these penalties may be defended in terms of an overall social policy toward illicit drugs, it has evidently failed as a means for either primary or secondary prevention.[10]

Scare Tactics and Negative Education

In the late 1960s, the suddenly widespread use of marijuana, amphetamines, barbiturates, LSD, and other hallucinogens, first among students on college campuses and later among youth at large, spawned a number of hastily designed programs based on the arousal of fear and exaggerated or blatantly inaccurate information about the risks involved. They were the products of panic rather than careful thought.

As might be imagined, such efforts turned young people *off* precisely at the time when they were turning themselves *on* to an array of exotic and seemingly innocuous drug-taking experiences. Professionals have called it the "reefer madness approach," an allusion to the government-sponsored movie of the 1930s that attempted to scare people away from experimenting with marijuana (see Chapter 7). These programs accomplished little, except to erode even further the credibility of the adult presenters in the eyes of youths who often knew (or thought they knew) a great deal more about drugs and their effects than their elders.[11]

Objective Information Approaches

At the opposite end of the emotional spectrum are programs designed to present information about drugs and their potential dangers in a straightforward, nonjudgmental way. Unfortunately, evaluations of this "just the facts, ma'am" approach have found that youths exposed to such primary prevention programs are no less likely to use drugs later in their lives and sometimes are *more* likely to use them. These programs tend to increase their curiosity about drugs in general, obviously something prevention program planners want to avoid.[12]

Despite these failures, however, it would be a mistake to dismiss the informational aspect of any ATOD prevention program completely out of hand, particularly when the information is presented in a low-fear atmosphere.[13] The overall value of an informational approach appears to depend on whether the target population consists of high-risk or low-risk children:

> *Providing information to low-risk youth on the health and legal implications of using illegal drugs often is enough incentive for them to avoid using drugs. When low-risk young people really understand the dangers of drugs, they choose to remain drug-free. High-risk youth may not be so easily dissuaded from using drugs, and for them additional intervention is necessary.*[14]

Magic Bullets and Promotional Campaigns

A variety of antidrug promotional materials such as T-shirts, caps, rings, buttons, bumper stickers, posters, rap songs, school assembly productions, books, and brochures is available and frequently is seen as "magic bullets" that can clinch success in an ATOD prevention program. Their appeal lies in their high visibility; these items give a clear signal to the public at large that something is being done. Yet, although they may be helpful in deglamorizing ATOD use and providing a forum for young people to express their feelings about drugs, promotional items are

Drugs . . . in Focus

Harm Reduction as a National Drug-Abuse Policy

To say that we are waging a "war on drugs" is, in effect, communicating how serious we are in dealing with the problems of drug abuse in the United States. Using the metaphor of warfare, we recognize that there is an acknowledged enemy (drug misuse and abuse), there are victims or casualties (us), there are resources at our disposal to fight the necessary battles (federal and state governments, communities, parents, etc.), and there is a high price to pay (billions of dollars of federal funds each year).

The implications of this real-life struggle, such as our overall strategy and ultimate goals, are also drawn in metaphorical terms. Do we want total victory and complete annihilation of the enemy? Or do we want some kind of negotiated settlement, some type of compromise that gives us some semblance of peace and tranquility? If it is the former, then we require a total elimination, often expressed as "zero tolerance" of abuse drug-taking behavior in America. If it is the latter, then we require a good deal less. We desire, in that case, only a reduction of the harmful consequences of abusive drug-taking behavior, knowing fully well that a total elimination is unrealistic and perhaps unattainable. The second alternative is referred to as the Harm Reduction approach. Whether we choose a harm-reduction approach or an approach based on zero tolerance is the essence of our deliberation on a national drug-abuse policy.

The harm-reduction approach in drug policy has its historical roots in the libertarian philosophy of the nineteenth-century philosopher John Stuart Mill, who argued that the state did not have the duty to protect individual citizens from harming themselves. As Mill expressed it,

> The only purpose for which power can be rightfully executed over any member of a civilized community, against his will, is to prevent harm to others. His own good, either physical or moral, is not a sufficient warrant. . . . Over himself, over his own body and mind, the individual is sovereign.

It is readily evident, however, that drug-taking behavior does indeed harm other people. The question, according to those advocating a harm-reduction strategy, is to look for policies that reduce the harm that drugs do, both directly to the drug user and indirectly to others.

Examples of the Harm Reduction approach include needle-exchange programs to lower the incidence of HIV infection among intravenous drug abusers (see Chapter 2), methadone maintenance programs for the treatment of heroin abusers (see Chapter 5), efforts to reduce the incidence of driving while under the influence of alcohol (see Chapter 10), and the use of nicotine patches to avoid the effects of cigarette smoking such as emphysema and lung cancer (see Chapter 12). A more controversial application of the Harm Reduction approach is the suggestion that we should attempt to reduce the level of heavy drug use down to a level of occasional use, rather than no use at all.

With regard to cigarette smoking and marijuana use, there is an indication that some teenagers may already be "harm reducing." In the University of Michigan survey, high school seniors engaging in occasional marijuana smoking and occasional cigarette smoking indicated a higher perceived risk of "regular substance use" than did high school seniors engaging in heavy use, even though there was no difference in the perceived risk of "occasional substance use." In other words, occasional users may have been moderating their behavior to minimize the harmful effects they associated with heavy drug-taking behavior. Whether a prevention program that emphasizes the risks of heavy drug use, as opposed to emphasizing the risks of any level of use, is the more successful strategy in reducing significant levels of drug-taking behavior is a question that advocates of the Harm Reduction approach will be investigating in the future with great interest.

Sources: Denning, Patt (2003). *Over the influence: The harm reduction guide for managing drugs and alcohol.* New York: Guilford Press. Des Jarlais, Don C. (2000). Prospects for a public health perspective on psychoactive drug use. *American Journal of Public Health, 90,* 335–337. How did we get here? History has a habit of repeating itself (2001, July 28–August 3). *Economist,* pp. 4–5. Quotation of John Stuart Mill on page 5. Levinthal, Charles F. (2003). Question: Should harm reduction be our overall goal in fighting drug abuse? *Point/Counterpoint: Opposing perspectives on issues of drug policy.* Boston: Allyn and Bacon, pp. 70–73. Marlatt, G. Alan (Ed.) (2002). *Harm reduction: Pragmatic strategies for managing high-risk behaviors.* New York: Guilford Press. Resnicow, Ken; Smith, Matt; Harrison, Lana; and Drucker, Ernest (1999). Correlates of occasional cigarette and marijuana use. Are teens harm reducing? *Addictive Behaviors, 24,* 251–266.

Self-Esteem Enhancement and Affective Education

In the early 1970s, several ATOD prevention programs were developed that emphasized the affective or emotional component of drug-taking behavior rather than specific information about drugs. In the wake of research that showed a relationship between drug abuse and psychological variables such as low self-esteem, poor decision-making skills, and poor interpersonal communication skills, programs were instituted that incorporated role-playing exercises with other assignments designed to help young people get in touch with their own emotions and feel better about themselves. This effort, called **affective education,** was an attempt to deal with underlying emotional and attitudinal factors rather than specific behaviors related to ATOD use (in fact, alcohol, tobacco, and other drugs were seldom mentioned at all). Affective education was based on the observation that ATOD users had difficulty identifying and expressing emotions such as anger and love. In a related set of programs called **values clarification,** specific moral values were taught to children, on the assumption that ATOD users frequently have a poorly developed sense of where their life is going and lack the moral "compass" to guide their behavior.

Difficulties arose, however, when parents, community leaders, and frequently educators themselves argued that the emphasis of affective education was inappropriate for public schools. In regard to values clarification, there was concern that a system of morality was being imposed on students without respecting their individual backgrounds and cultures. This kind of instruction, it was felt, was more suited for religious education settings.[16]

Beyond these considerations, the bottom line was that neither affective education nor values clarification was effective in preventing ATOD use. Some

inadequate by themselves to reduce ATOD abuse overall. They do, however, remain viable components of more comprehensive programs that will be examined later in the chapter.[15]

Designations of drug-free pledges are prominent features of many school-based drug prevention programs.

researchers have recently questioned the basic premise that self-esteem is a major factor at all. As a result, affective issues are no longer viewed as central considerations in primary or secondary prevention. Nonetheless, they can be found as components in more comprehensive prevention programs, discussed later, that have been more successful.[17]

---

affective education: An approach in ATOD prevention programs that emphasizes the building of self-esteem and an improved self-image.

values clarification: An approach in ATOD prevention programs that teaches positive social values and attitudes.

Hope and Promise: Components of Effective School-Based Prevention Programs

One of the major lessons to be learned from evaluations of previous ATOD prevention efforts is that there is a far greater chance for success when the programs are multifaceted than when they focus on only a single aspect of drug-taking behavior. We need to remember that success can be measured in various ways. A school-based ATOD program, for example, might be considered successful if it enjoys support from parents, administrators, and teachers. It might be considered successful if there is evidence of a change in a child's view toward ATOD use or in the child's stated inclination to engage in ATOD use in the future.

However gratifying these effects may be to the community, they do not impact on the core issue: Is the prevalence of ATOD use reduced? *The goal of any prevention program aimed at young people is to lower the numbers of new ATOD users or to delay the first use of alcohol and tobacco toward an age at which they are considered adults.* To be considered "research based," prevention programs must be evaluated against a control group that did not receive the intervention; otherwise, it is impossible to determine whether the effect of the program itself was greater than doing nothing at all.

Evaluations of ATOD prevention programs frequently have looked only at the "exit results" in the form of short-term effects, such as changes in how young people feel after the program has ended or how they think they will act in the future, rather than long-term effects such as actual ATOD use over an extended period of time. Obviously, we are far more interested in the latter measure. With these considerations in mind, it is useful to examine the components of programs that have been judged effective. The following are elements of school-based ATOD prevention programs that have been shown to work.

Peer-Refusal Skills

A number of school-based programs, developed during the 1980s, have included the teaching of personal and social skills as well as techniques for resisting various forms of social pressure to smoke, drink, or use other drugs (often referred to as **peer-refusal skills**). The emphasis is directed toward an individual's relationships with his or her peers and the surrounding social climate. Rather than simply prodding children and adolescents to "just say no," these programs teach them *how* to do so when placed in often uncomfortable social circumstances.

Primary prevention programs using peer-refusal skill training have been shown to reduce the rate of tobacco smoking, as well as alcohol drinking and marijuana smoking, by 35 to 45 percent. With respect to tobacco smoking, this approach has been even more effective for young people identified as being in a high-risk category (in that their friends or family smoked) than for other students.[18]

Anxiety and Stress Reduction

Adolescence can be an enormously stressful time, and ATOD use is frequently an option chosen to reduce feelings of anxiety, particularly when an individual has inadequate coping skills to deal with that anxiety. It is therefore useful to learn techniques of self-relaxation and stress management and to practice the application of these techniques to everyday situations.

Social Skills and Personal Decision Making

Peer-refusal skills are but one example of a range of assertiveness skills that allow young people to express their feelings, needs, preferences, and opinions directly and honestly, without fearing that they will jeopardize their friendships or lose the respect of others. Learning assertiveness skills not only helps advance the goals of primary prevention but also fosters positive interpersonal relationships throughout life. Tasks in social skills training have included the ability to initiate social interactions (introducing oneself to a stranger), offer a compliment to others, engage in conversation, and express feelings and opinions. Lessons generally involve a combination of instruction, demonstration, feedback, reinforcement, behavioral rehearsal, and extended practice through behavioral homework assignments.

A related skill is the ability to make decisions in a thoughtful and careful way. Emphasis is placed on the identification of problem situations, the formulation of goals, the generation of alternative solutions, and the consideration of the likely consequences of each. Lessons also focus on identifying persuasive advertising appeals and exploring counterarguments that can defuse them. Primary prevention programs using a social skills training approach have been shown to reduce the likelihood that a young person will try smoking by 42 to 75 percent and the likelihood that a nonsmoker will be a regular smoker in a one-year follow-up by 56 to 67 percent.[19]

A Model School-Based Prevention Program: Life Skills Training

One of the most well-researched efforts in school-based ATOD prevention is the Life Skills Training (LST) program developed by Gilbert Botvin at the Cornell University Medical College in New York City. It is directed toward seventh-grade students in a fifteen-session curriculum, with ten additional booster sessions in the eighth grade and five in the ninth grade.[20] Not

peer-refusal skills: Techniques by which an individual can resist peer pressure to use alcohol, tobacco, or other drugs.

surprisingly, the effective components of primary prevention discussed so far have been incorporated in this program. The major elements include the following:

- A *cognitive component* designed to provide information concerning the short-term consequences of alcohol, tobacco, and other drugs. Unlike traditional prevention approaches, LST includes only minimal information concerning the long-term health consequences of ATOD use. Evidently, it is not useful to tell young people about what might happen when they are "old." Instead, information is provided concerning immediate negative effects, the decreasing social acceptability of ATOD use, and actual prevalence rates among adults and adolescents. This last element of the lesson is to counter the myth that ATOD use is the norm in their age group, that "everyone's doing it."

- A *decision-making component* designed to facilitate critical thinking and independent decision making. Students learn to evaluate the role of the media in behavior as well as to formulate counterarguments and other cognitive strategies to resist advertising pressures.

- A *stress-reduction component* designed to help students develop ways to lessen anxiety. Students learn relaxation techniques and cognitive techniques to manage stress.

- A *social skills component* designed to teach social assertiveness and specific techniques for resisting peer pressure to engage in ATOD use.

- A *self-directed behavior-change component* designed to facilitate self-improvement and encourage a sense of personal control and self-esteem. Students are assigned to identify a skill or behavior that they would like to change or improve and to develop a long-term goal over an eight-week period and short-term objectives that can be met week by week.

Originally designed as a smoking-prevention program, LST presently focuses on issues related to the use of alcohol and marijuana as well as tobacco. During the program, students engage in peer interactions, demonstrations, exercises, and homework assignments (Figure 15.2). A series of studies has consistently shown its effectiveness in reducing tobacco, alcohol, and marijuana use, even in a long-range follow-up over a six-year period. In addition, reductions have been seen among inner-city minority students as well as white middle-class youths, an encouraging sign that primary prevention strategies can influence adolescents regardless of their social

backgrounds.[21] As Botvin has expressed it, these studies ultimately will "give us an intervention that we can use in cities and towns and villages across the United States without having to develop separate intervention approaches for each and every different population."[22]

The research concerning the effectiveness of LST has now spanned a period of as long as six years following exposure to the program, with outcomes being compared to controls. The effects have included a 50 to 75 percent decline in alcohol, tobacco, and marijuana use and a 66 percent decline in multiple-drug use. Pack-a-day smoking has been reduced by 25 percent, and decreased use of inhalants, opiate-based drugs, and hallucinogens has been noted.[23]

Drug Abuse Resistance Education (DARE)

The Drug Abuse Resistance Education program, commonly known as DARE, is undoubtedly the best-known school-based ATOD prevention program in the United States and perhaps the world. It was developed in 1983 as a collaborative effort by the Los Angeles Police Department and the Los Angeles United School District to bring uniformed police officers into kindergarten and elementary grade classrooms to teach basic drug information, peer-refusal skills, self-management techniques, and alternatives to drug use.

Quite rapidly, the DARE program expanded until today it has been established in all fifty U.S. states, in all Native American schools administered by the Bureau of Indian Affairs, the U.S. Department of Defense schools worldwide, and in school systems in many foreign countries. There are also teacher-orientation sessions, officer–student interactions at playgrounds and cafeterias, and parent-education evenings.[24]

Responses to Project DARE from teachers, principals, students, and police officers are typically enthusiastic, and it is clear that the program has struck a responsive chord for a public that has pushed for active prevention programs in the schools. Part of this enthusiasm can be seen as coming from the image of police departments shifting their emphasis from exclusively "supply reduction" to a larger social role in "demand reduction."

Yet, despite its success in the area of public relations, the evidence supporting the effectiveness of DARE in achieving genuine reductions in ATOD use is weak. In general, children who participated in the DARE program have a more negative attitude toward drugs one year later than children who did not, as well as

FIGURE 15.2

A sample homework assignment for the Life Skills Training program for ATOD prevention.

Source: Mathias, Robert (1997, March/April). From the 'burbs to the 'hood . . . this program reduces students' risk of drug use. *NIDA Notes,* pp. 1, 5–6. Reprinted with permission.

Whose Opinion Counts?
(Influences on Your Decisions)

1. Write a list of who or what you think about when you make a decision.

   _____

   _____

   _____

2. For each of the following decisions, check off all of the things that influence your choice. For example, when you decide what to wear, do you think about your own opinions, your friends' opinions, your mother's opinions, etc.? You can check more than one influence for each decision.

Influences

This → Influences This ↓	My Opinion	My Friends' Opinion	My Parents' Opinion	My Past Experiences, Successes, and Failures	What I See on TV	What I Read About	What It Costs (in Time, Money, Convenience)
What to Wear							
How to Cut My Hair							
What to Eat							
What Music to Listen to							
What Movies to See							
What I Like to Do							

Decisions I Make

Look at all of your answers. Where do you have the most checks? Your friends, parents, media? Sometimes you don't realize how much we worry about what other people think. Are you really making decisions that are right for you?

a greater capability to resist peer pressure and a lower estimate of how many of their peers smoked cigarettes. However, there are no significant differences between DARE and non-DARE groups in the level of ATOD use itself. Recent studies show few differences in drug use, drug attitudes, or self-esteem when young people are measured ten years after the administration of the DARE program.[25]

Why DARE remains popular when its effectiveness has been consistently challenged is an interesting ques-tion. Some health professionals in this field theorize that the popularity of DARE is, in part, a result of the per-ception among parents and DARE supporters that it *appears* to work, through a process of informally com-paring children who go through DARE against an imag-ined perception of those children who do not:

The adults rightly perceive that most children who go through DARE do not engage in problematic drug use. Unfortunately, these individuals may not realize

Understanding ATOD Prevention and Education

Check your understanding of ATOD prevention and education strategies by deciding whether the following approaches would or would not be effective (in and of themselves) in reducing ATOD use or delaying its onset, based on the available research.

	WOULD BE EFFECTIVE	WOULD NOT BE EFFECTIVE
1. Scare tactics	☐	☐
2. Life skills training	☐	☐
3. Peer-refusal skills training	☐	☐
4. Values clarification	☐	☐
5. Objective information	☐	☐
6. Anxiety reduction and stress management	☐	☐
7. Assertiveness training	☐	☐
8. Training in problem solving and goal setting	☐	☐

Answers: 1. would not   2. would   3. would   4. would not   5. would not   6. would   7. would   8. would

that the vast majority of children, even without any intervention, do not engage in problematic drug use. . . . That is, adults may believe that drug use among adolescents is much more frequent than it actually is. When the children who go through DARE are compared to this "normative" group of drug-using teens, DARE appears effective.[26]

In 2001, in response to the criticism leveled against its lack of impact on drug use, the DARE program was

impactors: Individuals in the community who function as positive role models to children and adolescents in ATOD prevention programs.

modified to become "enhanced DARE." In this new version, more emphasis has been placed on student interaction, providing more opportunities for children to participate rather than being lectured by police officers.[27] In effect, DARE has adopted many of the basic components of effective school-based prevention programs such as LST.

Community-Based Prevention Programs

Community-based prevention programs offer several obvious advantages over those restricted to schools. The first is the greater opportunity to involve parents and other family members, religious institutions, and the media as collaborative agents for change. The most important factor here is the comprehensive nature of such programs. They draw on multiple social institutions that have been demonstrated to represent protective factors in an individual's life, such as the family, religious groups, and community organizations. In addition, corporations and businesses can be contributing partners, in both a financial and nonfinancial sense. Undoubtedly, we are in a better position to tackle the complexities of ATOD use through the use of multiple strategies rather than a single approach.

Components of an Effective Community-Based Program

Typically, many of the prevention components that have been incorporated in the schools are also components in community-based programs, such as the dissemination of information, stress management, and life skills training. Other approaches can be handled better in a community setting. For example, although schools can promote the possibility of alternative student activities that provide positive and constructive means for addressing feelings of boredom, frustration, and powerlessness (activities such as Midnight Basketball and Boys and Girls Clubs), the community is in a better position than the schools to actually provide these activities.

There is also a greater opportunity in the community to elicit the involvement of significant individuals to act as positive role models, referred to as **impactors,** and to enlist the help of the mass media to promote antidrug messages in the press and on television. In addition, community-based programs can be more influential in promoting changes in public policy that foster opportunities for education, employment, and self-development.[28]

Alternative-Behavior Programming

It should not be surprising that it is easier to say no to drugs when you can say yes to something else. In community-based prevention programs, a major effort is made to provide the activities and outlets that steer people away from the high-risk situations associated with ATOD use. Owing to the fact that adolescents spend a majority of their time outside school, and it is outside school that the preponderance of ATOD use occurs, community programs have the best chance of providing the necessary interventions. In fact, adolescents at highest risk of engaging in ATOD use are the least likely even to be attending school on the days that prevention efforts are delivered.[29]

Table 15.1 gives a sampling of alternative behaviors corresponding to a particular individual's interests and needs. One way of thinking about alternative-behavior programming is that a person is trading a negative dependence (on alcohol, tobacco, or other drugs) that causes harm on a physical or psychological level for a positive dependence that causes no harm and taps into pleasures from within.[30]

The Influence of Mass Media

Adolescents spend a lot of time watching TV; in fact, by the time he or she graduates from high school, the average teenager has watched over the years an estimated 22,000 hours of TV.[31] It makes sense that the medium of TV should have a major role in ATOD prevention. Anti-drug messages, however, have been

---

TABLE 15.1

Alternative behaviors to drug use: Needs and motives

LEVEL OF EXPERIENCE	NEEDS AND MOTIVES	ALTERNATIVES
Physical	Physical satisfaction, more energy	Athletics, dance/exercise, hiking, carpentry, or outdoor work
Sensory	Stimulation of sensory experience	Sensory awareness training, sky diving, experiencing
Emotional	Relief from anxiety, mood elevation, emotional relaxation	Individual counseling, group therapy
Interpersonal	Peer acceptance, defiance of authority figures	Confidence training, sensitivity groups, helping others in distress
Social/environmental	Promotion of social change or identification with a subculture	Social service; community action; helping the poor, aged, handicapped; environmental activism
Intellectual	Escape from boredom, curiosity, or inclination to explore one's own awareness	Reading, creative games, memory training, discussion groups
Creative/aesthetic	Increase in one's creativity or enjoyment of images and thoughts	Nongraded instruction in visual arts, music, drama, crafts, cooking, gardening, writing, singing
Philosophical	Discovery of the meaning of life, organization of a belief system	Discussions, study of ethics or other philosophical literature
Spiritual/mystical	Transcendence of organized religion, spiritual insight or enlightenment	Study of world religions, meditation, yoga
Miscellaneous	Adventure, risk taking, "kicks"	Outward Bound survival training, meaningful employment

Source: Adapted from Cohen, Allan Y. (1972). The journey beyond trips: Alternatives to drugs. In David E. Smith and George R. Gay (Eds.), *It's so good, don't even try it once: Heroin in perspective.* Englewood Cliffs, NJ: Prentice Hall, pp. 191–192.

largely confined to public-service announcements, brief commercials, and limited program series. Even so, the impact can be substantial. A prominent example is a series of memorable and persuasive anti-drug advertisements on TV, on the radio, and in print. These ads, beginning in 1987, are sponsored by the Partnership for a Drug-Free America (PDFA), a non-profit coalition of professionals from the communications industry, whose mission is to reduce demand for drugs in America. In the early 1990s, a number of PDFA spots targeted inner-city children living in high-risk drug-use environments. A 1994 study of the responses of more than fifteen thousand New York City school children showed that anti-drug attitudes had gotten stronger, particularly among African American respondents and children attending schools in below-poverty-line areas.[32]

In 1998, the PDFA entered into a "public–private partnership" with the Office of National Drug Control Policy to coordinate anti-drug media messages. Since that time, media time has been purchased by the federal government rather than donated by network television or radio stations and other media outlets. Production costs incurred by advertising agencies are now reimbursed by public funds, but their creative expenditures are still offered free (*pro bono*) as a public service.

Unfortunately, despite the intensified efforts to publicize anti-drug information in the media, several factors have the potential to undermine these efforts. There are a rapidly growing number of Internet web sites devoted to information about marijuana cultivation, illicit drug use in general, and drug paraphernalia. These pro-drug outlets have greatly proliferated and are easily accessible through online search engines.[33]

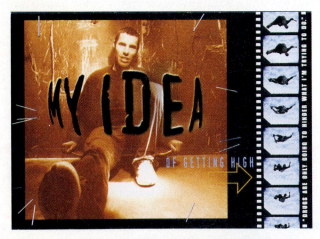

Skateboarding champion Andy Macdonald explains his way of getting high in this media message from the Partnership for a Drug-Free America.

A Model Community-Based Prevention Program: CASASTART

An intensive and coordinated program of preventive services and community-based law enforcement has been designed by the National Center on Addiction and Substance Abuse at Columbia University in New York, called CASASTART (the first part of the acronym referring to the center that designed it and the latter part standing for "Striving Together to Achieve Rewarding Tomorrows"). The target population for the program is defined as children between eight and thirteen years of age who have at least four risk factors for substance abuse problems. These risk factors may involve school (such as poor academic performance, in-school behavior problems, or truancy), family (such as poverty, violence at home, or a family member involved with gangs, drug use or sales, or a criminal conviction within five years), or the individual child (such as a history of known or suspected drug use or sales, past arrest, gang membership, or being a victim of child maltreatment).

In the CASASTART program, a case manager serving fifteen children and their families coordinates a variety of services, including social support, family and educational services, after-school and summer activities, mentoring, incentives, and juvenile justice intervention. The objective is to build resilience in the child, strengthen families, and make neighborhoods safer for children and their families. Relative to controls, CASASTART children have been found to be 60 percent less likely to sell drugs, 20 percent less likely to use drugs in the past thirty days, 20 percent less likely to commit a violent act, and more likely to be promoted to the next grade in school.[34]

Family Systems in Primary and Secondary Prevention

It can be argued that family influences form the corner-stone of any successful ATOD prevention program, just as we have seen the impact of the family on alcohol and drug abuse treatment. In effect, the family is the first line of defense against alcohol, tobacco, and other drugs (Figure 15.3 on page 396). Reaching the parents or guardians of youths at greatest risk, however, is a difficult task. Too often, ATOD prevention programs are attended by those parents or guardians who do not really need the information; those who need the information the most—parents who are either in denial, too embarrassed, or too out of control themselves—are notably absent. Other parents or guardians may need and gen-

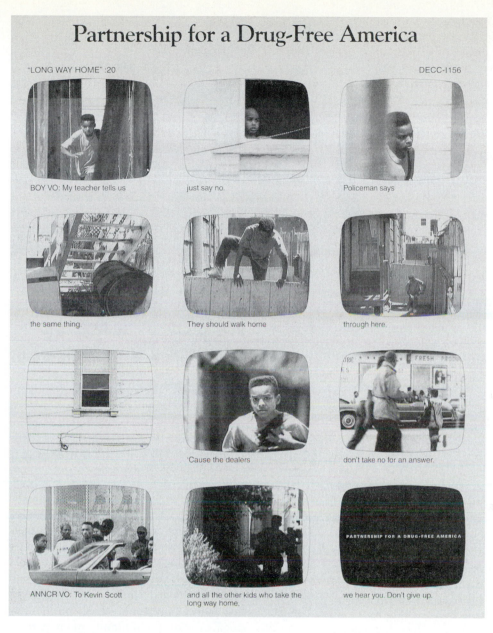

Partnership for a Drug-Free America

"LONG WAY HOME" :20   DECC-1156

BOY VO: My teacher tells us

just say no.

Policeman says

the same thing.

They should walk home

through here.

'Cause the dealers

don't take no for an answer.

ANNCR VO: To Kevin Scott

and all the other kids who take the long way home.

we hear you. Don't give up.

Scene segments from an anti-drug media message that aired on television in the 1990s and the voice-over (VO) script that accompanies the images. (Courtesy of the Partnership for a Drug-Free America, New York.)

uinely want to participate, but they may have difficulty attending because of lack of child care at home, lack of transportation, scheduling conflicts with their employment, or language differences. Several of the factors that prevent their attendance are the same factors that increase the risk of ATOD use among their children.[35]

Special Role Models in ATOD Prevention

Although obstacles exist, comprehensive ATOD prevention programs strive to incorporate parents or guardians, as well as other family members, into the overall effort. The reason lies in the variety of special roles they play in influencing children with regard to ATOD use:

- As role models, parents or guardians may drink alcoholic beverages, smoke, or drink excessive amounts of caffeinated coffee, not thinking of these habits as ATOD use. They can avoid sending their children signals about ATOD abstinence that are inconsistent at best, hypocritical at worst.

- As educators or resources for information, they can help by conveying verbal messages about health risks that are accurate and sincere.

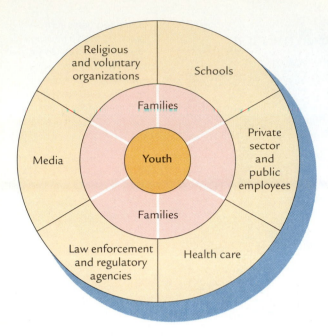

FIGURE 15.3

A schematic of various factors that impact upon families, and youth in turn, in ATOD prevention.

Source: Adapted from Fields, Richard (1998). *Drugs in perspective* (3rd ed.). Dubuque, IA: WCB McGraw-Hill, p. 309. Reprinted with permission of the McGraw-Hill Companies. Copyright 1998.

- As family policymakers and rule setters, they can convey a clear understanding of the consequence of ATOD use. If a parent or guardian cannot or will not back up family rules with logical and consistent consequences, the risk increases that rules will be broken.
- As stimulators of enjoyable family activities, parents or guardians can provide alternative-behavior programming necessary to steer youth away from high-risk situations.
- As consultants against peer pressure, parents or guardians can help reinforce the peer-refusal skills of their children. Children and adolescents frequently report that a strongly negative reaction at home is the single most important reason for their refusing alcohol, tobacco, and other drugs from their peers.

Dysfunctional Communication within the Family

The need for better lines of communication between parents and teenagers is illustrated in a PDFA survey. When asked whether they talked to their teenagers

The power of a Grandpa.

Children have a very special relationship with Grandma and Grandpa. That's why grandparents can be such powerful allies in helping keep a kid off drugs.

Grandparents are cool. Relaxed. They're not on the firing line every day. Some days a kid hates his folks. He never hates his grandparents. Grandparents ask direct, point-blank, embarrassing questions you're too nervous to ask:

"Who's the girl?"

"How come you're doing poorly in history?"

"Why are your eyes always red?"

"Did you go to the doctor? What did he say?"

The same kid who cons his parents is ashamed to lie to Grandpa. Without betraying their trust, a loving, understanding grandparent can discuss the danger of drugs openly with the child he adores. And should.

• The average age of first-time drug use among teens is 13. Some kids start at 9.

• 1 out of 4 American kids between 9 and 12 is offered illegal drugs. 22% of these kids receive the offer from a friend. And 10% named a family member as their source.

• Illegal drugs are linked to increased violence in many communities, to AIDS, to birth defects, drug-related crime, and homelessness.

As a grandparent, you hold a special place in the hearts and minds of your grandchildren. Share your knowledge, your love, your faith in them. Use your power as an influencer to steer your grandchildren away from drugs.

If you don't have the words, we do. We'll send you information on how to talk to your grandkids about drugs. Just ask for your free copy of *Keeping Youth Drug-Free*. Call 1-800-788-2800 or visit our websites, www.projectknow.com or www.drugfreeamerica.org.

Grandma, Grandpa. Talk to your grandkids. You don't realize the power you have to save them.

Office of National Drug Control Policy
Partnership for a Drug-Free America

Communication between grandparents and grandchildren can be an important tool in ATOD prevention.

about drugs at least once, 98 percent of parents reported that they had done so, but only 65 percent of teenagers recalled such a conversation. Barely 27 percent of teenagers reported learning at lot at home about the risks of drug use, even though virtually all their parents said they had discussed the topic. Justifiably, anti-drug media campaigns have focused on parent–child communication skills, specifically on the difficulty many parents have in talking to their children about sensitive subjects like drugs. There are recent indications that effective communication is on the rise.[36] Drugs . . . in Focus, however, examines an option that may be necessary when family communication breaks down.

The Triple Threat: Stress, Boredom, and Spending Money

ATOD prevention in young people sometimes can be simpler and more straightforward than we realize. A recent survey of teenagers aged twelve to seventeen measured the effects of three circumstances on the

A Test Kit for Drugs in the Home: Whom Can You Trust?

In 1995, a drug detection company introduced a commercial kit capable of testing for illicit drugs in the home. Marketed for parents who wish to check for possible drug abuse among their children, the kit consists of a 3-inch premoistened pad that can be wiped across desk tops, telephones, books, clothing, or other items. The pad is mailed to the company, where an analysis for the presence of cocaine, crack cocaine, heroin, methamphetamine, LSD, marijuana, and PCP is performed. The testing destroys the sample, so it cannot be used later in any court proceedings. The results of the analysis are then mailed to the parents.

The fact that the test kit is designed to be used by parents with or without their children's knowledge has raised a number of controversial issues. On the one hand, the kit is promoted as a potent new weapon in the battle against the increased levels of drug abuse among young people. From this point of view, parents are now able to get early help for their children before drug-abuse problems become too great. On the other hand, the kit can be viewed as a new weapon in the battle of the generations. Detractors argue that it sets up an atmosphere of distrust between parents and their children.

What do you think? If you were a parent, would you consider this new testing kit as a step forward or a step backward in the effort to prevent drug abuse in your family?

Sources: Kit to test for drugs at home (1995, March 29). *Newsday,* p. A8. Winslow, Olivia, and Lam, Chau (1995, March 30). Test fuels drugs debate. *Newsday,* pp. A6, A51.

likelihood that a teenager might engage in some form of substance abuse: (1) the degree of stress they feel they are under, (2) the frequency with which they are bored, and (3) the amount of money they have to spend in a typical week. High-stress teens (one-fourth of teens interviewed) were twice as likely as low-stress teens (a little more than one-fourth of teens interviewed) to smoke, drink, get drunk, and use illicit drugs. Teens reporting that they were frequently bored were 50 percent more likely than not-often-bored teens to engage in these behaviors. Teens with $25 or more a week in spending money were nearly twice as likely as teens with less spending money to smoke, drink, and use illicit drugs, and they were more than twice as likely to get drunk. Combining two or three of these risk factors (high stress, frequent boredom, and too much spending money) made the risk of smoking, drinking, and illicit drug use three times higher than when none of these characteristics was present (Portrait).[37]

Yes, You: ATOD Prevention and the College Student

In turning to the subject of ATOD prevention among college students, we first need to recognize that we are hardly speaking of a homogeneous population. U.S. college students represent all racial, ethnic, and socioeconomic groups and are likely to come from all parts of the world. They include undergraduate and graduate students, full-time and part-time students, residential students and commuters, students of traditional college age, and students who are considerably older.

In particular, there are marked differences in the objectives of a prevention program between those under twenty-one years of age and those who are older. In the former group, the goal may be "no use of" (or abstinence from) alcohol, tobacco, and other drugs, whereas in the latter group, the goal may be the low-risk (that is, responsible) consumption of alcohol and no use of tobacco and other drugs. The term "low-risk consumption" refers to a level of use restricted by considerations of physical health, family background, pregnancy risk, the law, safety, and other personal concerns.

With respect to alcohol, secondary prevention guidelines might stipulate that pregnant women, recovering alcoholics or those with a family history of alcoholism, people driving cars or heavy machinery, people on medications, or those under the age of twenty-one should not drink alcohol at all. Although the distinction between under-twenty-one and over-twenty-one preventive goals is applicable in many community-oriented programs, it is an especially difficult challenge for prevention efforts on a college campus when the target population contains both subgroups so closely intermingled.[38]

PORTRAIT

Meredith Poulten—A Counselor on the Front Lines

Since 1987, in the high school in Medway, Massachusetts, a quiet suburban town outside Boston, young people have had a place to go for help, for a referral, for a sympathetic ear, or just to sit and relax for a few minutes from the pressures of school, parents, and peers. It is called a Walk-in Center, with entrances both within the school and directly from the outside, and Meredith Poulten, its director and counselor, has been its driving force since its inception. The center deals with contemporary issues of teen suicide, depression, family conflicts, sexuality, alcohol and other drugs, self-esteem, physical health, and personal hygiene—not from a distance but as the daily reality of today's adolescents.

Out of an average of 150 student contacts per week in this center, more than half concern alcohol or other drug involvement at some level. Before the center was established,

such students were essentially on their own, "self-medicating" their problems, in the words of Poulten, rather than learning to handle the stresses of their lives. The school guidance department was oriented toward academic needs rather than day-to-day student problems, and many students have said that there was too great a stigma attached to talking to the school psychologist. As one student has expressed it, "I talk to Mrs. P. every day. She's more of a friend than a counselor. I can talk to her about anything." Another student admitted that were it not for the center, he would have been dead in less than a month.

The functioning of Poulten's Walk-in Center illustrates that the problems of today's youth do not fit into neat categories. They live in a world where drugs and sex are readily available and the pressure to indulge in both is high. The presence of alcohol and

other drugs has become "normalized" at parties and social gatherings. Ecstasy ("X") is pervasive, as are Adderall ("Addies"), OxyContin ("Oxy"), and Percocet ("Perks").

At the same time, society equates success with being first and being second-best with failure. For many students, communication with parents is next to impossible. Even when parents are open-minded about their child's circumstances, "You don't want to talk to your parents about your problems," says a student, "because you always want to please them."

Sources: Graham, Fiona (1989, October 11). A place to call their own. *The Country Gazette* (Medway, MA), pp. 1, 14. Hudson, Ted (1991, February 20). Letter to the Editor: Medway High Walk-in Center must be spared. *The Country Gazette* (Medway, MA), p. 3. Meredith Poulten, personal communication, 2007.

Changing the Culture of Alcohol and Other Drug Use in College

A major challenge with regard to prevention programs at colleges and universities comes from the widely regarded expectation that heavy alcoholic drinking, as well as some illicit drug use, during the college years represents something of a rite of passage. College alumni (and potential benefactors) frequently impede the implementation of drug and alcohol crackdowns, arguing that "we did it when we were in school."[39] Moreover, national surveys in 2006 indicate that by the end of high school, about 73 percent of all students have consumed alcoholic beverages, 56 percent have been drunk at least once, and 42 percent have smoked marijuana. Therefore, we cannot say that use of these drugs is a new experience for many college students.[40] Given this base of prior exposure, it is not surprising that further experimentation and more extensive patterns of ATOD use will occur. There is a compelling argument for secondary and tertiary prevention programs to be in place at this point.

The emphasis on most campuses is on the prevention and control of alcohol problems. However, it is less common for college administrators to focus on the problems associated with drugs other than alcohol. Although alcohol-abuse programs are virtually certain to be found on college campuses (Drugs . . . in Focus), attention directed toward comparable programs related specifically to drugs other than alcohol lags behind. Frequently, the only policy in place involves a procedure of punitive action if a student-athlete tests positive for an illicit drug. While no-smoking campuses are the norm, few if any programs are in place to help reduce the level of tobacco use among college students who smoke.

Prevention Approaches on College Campuses

On the positive side, college campuses have the potential for being ideal environments for comprehensive ATOD prevention programs because they combine features of

Alcohol 101 on College Campuses

A familiar experience among many students entering college for the first time is referred to by public health officials as the "college effect"—defined as an increase in drinking and negative behaviors associated with it (Chapter 10). One increasingly popular approach intended to minimize this phenomenon is a three-hour web-based online course called AlcoholEdu, developed by Outside the Classroom, Inc. More than 500 colleges and universities nationwide are currently participating in this program.

AlcoholEdu is oriented toward responsible drinking behavior rather than abstinence. Topics include an understanding of blood alcohol concentrations, activities that increase the likelihood of blacking out, discredited remedies for hangovers, as well as an appreciation of the alcohol beverage industry's role in fostering the image of alcohol consumption as a means for advancing social and interpersonal relationships. Participants are given an exam that tests their knowledge of the information provided in the course.

Colleges and universities have varying policies regarding students taking AlcoholEdu. Some require students to complete and pass the course with a minimum score on the exam prior to the first day of classes or prior to registering for the next semester. Others convey an expectation that the AlcoholEdu should be completed and warn that severe consequences will be imposed for those students who fail to finish the course and commit an alcohol violation in the future. There are early indications that student participation in AlcoholEdu results in significantly fewer negative consequences of drinking, such as missing class, attending class with a hangover, blacking out, and abusive behavior. Intensive studies of effectiveness, both short-term and long-term, however, need to be carried out.

In the meantime, additional programs addressing a wider range of alcohol problems on campuses have been developed. AlcoholEdu for Sanctions is an intervention program suited for students who have violated academic policies on alcohol, aimed at reducing recidivism rates. Alcohol Innerview is a brief motivational intervention tool for students who have experienced alcohol problems or are in alcohol-abuse counseling.

Sources: Fact sheet on alcohol issues, University of Colorado at Boulder (2004, August 11). Boulder, CO: Office of News Services, University of Colorado. Kesmodel, David (2005, November 1). Schools use web to teach about booze. *Wall Street Journal Online.* Outside the Classroom (2007), www.outsidetheclassroom.com.

---

school and community settings. Here are some suggested strategies for ATOD prevention on the college campus:

- Develop a multifaceted prevention program of assessment, education, policy, and enforcement. Involve students, faculty, and administrators together to determine the degree of availability and demand for alcohol and other drugs on campus and in the surrounding community and initiate public information and education efforts.

- Incorporate alcohol and other drug education into the curriculum. Faculty members can use drug-related situations as teachable moments, include drug topics in their course syllabi, and develop courses or course projects on issues relating to alcohol and other drugs.

- Ensure that hypocrisy is not the rule of the day. ATOD prevention is not a goal for college students only but is a larger issue that affects all members of the academic community, including faculty and administration.

- Encourage environments that lessen the pressures to engage in ATOD use. Foster more places where social and recreational activities can take place spontaneously and at hours when the most enticing alternative may be the consumption of alcohol and other drugs. A promising sign is the continuing popularity of drug-free dormitories on many college campuses, where student residents specifically choose to refrain from alcohol, tobacco, and other drugs.

The seriousness of the issue of ATOD use on college campuses could not be demonstrated more clearly than in the current trend toward promoting alcohol-free fraternities. At Northwestern University, for example, thirteen out of seventeen fraternities on campus have banned alcohol. Across the United States, at least thirty colleges, including such large universities as the

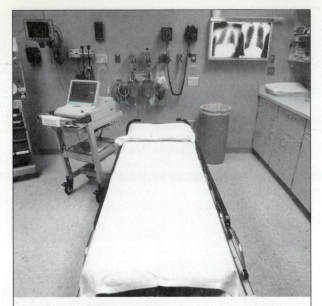

This Bed's For You.

Spring break in the ER, instead of on the beach?

There's no view of the beach and the food is terrible. You don't want your spring break to end in an emergency room.

Yet every year, that's where more and more students are winding up.

Alcohol poisoning. Car wrecks. Falls from balconies. Fistfights. Rape.

Why? Statistics show that half of male students – and 40 percent of females – drink

on spring break until they vomit or pass out. The average male student consumes 18 drinks daily. The average female downs 10.

The alcohol and tour industries are urging you on with free beer, all-you-can-drink parties, booze cruises and endless happy hours.

Don't fall for it. Enjoy a fun, safe spring break. And remember. Nobody looks good in a hospital robe.

This message is sponsored by **A Matter of Degree**

The National Effort to Reduce High-Risk Drinking Among College Students

AMOD is a project of the American Medical Association and campus-community partnerships across America • www.alcoholpolicysolutions.net

This ad, sponsored by the American Medical Association (AMA), appeared in college newspapers in 2004 in a campaign to discourage binge drinking, just prior to Spring Break. In 2007, the AMA called on the National Collegiate Athletic Association (NCAA) to eliminate alcohol advertising during radio and television broadcasts of college sports. The NCAA currently limits alcohol-related commercials to one minute per broadcast and encourages "responsibility themes and messages."

University of Iowa, the University of Oklahoma, and the University of Oregon, have banned alcohol in all their fraternity houses. The Arizona Supreme Court in 1994 has expressed the present-day concern in unmistakable terms:

> We are hardpressed to find a setting where the risk of an alcohol-related injury is more likely than from under-age drinking at a university fraternity party the first week of the new college year.[41]

Prevention and Treatment in the Workplace

The workplace has been recognized as an important focus for drug prevention and treatment. The 1988 Drug-free Workplace Act requires that all companies and businesses receiving any U.S. federal contracts or grants provide a drug-free workplace. Specifically, organizations must initiate a comprehensive and continuing program of drug education and awareness. Employees also must be notified that the distribution, possession, or unauthorized use of controlled substances is prohibited in that workplace and that actions will be taken against any employee violating these rules. Supervisors are advised to be especially alert to changes in a worker that might signal early or progressive stages in the abuse of alcohol and or other drugs. These signals include chronic absenteeism, a sudden change in physical appearance or behavior, spasmodic work pace, unexpectedly lower quantity or quality of work, partial or unexplained absences, a pattern of excuse-making or lying, the avoidance of supervisors or coworkers, and on-the-job accidents or lost time from such accidents.[42]

Employee and Member Assistance Programs

By executive order of President Reagan in 1986, all U.S. federal agencies were directed to establish an employee assistance program (EAP) for governmental employees. Nongovernmental organizations have since been encouraged (but not required) by the 1988 act to establish EAP services as well, so as to identify and counsel employees with personal problems that are connected to drug abuse or dependence and to provide referrals to community agencies where these individuals can get further help. Though not technically required to do so, steadily increasing numbers of American businesses have set up EAPs and are becoming committed to prevention and treatment. By the mid-1990s, approximately half of all private nonagricultural worksites with fifty or more full-time employees had ongoing EAP services. Traditionally, the emphasis in EAPs has been on problems resulting from alcohol abuse, which is understandable given that this category represents such a large proportion of drug abuse in general (see Chapter 11). This emphasis remains, but there is a growing awareness that the range of drug abuse problems is wider than alcoholism.[43]

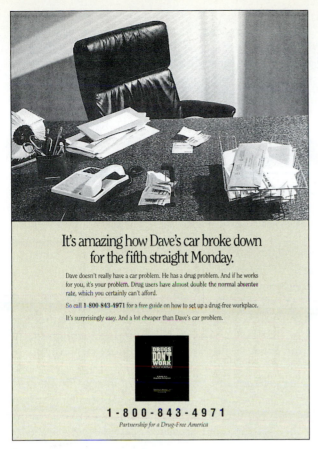

It's amazing how Dave's car broke down
for the fifth straight Monday.

Dave doesn't really have a car problem. He has a drug problem. And if he works
for you, it's your problem. Drug users have almost double the normal absentee
rate, which you certainly can't afford.

So call 1-800-843-4971 for a free guide on how to set up a drug-free workplace.

It's surprisingly easy. And a lot cheaper than Dave's car problem.

**DRUGS
DON'T
WORK**

1 - 8 0 0 - 8 4 3 - 4 9 7 1

Partnership for a Drug-Free America

Drug and alcohol problems are major sources of worker
absenteeism and decreased workplace productivity.

In the case of union-supported member assistance programs (MAPs), the treatment focus is on teams of volunteer peer counselors. These individuals undergo extensive training and, in some cases, are certified. An example is the MAP run by the New York City–based Steamfitters Union Local 638. Working against a deep-seated workplace drinking culture, MAP drug counselors emphasize the fact that the use of alcohol or other drugs on the job is a violation of union as well as occupational regulations.

> They let people know that off-the-job use of alcohol
> and other drugs that ultimately impair job function
> is unacceptable. For instance, if a worker violates
> the drug- and alcohol-related norms, a peer coun-
> selor reinforces what is acceptable behavior and
> urges the worker to comply voluntarily. If a worker
> is unable to comply to the standard voluntarily,
> then the MAP peer counselor may offer a referral
> for treatment.[44]

Drug Testing in the Workplace

The 1986 Executive Order also mandated preemployment drug screening of all federal employees as well as periodic, random schedules of drug testing afterward. Assuming the most commonly available EMIT urinalysis were used (see Chapter 9), drug testing refers to a screening for opiates, amphetamines, cocaine, benzodiazepines, and marijuana. (It is not known whether the president at the time or subsequent presidents since 1986 have been included in this requirement.)

As with the policy regarding EAPs under the 1988 Drug-free Workplace Act, statutes do not require drug testing for employees other than those working for the federal government. Nonetheless, as of 1996, according to a survey conducted by the American Management Association, seven out of every eight American companies, whether they are covered by the 1988 act or not, have established policies for drug-testing procedures either as part of the job application process or as a way of monitoring drug use among employees on a periodic basis.[45]

While it is easy to understand the rationale for drug testing in the workplace in the overall scheme of drug prevention, the procedure has raised a number of important issues regarding individual rights. Is the taking of a urine sample a violation of a person's freedom from "unreasonable search and seizure" as guaranteed by the Fourth Amendment to the U.S. Constitution? It turns out that if the government requires it, the decision rests on the question of whether there is reasonable or unreasonable cause for the drug testing to occur. In cases in which a threat to public safety is involved, the cause has been ruled as reasonable. However, if a private business requires it, the legal rights of employees are somewhat murky. An employee typically accepts his or her job offer with the assumption and agreement that periodic monitoring of drug use will take place, but whether this understanding is a form of implied coercion is an open question.

If you lose your job as a result of testing positive in a drug test, has there been a violation of your right to "due process" as guaranteed by the Fifth Amendment? The courts have ruled that this right would be violated only if the method of drug screening were unreliable, if the analysis and reporting were carried out in an unreliable manner, or if it could not be shown that the presence of any one of the screened substances had a relationship to job impairment. In general, screening methods are not perfectly reliable, the handling of drug tests is not perfectly controlled, and the relationship between drug use and a decline in job performance is not perfectly clear, but drug tests nonetheless have been judged to have met reasonable standards, and the practice is allowed. The bottom line is that drug testing, despite its obvious infringements on individual privacy, has become a fact of life in corporate America.[46]

Nonetheless, despite the increasing acceptance of drug testing as a tool for drug-abuse prevention in the workplace, there will always be questions about the impact on workers themselves. For example, the possibility of false positives (when an individual tests positive but has not been using a particular drug) or false negatives (when an individual who, on the basis of prior drug use, should test positive for a particular drug but does not do so) during drug testing can present unfortunate consequences. Consider this possible preemployment screening scenario:

Suppose that the EMIT test were 100 percent effective in spotting drug users (it is not) and that it has a false-positive rate of 3 percent (which is not unreasonable). In a group of 100 prospective employees, one person has recently taken an illegal drug. Since the test is 100 percent effective, that person will be caught, but three other people (the 3 percent false-positive rate) will also. Therefore, 75 percent of those who fail the test are innocent parties.[47]

Another problem is that companies are not required to follow up a positive EMIT test result with another more sensitive method, such as one using the GC/MS procedure (see Chapter 9). Some companies allow for retesting in general, but many do not. In the American Management Association survey mentioned earlier, 22 percent of the companies reported that workers who tested positive were immediately dismissed from their positions.[48]

The Prevalence and Economic Costs of Alcohol and Other Drug Abuse in the Workplace

When considering the scope of drug-abuse problems in the workplace, it is all too easy to look at high-profile instances of on-the-job accidents involving the effects of either illicit drugs or alcohol. In 1991, a New York subway operator crashed his train near a station in lower Manhattan, resulting in 5 deaths and 215 injuries. The operator admitted that he had been drinking prior to the crash, and his BAC level was measured at 0.21 percent, more than twice the legal limit of 0.10 percent in New York at that time. In 1987, a Conrail train brakeman and an engineer were found to be responsible for a collision that resulted in 16 deaths and 170 injuries. Drug testing revealed traces of marijuana in their systems, though it was not clear if they were intoxicated at the time of the accident.

These conspicuous examples do not accurately reflect the impact of alcohol and other drug abuse in the workplace for a number of reasons. First, the likelihood of an adverse effect is not adequately reflected in news reports, any more than the impact of drug toxicity on our society can be assessed by reading the news stories of public figures and celebrities who have died of drug overdoses (see Chapter 1). Second, in many cases, we are limited in determining the extent to which we can connect drug use with the tragic consequences of an accident because some drugs leave metabolites in the system long after they have stopped producing behavioral effects (see Chapter 9). In the case of the Conrail incident, the continued presence of marijuana metabolites for weeks after marijuana use can make the positive test results irrelevant. Nonetheless, we are greatly influenced in our thinking by the media coverage of such events.

Obviously, we must turn to estimates gathered from other sources of information. Unfortunately, these estimates are "soft," having large margins of error. Even so, they leave little doubt that the abuse of alcohol and other drugs has a major impact on workplace productivity. On the basis of its own studies, the federal Center for Substance Abuse Prevention (CSAP) estimates that, relative to nonabusers, abusers of alcohol and other drugs

- are 5 times more likely to file a workers' compensation claim
- are 2.5 times more likely to be absent from work for eight days or more
- are 3.6 times more likely to be involved in an accident on the job
- are 5 times more likely to be personally injured on the job
- are 3 times more likely to be late for work
- are 2.2 times more likely to request early dismissal from work or time off
- use 16 times more sick leave

Overall, the estimated costs of the loss in productivity as a result of such behavior amount to $60 to $100 billion each year.[49]

The Impact of Drug-Free Workplace Policies

Given the adverse effects of drug abuse on productivity, we should expect to see substantial economic and personal benefits when drug-free workplace policies are in place. In one well-documented case, a program developed by the Southern Pacific Railroad Company in the 1980s, extensive drug testing was required for all employees who had been involved in a company accident or rule violation. As a result, the annual number of accidents decreased from 911 to 168 in three years, and the financial losses from such accidents decreased from $6.4 million to $1.2 million. During the first few months of the new testing program, it was found that 22 to 24 percent of employees who had had some human-factor-related accident tested positive for alcohol or other drugs, a figure that fell to 3 percent three years later.[50]

It makes sense that drug-abuse prevention programs would have the greatest impact in companies within the transportation industry, owing to the close relationship between drug-induced impairments in performance and the incidence of industrial accidents. Beyond this application, however, it is widely recognized that a similar impact, if not one as dramatic in magnitude, can be demonstrated in any business setting. The reasons relate to the basic goals of prevention, as discussed earlier: deterrence and rehabilitation. The practice of testing for illicit drug use in the workplace functions as an effective deterrent among workers because the likelihood is strong that illicit drug use will be detected. In addition, EAP and MAP services can function as an effective rehabilitative tool because those workers who might otherwise not receive help with drug-abuse problems of all kinds now will be referred to appropriate agencies for treatment services.[51]

Multicultural Issues in Prevention

In the case of ATOD prevention efforts, it is important to remember that information intended to reach individuals of a specific culture passes through a series of **sociocultural filters.** Understanding this filtering process is essential to maximize the reception and acceptance of ATOD prevention information.

Prevention Approaches among Latino Groups

A good example of the need to recognize sociocultural filters is the set of special concerns associated with communicating ATOD information to Latinos, a diverse group of more than 41 million people living throughout the United States.[52] The following insights concerning elements of the Latino community have a strong bearing on an ATOD prevention program's chances of succeeding.

■ Because of the importance Latinos confer on the family and religious institutions, prevention and treatment efforts should be targeted to include the entire family and, if possible, its religious leaders. Prevention efforts will be most effective when counselors reinforce family units and value them as a whole.

■ Prevention programs are needed to help Latino fathers recognize how important their role or example is to their sons' and daughters' self-image regarding alcohol and other drugs. Because being a good father is part of *machismo*, it is important that the men become full partners in parenting. Mothers should be encouraged to learn strategies for including their husbands in family interactions at home.

■ Because a Latina woman with alcohol or other drug problems is strongly associated with a violation of womanly ideals of purity, discipline, and self-sacrifice, educational efforts should concentrate on reducing the shame associated with her reaching out for help. One particular web site that addresses the needs of the Latino community is sponsored by the National Latino Council on Alcohol and Tobacco Prevention (NLCATP).

Prevention Approaches among African American Groups

Another set of special concerns exist with regard to communicating ATOD information in African American communities.[53] Some basic generalizations have proven helpful in optimizing the design of ATOD prevention programs.

■ African American youths tend to use drugs other than alcohol after they form social attitudes and adopt behaviors associated with delinquency. The most common examples of delinquency include drug dealing, shoplifting, and petty theft. With regard to the designing of media campaigns, it is the deglamorization of the drug dealer that appears to be most helpful in primary prevention efforts among African American youths.

> **sociocultural filters:** A set of considerations specific to a particular culture or community that can influence the reception and acceptance of public information.

- Drug use and social problems are likely to be inter-related in primarily African American neighborhoods. The effects of alcohol and other drug use are intensified when other factors exist, such as high unemployment, poverty, poor health care, and poor nutrition.

- Several research studies have shown that most African American youths, even those in low-income areas, do manage to escape from the pressures to use alcohol and other drugs. The protective factors of staying in school, solid family bonds, strong religious beliefs, high self-esteem, adequate coping strategies, positive social skills, and steady employment all build on one another to provide resilience on the part of high-risk children and adolescents. As noted before, prevention programs developed with protective factors in mind have the greatest chance for success.

The Personal Journey to Treatment and Recovery

Individuals who seek help in a treatment program typically have been "jolted" by some external force in their lives. They may have no other option except imprisonment for drug offenses; they may be at risk of losing their job because their supervisor has identified an unproductive pattern of behavior; a spouse may have threatened to leave if something is not done; a friend may have died from a drug overdose or a drug-related accident. Any of these crises or others similar to them can force the question and the decision to seek treatment.[54]

The prospect of entering a treatment program is probably the most frightening experience the abuser has ever had in his or her life. Treatment counselors frequently hear the questions, "Couldn't I just cut down?" or "Couldn't I just give up drugs temporarily?" or "How will I be able to take the pain of withdrawal?" or "How will I be able to stand the humiliation?" Far from stalling tactics, these questions represent real obstacles to taking that crucial first step.[55]

precontemplation stage: A stage of change in which the individual may wish to change but either lacks the serious intention to undergo change in the foreseeable future or is unaware of how significant his or her problem has become.

Rehabilitation and the Stages of Change

Rehabilitation from drug abuse and dependence has three major goals. First, the long decline in physical and psychological functioning that has accumulated over the years must be reversed. Drugs take a heavy toll on the user's medical condition and his or her personal relationships. Second, the use of all psychoactive substances must stop, not simply the one or two that are causing the immediate problem and not merely for a limited period of time. Thus the motivation to stop using alcohol and other drugs and to remain abstinent on a permanent basis must be strong, and stay strong. Third, a life-style free of alcohol and other drugs must be rebuilt, from scratch if necessary. This frequently means giving up the old friends and the old places where drugs were part of an abuser's life, and finding new friends and places that reinforce a drug-free existence. A determination to stay clean and sober requires avoiding high-risk situations, defined as those that increase the possibility of relapse.[56]

We can understand the journey toward rehabilitation by examining five separate stages through which the recovering individual must pass.[57] These stages are (1) precontemplation, (2) contemplation, (3) preparation, (4) action, and (5) maintenance. Rather than thinking of these stages as a linear progression, however, it is more accurate to think of them as points along a spiral (Figure 15.4); more than likely, a person will recycle through the stages multiple times before he or she is totally rehabilitated. Unfortunately, relapse is the rule rather than the exception in the process of recovery. The following is an examination of each stage in detail.

- *Precontemplation.* Individuals who are in the **precontemplation stage** may *wish* to change but lack the serious intention to undergo change in the foreseeable future or may be unaware of how significant their problems have become. They may be entering treatment at this time only because they perceive that a crisis is at hand. They may even demonstrate a change in behavior while the pressure is on, but once the pressure is off, they revert to their former ways. It is often difficult for a counselor to deal with a drug abuser during the precontemplation stage because the abuser still feels committed to positive aspects of drug use. A principal goal at this point is to induce inconsistencies in the abuser's perception of drugs in general.

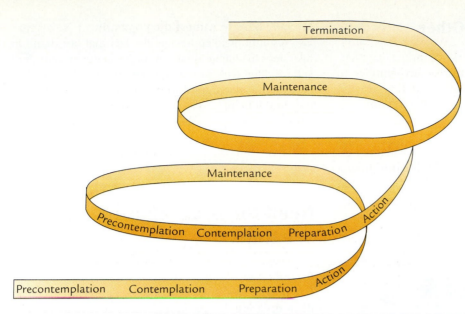

FIGURE 15.4

A spiral model of the stages of change in the recovery from drug abuse and dependence.

Source: Prochaska, James O., DiClemente, Carlo C., and Norcross, John C. (1992). In search of how people change: Applications to addictive behaviors. *American Psychologist, 47,* 1104. Copyright © 1992 by the American Psychological Association. Reprinted with permission.

- *Contemplation.* In the **contemplation stage,** individuals are aware that a problem exists and are thinking about overcoming it but have not yet made a commitment to take action. At this point, drug abusers may struggle with the prospect of the tremendous amount of effort and energy needed to overcome the problem. Counselors can help them by highlighting the negative aspects of drug use, making reasonable assurances about the recovery process, and building the self-confidence necessary to change.

- *Preparation.* Individuals in the **preparation stage** are defined as those who are seriously considering taking action in the next thirty days and have unsuccessfully taken action over the past twelve months. Alcohol abusers or tobacco smokers may at this point set a "quit date," or a heroin abuser may make a firm date to enter a therapeutic community within the next month. Because drug abusers are fully capable of stating a clear commitment to change at the preparation stage, counselors can begin to discuss the specific steps in the recovery process, strategies for avoiding problems or postponements, and ways to involve friends and family members in their decision.

- *Action.* The **action stage** is the point at which individuals actually modify their behavior, their experiences, and their environment in an effort to overcome their problem. Drug use has now stopped. This is the most fragile stage; abusers are at a high risk for giving in to drug cravings and experiencing mixed feelings about the psychological costs of staying clean. If they successfully resist these urges to return to drug use, the counselor should strongly reinforce their restraint. If they slip back to drug use temporarily then return to

abstinence, the counselor should praise their efforts to have turned their life around. An important message to be conveyed at this stage is that a fundamental change in life-style and a strong support system of friends and family will reduce the chances of relapse.

- *Maintenance stage.* Individuals in the **maintenance stage** have been drug-free for a minimum of six months. They have developed new skills and strategies to avoid backsliding and are consolidating a life-style free of drugs. Here, the counselor must simultaneously acknowledge the success that has been achieved and emphasize that the struggle will never be totally over. The maintenance stage is ultimately open-ended, in that it continues for the rest of the ex-user's life. Therefore, it may be necessary to have "booster sessions" from time to time, so that the maintenance stage is itself maintained.

contemplation stage: A stage of change in which the individual is aware that a problem exists and is thinking about overcoming it but has not yet made a commitment to take action.

preparation stage: A stage of change in which the individual seriously considers taking action to overcome a problem in the next thirty days and has unsuccessfully taken action over the past twelve months.

action stage: A stage of change in which the individual actually modifies his or her behavior and environment to overcome a problem.

maintenance stage: A stage of change in which the individual has become drug-free for a minimum of six months and has developed new skills and strategies that reduce the probability of relapse.

Stages of Change and Other Problems in Life

If these stages of change seem vaguely familiar to you, with or without a drug-related problem, it is no accident. Problems may take many different forms, but the difficulties that we face when we confront these problems have a great deal in common. We may wish to lose weight, get more exercise, stop smoking, end an unhappy relationship, seek out a physician to help a medical condition, or any of a number of actions that might lead toward a healthier and more productive life.

We only have to witness the popularity of New Year's Eve resolutions to appreciate the fact that our desire to take steps to change is part of simply being human. And yet, we often feel frustrated when our intentions do not prevail, and those resolutions are left unfulfilled. You may find it helpful to look at your own personal journey toward resolving a problem in your life in terms of the five stages of change.[58]

A Final Note: The Continuing Need for Drug-Abuse Treatment

According to U.S. government estimates, nearly 8 million people aged twelve or older need treatment for an illicit drug problem, but only 18 percent of them have received drug-abuse treatment at a specialty substance-abuse facility in the past twelve months. Among those who were not in treatment, about one-fourth report that they made an effort but were unable to receive proper care for their problem; the other three-fourths made no effort at all.

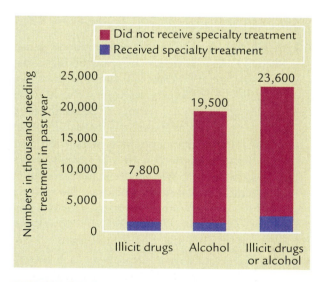

FIGURE 15.5

The gap between treatment needed and treatment received among individuals over the age of twelve in the United States.

Source: Substance Abuse and Mental Health Services Administration (2007). *Results from the 2005 National Survey on Drug Use and Health: National findings.* Rockville, MD: Office of Applied Studies, Substance Abuse and Mental Health Services Administration, pp. 76–82.

With respect to those identified as having a need for alcohol-abuse treatment, the picture is even worse. Approximately 19 million people aged twelve or older need treatment for an alcohol problem, but only 8 percent of them are receiving it. About one-third report that the reason for not receiving treatment was that no treatment program was available to them, even though they made the effort to seek one out; two-thirds made no effort at all.[59]

Figure 15.5 shows the wide gap between treatment needed and treatment received, in terms of the percentage of the total U.S. population over the age of twelve. As the statistics indicate, the solution is two-fold. First, we must increase the availability of diverse and effective treatment programs for alcohol and drug abuse. Second, we must find ways to enhance the motivation of those who should be in treatment so they can seek out the help they need.

Summary

Levels of Intervention in Drug-Abuse Prevention

- Drug-abuse prevention efforts fall into three basic levels of intervention: primary, secondary, and tertiary.

- Primary prevention focuses on populations that have had only minimal or no exposure to drugs. Secondary prevention focuses on populations whose drug experience has not yet been associated with serious long-term problems. Tertiary prevention focuses on populations who have entered drug treatment; the goal is to prevent relapse.

ATOD Prevention: Strategic Priorities, Goals, and Resilience

- The overall strategy for alcohol, tobacco, and other drug (ATOD) prevention and education is to minimize the risk factors in a person's life with respect to ATOD use and maximize the protective factors. The inclination to resist the effects of risk factors for ATOD use through the action of protective factors is referred to as resilience.

- The overall national policy for the control of drug use in the United States is coordinated by the White House Office of National Drug Control Policy (ONDCP). In a recent formulation of this policy, three priorities have been established as components of a national strategy: stopping drug use before it starts through primary prevention, healing America's drug users through tertiary prevention, and disrupting the market through efforts to reduce the availability of illicit drugs.

- In 1992, the federal program, Healthy People 2000, set specific objectives to be reached by 2000 regarding aspects of personal health, including those that pertain to ATOD use. More recently, a new program, Healthy People 2010, has begun to work on achieving objectives that had not yet been met previously.

Lessons from the Past: Prevention Approaches That Have Failed

- Several strategies have been largely unsuccessful in meeting the goals of ATOD prevention. They include the reliance on supply/availability reduction, punitive judicial policies, scare tactics, objective information, and affective education.

Hope and Promise: Components of Effective School-Based Prevention Programs

- Effective school-based programs have incorporated a combination of peer-refusal skills training, relaxation and stress management, and training in social skills and personal decision making.

- The Life Skills Training program is a model for programs incorporating school-based components for effective ATOD prevention.

Community-Based Prevention Programs

- Community-based programs make use of a broader range of resources, including community leaders and public figures as positive role models, opportunities for alternative-behavior programming, and the mass media.

- Recent efforts by the media have had a major impact on the image of ATOD use in both high-risk populations and others in the community.

- CASASTART is a model for programs incorporating intensive community-wide components of ATOD prevention.

Family Systems in Primary and Secondary Prevention

- Community-based prevention programs are increasingly mindful of the importance of the family, particularly parents, as the first line of defense in ATOD prevention efforts.

- A major emphasis in ATOD prevention has been on the special roles of parents, grandparents, guardians, and other family members. Improved lines of communication within the family are crucial elements.

Yes, You: ATOD Prevention and the College Student

- On college campuses, ATOD prevention programs are incorporating features of both school-based and community-based approaches. There is a compelling argument for the need to change the culture of alcohol and other drug use in college. There is the perception that heavy alcoholic drinking, as well as some illicit drug use, during the college years represents something of a rite of passage.
- ATOD prevention programs should involve faculty and administrators, as well as students, in an overall comprehensive strategy.

Prevention and Treatment in the Workplace

- Since the mid-1980s, a growing number of companies and other businesses have adopted measures to encourage a drug-free workplace. This involves, in part, the establishment of educational programs that increase workers' awareness of alcohol abuse, the abuse of illicit drugs, and the impact of these behaviors on productivity and the quality of the workers' lives.
- One element of most drug-free workplace programs is an employee assistance program (EAP), serving to help workers with abuse problems. Member assistance programs (MAPs) supplement and complement the work of EAPs, where unions exist. Another element is a policy of drug testing, serving to reduce illicit drug use among workers and employment applicants.
- Although employee assistance programs and drug testing have been readily accepted among U.S. businesses, questions about the extent to which drug testing violates personal privacy and individual rights still remain.

Multicultural Issues in Prevention

- Sociocultural filters are considerations that influence the reception and acceptance of public information by a particular culture or community.
- Considerations of this kind need to be made when communicating with specific subgroups such as Latino and African American individuals in order to facilitate drug-abuse prevention efforts.

The Personal Journey to Treatment and Recovery

- The road to recovery can be understood in terms of five stages of change: precontemplation, contemplation, preparation, action, and maintenance. It is possible to recycle through these stages multiple times in a kind of spiraling pattern before long-term recovery is attained.
- The five stages of change are applicable to the resolution of any life problems, not just those associated with drug abuse.

The Continuing Need for Drug-Abuse Treatment

- According to U.S. government estimates, nearly 8 million people, aged twelve or older, need treatment for an illicit drug problem; approximately 19 million people need treatment for an alcohol-related problem. A small fraction, however, have received treatment at a specialized facility in the past twelve months.
- About one-fourth of those who need treatment for an illicit drug problem and about one-third of those who need treatment for an alcohol problem have made an effort but were not able to receive proper care. The others have made no effort at all toward getting treatment.

Key Terms

action stage, p. 405
affective education, p. 388
contemplation stage, p. 405
impactors, p. 392

maintenance stage, p. 405
peer-refusal skills, p. 389
precontemplation stage, p. 404

preparation stage, p. 405
primary prevention, p. 382
resilience, p. 383
secondary prevention, p. 382

sociocultural filters, p. 403
tertiary prevention, p. 382
values clarification, p. 388

Endnotes

1. Foxhall, Kathryn (2001, June). Preventing relapse: Looking at data differently led to today's influential relapse prevention therapy. *Monitor on Psychology*, pp. 46–47. Swisher, John D. (1979). Prevention issues. In R. L. DuPont, A. Goldstein, and J. O'Donnell (Eds.). *Handbook on drug abuse*. Washington DC: National Institute on Drug Abuse, pp. 423–435.

2. Brook, Judith S., and Brook, David W. (1996). Risk and protective factors for drug use. In Clyde B. McCoy, Lisa R. Metsch, and James A. Inciardi (Eds.), *Intervening with drug-involved youth*. Thousand Oaks, CA: Sage Publications, pp. 23–44. Catalano, Richard F.; Kosterman, Rick; Hawkins, J. David; Newcomb, Michael D.; and Abbott, Robert D. (1996). Modeling the etiology of adolescent substance use: A test of the social development model. *Journal of Drug Issues*, 23, 429–455. Glantz, Meyer D., and Johnson, Jeannette, L. (Eds.) (2003). *Resilience and development: Positive life adaptations*. New York: Kluwer Academic/Plenum. Wills, Thomas A., and Yaeger, Alison M. (2003). Family factors in adolescent substance abuse: Models and mechanisms. *Current Directions in Psychological Science*, 12, 222–226.

3. Biglan, Anthony; Mrazek, Patricia J.; Carnine, Douglas; and Flay, Brian R. (2003). The integration of research and practice in the prevention of youth problem behaviors. *American Psychologist*, 58, 433–441. Office of National Drug Control Policy (2003, February). *National drug control strategy: Update*. Washington DC: White House Office of National Drug Control Policy.

4. McGinnis, J. Michael, and Foege, William H. (1993, November 10). Actual causes of death in the United States. *Journal of the American Medical Association*, 270, 2207–2212.

5. Public Health Service (1992). *Healthy People 2000: National health promotion and disease prevention objectives—Summary report*. Boston: Jones and Bartlett.

6. Marwick, Charles (2000). Healthy People 2010 initiative launched. *Journal of the American Medical Association*, 283, 989–990. Public Health Service (2000). *Healthy People 2010: National health promotion and disease prevention objectives: Conference edition*. Bethesda, MD: Public Health Service.

7. Office of National Drug Control Policy, *National drug control strategy*, p. 4.

8. Goode, Erich (1999). *Drugs in American society* (5th ed.). New York: McGraw-Hill College, pp. 385–387.

9. Hingson, Ralph W.; Scotch, Norman; Mangione, Thomas; Meyers, Allan; Glantz, Leonard; Heeren, Timothy; Lin, Nan; Mucatel, March; and Pierce, Glenn (1983). Impact of legislation raising the legal drinking age in Massachusetts from 18 to 21. *American Journal of Public Health*, 73, 163–170.

10. Goode, *Drugs in American society*, pp. 381–418. Steinberg, Neil (1994, May 5). The law of unintended consequences. *Rolling Stone*, pp. 33–34.

11. Funkhouser, Judith E., and Denniston, Robert W. (1992). Historical perspective. In Mary A. Jansen (Ed.), *A promising future: Alcohol and other drug problem prevention services improvement* (OSAP Prevention Monograph 10). Rockville, MD: Office of Substance Abuse Prevention, pp. 5–15.

12. Flay, Brian R., and Sobel, Judith L. (1983). The role of mass media in preventing adolescent substance abuse. In Thomas J. Glynn, Carl G. Leukenfeld, and Jacqueline P. Ludford (Eds.), *Preventive adolescent drug abuse*. Rockville, MD: National Institute on Drug Abuse, pp. 5–35. Swisher, John D.; Crawford, J.; Goldstein, R.; and Yura, M. (1971). Drug education: Pushing or preventing. *Peabody Journal of Education*, 49, 68–75.

13. Williams, R., Ward, D., and Gray, L. (1985). The persistence of experimentally induced cognitive change: A neglected dimension in the assessment of drug prevention programs. *Journal of Drug Education*, 15, 33–42.

14. Meeks, Linda, Heit, Philip, and Page, Randy (1994). *Drugs, alcohol, and tobacco*. Blacklick, OH: Meeks Heit Publishing, p. 201.

15. Ibid., p. 202.

16. McBride, Duane C., Mutch, Patricia B., and Chitwood, Dale D. (1996). Religious belief and the initiation and prevention of drug use among youth. In Clyde B. McCoy, Lisa R. Metsch, and James A. Inciardi (Eds.), *Intervening with drug-involved youth*. Thousand Oaks, CA: Sage Publications, pp. 110–130.

17. Schroeder, Debra S., Laflin, Molly T., and Weis, David L. (1993). Is there a relationship between self-esteem and drug use? Methodological and statistical limitations of the research. *Journal of Drug Issues*, 22, 645–665. Yuen, Francis K. O., and Pardeck, John T. (1998). Effective strategies for preventing substance abuse among children and adolescents. *Early Child Development and Care*, 145, 119–131.

18. Best, J. Allan; Flay, Brian R.; Towson, Shelagh M. J.; Ryan, Katherine B.; Perry, Cheryl L.; Brown, K. Stephen; Kersell, Mary W.; and d'Avernas, Josie R. (1984). Smoking prevention and the concept of risk. *Journal of Applied Social Psychology*, 14, 257–273.

19. Botvin, Gilbert J., and Botvin, Elizabeth M. (1992). School-based and community-based prevention approaches. In Joyce H. Lewisohn, Pedro Ruiz, and Robert B. Millman (Eds.), *Substance abuse: A comprehensive textbook* (2d ed.). Baltimore: Williams and Wilkins, pp. 910–927. Orlandi, Mario A. (1986). Prevention technologies for drug-involved youth. In Clyde B. McCoy, Lisa R. Metsch, and James A. Inciardi (Eds.), *Intervening with drug-involved youth*. Thousand Oaks, CA: Sage Publications, pp. 81–100. Schinke, Steven P., and Gilchrist, Lewayne D. (1983). Primary prevention of tobacco smoking. *Journal of School Health*, 53, 416–419.

20. Botvin, Gilbert J., and Tortu, Stephanie (1988). Preventing adolescent substance abuse through life skills training. In Richard M. Price, Emory L. Cowen, Raymond P. Lorion, and Julia Ramos-McKay (Eds.), *Fourteen ounces of prevention: A casebook for practitioners*. Washington DC: American Psychological Association, pp. 98–110.

21. Botvin, Gilbert J.; Baker, Eli; Dusenbury, Linda; Botvin, Elizabeth M.; and Diaz, Tracy (1995). Long-term follow-up results of a randomized drug abuse prevention trial in a white middle-class population. *Journal of the American Medical Association, 273,* 1106–1112. Botvin, Gilbert J.; Epstein Jennifer A.; Baker, Eli; Diaz, Tracy; and Ifill-Williams, Michelle (1997). School-based drug abuse prevention with inner-city minority youth. *Journal of Child and Adolescent Substance Abuse, 6,* 5–19.

22. Mathias, Robert (1997, March/April). From the 'burbs to the 'hood . . . this program reduces student's risk of drug use. *NIDA Notes,* pp. 1, 5–6. Quotation on p. 6.

23. Information courtesy of the Substance Abuse and Mental Health Services Administration, Rockville, MD.

24. Cavazos, Lauro F. (1989). *What works: Schools without drugs.* Washington DC: U.S. Department of Education, p. 38.

25. Clayton, Richard R., Cattarello, Anne M., and Johnstone, Bryan M. (1996). The effectiveness of Drug Abuse Resistance Education (Project DARE): 5-year follow-up results. *Preventive Medicine, 25,* 307–318. Lynam, Donald R.; Milich, Richard; Zimmerman, Rick; Novak, Scott P.; Logan, T. K.; Martin, Catherine; Leukefeld, Carl; and Clayton, Richard (1999). Project DARE: No effects at 10-year follow-up. *Journal of Consulting and Clinical Psychology, 67,* 590–593.

26. Lynam, Project DARE, p. 593.

27. Zernike, Kate (2001, February 15). Antidrug program says it will adopt a new strategy. *New York Times,* pp. A1, A29.

28. Wandersman, Abraham, and Florin, Paul (2003). Community interventions and effective prevention. *American Psychologist, 58,* 441–448. Winick, Charles, and Larson, Mary Jo (1997). Community action programs. In Joyce H. Lowinson, Pedro Ruiz, Robert B. Millman, and John G. Langrod (Eds.), *Substance abuse: A comprehensive textbook* (3d ed.). Baltimore: Williams and Wilkins, pp. 755–764.

29. Rhodes, Jean E., and Jason, Leonard A. (1991). The social stress model of alcohol and other drug abuse: A basis for comprehensive, community-based prevention. In Ketty H. Rey, Christopher L. Faegre, and Patti Lowery (Eds.), *Prevention research findings: 1988* (OSAP Prevention Monograph 3). Rockville, MD: Office of Substance Abuse Prevention, pp. 155–171.

30. Tobler, Nancy S. (1986). Meta-analysis of 143 adolescent drug prevention programs: Quantitative outcome results of program participants compared to a control group. *Journal of Drug Issues, 16,* 537–567.

31. Zeuschner, Raymond (1997). *Communicating today* (2d ed.). Boston: Allyn and Bacon, p. 372.

32. Partnership for a Drug-Free America (1994, July 12). New study shows children in NYC becoming more anti-drug, bucking national trends (press release). Partnership for a Drug-Free America, New York.

33. Center for Media and Public Affairs. Cited in Sussman, Steve; Stacy, Alan W.; Dent, Clyde W.; Simon, Thomas R.; and Johnson, C. Anderson (1996). Marijuana use: Current issues and new research directions. *Journal of Drug Issues, 26,* p. 714. Partnership for a Drug-Free America, New York. Wren, Christopher S. (1997, June 20). A seductive drug culture flourishes on the Internet. *New York Times,* pp. A1, A22.

34. Information courtesy of the Substance Abuse and Mental Health Services Administration, Rockville, MD.

35. Fields, Richard (2004). *Drugs in perspective* (5th ed.). Boston: McGraw-Hill. Kumpfer, Karol L. (1991). How to get hard-to-reach parents involved in parenting programs. *Parent training is prevention: Preventing alcohol and other drug problems among youth in the family.* Rockville, MD: Office of Substance Abuse Prevention, pp. 87–95. National Center on Addiction and Substance Abuse at Columbia University (1999). *No safe haven: Children of substance-abusing parents.* New York: National Center on Addiction and Substance Abuse. Kumpfer, Karol L., and Alvarado, Rose (2003). Family-strengthening approaches for the prevention of youth problem behaviors. *American Psychologist, 58,* 457–465. Seizas, Judith S., and Youcha, Geraldine (1999). *Drugs, alcohol, and your children: What every parent needs to know.* New York: Penguin Books.

36. Partnership for a Drug-Free America (1998). Partnership attitude tracking survey: Parents say they're talking, but only 27% of teens—1 in 4—are learning a lot at home about the risk of drugs. Partnership for a Drug-Free America (1999). Partnership attitude tracking survey: More parents talking with kids about drugs more often, and appear to be having an impact. Information courtesy of Partnership for a Drug-Free America, New York.

37. The National Center on Addiction and Substance Abuse at Columbia University (2003, August). *National Survey American Attitudes on Substance Abuse VIII: Teens and parents.* New York: National Center on Addiction and Substance Abuse at Columbia University.

38. Castro, Ralph J., and Foy, Betsy D. (2002). Harm reduction: A promising approach for college health. *Journal of American College Health, 51,* 89–91. Lewis, David C. (2001). Urging college alcohol and drug policies that target adverse behavior, not use. *Journal of American College Health, 50,* 39–41. Office of Substance Abuse Prevention (1991). *Faculty members' handbook: Strategies for preventing alcohol and other drug problems.* Rockville, MD: National Clearinghouse for Alcohol and Drug Information, National Institute on Drug Abuse, p. 4.

39. National Institute on Alcohol Abuse and Alcoholism (2002, October). Changing the culture of campus drinking. *Alcohol Alert,* No. 58. Rockville, MD: National Institute on Alcohol Abuse and Alcoholism. Task Force of the National Advisory Council on Alcohol Abuse and Alcoholism (2002, April). *A call to action: Changing the*

culture of drinking at U.S. colleges. Rockville, MD: National Institute on Alcohol Abuse and Alcoholism. Wechsler, Henry; Lee, Jae Eun; Gledhill-Hoyt, Jeana; and Nelson, Toben F. (2001). Alcohol use and problems at colleges banning alcohol: Results of a national survey. *Journal of Studies on Alcohol, 62,* 133–141.

40. Johnston, Lloyd D.; O'Malley, Patrick M.; Bachman, Jerald G.; and Schulenberg, John E. (2007). *Monitoring the Future national results on adolescent drug use. Overview of key findings, 2006.* Bethesda, MD: National Institute on Drug Abuse, Table 1.

41. Denizet-Lewis, Benoit (2005, January 9). Ban of brothers. *New York Times Magazine,* pp. 32–39, 52, 73. Quotation on p. 35. Office of Educational Research and Improvement (1990). *A guide for college presidents and governing bodies: Strategies for eliminating alcohol and other drug abuse on campuses.* Washington DC: U.S. Department of Education. Office of Substance Abuse Prevention. *Faculty members' handbook,* pp. 21–25.

42. Adapted from McNeece, C. Aaron, and DiNitto, Diana M. (1994). *Chemical dependency: A systems approach.* Englewood Cliffs, NJ: Prentice Hall, p. 153.

43. French, Michael T., Zarkin, Gary A., and Bray, Jeremy W. (1995). A methodology for evaluating the costs and benefits of employee assistance programs. *Journal of Drug Issues, 25,* 451–470.

44. Bacharach, Samuel B. (2007). Battling addiction: The workplace matters. Courtesy of HBO in the series *Addiction.*

45. Drug testing in the workplace (July/August 1996). *Prevention Pipeline,* p. 3. Meeks, Linda, Heit, Philip, and Page, Randy (1994). *Drugs, alcohol, and tobacco.* Blacklick, OH: Meeks-Heit Publishing, pp. 220–221. U.S. Department of Labor (1990). *An employer's guide to dealing with substance abuse.* Washington DC: U.S. Department of Labor.

46. Comerford, Anthony W. (1999). Work dysfunction and addiction. *Journal of Substance Abuse Treatment, 16,* 247–253. Engelhart, Paul F., Robinson, Holly, and Kates, Hannah (1997). The workplace. In Joyce H. Lowinson, Pedro Ruiz, Robert B. Millman, and John G. Langrod (Eds.), *Substance abuse: A comprehensive textbook* (3rd ed.). Baltimore: Williams and Wilkins, pp. 874–884. Normand, J., Lempert, R., and O'Brien, C. (eds.) (1994). *Under the influence? Drugs and the American work force.* Washington DC: National Academy Press.

47. Avis, Harry (1996). *Drugs and life* (3d ed.). Dubuque, IA: Brown and Benchmark, p. 256.

48. Avis, *Drugs and life.* Fishbein, Diana H., and Pease, Susan E. (1996). *The dynamics of drug abuse.* Needham Heights, MA: Allyn and Bacon. *Prevention Pipeline,* p. 3.

49. Center for Substance Abuse Prevention (1994). *Making the link: Alcohol, tobacco, and other drugs in the workplace.* Rockville, MD: Center for Substance Abuse Prevention. Substance abuse in the workplace (1996, July/August). *Prevention Pipeline,* p. 2.

50. National Transportation Safety Board (1988). *Alcohol/drug use and its impact on railroad safety: Safety study.* Washington DC: U.S. Department of Transportation.

51. Blum, Terry C., and Roman, Paul M. (1995). *Cost-effectiveness and preventive implications of employee assistance programs.* Rockville, MD: Substance Abuse and Mental Health Services Administration. Meeks, Heit, and Page, *Drugs,* p. 214.

52. Hernandez, Lawrence P., and Lucero, Ed (1996). La Familia community drug and alcohol prevention program: Family-centered model for working with inner-city Hispanic families. *Journal of Primary Prevention, 16,* 255–272. Office of Substance Abuse Prevention (1990). *The fact is . . . reaching Hispanic/Latino audiences requires cultural sensitivity.* Rockville, MD: National Clearinghouse for Alcohol and Drug Information, National Institute on Drug Abuse. U.S. Census Bureau (2005). *The Hispanic population in the United States: March 2004.* Washington DC: U.S. Department of Commerce.

53. Hahn, Ellen J., and Rado, Mary (1996). African-American Head Start parent involvement in drug prevention. *American Journal of Health Behavior, 20,* 41–51. Office of Substance Abuse Prevention (1990). *The fact is . . . alcohol and other drug use is a special concern for African American families and communities.* Rockville, MD: National Clearinghouse for Drug and Alcohol Information, National Institute on Drug Abuse.

54. Meeks, Heit, and Page, *Drugs,* p. 219.

55. Connors, Gerard J., Donovan, Dennis J., and DiClemente, Carlo C. (2001). *Substance abuse treatment and the stages of change: Selecting and planning interventions.* New York: Guilford Press. DiClemente, Carlo C., Bellino, Lori E., and Neavins, Tara M. (1999). Motivation for change and alcoholism treatment. *Alcohol Research and Health, 23,* 86–92. Schuckit, Marc A. (1995). *Educating yourself about alcohol and drugs: A people's primer.* New York: Plenum Press, pp. 131–153.

56. Schuckit, *Educating yourself,* pp. 186–216.

57. Dijkstra, Arie, Roijackers, Jolanda, and DeVries, Hein (1998). Smokers in four stages of readiness to change. *Addictive Behaviors, 23,* 339–350. Prochaska, James O., DiClemente, Carlo C., and Norcross, John C. (1992). In search of how people change. *American Psychologist, 47,* 1102–1114.

58. Norman, Gregory J.; Velicer, Wayne F.; Fava, Joseph L.; and Prochaska, James O. (1998). Dynamic typology clustering within the stages of change for smoking cessation. *Addictive Behaviors, 23,* 139–153. Prochaska, James O. (1994). *Changing for good.* New York: William Morrow. Velicer, Wayne F.; Norman, Gregory J.; Fava, Joseph L.; and Prochaska, James O. (1999). Testing 40 predictions

from the transtheoretical model. *Addictive Behaviors, 24,* 455–469.

59. Foxhall, Kathryn (2001, June). Adolescents aren't getting the help they need. *Monitor on Psychology,* pp. 56–58. Markel, Howard (2003, October 21). Treatment for addiction meets barriers in the doctor's office. *New York Times,* pp. F5, F8. Substance Abuse and Mental Health Services Administration (2007). *Results from the 2005 National Survey on Drug Use and Health: National findings.* Rockville, MD: Office of Applied Studies, Substance Abuse and Mental Health Services Administration, pp. 69–82.

Chapter 1: Page 2, © Campbell William/CORBIS; 3, © Spencer Grant/Stock Boston; 15, © Eugene Richards/Magnum Photos; 18, © Mitch Wojnarowicz/The Image works; 26, © Chuck Nacke/Woodfin Camp & Associates; 33 (top), AP Photo; 33 (bottom), © Patrick McCarthy/Newsday.

Chapter 2: Page 41, © Victor Englebert/Photo Researchers; 42, The National Library of Medicine, Bethesda; 44, © Bettmann/CORBIS; 47, © Hulton Archive/Getty Images; 48 (top), Courtesy Everett Collection; 48 (bottom), © Henry Diltz Photography.

Chapter 3: Page 71, Courtesy of Brookhaven National Laboratory; 72, © SSPL/The Image Works; 74, Native American Posters. Artwork courtesy of Blas E. Lopez; 75, © Sybil Shackman; 80, © JupiterImages/BananaStock/Alamy.

Chapter 4: Page 89, © Bettmann/CORBIS; 92, © Photofest; 95, © Spencer Grant/IndexStock Imagery; 98, © Rune Hellestad/CORBIS; 102, © Dan McCoy/Rainbow; 104, AP Photo/The Grundy County Herald, C. E. Jones.

Chapter 5: Page 115, © Marcelo Salinas; 117 (both), 120, © Bettmann/CORBIS; 135 (left), © 2001 Newsday. Reprinted with permission; 135 (right), © Andy Molloy/Kennebec Journal; 136, © Darren McCollester/Getty Images.

Chapter 6: Page 145, © Gene Anthony/Black Star/Stock photo.com; 146, © Frank Capri/SAGA/Woodfin Camp & Associates; 147, © David Hoffman; 151, © Vaugh Fleming/Science Photo Library/Photo Researchers; 153, © Francois Gohier/Photo Researchers.

Chapter 7: Page 166, © Gene Anthony/Black Star/Stock photo.com; 168, © fl online/Alamy; 169, Marijuana Tax Stamp images courtesy of Mystic Stamp Company, Camden, New York 13316 <MysticStamp.com>; 170, © Hulton Archive/Getty Images; 180, © Stacy Walsh/Rosenstock; 181, AP Photo/J. Scott Applewhite; 184, Marijuana Policy Project Foundation, www.MarijuanaPolicy.org; 185, © Kenneth Hayden/Black Star/Stock photo.com.

Chapter 8: Page 194, © Will McIntyre/Photo Researchers; 196, © Johnathan Kirn; 203, AP Photo/Eric Risberg; 204, © Amanda Friedman/Getty Images; 205, © Bettmann/CORBIS; 209, © Reuters News Media/ CORBIS; 211, Courtesy of the National Inhalant Prevention Coalition, Austin, Texas, 800-269-4237; 221both, AP Photo.

Chapter 9: Page 223, © Reuters New Media/CORBIS; 225, © Catherine Karnow/Woodfin Camp & Associates; 228, © NYT Graphics/ NYT Pictures; 233, © Tribune Media Services, Inc. All Rights Reserved. Reprinted with permission; 235, © Blair Seitz/Photo Researchers.

Chapter 10: Page 243, Courtesy of The Lewis Walpole Library, Yale University; 245, © George Steinmetz; 248, © Joe Raedle/Getty Images; 258, © Zuma Press/ZUMA/CORBIS; 259, Photo by Greg Davis/Courtesy of Alcohol Monitoring Systems, Inc.; 263, By permission of Mike Luckovich and Creators Syndicate.

Chapter 11: Page 271, National Clearinghouse for Alcohol & Drug Information; 275, © Bettmann/CORBIS; 278 top, © Martin M. Rotker/Photo Researchers; 278 (bottom), © Biophto Associates/ Science Source/Photo Researchers; 279, © George Steinmetz; 286, © Hank Morgan/Science Source/Photo Researchers; 287, Compliments of the Wilson House, East Dorset, VT.

Chapter 12: Page 297, © Bettmann/CORBIS; 300 (left), © John Coletti/IndexStock Imagery; 300 (right), Gaslight Advertising Archives; 302, © Reuters News Media/CORBIS; 311, National Library of Medicine; 314 (top), © Richard Hutchings/Photo Researchers; 314 (bottom), DOONESBURY ©1992 G. B. Trudeau. Reprinted with permission of UNIVERSAL PRESS SYNDICATE. All rights reserved; 316, AP Photo; 318, Yola Monakhov for The New York Times; 320, Courtesy of California Department of Health Services.

Chapter 13: Page 336, © Forest Johnson/CORBIS; 338, © Reuters News Media/CORBIS; 339, Photo Courtesy of the Drug Enforcement Administration; 340, AP Photo/David Maung; 343, AP Photo/Adam Butler; 346, © Owen Franken/CORBIS; 347, AP Photo/The Grundy County Herald, C. E. Jones.

Chapter 14: Page 361, © Les Stone/The Image Works; 362, © Rosemary Greenwood; Ecoscene/CORBIS; 363, AP Photo/Kathryn Cook; 364, © A&E/CORBIS SYGMA; 365, AP Photo/Hans Deryk; 373, © Bill Pugliano/Getty Images.

Chapter 15: Page 388, © Jim Pickerell/Stock Connection; 394, 395, 396, 398, Courtesy of Partnership for a Drug-Free America; 400, A Matter of Degree, a partnership of the American Medical Association Office of Alcohol and Other Drug Abuse and The Robert Wood Johnson Foundation. All Rights Reserved; 401, Courtesy of Partnership for a Drug-Free America.

INDEX

Alcohol dependence, 274
    professional's view of, 274
AlcoholEdu, 399
AlcoholEdu for Sanctions, 399
Alcoholic beverages
    alcohol equivalencies of, 246, 247
    production of, 242–43
    sources of, 244
Alcoholic cirrhosis, 277, 277–78
Alcoholic dementia, 278, 278–79
Alcoholic hepatitis, 277
Alcoholics
    children of (COAs), 66–67, 283
    controlled drinking for, 288
    types of, 284
Alcoholics Anonymous (AA), 272, 286,
        286–88, 289, 290
"Alcohol-in-combination" incidents, 26–27
Alcohol Innerview, 399
Alcoholism, 270, 270–73
    biologically based treatments of, 285–86
    costs of, 280–81
    demographics of, 270, 271, 281–82
    as disease, 285, 288
    emotional problems and, 272
    genetics of, 66–67, 283–84
    hiding problems of, 272–73
    physical problems associated with, 272
    preoccupation with drinking and, 270–72
    psychology of, 274
    self-survey for, 273
    SMART Recovery for, 288, 288–90
    vocational, social, family dynamics of, 272,
        282–83, 290
Alcohol withdrawal syndrome, 277
Aldactone, 257
Alpert, Richard, 145
Alprazolam, 27, 197
Alternative-behavior programming, 393, 396
Alzado, Lyle, 225–26
Alzheimer's disease, 198, 282
Amando Carrillo-Fuentes Organization, 339
Amanita muscaria, 12, 41, 142, 143, 155,
        155–57
Ambien CR, 201
Ambien (zolpidem), 200–201
American Bar Association, 184, 373
American Cancer Society, 309, 319
American Management Association survey
        (1996), 401, 402
American Medical Association, 42, 184,
        285, 400
American Psychiatric Association, 21, 273
American Psychological Association, 373
American Temperance Society, 275
Amitriptyline, 197
Ammonia as cigarette additive, 306
Amobarbital, 191, 192, 193, 195, 234
Amotivational syndrome, 176, 176–77
Amphetamine psychosis, 102
Amphetamines, 21, 88, 100, 100–108
    in 1960s and 1970s, 120
    acute and chronic effects of, 102–6
    brain and, 101–2

detection periods for, 234
forms of, 101
heroin combined with, street names
        for, 128
history of, 100–101
medical uses for, 106–8
molecular structure of, 101
neurochemical system in brain and, 68
patterns of abuse and treatment, 102–6
pharmacological violence and, 330
street names, 103
use among youth, 56
withdrawal from, 104
Amyl nitrite, 211, 212, 212–13
Amytal (amobarbital), 191, 192, 193, 195
Anabolic-androgenic steroids, 219. See also
        Anabolic steroids
Anabolic effects, 219
Anabolic Steroid Control Act of 2004, 52
Anabolic steroids, 218, 219–30, 220
    abuse patterns, 227–30
    adolescents' use of, 223, 226–27
    baseball and, 218, 223, 231
    black market for, 227–28
    cardiovascular effects of, 225
    counterfeit, 229–30
    currently available, 220
    dependence on, 228–29
    detection periods for, 234
    hazards of, 223–27
    hormonal systems and, 224–25
    liver and, 225
    masking drugs to hide, 234
    in modern Olympic Games, 220–22, 223
    in professional and collegiate sports,
        222–23, 224
    psychological problems and, 225–26, 227
    reasons for taking, 236
    signs of abuse, 229
    social context of, 235–36
    temptation to use, 236
    testing for, 234
    women's use of, 221, 225, 227, 229
Anabolic Steroids Control Act, 227
Anadrol (oxymetholone), 220
Analgesic drugs
    acetaminophen, 27, 133, 257
    aspirin, 40, 118, 133, 253
    ibuprofen, 27, 234
    narcotic, 7, 29
Anandamide, 173
Androderm transdermal system, 220
Androgenic drugs, 219
Android (methyltestosterone), 220
Android-50 (oxymetholone), 220
Androstenedione, 31, 231
Anesthesia
    barbiturates used in, 192
    nitrous oxide as, 204
    Rohypnol for surgical, 200
Anesthetics
    cocaine as, 90, 91, 93
    ketamine as, 351
    PCP as, 350

Angel dust. See Phencyclidine (PCP)
Angina, 311
Angiotensin-converting enzyme (ACE), 222
Anhydrous ammonia, methamphetamine
        manufacture using, 103
Anodyne, 205
Anomie, 73, 73–75
Anomie/strain theory, 73–75
Anorexia, endorphins and, 125
Anslinger, Harry, 46, 48, 169
Antabuse (disulfiram), 257, 285
Antagonistic effect, 14
Antianxiety drugs, 27, 28, 70, 191. See also
        Benzodiazepines
    buspirone, 202
    development of, 195–96
    ethnicity and, 17
    zolpidem, 200–201, 201
Antibiotics, 257
    quinolone, 234
Anticholinergic drugs, 157–58
Anticoagulants, alcohol mixed with, 256
Anticonvulsants, alcohol mixed with, 256
Antidepressants, 21, 27
    for anxiety disorders, 202
    selective serotonin reuptake
        inhibitors, 202
Antidiuresis, 256, 257
Antidiuretic hormone (ADH), 255, 255–56
Anti-Drug Abuse Acts (1986 and 1988),
        51, 52, 374
Anti-drug campaigns, 2
Antihistamines, 257
Antihypertensives, 257
Antimarijuana crusade, 168–70
Anti-Opium Smoking Act (1875), 52
Antipsychotic drugs, 21
    ethnicity and, 17
Anti-Saloon League, 275
Antisocial personality disorder, 73
Antitussive drug, 133
Anxiety, 195–96. See also Antianxiety drugs
    as precursor to drug abuse, 73
Anxiety disorders, 197
Anxiety reduction, 389
Appalachia
    marijuana industry in, 346, 347
    methamphetamine produced in clan
        labs, 348
Appetite, marijuana's effect on, 171
Appetite suppressants, 100
Apresoline, 257
Aqua vitae, 243
Arellano-Félix, Benjamin, 339
Arellano-Félix, Francisco Javier, 339
Arellano-Félix, Ramon, 339
Arellano-Félix Organization, 339, 340
Arizona Proposition 200 (1996), 52
Arizona Supreme Court, 400
Arrestee Drug Abuse Monitoring (ADAM)
        Program, 55, 329
Arrest rates for drug-related violations,
        371–72
Arteriosclerosis, 308

Cocaine (*cont.*)
  drug laws and, 44, 45
  drug-related deaths from, 27, 28, 29
  ED visits for, 27
  extraction process, 94
  fatal effects of, 89, 92
  federal penalties for, 374
  free-base, 95, 97
  Freud and, 87, 88, 90–91
  genetic factors in use of, 66
  heroin combined with, 94, 122, 128
  history of, 40, 42, 44, 47, 50–51, 88–91
  hotline for, 97, 106
  intravenous, 94
  legalization of drugs and, 377
  LSD combined with, 95
  mandatory minimum sentencing for
    selling, **372,** 372–73
  marijuana mixed with, 347
  medical uses of, 90, 91, 93
  methadone clients' abuse of, 131
  methamphetamine abuse
    compared to, 104
  neurochemical system in brain and, 68
  Pavlovian conditioning and associations
    with, 72
  penalties for crack possession vs., 374
  pharmacological violence and, 330
  physical signs of abuse, 97
  possession as drug-defined
    offense, 328
  precursor chemicals, 362
  price of, 96, 341
  production of, 335
  psychological dependence on, 20, 21
  risk of toxicity, 24
  smuggling methods for, 363
  snorted, 91, 93, 94
  source of, 40
  speedball, mixture of heroin and, **341**
  street names, 95
  street purity of, 341
  trafficking of, 100, 335, 336–41, 353
  treatment for abusers, 97–100
  use among adults aged 26 and older, 59
  use among American youth, 54, 56, 57
Cocaine Anonymous, 99, 104, 287
Cocaine hydrochloride, 94
Cocaine psychosis, 93
Coca leaves, chewing of, 88
Coca paste, 94
Codeine, 114, 118, 133
  combined with Doriden, street
    names for, 128
Code of Hammurabi, 243
Codependency, 283
Cognitive-behavioral therapy for cocaine
  abusers, 99
Cognitive-expectation theory, 261–62
Cold medications
  containing pseudoepinephrine, limiting
    sales of, 103
  detection periods for, 234
  dextromethorphan in, 33, 34

College students, drug use among, 56–57,
    58. *See also* Youth, drug use among
  alcohol, 248–50
  prevention of, 397–400
  smoking, 313
Collegiate sports, steroid use in, 222–23
Colombia, 53, 100, 337–39, 341
  cocaine cultivation in, 335, 336–37
  cocaine trafficking, 336–41
  crop eradication in, 360, 360–61
  marijuana from, 345
  Medellin and Cali drug cartels, 337,
    337–39, 360
  money laundering by traffickers in, **352**
  opium and heroin from, 122, 126, 344
  revolutionary guerilla groups in,
    337–39, 344
Columbus, Christopher, 296
Combat Methamphetamine Epidemic Act
    (2005), 52, 348
Commit, 319
Commitment (social bond), 75
Communication within family,
    dysfunctional, 396
Communism, 48
Community-based prevention, 392–94
  alternative-behavior programming,
    393, 396
  CASASTART, 394
  role of mass media in, 393–94, 395
Compassion Use Act (1996, California), 183
Comprehensive Crime Control Act of 1984,
    51, 52
Comprehensive Drug Abuse Prevention
    and Control Act of 1970, 47, 49, 52,
    184, 185, 351, 370
Comprehensive Methamphetamine Control
    Act (1996), 52
Comprehensive Textbook of Psychiatry, 94
Compulsive behavior
  economically compulsive crime,
    331, 333
  neurochemical system in brain and, 68, 69
Concerta, 107
Concordance rate, 284
Conditioned cues, 72–73, 99
Conditioned-learning effects, heroin
    abuse and, 127
Conditioned tolerance, 15–16
  heroin abuse and, 128
Conditioning, Pavlovian, 15–16, 72
Confabulation, 279
Confessions of an English Opium Eater
    (DeQuincey), 117
Confiscation Act of 1862, 370
Conformity
  adaptation to anomie, 74
  social bonds promoting, 75
Congeners, 257
Consent search, 369
Constipation, heroin abuse and, 123, 132
Constitution, U.S.
  Eighteenth Amendment, 45–46, 52, 275
  Fifth Amendment, 401

Fourth Amendment, 366, 401
  Twenty-first Amendment, 46, 52, 276
Consultants, parents or guardians as, 396
Contemplation stage of rehabilitation, **405**
Contraband, 370
Contraceptives, smoking and, 311–12
Controlled buy, 368
Controlled Substance Act. *See*
    Comprehensive Drug Abuse
    Prevention and Control Act of 1970
Controlled Substance Analogue
    Act (1986), 121
Controlled substances, schedules of, 49
COPD (chronic obstructive pulmonary
    disease), 309, 316
Copenhagen (chewing tobacco), 315
Coricidin HBP Cough and Cold pills, 33
Coronary heart disease (CHD), 263, **308,**
    316, 318
Correctional system, 371–75
  cost of building and maintaining
    prisons, 51, 373
  drug use among inmates, 329–30, 332
  percentage drug offenders in, 373
Cortisone, 220
Coughing, narcotic drugs to treat, 133
Coumadin (warfarin), 257
Counterconditioning, 72
Couriers, drug, 340, 344
  "mules," 340, 363
Courts, drug, 374, 374–75
Crack cocaine (crack), 29, 50–51, **95,** 97,
    101, 341
  economically compulsive crime and, **331**
  federal penalties for, 374
  freelance sale of, 335
  heroin mixed with, 122, 128
  legalization of drugs and, 377
  marijuana mixed with, 347
  PCP combined with, 95
  pharmacological violence and, 330
  systemic violence and, **332,** 332–33, 336
  use among adults aged 26 and older, 59
  use among American youth, 54, 57
  withdrawal from, 330
Crack dealing organizations, 336
CrackGen subculture, 334
Crack houses, 331, 341
"Crank," 348
Creatine, 31, 231
Creativity
  LSD and, 149
  marijuana and, 171
Crime, 327–58
  crack cocaine and, 95
  deviant life-style and, 332–33
  drug-defined offenses, 328
  drug-related offenses, 328
  drug trafficking. *See* Drug trafficking
  drug use and, 328–34
  economically compulsive, 331, 333
  heroin abuse and, 120, 129
  incarceration rates of drug offenders, 328
  LSD use and, 150–51

Preparation stage of rehabilitation, 405
Presley, Elvis, 25
Prevention strategies, 382–404. *See also*
ATOD prevention
against alcohol use during pregnancy, 280
college students and, 397–400
community-based, 392–94
family and, 394–97
"magic bullets" and promotional
campaigns, 385–88
multicultural issues, 403–4
objective-information approach, 385
primary, 382, 383, 389, 390, 394–97
punitive measures for drug addicts, 385
reducing availability, 385–86
scare tactics and negative education, 385
school-based, 58, 388–92
secondary, 382, 383, 394–97
self-esteem enhancement and affective
education, 388
tertiary, 382, 383–84
unsuccessful, 385–88
in workplace, 400–403
Priapism, 224
Prices, economically compulsive crime
and drug, 331
Primary deviance, 77, 77–78
Primary prevention, 382, 383, 389,
390, 394–97
resilience and, 383
Prisoners
drug use among inmates, 329–30
drug use prior to first crime, 332
in federal prison by type of
offense, 372
incarceration rates, 328, 371
percentage drug offenders, 372
Prison system, cost of building and
maintaining, 51, 373
Probenecid, 234
Productivity, legalization of drugs
and, 376–77
Professional sports, steroids use in, 222–23
suspension penalties, 224
Profiling and drug-law enforcement, 366–67
Prohibition, 45–46, 46, 275–76
marijuana's popularity during, 168
Promotional campaigns, prevention
through, 385–88
Proof of distilled spirits, 243
Propane, 206, 208
Propanolol, 202
Property crime and price of heroin, 331
Propoxyphene, 130, 133, 134
Proprietary and Patent Medicine Act of
1908, 90
ProSom (estazolam), 197
Prostitution, 331, 332, 333
Protective factors, 79, 80–81
Protropin (genetically engineered hGH), 230
Provigil (modafinil), 108
Pseudoephedrine, 362
cold remedies containing, 103
methamphetamine manufacture
and, 103, 348

Psilocin, 151
Psilocybe mexicana, 151
Psilocybin, 142, 145, 146, 151, 151
effects of, 151
Psychedelic drugs. *See* Hallucinogens
Psychedelic era, beginning of, 144–46
Psychoactive drugs, 3. *See also* Inhalants;
Alcohol
biochemistry of, 69–70
drug dependence and, 4
in early times, 40–41
Psychoanalytic explanations, 70, 70–72
Psychodysleptic drugs. *See* Hallucinogens
Psychological dependence, 19–21, 20
on alcohol, 254
on cocaine, 20, 21
on crack cocaine, 95
on heroin, 20, 21
on marijuana, 175
neurochemical basis for, 68
Psychological effects, 17–19
of anabolic steroids, 225–26, 227
of marijuana, 171–73
Psychological perspectives on drug
abuse, 68–73
Psycholytic drugs. *See* Hallucinogens
Psychosis
amphetamine, 102
cocaine, 93
Korsakoff's, 279
LSD, 148–49
Psychotherapeutic medications, nonmedical
use of, 59
Psychotomimetic drugs. *See* Hallucinogens
Public Health Model, 384–85
Public Health Service, 384
Pulse Check, 55
Punitive measures for drug addicts, 385. *See
also* Crime; Criminal justice system,
drugs and
Pure Food and Drug Act (1906), 44, 52, 90
"Push down, pop up phenomenon" of crop
eradication programs, 361
Pyramiding pattern of steroid abuse, 228

Quaalude (methaqualone), 195, 234
Quid (pinch of snuff), 315
Quinolone antibiotics, 234

R. J. Reynolds Tobacco, 316, 317
Race and ethnicity, 57
alcohol metabolism and, 253
cancer mortality and, 309
cocaine use and, 92
drug effects and, 17
drug laws and, 42–47
drug use among youth, 56
heroin abuse and, 120
inhalant use by, 209
penalties for cocaine vs. crack possession
and, 374
racial profiling and, 366
smoking and, 313
Racial profiling, 366
Racism, 44

Raich, Angel McClary, 183
Raich v. *Ashcroft*, 183
Raleigh, Sir Walter, 296
Rametton, 201
Ramone, DeeDee, 25
Randolph, Elmo, 366
Rape
alcohol intoxication and, 331
drugs used for, 160, 200, 202–4
Rape, Abuse, and Incest National Network
(RAINN), 204
Rapid-eye movement (REM) sleep, 193
alcohol and reduction of, 256
Rational emotive behavior therapy
(REBT), 290
RAVE (Reducing American's Vulnerability
to Ecstasy) Act (2003), 156
Rave subcultures, 52, 76, 348
Reagan, Nancy, 51
Reagan, Ronald, 51, 400
Rebellion, as adaptation to anomie, 75
REBT, 290
Receptor binding, 69
Receptors
benzodiazepine, 198–99
dopamine, 68, 71, 93
endorphin-sensitive, 127
GABA, sensitivity to alcohol, 254
glutamate, 159, 160
morphine-sensitive, 123, 173
nicotinic, 306
serotonin-sensitive, 148
THC-sensitive, 173
Recidivism rate for drug court participants
vs. nonparticipants, 375
Recovery, personal journey to, 404–6
Recreational use, 6, 7
Recruitment and socialization theory,
subcultural, 76, 76–77
Red Man, 315
Red Rum, 345
Reducing American's Vulnerability to
Ecstasy Act (RAVE) of 2003, 156
Reefer, 170. *See also* Marijuana
Reefer madness approach, 385
Reefer Madness (film), 46, 169
Regulation, 42–47
of alcohol, 45–46, 274–76
of anabolic steroids, 227
lack of, in 19th century, 42
of marijuana, 169, 184–85
minimum-age, for smoking, 314–15
of narcotics, 45, 48
states' rights and, 42
tobacco, economics and, 303–4
Rehabilitation, stages of change
and, 404–5
Rehnquist, William H., 366
Reinforcement
behavioral theory of, 72, 72–73
dopamine and, 70
negative, 72
positive, 72
Religious Freedom Restoration Act
of 1993, 154